Wall to Wall

The Second Great Wall of China and Hadrian's Wall Management Seminar Proceedings

双墙对话

第二届中国长城与哈德良长城保护管理研讨会文集

英格兰遗产委员会
Historic England
中国文化遗产研究院
Chinese Academy of Cultural Heritage
编著

文物出版社

图书在版编目（CIP）数据

双墙对话：第二届中国长城与哈德良长城保护管理研讨会文集：汉英对照 / 英格兰遗产委员会，中国文化遗产研究院编著. -- 北京：文物出版社，2021.10
ISBN 978-7-5010-7157-9

Ⅰ.①双… Ⅱ.①英… ②中… Ⅲ.①长城－文物保护－中国－国际学术会议－文集－汉、英②城墙－文物保护－英国－国际学术会议－文集－汉、英 Ⅳ.
① K878.34-53 ② K885.618.34-53

中国版本图书馆 CIP 数据核字（2021）第 138244 号
审图号：GS（2021）8859 号

双墙对话：第二届中国长城与哈德良长城保护管理研讨会文集
Wall to Wall: The Second Great Wall of China and Hadrian's Wall Management Seminar Proceedings

编　　著：英格兰遗产委员会
Historic England
中国文化遗产研究院
Chinese Academy of Cultural Heritage
责任编辑：李　睿
封面设计：王文娴
责任印制：苏　林

出版发行：文物出版社
Cultural Relics Press
地　　址：北京市东城区东直门内北小街 2 号楼
Building No.2, Dongzhimennei Beixiaojie, Dongcheng District, Beijing
网　　址：www.wenwu.com
邮政编码：100007
经　　销：新华书店
印　　刷：宝蕾元仁浩（天津）印刷有限公司
开　　本：889mm × 1194mm　1/16
印　　张：24　插页：1
版　　次：2021 年 10 月第 1 版
印　　次：2021 年 10 月第 1 次印刷
书　　号：ISBN 978-7-5010-7157-9
定　　价：380.00 元

乌鲁木齐
新疆
Xinjiang
玉门关
Yumen Pass
嘉峪关
Jiayu Pass
西宁
兰州
青海
Qinghai
甘肃
Gansu
西藏
Xizang
拉萨
四川
Sichuan
成都
昆明
云南
Yunnan
图例
Legend
首都 Capital
省级行政中心
Provincial administrative center
国界 International boundary
未定国界
Undefined international boundary
省级界 Provincial boundaries
特别行政区界 Boundary of SAR
河流 River
湖泊 Lake
比例尺(Scale) 1:18 000 000
专题图例
Special Legend
关
fortified pass
堡
fort and fortress
烽火台
beacon tower
墙体
wall
山险
cliff wall
界壕壕堑
trench
注：各时代的长城资源要素颜色设置如下
春秋战国（5th-3rd B.C.）
秦（3rd B.C.）
汉（3rd B.C.-3rd A.D.）
魏晋南北朝（3rd -6th A.D.）
隋唐至辽（6th-12th A.D.）
金（12th-13th A.D.）
明（14th-17th A.D.）

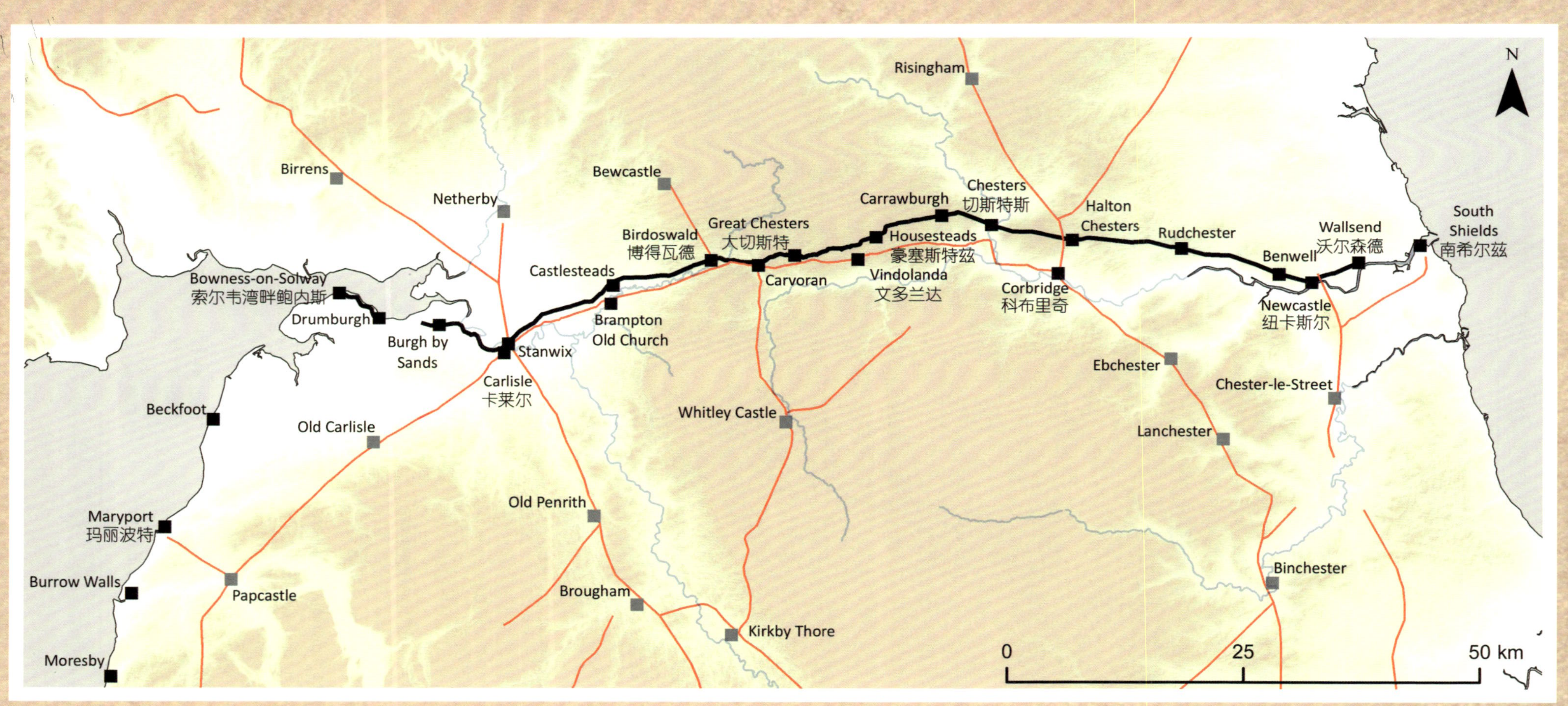

英国哈德良长城地图（版权：哈德良长城社区考古项目）
Hadrian 's Wall Map (© Wall CAP)

罗马帝国边疆防御体系分布图（公元二世纪中期，版权：文化 2000 年，罗马帝国边疆项目

Map of Frontiers of the Roman Empire (© Culture 2000 Frontiers of the Roman Empire projec

中国长城分布示意图（版权：国家文物局；制图：国信司南）

Map of the Great Wall of China (© NCHA; drawing: Geo-Compass)

主　编　Editors in Chief

大卫・布劳夫 David Brough
于 冰 Yu Bing

副主编　Assistant editors

汉佛瑞・维尔法 Humphrey Welfare
刘文艳 Liu Wenyan
卡罗尔・派拉 Carol Pyrah

翻　译　Translators

黄思源，李默识，马艳鑫，徐逢时
Huang Siyuan, Li Moshi, Ma Yanxin, Xu Fengshi

第二届中国长城和英国哈德良长城双墙对话研讨会暨长城保护联盟第二届年会由滦平县人民政府及金山岭长城管理处于 2019 年 11 月承办。

The 2nd Great Wall of China and the Hadrian's Wall Management Seminar & 2nd Great Wall Alliance Annual Conference was hosted by the People's Government of Luanping and Jinshanling Great Wall Cultural Relics Management Office.

文集编辑、排版和论文中英双语互译由英格兰遗产委员会资金支持。

The editing and design of the publication, and the translation of original texts were funded by Historic England.

文集排版由英国牛津 Archaeopress 出版公司承担。

Design of the publication was undertaken by Archaeopress Publishing Limited, Oxford, UK.

文集正式出版印刷由中国文化遗产研究院资金支持。

The formal publication and printing is funded by CACH.

CONTENTS

目录

CHAPTER 4: CONSERVATION PRINCIPLES AND PRACTICES

CHAPTER 5: VISITOR ACCESS AND PUBLIC ENGAGEMENT

第四单元　长城保护维修理念与实践

第五单元　长城开放利用与社会参与

FOREWORD

China and the UK are privileged to be custodians of two of the world's finest examples of frontier heritage. The Great Wall and Hadrian's Wall embrace over two thousand years of human achievement and are remarkable archaeological, landscape and cultural resources. Despite differences in scale, their similarities of challenge and opportunity provide considerable scope for shared learning, and for building appreciation and understanding of our common heritage.

The idea of a Wall to Wall collaboration between these great World Heritage Sites emerged in 2017. It has been heartening to see the progress that has been made since then. First of all, China and the UK signed a Memorandum of Understanding which established a formal dialogue about cultural heritage. In 2018 the UK hosted a seminar in Newcastle to share our real-life experiences in managing and celebrating these great assets.

This publication collates the papers given at the second Wall to Wall seminar at Jinshanling in 2019, which marked the next step on our collaboration. The event was hosted by the Chinese Academy of Cultural Heritage, co-organised with Historic England and supported by the National Cultural Heritage Administration of China, the British Council and UNESCO. Here we have brought together the seminar contributions of experts and practitioners from both countries, through which several major themes are interrogated.

We examine how both our differences and similarities in conservation and management practices can help inform future protection of these sites. In particular, we reflect on ways in which heritage and tourism can work in harmony.

We discuss how to harness our emerging methods of archaeological research, survey and comparative studies to improve our understanding of the two Walls. By sharing our technological expertise in investigation and analysis, we can better tackle the important questions of why, how and when they were built and adapted over time.

We also explore ways of delivering improved and innovative public access to tell the fascinating stories about our special places. Our heritage will only be safe if it can continue to be understood, valued and enjoyed by wider audiences.

Several specific collaborative projects have emerged as a result of our fruitful dialogue in Jinshanling. These will ensure the practical application of our learning to strengthen our bi-lateral understanding and partnership, and secure mutually beneficial results for these treasured symbols of our nations' history.

DUNCAN WILSON OBE
Chief Executive
Historic England

CHAI XIAOMING
Director
Chinese Academy of Cultural Heritage

前言

中国和英国十分荣幸地成为世界上两个最杰出边疆遗产的守护者。中国长城和英国哈德良长城见证两千多年的人类成就，是非凡的考古、景观和文化资源。它们尽管规模不同，但在挑战和机遇方面存在相似之处，为我们共同遗产的分享、交流和理解提供了巨大空间。

这两处世界遗产之间的“双墙对话”合作意向始于2017年。自那时以来所取得的进展令人振奋。首先，中英两国签署了《谅解备忘录》，开启文化遗产的正式对话。2018年，英方主办在纽卡斯尔召开研讨会，分享了双方在管理和弘扬这些伟大遗产方面的实际经验。

2019 年召开了第二届金山岭双墙对话研讨会，会议论文汇编成为本文集。金山岭研讨会标志着我们合作在继续推向深入。该活动由中国文化遗产研究院与英格兰遗产委员会共同主办，并得到中国国家文物局、英国文化协会和联合国教科文组织的支持。参加本研讨会的人员包括来自两国的专家和从业人员，其论文涉及双墙各个主题。

文集探讨我们在双墙保护和管理实践上的差异和相似，以及如何为双墙的未来保护提供帮助。我们还特别反思了遗产与旅游业融合的各种形式。

文集讨论如何利用最新的考古研究、调查和比较研究方法来增进我们对双墙的认知。分享双方在调查和分析方面的技术经验，有助于我们更好地回答双墙为什么修建、如何修建、以及如何随时间不断变化等重要问题。

文集还探索改进和创新双墙开放利用、讲述生动故事的方式。只有继续得到更广泛公众的认知、珍爱和享受，我们的文化遗产才会是安全的。

我们在金山岭进行了卓有成效的交流沟通后，形成了一些具体合作意向。开展具体合作有益于将双方分享交流体会真正落实于实际工作之中，有益于加强双方相互理解和建立更密切伙伴关系，有益于我们国家历史上这些珍贵的象征性遗产均得到良好保护。

邓肯·威尔逊
行政总裁
英格兰遗产委员会

柴晓明
院长
中国文化遗产研究院

INTRODUCTION

DAVID BROUGH
Newcastle University - Newcastle upon Tyne - UK

YU BING
Chinese Academy of Cultural Heritage - China - Beijing

This publication is based on papers presented at the Second Great Wall of China and Hadrian's Wall Management Seminar and the Second Great Wall Alliance Annual Conference, held at Jinshanling Great Wall, Hebei, between 4th to 7th November 2019. At the Seminar the papers from the first Great Wall of China and Hadrian's Wall Management Seminar, held at Newcastle University in March 2018, were published and presented. These seminars are major steps in the collaboration between the two World Heritage Sites, led by the Chinese Academy of Cultural Heritage and English Heritage, that began in 2017 and which is known as the 'Wall to Wall' programme.

The seminar held at Newcastle was the first major meeting between those responsible for managing the two World Heritage Sites. Its primary objective was to provide an overview of the archaeological resources of each Site and of the principal issues and challenges that their managers face. The objectives of the seminar at Jinshanling were twofold. First to provide greater detail and insight about those issues and challenges, and how they are currently addressed, and second to identify specific areas of opportunity and interest for more detailed collaborative working. The papers included in this publication reflect the first objective and, it is hoped, will inform our thinking about how the Wall to Wall programme should be taken forward. The papers presented demonstrate the wide range and complexity of the issues involved in managing the two Sites. They are presented in chapters, under five broad subject headings.

Chapter 1 is about the management context of each Site, starting with David Brough's discussion on the concept of management planning as it is practised in the UK, and an outline of how it has evolved on Hadrian's Wall. Yu Bing and her colleagues then provide an overview of current management practice and experience on the Great Wall, highlighting the principal results of the Great Wall Protection Report 2017-18. The current development of the Great Wall, highlighted in this paper, as an potential exemplar of heritage conservation and regional development, and as a flagship of cultural and tourism integration is illustrated further in the following paper by Wang Yuwei. In his paper, he explains the ongoing Great Wall Cultural Belt initiative in Beijing Municipality and its aspirations, objectives, and policies, whilst stressing the need for a stricter protection zoning regime, clearer institutional responsibilities and a greater emphasis on public benefits. The chapter concludes with Carol Pyrah's explanation of the role and significance of the Third Sector in heritage management in the UK.

The second chapter concentrates on the archaeological and historical research on which our understanding of the two Sites is based, and which underpins their management and conservation. The long history of research into Hadrian's Wall, and on Roman frontiers more broadly, is set out by David Breeze who emphasises the breadth of the archaeological research that has been undertaken and the longstanding tradition of collaboration between scholars across many countries. Li Yan then provides a comparison between the military and physical structures of the frontier defence systems - the Ming Great Wall and those of Imperial Rome - drawing out the similarities and the significant differences between the two. This is followed by Tony Wilmott's description of the process of developing the Hadrian's Wall Research Framework, and the benefits that it has provided in the assessment of archaeological understanding and in informing the identification of future research priorities. As a part of the description of research into wider Roman frontier systems, Rob Collins then explains the concept of landscape archaeology and shows how it has been applied to developing our understanding of Hadrian's Wall in the broader context of Roman Britain.

Two further papers describe recent research projects on the Great Wall. The findings of the research on the rammed-earth structures from the Han and Ming Great Walls in Gansu Province are presented by Zhang Bin, whilst Guo Zhongxing details the variety of bricks found on the Jinshanling section of the Great Wall and their conservation. A contrast is then provided between

引言

大卫·布劳夫—纽卡斯尔大学—纽卡斯尔—英国
于冰—中国文化遗产研究院—北京—中国

2019 年 11 月 4 日至 7 日，第二届中国长城与英国哈德良长城管理研讨会暨第二届中国长城联盟年会在河北金山岭长城召开。本论文集主要汇编了研讨会发言内容撰写的文章。会上还发布了第一届中国长城和英国哈德良长城管理研讨会论文集。第一届研讨会于 2018 年 3 月在纽卡斯尔大学召开。这两次研讨会是 2017 年启动的“双墙对话”合作框架下的重要活动，由中国文化遗产研究院和英国遗产委员会牵头组织。

在纽卡斯尔举行的第一届研讨会上，两大世界遗产地的保护管理人员第一次面对面交流。其主要目的是交流双墙的资源概况和在管理过程中面临的主要问题和挑战。到了金山岭研讨会，则有两方面的目标。第一，进一步深入交流两处遗产地保护管理问题和经验；第二，探讨双方感兴趣的具体领域，寻找开展深入合作的机会。本论文集中的文章紧紧围绕第一个目标而组织，也希望它们能够启发如何继续推进双墙对话项目合作。论文集收录的文章反映出两大遗产地管理中面临的问题广泛且复杂，将它们按大的主题共分为五章。

第一章是英国哈德良长城和中国长城各自相关的宏观管理情况。大卫·布劳夫首先等讨论了英国管理规划的概念及其在实践中的应用，以及哈德良长城管理规划的编制和修订历程。于冰等概述了2017–2018 年度中国长城保护报告的主要内容，反映近年来中国长城的保护管理成就和最新动态。文中指出，长城开放利用成为综合区域资源、实现文物保护与区域协调发展的热点，成为我国大型线性文化遗产开放利用与文化旅游融合的先锋示范。这一趋势在随后王玉伟的论文中得到进一步阐述，他描述了正在实施的北京市长城文化带战略，介绍了其愿景、目标和政策，同时建议细化分区管理和保护，明确机构职责，坚持公共属性。第一章最后卡罗尔·派拉的文章概述了英国社会组织在遗产管理中扮演的角色及其重要作用。

第二章的主题是两座长城的考古和历史研究，这些研究深化了对长城的认知，也是长城保护管理的基础。大卫·布雷兹概述了哈德良长城以及更大范围内的罗马边疆研究的悠久历史，从中可以了解相关的研究题材相当广泛，多国学者的合作研究也形成传统。随后李严等对比了明代长城防御体系和罗马帝国边疆防线的军事组织和防御设施体系，展现了两者的相似之处和显著的区别。接下来托尼·威尔莫特介绍了哈德良长城研究框架的编制过程，以及该框 架在评估考古成果和确定未来考古研究重点中发挥的积极作用。为了说明更大范围内的罗马边疆体系研究 成果，罗伯·柯林斯随后解释了景观考古的概念，并展示如何应用景还有观考古使我们更好地在不列颠罗马帝国的大背景下理解哈德良长城。

还有两篇论文分享了中国长城的近期研究成果。张斌在文章中展示了甘肃省汉代和明代夯土长城的调查研究成果。郭中兴详细描述了河北金山岭长城各种形式的长城砖以及对它们的保护。随后的两篇文章对

some of the inscriptions found on the two monuments, as Feng Ying explains how the inscribed bricks found at Shanhaiguan can contribute to dating different periods of its construction or repair, and Paul Bidwell gives an insight into the wealth of historical information contained in inscriptions found across Hadrian's Wall.

Chapter 3 then considers recent approaches to the survey and monitoring of archaeological remains. Chai Xiaoming summarises the findings of the National Great Wall Resources Survey, conducted between 2006 and 2011, focusing on the extant architectural and archaeological remains of the Ming Great Wall. Liu Wenyan then sets out her analysis of the Survey's findings in respect of the beacon towers in Liaodong Province and their distribution, design, and the materials used in their original construction. They are followed by papers introducing how remote sensing and digital technologies are applied on both walls. Matt Oakey and Zhang Jing present interesting parallels, on the national level, in the long-term development of the integrated application of new technologies with traditional approaches in survey and recording to inform decision-making on the two World Heritage Sites. This chapter ends with Zhang Jianwei who shows how digital technologies have helped tracking, recording and informing management of the conservation project at Jainkou.

Contrasting methodologies, principles and practice in relation to conservation are discussed in Chapter 4. Tang Yuyang reflects on some of the key ideas and principles involved in the development of appropriate conservation strategies on brick and stone walls, whilst Lan Lizhi describes how the principle of minimum intervention has been applied to the conservation of earthen walls, using the Yaotan section of the Great Wall in Ningxia Hui Autonomous Region as a case study. Mike Collins then explains how conservation works are undertaken and managed on Hadrian's Wall, and Zhao Peng sets out the processes through which the conservation project at the southern section of Jiankou Great Wall was conducted. The chapter concludes with Bill Griffiths and Mike Collins each offering different perspectives on the reconstruction of archaeological sites in the UK: Griffiths emphasises the interpretive benefits which reconstructions can provide, whilst Collins explains how official policy has been evolving into more balanced approaches between different considerations while maintaining the principles of authenticity.

The final chapter presents a number of papers about initiatives to improve visitor access to the two Sites and to increase public engagement with them. Julia Datow-Ensling and David Brough describe the development of the German Limes Strasse initiative, and how it has provided greater access to the remains of the Roman frontier in Germany through its motoring, walking and cycling routes. As a comparison, the experience of the establishment of the Hadrian's Wall Path National Trail is explained by Humphrey Welfare. Recently completed research into current patterns of tourist visits to the Great Wall is then presented by Zhou Xiaofeng and her colleagues, suggesting that policies for opening up to visitors should be carefully scrutinised based on the condition of different sections of the monument and their suitability for different types of access. English Heritage has undertaken research on the visitors to the sites that it manages along Hadrian's Wall, and Joe Savage explains how this has been used to inform how these sites can be interpreted for the public. The very important objective of enhancing public engagement in the two Walls is discussed in the final three papers. Patricia Weeks explains the Rediscovering the Antonine Wall Project, currently being undertaken by Hadrian's Wall's sister Site in Scotland, and describes the variety of ways in which it enables local communities to get involved. The experiences of a volunteer who became a Great Wall Patroller are then recounted by Liang Qingli and Liu Wenyan; these not only explain Liang Qingli's core responsibility of patrolling a section of the Great Wall but also his work in engaging directly with surrounding communities. Finally, Barbara Birley describes the long-established and extensive volunteer programmes developed by the Vindolanda Trust and the range of opportunities they present for local, national and international volunteers to actively participate in different aspects of the Trust's work.

The publication concludes with some reflections from Yu Bing and from Humphrey Welfare on the seminar at Jinshanling and the progress made to date in the overall Wall to Wall collaboration. Acknowledgement is also made that the Wall to Wall collaboration has now moved into a second stage in which specific areas for future collaborative working are being developed on a project-by-project basis within a broader co-ordinated framework.

The success of both of the seminars that we have held to date has been due to a lot of hard work by many people in China and in the UK. Similarly, the production of this bilingual publication has only been possible due to the enormous contributions of its translation and editorial teams.

中国长城和哈德良长城的文字砖进行介绍。冯颖分析了山海关发现的文字砖可以帮助确定不同的建造和修筑时间，而保罗·彼得维尔详细展示了哈德良长城沿线发现的刻字石中包含的丰富历史信息。

第三章集中讨论双墙调查和监测的最新进展。柴晓明总结了在 2006 到2 011 年中国长城资源调查成果，重点介绍了明长城遗存分布状况。刘文艳则专题分析了长城资源调查中有关辽东镇烽火台的成果，包括烽火台的分布、结构以及建筑材料。随后的文章介绍了遥感技术和数码技术在双墙中的应用。马修·奥基和张景的文章展现出遥感技术在双墙应用中有趣的相似性，两国都长期在国家级开展新技术应用与传统方法结合，对长城进行调查和记录，并为长城的保护管理决策服务。本章最后张剑葳等的文章描述如何在箭扣长城修复项目中应用数字技术辅助进行跟踪、记录和管理施工过程。

第四章侧重于长城保护维修的理念和实践的对比分析。汤羽扬对砖石质长城保护维修中的理念和原则进行了深入思考，兰立志等以宁夏回族自治区姚滩长城为例，解释如何应用最小干预原则开展土长城维修。麦克·考林斯分享了哈德良长城如何实施和管理保护维修工作。赵鹏则展示了箭扣长城南段的修复过程。 本章最后，比尔·格里芬和麦克·考林斯分别从不同角度论述了英国考古遗址的重建问题。格里芬强调古迹重建对遗产阐释的积极作用，考林斯则总结相关的官方政策的不断演变过程，以更为稳健和透明的方式在考量多方诉求和保持真实原则中不断寻求平衡。

最后一章的文章主要涉及双墙各自推动开放利用和公众参与的经验。尤利娅·达托–恩斯林和大卫布劳夫介绍了德国界墙之路计划的发展历史，以及它是如何通过步道、自行车道以及机动车道为游客提供更便捷游览德国境内的罗马遗迹的条件。作为对比，汉佛瑞·维尔法分享了建立哈德良长城国家步道的经验。周小凤等分享了长城开放利用的最新调研成果，指出应针对长城资源类型和开放形式进行认真评估，从而制定相应的游客开放政策。英国遗产委员会对其负责管理的长城沿线遗址景区游客参观状况进行了调查研究，乔·萨维奇阐述如何应用该调研结果调整不同遗址景区的阐释策略。最后三篇文章集中讨论了哈德良长城和中国长城如何实现公众参与这一重要目标。帕特丽夏·威克斯介绍了“安东尼长城再发现”项目，该项目位于哈德良长城的苏格兰姊妹遗产地，她分享了为鼓励当地社区参与采取的多种不同方式。梁庆立和刘文艳讲述了一名长城志愿者成长为长城保护员的故事，文章不仅介绍了梁庆立作为长城保护员的主要职责，而且也分享了他在长城家乡积极动员公众参与长城保护工作的经验。最后，芭芭拉·博利展示了文多兰达信托长期以来开展的大规模志愿者项目，以及为本地、全国乃至国际志愿者提供的一系列志愿活动，志愿者活跃在文多兰达信托的各个领域工作中。

本论文集的最后，于冰和汉佛瑞·维尔法分享了他们在金山岭研讨会中的一些思考，以及回顾了双墙对话这一合作项目中取得的成就。另外还介绍双墙对话合作项目已经进入到第二阶段，重点是在宏观合作框架内推进多个领域具体合作项目的落实。

迄今为止两次研讨会的圆满召开离不开中国和英国许多工作人员的通力合作。同样，本部双语论文集的结集出版也离不开翻译团队和编辑团队的巨大付出。

GLOSSARY
术语表

于冰, 大卫・布劳夫, 汉佛瑞・维尔法
YU BING, DAVID BROUGH, HUMPHREY WELFARE

INTRODUCTION
介绍

The tables below are divided into four sections.
以下表格分为四部分。

Section 1.1 includes English translations and explanations of some specific terminology related to the archaeology of the Great Wall.
1.1部分包括与长城考古相关的一些特定术语的英文翻译和解释。

Section 1.2 includes English translations and explanations of key regulatory, administrative, conservation and heritage management organisations and terminology related to the management and conservation of the Great Wall of China.
1.2部分包括与中国长城管理和保护相关的监管、行政、保护、遗产管理组织的关键术语的英文翻译和解释。

Section 2.1 includes Chinese translations and explanations of some specific terminology related to the archaeology of Hadrian's Wall together with some further terminology specific to its management and conservation.
2.1部分包括与哈德良长城考古相关，以及一些特定于其管理和保护的术语的中文翻译和解释。

Section 2.2 includes Chinese translations and explanations of key regulatory, administrative, conservation and heritage management policies and organisations related to the management and conservation of Hadrian's Wall.
2.2部分包括与哈德良长城管理和保护相关的监管、行政、保护、遗产管理政策以及相关组织的中文翻译和解释。

This glossary is an updated version of that which appeared in *Wall to Wall: the Hadrian's Wall and Great Wall of China Management Seminar Proceedings*, published in 2019 by the Chinese Academy of Cultural Heritage and Historic England. It includes some additional terms and some revision of definitions and recommended translations of several others.
在2019年由中国文化遗产研究院和英格兰遗产委员会主编的《双墙对话——哈德良长城与中国长城保护管理研讨会文集》中术语表的基础上，本术语表有所补充和修改。

1. ENGLISH GLOSSARY OF CHINESE TERMINOLOGY
1.中文术语的英文对照表

1.1 与长城相关的专用术语与词汇
Section 1.1 Great Wall specific terminology and vocabulary

Original Chinese (Hanzi and Pinyin) 中文原文（加拼音标注）	Meaning in Chinese 中文释义	(Recommended) English translation 英文翻译	Meaning / Description in English 英文释义
边 Bian	长城沿线的区域性边境军事指挥区。	*Bian*	A regional frontier or boundary military command area along the Great Wall.
堡 Bu or Bao 镇城 Zhencheng 路城 lucheng 卫城 Weicheng 所城 Suocheng 堡城 Bucheng	筑有城、围的屯兵、居住地，为长城防御体系的重要组成部分，与墙体不发生直接关联。 根据军事级别分为镇城、路城、卫城、所城和堡城。	fort fortress *Zhen*-fort *Lu*-fort *Wei*-fort *Suo*-fort *Bu*-fort	A defended enclosure containing barracks or living quarters, constituting an integral part of the Great Wall defence system but not attached to the Wall itself. According to military hierarchy, they comprise of *Zhen*-forts, *Lu*-forts, *Wei*-forts, *Suo*-forts and *Bu*-forts.
长城 各时代长城 各段长城 Changcheng Geshidai changcheng Geduan changcheng	分布于全国15个省、自治区、直辖市，由不同朝代建立的长城防御体系的统称。既可作为通用术语，也可作为特指用语，指特定时期（如楚长城，指由楚国建造的长城），或特定点段（如金山岭长城，指金山岭段长城），或特定地区（如北京长城，指北京市境内长城段落和相关设施）。	the Great Wall	A collective term for each of the Great Wall defence systems built by different kingdoms and dynasties across 15 present day Provinces, Direct Municipalities and Autonomous Regions in China. It is used either as a general term, or a specific term for a specific time (the Chu Great Wall which means the Great Wall of the Chu State), or for a specific section or site (the Jinshanling Great Wall which means the Jinshanling section of the Great Wall) or a specific region (the Beijing Great Wall which means the sections and related facilities of the Great Wall within Beijing Direct Municipality).
长城地带 Changcheng didai	指长城及其附属设施所分布的宽阔地域。	the Great Wall Zone / Corridor	The broad band of territory across which each of the different Great Wall systems were built.
长城资源认定分类 Changcheng ziyuan rending fenlei 墙体qiangti 壕堑 haoqian 单体建筑danti jianzhu 关堡guanbu 相关设施 xiangguan sheshi	2012年国家文物局组织的长城资源认定分以下几类： －墙体，包括人工墙体和自然险 －壕堑，壕堑和界壕 －单体建筑，包括敌台、马面、水关、烽火台、铺房等 －关堡，包括关和堡 －相关设施，包括挡马墙、品字窖、壕沟。	The Great Wall Resource Rectification categories: - Walls - Trenches - Individual components and structures - Passes and forts - Other features	The Great Wall Resource Rectification organized by SACH in 2012 uses the following categories: Walls: including man-made walls and natural barriers; Trenches: including trenches and the Trench-Wall; Individual components and structures: including defence towers, horse faces, water gates, beacon towers, sentry houses, etc.; Passes and forts: including fortified passes, strategic passes, forts and fortresses; and Other features: including horse walls, pin-shape pits, and ditches.

Original Chinese (Hanzi and Pinyin) 中文原文（加拼音标注）	Meaning in Chinese 中文释义	(Recommended) English translation 英文翻译	Meaning / Description in English 英文释义
城楼 Chenglou 其他名称 门楼Menlou 战棚Zhanpeng 楼子Louzi 敌团Dituan 堞楼Dielou	建于长城墙体上用于瞭望和射击的建筑物。	gate tower	Buildings built above gates within walls for observation and defence.
挡马墙Dangmaqiang 其他名称 羊马垣Yangmayuan 副墙Fuqiang 小长城Xiaochangcheng	构筑在长城墙体外，平行于长城墙体或护城壕的墙体,多用于抵挡骑兵。	horse wall	An external wall parallel to the Wall or trench wall, often used to prevent or impede cavalry attacks.
敌台Ditai 其他名称 敌楼Dilou 墩台Duntai	突出于城墙的防御型高台，可分为空心和实心两种。	defence tower	A tower built along the Great Wall itself to protect against attacks, which can be either chambered or solid.
垛口 Duokou 其他名称 女口Nvkou 雉堞Zhidie 垛口墙Duokouqiang	城墙顶部外侧连续凹凸的矮墙。	battlement	The crenellated parapet on top of the Wall.
烽火台 Fenghuotai 其他名称 烽燧Fengsui 墩台Duntai 烽堠Fenghou 烟墩Yandun 狼烟台Langyantai 狼烟墩Langyandun	指在长城沿线用于点燃烟火传递重要信息的高台，是长城防御体系的重要组成部分。	beacon tower	A high platform on the top of which a signal beacon could be placed, constituting an integral part of the Great Wall defence system.
关 Guan 其他名称	一般指筑有城、围的屯兵地，一般依托于墙体。	Pass (for place-names) fortified pass (as a noun)	A fortification system guarding a mountain pass.
壕堑 Haoqian	包括壕和界壕。	trench trench wall	Can mean either the Trench Wall of the Jin Dynasty or a trench accompanying an earthen, brick or stone walll.
空心敌台 Kongxinditai	内部中空的敌台，更适于保护守城士兵。	chambered tower	A type of defence tower, with internal rooms offering greater protection to soldiers guarding the Great Wall.
马面 Mamian 其他名称 城垛Chengduo 墙台Qiangtai 墙垛Qiangduo	依附于城墙外侧、与城墙同高的台子。	horse face	A terrace attached to the exterior and at the same height as the Wall.

Original Chinese (Hanzi and Pinyin) 中文原文（加拼音标注）	Meaning in Chinese 中文释义	(Recommended) English translation 英文翻译	Meaning / Description in English 英文释义
马道 Madao	墙体内侧供人、马上下通行的道路。	horse path	A road on the inner side of the Wall for people and horses going to and from the Wall.
炮台 Paotai	建于长城墙体上设置火炮的平台。	artillery platform	Platforms built on top of the Wall as artillery emplacements.
铺舍 Pushe 其他名称 楼橹Loulu 铺房Pufang	建于城墙或者敌台上，供守城士兵巡逻放哨时遮风避雨的建筑物，也是戍卒休息和储备军用物品的场所。	sentry house	A building built on city walls or on defensive towers for the patrolling soldiers to find shelter from harsh weather, also used by garrison soldiers to rest and store material.
山险墙 Shanxianqiang	利用险要，经人为加工形成的险阻。	cut wall	Sections of the Wall created by cutting away sections of hills or mountains.
石墙Shiqiang	构筑时外观以石筑为主的墙体。	stone wall	Refers to wall whose exterior at the time of construction was mainly built with stone.
水门 Shuimen 其他名称 水窦Shuidou 水关Shuiguan	墙体上开设的便于下方河流和墙上积水排泄的设施。	water gate	A channel built into the Wall to allow streams to pass underneath and rainfall to be drained from the Wall.
土墙Tuqiang	构筑时外观以土筑为主的墙体。	earth wall	Refers to wall whose exterior at the time of construction was mainly built with earth.
坞墙 Wuqiang	敌台外侧的低矮围墙，上有箭孔用于防御。	outskirt wall	A low wall built surrounding some defence towers, with arrow slits to bolster the defence.
战台Zhantai	升起的建于长城外侧的进攻平台，可从上攻击来敌，为金山岭长城较典型设施。	battle platform	A raised platform, typically on a branch wall exterior to the Great Wall, from which the advancing enemy could be attacked, a typical facility at Jinshanling section.
障墙 Zhangqiang	为防止守城士兵暴露于敌人的视线和射程之内而构筑在墙体上横向防御的短墙。多建于墙体陡峭处。	barrier wall	A series of short walls constructed on the Wall perpendicular to the battlement to prevent the defending soldiers from being exposed to enemy vision and fire, usually only built on steep parts of the Wall.
镇 zhen	明朝年间，北部边境沿长城防线设立九边，即区域性军事指挥区，每边设一军事指挥所，称为镇，有时"边""镇"通用。	*Zhen*	During the Ming Dynasty, there were nine *Bians*, or regional military frontier or boundary areas along the Great Wall, a *Zhen* was where the headquarters of each *Bian* was located. Sometimes *Zhen* is also used interchangeably with *Bian*, denoting a military region.
砖墙 Zhuanqiang	构筑时外观以砖筑为主的墙体。	brick wall	Refers to wall whose exterior at the time of construction was mainly built with brick.
自然险 Ziranxian	指在地势险要之处，与墙体共同构成防御体系的山体、河流、沟壑等自然地物。	natural barriers	Natural features such as mountains, rivers, and gullies which, together with the Wall, constitute a defensive system.

1.2 与长城相关法规、行政管理、保护和管理机构相关的用语
Section 1.2 Chinese Regulatory, administrative, conservation and heritage management organisations and terminology related to the Great Wall

Original Chinese (Hanzi and Pinyin) 中文原文（加拼音标注）	Meaning in Chinese 中文释义	(Recommended) English translation 英文翻译	Meaning / Description in English 英文释义
保养维护 Baoyang weihu	对文物的轻微损害所作的日常性、季节性的养护。	maintenance	Routine and daily repair to minor damages.
不改变原状 Bu gaibian yuanzhuang	真实、完整地保护文物古迹在历史过程中形成的价值及体现这种价值的状态，有效地保护文物古迹的历史、文化环境，并通过保护延续相关的文化传统。	no change to the historical condition no change to the historical fabric	To conserve authentically -the values accumulated through history and their status embodied in monuments and sites, protect effectively their historical and cultural environment, and sustain their related cultural traditions through conservation and protection.
长城保护管理工程（2005-2014） Changcheng baohu guanli gongcheng	由国务院批准，国家文物局组织实施的10年项目，旨在提升长城保护和管理。	the Great Wall Conservation Programme (2005-2014)	A 10 year programme launched by the State Administration for Cultural Heritage (SACH) under the support of the State Council in 2006 to strengthen conservation and management of the Great Wall.
长城保护条例 Changcheng baohu tiaoli	2006年由国务院颁布，是中国为专门文物颁发的最高法规。	the Great Wall Protection Regulation	A regulation promulgated by the State Council in 2006, the only one in China for a specific cultural heritage site.
长城保护员 Changcheng baohuyuan	受各地政府聘用的兼职人员，职责包括巡视长城保护状况及向有关部门上报长城损坏情况。	the Great Wall Patrollers	Part-time workers recruited by local authorities who monitor the condition of the Great Wall and report any damage or destruction to its fabric to the authorities.
长城资源调查 Changcheng ziyuan diaocha	2006-2012年间，由国家文物局组织实施的对长城全线的首次调查，属于"长城保护工程（2005-2014年）总体工作方案"一部分。	the Great Wall Resource Survey	The first ever national-level Wall-wide survey of all surviving elements of the Great Walls in China, organized by SACH between 2006- 2012, as part of tasks provided in the Great Wall Conservation Programme (2005-2014).
公益组织 Gongyi zuzhi	非政府、非营利性质的提供公益性服务的机构。	the third sector	Often literally translated as 'public interest' organisations which are neither government led nor for-profit organisations and provide services for public purposes and benefits.
国家文物局 Guojia wenwujv	国务院文物主管部门2018年之前官方英译为 the State Administration of Cultural Heritage (SACH), 2018年后官方英译为 the National Cultural Heritage Administration (NCHA) in 2018.	the State Administration of Cultural Heritage (SACH) before 2018; the National Cultural Heritage Administration (NCHA) from 2018 onwards.	The State Council governmental department in charge of cultural heritage in China. Its official English translation was the State Administration of Cultural Heritage (SACH) before 2018 and changed to the National Cultural Heritage Administration in 2018.
国务院 Guowuyuan	中国中央政府最高国家权力的执行机关。	the State Council	The highest executive body of China's central government.

Original Chinese (Hanzi and Pinyin) 中文原文（加拼音标注）	Meaning in Chinese 中文释义	(Recommended) English translation 英文翻译	Meaning / Description in English 英文释义
IP	中国国内最新流行的概念，意思是一个符号、品牌、或想法有市场营销和商业化的创意产业潜力，利于新品牌产品的开发，如手机app、游戏、卡通、电影、纪念品以及其他商品。	IP branding	A very popular new concept now in China which means a symbol, brand, or an idea that has marketing and commercialization potential for creative industries for the development of new branded products such as mobile apps, games, cartoons and movies, as well as souvenirs and other merchandise.
考古清理 Kaogu qingli	以专业考古学家为主导进行的考古发掘和现场清理。	archaeologically led site clearance	Work by professional archaeological organisations to identify the original archaeological remains and direct the clearance of debris and vegetation and site preparation prior to conservation.
利用 Liyong	《文物保护法》用语。根据《中国文物古迹保护准则》，利用包括研究、展示、延续原有功能和赋予文物古迹适宜的当代功能等各种利用方式，保持文物古迹在当代社会生活中的活力。	use utilisation	This is a term used in the Cultural Relics Protection Law (CRPL) CRPL. According to the China Principles uses include research, presentation, keeping original functions, or reviving proper contemporary functions of monuments and sites, aiming to maintain their vitality in contemporary social life.
抢险加固 Qiangxian jiagu	指文物突发严重危险时，由于时间、技术、经费等条件的限制，不能进行彻底修缮而对文物采取具有可逆性的临时抢险加固措施的工程。	emergency stabilisation and consolidation	Refers to reversible and temporary measures taken to rescue and reinforce those cultural relics in serious danger which cannot be reinstated due to time, technical issues, funding and other constraints.
社会组织 Shehui zuzhi	根据中国相关法规，社会组织指在不同级别的政府民政部门注册的社会团体、基金会、民办非企业实体三类公益组织。	Social Organisations	Social Organisations, according to Chinese regulations, refer to three types of organisations, i.e. social groups, foundations, and private non-enterprise entities registered with government civil affairs departments of different levels.
“四有”工作 “Siyou” gongzuo	《文物保护法》要求文物保护单位应当具备的四项基础工作：划定必要保护范围，作出标志说明，建立记录档案，并区别情况分别设立专门机构或者专人负责管理。	the Four Haves	The four legal prerequisites for designated Protected Units of Cultural Relics (PUCRs) in China, which require each site to have: demarcated boundaries; an official plaque stating its name, its level and date of designation; an archive cataloguing its protected elements and activities; a dedicated organization or person(s) responsible for its daily management.
文物 Wenwu	中国基本概念和法律术语，涵盖所有可移动和不可移动物质文化遗产，因其历史、艺术、科学价值而受到保护。	cultural relic(s)	A basic legal term and fundamental concept in China. It is used to cover all movable and immovable material objects of cultural heritage that should be protected for their historic, artistic or scientific values.

Original Chinese (Hanzi and Pinyin) 中文原文（加拼音标注）	Meaning in Chinese 中文释义	(Recommended) English translation 英文翻译	Meaning / Description in English 英文释义
文物保护单位 Wenwu baohu danwei	根据《文物保护法》，不可移动文物根据其价值，可以公布为国家、省、市、县级文物保护单位。中国已公布 8 批全国 重点文物保护单位，共5058个。文物保护单位约相当于英国录登古迹 和注册建筑。	Protected Units of Cultural Relics (PUCR)	According to CRPL, immovable cultural relics can be designated, according to their significance, as national, provincial, municipal and county levels of Protected Units of Cultural Relics. There have been designated eight batches of National Key Protected Units of Cultural Relics (NKPUCR) with a total of 5058 in China. PUCRs are approximately the equivalent of Scheduled Monuments in the UK.
文物保护工程 Wenwu baohu gongcheng	根据中国相关文物保护工程管理办法，包括保养维护工程、抢险加固工程、修缮工程、保护性设施建设工程、迁移工程等类型。	cultural relics conservation project	The term used in related Chinese regulations, to refer to conservation projects in the following categories: maintenance; emergency stabilisation and consolidation; conservation; protective facility construction; and relocation of cultural relics.
文物部门 Wenwu bumen	省、市、县级政府部门及其下属机构，主要负责本辖区内所有文物的保存、维护和管理。	Cultural Relics Departments	The departments at Provincial, Municipal and County-level governments, together with their subordinate agencies, with principal responsibility for administration and management of protection and conservation of all cultural relics within their jurisdiction.
修缮 Xiushan	指为保护文物本体所必需的结构加固处理和维修，包括结合结构加固而进行的局部复原工程。	conservation	Refers to the structural consolidation and repair measures necessary to protect the fabric of the cultural relic, including partial reinstatement in conjunction with structural consolidation.
中国文化遗产研究院 Zhongguo wenhua yichan yanjiuyuan	国家文物局直属的唯一国家级文化遗产保护科学技术研究机构。	the Chinese Academy of Cultural Heritage	The sole national academic body providing technical and policy advice on the management and conservation of cultural relics which reports to NCHA.
中国文物保护基金会 Zhongguo wenwu baohu jijinhui	成立于1990年，由国家文物局主管的具有独立法人地位的全国公募性公益基金组织于2017年成为注册慈善组织。	the China Foundation for Cultural Heritage Conservation	A national charitable foundation founded in 1990, with independent legal status under the supervision of the National Cultural Heritage Administration (NCHA), and accredited as a registered charity in 2017.
中国文物古迹保护准则 Zhongguo Wenwu Guji Baohu Zhunze	2000 年，由中国国家文物局推荐，国际古迹遗址理事会中国国家委员会（中国古迹遗址保护协会）与美国盖蒂保护所、澳大利亚遗产委员会合作编制《中国文物古迹保护准则》，2015 年经中国古迹遗产保护协会组织修订发布。	Principles for the Conservation of Heritage and Sites in China (China Principles)	The Principles for the Conservation of Heritage and Sites in China was drafted by the National Committee of China ICOMOS, in cooperation with Getty Conservation Institute and the Australian Heritage Commission. As the most authoritative rules and major standards in the cultural heritage sector, it was issued in 2000 at the approval by SACH and revised by ICOMOS China and re-issued in 2015.

Original Chinese (Hanzi and Pinyin) 中文原文（加拼音标注）	Meaning in Chinese 中文释义	(Recommended) English translation 英文翻译	Meaning / Description in English 英文释义
中华人民共和国文物保护法 Zhonghua renmin gongheguo wenwu baohu fa	最早颁布于1982年，并于2002年修订。总共八章，包括总则、不可移动文物、考古发掘、馆藏文物、民间收藏文物、文物出境进境、法律责任、附则。	Cultural Relics Protection Law of the People's Republic of China (CRPL)	First promulgated in 1982 and revised in 2002. There are 8 chapters including: general provisions, immovable cultural relics, archaeological excavations, cultural relics in museums, private collections of cultural relics, import and export of cultural relics, legal responsibilities, supplementary provisions.
最低限度干预 Zuidi Chengdu ganyu	把干预限制在保证文物古迹安全的程度上。	minimum intervention	Intervention should be limited to ensuring the structural stability of monuments and sites.

2.0 CHINESE GLOSSARY OF ENGLISH TERMINOLOGY 英文术语的中文对照表

Section 2.1 Hadrian's Wall specific terminology and vocabulary 2.1与哈德良长城相关的专用术语与词汇

English 英文原文	Meaning / Description in English 英文释义	(Recommended) Translation in Chinese (Hanzi and Pinyin) 中文原文（加拼音标注）	Description in Chinese 中文释义
the Broad Wall	The original specification for Hadrian's Wall, only partly completed, measuring approximately 3m wide.	宽墙 Kuanqiang	哈德良长城最初规格，仅部分建成，宽约 3 米。
the Clayton Wall	The stretches of the Wall purchased and partly rebuilt by antiquarian John Clayton in the 19th century.	克莱顿长城 Kelaidun changcheng	由古物研究者约翰・克莱顿购买并部分重建的哈德良长城部分。
earthworks	A generic term to describe archaeological features made from earth or turf, including those mounded up into banks or wall and those created by digging out earth, such as ditches. The Vallum represents a combination of both.	土质工事 Tuzhi Gongshi	用于描述用土或草皮建成的考古遗址的统称，包括堆筑起来的堤岸或墙体，及挖掘出来的沟堑。南部壕沟即属于两者的结合
fort	Defended Roman military constructions for infantry and cavalry garrisons. They were built to standardised designs throughout the Roman Empire, although their sizes varied.	要塞 Yaosai	为罗马步兵和骑兵提供防御的军事建筑。在罗马帝国内其建筑设计标准统一，而规模有所不同。
fortlet	A small fort.	小要塞 Xiaoyaosai	小型要塞。
Hadrian's Wall	The continuous linear barrier (and its associated infrastructure) built across the north of England upon the orders of the Emperor Hadrian from AD122.	哈德良长城 Hadeliang changcheng	始建于公元 122 年罗马哈德良皇帝时期，建于英格兰北部的防御工事（及其附属设施）。
the Limes	A generic Latin term for the Roman imperial frontier system.	界墙 Jieqiang	罗马帝国边疆防御体系的拉丁语通称。

English 英文原文	Meaning / Description in English 英文释义	(Recommended) Translation in Chinese (Hanzi and Pinyin) 中文原文（加拼音标注）	Description in Chinese 中文释义
milecastle	A fortlet that provided a gate through Hadrian's Wall, and which housed 15 to 30 soldiers. Milecastles were built at intervals of approximately 1 Roman mile, and each one has been numbered by archaeologists sequentially from east to west.	里堡 Libao	城墙上每隔大约1罗马里（1479米）修建的小要塞，设出入口，能容纳15-30名士兵，每处里堡均由考古学家从东至西依次编号。
the Military Way	The Roman military road, usually built between the Wall and the Vallum, that linked the forts.	军道 Jundao	罗马帝国的军事道路，常建于哈德良长城墙体和南部壕沟之间，沟通各要塞。
the Narrow Wall	The second specification for Hadrian's Wall measuring approximately 2 to 2.5m wide – an economy measure.	窄墙 Zhaiqiang	出于节约成本考虑，哈德良长城采用的第二种建设规格，宽约2-2.5米。
the Stanegate	The Roman road which ran east - west between the Roman towns at Corbridge and Carlisle, south of Hadrian's Wall. The road and the Roman forts built along it pre-date the construction of Hadrian's Wall.	石路 Shilu	考布里奇和卡莱尔罗马城镇之间，哈德良长城以南东西走向的罗马道路。该道路及其沿线的罗马要塞比哈德良长城建设时间更早。
temporary camp	A Roman military earthwork enclosing a unit of soldiers when they were on the move or while they were constructing more permanent features such as roads, forts and Hadrian's Wall itself.	临时营地 Linshi yingdi	罗马军团行军时，或建设长期设施如道路、要塞、哈德良长城墙体时，保护部队的临时土质防御工事。
the Turf Wall	The early form of Hadrian's Wall in the west, running from the Irthing river to the Solway Firth. It was built from cut blocks of turf, and measured approximately 6m wide and 3.5m high. It was subsequently rebuilt in stone.	草被长城 Caobei changcheng	哈德良长城西段的早期形态，从厄辛河延伸到索尔维狭湾。由切割好的草皮块建成，宽约6米，高3米，之后改用石块重建。
turret	Small observation and signalling towers built into the Wall at regular intervals of approximately 1/3 of a Roman mile. The two turrets between each Milecastle are numbered according to their Wall-mile, sequentially A and B, east to west.	塔楼 Talou	小型观察塔和信号塔，在墙体上每 1/3 罗马里等距修建。每个里堡之间的两个塔楼根据其区段，从 A和B顺序编号。
the Vallum	A broad ditch, flanked by banks, forming an additional barrier on the interior side of the Wall. Translated here as "southern ditch" to differentiate from "ditch", which is on the northern (exterior) side of the Wall.	南部壕沟 Nanbu haogou	宽阔的壕沟，两侧为堤岸，在城墙内侧形成一道额外的障碍。为区别于墙体北侧（外侧）的 ditch，特译为南侧壕沟。
vicus	A civilian settlement outside a Roman fort.	平民聚落 Pingmin jvluo	罗马要塞外围的居民居住点。
wall-mile	The name given by archaeologists to identify sections of Hadrian's Wall between Milecastles. Each Wall-mile is numbered sequentially from east to west.	区段 Quduan	考古学家为辨识哈德良长城里堡之间墙体段落而起的指定名称，从东往西顺序编号。
the Whin Sill	A distinctive geological feature of volcanic rock, forming ridges along which much of the central sector of Hadrian's Wall was constructed.	暗色岩床 Anse yanchuang	火山岩的独特地质特征，形成了哈德良长城中央部分沿线的山脊。

Section 2.2 UK heritage organisations and related regulatory, administrative and conservation terminology related to Hadrian's Wall
与哈德良长城相关的英国法规、行政管理、保护和管理机构相关的用语

English 英文原文	Meaning / Description in English 英文释义	(Recommended) Translation in Chinese (Hanzi and Pinyin) 中文原文（加拼音标注）	Description in Chinese 中文释义
the Antonine Wall	The section of the Frontiers of the Roman Empire World Heritage Site in Scotland. It runs from the Firth of Forth to the Firth of Clyde, north of Edinburgh and Glasgow respectively and was occupied for about 25 years in the mid 2nd century AD.	安东尼长城 Andongni changcheng	位于苏格兰的罗马帝国边疆世界遗产区段。从爱丁堡以北的福斯湾延伸到格拉斯哥以北的克莱德湾，在公元2世纪中期使用了约25年。
Area of Outstanding Natural Beauty (AONB)	A formal designation of natural heritage landscapes of particular beauty that are protected from development.	突出自然风景区 Jiechu ziran fengjingqu	正式公布的，具有特殊美学价值的自然遗产景观，以免受开发破坏。
community archaeology	Archaeological excavation and survey projects designed to involve volunteers from local communities working alongside professional archaeologists.	社区考古 Shequ kaogu	由当地社区志愿者与专业考古学家一起开展的考古发掘和调查项目。
conserve as found	The prevailing principle in UK archaeological conservation, through which surviving original archaeological remains are simply stabilised in the form in which they are discovered, rather than reconstructed or reassembled.	按发现时状态保护 An faxianshi zhuangtai baohu	英国考古遗址保护中的主要原则，即只将幸存的考古遗迹稳定在其被发现时的状态，而不进行重建或规整。
Conservation Principles, Policy and Guidance	The principal UK policy document concerning cultural heritage conservation, published by English Heritage in 2008.	保护原则、政策和指南 Baohu yuanze, zhengce he zhinan	英国文化遗产保护的主要政策文件，由英格兰遗产委员会于2008年出版。
Department of Digital, Culture, Media and Sport (DCMS)	The UK Government Department with ultimate responsibility for cultural heritage conservation and management policy.	英国数字、文化、媒体和体育部 Yingguo shuzi wenhua meiti he tiyu bu	对文化遗产保护和管理政策负有最终责任的英国政府部门。
English Heritage	The informal name for 'The English Heritage Trust', established in 2012 to manage historic sites in England owned by the UK Government. Prior to 2012 English Heritage was a non-departmental public body which included the responsibilities of what is now Historic England.	英格兰遗产信托 Yinggelan yichan xintuo	"英格兰遗产信托"的简称，成立于2012年，负责经营管理英国政府拥有的英格兰历史古迹。2012 年之前，指现在的非部门公共机构英国遗产委员会。
generic consent	A scheme, first developed on Hadrian's Wall, through which minor routine maintenance and conservation work to Scheduled Monuments can be licenced without individual consent.	通用登录古迹许可 Tongyong (denglu guji) xuke	最初应用于哈德良长城的一种许可，可在未经单独批准的情况下对登录古迹开展一系列小型日常维护和保护工作。
Hadrian's Wall World Heritage Site	The protected elements of the Roman frontier defence system, inscribed in 1987. It is now a part of the Frontiers of the Roman Empire World Heritage Site.	哈德良长城世界遗产地 Hadeliang changcheng shijie yichandi	于1987年列为世界遗产的罗马边疆体系。现在是罗马帝国边疆世界遗产的一部分。

English 英文原文	Meaning / Description in English 英文释义	(Recommended) Translation in Chinese (Hanzi and Pinyin) 中文原文（加拼音标注）	Description in Chinese 中文释义
Hadrian's Wall Cycleway	One of a network of National Cycle Routes across the UK. Opened in 2007, it runs from Ravenglass on the Cumbrian coast to Wallsend.	哈德良长城自行车道 Hadeliang changcheng zixingche dao	英国国家自行车路线网络之一。于2007年开业，从坎布里亚海岸的雷文格拉斯延伸到沃森德。
Hadrian's Wall Path National Trail	One of a network of National Trails, it was opened in 2003 and follows the line of Hadrian's Wall from Wallsend in the east to Bowness-on-Solway in the west.	哈德良长城国家步道 Hadeliang changcheng guojia budao	国家步道网络之一，于2003年开放，沿哈德良长城尽东的沃森德延伸到西部的波尼斯-索尔维。
Hadrian's Wall Research Framework	An assessment of archaeological knowledge of Hadrian's Wall, published in 2009, which identifies academic priorities for further research. This assessment is currently being updated.	哈德良长城研究框架 Hadeliang changcheng yanji ukuangjia	2009年发表的对哈德良长城考古研究的评估，确定了进一步的学术研究重点，目前正在更新中。
Hadrian's Wall World Heritage Site Interpretation Framework	A set of principles and guidelines for the development of interpretation at sites and museums across Hadrian's Wall.	哈德良长城世界遗产地阐释框架 Hadeliang changcheng shijie yichandi chanshi kuangjia	为哈德良长城沿线遗址和博物馆开展遗产阐释制定的一系列原则和指南。
Hadrian's Wall World Heritage Site Management Plan	The document which sets out the priority issues facing the management of the World Heritage Site, and the agreed policies and actions necessary to address them. This document is reviewed and updated every 5 to 6 years.	哈德良长城世界遗产地管理规划 Hadeliang changcheng shijie yichandi guanli guihua	文件包括世界遗产管理所面临的优先问题，以及为解决这些问题而达成一致意见的政策和行动。每5至6年审核和更新。
Hadrian's Wall World Heritage Site Management Plan Co-ordinator	The individual responsible for co-ordinating the activities of partner organisations involved in managing and conserving the World Heritage Site.	哈德良长城世界遗产地管理规划协调员 Hadeliang changcheng shijie yichandi guanli guihua xietiaoyuan	负责协调参与管理和保护世界遗产地合作组织的活动的人。
The Hadrian's Wall World Heritage Site Partnership Board	The body which oversees the policies, objectives and actions for the conservation and management of the World Heritage Site.	哈德良长城世界遗产合作委员会 Hadeliang changcheng shijie yichandi hezuo weiyuanhui	负责统筹世界遗产保护和管理的政策、目标和行动的机构。
Heritage at Risk Register	A list of heritage sites at risk of damage or destruction, compiled by Historic England in collaboration with Local Authorities.	濒危遗产名录 Binwei yichan minglu	由英格兰遗产委员会会同地方政府编制的有受损或毁坏风险的遗产地点清单。
Historic England	The informal name for 'Historic Buildings and Monuments of England' the national non-departmental public body responsible for advising national and local government about the conservation and management of heritage sites and historic buildings.	英格兰遗产委员会 Yinggelan yichan weiyuanhui	"英格兰历史建筑和古迹委员会"的简称，是负责向国家和地方政府提供有关遗产地和历史建筑的保护管理建议的国家非部门公共机构。

English 英文原文	Meaning / Description in English 英文释义	(Recommended) Translation in Chinese (Hanzi and Pinyin) 中文原文（加拼音标注）	Description in Chinese 中文释义
Local Authority	The general name given to municipal and county level local government.	地方政府 Difangzhengfu	对市、县级地方政府的统称。
National Planning Policy Framework (NPPF)	The national guidance document which sets out Planning policies and principles across England.	国家规划政策框架 Guojia guihua zhengce kuangjia	制定整个英格兰的规划政策和原则的国家指导文件。
Natural England	The national non-departmental public body responsible for advising national and local government about the conservation and management of the natural environment.	英格兰自然委员会 Yinggelan ziran weiyuanhui	国家非部门公共机构，负责向国家和地方政府提供有关自然环境保护和管理的建议。
Planning Authority	The generic name for local government which has specific responsibility for authorising new development.	规划部门 Guihua bumen	对负责审批新开发建设项目的地方政府部门的统称。
scheduled monument	Cultural heritage sites which are officially designated as protected by law.	登录古迹 Denglu guji	官方公布的受法律保护的文化遗产地。
Scheduled Monument Consent	The official authorisation required for any work on, or alterations to, a Scheduled Monument.	登录古迹许可 Denglu guji xuke	对登录古迹进行任何施工或变动所需的官方批准。
Site of Special Scientific Interest (SSSI)	A designated area protecting biological or geological sites of national importance.	具特殊科学价值地点 Jv teshu kexuejiazhi didian	为保护有国家级重要性的生物或地质遗址而设的指定区域。
the Frontiers of Roman Empire	The collective term used to describe the border regions of the Roman Empire from the 2nd Century AD onwards.	罗马帝国边疆 Luomadiguo bianjiang	用于描述公元2世纪以来罗马帝国的边界地区的统称。
the Frontiers of the Roman Empire World Heritage Site	The serial transnational World Heritage Site, first established in 2005, comprising Hadrian's Wall (inscribed in 1987) the Upper-German Raetian Limes (inscribed in 2005) and the Antonine Wall (inscribed in 2008).	罗马帝国边疆世界遗产地 Luomadiguo bianjiang shijie yichandi	系列跨国世界遗产，最初于2005年公布，包括哈德良长城（1987年列入）、上日尔曼-雷蒂亚长城（2005年列入）和安东尼长城（2008年列入）。
The National Trust	The third-sector body responsible for the management of over 500 cultural and natural heritage sites within the UK.	国家信托 Guojia xintuo	负责管理英国500多个文化和自然遗产地的第三部门机构。
the Third Sector	The term used to describe all those organisations which are neither publicly owned nor privately owned. This includes not-for-profit organisations, charitable trusts, and other groups and associations.	公益组织 Disan bumen	用于描述所有非公共也非私有的组织，包括非营利组织，慈善信托以及其他团体和协会。
the Upper-German Raetian Limes	The section of the Frontiers of the Roman Empire World Heritage Site in Germany which runs from the River Rhine to the upper Danube.	上日尔曼-雷蒂亚长城 Shangri'erman-leidiya changcheng	在德国部分的罗马帝国世界遗产边疆，从莱茵河延伸到多瑙河上游。

Chapter 1:

General Management

Turret 41a (Caw Gap), looking east along the crags toward Housesteads. This is an example of a turret that was demolished in the later second century, leaving only the first course of stonework to be 'discovered' by archaeologists. (© Matthew Symonds).

41a号塔楼（科盖普），沿峭壁向东边的豪塞斯特兹方向拍摄。在这个典型案例中，塔楼在公元2世纪晚期被毁，后被考古工作者“发现”，仅存一层砌石结构（© 马修·西蒙德）。

第一单元

长城宏观管理

The Jinshanling Great Wall, Hebei, is a representative section of the Ming Dynasty Great Wall built of brick and stone. The Second Hadrian's Wall and Great Wall of China Management Seminar was held at the foot of Jinshanling (photograph by Ji Zhengquan).

河北金山岭长城，中国明长城砖石质长城的典型代表段落，第二届中国长城和哈德良长城保护管理研讨会即在金山岭长城脚下召开（摄影：纪正权）。

1.1 MANAGEMENT PLANNING FOR UK WORLD HERITAGE SITES

DAVID BROUGH
Newcastle University - Newcastle upon Tyne - UK

Abstract

In 1996 Hadrian's Wall became the first UK World Heritage Site to produce a Management Plan; since then all UK World Heritage Sites have each developed such a Plan. This paper explains how the concept of Management Planning for World Heritage Sites emerged in the UK. Whilst acknowledging that UK WHS Management Plans vary in their structure and in their content, the paper provides a summary of the primary elements which feature in most UK WHS Plans. It then outlines the principal benefits of Management Planning for World Heritage Sites, with particular emphasis on the benefits of a participative process in Management Planning, which it also describes. The issues discussed are illustrated through the experience of Hadrian's Wall WHS in the development of its successive Management Plans over the last 25 years.

Keywords: World Heritage Sites, Management Plan, Management Planning, Hadrian's Wall

THE EMERGENCE OF MANAGEMENT PLANNING FOR WORLD HERITAGE SITES IN THE UK

The first UK World Heritage Sites (WHSs) were inscribed in 1986, but it was not until 1996 that Hadrian's Wall, inscribed in 1987, became the first to publish a formal Management Plan. Although Avebury WHS had produced a 'Management Statement' in 1992, there had been very little documentation of how the Sites were managed or how their management was determined and planned. In the 1980s and 1990s the documentation prepared in support of Sites' nominations for World Heritage inscription had typically included almost no reference to how they were currently managed, or how they were to be managed post-inscription. It was not until 2000 that the inclusion of a Management Plan became compulsory for all UK Sites wishing to be nominated for World Heritage status.

The concept of Management Planning for World Heritage Sites emerged from a number of changes in public-sector management in general and, more particularly, in the changing context in which the heritage sector was operating. The management of public-sector organisations was becoming increasingly influenced by business planning within the private sector. Within the heritage sector, the established practices of planning for research and conservation were, by the 1990s, added to by an increasing focus on project planning. This was because more and more public funding was being provided to heritage management organisations on a project-by-project basis to meet specific objectives, rather than through annual allocations. These changes began in a context of increasing scrutiny of how public funding was spent, and growing demands from both government and the public that expenditure on non-statutory activities by public bodies should be justified by the extent to which investment would meet the objectives of agreed policies or strategies; these included the delivery of economic, social, community and educational benefits. Justification was typically required to be presented through either a business case or a project plan.

In parallel with these developments, the 1990s saw increasing concerns about the provisions for the legal protection of WHSs, as there was then (and still remains) no specific UK legislation for their protection. By the early 1990s Hadrian's Wall had experienced three major planning enquiries into specific development proposals within

1.1 英国世界遗产地管理规划

大卫・布劳夫
纽卡斯尔大学—纽卡斯尔—英国

摘要

1996 年，哈德良长城成为英国第一处出台管理规划的世界遗产地。在此之后，英国境内所有世界遗产地全部出台了各自的管理规划。本文探讨英国境内世界遗产地“管理规划”这一概念是如何产生的。英国各遗产地的世界遗产管理规划在结构和内容上各不相同，本文梳理的是出现在大部分管理规划中的主要构成元素。之后，本文将简要阐述世界遗产管理规划的几大益处，尤其是强调编制过程多方参与的益处。以上内容将通过梳理过去 *25* 年间哈德良长城世界遗产地管理规划的编制过程而展开。

关键词：世界遗产地　管理规划　哈德良长城

英国境内世界遗产地“管理规划”的产生

英国第一处世界遗产地于1986年入选。然而直到1996年，1987年入选世界遗产地的哈德良长城才率先颁布正式的管理规划。尽管早在1992年，世界遗产地埃夫伯里新石器墓葬群（Avebury WHS）就编制过一份“管理声明”，但当时关于遗产地如何管理以及如何制定管理决策和管理计划的资料很少。在20世纪80和90年代，申遗材料几乎不会涉及任何当前管理情况或申遗成功后将如何管理的内容。直到 2000 年，英国所有申遗项目才都必须提交一份管理规划。

世界遗产地管理规划的概念诞生于一系列变化因素，当时的公共事业领域的宏观管理发生变革，尤其是遗产领域运营环境持续变化。公共事业组织的管理模式日益受到企业领域商业计划的影响。到20世纪90年代，遗产业内既有的研究计划和保护计划编制工作开始引入项目规划理念。这是因为，越来越多的公共资金投入到各遗产管理组织中，这些资金以项目为单位进行投入，为的是完成具体目标，而不是按年度进行分配。这些变化发生的背景是社会对公共资金支出的监督日益严格，政府和公众都日益要求公共组织说明其用于法定职能以外活动开支的理由，说明该笔投入能在多大程度上完成既定政策目标或战略目标，包括是否能带来经济、社会、社区及教育方面的效益。说明通常要求采用项目申请书或项目计划书的形式。

与此同时，在90年代，为世界遗产地提供法律保护的需求日益迫切，因为当时英国没有（至今仍然没有）专门立法保护世界遗产。至90年代早期，哈德良长城已经就遗产地范围内的具体建设项目方案开展了三轮大型规划许可论证。每一轮论证最终都以拒绝许可告终，但英格兰遗产委员会意识到有必要出台文件，进一步明确诠释世界遗产地的价值，阐释保护反映这些价值的属性要素的重要性。世界遗产管理规划概念由此产生，它将成为管控遗产区及其缓冲区建设的文件依据。

同时，世界范围内对世界遗产地管理效果的担忧日益凸显，尤其是在遗产地保护方面，越来越多遗产地被联合国教科文组织列为“濒危遗产”。这也使得第一套世界遗产地管理指引文件正式出台（菲尔顿和

the setting of the WHS. Although each was refused permission, it was recognised by English Heritage that further articulation and documentation was needed of the value of the WHS, and of the importance of protecting the attributes which conveyed that value. The concept of a WHS Management Plan therefore emerged as a document which could be cited in the control of development within the WHS and its buffer zone.

At the same time, there was a growing international concern about the effectiveness of the management of WHSs, particularly with regard to their conservation, with an increasing number of them being listed by UNESCO as 'in danger'. This led to the publication of the first set of formal guidance on the management of WHSs (Fielden and Jokhilehto 1993), although the primary focus of this was on management systems rather than on Management Planning.

STRUCTURE AND CONTENTS OF UK WHS MANAGEMENT PLANS

Official guidance

Prior to 2005, UNESCO's Operational Guidelines for the Implementation of the World Heritage Convention made very little reference to the management of WHSs stating only that those submitting nominations for World Heritage status:

> '... are encouraged to prepare plans for the management of each natural site nominated and for the safeguarding of each cultural property nominated'. (UNESCO 2002, paragraph 21)

This clearly reflected the prevailing view that the focus of responsibility of those managing cultural WHSs should primarily be the protection of their Site. The management requirements in the 2005 update of the Operational Guidelines were, and have since remained, very general and non-specific, stating simply that each WHS should have:

> '... an appropriate management plan or other documented system' (UNESCO 2019, paragraph 108)

The Guidelines do not demand that WHSs produce Management Plans as such, nor do they specify their scope or what form or structure any Management Plan should take. This is an acknowledgement that because every WHS is different in its attributes (which define its outstanding universal value) and in the context in which it is managed, it follows that what may constitute an appropriate Management Plan or system will differ for each WHS, and:

> '... depends on the type, characteristics and needs of the property and its cultural and natural context ...' (ibid. paragraph 109)

Reflecting this acknowledgement, there is no set form or structure for WHS Management Plans in the UK.

Common components of UK WHS Management Plans

It is nevertheless possible to identify some components which most UK WHSs include in their Management Plans (Table 1).

Although UK Management Plans are typically updated every five years, the sections describing the Site, identifying its stakeholders and explaining its values generally require little revision in each new edition. The assessment of the management of the Site will normally concentrate on activities undertaken in the period since the previous plan was published. The identification of the principal issues and challenges facing the management of the Site, and of appropriate policies and actions to address them, may, however, involve a substantial revision of the preceding version of the plan because new challenges will often have emerged over the intervening five years. As the wider social, political, environmental, economic and technical contexts in which the Site is managed undergo change, the responses required to meet the new challenges must be altered, including management systems, responsibilities and implementation arrangements. Management Planning for a WHS should not therefore be seen as a one-off process, but as evolutionary and iterative.

乔其列托，1993），但该文件的关注点主要集中在管理体制，而非“管理规划”。

英国世界遗产管理规划的结构和内容

官方导则

2005年之前，联合国教科文组织的《保护世界自然与文化遗产公约操作指南》几乎没有涉及世界遗产管理，而只指出在提交申遗材料时，

“鼓励各遗产地在申报时为每一处自然遗产地的管理和每一处文化遗产地的保护编制相应的规划。”

（UNESCO 2002, 第 21 段）

这清晰地体现了当时的主流观点，即文化遗产地管理者的首要职责应当是遗产地的保护。2005版《操作指引》更新了对管理的要求，但仍然非常笼统，仅仅提到每处文化遗产地应当具有

“适当的管理规划或其他文件制度”（*UNESCO 2019*, 第 *108* 段）

《操作指南》并未要求世界遗产地必须编制管理规划，也没有明确管理规划的范围、形式或结构。这是考虑到每个遗产地特点不同（这些特点也决定了遗产地的“杰出普遍价值”），遗产地管理背景不同，因此每个遗产地适用的管理规划或管理体系的内容也不应相同，应：

“……取决于遗产地的类型、特点、需求，以及文化和自然背景……”（*UNESCO 2019*，第 *109* 段）

出于同样的考虑，英国的世界遗产管理规划也没有固定的形式或结构。

英国世界遗产管理规划的常见内容

尽管如此，大多数的英国世界遗产管理规划会涵盖一些共同的内容（表 1）。

在英国管理规划一般每五年更新一次，但遗产地描述、利益相关方和价值阐述等几个方面的内容在每次更新中几乎无需改动。遗产地管理评估一般侧重于上一版管理规划发布之后遗产地开展的活动。可能会较前版管理规划有更大修改的，是明确遗产地管理中的主要问题、挑战，以及适宜的政策和行动这部分内容，因为过去五年很可能出现了新的挑战。如果该遗产地的宏观社会、政治、环境、经济和技术环境发生改变，则遗产地所需采取的应对措施也必须进行改变，包括管理体制、职责划分和计划实施等。因此，世界遗产管理规划不该视作一次性工程，而是应当不断发展和迭代。

不少英国世界遗产管理规划还包括其他要素，比如各阶段遗产地的一系列管理目标。“行动”主要阐述遗产管理的一个长期方向（一般以30年为限）；“目标”或“成果”是一系列中期希望完成的工作（5到10年）；“目的”或“产出'则是更为短期的目标（3到5年），指的是需要执行和完成的具体计划，指的是需要执行和完成的具体计划，而“行动”通常是指每年的重点运行工作。

实际操作中，大部分英国管理规划将重点放在 5 年规划周期内的短期目标。很多英国规划侧重于政策和计划的评估和编制，而不涉及具体行动内容。这是因为人们意识到具体行动会随着政策的执行而变化，如果在一个为期五年的规划中明确出具体行动，那么可能某些行动在一开始实施就过时了。

管理规划的益处

如前文所述，联合国教科文组织没有要求世界遗产地必须编制管理规划。同样，英国也没有相应法规

Other elements which feature in many UK WHS Management Plans include the identification of a series of goals for the management of the Site over different time periods. A 'vision', is typically a statement of what management wants to achieve in the long term (usually defined as 30 years); a series of 'objectives' or 'outcomes' sets out the work to be accomplished in the medium term (5 to 10 years); more immediate (3 to 5 year) goals, sometimes referred to as 'aims' or 'outputs,' describe specific initiatives to be implemented and completed; whilst 'actions' typically describe operational priorities for each year.

In practice, most UK Management Plans concentrate their attention on shorter term objectives for the five-year lifetime of the Plan. Many UK Plans now focus on the review and development of policies and initiatives, and omit discussion of specific actions. This because it is recognised that specific actions will evolve as policies are implemented, and that their inclusion in a plan for a five-year period would render part of it almost immediately obsolete.

THE BENEFITS OF MANAGEMENT PLANNING

As described above, there is no absolute requirement from UNESCO that WHSs should produce Management Plans, as such. Similarly, there is no statutory requirement in the UK that WHSs inscribed before 2000 should produce Management Plans nor that they should be periodically updated. All UK WHSs have nevertheless now produced Management Plans, and they periodically update them because they each recognise the benefits of doing so. It has become accepted as 'good practice'. The principal benefits of Management Planning can be broadly defined under two headings: the benefits of having a published plan, and the benefits of the process of producing it, particularly if that process is participative.

The benefits of the Plan itself

One of the earliest motivations for WHSs producing Management Plans was to provide published documentation which could be used to restrict inappropriate development within a WHS and its surrounding landscape setting. Plans do this by detailing a Site's boundaries and components and by articulating why the Site is of importance and should be protected. The latter is normally done by defining a range of 'values' which a Site's possesses and by identifying how these values are expressed through its individual and collective elements. Such values may be economic, environmental and natural, scientific, academic and educational, spiritual, aesthetic, or based on community and amenity benefits. All WHSs will possess combinations of several of these different types of values.

A Plan also acts as a tool of management. It identifies goals and objectives, defines specific issues to be addressed and appropriate policies to address them. It thus aids the prioritisation of activities and helps to inform decision-making. In particular, it provides individual managers and staff with an overview of all of the interests and stakeholders, issues and policies related to the management of the Site, aspects which otherwise might be beyond their individual areas of knowledge, experience, understanding and responsibility. In so doing, it enables individuals to make decisions and undertake actions with a better appreciation of the affects that these may have on different (and sometimes conflicting) interests, and which need to be weighed and balanced in managing a WHS. A Management Plan also provides a reference point against which management performance can be assessed.

In addition, Management Plans provide broader, more externally focused, benefits. They can contribute significantly to raising public awareness and understanding of the Site itself and the complexity of its management. This can help reduce ill-informed criticism of or opposition to some management decisions and actions, not only within a Site's own local communities but also within different industry bodies, special-interest groups and amongst policy-makers, locally, regionally and nationally. In preparing a Plan it is therefore worth considering the potential range and variety of the different audiences that may read it, and therefore how it might be best presented.

Table 1: Common components of UK WHS Management Plans.
表1: 英国世界遗产管理规划的常见内容。

Description: definition and delineation of components of the Site
遗产地描述： 确定遗产地构成的边界和范围
Interests: identification of all the Site's stakeholders
利益方： 列出遗产地所有的利益相关方
Values: explanation of why the Site is important to different stakeholders
价值： 阐述遗产地对不同利益相关方的各类价值
Review: an updated assessment of management of the Site
评估： 对遗产地管理进行的最新评估
Issues, Policies and Actions: the identification of what needs to be done
问题、政策及行动： 明确需要开展的工作
Management and Implementation: a description of how required actions will be undertaken
管理和执行： 阐述所列工作将如何展开

要求 2000 年以前的世界遗产地编制管理规划，也不要求其定期更新规划。然而，如今所有的英国境内世界遗产地都已制定管理规划，并且定期更新，因为大家都意识到这样做的好处。制定管理规划已经成为‘良好惯例’被认可。管理规划的主要好处可以分为两类：第一是作为正式文件本身的好处，第二是规划编制过程，尤其是参与性强的编制过程带来的好处。

规划本身的益处

世界遗产地编制管理规划，最初可能是因为规划可以用于遏制遗产区内及周边环境中的不当建设。为此，规划详细描述遗产地的边界和构成，明确遗产地的价值及其保护的必要性。对于遗产价值，规划通常列出遗产地的一系列“价值”，并明确这些价值是如何通过每个构成要素及其组合来体现的。这些价值可以体现在经济、自然环境、科学、学术与教育、精神、美学方面，或者是社区和休闲方面的。所有遗产地都或多或少都有着上述价值的各类不同组合。

管理规划也是一种管理工具。规划指出工作目标和方向，明确有待解决的具体问题以及适宜的应对政策。这样，规划有助于确定工作优先顺序，指导决策。尤其是，规划为遗产地的每个管理者及员工提供与遗产地管理有关的整体情况，包括所有诉求及利益相关方，以及所有问题及相关政策，这是受个人知识、经验、理解程度和职责所限可能无法全面认识的。通过这种方式，规划让每个人在做出决策、采取行动之前，更好地了解其决定对各种（有时是冲突的诉求）诉求可能产生的影响，从而以更加全面、均衡的方式管理遗产地。管理规划同样还为管理绩效评估提供参照。

此外，管理规划还提供更广泛的、外在的益处。它们可以极大地促进公众认识和理解遗产地自身价值及其管理复杂性。这有助于减少外界对遗产地管理决策和措施的不当批评和反对，这些批评和反对不仅可能来自遗产地当地社区，也可能来自不同行业、特殊利益集体，以及地方、区域和国家政策制定者。因此，在编制管理规划时，应当考虑其潜在的读者范围和不同读者群体，并据此决定规划的呈现方式。

The benefits of a participative process in the preparation of Plans

The process of preparing Management Plans for each UK WHS has steadily evolved since the first of them were prepared in the late 1990s (Fig.1). (The principal features of the evolution of the Management Plan for Hadrian's Wall are described later in this paper.) At first, the process involved a very limited number of people in national organisations or local government, sometimes assisted by externally contracted consultants; often the work was done behind closed-doors and with only limited contact with, or input from, wider stakeholders and interests. These approaches had a number of adverse effects. Whilst the authors were normally experts, their expertise tended to be restricted to specific topics. As a result, Plans were frequently weighted towards the specialism of the principal author, be it in conservation, archaeology, architecture, or tourism, etc. Given that the values of any Site are typically more numerous and varied than a single area of interest, the full values of a Site were not adequately expressed, and therefore potentially not sufficiently considered in the subsequent management of the Site. Furthermore, the inadequate consideration of wider interests encouraged distrust or opposition to the Plan and to the overall management of the Site.

The process of development of a Plan was often not visible to stakeholders until a first draft had been published for consultation. This could lead to the draft being seen as a *fait accompli*, and the impression being given that the consultation itself was not genuine and that any responses to it would not be seriously considered in the final version. Plans developed on this basis could be viewed as being imposed on stakeholders, and might therefore be rejected either in part or as a whole. As the day-to-day functioning of most WHSs is dependent on the input of, and cooperation between, a number of individuals and organisations, the alienation of stakeholders could make the implementation of a Plan very difficult.

Such approaches have now been replaced by much more participative processes: there is widespread early involvement of stakeholders in consultation and their increased direct involvement in the preparation of Plans. This has improved the relevance, appropriateness and overall quality of the Plans and, consequently, the management of Sites.

Participative Management Planning processes start with the identification and recognition of the principal interests and stakeholders concerned with a Site. The consultation of those best placed to represent those interests begins early in the Management Planning process and continues throughout it or at different intervals. Consultation should extend beyond the managers of different stakeholder organisations to include the input of front-line staff involved in the day-to-day functioning of the Site. In addition, this consultation must be genuine, in the sense that the responses it generates will be seriously considered. This does not mean that all responses will be incorporated in the final Plan, but rather that they will be reflected in the necessary balancing of different interests required in planning the future management of the Site. From the start of the consultation process, the expectations of different interests and stakeholders of the process must be managed.

An important element of the process is that different stakeholders and interest groups share their perspectives. Whilst this can be done through public meetings, it is most effectively done by bringing together representatives of the different interests to discuss the management of the Site as a whole, not just those sections of the prospective Plan which might address their particular area of focus. This interaction generates greater understanding between different interests of each other's perspectives, and the risk of mistrust between interests is reduced. This early management of stakeholders' expectations, and the recognition that a degree of compromise on all sides will be required, naturally results in a Plan's policies, and the aspirations of individual interests, becoming more realistic. The establishment of the necessity of balancing different interests can then benefit the day-to-day management of the Site.

An example of this on Hadrian's Wall involved a dispute concerning the course of one section of the National Trail. Environmentalists had raised concerns that a particularly rare and vulnerable micro-ecology was being damaged by walkers. Archaeologists were then alarmed that the new route suggested would damage the archaeological remains lying immediately below it, but their alternative proposals were resisted by Trail managers who felt this would be an unacceptable detour which walkers would ignore. Eventually a compromise was agreed between these

加强参与性规划编制的益处

从20世纪 90 年代晚期首批规划编制开始，英国各处世界遗产地管理规划的编制过程就不断演变。（各期哈德良长城管理规划主要特点的变化将在后文阐述）。起初，编制过程只有少数国家级组织或当地政府的人员参与，有时会外聘顾问提供协助，而整个编制工作都是关起门来进行，与利益相关方和其他利益方面只有少量的接触或者沟通。这些方法带来了一些负面效果。尽管作者一般都是专家，但他们的专长往往只局限于某个具体领域。因此，管理规划常常偏重主要作者的专业领域，比如保护、考古、建筑、旅游等。既然任何一处遗产地的价值都是多元的、变化的，而不是单一的，那么如此规划编制方式无法充分体现遗产地的价值，也就无法充分考虑到后续遗产地管理工作的方方面面。此外，对更大范围内的诉求缺乏充分考虑还可能引起对规划的不信任或者反对，乃至制约整个遗产地管理。

对利益相关方来说，在规划初稿发布征求意见之前，整个规划编制过程都是“隐形”的。因此，他们可能视规划草案为“既成事实”，认为征求意见只是走过场，任何意见都不会在最终定稿中得到认真考虑。如此形成的规划会被视为强加于利益相关方头上，因此会遭遇部分甚至全盘的否定。实际上大部分世界遗产地的日常运作都依赖于大量个人和组织的协助和合作，因此置利益相关方的声音于不顾会为规划的实施平添困难。

这样的编制方法已经被更具参与性的流程取代。在早期阶段就广泛征求利益相关方的意见，并请利益相关方更多地直接参与规划编制。这种做法增加了规划的针对性和合理性，提高了规划的整体质量，最终可以改善遗产地管理。

参与性的管理规划编制过程从明确遗产地的主要利益诉求和利益相关方开始。从编制管理规划的最早期，征求意见就开始面向最能代表这些利益的人员，并贯穿整个过程或在各个环节持续进行。征询过程还应当走出利益相关方的机构管理层，倾听从事遗产地日常管理一线员工的意见。此外，征求意见应当真心诚意，也就是说对听到的意见应当予以认真考虑。这并不意味着所有意见都会整合至规划最终稿中，但在规划遗产

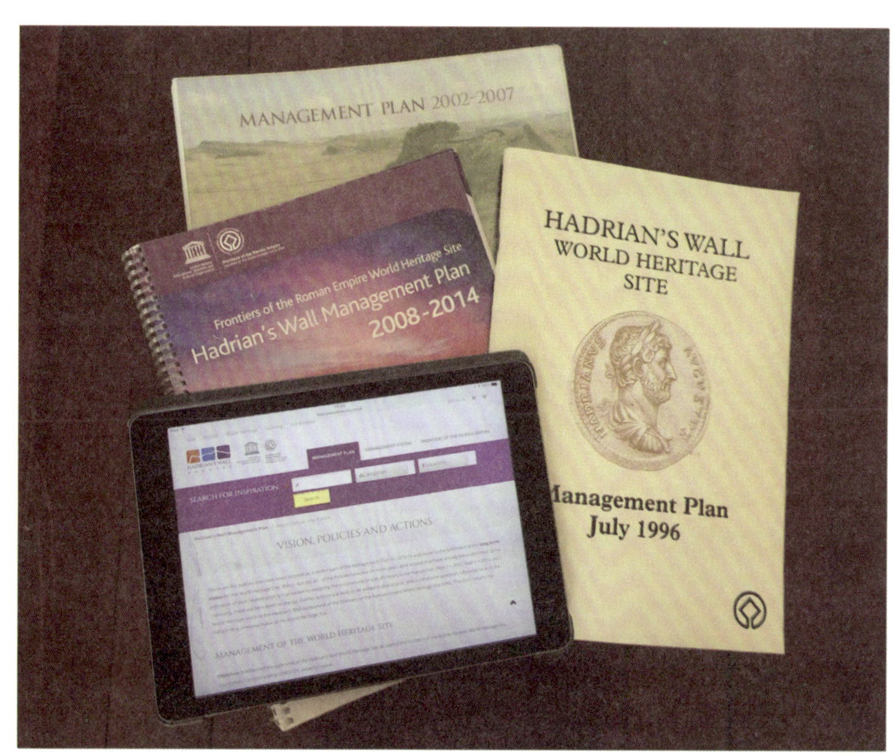

Fig.1 The first four iterations of the Hadrian's Wall World Heritage Site Management Plan (© Humphrey Welfare).
图 1 哈德良长城世界遗产地管理规划前四版（© 汉佛瑞·维尔法）。

conflicting interests, using alternative construction materials which minimised potential damage to both the natural and archaeological environments. It is unlikely that this consensus would have been reached without the broader respect for other interests that had been generated through the Management Planning process.

The participative principle can also extend to the actual drafting of the Plan. Many UK Sites now invite a number of individuals to write specific sections of the plan according to their expertise and experience. This enables the plan preparation process to draw upon a wider pool of knowledge and understanding than may be provided by a single author or organisation. It also results in responsibility for the plan being shared between a range of different stakeholders. As a result stakeholders feel that they have ownership of the plan as a whole and therefore feel both obliged and willing to support its implementation. This approach to the drafting of a plan does however require oversight and co-ordination, which is typically provided by the assignment of a central overall editorial responsibility.

Although participative approaches to the preparation of Management Plans can provide real benefits, these come at some cost. The most obvious is the time required to undertake such a process. The timescales required vary between different Sites, depending on the number of stakeholders and interests concerned, and in the UK range from nine to eighteen months. The preparation of a Site's first Management Plan as part of their nomination can be a lengthy process, but the timescale required for each periodic revision will be substantially reduced.

Participative approaches do require significant amounts of project planning, management and co-ordination. This has major implications for those responsible for the ongoing management of Sites which can be significantly disrupted by the Management Planning process; additional management and staffing resources may therefore be needed by Sites for the duration of the process, and this may equally apply to the stakeholder organisations.

THE EVOLUTION OF MANAGEMENT PLANS FOR HADRIAN'S WALL WHS

Context

Hadrian's Wall extends for more than 150 miles, crossing eight local government areas. It includes over 200 Scheduled Monuments, 12 visitor sites and museums managed by a number of different organisations, two National Parks, and numerous environmentally sensitive protected areas. It passes through a range of different landscapes and communities, including urban areas around the cities of Newcastle and Carlisle, lowland arable farms, and livestock farming in the uplands. The land on which it is situated is in multiple private ownership in urban areas, and its rural sections are owned and managed by over 700 farmers. Its stakeholders are therefore multiple and include: local residents and communities; farmers and landowners; tourism and other businesses; local and national government bodies; private trusts; academia; and tourists.

Coordinating the management of the Site is therefore enormously complex and challenging, as is the process of preparing each Management Plan for the Site.

The first Plan - 1996

The preparation of the first Management Plan for Hadrian's Wall WHS was led by English Heritage (now Historic England) and began in late 1993. At that stage its authors had little or no official guidance regarding what a Management Plan should contain. The Site's nomination documentation in 1987 had made almost no reference to its management and no other UK WHSs had produced Management Plans which it could emulate. A steering group involving representatives of different partners and stakeholders was established in early 1994 and various consultative workshops were held over the following year. In addition to the steering group, which met eight times during that period, a number of subordinate working groups were established and met frequently to work on specific issues. This resulted in a first draft of the Plan being published for consultation in May 1995.

Approximately 200 copies of the draft were circulated to stakeholders and around 35,000 explanatory leaflets were posted to households within the immediate vicinity of the WHS. This consultation generated over 200 written

地未来管理时会对这些意见作出必要的平衡。从意见征询过程开始，就必须管理好不同利益和利益相关方的期望。

参与过程的一个重要内容就是不同利益相关方和利益群体沟通和分享他们的观点。公开会议是一种方式，最有效的方法是将不同利益的代表召集在一起，就整个遗产地的管理展开讨论，而不仅仅是就规划中可能涉及他们的特定领域进行讨论。这种互动会在彼此的不同利益之间产生更大的理解，并且降低了利益集体之间互不信任的风险。对利益相关方的期望进行早期管理，以及认识到在各方面做出一定程度的妥协的必要性，自然会使得规划制定的原则和各自利益实现的预期变得更加现实。认识到平衡不同利益的必要性有助于遗产地的日常管理。

哈德良长城上的一个例子就是某段国家步道引发的争议。环保主义者担心游客会破坏一种特别稀有和脆弱的微生态。考古学家也发现，所选线路方案直接从考古遗迹上方穿过，可能的威胁引起了他们的警觉。但他们的替代方案遭到了步道管理者的抵制，他们认为该方案绕了一个大圈，游客是不会走的。最终，一个折衷方案在这些冲突的诉求间产生，即采用替代的建筑材料，最大限度地减少对自然环境和考古环境的潜在损害。如果没有更广泛地尊重管理规划制定过程产生的各种诉求，就不可能达成这种共识。

广泛参与的原则还可以扩展到规划的实际起草工作中。现在，不少英国遗产地都邀请许多专家根据其专业知识和经验编写计划的特定部分。与单个作者或机构相比，这一新的编写模式能够为编制过程提供更全面的知识和理解。另一个结果是，规划编制工作可以由一系列不同的利益相关方共同承担。于是，利益相关方对整个规划有了主人翁意识，因此既有责任感也有意愿支持规划的实施。不过，这种规划起草模式确实需要统筹和协调，通常安排专人承担统筹编纂的职责。

尽管采用广泛参与的方法来制定管理规划可以带来实在的益处，但要付出一定的代价。最明显的是这一过程耗时日久。不同遗产地所需的时间有所不同，具体取决于利益相关方和涉及利益的多少。在英国，编制过程花费时间从 9 个月至 18 个月不等。作为申遗材料的一部分，遗产地第一版管理规划的准备过程可能相当漫长，不过后续每次修订所需的时间将大大减少。

集体参与的编制模式确实需要大量的项目计划、管理和协调工作，会给负责遗产地日常管理的工作人员带来巨大影响，因为编制管理规划可能会严重打乱日常管理工作。遗产地在此过程中可能需要配备额外的管理和人力资源，利益相关方的机构或许也同样需要额外支持。

哈德良长城世界遗产地管理规划的演变

背景

哈德良长城全长超过 150 英里[1]，横跨八个地方政府辖区。沿途有 200 多处登录古迹、12 座由不同机构管理的遗址景区和博物馆、两座国家公园以及众多环境脆弱的保护区。它穿越了一系列不同的景观和社区，包括纽卡斯尔和卡莱尔市周围的城市地区，地势较低的大片耕地，以及地势较高的牧场。长城土地在城市地区属于多个私人产权人，在农村地区则由 700 多位农户持有和经营。因此，其利益相关方众多，包括当地居民和社区、农户和土地所有者、旅游从业机构和其他企业、地方和国家政府机关、私人信托基金、学术界和游客等。

1 约合 241.4 千米——译者注

responses, from which a number of principal criticisms were identified. Most significantly, concerns were expressed by farming communities that World Heritage status would enforce damaging restrictions on traditional farming practices. Farmers were also concerned that their work would be further disrupted by increases in visitor numbers crossing their land as a result of the proposed establishment of the National Trail. In contrast, local tourism bodies felt that the draft Plan did not give enough emphasis to the importance and potential of tourism, and that it focused too narrowly on the conservation agenda. Following this consultation, the draft was revised, but only in very minor ways, and the finalised Plan was formally published in July 1996. The Plan was greeted with little enthusiasm by local stakeholders, and, despite the extensive consultations during its preparation, it was viewed with suspicion by some stakeholders and was opposed by others.

The second Plan - 2002

Prior the 2002 updating of the Management Plan a major review was undertaken into the effectiveness of the 1996 Plan. This reported that steady but differing degrees of progress had been made in addressing the issues identified in the first Plan, and that this had been achieved through the development of collaborative working between different partners and stakeholders. This was widely attributed to the establishment in 1996 of the Hadrian's Wall Management Plan Committee (MPC), made up of over 30 different stakeholder bodies. The primary function of the MPC was to oversee and monitor the implementation of the Plan. The experience of greater collaboration between stakeholders, through day-to-day working and through the MPC, meant that the process of consulting on and drafting the second Plan was much less contentious than for the first one. This also enabled the revised Plan, published in 2002, to include more detailed policies and actions, which is '... only possible in a Management Plan of this sort because stakeholders are prepared to agree to them' (Young 2014, 30).

This second Plan was also broader in its scope than the first and included more emphasis on the natural environment, on the economic value of tourism, and on the sustainable use of the Site. This represented an acknowledgement of the wider values of the Site beyond its archaeological significance for which it was originally inscribed as a WHS.

The third Plan - 2008

The preparation of the third Plan took place in the changed context of a new structure for the management of the WHS. While the oversight of the MPC continued, the Site's operational management, previously dispersed across a number of partner organisations, was brought together under a stand-alone management organisation. Although this change had itself caused some disquiet amongst stakeholders and partners, this did not impede the process of consultation and preparation of the new edition of the Plan. Indeed, that process saw an even greater devolution of authorship responsibilities for the Plan through the establishment of a number of 'interest groups' to undertake the drafting of sections of most relevance to them. This also involved a degree of joint working between different interest groups on issues of common concern. This arrangement greatly reduced the burden of the consultation, because the majority of stakeholders and interests had already been either directly or indirectly involved in its preparation.

The new Plan included a further expansion of the range of values of the Site and further increases in the number and detail of policies it presented and of the actions identified to implement them. The Plan also set out in greater detail than previously how it was to be implemented.

The fourth Plan - 2015

When preparation of the fourth edition of the Plan began the centralised management body for the WHS had been dissolved, following a significant reduction in the funding of regional development by central government. It also had been impossible to adapt the static, printed version of the previous edition of the Plan to the drastic changes brought about by the global financial crash of 2008-9, which had made its hugely ambitious aspirations

因此，协调遗产地管理非常复杂，挑战严峻，每一版遗产地管理规划的编制过程也是如此。

第一版规划 - *1996* 年

第一版哈德良长城世界遗产地管理规划由英格兰遗产委员会主持编制，于 1993 年底开始。当时，对于管理规划应当包含的内容，编者几乎没有任何官方文件可以参考。哈德良长城在 1987 年的申遗材料中几乎没有提及管理，英国境内其他世界遗产地也没有出台任何管理规划可供借鉴。1994 年初，来自各合作伙伴和利益相关方的代表组成领导小组，并于次年举行了各种协商研讨会。领导小组在此期间召开了八次会议，除此之外，还成立了数个专题工作组，经常举行会议，就具体问题开展工作。管理规划初稿于 1995 年 5 月发布，征求意见。

大约有 200 份初稿印发给利益相关方，并在紧邻遗产地的居民区张贴了约 35,000 张说明性传单。本轮征求意见收到了 200 多份书面答复，其中有一些主要的批评性意见。反响最为强烈的是农户群体，他们担忧，世界遗产地的特殊身份将限制传统的农作方式，对农业造成破坏性影响。农户同样担心拟建立的国家步道会使得越来越多的游客穿越其土地，进一步打乱他们的工作。与此相反，当地的旅游机构则认为，规划初稿并未充分强调旅游业的重要性和潜力，却将关注点过于狭隘地放在了保护工作上。

经过此轮意见征求，草案只进行了少量的修订，便于 1996 年 7 月形成最终版本，正式颁布。该计划遭到当地利益相关方的冷遇。尽管在编制过程中进行了广泛的协商，但一些利益相关方还是心存疑虑，而另一些利益相关方则表示反对。

第二版规划 - *2002* 年

在 2002 年修订管理规划之前，首先对 1996 版管理规划的实施效果开展了认真评估。评估结果指出，第一版规划中发现的种种问题已经稳步得到解决，虽然解决的程度不一，但与不同合作伙伴和利益相关方之间发展协作关系十分重要。之所以取得这样的成绩，人们普遍将其归功于 1996 年成立的哈德良长城管理规划委员会（Management Plan Committee, 缩写为 MPC）。该委员会由 30 家不同利益相关机构组成。MPC 的主要职能是统筹和监测规划的实施。通过日常工作和 MPC 的统筹监测，利益相关方之间合作得以加强，也意味着第二版规划的意见征询及起草过程所遇到的争议远比第一版规划少得多。2002 年修订版规划也因此包含更为具体的政策和行动措施，这些内容“……只有通过广泛参与的方式才可能写进来，因为它们已经是利益相关方认可的”（杨，2014: 30）。

第二版管理规划范围也比第一版更为广泛，更加强调自然环境、旅游相关的经济价值和遗产地的可持续利用。这表明哈德良长城遗产地更广泛的价值得到认可，尽管它最初仅以其考古价值而列入世界文化遗产的。

第三版规划 - *2008* 年

第三版规划编制时，世界遗产地管理体制发生重大变化。MPC 仍继续承担监督职责，但遗产地的日常运营管理从之前多个分散机构合并为一个专门的管理机构。尽管这一变化本身引起了利益相关方和合作伙伴的些许不安，但这并没有妨碍新版规划的协商和编制进程。参与规划编制的团体更为广泛，成立了多个“利益小组”来起草与他们最相关的部分。同时，这种编写方式要求不同的利益小组在他们共同关心的问题上一起讨论。这种方式大大减轻了后期意见征求的负担，因为规划的编制过程本身已经直接或间接地照顾到大多数利益相关方及诉求。

virtually meaningless. The interest groups established by the third Plan had nevertheless continued to work together and, under the umbrella of the MPC, had steadily developed and refined the Plan's policies, and adapted its actions to these changed contexts in which the WHS was managed.

This meant that the process of reviewing and updating the Plan was, although still a major undertaking, relatively straightforward and encountered little dispute or contention. A public consultation was again undertaken, but for this fourth Plan it was more focused on the views of local communities and individual businesses. This reflected the fact that, by this stage, the representation of partner organisations and stakeholder bodies had been firmly established within the management of the Site through the MPC and the interest groups.

As there was also now no budget for the printing of the Plan in hard copy, it was decided that the new edition would only be published online.[1] This had two major benefits: it saved a lot of money in printing costs but, more importantly, it enabled the Plan to become a dynamic document, continuously updated by the MPC (and by the succeeding Partnership Board) whenever appropriate. As a result, the process of preparing for a fifth edition of the Plan, started in 2020, is likely to be even more straightforward than was that for the fourth edition.

References
参考文献

Feilden, B.M. & Jokhilehto, J. 1993. *Management Guidelines for World Cultural Heritage Sites*. ICCROM, Rome.

B.M·菲尔登，J·乔基尔莱特. 1993. 世界遗产地管理准则. 罗马：国际文物保护与修复研究中心.

UNESCO. 2002. *Operational Guidelines for the Implementation of the World Heritage Convention*. UNESCO, Paris.

联合国教科文组织. 2002. 世界遗产公约履行操作准则. 巴黎：联合国教科文组织.

UNESCO. 2019. *Operational Guidelines for the Implementation of the World Heritage Convention*. UNESCO, Paris.

联合国教科文组织. 2019. 世界遗产公约履行操作准则. 巴黎：联合国教科文组织.

Young, C. 2014. 'The need for a Management Plan and the 1st and 2nd Plans,' *in* P. G. Stone and D. Brough (eds) *Managing, Using, and Interpreting Hadrian's Wall as World Heritage*, London.

C·杨. 2014. 管理规划的必要性和第一、第二版管理规划，见于P.G·斯通、D·布劳夫（编）哈德良长城作为世界文化遗产的管理、利用和阐释. 伦敦.

1 http://hadrianswallcountry.co.uk/hadrians-wall-management-plan

新修订的规划中，遗产地价值范畴得到进一步扩充，提出的政策数量和行动措施也进一步丰富和细化。相比之前一版，新规划在实施手段上给出了更为具体的描述。

第四版规划 - *2015* 年

在开始编制第四版规划时，由于中央政府大幅减少了对地区发展的资金投入，世界遗产地的统一管理机构已经解散。这时已经不再可能采取原来的静态、纸质的规划形式，因为 2008-2009 年全球金融危机带来的巨大变化，使原来规划中那些宏伟目标事实上已经毫无意义。尽管如此，第三版规划时设立的利益小组仍继续合作，在 MPC 的统筹协调下，顺利制定和完善了规划的政策，并根据遗产地管理大环境的变化调整了相应的行动措施。

由此看来，虽然规划的评估和修订任务重大，但完成起来还是相对顺利的，几乎没有争议或争论。第四版规划再次向社会各界征求意见，不过新版规划更注意倾听当地社区和各家企业的声音。通过多次规划编制的长期磨合，合作机构和利益相关机构的参与机制已借由MPC和利益小组的形式稳固地扎根于遗产地管理工作。

由于缺乏规划付梓的预算，新版规划决定只在线上发布。这有两个主要好处：一是显著节省印刷成本，但更重要的是，规划得以成为一份动态文件，可以在适当时由 MPC（现已由合作伙伴委员会接手）持续更新。由此, 2020 年开始的第五版管理规划编制过程可能会比第四版更为简单顺畅。

1.2 中国长城保护：2017–2018

于冰，刘文艳，许慧君，冯双元
中国文化遗产研究院—中国—北京

张朝枝
中山大学旅游学院—中国—广州

摘要

2016 年，在《长城保护条例》实施十周年之际，国家文物局首次发布《中国长城保护报告》。本报告继而聚焦 2017 年和 2018 年，总结中国长城在考古与价值研究，法规建设与管理，项目管理与预防性保护，以及价值共建共享与文旅融合方面的最新成绩。

关键词： 中国长城　保护　双年报告

一、长城考古与价值研究

（一）长城考古调查与发掘

近年考古在长城研究和保护中的重要性开始受到关注。据初步统计，2017–2018 年全国共开展 4 项长城考古发掘项目，以配合文物修缮项目及配合基建工程为主，为科学制定保护维修方案提供重要依据。例如，北京延庆岔道城长城北侧 1–6 号烽火台及边墙考古发掘（图 1）、河北唐山喜峰口西潘家口段长城 4 号敌台及两侧城墙遗址考古发掘、河北大城县旺村镇津石高速公路东段燕南长城遗址考古发掘、宁夏固原市西南郊吴庄段长城遗址考古发掘项目。

此外，国家文物局加强长城保护维修项目前期勘察和设计中的考古工作要求。长城保护维修工程也开展考古清理工作。例如，2018 年，由文物保护基金会资助的箭扣长城保护维修项目中，考古清理工作出土了大量建筑构件、守城武器以及守城官兵生活用品，对研究明代建筑技术、军事史以及守城官兵生活状态提供了重要的实物资料。

但也可以看出，有计划的考古工作仍是长城保护中最为薄弱的领域，需要系统性加强。

（二）长城遗产研究

2017–2018 年，随着长城资源调查报告的陆续出版以及考古发掘工作的开展，长城研究工作取得推进。除中国文化遗产研究院、各地文博单位及大学长城研究课题组继续发挥重要作用外，作为专职机构的内蒙古长城保护中心、嘉峪关丝路（长城）研究院以及长城保护联盟相继成立，在一定程度上推动了长城研究的加强。据不完全统计，在各科研院所及科研人员的共同努力下，长城研究工作取得了较重要的进展，共出版调查报告 5 部、研究论著 6 部，长城文化科普宣传书籍 7 部、发表各类研究论文 150 余篇。

1.2 CHINA'S GREAT WALL PROTECTION REPORT 2017-2018

YU BING, LIU WENYAN, XU HUIJUN, FENG SHUANGYUAN
The Chinese Academy of Cultural Heritage - China - Beijing

ZHANG CHAOZHI
Sun Yat-sen University - China - Guangzhou

Abstract

In 2016, at the tenth anniversary of the implementation of the Great Wall Protection Regulation, the then State Administration for Cultural Heritage (SACH)[1] published the first Great Wall Protection Report. The Chinese Academy of Cultural Heritage (CACH) has continued the process of reviewing work on the protection of the Great Wall and has now reported on work done in the years 2017 and 2018. This paper, based on that report, now summarises the latest achievements in relation to the Great Wall in archaeology and research, regulation and management, project management and preventive conservation, public access and engagement, and in integration with cultural tourism.

Keywords: The Great Wall, protection, biennial report.

ARCHAEOLOGY AND RESEARCH

Archaeological Survey and Excavation of the Great Wall

In recent years, the importance of archaeology in research and protection of the Great Wall has begun to receive more attention. In 2017 and 2018, 4 Great Wall archaeological excavations were carried out across the country, mainly in conjunction with conservation and development projects, to formulate scientific conservation and protection plans. These excavations include Beacon Towers No.1 to No.6 and the Wall north of Chadao Fort at: Yanqing, Beijing (Fig. 1); Defence Tower No.4 and adjacent walls at Xifengkou on the West Panjiakou Section of the Wall in Hebei Province; South Yan State Great Wall Site at the East Section of the Jinshi Expressway, Wangcun Town, Dacheng County, in Hebei Province; and the Wuzhuang Section Wall in the southwest suburb of Guyuan in Ningxia Hui Autonomous Region.

In addition, NCHA has strengthened the requirement for archaeological work as part of the preliminary survey and design stages of conservation projects on the Great Wall. Archaeologically-led site clearance work has also been carried out for some conservation projects. For instance, in 2018, components of buildings, weaponry and artefacts from soldiers' daily lives were found in large quantity in the archaeologically led site clearance work during conservation work at Jiankou funded by the China Foundation for Cultural Heritage Conservation (CFCHC). These finds provide important physical data for research on architectural techniques, military history and the living conditions of soldiers in the Ming Dynasty.

Research on the archaeology and the current management of the Great Wall

From 2017 to 2018, with the publication of more Great Wall Resources Survey Reports and archaeological excavations, research on the Great Wall also advanced. In addition to the significant role played by the Chinese

1 In 2018 SACH was renamed as the National Cultural Heritage Administration (NCHA). (Editors' note).

图 1 延庆岔道城长城 6 号烽火台遗址考古发掘鸟瞰，北京（图片来源：北京市文物研究所）。
Fig.1 Aerial view of the archaeological excavation at Beacon Tower No. 6, north of Chadao Fort at Yanqing, Beijing (photograph by Beijing Archaeological Research Institute).

二、长城法规建设与管理

2017–2018 年长城保护管理工作更加注重长城依法行政基础工作的制度化、精细化，结合长城沿线各地实际情况不断创新探索有效工作机制，同时强调人员队伍培训建设和经费保障。

（一）长城法规体系建设

2017 年和 2018 年，各地出台（包括修订、升级）的长城保护法律法规共有 7 部，包括新增 5 部，修订 1 部，提高法规级别 1 部，地区主要集中在北京市、河北省、内蒙古自治区和甘肃省。截至 2018 年底，全国现行涉及长城各级专门法规和规范性文件的共有 28 部。

（二）长城文物保护单位公布

2017 和 2018 年，辽宁、陕西和新疆等 3 个省（自治区）补充公布一批长城点段为省级文物保护单位。截至 2018 年底，共有河北、山西、内蒙古、黑龙江、山东、河南、陕西、甘肃、青海、宁夏、陕西等 10 个省（自治区）长城认定资源全部公布为省级以上文物保护单位。

Academy of Cultural Heritage (CACH), professional heritage institutions and research teams in universities, the newly established of the Inner Mongolia Great Wall Conservation Centre, the Jiayuguan Silk Road Culture Research Institute (Great Wall) and the Great Wall Alliance have improved research capability. According to the partial statistics available, with the joint efforts from various institutes and researchers, recent studies on the Great Wall include five Great Wall Survey reports, six academic publications, seven promotional and educational books on the heritage of the Great Wall and its culture, and more than 150 related research papers have been published.

Generally speaking, archaeological and research work on the Great Wall is still very weak and fragmented, and more systematic and sustained work is required to address these deficiencies.

REGULATION AND MANAGEMENT

In 2017 and 2018, more efforts were made in capacity building and in improving regulations concerning the Great Wall. Innovations in, and exploration of, effective working mechanisms based on local practice have emerged along the Wall. At the same time, training and funding have also been strengthened.

Development of the Great Wall legal system

In 2017 and 2018, seven Great Wall-related laws and regulations were promulgated, mostly in Beijing, Hebei, Inner Mongolia and Gansu. Five of them were newly published laws; one was an amendment and the other was an upgrading of an existing regulation. By the end of 2018, there were 28 special laws and regulatory documents referring to the Great Wall at different administrative levels.

Designation of Protected Units of Cultural Relics

In 2017 and 2018, Shaanxi, Liaoning, Xinjiang announced additional batches of Protected Units of Cultural Relics (PUCRs) at provincial level. By the end of 2018, 10 out of 15 provincial-level administrations including Hebei, Shanxi, Inner Mongolia, Heilongjiang, Shandong, Henan, Shaanxi, Gansu, Qinghai and Ningxia, had designated all of their verified Great Wall resources as PUCRs at or above the provincial level as required by the Great Wall Protection Regulation.

Enforcement and supervision

In 2017, in response to the problems found in the previous year's inspection of law enforcement inspection on the Great Wall, SACH organised a special review of how policies of the previous inspection were being implemented and how the problems it identified were being addressed. The inspection focused on how government authorities performed their responsibilities for protection of the Wall and whether all verified Great Wall resources were designated as PUCRs as required. It also examined how well the four legal prerequisites for designated PUCRs ('the Four Haves') were fulfilled. These require each site to have: demarcated boundaries; an official plaque stating its name, its level and date of designation; an archive cataloguing its protected elements and activities; and a dedicated organisation or person(s) responsible for its daily management. In addition the inspection also reviewed whether authorities have established mechanisms for law enforcement and for the investigation and prosecution of cultural relics-related crimes involving the Great Wall.

The *Special Rectification Action against Legal Entity Law-breaking Cases Involving Cultural Relics (2016 to 2018)* launched by SACH also targeted cases that damaged the fabric of the Wall and its historic features. A number of major cases of damage to the Great Wall were investigated and perpetrators prosecuted.

Planning of Great Wall Protection

At the end of 2018, the Great Wall Protection Master Plan was completed. With the consent of China's State Council, the Ministry of Culture and Tourism and NCHA officially published it on 22nd January 2019. The Master

（三）长城执法与督察

2017 年，针对上年长城执法专项督察中发现的问题，国家文物局组织开展了长城执法专项督察“回头看”，持续抓问题整改、抓措施落实，着力对政府长城保护主体责任落实情况、长城核定公布为省级以上文物保护单位情况、长城“四有”等基础工作落实情况、长城监管与执法常态化机制建立情况、涉及长城的文物违法犯罪案件查处情况等五个方面进行了再督察。

国家文物局开展文物“法人违法案件专项整治行动（2016–2018 年）”，将破坏长城本体及其历史风貌案件作为主要任务之一。一批涉及长城重大违法案件受到查处。

（四）长城保护规划编制

2018 年底完成《长城保护总体规划》全部工作。经国务院同意，2019 年 1 月 22，文化和旅游部、国家文物局正式印发《长城保护总体规划》。《长城保护总体规划》为建立长城保护传承利用长效工作机制，督促各省（区、市）将长城保护作为一项长期任务持之以恒地抓下去提供了重要遵循。同时，省级长城保护规划的编制工作也得到推进。目前已完成15省的19部省级规划初稿。下一步将根据已经公布的《长城保护总体规划》进行衔接和细化完善。

（五）长城“四有”基础工作

2017 年和 2018 年，有 5 省（自治区，直辖市）新公布长城保护范围和建设控制地带，9 个省（自治区，直辖市）新设置了保护标志，吉林省、河南省、陕西省、青海省、新疆维吾尔自治区建立健全长城四有档案，实现了对辖区内长城资源的全覆盖。内蒙古自治区、辽宁省和甘肃省等一些地方加强长城保护管理机构专门机构建设，新设立 4 个长城保护管理专门机构。

（六）长城保护管理培训组织

2017– 2018 年，各级文物部门加强长城保护管理培训工作，培训既涉及综合性内容，也涉及保护技术、“四有”工作、执法等专题性内容。参加学员大都是来自基层长城保护一线的文博工作者和长城保护员，培训形式既有专家授课，也有现场研学交流，同时发放法规制度资料和工作装备等，更加注重针对性、操作性和实效性。其中国家文物局相继组织开展了第二期和第三期（图 2）全国长城保护管理培训班，天津、河北、内蒙组织了省

图 2 2018 年国家文物局砖石质长城保护管理培训班现场教学,2018 年 9 月，河北山海关长城（图片来源：山海关区文物局）。

Fig.2 On-site training session organised by NCHA on the protection and management of the brick and stone Wall at Shanhaiguan, Hebei Province, Sep. 2018 (photograph by the Cultural Relics Administration Bureau of Shanhaiguan District).

Plan sets out important guidelines, which will serve as common goals for all stakeholders, for protection and conservation of the Great Wall, and for the enhancement of the benefits to society which the Great Wall provides. In parallel with this, provincial Great Wall protection planning has also been pushed forward at a faster pace. So far, preliminary drafts for 15 out of 19 provincial level plans have been completed. These plans will now be finalised and integrated with the new Master Plan.

The 'Four Haves'

In 2017 and 2018, five provincial level administrations published their demarcated boundaries for the protection and development control areas surrounding the Great Wall. Nine administrations put up more protection plaques and the Provinces of Jilin, Henan, Shaanxi, Qinghai and Xinjiang Hui Autonomous Region have established and improved their archives to cover all Great Wall resources in each region. Furthermore, Inner Mongolia Autonomous Region, and Liaoning and Gansu Provinces have strengthened protection by the creation of four specialised agencies or institutes to manage and protect the Great Wall.

Training on protection management

From 2017 to 2018, Cultural Relics Departments at all levels strengthened training in the protection of the Great Wall. The training covers general conservation and protection topics as well as more technical subjects such as conservation techniques and technologies, the Four Haves and law enforcement. Most of the participants were people who worked as the front-line protectors of the Great Wall. Some of them were staff from professional heritage institutions, and some were Great Wall Patrollers. Lectures were given by experts, as well as field seminars, with targeted subjects, during which guidance on regulations and work equipment were issued to participants, all of which aimed to make the training provided more practical and relevant for the participants. In the same period NCHA organised the second- and third- phase national training courses on the protection and management of the Great Wall (Fig. 2) and Tianjin, Hebei and Inner Mongolia organised training sessions at provincial levels.

CONSERVATION PROJECT MANAGEMENT AND PILOT PROJECTS FOR PREVENTIVE CONSERVATION

Five guiding principles for conservation have been gradually established during the implementation of conservation projects on the Great Wall. As stipulated clearly in the Great Wall Protection Master Plan, these principles are:

- no change to the historical fabric;
- minimum intervention;
- preventive conservation projects should be prioritised;
- protection according to the classification of heritage resources;
- protection according to the current state of conservation (Ministry of Culture and Tourism & NCHA 2019).

Management of protection projects

NCHA strengthened the regulatory processes for approving proposals for repair and conservation of sections of the Wall that are classified as PUCRs at state level. In 2017 and 2018, the number of applications for approval of Great Wall conservation and repair projects increased, but the approval rate dropped significantly. During this period, 31 projects proposals have been approved, with distinct differences in the numbers from different regions along the Great Wall.

In 2017 and 2018, 36 Great Wall conservation project designs were approved by NCHA. Compared with the period between 2014 to 2016, stricter assessments were undertaken with emphasis on the design's provision for prior

级长城保护培训。

三、长城保护项目管理与预防性保护监测试点

在长城保护中逐渐明确五大保护原则，即不改变原状、最低程度干预、预防为主、分类保护和分级保护原则。

（一）长城保护项目管理

国家文物局加强对全国重点文物保护单位的长城点段保护维修方案的严格审批。2017 年和 2018 年全国长城保护维修项目申报立项数量有较大增加，但立项计划通过率明显下降。2017 年和 2018 年共批复立项计划 31 项，从地域分布情况看数量差异较大。

2017 和年 2018 年，由国家文物局审批的长城保护维修方案共计 36 项，地区分布也差异较大。与之前 2014-2016 年 3 年情况相比，更加重视工程实施前的考古勘察、病害调查，依据最小干预原则，对长城保护维修方案的审批更加严格。

（二）加强预防性保护

近年来，长城保护工作重点逐渐从修缮转变为采取一系列管理措施加强“预防性保护”，防范风险的发生与发展，取得积极成果。

2018 年汛期之前，长城沿线各省（自治区、直辖市）根据国家文物局要求，对长城险情进行了全面排查，及时采取临时性加固措施。长城日常养护的也日益受到重视，一些地方已经开始探索调整配套政策，切实推动长城向预防性保护转变。例如，河北省总结经验教训，调整工作思路，近年来有意识的将长城保养维护项目列为长城保护重点。

2017-2018 年，各级各地文物部门和研究机构通过建立监测预警平台、采用无人机、便携式移动设备、安装前端监测设备、卫星影像对比、开发手机 APP 等监测技术开展了大量的监测实践工作，为系统开展长城监测进行了有益地经验探索。

（三）编制保护维修技术规范

为提升长城保护维修项目设计水平，深入对长城保护维修理念的探索与实践，在《长城保护维修工作指导意见》基础上, 2017 年和 2018 年期间，国家文物局委托专业机构组织开展了《长城维修工程施工技术规程》、《砖石质长城保护维修指导性文件》等具有针对性的长城保护维修技术规范编制工作。

四、长城价值共建共享与文旅融合

2017 年和 2018 年期间，一系列长城重大政策与改革行动陆续推出，政府和社会携手，文化与旅游融合，共同保护长城安全，弘扬长城文化，传播长城价值，带动长城区域社会发展。

（一）长城开放利用新形势

2018 年政府机构改革，文化部和国家旅游局合并成立文化和旅游部.全国各地纷纷出台加快文化和旅游融合发展的意见，拉开了文旅融合的时代序幕。在此背景下，长城开放利用迎来了新的发展契机。

archaeological survey, and damage investigation and analysis to ensure that the minimum intervention principle would be upheld.

Preventative conservation

In recent years, the focus of Great Wall protection work has gradually shifted from restoration to adopting a series of management measures to strengthen proactive conservation. Aimed at preventing damage and slowing deterioration of the Wall structure, these measures have achieved positive results.

Before the flood season in 2018, under the direction of NCHA, provinces, autonomous regions and direct municipalities along the Great Wall carried out a thorough screening of potential structural risks and implemented pre-emptive temporary reinforcement measures. The daily maintenance of the Wall has also received increasing attention. Some places have begun to explore and change policies to promote the transition to preventive conservation. For instance, based on lessons learnt from past experience, Hebei Province has in recent years consciously included maintenance work into their funding programme in addition to major stabilisation and conservation projects.

From 2017 to 2018, cultural relics departments and research institutions at all levels explored various methodologies to improve monitoring of the Great Wall. These included: establishing monitoring and early warning platforms; using drones, portable mobile devices and installing front-end monitoring equipment to gather data; comparing satellite images; and developing mobile phone apps. These practices provided valuable experience to inform subsequent future systematic monitoring of the Great Wall.

Compiling technical regulations for the implementation of repair projects

To improve the standards of conservation and repair projects and advance theoretical and practical understanding of conservation of the Great Wall, NCHA commissioned specialised institutions to compile technical regulations on specific subjects. These included Technical Regulations for the Implementation of the Great Wall Conservation and Guidelines for the Conservation of Brick and Stone Walls, each in accordance with The Guidelines of the Great Wall Conservation Project issued by SACH in 2014.

CO-CREATION OF SHARED VALUES AND INTEGRATION WITH CULTURAL TOURISM

In 2017 and 2018, a series of major policies and reforms related to the Great Wall were launched which aimed to promote cooperation between government and society to facilitate the integration of culture and tourism so that they can together protect the Great Wall, promote its culture and communicate the value of the Great Wall to larger audiences and contribute to the development of its surrounding communities.

Recent developments in the opening up of the Great Wall for tourism

In 2018, China's government agencies were restructured. The former National Tourism Administration and the Ministry of Culture were merged to form the Ministry of Culture and Tourism. This has led to a surge of new policies across the country on accelerating the integration of culture and tourism. This has marked a new era in the development of cultural tourism. With this general momentum, greater public access to the Great Wall has ushered in new opportunities.

New developments in Great Wall tourism

Public access is extending more widely and cultural tourism is becoming more diversified along the Great Wall. The traditional tourism model was dominated by individual scenic spots. There is now a process of integration that tries to link up individual sites and promote regional, and even cross-regional, co-operation. In 2017 and

（二）长城开放利用的整体格局

长城开放利用和文化旅游的深度与广度不断拓展与延伸，长城由点式景区为主的传统开放利用形式，逐渐向“以点呈线、以线连域、跨行政区、跨国家合作”的全方位发展整体格局发展。2017 年和 2018 年，长城开放利用开始提出一系列长城国家文化公园、长城文化带、全域旅游等视阈下的专题新型文旅融合概念和形式。长城开放利用成为综合区域资源、实现文物保护与区域协调发展的热点，成为我国大型线性文化遗产开放利用与文化旅游融合的先锋示范，同时也对长城开放利用管理提出了新要求。

（三）政府和文物部门开展长城宣传

2017–2018 年，各级政府部门及文物保护专业机构通过文化遗产日主题活动、校园公开课、文化节、长城专题展览、普法宣传教育讲座等各种形式开展了内容丰富的保护长城系列宣传教育活动。

（四）社会参与长城保护利用

2017– 2018 年，社会各界参与长城保护的活动丰富，与往年相比更具有目的性、组织性和计划性，长城沿

图 3 长城保护联盟成立大会照片，2018 年 6 月 6 日，北京怀柔慕田峪长城（摄影：张俊）。
Fig.3 The founding ceremony of the Great Wall Alliance, at the Mutianyu Great Wall in Huairou District, Beijing, 6th June 2018 (photograph by Zhang Jun).

2018, such new initiatives as the Great Wall National Cultural Park (General Office of the CCP 2017) and the Great Wall Cultural Belt (People's Government of Beijing Municipality 2017) were launched, together with other holistic tourist destination development strategies involving the Great Wall in the regions. The Great Wall has become the focus of greater attention in these contexts, as a multi-faceted resource rather than simply a historic site, and as an potential exemplar of sustainability between regional development and heritage conservation, and as a flagship of cultural and tourism integration in heritage management. Consequently, this also poses new demands on the existing management of the Great Wall.

Developing public awareness

Throughout this period, government agencies at all levels and cultural heritage conservation institutions carried out a series of public awareness raising and education activities. These included celebrating Cultural Heritage Day with the Great Wall as a special theme, giving public lectures on campuses, organising cultural festivals, and holding thematic exhibitions as well as delivering lectures on the basic laws and regulations related to the protection of the Wall.

Social engagement

A wide range of organisations have participated in activities contributing to the protection of the Great Wall and these activities have been more focused, and better organised and planned than in previous years. A cross-regional, multi-industry, multi-level organisation for the coordination of the protection and the enhancement of the benefit to society of the Great Wall has also been established. In 2018, the Great Wall Alliance was initiated by CACH, the CFCHC, the Tencent Charity Foundation and other institutions. The Great Wall Alliance, pools resources from 41 research and professional institutes, Great Wall management agencies, major scenic areas, private enterprises, government institutions as well as social groups. Its purpose is to enhance protection of the Wall; to share knowledge and understanding of the monument; to share experience of its conservation and of enhancing its benefits to society; and to promote its cultural recognition and development of high quality tourist experiences.

International dialogue on the protection and management of the Great Wall

In December 2017, CACH and Historic England signed the Collaboration Agreement for Hadrian's Wall and the Great Wall of China (Fig.4). In March 2018, hosted by Newcastle University and organised by CACH and Historic England, the first 'Wall to Wall: The Great Wall of China and Hadrian's Wall Management Seminar' was held, during which participants on both sides exchanged ideas on a broad range of issues and discussed opportunities for cooperation.

In March 2017, the Jiayuguan Great Wall and Petra in Jordan agreed to become sister cultural World Heritage Sites and signed a cooperation agreement.

CONCLUSION

Looking back on 2017 and 2018, great achievements have been made in the protection and management of the Great Wall. Yet at the same time, there were also many issues to be addressed. For example, archaeological research is still insufficient to inform either the conservation of the Great Wall or understanding and promotion of its value. Fundamental capacity building in Great Wall conservation needs to be strengthened further. Conservation interventions need to be followed-up to evaluate their effectiveness in a more scientific and systematic way. The daily maintenance of the Great Wall should be more prioritised in terms of resource allocation. In addition, there is a need to face the new developments in public access and tourism development in a more responsive and open-minded way. The principles for landscape and ecological protection of the Wall also still need to be translated into feasible policies.

线跨区域、跨行业、跨层级的长城保护利用协作性组织成立。2018年，中国文化遗产研究院、中国文物保护基金会、腾讯公益慈善基金会等机构发起成立长城保护联盟，41家长城专业研究机构、部分重要点段保护管理机构、主要景区、企事业单位和社会团体加盟，旨在进一步加强长城保护工作，共享各地长城保护、研究与利用成果，促进长城文化传播，提升长城旅游品质。

（五）国际交流对话长城保护管理

2017年12月，中国文化遗产研究院和英格兰遗产委员会签署《哈德良长城和中国长城全面合作协议》（图4）。2018年3月，中国文化遗产研究院与英格兰遗产委员会主办，纽卡斯尔大学承办第一届“双墙对话—中国长城与英国哈德良长城保护管理研讨会”，中国长城和罗马帝国长城开启了有组织的广泛对话，并积极探讨各种合作方式。

2017年3月，中国长城嘉峪关与约旦佩特拉古城缔结为姊妹世界文化遗产地，签订合作协议。

五、结语

回顾2017年和2018年，长城保护管理取得很大成绩，同时也存在不少问题，如考古研究对保护利用支撑不足，长城基础工作仍普遍较为薄弱，长城保护维修项目实施效果缺乏科学管理和评估，长城日常养护缺乏政策保障，面对长城开放利用新形势的统筹管理滞后，长城景观和生态保护有待落实。

根据《长城保护总体规划》要求，应加强长城行政管理、保护维修、宣传教育、参观开放和专题研究，以实现长城保护总体目标：传承弘扬长城精神，宣传推介长城文化，保护长城建筑遗产，延续长城文化景观。

参考文献
References

Ministry of Culture and Tourism & National Cultural Heritage Administration. 2019. *The Great Wall Protection Master Plan.*

文化和旅游部, 国家文物局. 2019. 长城保护总体规划.

People's Government of Beijing Municipality. 2017. Beijing Municipality Master Plan (2016-2035).

北京市人民政府. 2017. 北京城市总体规划 (2016年—2035年).

General Office of CCP and General office of the State Council. 2017. *National Cultural Development and Reform Planning Framework for the '13th Five Year Period'.*

中共中央办公厅, 国务院办公厅. 2017. 国家“十三五”时期文化发展改革规划纲要.

图 4 中英签署《全面合作协议》，2017 年 12 月 7 日，英国伦敦（图片来源：英格兰遗产委员会）。

Fig.4 Signing of the Collaboration Agreement for Hadrian's Wall and the Great Wall of China, 7th December, 2017 (photograph by Historic England).

As stipulated by the Great Wall Protection Master Plan, major efforts should be made to reinforce the Wall's administrative systems, maintenance and conservation practices, public engagement and educational initiatives, public access provisions, and further thematic studies should be undertaken. Together these will help realise the ultimate goals of passing on the Great Wall's spiritual legacy, the promotion and enhancement of the culture of the Great Wall, the protection of the Great Wall's architectural heritage, and sustaining the cultural landscape of the Great Wall (Ministry of Culture and Tourism & NCHA 2019).

1.3 北京长城文化带建设与展望

王玉伟
原北京市文物局—中国—北京

摘要

北京长城文化带建设是北京市全国文化中心建设重要组成部分，列为北京市重点工作之一。根据北京长城保护利用工作现状及存在的突出问题，从社会参与、机制创新、资源整合三个方面阐述了长城文化带建设工作的主要内容，并结合长城保护管理工作的实践，提出相应的对策建议。长城文化带建设不仅是北京市推进长城保护利用、文化传承的一项重要举措，也是利用长城文化资源优势，为激发遗产地所在区域社会经济活力而提供的又一难得的发展机遇。

关键词：北京长城文化带　建设　展望

引言

多年来，北京市持续投入巨资对市级以上文物保护单位进行抢险修缮，极大缓解了文物建筑长期存在的安全隐患，基本上扭转了文物建筑年久失修的被动局面。

同时，大型线性世界文化遗产长城的保护状况也得到了不断改善，但由于历史欠账过多，保护和管理难度过大，随着北京社会经济的快速发展，管理中的一些问题也逐渐显露出来，特别是一些未开放地段长城，由于游人攀爬与日递增，墙体险情逐渐加剧，抢修工作迫在眉睫。而已开放景区则分布不均，普遍存在着开放展示形式单一，研究力量薄弱，价值阐释深度不到位等问题。一些规模较大景区为提高经营收入呈现走“高端”寻求出路的趋势，使长城利用强度过大。而较小景区则因资金等因素导致基础服务设施落后整体水平难以提升而门可罗雀。加之一些历史原因形成的部门设置交叉重叠多头管理协调困难等问题，传统的管理模式越来越难以应对当前文化遗产保护的需要。管理工作的压力越来越大，保护状况仍然不容乐观。长城作为社会公共资源社会效益尚未得到充分发挥。

针对这些突出问题和长城文化带区域的实际情况，北京市广泛听取各方面专家的意见，在充分调研的基础上，于 2015 年提出了长城文化带建设的初步设想。由北京市文物局牵头组织编制完成《北京市长城文化带保护发展规划（2018 年–2035 年）》（以下简称《规划》）经专家论证，2019 年 3 月由北京市推进全国文化中心建设领导小组批准印发相关单位。文化带建设以抓好文化遗产保护的保护利用为核心，以加强文物抢险、文化传承、资源整合，建立完善的长城保护利用统筹协调机制为主要工作内容，旨在利用文化带区域资源整体优势驱动遗产地社会、文化、经济更快发展。

1.3 ESTABLISHMENT AND FUTURE DEVELOPMENT OF THE BEIJING GREAT WALL CULTURAL BELT

Wang Yuwei
Beijing Cultural Relics Bureau - China - Beijing

Abstract

The Beijing Great Wall Cultural Belt is a key project in turning Beijing into the national centre of culture. Therefore, it is listed as one of the priority projects of the municipality. Based on the progress of the conservation of the Great Wall in Beijing and the major issues which have emerged from this process, this paper elaborates on the project from the aspects of community engagement, reform of management systems and resource integration. It then identifies solutions to address issues in current conservation practice. Developing the Cultural Belt not only promotes the conservation of the Wall as a cultural heritage site but also provides a significant opportunity to boost vibrancy in the local economy and in communities.

Keywords: Beijing Great Wall Cultural Belt, establishment, future development

INTRODUCTION

For many years the municipal government of Beijing has been investing heavily in the rescue of Protected Units of Cultural Resources (PUCRs) at the municipal level or above. It has largely reduced the risks these sites were facing and has essentially broken the vicious cycle caused by overdue repairs. As a result, the Great Wall as a massive linear World Heritage Site has become better preserved. However, a combination of accumulated issues have remained unaddressed which have made its conservation and management even more difficult. This is exacerbated by rapid social change and by economic development in Beijing. Mismanagement has been gradually revealed, especially in sections of the Great Wall not yet open to the public. The increase of unlawful climbing on these sections has put them in imminent danger and immediate intervention is required. Those sections already open to the public are unevenly distributed and already face their own challenges. These include a lack of exhibitions, limited research capability, and an absence of in-depth interpretation of the value of the Great Wall. A few larger sites seek to increase their operating income through encouraging higher visitor spending, which leads to over exploitation of the Wall. In contrast, the smaller sites are relatively unvisited due to their lack of funding and poorer visitor facilities and services. In addition, long-term issues such as overlapping administrative responsibilities and difficulties in coordination between different authorities have made the traditional management models increasingly inadequate to meet the demands of cultural heritage preservation today. The challenges for management are growing greater, yet the state of conservation of the monument must continue to be improved. The full potential of the Great Wall as a communal resource that brings benefits to the public has not yet been realised.

To address these issues, the municipal government of Beijing consulted with a range of experts from different fields, and, in 2015, after careful deliberations, developed a preliminary plan of the Great Wall Cultural Belt (GWCB). *The Preservation and Development Plan of the Beijing Great Wall Cultural Belt 2018 - 2035* (referred to as '*The Plan*' hereafter), was then compiled by a team led by the Beijing Cultural Relics Bureau. In March 2019, after an expert review, the Plan gained the approval of the Steering Group for Promoting Beijing as a National Cultural Area for it to be

一、 加强本体保护鼓励社会参与

北京长城墙体有迹可寻的约 520 千米，敌台、马面、水关（门）、铺房、烽火台等 5 种类型，计 1742 座（《规划》第 8 条），目前长城墙体保存状况相对较好约占三分之一，尚有三分之一保存状况较差，已实施过不同程度修缮的仅为十分之一左右，部分地段安全隐患严重。为此，长城文化带建设中市文物部门加强政策指导和监管，工作重心下移，进一步下放管理权限，强化属地责任。推行网格化管理模式，全面落实专职长城保护员管理制度，调动各方面的积极性，争取更多社会力量参与长城的保护。

长城抢险项目关口前移，争取简化审批手续，由区文物主管部门牵头组织拉网排查，按照“先救命后治病”（《规划》第 19 条）原则，制定计划分轻重缓急加快实施。同时，加强科学管理，探索建立遗产预防性保护机制和市区两级长城监测体系（《规划》第 32 条），努力做到早预防、早发现、早干预。

二、 建立统筹协调机制

北京长城文化带所处区域用地权属复杂，涉及众多部门管理，产权、管理权、使用权分散，加上长城部分地段与天津市、河北省存在跨界管理的问题，保护利用方面协调管理难度大。为此，北京市成立了由市文物局、市发展和改革委员会、北京市规划和自然资源委员会、市住房和建设委员会、市园林绿化局、市文化和旅游局、市财政局及相关区等部门组成的“长城文化带建设组”（《规划》第 92 条），建立市区统筹、部门联动机制和京津冀长城保护利用协商制度，共同协调解决长城维修、长城文化资源保护利用等方面的一些重大问题，为区域协同发展提供保障。

三、整合资源促进区域发展

北京长城沿线文化遗产和自然资源十分丰富，军防村镇乡土民俗、农业种植、交通驿道等传统村落等共 624 处，生态资源 40 片（《规划》第 13 条），展现出这一地带丰富的文化多样性特征，存在着巨大的文旅资源潜力。然而，由于各部门在管理和利用上“各司其职，单打独斗”，远没有形成合力，制约了长城文化的挖掘、研究和合理利用，致使资源优势未能充分体现。

20 世纪末，随着文化线路、乡土建筑等新型文化遗产进入人们视野，文物保护视角从传统上的本体保护逐步拓展到与其相关的非物质文化及周边历史环境的保护。由于文化遗产保护理念认识的不断深入，北京市力求通过长城文化带建设搭建政府部门携手合作平台，共同承担起新时期赋予我们遗产保护更加复杂、更加艰巨的历史使命。以通过组织长城文化带区域利益相关者的广泛参与，整合文化资源，共同推进北京乃至京津冀地区以长城为主线的极具特色的生态涵养区建设，发挥独特的历史文化资源优势，满足社会日益增长精神文化需求，通过不断开拓历史文化旅游和生态休闲场所，使公众能够享受更多的遗产保护成果。

《规划》明确提出长城文化带建设“一线五片多点”整体空间结构的发展定位和规划 目标（《规划》第 30 条），北京长城文化带总面积达 4929.29 平方千米，接近北京全市面积的三分之一，其中核心区占 2228.02 平方千米。

文化带将呈线型分布的长城遗存及周边，划分成五处核心组团片区和近百处城堡、传统聚落等点段，把文化及生态环境组合为一体统一规划。以实现长城本体和载体全线无险情，城村镇基础设施完善，长城

issued to relevant departments. The core objective of the Cultural Belt is the conservation of cultural heritage and the enhancement of its value to society. The priorities include emergency stabilisation, the preservation of cultural inheritance, resource integration and the establishment of a mechanism of improved management and coordination of conservation and utilisation of the Great Wall. The aim is to use the rich resources within the region to boost the development of local communities and their culture and economy.

STRENGTHENING WALL PRESERVATION AND ENCOURAGING SOCIAL ENGAGEMENT

Around 520km of the Wall in Beijing is visible. The 1,742 structures on this section fall into five categories: defence towers; horse faces; water gates; sentry houses; and beacon towers (Article 8, *The Plan*). Roughly a third of the section is well preserved, but the condition of another one-third gives rise to concern. Only a tenth of the Wall has been subject to repair (to different degrees) and some parts of the section are at high levels of structural risk. In this context, and within the framework of GWCB, while the municipal cultural relics authorities have augmented their policies, guidelines and supervision mechanisms, more emphasis has been put on delegating more authority to the local level. As a result, the entire area is broken down into managerial grids. Great Wall patrollers have been appointed and social engagement is encouraged to involve more participants from wider communities.

Emergency stabilisation projects are to be prioritised through a streamlined approval process, wherever possible. In order to expedite the process, district cultural relics authorities will proactively lead thorough site investigations and develop intervention plans for the prioritisation of projects according to the rule of 'saving endangered sites before repairing already damaged ones' (Article 19, *The Plan*). Meanwhile, management decisions will be based on better-informed understanding of the remains. Tentative moves will be taken to establish a mechanism of preventive preservation and Great Wall monitoring systems at both the municipal and district levels (Article 32, *The Plan*). The objective is to prevent anticipated damage from occurring and to ensure early detection and intervention when unanticipated damage does occur.

SETTING UP A COORDINATION MECHANISM

Land use rights within the GWCB area is complex, involving numerous authorities and fragmented ownership and usage rights. This situation is further complicated because several stretches of the Wall function as the boundaries between Beijing Municipality and Tianjin Municipality and between Beijing Municipality and Hebei Province, making it even more difficult to coordinate between different jurisdictions' heritage authorities. To address this issue, the municipal government set up the GWCB Development Group, made up of: the Beijing Cultural Relics Bureau; the Municipal Commissions of Development and Reform, Planning and Natural Resources, Housing and Urban-Rural Development; the Municipal Bureaux of Gardening and Greening, Culture and Tourism, and Finance; and district governments along the Wall (Article 92, *The Plan*). This is to set up a consultation system that can address prominent issues such as the conservation and utilisation of the Great Wall, and ensure coordination across municipal and district levels, across different government departments, and between the Beijing-Tianjin-Hebei regions.

INTEGRATING RESOURCES TO BOOST REGIONAL DEVELOPMENT

The Beijing section of the Wall is rich in cultural and environmental resources. There are 624 villages featuring military forts, folk culture, traditional agriculture and historical transport routes, alongside 40 areas of ecological importance (Article 13, *The Plan*). These show the cultural diversity in the area as well as the great potential for tourism. However, different authorities have been working separately on managing and utilising their heritage, and consequently they have failed to make the most out of these resources. Such a lack of joint working holds back the

沿线整体统筹分段管理的目标，是一次突破当前文物保护利用瓶颈的大胆尝试，也是探索区域经济与长城文化融合的创新型模式。

四、落实实施建议

长城文化带建设以文化与自然资源保护为前提，建立管理与运行的长效机制为保障，带动长城沿线区域社会、文化、经济活力的整体提升为出发点，充分体现了北京市保护文化遗产的决心与信心。现结合当前北京长城保护利用中一些难点问题，提出以下五点建议：

一是继续加大宣传力度。充分利用文化和自然遗产日、新媒体等国家公共资源，通过社区、学校等社会公益活动鼓励更多的社会力量参与长城保护，投身到长城文化带建设中去。

二是加强法规建设，落实实施主体。建议制定北京长城文化带保护利用专项管理办法，为长城文化带建设提供法律保障。同时，尽快在长城文化带组织领导机构的框架下，组建由发展改革委、规划和自然委员会、文物部门牵头，各区文化旅游部门参与的长城文化带建设工作执行机构，落实人员分工、明确任务责任。防止出现多头管理或推诿扯皮的现象。

三是创新项目运行管理机制。长城为大型遗址类文化遗产，调查研究、保护维修、资源挖掘中做好常被忽视的考古工作尤为重要。建议制定长城考古工作专项规划，探索建立以建筑考古为基础的长城保护项目新型管理模式。鼓励以购买服务方式引进适合长城项目管理的咨询服务制度，以弥补项目甲方专业技术人员不足，管理不规范不到位等问题。借鉴国际项目先进的管理经验，在具备条件的项目中试行设计总承包制，尝试以研究为基础，设计、采购、施工密切配合为一体的管理保障模式，使保护项目管理更加精细、科学、合理。

四是优化区划管理。北京段长城保护区划标准高、出台早，2003 年 7 月，北京市文物局《关于划定长城临时保护区的通知》（京文物 [2003] 428 号）就要求长城非建设区（保护范围）为长城墙体两侧 500 米，限制建设区（建设控制地带）为长城墙体两侧 500—3000 米。这对今天长城良好的环境保护起到了极其重要的作用。但由于历史原因，目前除长城本体外，绝大多数保护范围内的土地权属不归文物管理使用单位，给文物维修及展示利用带来极大不便，长城本体也因此常常面临着严重的安全隐患。最好的解决办法是由城市规划和自然委员会牵头，将长城两侧及附属遗存周边一定范围的农业或林业等用地施划长城保护利用红线，在保护范围内增设一条确保长城本体安全的隔离地带。红线内可设巡视考察步道，展示休憩平台及安装说明、警示标识等。如果再建硬化道路、种植果树林木及农作物等必须避让红线。红线内用地可选择在土地确权、规划建设和旧村改造时采取征收、置换或租用等方式逐步退让，现有的植被根据长城保护需要予以优化。

五是进一步突出长城文化带公益性特点。长城文化与自然生态为国家公共资源，应充分显现政府主导公众参与、服务于研究、教育、休憩的公益性特点。长城保护及公共服务等基础设施，应坚持以政府财政、社会公益基金投入为主的原则。购买服务形式的托管及文化创意产品特许经营等不得以盈利为目的。郊野性质的长城遗址区域集体或企业圈地经营开发方式应严格控制。在确保长城安全的前提下，鼓励长城具备开放的区域以多种形式向公众开放，使老百姓能够更多的享受到文化遗产保护成果，不能仅靠设置“禁止攀登”警示或采取“门票杠杆”等简单控制手段替代管理上的缺失。

research, assessment and appropriate utilisation of the cultural resources of the Wall.

At the end of the 20th century, the focus of heritage preservation gradually extended from simply preserving the site itself to preserving all of its related intangible heritage and the surrounding historical landscape, while at the same time the definition of cultural heritage was broadening to include cultural routes and folk architecture. Against this background, the strategy of the GWCB has been is initiated by the Beijing Municipality to establish a collaboration platform through which all government agencies can together take on the increasingly complex and challenging duty of heritage preservation. The GWCB promotes the establishment of an ecological preservation area combined with cultural resources in Beijing and its surrounding areas in which the Great Wall is situated. Through more holistic enhancement of the unique historic resources and wider engagement of all stakeholders in the GWCB, it aims to serve the increasing demand for cultural activities by the public to provide more access by developing new forms of tourism including ecological areas for both leisure and tourism.

The Plan has clearly set out the development framework of 'one line, five clusters and various sites' (Article 30, *The Plan*). The Beijing section of the GWCB will cover 4,929km^2 - a third of the entire area of the municipality; the core area consisting of the five clusters covers 2,228km^2.

The GWCB divides the line of the Wall and its surrounding areas into five core clusters linked together by almost a hundred forts and folk settlements. Its cultural and ecological components are all incorporated into this plan. The goals are to eliminate the structural risks in the Wall itself and its foundations, to improve the infrastructure in the towns and villages along it, and to manage the Wall through a localised yet coordinated mechanism. The establishment of the GWCB is a bold attempt to break the longstanding challenges in current cultural heritage conservation and utilisation, as well as being a new initiative to explore the possibility of integrating the local economy with the cultural significance of the Great Wall.

ADVICE ON IMPLEMENTATION

The GWCB initiative shows the determination and confidence of the Beijing Municipality to focus on the preservation of the Great Wall's cultural and natural resources, to develop long-term management and operational mechanisms and to comprehensively boost the vitality, culture, and economy of communities along the Wall. From long observation of the challenges we face in our work, I would like to propose the following five suggestions for the implementation of the GWCB development initiative.

Firstly, we need to continuously raise public awareness. The appropriate authorities should make full use of opportunities for public engagement such as the Cultural and Natural Heritage Day and new media, and should launch public engagement campaigns in local communities and schools. This is to encourage wider social involvement in Great Wall preservation and in the establishment of the GWCB.

Secondly, it is important to have appropriate laws and regulations in place, and specific entities should be appointed to enforce them. I suggest that dedicated regulations for the conservation and utilisation of Beijing GWCB should be established to provide an appropriate legal framework. Meanwhile, a GWCB executive body should be set up as soon as possible, which should be led by the Municipality's Commission of Development and Reform, the Commission of Planning and Natural Resources, and Cultural Relics Bureau, consisting of participants from cultural and tourism departments in the districts. In this way, responsibilities can be clearly assigned to individuals, which would prevent the situation where the management duties overlap or are passed between different authorities.

Thirdly, it is time to reform the mechanisms for the management of conservation projects. The Great Wall is an enormous collection of archaeological ruins, and this makes it particularly important to carry out archaeological work properly before implementing any survey and investigation, conservation or utilisation projects; yet this crucial proviso is often neglected. My suggestion is to develop a dedicated plan for Great Wall archaeology as the basis for a new management model for conservation projects on the Wall. Hiring external consultancies to support

结束语

长城是北京最重要的一条历史文脉，几乎覆盖整个北京西部、北部区域。长城文化带建设立足于首都城市战略定位，以长城保护为前提，以传统文化为引领，破解长城保护过程中长期存在的保护与研究脱节、保护与公众脱节、保护与遗产地社会经济发展脱节的难题。通过整合长城文化资源，建立一个统一规范、高效的运营管理体制，弘扬遗产价值,优化生态环境，带动区域文化和社会发展，实现长城文化遗产的整体保护、合理利用，惠及百姓，服务未来的宏伟目标。

参考文献
References

The Steering Group of Promoting Beijing as a National Cultural Area. March 2019. *The Preservation and Development Plan of the Beijing Great Wall Cultural Belt (2018 - 2035).* (Beijing Cultural Establishment Notice [2019] No.3.

北京市推进全国文化中心建设领导小组. 2019 年 3 月. 北京市长城文化带保护发展规划（2018 年-2035 年）.（京文建发 [2019] 3 号）.

the management of projects is a desirable way to bring in expertise and to make up for insufficient professional management capacity. We should learn from best practice all over the world and conduct pilot projects, when appropriate, that bring in a process of whole-project contracting, through which projects are led by the lead designer, and which links together the initial stage of scientific research with the subsequent stages of design, procurement and construction. All these efforts can help make us better informed and hence enable us to make wiser decisions in conservation projects.

Fourthly, we need to refine zoning regulations. In July 2003, in the *Notice of Temporary Great Wall Protection Zone Designation* (Beijing Cultural Relics Bureau Notice [2003] 428) the Beijing Cultural Relics Bureau ruled that the non-construction zone (the protection zone) extends for 500m on both sides of the Wall. The restricted area (the construction control zone) extends beyond the non-construction zone to 3,000m from the Wall. This early and strict legislation has played a significant role in preserving the landscape setting of the Wall. However, the rights to use most of the land within the protection zone do not belong to the cultural relics management agencies. This has been a long-standing issue, which has caused great inconvenience both for conservation and for utilisation of the Wall, and it means that the fabric of the Wall is often still at serious risk. The best solution would be to have the Municipal Commission of Planning and Natural Resources set up an additional 'red-line' zone along the Wall within the boundary of the protection zone to exert stricter control over agricultural and forestry land use and further enhance the protection of the Wall. Within the new zone, apart from for inspection trails for Patrollers, visitor terraces at vantage points, information plaques and signs, no other construction and no forestry or agricultural activities should be permitted. Land within the new zone could be transferred gradually by requisition, land exchange or leaseholds as a part of rights identification, planning, and village regeneration. The vegetation would also need to be managed to meet the needs of conservation.

Fifthly, we need to emphasise the public benefits of the GWCB. The Great Wall cultural and natural eco-system is a national resource, and this should be reflected in governmental leadership, public engagement activities and the promotion of research, education and public amenity. Any outsourcing of the operation of visitor services or cultural products concessions should be for non-profit purposes. Commercial enclosure and development of the Wall sites in rural areas by local community councils and companies should be strictly controlled. Public access should be encouraged through providing a variety of alternative ways to visit the Great Wall, provided that they do not damage the archaeology. This would allow the public to enjoy and appreciate the results of good heritage preservation, and no longer be excluded by traditional management practices, such as putting up signs saying 'climbing forbidden' or applying excessive ticket prices.

CONCLUSION

The Great Wall is one of the most important cultural heritage sites in Beijing, covering the entire western and northern parts of the municipality. The GWCB is a strategic initiative of capital city level status which is led by the conservation and protection of its cultural heritage site and by its traditional culture. The initiative will remove the long-standing disconnections between conservation and research, on the one hand, and accessibility, utilisation, and the economic development of the site and its communities, on the other. By integrating the Great Wall's cultural resources, we can build a holistic and efficient management system that can promote the value of the Wall, improve the environment and boost the development of local culture and society. Ultimately, it serves the great vision of the comprehensive preservation and utilisation of the site that will bring benefits to everyone in the future.

1.4 THE THIRD SECTOR IN HERITAGE MANAGEMENT

CAROL PYRAH
Historic Coventry Trust - Coventry - UK

Abstract

This paper explores the background and development of the thriving third sector in heritage management in the UK. It looks at the cultural origins of the third sector, the development of interest in heritage and conservation, and the role of the third sector on Hadrian's Wall. Through the case study of Historic Coventry Trust, it explores the role and opportunities for charities today.

Keywords: third sector, voluntary organisations, charitable trusts, charities, community, conservation

INTRODUCTION

The third sector in the UK is an increasingly important part of the social and economic ecosystem of the country. It is distinctive from both the public sector (comprising national and local government, and or government-sponsored but independently managed organisations) and the private sector (commercial companies run by individuals primarily for profit which are entirely independent of government). The term 'the third sector' refers all other organisations, ranging from informal voluntary groups and associations to organisations with formal legal status. The latter are predominantly constituted as charitable trusts ('charities') and can be either fully professional or purely volunteer-run bodies, but typically are a combination of both. The third sector plays a major role in heritage protection and management, often channelling community passion for a place or activity. This paper explores the origins of voluntary interest in heritage, the third sector's role in heritage management today and the characteristics and governance of UK charitable trusts. As well as looking at the third sector on Hadrian's Wall, the paper uses the case study of Historic Coventry Trust to explore some of the opportunities in caring for heritage via a charitable trust.

THE EUROPEAN ENLIGHTENMENT AND THE BIRTH AND GROWTH OF THE THIRD SECTOR

To understand the place of the third sector and the deep roots which it has in UK culture we need to look at its history. The period from the late 17th century to the end of the Napoleonic Wars in 1815 is known in Europe as 'the Enlightenment' or the 'Age of Reason.' This was a period of great development of scientific, political and philosophical ideas. A key element of the Enlightenment culture was the rise of the 'public sphere' *i.e.* public debate on matters of morality, science, economy and society. This was fuelled by a large increase in printed books, the wealth to buy them, and increasing literacy. Informing this public debate was a belief in 'reason' as a basis for thought, in the importance of independence from the state, of the openness of debate, and of all ideas being open to criticism.

One result of this period was the creation of a network of independent intellectual, scientific and benevolent organisations by an increasingly literate middle and upper class who were thirsty to gain and share knowledge. At the same time there was a growth of interest in geology, archaeology, fossils and natural history, and many independent organisations were set up to promote the study of these subjects. The Society of Antiquaries of

1.4 文化遗产管理的第三部门

卡罗尔·派拉
考文垂历史信托—考文垂—英国

摘要

本文介绍了英国繁荣的文化遗产管理第三部门的背景及发展历程，探究了第三部门的文化起源，其对遗产及遗产保护日益关注的过程，以及其在哈德良长城中扮演的角色。通过考文垂历史信托的案例分析，该文阐述了当今慈善机构担当的角色和面临的机遇。

关键字：第三部门　志愿团体　慈善信托机构　慈善　社区　保护

引言

在英国，第三部门（third sector）正在成为国家社会和经济生态系统中越来越重要的一部分。它有别于公共机构（包括国家和地方政府，以及由政府资助但独立运营的机构）和私营组织（由个体运营、以营利为主要目的且独立于政府的商业公司）。第三部门指除公共机构和私营组织外的所有其他组织机构，包括非正式的志愿团体和协会，以及拥有正式法人地位的机构。后者主要由慈善信托机构组成，可能以专业人士为主，也可能以以志愿者为主组建，但通常情况下两者都有。第三部门在遗产保护和管理中扮演着重要角色，常为某地或某活动注入来自社区的活力。本文将探讨志愿团体的自发参与究竟由何而来，介绍第三部门的现状和英国慈善信托机构的治理。同时，本文不仅介绍了哈德良长城的第三部门概况，还通过对考文垂历史信托的案例分析，探讨慈善信托机构如何参与遗产保护。

欧洲启蒙运动与第三部门的诞生和发展

想要了解第三部门以及它与英国文化相关的深层渊源，首先要了解它的历史。自 17 世纪晚期到 1815 年拿破仑战争结束，欧洲经历了启蒙运动，又称“理性时代”，其间科学、政治、哲学思想得到长足发展。“公共领域”的兴起是启蒙文化最关键的要素之一，人们开始公开辩论道德、科学、经济与社会等方面的问题。这一现象源于印刷书籍的大幅普及，书籍购买力的增长与识字率的提高。人们崇尚将“理性”视作思想的基础，提倡独立于政府，提倡公开辩论，提倡批判一切的精神，使公开辩论十分活跃。

由此，启蒙时代出现了一系列独立的知识、科技和行善的组织，文化程度越来越高的中产阶级和上层阶级创办这类组织，渴望获得并分享知识。与此同时，人们对地质学、考古学、化石和自然历史产生了浓厚兴趣，许多相关的独立机构也应运而生，推动这些学科的研究。例如，伦敦古董协会就是在 1707 年成立的，旨在“鼓励、发展和深化对本国及其他国家的古董历史知识研究”（https://www.sal.org.uk/about-us/who-we-are/our-history/）。协会一直延续至今，属于登记注册的慈善机构，拥有超过 3000 名会员（因学术能力优秀而经选举入会的成员），致力于促进公众对遗产的认知，支持相关研究，并影响历史环境公共政策的制定（https://www.sal.org.uk/about-us/）。

London is an example, which was founded in 1707 for 'the encouragement, advancement and furtherance of the study and knowledge of the antiquities and history of this and other countries' (https://www.sal.org.uk/about-us/who-we-are/our-history/). Still in existence today, the Society of Antiquaries is now a registered charity with over 3,000 'Fellows' (members who are elected to join because of their academic expertise) and it exists to foster public understanding of heritage, to support research and to influence public policy on the historic environment (https://www.sal.org.uk/about-us/).

Many other towns and cities around the country set up similar organisations in the 18th and early 19th centuries. A good example is the Society of Antiquaries of Newcastle upon Tyne which is the oldest provincial antiquarian society in the country. It was founded on 23 January 1813 when 17 men met in a local pub to discuss how to study local antiquities. They decided to form a society. The membership subscription was 1 guinea (a gold coin then in use in England worth roughly £1) and they met on the first Wednesday of every month. Like many similar organisations, the Society developed a library and museum, carried out field trips and archaeological excavations, and provided a focus for sharing knowledge and debate on ideas (http://www.newcastle-antiquaries.org.uk/index.php?pageId=277).

As interest and knowledge of history and landscape grew through the learned societies, so did a concern for conservation. From the late 18th century onwards increasing urban expansion, industrialisation and new transport links were destroying archaeological sites, landscapes and historic buildings. Concerns for the future of the landscape and historic sites resulted in the establishment of new campaigning bodies for their protection.

The first conservation body in the UK was the Commons Preservation Society, founded in 1865 to protect public open spaces from development and to retain them as places of recreation (https://www.oss.org.uk/about-us/). Two of the founders of this Society, Sir Robert Hunter and the social reformer, Octavia Hill, went on to set up the National Trust for Places of Historic Interest and Natural Beauty, together with Hardwicke Rawnsley. The National Trust, founded in 1895, is one of the earliest, and is today the largest and best known, of the third-sector heritage conservation organisations in the UK. It was, and remains, an independent charity funded by its members' subscriptions, by donations and by income earned from public visits to its historic houses and landscapes (https://www.nationaltrust.org.uk/about-us).

Throughout the late 19th century and the first half of the 20th century many heritage conservation charities developed. These ranged from organisations to save individual buildings or to champion conservation in particular places (such as civic amenity societies like the City of Durham Trust, which was set up in 1942), to national organisations such as the Society for the Protection of Ancient Buildings (https://www.spab.org.uk/) founded by William Morris in 1877 to campaign against the restoring zeal of Victorian architects, and the Council for British Archaeology (https://new.archaeologyuk.org/), set up in 1944 to campaign for improved protection for archaeology.

THE ROLE OF THE THIRD SECTOR TODAY

As described above, the third sector includes all organisations which are neither government owned and controlled nor privately owned businesses. It includes all forms of voluntary organisations and groups, which are typically run by their members. Some are informal associations, clubs or community groups which have rules and constitutions but no formal legal status. Many others have formal legal status as charities (also known as charitable trusts) or as companies limited by guarantee or as community-interest companies.

There are now well over 4,000 UK-based charities focusing on cultural heritage, over 300 building preservation trusts, and thousands of voluntary organisations such as local history groups, civic societies and archaeological groups. In fact, probably every settlement in the UK with a population of over *c.*700 people has some kind of local

18 世纪到 19 世纪早期，英国各地许多其他乡镇和城市也相继建立起类似的组织。泰恩河畔纽卡斯尔古物协会就是一个很好的例子，它是全英最古老的省级古物协会。协会成立于 1813 年 1 月 23 日，当天有 17 个人在一家当地酒吧聚会，探讨如何研究当地的古物。于是，他们决定要组建一个协会，会费为 1 基尼（当时英国流通的一种金币，约值 1 英镑），规定每个月的第一个星期三开会。与许多类似组织相同，协会建起了博物馆和图书馆，进行实地考察与考古发掘，并组织分享知识、讨论思想（http://www.newcastle-antiquaries.org.uk/index.php?pageId=277）。

通过这些学习知识类协会，人们对历史和景观的兴趣愈发强烈、了解越来越深入，对遗产保护的关注也不断增强。自 18 世纪晚期，城市不断扩张，工业化与新的交通基础设施建设破坏了考古遗址、景观和以及历史建筑。由于对景观和历史遗迹的未来深感担忧，新的保护机构应运而生。

英国第一个保护机构是公共用地保护协会。该协会于 1865 年成立，最初目的是保护公共开放空间不受建设破坏，成为民众休闲娱乐的场所（https://www.oss.org.uk/about-us/）。随后，该机构的两位创始人罗伯特·亨特爵士和社会改革家奥克塔维亚·希尔与哈德威克·罗恩斯利一道于 1895 年又建立了国家历史古迹及自然名胜信托，简称国家信托。这是英国历史最悠久、也是现在最大最知名的文化遗产第三部门保护机构之一。一直以来，国家信托都是独立的慈善组织，资金来源于会员交纳的会费、其他善款以及公众参观历史建筑和景观所获得的收入（https://www.nationaltrust.org.uk/about-us）。

19 世纪晚期到 20 世纪上半叶，遗产保护机构不断发展。这些组织的类型多种多样，从致力于保护单个建筑体的专门机构或地方特设的遗产保护机构（如 1942 年成立的杜伦市信托这类公民休闲组织），到诸如古建筑保护协会的全国性组织（https://www.spab.org.uk/），不一而足。古建筑保护协会创建于 1877 年，其创始人威廉·莫里斯致力于抵制维多利亚时期建筑的“复辟”热潮，于 1944 年成立英国考古委员会（https://new.archaeologyuk.org/），致力于推动考古保护的发展。

当今第三部门的角色

如前所述，第三部门指所有既非政府所有和管控、也非私有的机构。它包括所有形式的志愿组织和团体，主要由其成员负责运营。有一些是非正式的协会、俱乐部或社区团体，虽然制定了制度章程，但不具有正式的法人地位。其他多数为拥有正式法人地位的慈善机构（即慈善信托机构）、担保责任有限公司或社区利益公司。

目前，有超过 4000 家总部位于英国且与文化遗产相关的慈善机构，300 多家建筑保护信托机构，以及数千个志愿组织，包括当地的历史团体、公民组织和考古团体。事实上，只要当地人口超过 700 人，那里就会有某种形式的历史团体或协会。

根据兴趣的不同，英国的文化遗产第三部门的性质也有所区别，但是他们秉承的共同精神由“公民声音”很好地提炼出来：

为其珍爱的地方，公民组织可以表现得积极、顽强、富于创新而又直言不讳。它们是独立的草根组织，仿佛是蚌中的一粒沙，激励人们不断思考，拓宽视野。它们鼓励并提倡积极行动，坚决抵制破坏行为（http://www.civicvoice.org.uk/about/civic_movement/）。

公民声音是众多公民组织的共同联盟。英国的公民组织一般以社区为中心，目标是让人们所居住的市

history group or association.

The nature of third sector heritage organisations in the UK is as varied as their interests, but a description which captures the spirit of many volunteer heritage organisations comes from Civic Voice:

'Civic societies can be provocative, stubborn, forceful, inspiring and outspoken on behalf of the places they care about. They are fiercely independent grassroots organisations, often providing the grit in the oyster which stimulates people to think, reconsider and widen their horizons. They will celebrate and encourage positive action and be forthright in resisting' (http://www.civicvoice.org.uk/about/civic_movement/)

Civic Voice is the umbrella group for civic societies. A 'civic society' in the UK is generally a place-based community organisation that campaigns to make a village, town or city better for its citizens. This often means trying to save historic buildings, commenting on development proposals, and carrying out small repair and restoration projects on features of community value such as village ponds, green spaces, war memorials and statues.

Third-sector organisations in the UK have a number of core principles in common, although their areas of work vary greatly. The National Council for Voluntary Organisations in the UK identifies six key criteria which define 'third sector' organisations (https://www.ncvo.org.uk/):

- Formality: they are formal entities with a recognisable structure and a constitution or set of rules;
- Independence: they are separate from the state and from the private sector;
- Non-profit distributing: most make no profit, but more importantly, any surplus/profit is reinvested in the organisation or used for the benefit of the community;
- Self-governance: they are truly independent in determining their own course;
- The voluntary principle: they involve a meaningful degree of voluntary participation, e.g. through having a unpaid board of Trustees, and volunteers and donations from the public;
- Public benefit: they have social objectives and work to benefit the community.

CHARITABLE TRUSTS

The majority of larger third sector organisations in England and Wales are registered charities regulated by the Charity Commission (under the Charities Act 2011). The Charity Commission was set up on 1853 https://www.gov.uk/government/organisations/charity-commission/about). Only organisations which have defined, non-political, charitable purposes which are for the public benefit can register as a charitable trust. Charities can only spend their money on achieving their aims, they cannot make a distributable profit, nor can they have owners or shareholders who benefit financially from the charity.

A charity is governed by Trustees (usually unpaid volunteers who are interested in the charity's work). The Board of Trustees has overall responsibility for everything the charity does. An estimated 850,000 people in the UK volunteer for a total of 950,000 trustee board roles.

There are about 168,000 charitable trusts in the UK. Their total annual turnover of is *c.*£48bn, and they employ around 880,000 people. Charities contribute over £15.3bn a year to the UK economy, representing 0.8% of total GVA, which is more than agriculture (£8.5bn) or the arts (£8.5bn) (https://nfpsynergy.net/free-report/facts-and-figures-uk-charity-sector-2018), but 80% of UK charities have an income of less than £100,000 a year. Each year about 5,000 new charities are registered (https://howcharitieswork.com/about-charities/how-many-charities/).

Funding for charitable trusts in the UK comes from a range of different sources. These include:

- **Membership fees:** the National Trust has more than 5 million members providing a membership subscription income of over £243,425,000 (National Trust Annual Report 2018/19). At the other end of the scale, many small archaeological societies and civic societies which are also charitable trusts have far fewer members and far less income from annual membership fees.
- **Fundraising/donations from the public:** Many charities in the UK raise funds from the public in a

镇村庄发展得更好、更宜居。为此，公民组织经常努力拯救历史建筑，对建设项目方案提供意见和建议，对具有社区价值的设施开展小型修缮，诸如村里的池塘、绿地、战争纪念碑和雕像等。

在英国，尽管第三部门各组织的工作领域大不相同，它们却有着许多共同的原则。英国国家志愿组织委员会提出了定义第三部门组织的六个关键标准（https://www.ncvo.org.uk/）：

- 正规性：具有清晰组织架构与规章制度的正式实体；
- 独立性：独立于任何政府与私人企业；
- 非营利性分配：大多数不营利；更重要的是，任何盈余/利润全部再投入该组织中，或用于服务社区；
- 自治性：真正做到独立，自行决定发展方向；
- 自愿原则：鼓励志愿参与，例如设立无偿的受托人董事会，招募志愿者和鼓励公众捐赠；
- 公共利益为宗：旨在实现社会目标，努力造福社区。

慈善信托机构

在英格兰和威尔士，大多数第三部门机构都是注册的慈善机构，由慈善事务委员会（依据 2011 年慈善法）负责监管。该委员会成立于 1853 年（https://www.gov.uk/government/organisations/charity-commission/about）。只有出于公共利益、为了实现慈善目标、为公众谋福利的非政治团体才可注册成为慈善信托机构。慈善机构必须把所有的资金用于实现慈善目标上，不得追求以分配为目的利润，其所有者或股东不得通过慈善机构获得财务利益。

慈善机构由受托人管理，通常由对慈善工作感兴趣的志愿者无偿担任。受托人董事会全权负责慈善机构所有事宜。据估计，英国约有 85 万人担任 95 万个受托董事职务。

全英共有约 16.8 万个慈善信托机构，它们的年营业额约为 480 亿英镑，员工共计 88 万人。慈善业每年为英国经济创收超过 153 亿英镑，占总增加值的 0.8%，超过农业或艺术（各 85 亿英镑）的贡献（https://nfpsynergy.net/free-report/facts-and-figures-uk-charity-sector-2018）。然而，英国 80 %的慈善机构年收入却不足 10 万英镑。每年新增注册慈善机构大约在 5000 个左右（https://howcharitieswork.com/about-charities/how-many-charities/）。

在英国，慈善信托机构的资金来源十分广泛，具体包括：

- **会费**：国家信托慈善机构拥有超过 500 万名会员，每年交纳的会费能为信托机构带来超过 2 亿 4342.5 万英镑的收入（国家信托年报 2018/19）。但另一方面，同样身为慈善信托机构，许多小型考古学会和公民组织的会员数可谓少之又少，会员交纳的年费带来的收入也非常有限。
- **公共筹资或捐款**：英国很多慈善机构以各种各样的方式向公众筹集资金。有些机构会开展街头募捐或线上众筹，还有一些会举办筹资活动（如抽彩或有赞助的赛跑），或者获得个人捐赠。在英国，慈善募捐须受募捐监管机构监督管理，后者为独立非法定机构（https://www.fundraisingregulator.org.uk/）。
- **拨款**：英国政府会拨款支持那些为社会带来积极影响的活动。通过国家彩票遗产基金会等若干半公共的彩票机构，全国性彩票每周会为公共事业提供约 3000 万英镑（https://www.heritagefund.org.uk/）的资金。此外，还有各种各样的私有信托和基金会（通常由资产雄厚的个人或组织会成立），慈善机构可以申请其资金支持，它们有各自重点资助的领域、各自的资金申请流程和决策机制。

number of different ways. Some charities run street collections or online crowd-funding campaigns, while others undertake fundraising events (such as raffles or sponsored runs) or receive donations from private individuals. Charitable fundraising in the UK is regulated by the Fundraising Regulator, which is an independent, non-statutory body (https://www.fundraisingregulator.org.uk/).

- **Grants:** In the UK the government gives out grants for activities that produce beneficial social impact. Separately, a national lottery gives out around £30M a week to good causes through a number of semi-public lottery organisations such as the National Lottery Heritage Fund (https://www.heritagefund.org.uk/). There is also a wide range of private grant-giving trusts and foundations (often established by wealthy individuals or organisations) to which charities can apply. Each has its own priorities for funding, its own application procedures and its own decision-making mechanisms.
- **Earned income:** Many heritage charities which look after historic buildings and sites open them to the public and charge an entrance fee, as well as having cafes and shops which earn valuable income.

The charitable trust model has a number of advantages and disadvantages.

Charities can be a means to empower local voluntary action. When they are rooted in a local community or place, or allow a community to rally around a shared cause, they can build wider public support and commitment for the purpose of the charity. Charities can also be inventive and make things happen quickly; as independent organisations they are free from government and public-sector constraints. They can raise money from a wide range of sources and they benefit from some tax relief. Private donations to charities can reduce an individual's personal income tax liability and the national 'Gift Aid' scheme enables individuals to declare their payment of entrance fees as donations, meaning that a charity can receive a further 25% of the 'donated' fee from government tax revenues. Gift Aid also applies to donations, sponsorship and membership fees. Bequests to charities are exempt from inheritance tax, and charities are also partly exempt from paying purchase tax on their expenses, thus reducing some of their operating and capital project costs.

There are, however, some disadvantages to the charity model. Sustaining a charity in the long-term is a challenge; it requires a consistency of purpose and energy that is easy to maintain in the early phase of a charity, but that tends to diminish over time. Finding suitable trustees and enough volunteers is increasingly difficult as people have less free time. In the UK the charity 'brand' has been tarnished in recent years due to a number of fundraising and other scandals in major charities. These led to new charity fundraising rules being introduced by government. Fundraising is also a constant effort for most charities, and very hard work.

The charity sector is nevertheless widely trusted and highly successful in the UK and it enables a wide range of valuable activities that could not be carried out by government or commercial companies.

HADRIAN'S WALL AND THE THIRD SECTOR

There is a thriving and long-established third-sector involvement in the management of Hadrian's Wall. Some key sites are owned by independent conservation charities, from the Vindolanda Trust (established formally in 1970, but where excavation and research had been carried out independently since Eric Birley bought Vindolanda in 1929) to the National Trust (at Housesteads) and the Cultura Trust at Camp Farm, Maryport.

Across the Hadrian's Wall landscape there are many charitable trusts and voluntary organisations such as archaeological societies and history groups who carry out research, do fieldwork, publish articles and set up lectures and events. These range from the long-established organisations, such as the Cumberland & Westmorland Antiquarian and Archaeological Society and the Society of Antiquaries of Newcastle upon Tyne, to smaller groups like the Tynedale North of the Wall Archaeology Group.

There are also local history groups along the Wall corridor, which are interested in all periods of history in their area. These include the Hexham Local History Society and the South Shields Local History Group. Many of the museums

- **运营收入：**很多慈善机构会将其负责运营的历史建筑和遗址向公众开放，并收取门票费，还通过运营咖啡厅与商店获得收入。

慈善信托机构的模式既有优点也有缺点。

慈善信托机构能够成为推动当地志愿活动的有效途经。这些机构植根于当地社区，使整个社区因共同事业团结在一起，有助于为该事业赢得更广泛的公众支持与群众基础。作为独立机构的慈善信托机构不受政府与其他公共部门的约束，因此具有更强的创造力和更高的效率。此外，它们不仅能通过多种渠道筹集资金，还可享受税收减免。私人慈善捐款能够抵扣个人所得税，而国家“馈赠资助”计划则视个人支付的门票为慈善捐款，意味着慈善信托机构可以另外获得捐款金额 25% 的返还税款。“馈赠资助”计划同样适用于捐赠、赞助和会员年费。此外，向慈善信托机构进行遗赠无需缴付遗产税。机构的支出也能享有部分购置税减免，从而减少了运营成本和投资成本。

然而，慈善信托机构也存在一些缺点。如何维持其可持续发展是一个挑战。保持目标和行动力持续不变在慈善信托机构发展的初期并不难做到，但时间一久，往往难以为继。随着人们的空闲时间越来越少，找到合适的受托人与足够的志愿者也愈发困难。近年来，英国几家大型慈善信托机构出现了多起募捐和其他方面的丑闻，名声受损。对此，政府也新出台了若干慈善募捐的规定。另外，对于绝大多数慈善信托机构而言，募集资金是一项持续不断的工作，也十分艰巨。

尽管如此，慈善行业在英国还是赢得了广泛的信任，取得极大的成功，更开展了各种各样政府和商业公司无法牵头却意义非凡的活动。

哈德良长城与第三部门

第三部门一直积极参与哈德良长城的管理，历史十分悠久。一些主要长城遗产地由独立的慈善保护组织所有。比如，文多兰达罗马遗址为文多兰达信托所有。该信托正式创建于 1970 年。不过自遗迹于 1929 年被埃里克·伯利购买后，所有发掘与研究工作皆独立开展。豪塞斯特兹罗马要塞为国家信托所有，而位于玛丽波特的营地农场则为文化信托所有。

哈德良长城沿线有许多慈善信托机构和志愿团体，如考古协会与历史学会，对其展开研究和实地考察，发表文章，并组织讲座与活动。其中，有历史悠久的坎伯兰与西莫兰文物考古学会、泰恩河畔纽卡斯尔古文化研究者学会，以及规模相对较小的泰恩河谷北部长城考古学会等。

长城沿线地区还有很多地方的历史学会，他们对本地长城各时期的历史都很感兴趣，例如赫克瑟姆历史学会和南谢尔德历史学会。长城沿线许多博物馆也是由独立的慈善组织运营的，如卡莱尔的图利别墅博物馆与美术馆。

蓬勃而多样的慈善信托和志愿团体的好处，在于它们的独立、草根特性，以及其兴趣和工作的多样化。当然这也为协调哈德良长城全线的相关活动带来困难。

考文垂历史信托案例分析：一个英国现代第三部门机构

在英国，遗产慈善行业不断发展，最有趣的趋势之一就是“遗产开发信托”的壮大。它们是新的企业型慈善机构，自成规模，致力于修复历史建筑并寻求发现它们的新用途。它们旨在将社区支持和商业方式相融合，确保这些建筑能获得收入，维持其长期的发展。其中规模最大之一要属考文垂历史信托。

along the Wall are also run by independent charities, for example Tullie House Museum & Art Gallery in Carlisle.

The benefit of this rich ecosystem of charities and voluntary effort is the independence, grassroots character and variety of their interests and work. However, it can make attempts to co-ordinate activity across the Wall difficult.

CASE STUDY: HISTORIC COVENTRY TRUST, A MODERN UK THIRD-SECTOR ORGANISATION

The heritage charity sector in the UK is evolving and one of the most interesting trends is the growth in 'heritage development trusts'. These organisations are a new breed of entrepreneurial charities working at scale to repair and find new uses for a collection of historic buildings. They aim to blend community support for a cause with a commercial approach to ensure that the buildings have an income to sustain them in the long-term. One of the largest examples of this is Historic Coventry Trust.

In the 15th century Coventry was one of the most important and wealthy cities in England. Subsequently it became best known for watchmaking (in the 18th and 19th centuries), and for bicycles and the car industry (19th and 20th centuries). The city suffered extensive damage in World War II during the Blitz in November 1940. This, and the post-war policies of the City Council. led to the loss of many of the fine medieval stone and timber-framed buildings that the city had been rich in.

One of the surviving gems is the Charterhouse, one of only two surviving Carthusian monasteries in England (Fig.1). A community campaign against the sale of the site in 2011 led to the creation of the Coventry Charterhouse Preservation Trust, a charity to save and look after the Charterhouse site. The new trustees of the Charity soon realised that Coventry had many other historic buildings in need of a new future, and Historic Coventry Trust was born. Coventry City Council has agreed to give 22 publicly-owned historic buildings to the Trust (on 250-year leases). The Trust is responsible for finding new uses for these buildings, raising funds, carrying out repairs, and then looking after the buildings in perpetuity. This process of community-asset transfer is relatively common in the UK, but the scale of the transfer in Coventry is nationally unique.

Historic Coventry Trust's mission is to be the champion of all heritage at risk in Coventry and to become its permanent guardian. It aims to: acquire, restore, re-use and regenerate Coventry's heritage buildings for the benefit of the public; to ensure a sustainable future for each building as part of a portfolio approach, enabling cross-subsidy between different heritage assets; to be a safe haven for the city's heritage in perpetuity; and to be an active partner in the city's regeneration using heritage as an economic driver.

Historic Coventry Trust is a very small charity with an ambitious programme of projects. It has, to date, raised over £20m, and in 2021 it will be opening the Charterhouse to the public as a visitor attraction, the Draper's Hall as a music venue, and the two remaining city gates (Fig.2) and a row of timber-framed cottages as holiday accommodation for visitors. In addition, the Trust will compete a high-street regeneration programme on Hales Street and the Burges area later in 2020 (Figs.3 & 4).

Coventry will be the UK City of Culture in 2021. This is a designation awarded by the government every four years to one city in the UK. The aim is to bring social and economic benefits through a year-long festival of cultural activity. This is a great opportunity for the Trust, but also means that many more projects need to be completed by 2021, which is a very challenging timescale.

The ability of Historic Coventry Trust to take on an ambitious programme of work relies on a number of key factors. First, the trustees of the charity have a wide range of valuable skills, experience and contacts. The Chairman is a property developer, and other trustees include bankers, business people, lawyers and property managers. This has led to an entrepreneurial approach which brings valuable private-sector thinking into the charity sector. Second, is the Trust's partnership with Coventry City Council. The Council has been bold in agreeing an overall property transfer framework, and the Trust has strong support both from elected politicians

15 世纪，考文垂是英格兰最重要也是最富裕的城市之一。随后，考文垂又以制表业（18 世纪至 19 世纪）和自行车与汽车制造业（19 世纪至 20 世纪）闻名。二战时期，1940 年的闪电战[1]令考文垂遭受重创，加上战后市议会的政策，令考文垂失去了大量精美的中世纪石木建筑。

所幸，卡尔特修道院免于此难，它也是英格兰幸存下来的仅有的两座天主教加尔都西会教士修道院之一（图 1）。2011 年，在一场反对出售卡尔特修道院的社区运动中，考文垂卡尔特修道院保护信托应运而生，旨在拯救和守护卡尔特修道院。很快，新上任的受托董事们便意识到考文垂还有很多其他的历史建筑亟待保护。于是，考文垂历史信托就此成立。市议会同意将 22 座公有历史建筑移交给考文垂历史信托（租期为 250 年）。考文垂历史信托负责开发这些建筑的新用途，筹措资金，开展修复工作，并看护这些建筑使其永久保存。类似的社区资产移交在英国相对普遍，然而考文垂这种规模的移交可谓绝无仅有。

考文垂历史信托肩负的使命是成为考文垂所有濒危遗产的捍卫者和永远的守护者。其宗旨是收购、修复、重新利用和活化考文垂的历史建筑，造福社会；通过其资产组合中各项遗产资产的交叉补贴，确保每栋建筑运营的可持续；成为考文垂市遗产永远的避风港；发挥遗产推动经济增长的作用，积极推动城市复兴。

考文垂历史信托是一个小型慈善机构，但拥有实施众多项目的雄心壮志。信托截至目前已筹集善款超过 2000 万英镑，并将于 2021 年向公众开放若干历史建筑，包括卡尔特修道院作为旅游景点、德雷珀大厅作为音乐厅、两处遗留下来的城门（图 2），以及一排木质结构的村舍为度假住宿。此外，信托还会在 2020 年完成商业街重建项目，涉及黑尔斯街和伯吉斯地区（图 3 & 4）。

考文垂将成为 2021 年的英国文化之城。英国政府每四年将这一荣誉授予一个城市，并在该城市举行长达一年的文化节，旨在推动当地社会与经济的发展。这对于考文垂历史信托而言是个极好的机会。但另一方面，这意味着很多项目需在 2021 年前完成，任务十分艰巨。

考文垂历史信托开展众多项目的雄心壮志与若干关键因素密不可分。第一，慈善信托机构的受托人拥有各种各样的宝贵技能、经验和人脉。董事会主席是一名地产开发商，而受托董事来自各行各业，包括银行家、商人、律师和地产经理，他们将宝贵的企业思维引入慈善界，用经营企业的方法管理着信托。第二，考文垂历史信托和考文垂市议会建立了伙伴关系。市议会大力促成地产移交整体框架的确立，而信托也获得了当选政客和议会官员的有力支持。最后，虽然规模小，考文垂历史信托既灵活又敏捷，固定成本也很少；还能迅速决策，高效实施。慈善信托机构的性质与企业模式的结合为英国促进遗产地保护创造了巨大潜力。

英国文化遗产管理第三部门当今及未来面临的挑战

近十年来，英国许多政府或地方当局将原来由其承担的职能都“外包”给了慈善信托机构，现在由后者负责运营。其直接原因在于政府资金的削减，并尝试在文化和遗产服务的可持续发展方面寻求创新。从长远角度来看，还不能确定这种模式是否可行。公共资金减少、部分社区并无运营能力意味着一些尝试很有可能失败。可以确定的是，志愿精神在英国有着很深的基础。自 18 世纪晚期以来，第三部门一直处于独立状态，自力更生，不断发展。这些第三部门机构由真正热衷于某个领域或某一地区的人发起，他们往往在激发他人热情，为其事业争取公众支持和捐款方面非常成功。

1 闪电战指第二次世界大战期间德国对英国的伦敦、考文垂和其他城市的一系列密集的轰炸袭击。出自德语的“闪电”一词——译者注。

Fig.1 Coventry's 14th-century Charterhouse monastery, saved by community action and now in the ownership of Historic Coventry Trust (© Historic Coventry Trust).

图 1 考文垂卡尔特修道院，始建于14世纪，通过社区运动获得保护，现今属于考文垂历史信托（© 考文垂历史信托）。

Fig.2 Swanswell Gate, one of the two remaining 14th-century gatehouses from Coventry's medieval city walls (© Historic Coventry Trust).

图 2 斯万维尔城门，考文垂中世纪城市城墙中，现存两座14世纪城门中的一座（© 考文垂历史信托）。

Fig.3 High-street regeneration in Coventry before and after: the Burges in Coventry (© Historic England Archives).
图 3 考文垂商业街重建前后对比：考文垂伯吉斯（© Historic England Archives)。

Fig.4. An artist's impression of the Burges after regeneration work led by Historic Coventry Trust (© Corstorphine and Wright).
图 4 考文垂历史信托带领下的重建伯吉斯工作完成后，一位艺术家的作品（© 克里斯托芬和怀特）。

and from officers of the Council. Finally, as a small organisation, Historic Coventry Trust is able to be flexible and agile, and has few fixed costs; decisions can be made very quickly and projects can begin to progress soon afterwards. This blend of charitable status with entrepreneurialism offers great potential in the UK for helping to look after heritage sites.

CURRENT AND FUTURE CHALLENGES FOR THE THIRD SECTOR IN UK HERITAGE MANAGEMENT

In the last decade in the UK many functions previously carried out by government or local authorities have been externalised and are now run by charitable trusts. This has been a direct result of cuts in government funding and of subsequent attempts to find new ways of sustaining cultural and heritage services. Whether this works in the long term is not clear; some initiatives are likely to fail as public funding reduces, or where there is a lack of community capacity to run them. What is clear is that the voluntary principle in the UK has deep roots. Since the late 18th century the third- sector has been independent, self-generating and growing. Those organisations which develop from a group of people with a passionate interest in a subject or a place have been very successful at enthusing others, in gaining support for their cause and in raising funds from the public.

The third sector does, however, face many challenges. Charities need to keep evolving as wider circumstances, and the interests of the general public, change. In particular, traditional heritage charities need to appeal to more younger people and to the diverse communities that now live in urban areas, if they are to succeed in the next 100 years.

There are opportunities here too: heritage charities provide a way to connect people to a place and a community at a time of increasing globalisation. Technology also provides new ways of engaging people, although it requires new skills which some of the traditional smaller community heritage charities may struggle to source.

CONCLUSION

The UK has a long history of third sector heritage activity which is rooted deep in its culture and community. Many of the charities which are thriving today, such as Historic Coventry Trust, have developed creative and entrepreneurial ways of working, new partnerships with local government, and imaginative ways of engaging people of all ages.

A number of today's charities working on Hadrian's Wall are long-established and follow in the historical traditions of the learned societies created in the late 18th and early 19th centuries. Without such organisations, Hadrian's Wall would be less well understood, less well conserved and less valued. The charities provide a vital mechanism to connect local people to the World Heritage Site.

The third-sector model is one that it would be interesting to explore in the context of the Great Wall of China, particularly in areas where there is a desire to involve local communities in conservation. The exemplary of use of modern technology on the Great Wall, and work with Tencent Corporation to engage young people also has much learning to offer the UK charity sector on Hadrian's Wall.

但是，第三部门确实也面临诸多挑战。随着更广泛的环境和公众利益不断变化，慈善组织需要与时俱进。尤其对传统的文化遗产慈善机构来说，要想在未来 100 年内取得成功，就必须吸引更多的年轻人，吸引现在城市地区更加多元化的社区参与。

机遇同样存在：在全球化日益发展的时代，遗产慈善组织作为一个纽带，将人们与某个地方或社区联系起来。科技进步也提供了吸引人们的新方法，但这对传统的小型地方性遗产慈善组织提出挑战，需要他们努力掌握这些新技能。

结语

英国的第三部门参与文化遗产保护由来已久，深深根植于其文化和社区之中。当今蓬勃发展的许多慈善组织研究出很多富有创意和企业思维的工作方法，与当地政府建立新的伙伴关系，并开创诸多富有想象力的吸引各年龄段公众的方案。考文垂历史信托就是其中之一。

当今与哈德良长城相关的慈善机构中有些机构有着悠久历史，并遵循着学术团体在 18 世纪晚期和 19 世纪早期建立的历史传统。正是这些机构促进了公众对哈德良长城的理解与保护，更珍惜它的价值。慈善机构提供了将当地群众与世界遗产地关联起来的关键机制。

第三部门模式在在中国长城也是一个重要领域，尤其对那些希望让当地社区更多参与到长城保护中的地区而言更至关重要。现代技术在中国长城的示范应用，以及与腾讯合作来吸引年轻人了解长城也同样十分值得英国哈德良长城相关的第三部门学习借鉴。

Chapter 2:

Historical and Archaeological Research

Excavation of Hadrian's Wall at Wallsend (© Tyne and Wear Archives & Museums).
哈德良长城考古发掘，沃尔森德（©泰恩·威尔地区档案及博物馆）。

第二单元

长城考古与历史研究

Excavation of the Chu Great Wall (west-east), Wulipo, Henan (photograph by Li Yipi).
楚长城墙体发掘现场（西–东），五里坡，河南（摄影：李一丕）。

2.1 RESEARCH ON HADRIAN'S WALL AND ON ROMAN FRONTIERS

DAVID J BREEZE
Edinburgh - UK

Abstract

Research into Roman military remains began in Europe over five centuries ago. Visible remains were recorded, the literary sources studied and artefacts brought together in private collections and then museums. Today, we have a wide range of techniques available to help us understand the frontiers of the Roman Empire better. International cooperation took off in the late 19th century and continues even more strongly today, supported through European Union projects.

Keywords: Hadrian's Wall, Roman frontiers, museums, international cooperation, presentation of archaeological sites

The serious study of the remains of Roman frontiers in Europe started in the 16th century. From that time some landowners in the United Kingdom collected altars and other items of sculpture found on their land. Some laid out archaeological parks to display such items. Many owners displayed their discoveries in their own grand houses and encouraged visitors to come and admire them. Most such collections are now in museums. Along Hadrian's Wall these include the museum at Chesters, displaying the great collection of John Clayton, and Maryport containing the discoveries of the Senhouse family. Today these museums, and others such as Aquincum in Budapest, in Hungary, are essentially great storehouses of information for archaeologists, always available for further study leading to greater understanding of life on Roman frontiers (Fig.1).

Amongst the many records that survive from earlier days are 19th-century paintings of Hadrian's Wall which show what the monument looked like nearly 200 years ago (Breeze 2016). They can also show what we have lost since that time. For instance, a tower was discovered on Hadrian's Wall in 1883 but it was destroyed by quarrying soon afterwards. By that time, however, it had been photographed and drawn, and then published. The record of the turret, now known as Turret 45b (Walltown West), remains a valuable part of the Hadrian's Wall archive today.

Research on Roman frontiers at an international level began with the writings of the great German ancient historian Theodor Mommsen. In his book, *The Provinces of the Roman Empire*, published in 1885, he offered comparisons between different frontiers and sought to explain these differences.

Cross-border links were strengthened by correspondence and by visits, notably that of Oskar von Sarwey of the German Reichs Limes Kommission to Hadrian's Wall and the Antonine Wall in 1893, as well as visits to the German frontier by British archaeologists.

In 1907 Lord Curzon, previously Viceroy of India, gave the Romanes Lectures at the University of Oxford, on the subject of Frontiers. He cast his net widely, extending the study of frontiers well beyond the borders of the Roman Empire. The Great Wall of China had entered the consciousness of British ancient historians in the 18th century and since then it has been suggested on several occasions that Hadrian's Wall was modelled on its eastern counterpart, information on the Great Wall having been brought to the Roman emperors by travellers.

In 1949 the first International Congress of Roman Frontier Studies was held on Hadrian's Wall (Fig.2). The Congress is now held every three years. These meetings not only allow archaeologists to discuss new research and to review old problems, but also to visit other frontiers and learn about their different histories and the different landscapes in which they were constructed.

2.1 哈德良长城及罗马帝国边疆的研究

大卫・J・布里兹
爱丁堡—英国

摘要

在欧洲，对古罗马军事遗迹的研究始于 5 个多世纪前。可见遗迹被记录下来，文献资料被加以研究，人工制品则被私人收藏起来，后来又建成多家博物馆。如今，一系列科技手段帮助我们更好地理解罗马帝国边疆。国际合作起步于 19 世纪末，延续至今并不断加强，得到欧盟项目的大力支持。

关键词：哈德良长城　罗马帝国边疆　博物馆　国际合作　考古遗址展示

在欧洲，对罗马边疆遗迹的严肃研究始于 16 世纪。从那时起，英国的一些土地主把自已领地里发现的祭坛和其他雕刻品收藏起来。有些人修建起了考古公园，以展示这些文物。不少土地主在自已的大宅中展出他们发现的文物，鼓励游客前来观赏。如今这些藏品大都已收于各家博物馆中。哈德良长城沿线有位于切斯特的博物馆，陈列着约翰・克莱顿（John Clayton）精美绝伦的收藏，有位于玛丽波特（Maryport）的博物馆，陈列着森豪斯家族（Senhouse）的发现等。如今这些博物馆，加上匈牙利布达佩斯的阿奎肯（Aquincum）等其他博物馆，本质上就是考古学家们的巨大信息库，成为进一步研究和理解罗马边疆生活的不竭源泉（图 1）。

在诸多保存下来的早期记录中，很多 19 世纪的哈德良长城油画描绘了近 200 年前长城当时的形态（布里兹，2016）。通过这些油画也揭示出 200 年后，多少遗存已经消失。比如，1883 年哈德良长城上发现一座塔楼，但不久便因采石而被毁。不过，在毁坏之前，该塔楼已经被拍照和绘图，并且出版。这座塔楼现被称为 45b 号塔楼，位于诺森伯兰郡沃尔顿西（Walltown West）。有关 45b 号塔楼的记录今天成为哈德良长城档案的珍贵组成部分。

在国际层面上研究罗马边疆始于伟大的德国古代史学家西奥多・莫姆森（Theodor Mommsen）的著作。在他 1885 出版的专著《罗马帝国各行省》（*The Provinces of the Roman Empire*）中，莫姆森比较了边疆各地的不同之处，并试图对这些差异加以解释。

书信往来与实地造访加强了跨国交往。其中比较著名的是 1893 年由奥斯卡・冯・萨尔维（Oskar von Sarwey）代表德意志帝国边墙委员会（the German Reichs Limes Kommission）考察哈德良长城和安东尼长城；英国考古学家也多次考察德国的罗马边疆遗址。

1907 年，曾任印度总督的寇松勋爵（Lord Curzon）在牛津大学作罗曼讲座[1]，主题为古罗马帝国边疆。他将罗马边疆的研究进一步拓展，远远超出了古罗马帝国的边境线。中国的长城自 18 世纪便进入了英国古代史学家的视线。自此以后，学者曾在不同场合指出哈德良长城借鉴了来自东方的做法，因为罗马皇帝们很早就从旅人那里获知了中国长城的情况。

1 牛津大学罗曼讲座于 1892 设立，每年举办一次，是向公众免费开放的高水平学术讲座。——译者注

Fig.1 The museum in the archaeological park at Aquincum, Hungary, opened in 1894 (© David J Breeze).
图 1 匈牙利阿奎肯考古公园内的博物馆. 1984 年开馆（© 大卫・布雷兹）。

Understanding the landscape is an essential element in appreciating how Roman frontiers operated. In all frontier regions we can see that the military installations related closely to landscape features, be they rivers, mountains, rough terrain or deserts (Breeze 2019).

For a deeper appreciation of the function and operation of Roman frontiers we must turn to archaeology, and in particular to archaeological excavation. Excavations on Hadrian's Wall began exactly 200 years ago (Breeze 2014). The records of these early excavations are still important in providing information not otherwise available. Sometimes buildings recorded long ago survive now only in part, such as the few surviving stones of the north gate at Maryport which were first recorded in the 17th century.

The modern era of excavation began in 1892 and has continued uninterrupted since. Excavations have followed two main lines of action. Research excavations, which seek to answer specific questions, and rescue or salvage excavations which are reactions to developments such as roads, houses, factories and so on, where it is important to record the archaeological remains before they are destroyed. One of the most important research excavations was at Birdoswald on Hadrian's Wall in 1929 when part of a barrack-block was examined (Fig.3). The results were of major importance because they led to the definition of four phases of occupation, two of which were dated by inscriptions. At the same time, towers, milecastles, and even parts of forts, were being examined in advance of the improvement of the main road leading west out of Newcastle.

Excavations of smaller installations such as milecastles, and of forts such as Benwell and Halton Chesters, allowed the complicated history of Hadrian's Wall to be worked out. From the beginning of archaeological excavations, coins of the Roman emperors have helped date the main periods of occupation of Hadrian's Wall.

In particular, excavations have enabled us to trace the changes to Hadrian's Wall during its building programme (Fig.4). We can date the precursor to Hadrian's Wall, which was a line of forts across the island of Britain. It was then planned to build Hadrian's Wall to the north of these forts. This plan was changed during the

1949 年，首届国际罗马边疆研究大会于哈德良长城举行。如今，大会每三年举办一次。这些会议不仅使考古学家可以总结旧问题，探讨新进展，更可以访问其他边疆遗址，了解不同边疆的历史以及边疆周围的景观（图 2）。

Fig.2 Some of the archaeologists attending the first International Congress of Roman Frontier Studies held in Newcastle, UK in 1949.
图 2 部分参加英国纽卡斯尔首届国际罗马帝国边疆研究大学的考古学家。

理解景观是理解罗马边疆运行机制的基础。在所有边疆地区，我们都会看到军事设施与周边地势紧密相关，无论是河流高山，亦或是丘陵大漠（布里兹, 2019）。

要更深入地理解罗马边疆的功能和运作机制，我们必须求助考古学，尤其是考古发掘。哈德良长城的考古发掘迄今已走过整整 200 年的历程（布里兹，2014）。这些早期发掘记录至今仍在为我们提供无可替代的信息，十分重要。有时，多年前记录的建筑如今只有部分幸存，比如玛丽波特北门遗址。17 世纪，该遗址第一次进入考古记录，可如今仅存零星散石。

现代意义上的考古发掘始于1892年，延续至今没有间断。发掘工作遵循两条主线。一是研究性发掘，旨在解决具体问题，二是抢救性发掘，即在修建道路、房屋、工厂等建设项目时开展的配合性工作，旨在被毁坏前对遗迹进行记录。最重要的研究性发掘项目之一是 1929 年哈德良长城博得瓦德（Birdoswald）对一处兵营遗迹进行的局部发掘。此次发掘结果至关重要，因为确定了四个使用时期，其中两个时期留下了明确的铭文纪年（图 3）。与此同时，在纽卡斯尔向西出城的主要道路整治前，开展了对各座塔楼、里堡甚至部分要塞的发掘工作。

对体量稍小的设施——诸如里堡以及本维尔（Benwell）和霍尔顿切斯特（Halton Chesters）等要塞——进行发掘，使我们能梳理出哈德良长城复杂的历史。从考古发掘之初起，罗马皇帝发行的硬币便帮助判断哈德良长城主要的使用年代。

值得一提的是，考古发掘使我们能追溯哈德良长城在建造过程中发生的变化（图 4）。我们确定了哈德良长城前身修建的年代，那是横跨不列颠岛的一连串要塞。之后才规划在这些要塞北部修建哈德良长城。该规划又在后续修建过程中发生变动，在长城墙体上建起数座新要塞。这些变动帮助我们理解哈德良长城的修建目的以及设想的运作方式。

如今，考古发掘过程非常仔细，并使用更多的科技手段。在我本人发掘安东尼长城位于比尔斯登（Bearsden）的一处要塞时，通过大规模采样来帮助理解罗马军队抵达时的周围环境，并通过分析要塞厕

Fig.3 The 1929 excavation at Birdoswald on Hadrian's Wall. From left to right: John Charlton, Eric Birley, a student, F. G. Simpson, a student, Kurt Stade, Shimon Applebaum and R. G. Collingwood

图3 1929年哈德良长城博得瓦德要塞发掘人员合影。
从左至右：约翰·查尔顿、埃里克·博尔利、学生、F.G·辛普森、学生、科特·斯泰德、西蒙·爱泼博姆及P.G·柯林伍德。

construction of the Wall and new forts were erected on the line of the Wall itself. These changes help us understand both the purpose of Hadrian's Wall and how it was intended to function.

Today, excavations are carefully undertaken and with the greater use of scientific techniques. At my own excavation of the fort on the Antonine Wall at Bearsden, extensive sampling allowed us to create an understanding of the environment at the time of the arrival of the Roman army, as well as to learn about the diet of the soldiers through the analysis of the sewage from the fort's latrine. Through plotting the distribution of pottery found within the fort, we were able to suggest that the Roman soldiers prepared, cooked and ate their food in their barrack rooms. Some of that food was gathered locally, but other items, such as figs, came hundreds of kilometres from continental Europe including modern Germany, France and Spain. Olive oil and wine came to this north-west frontier from the Mediterranean lands.

Other new scientific techniques such as geophysical survey can not only help us map out the interior of forts but can place forts in their wider setting. This includes the location and extent of external civil settlements but also what lies beyond those, including rural farms.

The comparisons between different sections of Roman frontiers have become an important part of Roman frontier studies. We can compare and seek to understand the reasons for the use of different materials along different frontiers: for instance, timber and stone were sometimes both used in the same frontier. Hadrian's Wall was built of stone, turf and timber. Was this the result of using the materials that were available locally or did it depend on imperial decree?

Hadrian's Wall was designated a World Heritage Site in 1987. It was followed by the Upper German-Raetian Limes in 2005 and the Antonine Wall in Scotland in 2008. These three sites now form the Frontiers of the Roman Empire World Heritage Site. Each of them has its own Management Plan, and within each Plan specific principles and policies are set out concerning their respective Research Strategies. The current Research Strategy for Hadrian's Wall was published in 2009. A new Management Plan and an updated Research Strategy are now under consideration.

There is no requirement that these Research Strategies should each follow the same framework, and it would be surprising if they did as each country in Europe has its own traditions and approaches to research. Indeed, within the United Kingdom, Scotland, which looks after the Antonine Wall, has different traditions from England, which manages Hadrian's Wall. These different approaches have been recognised by the World Heritage Centre in Paris.

Fifteen years ago, archaeologists working on Roman frontiers in Europe came together to discuss how to create

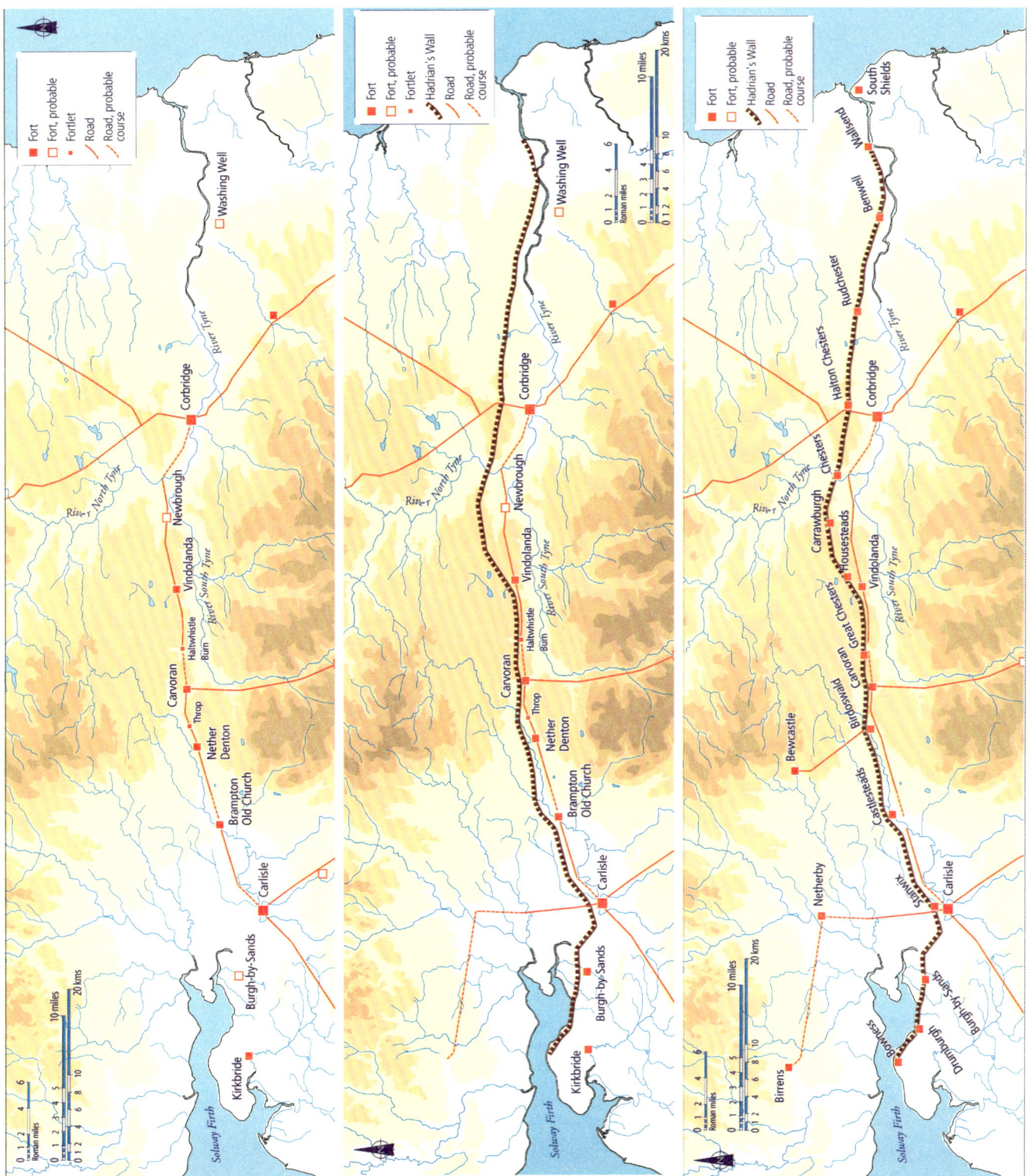

Fig.4 The development of the Roman frontier in Britain during the reign of Hadrian (AD 117-138). The military installations across the Tyne-Solway isthmus at the beginning of the reign (top). The first plan for Hadrian's Wall (middle). The completed plan (bottom) (© David J. Breeze).

图 4 哈德良皇帝统治时期（公元117－138 年）不列颠罗马边疆的修筑变迁。哈德良统治初期横跨泰恩–索尔韦地峡的一系列军事设施（上）；哈德良长城初始规划（中）；哈德良长城最终规划（下）（© 大卫 · 布里兹）。

Fig.5 The Culture 2000 Frontiers of the Roman Empire project team (© David J. Breeze).
图 5 文化 2000——罗马帝国边疆项目团队成员合影（© 大卫·J·布里兹）。

an all-embracing research strategy (Breeze and Jilek 2008). We failed in this task. We did undertake more research in our own countries. In particular, in Scotland several geophysical surveys at locations along the Antonine Wall were undertaken in order to improve our understanding of what should be included within the proposed World Heritage Site. (The Antonine Wall successfully achieved World Heritage Site status in 2008). Extensive survey and mapping work has now also been undertaken in the other countries in Europe that are seeking to nominate different sections of the Roman frontier system for World Heritage status.

That attempt to create a research strategy for the European frontiers of the Roman Empire was also important in teaching us how to work together; this has been of enormous help in planning and undertaking new projects and will be of value when we return to the task of creating the research strategy.

One important result of our collaboration was to produce a new map of the frontiers of the Roman Empire (see maps section of this publication). This has been accompanied by the preparation of detailed maps of all sections of the frontiers (Breeze 2019).

At our meetings we were able to share our experiences and our knowledge of new discoveries. We explored different methods of conservation. Hungary, for example, has a very different approach from the United Kingdom but neither is necessarily right or wrong. We shared our different approaches to presentation, acknowledging that different conditions lead to different solutions. The bath-house at Bearsden, for example, sits in a housing estate in Scotland, while the much larger bath-house in Budapest, Hungary, lies under a fly-over.

For all archaeologists the dissemination of research is of vital importance. Roman archaeologists are very good

所（latrine）下水道了解当时士兵的饮食情况。通过标记要塞内发现的陶器分布，我们得以判断罗马士兵是在营房内备菜、做饭、就餐的。有些食物来自本地，而其他食物，比如无花果，来自几百千米之外的欧洲大陆，覆盖今天的德国、法国和西班牙。橄榄油和葡萄酒则是从地中海地区运抵帝国西北边疆的。

其他新兴科技手段，诸如地球物理调查等，不仅能帮助我们绘制要塞内部布局，更可以将要塞定位于更大范围的环境中，包括军事设施外的平民聚落的位置和范围，以及更远的环境，比如乡村农场。

比较罗马边疆不同区段也成为罗马边疆研究的重要组成部分。我们通过比较可以试着理解为什么边疆各区段都存在多种建材共用的现象。比如，在同一处边疆区段，有时会同时使用木头和石头修建。哈德良长城就是由石、草、木修筑。这是就地取材的结果，还是皇帝敕令的结果?

1987年，哈德良长城成为世界遗产地。此后，上日耳曼—雷蒂亚界墙和苏格兰安东尼长城分别在 2005 年和 2008 年成为世界遗产地。现在，这三处遗产地联合构成"罗马帝国边疆世界遗产地" 。其中每处遗产地都有自己的管理规划，每部规划中都就各自的研究策略制定具体原则和政策。现行哈德良长城研究策略于 2009 年出版，新版管理规划及更新版研究策略正在酝酿中。

遗产地各自的研究策略是否遵循同一框架并无规定。若是真的遵循反倒不同寻常，因为每个欧洲国家都有各自的传统和研究方法。即便在英国内部，负责管理安东尼长城的苏格兰也与负责管理哈德良长城的英格兰有着不同的传统。这些不同方法都得到了巴黎世界遗产中心的认可。

15 年前，欧洲各国研究罗马边疆的考古学家汇聚一堂，探讨如何制定融各家于一炉的研究策略（布里兹和基列克, 2008），结果以失败而告终。但这确实促进了各国各自开展更多的研究工作。具体来说，在苏格兰，在安东尼长城沿线进行了若干地球物理调查，旨在更科学地确定申报世界遗产的构成范围。（最终安东尼长城于 2008 年成功申遗）。目前，欧洲其他国家也在开展广泛的勘察和测绘工作，他们希望将各自罗马边疆区段纳入世界遗产名录。

制定全欧洲罗马帝国边疆研究策略的尝试也为我们该如何合作上了重要一课。在制定和实施新项目的过程中起到了巨大作用，若今后制定研究策略再次提上日程，这次尝试也将提供宝贵经验。

我们合作的一项重要成果就是绘制了新的罗马帝国边疆地图（请见本文集地图插页），并配有边疆各区段详图（布里兹, 2019）。

通过各类集会，我们分享各自的经验及新发现。我们探索不同的遗产保护手段。比如，匈牙利的手段与英国截然不同，两者却未必有对错之分。我们还分享各自不同的展陈手段，承认不同情况下解决方法也会不同。比如，比尔斯登的罗马浴室坐落于苏格兰一处居民区，而布达佩斯的罗马浴室体量更大，横卧在高架桥下。

对全体考古学家而言，宣传考古研究至关重要。研究古罗马的考古学者非常善于出版面向不同层次人群的相关成果，从单个遗址的导览手册和区域概述，到省级、州级、国家级乃至国际的各类专著。其中一个重大项目是罗马帝国边疆多语种系列丛书的出版，全面介绍了从布列颠延伸至中东，向南直抵撒哈拉沙漠的边疆全貌。

这一项目萌芽于"文化 2000——罗马帝国边疆"项目，当时以多语种出版了CD，面向全欧洲学校发行。现在，我们跟随潮流研发了手机 APP, 不少手机还是中国制造的。

最重要的是，罗马帝国边疆项目的同仁们在工作中互相了解，学会合作。简而言之，项目主要成果促进了考古学家间的交流，促进了考古学家与罗马帝国边疆遗址管理者的交流。这也正是我们希望通过

at producing books on their subject, and at different levels: from individual site guides and regional overviews, to treatises at provincial, state, national and international level. An important initiative is the series of multi-language books on all Roman frontiers from Britain to the Middle East, and south to the Sahara Desert.

This initiative sprang out of the Culture 2000 Frontiers of the Roman Empire project, as did a CD in several languages which was distributed to schools across Europe. Now of course we are into apps, produced for mobile phones, many made in China.

Most of all, we in the Roman frontiers project got to know each other and learnt how to work together. In short, the main result was that we improved communications between archaeologists, and between archaeologists and the people who manage the physical remains of the frontiers. This, after all, is what we are seeking to do with the Wall to Wall project. The network of frontier archaeologists in Europe is a great aid to research of all kinds and to the dissemination of knowledge (Fig. 5).

There are many similarities between the Great Wall and Hadrian's Wall and other Roman frontiers. Both were built to protect the people of their countries. Both survive today for many kilometres as visible monuments. Both are visited by many people who want to be informed about what they are looking at. Both therefore require active research to aid our understanding of their history and role, active preservation and conservation measures, and the use of the most up-to-date presentation techniques. In all of these tasks we can learn a lot from each other about how to protect, preserve, conserve, manage and present these tangible remains of our wonderful heritage.

（和中国）“双墙对话”项目达到的目的。欧洲的罗马边疆考古学家构建的网络为各类研究和知识传播提供了莫大的帮助（图 5）。

中国长城与哈德良长城及其他罗马边疆间有着诸多相似性。二者同为保护本国人民而建。二者均保存至今，遗迹绵延横亘。二者均有大量参观者，希望能在参观时获得更多的知识。这也就需要二者主动开展更多研究，了解长城的历史和作用，主动采取保存和保护措施，采用最先进的展陈方式。在上述各个方面，我们都可以相互借鉴，学习如何保护、保存、修缮、管理和展示我们杰出遗产的有形遗存。

References
参考文献

Breeze, D. J. 2014. *Hadrian's Wall: A History of Archaeological Thought*. Kendal.
D . J . 布里兹. 2014 . 哈德良长城：一部考古思想史 . 肯达尔.
Breeze, D. J. 2016. *Hadrian's Wall. Paintings by the Richardson Family*. Edinburgh.
D . J . 布里兹. 2016. 哈德良长城： 理查德森家族创作的绘画 . 爱丁堡.
Breeze, D. J. 2019. *The Frontiers of Imperial Rome*. Barnsley.
D . J . 布里兹. 2019. 罗马帝国的边疆 . 巴恩斯利.
Breeze, D.J. and Jilek. S. 2008. *Frontiers of the Roman Empire. The European Dimension of a World Heritage Site*. Edinburgh.
D . J . 布里兹，S . 基列克. 2008 . 罗马帝国边疆：世界文化遗产的欧洲维度. 爱丁堡.

2.2 古罗马长城与明长城防御体系比较

李严，张玉坤，李哲
天津大学建筑学院—中国—天津

摘要

虽然古罗马与明代在时间上相差一千多年，但是古罗马长城的防御体系与明长城在防御体系的建设、城池布局、城池内部空间结构有诸多相似之处，同时也有显著的不同，明长城的防御体系更复杂。本文以明长城和古罗马长城全线实地踏勘为基础，从防御体系的建设、城池布局、城池内部空间结构三方面比较古罗马长城与明长城防御体系和军事聚落的异与同。[1]

关键词： 古罗马长城　明长城　比较

古罗马长城是世界上唯一在体量上可以与中国长城相比拟的古代军事工程，现存较好的两段分别为英国哈德良长城（Hadrian's Wall）与德国上日耳曼-雷蒂安边墙（Limes），两者并称为世界遗产——罗马帝国的边境（Frontiers of the Roman Empire）。虽然古罗马与明代在时间上相差一千多年，但是古罗马长城与明长城在防御体系、城池布局、城池内部空间结构有诸多相似之处。

一、防御体系的比较

（一）明长城防御体系的空间布局和层次体系

明初，军事制度的演变是从卫所制开始的，卫所制保证了九边地区重兵力部署，所驻城池分别为卫城和所城。为了更好的经营边疆防务，在边疆地区设置了九个军事重镇，分段防守，出现了九边总兵镇守制，承担边防前线的预警、戍守和作战任务（赵现海，2005）。

明代九边重镇防御体系东西跨度 8800 多千米，九边总兵镇守制下分十一军镇、四十五路防守。十一军镇从东到西分别为：辽东镇、蓟镇、昌镇、真保镇、宣府镇、大同镇、山西镇、榆林镇、宁夏镇、固原镇和甘肃镇，所辖区域与现省界接近但不完全重合。诸镇的内部结构基本相同，略有差异。①镇：由总兵统辖，驻镇城，统辖全镇兵马，总掌防区内的战守行动。②路：镇下分路。每个军镇下分三路到八路不等，各路分设路城，内驻参将，负责本路地段的战守。③堡：路下分堡，每路辖几个至十几个军堡，内驻守备，负责本地段的战守；各路之间有游击堡，内设游击将军，往来策应，既分段防守又互相连结、各负其责（艾冲，1990）。

五类城池按照级别高低和规模大小共有分为五级：镇城——各镇总兵驻地、路城——各路守将驻地、

1 本文受国家自然科学基金 51878437/51878439/51908179、教育部人文社科 17 YJCZH095 及河北社科 HB19YS036 支持。

2.2 THE FRONTIER DEFENCE SYSTEMS OF ANCIENT ROME AND THE MING DYNASTY: A COMPARISON

LI YAN, ZHANG YUKUN, LI ZHE
Tianjin University - China - Tianjin

Abstract

The defence systems of the Roman Empire and the Ming Empire share many similarities in their components and structures, and in the internal layout of their forts, despite there being a thousand years of time between them. However, there are noticeable differences. Specifically, the Ming system is more complicated. This paper compares the Roman frontiers system with the Ming defence system, and its fortresses, in the three aspects mentioned; this is based on on-site investigations along Hadrian's Wall and the Great Wall of China.[1]

Keywords: Roman walls, the Ming Wall, comparative study

INTRODUCTION

The Roman frontier defence system is the only ancient military defence system that matched the Great Wall of China in size. Two well preserved sections of this system are Hadrian's Wall in Britain and the Upper German-Raetian Limes, which are now two components of the Frontiers of the Roman Empire World Heritage Site. The defence systems of the Roman Empire and the Ming Empire share many similarities in their components, structures, and internal layouts of their forts, despite a thousand years of time between them

A COMPARISON IN THE DEFENCE SYSTEMS

The structure and hierarchy of the Ming defence system

The evolution of the military command during the Ming Dynasty started with the two-level hierarchy of the *weisuo* system To impose better control over military strength across the empire, the imperial government divided the empire into several military provinces or regions and created several *dusi*, local administrations led by non-military officials reporting to the central government (Zhao 2005). In each province or region, the top level of military command, also appointed by the imperial government, was the *zhen,* below which the army was divided into *wei* and *suo*[2] Across the interior of the empire, troops were stationed in *zhen*-forts, *wei*-forts and *suo*-forts, and the role of these units was primarily to maintain internal security (Ai 1990).

In addition to these military command-structures of the imperial interior, across the northern frontier nine regional military defence commands, or *bians,* were established; these were led by officers who were appointed by the central government for their military capability. Stretching over 8,800km from east to west, the nine *bians*

1 This study is funded by National Natural Science Foundation of China (51878437/51878439/51908179), Humanities Division, Ministry of Education (17YJCZH095) and Hebei Social Science (HB19YS036).

2 *Wei* or guards were made up of around 5,600 men. Each guard consisted of five *suo* or battalions of 1,120 men made up of ten companies of 112 men. Commands of these units were generally hereditary titles held by military families (Editors' note).

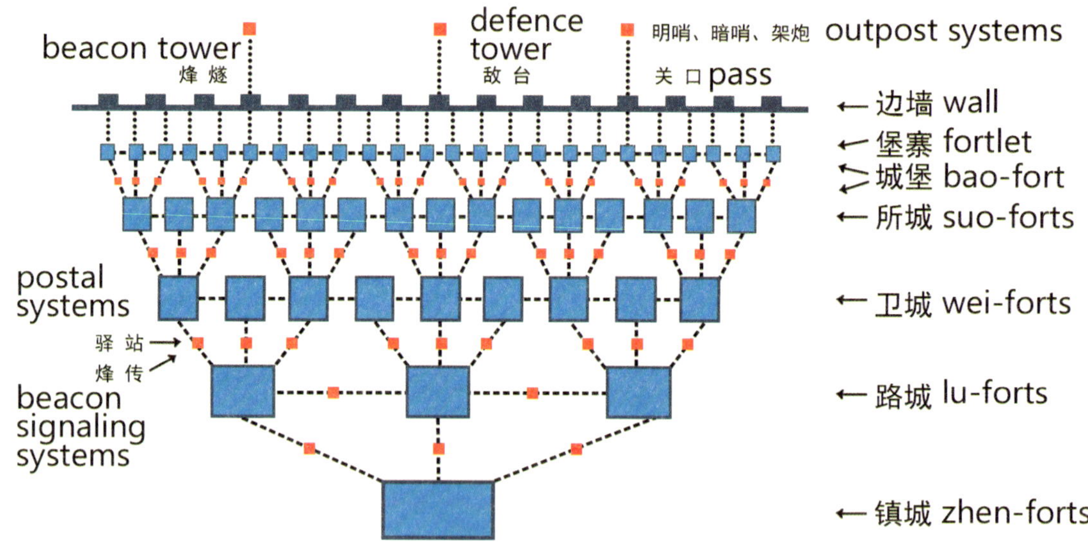

图 1 明长城军事聚落分布图及明长城防御体系示意（绘制：李严）。
Fig.1 Ming military units and defence system (drawn by the authors).

卫城——各卫守将驻地、所城——各所守将驻地和堡城——各堡守将驻地，最第一级防御单位。这些城池共同履行卫所制下屯兵屯粮、治安管理和九边总兵镇守制下预警戍守、出兵作战的军事任务。

预警、烽传和驿传系统是长城墙体和各城池之间的连接体和生命线预警系统，包含明哨——暗哨——架炮——墩堠，总称为前哨，负责侦探情报并迅速回传。烽传系统通过旗、火、烟和炮的“声色语言”将军情由沿边烽火台传递给所属边堡，再传递给上级路城、镇城，形成整个防御体系复杂通达的空中信息传递网络。驿传系统由水马驿、递运所和急递铺三大机构组成，承担了宣传政令、飞报军情与物资运送的任务（李严，2018）（图 1）。

（二）古罗马长城防御体系的空间布局和层次体系

英国哈德良长城东西跨度 80 罗马里，约 117 千米，包括 16 座要塞、79 个里堡、160 个塔楼，还有与长城平行的北侧壁垒、南侧壕沟、军用道路和坎伯里亚（Cumbrian）海岸的海防。（William Hutton, 'The History of the Roman Wall' (1802)。军事城堡分为：前线城池（Wall forts，沿长城东西向）、前哨城池（Outpost forts）、道路城池（Stanegate forts）、后勤补给城池（Supply forts）和海防城池（Coast forts，从北到南）（表 1）（菲尔兹，2003）。

德国日耳曼长城指罗马帝国在上日耳曼行省（Germania Superior）和雷蒂安行省（Raetia）内修建的一段边境防御工事，总长568千米，修筑于 83 年到260年间，包括至少 60 座堡垒和900座瞭望塔（Watchtower）大致呈“之”字形分布，堡垒分军团（Legionary fortress）和城堡（Fort）两级（英格兰遗产委员会，2006）。与哈德良长城不同的是没有里堡（Mile castle）和塔楼（Turrets），但也有连续防御设施（physicalbarrier）和附属道路（associatedroad）两个系统，并且在边墙内侧设置了一系列瞭望塔（M.罗伊特，A.蒂尔，2015）。通过英国哈德良长城和德国

consisted of eleven *zhens* and 45 *lus*. The eleven *zhens*, starting from the east, were: Liaodong *Zhen*, Ji *Zhen*, Chang *Zhen*, Zhenbao *Zhen*, Xuanfu *Zhen*, Datong *Zhen*, Shanxi *Zhen*, Yulin *Zhen*, Guyuan *Zhen* and Gansu *Zhen*. Their jurisdictions were close, though not identical, to modern provincial jurisdictions. Despite some slight differences, these *zhens* shared similar command-structures. Each one was led by a *Zongbing*, based in a *zhen*-fort. The commander was responsible for all the military operations within his territory, and for the deployment of troops for active combat. Each *zhen* was broken down into three to eight *lus*; these had their headquarters in *lu*-forts and were commanded by a *Canjiang*. Each *lu* was composed of up to twenty *baos*, based in *bao*-forts which were garrisoned for local defence. Within each *lu* some of the *baos* were both defensive and mobile units, defending their local area and also supporting the defence of other areas (Ai 1990).

There were thus five levels in the hierarchy of fort types, in terms of rank and size, across the nine *bians*: *zhen*-forts being regional command centres; *lu*-forts and then *wei*-forts, being area command garrisons; district command centres stationed at *suo*-forts; and local defence units at *bao*-forts. Together, these forts fulfilled both the administrative and internal security responsibilities of the *dusi-wei-suo* system and the combat role of the *zhen-lu-bao* system.

The warning and beacon signalling systems, and the postal and supply services, provided the vital connection between the Wall and the forts. The warning system, also known as the outpost system, included sentry stations, scout-patrol stations, gun-signalling carriages, and watchtowers, and was responsible for gathering and promptly relaying intelligence. The beacon signalling system sent messages from the beacon towers to their hinterland fortresses through visual and acoustic signals such as flags, fire, smoke and gunfire. The messages were passed to the *lu*-forts and then on to the *zhen*-forts. This formed the sophisticated information network of the defence system. The postal and logistics service was made of a courier service (using boats and horses), a transport system for the supply of food, and an urgent delivery service. These elements (Fig.1) worked together to distribute executive orders, to report intelligence and to deliver supplies (Li 2018).

The structure and hierarchy of the Roman defence system

Hadrian's Wall stretches for 80 Roman miles (approximately 117km) from east to west, and includes 16 forts, 79 milecastles, 160 turrets along its curtain Wall, a ditch to the north, and the Vallum to the south, the Stanegate road, and the defences along the Cumbrian coast. The forts can be categorised into Wall forts (from east to west along the Wall), outpost forts, Stanegate forts, supply forts, and coastal forts (listed from north to south). See Table 1 (Fields 2003).

The German Limes is the name given to the border defence of the Roman Empire in Upper Germany and Raetia. In operation between AD 83 and 260, this z-shaped fortification is 568km long, including at least 60 forts and fortlets and 900 watchtowers. There are two classes of forts: legionary fortresses and forts (English Heritage 2006) . As with Hadrian's Wall, the German Limes also has a physical barrier and associated roads, but it does not have milecastles or turrets, instead it had a series of watchtowers placed immediately behind the barrier (Reuter & Thiel 2015). The Roman defence system, summarised from Hadrian's Wall and the German Limes, includes the physical barrier, the forts along it, outpost forts, forts along roads (including the Stanegate forts and supply forts), military roads and, further into their hinterland, the legionary fortresses which were the top of the hierarchy of military command (Fig.2).

The defence system on the Roman walls is remarkably similar to its Ming counterpart. The function of the legionary fortresses is close to that of the *bian*-forts on the Ming Wall, and there were broad similarities between the Roman and Ming outpost forts, the forts on the Roman roads and the Ming postal stations, and the Roman supply forts and the Ming *wei*-forts and *suo*-forts. On Hadrian's Wall, some of the forts, like those on the Ming Wall, were at strategic crossing-points, but almost all of them were attached to the Wall itself (English Heritage 2006). In general, however, the Ming Wall defence system had more levels in its hierarchy and was therefore more complex.

表1：哈德良长城城池层级
Table 1: Forts of Hadrian's Wall

屯兵城 Wall Forts (East to West)	Wallsend (Segedunum), Newcastle, Benwell, Rudchester, Haltonchesters, Chesters, Carrawburgh, Housesteads, Great Chesters, Carvoran, Birdoswald, Castlesteads, Stanwix, Burgh-by-Sands, Drumburgh, Bowness-on-Solway
前哨城池 Outpost Forts	Risingham, High Rochester, Bewcastle, Netherby, Birrens
道路城池 Stanegate Forts	Corbridge, Newbrough, Chesterholm (Vindolanda), Haltwhistle Burn, Carvoran, Throp, Nether Denton, Castle Hill Boothby, Brampton Old Church, Carlisle
后勤补给城池 Supply Forts	South Shields (Arbeia)
西部海防 Forts on the West coast	Beckfoot, Maryport, Burrow Walls, Moresby, Ravenglass

日耳曼长城的空间布局总结抽象出古罗马长城的防御体系，主要包括长城墙体及其内外的防御设施、前哨城池、道路城池（包括道路城池和后勤给养城池）、军用道路和最高级别城池——军团（图2）。

古罗马长城与明长城的防御体系有很大相似之处：前线城池与明长城边堡功能类似，前哨城池与明前哨类似，道路城池与明驿站类似，给养城池与明卫所类似。哈德良长城与明长城相类似，在长城与道路交叉口设置关津要塞，依附长城设置。明长城防御体系的层次更多，更复杂。

二、城池布局

（一）明长城

明长城镇、路、卫、所、堡各城池在规模、功能、选址和防御设施上不尽一致，实土卫所内既有行政衙署又有军事衙署，军管型政区所在城池内只有军事衙署，没有行政衙署，如宁夏镇城，这类城池更强调军事特征。

镇城，规模最大，周长在12里（约7000米）以上，城门数量最少为四门、多者八门，道路可分为干道、一般街道、巷三级。路城，周长在 2000-4000 米左右，道路分两级，十字形主路和巷，城多开四门，也有的开两门。卫城，以驻屯兵粮为主，周长四里至七里，二门到四门不等，道路结构布局多为十字街，也有的呈一字形，道路分为街及巷二级。所城，周长 2000 米左右，大多只有三门、无北门，主要道路也呈十字形或一字形，然后再分设巷道。堡城，屯兵系统的最小单位，纯粹的军事设施，周长一里到四里不等，即 2000 米以下，大则十字街，小则一字街，形状规则的堡城呈方形或长方形，不规则的形状各异，开一门、二门或三门不等（图3）。

（二）古罗马长城

古罗马军事城池分为三个等级：Fortress（城池），Fort（城堡），Fortlet（小城）。城池（Fortress）是可容纳两个军团的持久性工事；城堡（Fort）是专供辅助军团的持久性军事堡垒；小城（Fortlet），修筑在前线防御系统的中间的位置，沿着道路或者在河流交叉口，通常是用来为百人团（century）或者辅助步兵队列（auxiliary cohort）提供的住处，内驻扎的士兵来自于非罗马公民（英格兰遗产委员会，2006）。Fortlet 不同

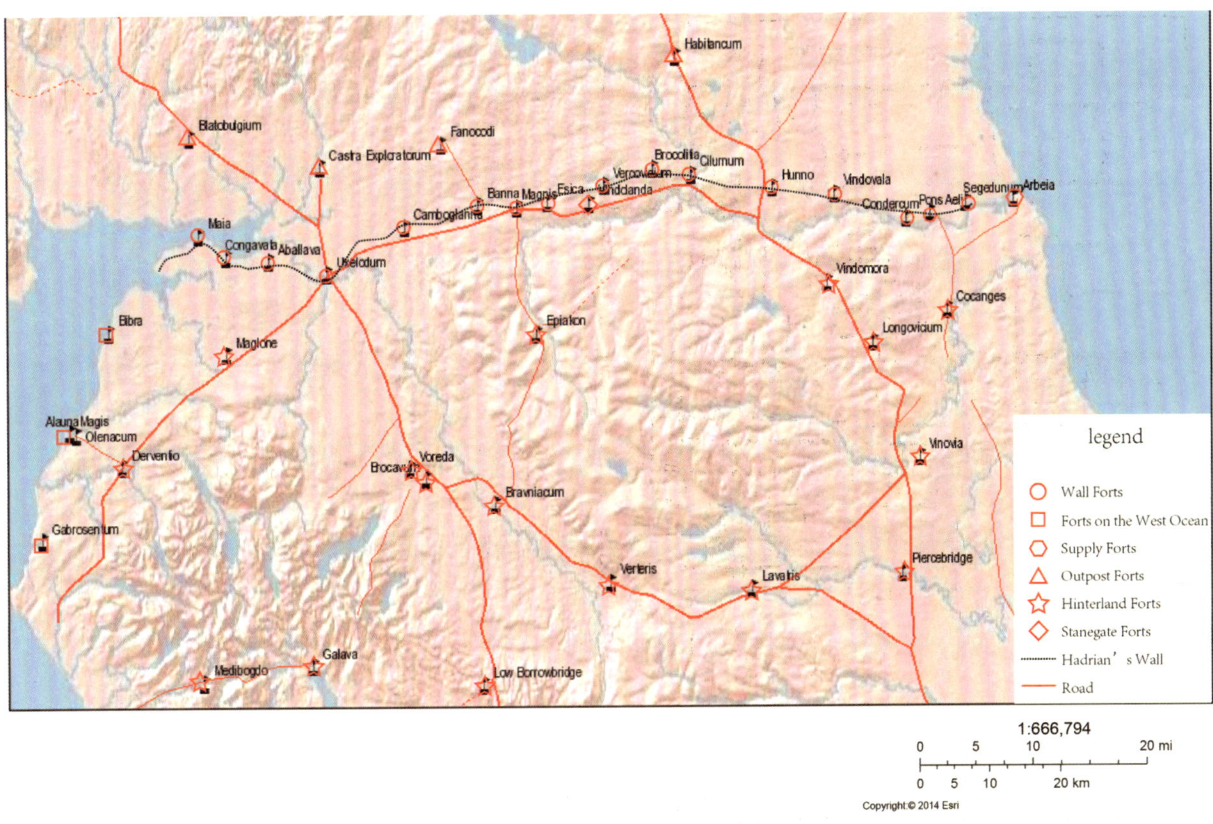

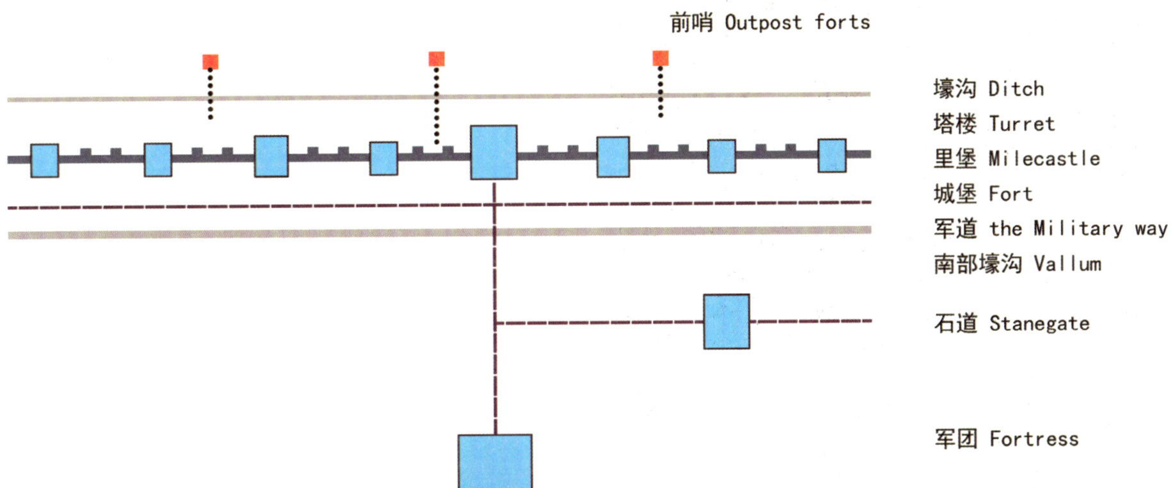

图 2 哈德良长城军事聚落分布图及防御体系示意（作者绘制：作者基于DARMC 1.3.1 地图绘制）。
Fig.2. Locations of the Roman military units and the defence on Hadrian's Wall (drawn by the authors based on the Digital Atlas of Roman and Medieval Civilisations 1.3.1 map).

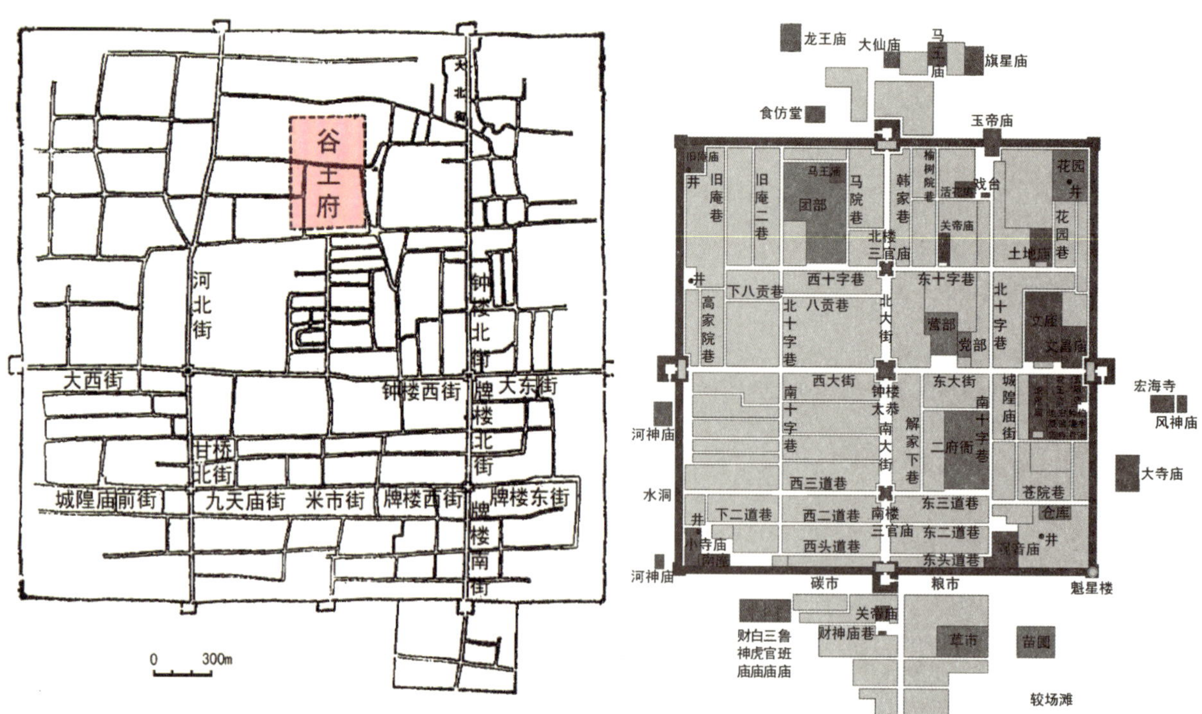

图 3a 镇城—宣府镇宣化镇城。

Fig.3a Xuanhua zhen-fort, Xuanfu Zhen.

图 3b 路城—榆林镇神木城。

Fig.3b Shenmu lu-fort, Yulin Zhen.

图 3d 所城—辽东镇中前所城。

Fig.3d Zhongqian suo-fort, Liaodong Zhen.

图 3e 堡城—宁夏镇红山堡。

Fig.3e - Hongshan bao-fort, Ningxia Zhen

图 3 明代各级军事聚落平面示意（图 3c 来自：刘谦《明辽东镇长城及防御考》，其余来自作者）。

Fig.3. Plans of all levels of Ming forts (credit for 3c: Examining the Ming Wall and defence in Liaodong Zhen by Liu Qian; all others by the authors).

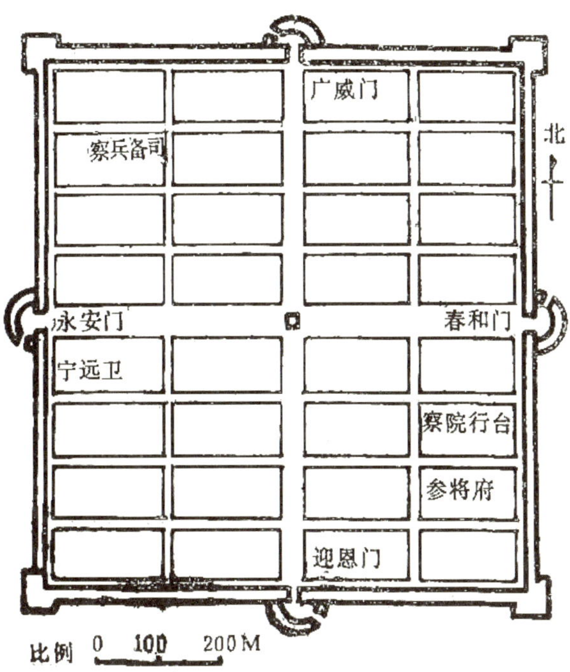

图 3c 卫城—辽东镇宁远卫城。
Fig.3c Ningyuan wei-fort, Liaodong Zhen.

THE LAYOUT OF THE FORTS

The layout of the Ming forts

The scale, function, location, and form of the fortifications varied between *zhen*, *lu*, *wei* and *suo* forts within the Ming defence system. There were both administrative and military officials in autonomous *weis* and *suos.* In military areas, such as Ningxia *Zhen*, there were no administrative officials, only military ones, as the forts were designed specifically for military purposes

Zhen-forts (Fig.3a) were the largest in size, with a perimeter of about 12 *li*[3], or 7km. These forts had at least four gates, with some having up to eight. The streets inside were classified into main streets, secondary streets and alleyways *Lu*-forts (Fig.3b) were 2km to 4km in perimeter with two classes of streets: cross-shaped main streets and alleyways. Most of the *lu*-forts had four gates, but some had only two *Wei*-forts (Fig.3c) are 4 to 7 *li* or 23km to 4km in perimeter, with two to four gates. These forts are usually divided by several cross-shaped streets (i.e. a grid), with a few exceptions divided simply by parallel streets. Secondary to streets are alleyways *Suo*-forts (Fig.3d) were about 2km in perimeter. Most of them had only three gates with no north gate. Again, the main streets were either in a grid or parallel to each other, branching off into alleyways. *Bao*-forts (Fig.3e) were the smallest unit in the system of stationing troops, and they were built and designed for purely military purposes. They were between 1 to 4 *li* in perimeter, that is, normally less than two kilometres. The main streets were in a grid within the larger ones and parallel in smaller ones. Regular-shaped *bao*-forts were square or rectangular, but there were irregular variations also. These forts had up to three gates (Fig.3).

The layout of the Roman forts

Roman forts can be graded into fortresses, forts and fortlets. Fortresses provide permanent fortification for up to two legions, whilst forts were built for auxiliary units. Fortlets were usually built in the middle of the frontline defence system, or along a road or at a river crossing, providing lodgings for small detachments. The soldiers stationed in forts and fortlets were auxiliary troops who were not Roman citizens (English Heritage 2006) . Fortlets may have only one or two gates. Over the gate there was a tower built of stone or timber, and the outer defences may consist of one or two ditches.

The Ming forts had a clear hierarchy, determined by the rank of the commander stationed there. The rank of a Roman fort is decided by size, complexity, and the status of the garrison; legions or auxiliaries. The Ming forts were evenly distributed in a general sense, though with exceptions due to geographical considerations, and the Wall forts and milecastles on Hadrian's Wall were sited at a fixed distance. The Ming forts were usually built on the inner side of the Wall to house soldiers and supplies. Only fortified passes were built riding on the wall as defensive

3 A *li* is about a third of a mile (Editors' note).

于Fort的是只有一个或两个门通过障墙，门的上面有一个木质或石质塔楼，旁边有一道或两道沟渠。

明长城军堡有层次分明的等级关系，城内驻扎将领的级别决定了城池的级别；而古罗马城池的级别与城池规模、复杂性和驻军状态、即士兵来自于军团还是辅助军团划分的。明长城军堡之间的距离受高山沟谷等复杂地形限制不严格等距，但也相对均匀，而哈德良长城上的屯兵城（Wall Forts）和里堡基本上等距离设置。明军堡多为与长城内侧，起到屯兵屯粮的作用，只有关口、关城才跨长城墙体而建，起到“一夫当关、万夫莫开的”防守作用，同时也具有关卡的作用，哈德良长城沿线的城池则穿墙而建。

三、城池内部空间结构

明代军事城池于清前期“撤卫设县”被改民堡了，也有军堡被遗弃，至今被完整做过考古挖掘的寥寥无几，很难有考古资料证实，本文在大量实地调查的基础上，以民国年间神木路城测绘图为原型，推测堡内部结构的基本特征：①城内主街呈十字形、丰字型或一字形等，道路通畅。②四周城墙，墙内部有环涂，便于迅速调配兵力。③每边墙上设墩台角处设角墩台；④城开一到四门，门设瓮城，城门和瓮城门上有城楼；⑤城中央十字街交叉处设镇中央楼；⑥城内庙祠和牌坊众多；⑦内设井若干；⑧城内设将领的署地或 行政部门衙署。⑨城外设校场、演武厅等。

Polybius and Pseudo-Hyginus: Fortification of the Roman Camp 这本书介绍了两个古代历史学家记述的古罗马军营的布局：①军营的地点要便于执行官发布命令、俯瞰全营，先在地上插上一个旗帜，然后以这个地点为中心，画一个方形，方形的四边距中心点 100 英尺，这样整个地块共 4 亩（iugera）。（实际上，哈德良时期大多数城池都是长方形平面，带有圆弧形转角，类似扑克牌形状）②执行官与军事法庭位于中央区域，便于发布命令、俯瞰全营；③中央区域除了指挥部还有粮仓，粮仓里储存的粮食够全城士兵一年的给养；④骑兵营房占据了距离军事法庭最近的位置，往外是步兵营房；⑤通过中央指挥部有南北向两条宽阔通道连接了城池的四个城门；⑥对于较大规模的城池，从中心往四周城池中要容纳执政官、财政官、使者、骑兵、步兵、特种兵和后备兵等（M.C·J 米勒，J·G 德沃托，1993）（图 4）。

两者皆有坚固城墙和城壕作为最外围围护结构，通常会在城墙上开四门便于进出，级别越高，城门数量越多。城池内部会以城门为轴线做通路，分主街和次巷。高级别建筑居城池最安全区域，如古罗马城池中中央指挥部、驻军指挥官和仓库居于城中；明军堡的军事衙署居于城中。城中或城外附近有井用于生活和生产。

四、小结

城防系统的层次性设置、屯兵城内的空间布局，也有高度的相似性，都有力地展示了她们都曾经在边疆沿线发挥过坚不可摧的重要防御任务。通过比较，增强了我们对古人军事智慧的敬畏，也敦促我们在更深层次上理解蕴含在古代城防系统中的军事思想。

strongpoints and checkpoints. The milecastles and the Wall forts on Hadrian's Wall, though, were almost all built attached to the Wall.

THE INTERNAL LAYOUT

The Ming forts were largely lost in the civilianisation movement in the early Qing Dynasty, and those not built over were abandoned. Few have been adequately excavated, which means that very little archaeological information about them has been produced. Based on the on-site investigations and the plan of Shenmu *Lu*-Fort, this paper infers that a fort would have the following components:

- Cross-shaped, 丰-shaped or parallel main streets to facilitate movement within the fort.
- Curtain walls surrounding the fort with walkways on the top for the rapid deployment of troops.
- Beacon towers on each side and at each corner.
- Up to four gates, reinforced by barbicans and gatehouses.
- A central building at the joint of the cross.
- A considerable number of temples and memorial arches.
- Several wells.
- The residence of the general or the administrative office.
- Training grounds for officers and soldiers in the outskirts.

Polybius, and Pseudo-Hyginus (Miller & De Voto 1993), the authors of two Roman military manuals, provided an idealised outline plan of a Roman fort, which was infinitely adapted to local circumstances:

- The camp was outlined by setting up a flag on the ground as the centre before drawing a square around it. The four sides were exactly 100ft from the centre, so that the entire block covers a four-*iugera* area. (In practice, however, by the time of Hadrian, most forts were rectangular with rounded corners, like playing cards).
- The headquarters and the tribunal occupied the central area to allow officers to give orders and rulings, and to have a better overview of the camp.
- The granaries, which stored food for the soldiers, were also situated in the central area.
- The cavalry barracks lay closest to the tribunal, and beyond them were the infantry barracks.
- Two wide streets intersected at the headquarters, connecting the four gates north to south.
- Some larger forts needed to accommodate, starting from the centre, the commander (*praefectus*), the treasurer (*quaestor*), messengers (*legati*), the cavalry (*equites*), the infantry (*pedites*), special forces (*extraodinarii*) and military reserves (*auxilia*) (Fig.4).

Archaeology – not least on Hadrian's Wall – has clarified and amplified these ideal arrangements. Both the Ming fort and the Roman fort were reinforced by robust curtain walls and ditches. The fort is usually equipped with four gates built in the wall. The more important the fort, the more gates. The opposite gates form axes for streets, which can be a main street or an alleyway. The important buildings, i.e. the headquarters, the commanding officer's house, and the granary for the Roman forts, and the military office of the Ming forts, are placed in the safest place of the fort. Wells were dug both inside and outside the fort.

CONCLUSION

The highly similar hierarchies and planning of the defence and the forts demonstrate the duties they once carried out on the frontiers. The comparison intensifies the respect to the military wisdom of our ancestors, urging us to obtain a better understanding of the military agenda in the ancient defence systems.

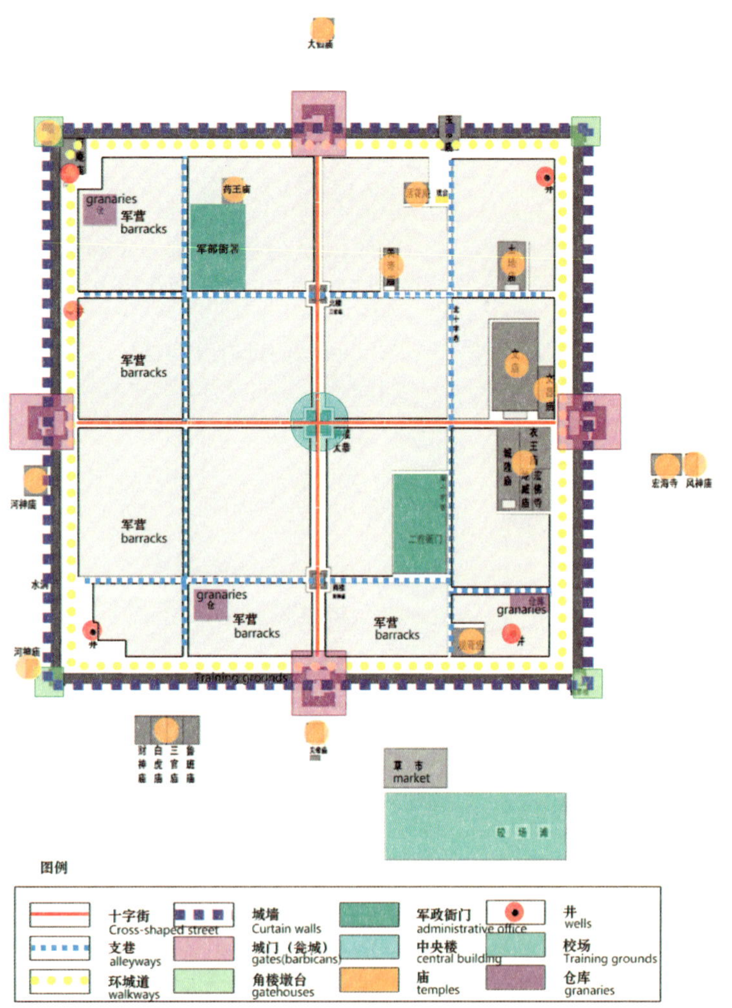

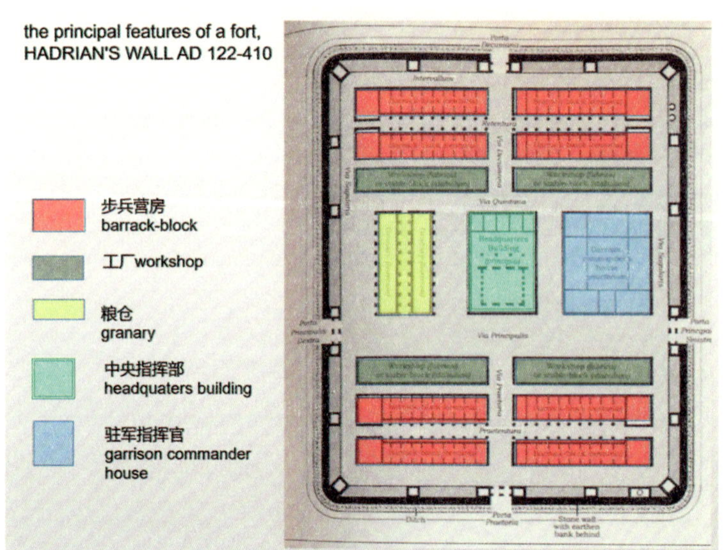

图 4 军事聚落空间结构示意，明长城（以上）；古罗马长城（下面），底图来源：Fields 2003）。

Fig.4. Plans of a Ming fort (above) and a Roman fort (below)(credit Fields 2003).

参考文献
References

Al Chong. 1990, *The Ming Wall in the Four Zhens of Shaanxi*. Xi'an: Shaanxi Normal University General Publishing House.

艾冲. 1990 . 明代陕西四镇长城. 西安： 陕西师范大学出版社.

English Heritage. *Hadrian's Wall*. English Heritage, 2006.

英格兰遗产委员会. 2006. 哈德良长城.

Fields, N. 2003. *Hadrian's Wall AD122-410,* Osprey Publishing Ltd.

N . 菲尔兹. 2003. 哈德良长城 AD 122-410. 鱼鹰出版公司.

Li Yan, Zhang Yukun, Li Zhe. "A Study on the Ming Wall Defence System and Its Fortresses" in *Architecture Bulletin*, 2018, 596(5), 69-75.

李严， 张玉坤， 李哲. 2018 . 明长城防御体系与军事聚落研究. 建筑学报, 596（5）, 69-75.

Polybius and Pseudo-Hyginus: Fortification of the Roman Camp, translated and edited by M. C. J. Miller and J. G. De Voto, 1993. Chicago, Ares Publishers.

波利比乌斯， 伪许癸努斯. 1993. 罗马兵营要塞. M . C . J · 米勒， J . G · 德沃托 （翻译和编辑）. 芝加哥： 阿瑞斯出版社.

Reuter, M. & Thiel, A. 2015. *Der Limes: Auf Den Spuren Der Romer*. Wissenschaftliche Buchgesellschaft.

M . 罗伊特， A . 蒂尔. 2015. 边墙： 罗马人的脚步. 科学图书协会.

Zhao Xianhai. 2005. *The Study of the Ming Nine Bian System*. Changchun: Northeast Normal University, 28.

赵现海. 2005. 明代九边军镇体制研究. 长春： 东北师范大学, 28.

2.3 HADRIAN'S WALL RESEARCH FRAMEWORK: METHODOLOGY AND RESULTS

TONY WILMOTT
Historic England - Cumbria - UK

Abstract

There have been great changes in the nature, circumstances, and quantity of archaeological work in the UK. The increase in archaeological data recovered made it essential to develop frameworks for research in order to focus the work of researchers. In 2009 a cross-regional framework was developed for the Hadrian's Wall World Heritage Site. The creation of the Framework included as wide a cross-section of interested parties as possible, and was wholly inclusive. It consisted of three elements. The Resource Assessment established existing knowledge. The Research Agenda highlighted gaps in knowledge that would be desirable to fill. The Research Strategy prioritised research objectives, and the ways that these might be met.

Keywords: Hadrian's Wall, Archaeology, Research, Assessment, Strategy, Agenda

INTRODUCTION

In the UK the nature and circumstances of archaeological fieldwork have changed radically over the past century. From an amateur pursuit, archaeology became increasingly concerned with rescue excavation, first in the cities after the devastation of the Second World War, and then with the pace of development and the growth of infrastructure thereafter. A large volunteer element provided much of the archaeological workforce at that time, and volunteer participation remains significant. During the 1970s, government funding increased greatly, and archaeology became more professionalised with, for example, the development of publicly funded regional archaeological units. In 1990 this changed with the implementation of *Planning Policy Guidance Note 16* (PPG16: Department of the Environment 1990) which identified archaeology as a material consideration in the planning process. PPG 16 also introduced the concept of 'the polluter pays', whereby development proposals are assessed by regional archaeological curators to determine the impact of the development on archaeological remains. Where appropriate, an archaeological condition is placed upon planning consent for the development, and the developers themselves provide funding for investigation, excavation and recording on their sites. As a result, the professionalisation of archaeology has continued, and archaeology has become an integral feature within the development process, under PPG 16 and its successor policies.

The availability of developer funding has meant that the number of archaeological interventions carried out has increased enormously (Fig.1). Archaeological work undertaken in response to development is, of course, not driven by research priorities, but by the need to record the archaeological deposits and structures that will be destroyed partly or wholly by the development. This has meant that the vast quantity of archaeological data gathered by these works has remained just that - data - usually not published, but available in the archives managed by the local Historic Environment Records (HERs). The very quantity of data held on individual sites makes it difficult to access,

2.3 哈德良长城研究框架: 方法与成果

托尼·威尔莫特

英格兰遗产委员会—坎布里亚—英国

摘要

不论从性质、境况还是数量上来说，英国的考古工作出现了诸多变化。随着考古发掘资料和数据日益增加，很有必要制定一个研究框架，以便能够将研究人员的精力集中于重点领域。2009年，针对哈德良长城世界遗产地的跨区域研究框架正式发布。该框架尽可能广泛地容纳各个领域有兴趣的方面参与进来，极具包容性。框架包括三个部分。“资源评估”整合已有知识成果。“研究议程”指出需要填补的知识空白。“研究策略”排列优先的研究目标及可能的实现方法。

关键词：哈德良长城　考古　研究　评估　策略　议程

绪论

近一个多世纪以来，英国田野考古工作的性质与境况经历了翻天覆地的变化。起初，考古只属于业余爱好。后来，二战炮火摧毁了众多城市，导致后续城市发展和基础设施建设，使考古工作日益重视抢救性发掘。当时，志愿者就为考古工作提供了许多人力。如今，志愿者仍发挥着重要的作用。20 世纪 70 年代，政府资助显著增加，诞生了一批公共资助的地方性考古机构，考古的专业性逐渐提升。1990 年,《规划政策指南注解 16》（PPG 16: 英国环境部, 1990 年）的颁布与实施改变了这一状况。PPG16 将考古工作列为规划编制程序中的关键环节。此外，PPG16 还提出“谁污染，谁付费”原则，这意味着建设项目方案需要得到地方考古机构管理人员的评估，判断建设项目是否将对考古遗存造成影响。某些情况下，颁发建设规划许可附有保护考古遗存的条件，相关勘探、发掘与记录费用由建设方负担。于是在 PPG16 与后续政策的推动下，考古工作进一步专业化，并成为建设开发中不可或缺的一部分。

来自建设方的资金促使考古干预项目的数量大幅提升（见图 1）。当然，配合建设项目展开的考古工作并非出于研究目的，而是旨在记录即将因建设遭到全面或部分损坏的考古遗存和遗迹结构。这意味着这些考古工作所收集的大量信息只停留在数据层面，通常并不公开发表，但可以在地方历史环境记录局（HERs）管理的档案库中查到。然而，庞大的数据分散保存在每个遗址上，难以查询、关联、整合和解读。

梳理与发表

针对上述情况，英格兰遗产委员会对英格兰已有的各种研究框架展开调查评估。这些研究框架都列出了各自的研究重点。调查结果显示，已有的研究框架在结构与重点上各自为政，缺乏协调。这些国家级的研究框架编制于不同时期，主要由专门研究某一历史时期的不同研究团体制定，有许多其他历史时期、专

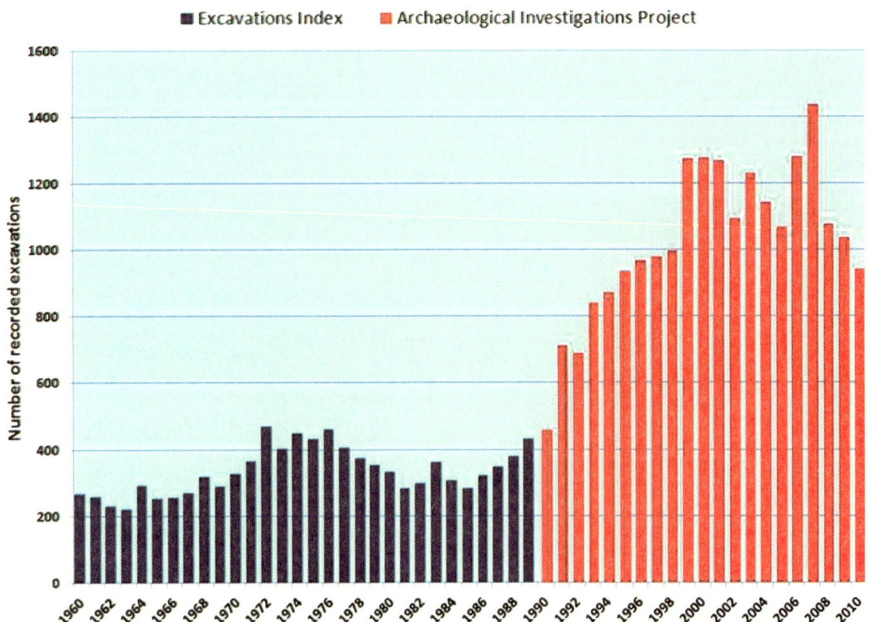

Fig.1 Archaeological events comprising or including excavation in England, 1960-2010, showing the increase in work following the publication of PPG 16 in 1990 (© Historic England).
图 1 1960 年至 2010 年在英格兰展开的发掘及其他考古活动，显然在 1990 年 PPG 16 颁布后考古工作数量有所增加（© 英格兰遗产委员会）。

Legend 图例:		
	Excavation Index	发掘项目
	Archaeological Investigation project	考古项目
	Number of recorded excavations	考古记录数量

contextualise, synthesise and interpret.

REVIEW AND PUBLICATION

This situation prompted a survey by English Heritage into the range of frameworks for research, each listing their own priorities, that already existed in England. The survey found that such frameworks were inconsistent in their structure and emphasis. There were national frameworks for different periods, largely produced by the Societies interested in specific archaeological periods, but many periods, specialisms and subjects were under represented. Furthermore, often the existing frameworks represented the particular interests of single authors, or small groups of authors.

The review resulted in the production in 1996 by English Heritage of a document entitled *Frameworks for our Past* (Olivier 1996). This established that it was desirable to create regional research frameworks covering all periods of the history of a region and establishing the research priorities both on a regional and chronological basis.

Among the regional frameworks created and published in 2006 were those for the north west and north eastern regions of England (Brennand 2006; Petts and Gerard 2006) – the regions through which Hadrian's Wall runs. Within the regional frameworks, although the Roman Period was dealt with regionally, the specific needs of Hadrian's Wall were not tackled, as it was clear that a holistic research framework was needed to take into account the special status of Hadrian's Wall as a monument which transcended regional boundaries and which, furthermore, was a World Heritage Site.

The research framework for Hadrian's Wall, *Frontiers of Knowledge*, was published in 2009 (Symonds and Mason 2009) after a process of consultation and academic discussion (described below) which took two years. The main components of the framework relate to past, present and future. The Resource Assessment looks at past research leading to the Agenda, which relates to where we are now, while the Strategy examines options for the future.

RESOURCE ASSESSMENT

This is the first step – to establish the starting point – i.e. what we know, or what we think we know, and where the

业方向与研究主题却未得到充分关注。此外，已有框架通常只代表某个学者或某个小学术团队的具体研究取向。

作为调研成果，英格兰遗产委员会于 1996 年发表了题为《历史研究框架》（奥利维尔，1996）的文件。这份文件提出，有必要制定一个涵盖各个地区所有历史时期的研究框架，并以地区和时代为纲提出重点研究目标。

2006 年，英格兰各大地区发布了研究框架，其中包括哈德良长城所在西北地区和东北地区（布伦南德，2006；佩茨&杰拉德，2006）。尽管各地区的研究框架都各自将罗马时期作为研究重点，但并没有针对哈德良长城研究的特点。显然，需要建立一个整体性研究框架，以满足哈德良长城这一跨区域遗产、特别是作为世界遗产的特殊研究需求。

经过长达两年的咨询与学术讨论后，哈德良长城研究框架《知识前沿》（西蒙兹&梅森）（下简称《框架》）于 2009 年正式发表。这一框架主要包括过去、现在与未来。"资源评估"部分回顾过去的研究，紧随其后的"研究议程"涉及当前的研究，"研究策略"则探讨未来的方向。

资源评估

资源评估是第一阶段，它建立《框架》的起点，即哪些是已经解决的问题，哪些是学者们自认为已经解决的问题，哪些是需要填补的知识空白。以前哈德良长城的研究缺乏协调，各个学者根据各自的学术目标展开研究，或是配合建设项目展开抢救性工作。评估阶段总结和分析现有成果基础，包含发掘资料、调查数据、实物遗存、博物馆器物与出土文物等现有成果。

"资源评估"的撰写尽可能地展开了广泛咨询，覆盖与哈德良长城研究相关的各个方面。虽然这项调研由英格兰遗产委员会出资，但要求不能局限于委员会自身的研究，而要包括长城沿线的所有考古团体。如果没有如此大的包容性，该《框架》可能被视为一个自上而下、由官方规定的做什么或不做什么的强制性文件。广泛吸收各方意见，使整个长城学术界对《框架》产生了主人翁意识与责任感，从而调动他们积极参与《框架》规划的相关学术活动。

初期的讨论一直试图在很广泛的研究主题中划定范围，包括在成果评估的基础上，如何划定时间的范围，是否应该涵盖哈德良长城所在地区遥远的史前、以及中世纪与后中世纪时期发展相关史料。《框架》文件决定，上述历史时期已经涵盖在各大区研究框架中，因此最终的研究主题将涵盖下列内容：

- 哈德良长城历史框架；
- 前罗马帝国时代（铁器时代）泰恩-索尔韦海湾考古；
- 哈德良大帝以前边疆与石路（Stangegate)；
- 哈德良长城本体；
- 要塞与长城外聚落；
- 地貌环境与景观；
- 生产与采购；
- 生活与社会；
- 后罗马时代公元 400-1000 年的哈德良长城考古。

上述主题领域都有三十多名学者在不同但又相互交叉的研究团队中开展。这些团队的研究成果都在网

gaps in knowledge are. Research on Hadrian's Wall had been uncoordinated, often following the research objectives of individual scholars, or being undertaken as rescue work in the face of development. This phase summarised and assessed the existing knowledge base, be that in terms of excavation evidence, survey data, the physical remains of the monument, or collections of artefacts in museums and excavated collections.

The compilation of the Resource Assessment was undertaken with the widest possible consultation, ranging across the whole range of shareholders in knowledge of the Wall. Although funded by English Heritage, a prerequisite was to ensure that the process was not exclusive but wholly inclusive of the archaeological community of the Wall. Without this inclusivity the framework might be seen as top-down and imposed – a self-appointed or official group 'dictating' what research should and should not be done. Inclusivity of contribution meant that the entire Wall research community could feel a sense of ownership of the resulting publication, and thus would fully participate in the activities engendered by the framework.

Preliminary meetings struggled with finding a series of themes within which to assess the material, and in particular the time frame and whether we were to consider the remote prehistory of the Wall zone, and medieval and post medieval developments. It was decided that these aspects were covered in the overlapping regional research frameworks, so the final list of themes was:

- The historical framework of Hadrian's Wall;
- The pre-Roman (Iron Age) archaeology of the Tyne-Solway isthmus;
- The pre-Hadrianic frontier and the Stanegate;
- The Wall;
- The forts and extramural settlements;
- Landscape and environment;
- Production and procurement;
- Life and society;
- The post-Roman archaeology of Hadrian's Wall AD 400-1000.

These themes were studied by over 30 colleagues in different but overlapping groups, and documentation produced by the groups was made available on the internet, so that interested parties not in the thematic groups could contribute. These groups assessed the data within their own themes and summarised these data in chapters in the Resource Assessment document (Fig.2). This led to the identification of gaps in knowledge in the different areas, contributing to the production of a Research Agenda (Fig.3).

RESEARCH AGENDA

This stage attempted to identify the main gaps in knowledge within each theme. It was clear that some themes had more gaps than others, and that gaps differed widely in scale, ranging from major conceptual issues which could only be resolved by large scale research projects, to minor lacunae which might be resolved by small scale work in the field or in archives. Although the range of gaps was different within each theme, many gaps, unsurprisingly, transcended individual themes. Many of the interpretative questions in the Agenda were issues that had been challenging scholars for up to a century, and could clearly not be resolved by quick and easy responses.

The Agenda is then a point-in-time statement of the gaps in knowledge that it would be desirable to fill. It was based on current knowledge, and it was clear that further research would generate new questions and would change the emphases of the Agenda. For this reason this is seen as a 'live' document, which needs to be open to review and revision in order to keep it up to date. The identification of the gaps in knowledge led to the development of a Research Strategy.

RESEARCH STRATEGY

This stage is intended to enable a prioritised set of research objectives to be identified, and to identify ways

上公布，以便那些不在研究团队中、但有兴趣的学者参与。这些研究团队根据公布的成果结合各自的研究领域进行了评估和总结，并汇总编制成“资源评估”中的章节（见图表 2）。通过这一过程梳理出各领域需要填补的研究空白，为“研究议程”的编写奠定基础（见图表 3）。

研究议程

这一阶段旨在明确每个主题下需要填补的主要研究空白。显而易见，各个主题有待研究的空白程度不一，而且空白的研究课题范围差别很大。有些涉及概念性问题，需要依靠大型研究项目才能解决，有些则属于小型研究课题，通过小规模实地考察或查阅文献就可以完成。尽管各主题下有待研究领域各不相同，但毫不意外的是，很多研究问题超越不同专题，拥有交叉共性。“研究议程”中的许多阐释性与解读性的问题往往已困扰学术界数十年，恐难在短时间内轻易解决。

研究议程是基于当下、明确需要填补的研究空白。因此，研究议程的基础是现有的知识成果，可以想见随着研究不断深入将产生更多新问题，从而改变研究日程的重点。正是因此，“研究议程”被视作一份“活的”文件，需要随时评估和修订，以保持与时俱进。明确研究空白之后，下个阶段就是确定“研究策略”。

Fig.2 The Hadrian's Wall Research Framework – Cover of Vol 1, the Resource Assessment
图 2《哈德良长城研究框架》卷一：资源评估封面。

Fig.3 The Hadrian's Wall Research Framework – Cover of Vol 2, the Research Strategy and Agenda.
图 3《哈德良长城研究框架》卷二：研究议程与策略封面。

in which these objectives might be met. As well as thematic objectives, the Strategy also identifies key universal priorities which were identified by a majority of the thematic groups. They are:

- An audit of existing material: which would identify all relevant data, possibly in a GIS format, and which would need to be kept continuously up to date.
- Risk Assessment for Hadrian's Wall: to identify potential threats from both human and natural activities.
- Development of a layered Hadrian's Wall GIS System – an obvious means to create a valuable management tool.
- Chronology: there is still inadequate chronological information available for the features in the frontier zone. In particular the many features which appear to be Iron Age or Roman on morphological grounds have been independently dated.
- Communicating knowledge, raising awareness, and improving public understanding: by publishing on many levels including annual magazines, ensuring publication and dissemination of research beyond the HER archive.
- To produce information at a level where it is accessible by both academic and non-academic researchers.
- Specialist succession planning: to identify relevant specialisms, and to ensure these are taken up by the next generation, so that study continues at the same or a higher level.
- The establishment of a Discussion Group (or Forum) for the further sharing of research and ideas.
- The initiation of flagship strategic projects in specific identified subjects where themes overlap and are complementary.

Although the Framework was published at a particular point in time, in order to maintain relevance it requires regular review and updating. The Strategy includes both long term (30 years) and short term (5 years) objectives, and it is important to periodically examine whether progress on these objectives has been made. The target for this has been to undertake a review every five years. In practice this has proved not to be simple, and progress in any area is dependent on resource having been available for research to take place.

RESULTS

Although progress has been fairly slow, simply because not a huge amount of research has taken place, nevertheless, where opportunities for research have occurred, projects have been designed specifically with a view to addressing the Research Framework priorities. In this respect all practitioners have a common group of objectives at which to aim.

Responsibility for the suggested Discussion Group is now held under the Hadrian's Wall Management Plan by the Archaeological Research Delivery Group – one of a number of Delivery Groups which report to the WHS Partnership Board. Under Objective 9 of the Management Plan, the aims of the Delivery Group are to:

- Seek to promote high-quality research into the archaeology of the Hadrian's Wall frontier and its cultural history.
- Provide coordination for this through the promotion, support, and periodic review of the *Hadrian's Wall Research Framework.*
- Provide research input into wider World Heritage Site management on the Wall, aiming to provide a forum and voice for researchers to become involved with and impact upon wider WHS management.
- Seek to disseminate this research both within the archaeological community and to involve the wider public.

An action which has fostered and encouraged public participation in the archaeological research on the Wall is WallCAP (Hadrian's Wall Community Archaeology Project), which has developed a community group, trained and guided by heritage professionals and archaeologists, to undertake a variety of work to:

研究策略

研究策略旨在明确优先研究目标，以及研究目标的实现方式。除了确定各个研究主题的目标外，大部分研究主题团队还在“研究策略”中提出共性的优先研究领域，即：

- 分类整理、罗列已有材料，收集所有相关数据，可能需要通过地理信息系统（GIS）加以汇总，并持续更新；
- 哈德良长城风险评估，明确人类活动与自然活动对长城带来的潜在危险；
- 哈德良长城多图层GIS系统建设，作为高效的管理工具；
- 编年序列，目前罗马疆域所有年代序列的特征信息尚不完整，特别是很多具有铁器时代或罗马时代形态学现象的遗迹还缺乏测年研究；
- 传播知识，提高认知，完善公众理解：通过在年度杂志等各层次的书籍报刊出版和传播，提高研究成果认知度，而不是孤立地存在于HER管理的档案馆中；
- 确保学术研究人员与非学术研究人员都能浏览并使用整理好的信息；
- 开展“专业接班人计划”，首先确定特定研究方向，确保研究这一领域的学者“后继有人”，以便研究得以延续与提升；
- 成立讨论组或论坛，以进一步共享研究成果和研究思路；
- 发起“旗舰战略项目”：即那些研究主题中交叉或互补的项目。

尽管《框架》是在某一特定时间发布的，但为了保持其有效性，需要定期对其评估与更新。“研究策略”中包括 30 年的长期目标与 5 年短期目标，定期检查这些目标是否取得进展至关重要。因此，计划每五年对《框架》进行一次评审，但能否真正落实并非易事，每个领域取得进展都需要足够的研究资源。

成果

《框架》实施的进展相当缓慢，因为开展的研究项目还不是很多。但是，只要出现研究机会，确定研究项目方案时都会特别考虑《框架》所明确的优先研究主题。这样一来，所有研究者就都有了共同的目标。

目前，上文提及的讨论组计划已经列入《哈德良长城管理规划》，正在由考古研究执行组负责实施。考古研究执行组和其他几个执行组一起，由哈德良长城世界遗产合作委员会负责管理。在《管理规划》的第九项目标中，指出考研研究执行组的目标为：

- 推进哈德良长城罗马帝国边疆及其文化历史的高质量考古研究；
- 为实现这一目标，通过倡导、支持和定期评估《哈德良长城研究框架》而发挥协调作用；
- 为涵盖内容更加广泛的哈德良长城世界遗产管理提供科研支持，为研究人员参与并影响世界遗产地管理提供平台；
- 宣传相关研究，不仅在考古学术界，还包括更广泛的公众群体。

哈德良长城社区考古项目成功地吸引并鼓励公众参与有关哈德良长城的考古研究之中，组建起社区小组，在文化遗产专业人士与考古学家的指导下开展了一系列工作：

- 深化对哈德良长城当前与历史上曾面临的威胁的理解，努力为后代保护这一遗产。

- Improve our understanding of the current and historic risks to Hadrian's Wall so as to secure its heritage for future generations.
- Undertake research to better understand the historic use of Hadrian's Wall in the Roman era and across successive centuries.
- Engage and empower local communities in the heritage of the Wall, locally and across the WHS, for the duration of the project and beyond.

Although the existence of the Framework does not provide any additional resource for research, its main purpose is to identify a range of research objectives which are agreed by the entire Wall community, so that when resources are available, work can be aimed towards fulfilling these specific objectives. Since the Framework was published research has been so aimed, and current and future project proposals and projects will continue to do so.

- 深入研究罗马帝国时期及以后各个时期哈德良长城在历史上的使用情况。
- 在项目实施的整个过程中以及结束后，鼓励各社区群体融入当地的哈德良长城，融入整个哈德良长城世界遗产地，为社区参与赋能。

尽管《框架》并未提供额外的研究资源，但它明确了一系列哈德良长城研究界公认的研究目标。这样一来，一旦资源到位，便可迅速展开工作，以便实现这些目标。自《框架》发布以来，相关研究便依照上述目标展开，未来的研究选题和研究项目也将坚持如此。

References
参考文献

Brennand, M. (ed.). 2006. *The Archaeology of North West England; An Archaeological Research Framework for the North West Region* (*Archaeology North West*, 8), Council for British Archaeology: Manchester.

M·布伦南德（编）. 2006. 西北英格兰考古：西北地区的考古研究框架（西北考古局, 8）. 曼彻斯特：英国考古委员会.

Department of the Environment. 1990. *Planning Policy Guidance Note 16: Archaeology and Planning.*

英国环境部. 1990. 规划政策指南注解16（PPG16).

Olivier, A. C. H. 1996. *Frameworks for our Past*, English Heritage: Portsmouth.

A.C.H·奥利维尔. 1996. 历史研究框架. 普特茅斯：英格兰遗产委员会.

Petts, D. and Gerrard, C. 2006. *Shared Visions: The North East Regional Research Framework for the Historic Environment*, Durham County Council: Durham.

D·佩茨，C·杰拉德. 2006. 共同愿景：东北地区历史环境研究框架. 杜伦：杜伦郡会议.

Symonds, M. F. A. and Mason, D. J. P. 2009. *Frontiers of Knowledge: A Research Framework for Hadrian's Wall, part of the Frontiers of the Roman Empire World Heritage Site*, Durham County Council: Durham.

M.F.A·西蒙兹，D.J.P·梅森. 2009. 知识前沿：哈德良长城的研究框架——罗马帝国边疆世界遗产的一部分. 杜伦：杜伦郡会议.

2.4 UNDERSTANDING HADRIAN'S WALL THROUGH LANDSCAPE ARCHAEOLOGY

ROB COLLINS
Newcastle University - Newcastle upon Tyne - UK

ABSTRACT

Hadrian's Wall is not only a monument, but a landscape. The concept of landscape is fundamental not only to understanding the Wall, but also other frontiers in the past, and their archaeological and architectural survival (or not) into the present. In this paper, landscape archaeology is defined, followed by a discussion of Roman frontiers as landscapes. Hadrian's Wall itself is de-emphasized in a brief case study that highlights the economic networks of the late Roman frontier of the 4th century AD, and our understanding of the monument from a broader landscape perspective.

Keywords: frontier, landscape, supply

INTRODUCTION

'Hadrian's Wall' can be taken to mean simply the monumental structure that bears the name, but for most visitors and researchers, the Wall includes not only the surviving archaeology but also the environment and topography where it is located. Hadrian's Wall is not only a monument, but a landscape. Indeed, the relationship between the built frontier works and the land on which they stand is integral to nearly all modern interpretations of Hadrian's Wall.

LANDSCAPE ARCHAEOLOGY

The common conception of landscape is the discrete combination of climate with the vegetation, wildlife, and topography of a particular location, such that an individual may photograph or paint a landscape. Among academics and heritage managers, however, landscape is a trans-disciplinary concept that includes cultural and physical aspects as 'an area, as perceived by people, whose character is the result of the action and interaction of natural and/or human factors' (ELC 2000). In spanning the natural sciences, social sciences, and humanities, landscape has 'come to occupy a place of central importance for archaeology in recent decades' (Turner *et al.* 2019, 155; see also Gamble 2001; David and Thomas 2008). Furthermore, landscape is not static, and it is continuously shaped by the activities occurring within it (such as agriculture). These activities and their social significance shape perceptions and values of a given landscape.

These recursive relationships are complex and entangled haecceities that can be difficult to distinguish. Different approaches to landscape research make greater or lesser use of different data sets (Turner *et al.* 2019, 156-161). For example, historical geography and landscape history have focused on textual and visible remains of human activities in the landscape, often using the concept of palimpsest to describe the layered accumulation of human modifications to landscape. In contrast, the analysis of physical remains and formation of landscapes, including spatial analyses, make use of more traditional scientific data sets for soils, flora, and fauna, as well as anthropogenic data. More recent decades have also seen the growing influence of social, cultural, and material landscape research that focus on relational interpretive models, and emphasise landscapes as dynamic spaces and contested places.

2.4 通过景观考古学理解哈德良长城

罗伯·柯林斯
纽卡斯尔大学—纽卡斯尔—英国

摘要

哈德良长城不仅仅是古迹，它还是景观。景观是一个核心概念，无论是对于认知哈德良长城及其他边疆防御体系，还是认知保存至今（或已消失）的相关考古遗址和建筑遗存，都至关重要。本文定义了景观考古学的内涵，之后从景观角度探讨罗马帝国边疆。在随后简要的案例分析部分，哈德良长城本体退居次位，而聚焦公元4世纪晚期罗马帝国边疆的经济网络，以及如何从更宏观的景观角度看待哈德良长城。

关键字：边疆　景观　物资供应

引言

“哈德良长城”可以仅指其建筑结构本体。但对于绝大多数的游客和研究人员而言，长城包括的不仅是考古遗存，还有它所处的环境和地形。哈德良长城不仅仅是古迹，它还是景观。的确，长城本体与其所附土地这二者之间的关系已成为几乎所有关于哈德良长城的现代阐释中必会探讨的问题。

景观考古

在一般认知中，景观是某个地点的气候与植被、野生生物和地形的离散组合，就如在该地点拍照或写生中所呈现的那样。然而，学者和遗产管理者则认为，景观是一个跨学科的概念，包含文化与物质两方面，是“一个区域，是人们的感知，其特征是自然因素和/或人为因素的作用及相互作用的结果（ELC 2000）”。景观涵盖了自然科学、社会科学和人文科学，“近几十年来开始在考古学中占据着至关重要的位置（特纳等 2019,155；另见甘布勒 2001；大卫和托马斯 2008）”。此外，景观不是静态的，它因其中发生的各类活动（如农业生产）而不断地得到塑造和改变。这些活动及其社会影响决定着该景观在人们心目中的感受和意义。

这些递归关系是错综复杂的，往往很难加以区分。景观研究的各类方法或多或少地使用了不同的数据集（特纳，等2019，156–161）。例如，历史地理学和景观历史学重点研究景观中人类活动遗留下来的文字记载和实物遗迹，通常运用“覆写”这一概念来描述人类对景观改造带来的多重地层积累。相比之下，对物质遗存和空间解析等景观形成分析，则利用土壤、动植物以及人类学等更为传统的科学数据。近几十年来，社会、文化和物质景观研究也愈发具有影响力，重视建立关系阐释的模型，强调景观作为动态空间和争夺场所的意义。

ROMAN FRONTIERS AS LANDSCAPES

The diverse physical geographies and environments encompassed by Roman frontiers should be understood as landscapes that were fundamentally created by and sustained for the Roman army, including territory to either side of a delineated border. The Roman army dominated and frequently dictated the cultural geography of the frontiers, from the positioning of military installations to the disposition of the road network. Even non-military settlement, be it Roman provincial or barbarian, was influenced by these factors. Around Hadrian's Wall and other Roman frontier regions, the requirements of the army, and the infrastructure that was imposed, physically shaped the landscape and influenced activities undertaken within it.

The location of military installations in the early Roman Empire was a compromise between tactical value and broader strategic-logistical considerations. Smaller installations, such as towers, were employed for their tactical value in local landscape observation and control of communications (Symonds 2017). Legionary fortresses and auxiliary forts were located more strategically, to provide support and reinforcement for smaller installations, and to take advantage of topography and infrastructure that facilitated supply, a key and constant concern for any army. The consolidation of Rome's frontiers under Hadrian between AD 117-138 resulted in a banded linear deployment of the army around the peripheries of the Empire, defined and reinforced by constructions like Hadrian's Wall and natural features like the Rivers Rhine and Danube. Walls and rivers were linear foci, but these lines were not the frontiers in themselves. Each frontier was in reality a deeper zone comprising the immediate provincial hinterland, or inner frontier, the linear border feature, and the adjacent and more distant barbarian territories, or outer frontier (Whittaker 1994; Lattimore 1940). The frontiers in North Africa aptly demonstrate this principle on the ground, where the disposition of the Roman army followed an amorphous branching out of provincial heartlands rather than following a strictly linear cordon (Rushworth 2015).

The consolidation of the frontiers as long-term border regions for the Roman Empire conferred two key benefits. As army installations were constructed in stone, they were suitable for long-term use, creating a more permanent settlement situation. This attracted the broader civilian elements of the military community which established settlements outside forts and fortresses, many including temples, baths, taverns, and workshops as well as homes. These settlements and more permanent garrisons in turn enabled more systematic management and exploitation of land for agriculture, for quarrying and mineral extraction, and for trade. This contrasted with the disorder induced by transient campaigning armies. These fixed locations also fixed supply lines, making it possible to organize and plan the provision of goods and materials, thus contributing to the stability of each frontier. Merchants and traders had access to a stable and relatively well-paid consumer market of Roman military personnel, and to secure infrastructure for the transportation, storage and sale of goods. This enabled the needs of soldiers and their dependents to be met locally, reducing the need to travel further afield for some goods and services.

However, the fixed position of frontiers tied the army down to known locations, providing either a clear target or an identified obstacle for hostile barbarians. This danger was minimised by the army's choice of locations for border fortifications. The Sahara, the Danube, and the Rhine could be substantial natural obstacles to barbarian attack, whilst military installations were placed to control key access points through the landscape. Linear fortifications, like Hadrian's Wall, reinforced these strongpoints, and regular patrols and the use of scouts and spies provided advance warning of major attacks (Austin and Rankov 1995). These installations and routines provided visible markers of the Empire, which attracted the attention of its barbarian neighbours in different ways. The concentrations of resources attracted barbarians seeking plunder, but also those wanting to access the trading and commercial opportunities of the Empire. As Roman goods moved outwards across the borders, people, objects and raw materials also moved into the Empire (Whittaker 1994, 113-121).

The presence of the army significantly changed the demography across the wider corridors of the frontiers. Added

罗马帝国边疆景观

可以这么说，罗马帝国边疆所涵盖的多元的自然地理和环境，包括边境的两侧领土在内，本质上都是由罗马军队创造和维护的景观。从军事设施的选址到道路网络的布局，罗马军队统治并经常支配着边疆的文化地理发展。甚至罗马行省或蛮族的非军事聚落都会受到上述因素的影响。在哈德良长城和其他罗马边疆地区周围，军队的需求及军队修筑的基础设施从根本上塑造了该地景观并影响着其中的活动。

罗马帝国早期的军事设施布局是在军事目标和更广泛的战略–供给因素之间平衡的决策结果。塔楼等小型军事设施的修建主要考虑的是局部景观瞭望和通讯控制等军事因素（西蒙兹 2017），而军团要塞及附属堡垒的布局则更具战略意义，不仅要支持和加强那些小型军事设施，而且还要考虑保障补给的地形因素和基础设施建设需求，因为军需补给历来为兵家之重。公元117年至138年间，哈德良皇帝巩固了罗马边疆，其军队在帝国外围呈带状线性部署，并利用哈德良长城等一系列人造设施以及莱茵河和多瑙河等自然地貌划定并巩固防线。长城和河流是线性的，但罗马边疆不仅仅是这些线性设施和自然地貌。每个地区的边疆实际上都是一片更深更广的区域，包括省内腹地（即内部边疆）、线性边境要素，以及临近和更远处的蛮族领土（即外部边疆）（惠特克 1994；拉蒂摩尔 1940）。位于北非的边疆提供了很好的证明，罗马军队的部署以行省的心脏地带为中心向外辐射，而并非严格的线性布局（鲁什沃斯 2015）。

通过巩固边疆设防，这些区域成为罗马帝国长期的固定边境，这带来了两个主要好处。军事设施都是由石头筑成，适合长期使用，为永久定居创造了更有利的条件。因此，以要塞和堡垒为中心，在其外围吸引形成了包含更多平民要素的军事聚落，除居所以外还建有神庙、浴场、酒馆和作坊。这些聚落和更多永久性军营反过来又推动了农业、采石、采矿和贸易用地的系统性管理和开发。这同短暂的军事活动带来的混乱无序形成了鲜明的对比。当这些地点固定下来，补给线路也随之固化，因而可以有计划地组织货物和材料的供给，进而促进各个边疆地区的稳定。商贸人员得以进入罗马军人形成的稳定优渥的消费市场，货物运输、仓储和销售所需的基础设施也都能够得到保障。这样一来，士兵及其家属的需求在当地就可以得到满足，不再需要长途跋涉采购物资或寻求服务。

然而，边疆的固定也意味着军队安营扎寨的位置固定下来，成为敌对蛮族的明确打击目标或是进入帝国腹地的障碍。将防御工事建在合适的位置能够最大程度地降低这一危险。撒哈拉沙漠、多瑙河和莱茵河成为蛮族攻击的主要天然屏障，而人造军事设施能够对景观的关键通道进行严格管控。像哈德良长城这样的线性防御工事则加强了这些战略据点的防御能力，而派遣侦察兵定期巡逻，配合使用间谍能在重大袭击来临时提供预警（奥斯汀和兰科夫 1995）。这些军事设施和日常活动成为罗马帝国的明显标志，以各种各样的方式吸引了隔壁蛮族的注意。资源的集中不仅吸引了想要掠夺的蛮族，也吸引了那些想要抓住帝国贸易和商业机会的人们。随着罗马的货物跨越边境向外输出，人员、物品和原材料也源源不断地涌入帝国（惠特克 1994, 113–121）。

军队的存在极大地改变了整个边疆廊道地区的人口结构。除了一般的罗马行省社会的奴隶、自由农户、工匠和当地精英，这里还有各种军事人员，以及由众多商人家属和士兵家属组成的“营地随行人员”。这些非军事人员中，很多人在要塞之外毗邻而居。再后来，他们移居至塞内。外部边疆是各蛮族族群的大本营，他们归属于部落，并经常与罗马帝国开展合作。这意味着在行省平民和宗教上流社会中，还汇聚了具有同样高社会地位的军事精英和蛮族首领，各自带来不同的军事、政治和经济思想。

罗马军队的组织结构也对当地和整个区域带来了重大影响。边防司令和各军队指挥官除了负责战术和

to the mix of slaves, free farmers, craftsmen and local elites that composed normal Roman provincial societies was the diverse range military personnel, and their numerous 'camp followers' of merchants and soldiers' dependents. Many of those civilians lived immediately outside the forts or, in later periods, within the forts. The outer frontiers were home to diverse barbarian groups, ascribed to tribes, which often collaborated with the Empire. This means that the standard provincial civil and religious elites were added to by similarly high social status military elites, and barbarian chiefs, each of whom brought with them a range of military, political and economic perspectives.

The structural organization of the Roman army also had strong local and regional impacts. As well as dealing with tactical and strategic matters, generals with frontier commands, and unit commanders, were tasked with sustaining their soldiers. They were supported by praetorian prefects and provincial governmental officials responsible for collecting the *annona militaris*, a tax directly supporting the army (Jones 1964, 458-460). Sources indicate that the army sought to maximise local or regional self-sufficiency in supply, as far as the local resources of each frontier would allow. A considerable amount of supplies could often be sourced locally through taxation in-kind, for which detailed accounts have survived from the provinces of Syria and Egypt (Alston 1995; Pollard 2000). Furthermore, each fort or larger installation could draw on its associated *territorium*[1], to provide at least some of the core needs of a garrison, notably food, firewood, fodder, and pasture (le Bohec 2000, 219-220). These military estates are not well documented, and consequently are poorly understood. The implication is however clear that generals and local commanders would be expected to organize and manage these lands. An army garrison was not merely a concentration of consumers; the army and its broader military community had considerable capacity for production and provision of materials, goods, and services (Collins 2012, 57-66).

Roman frontiers, then, should be understood as complex, constructed landscapes of defence. While they were spatially peripheral to the political centre of the Empire, the frontiers benefitted from effective communications with imperial officials concerning the transfer of officers and soldiers, and the provision of supplies. Indeed, this supply network and the heavy financial commitment of paying the army was a material recognition that the preservation of the peripheries was key for the core of the Roman Empire and its imperial elite. Considering Roman frontiers as re-shaped landscapes provides a foundation for understanding the context within which specific frontier sites and monuments, like Hadrian's Wall, can be understood in ecological, geographical, and socio-political terms.

A LATE ROMAN FRONTIER LANDSCAPE: AN ECONOMIC PERSPECTIVE

The northern frontier of *Britannia*, focused on the monumental complex of Hadrian's Wall, offers a rich dataset for a landscape approach (Fig. 1). Roman Britain, and especially the Wall, has benefitted from centuries of investigation by antiquarians and archaeologists, with each successive generation enhancing knowledge with improved methods of enquiry and recording (Breeze 2014). However, to understand the frontier, we must also zoom out from the Wall. Considering the frontier from an economic perspective is simply one manner in which a landscape approach can be applied.

Regional overview

The northern frontier of *Britannia* largely corresponds to the late Roman province of *Britannia secunda*; this covered most of present-day northern England from the Humber up to Hadrian's Wall, with its provincial capital at York (Mattingly 2006, 228), and also the barbarian territories in southern Scotland. Within the province, there are only three known *civitates*[2], two in present day Yorkshire and one at Carlisle, and a further number of smaller towns.

---

1 *Territorium* is the Latin for the English word territory. However, it has a legal meaning and implication that is not well understood, so it is more accurate to retain the Latin usage rather than 'territory', which has a more generic meaning in English.

2 A *civitas* (the singular plural is *civitates*) is a Latin term for a town and its territory with a defined political status, equivalent

战略事务，还肩负着维持军队供给的任务。禁卫军长官和行省的政府官员通过征收军事税[1]，也为军队将领提供支持（琼斯 1964, 458–460）。多种资料表明，在边疆各处的本地资源允许的范围内，罗马军队都尽可能在本地或当地区域内做到自给自足。通常，军队可以实物税收的方式在当地获得大量物资。这在叙利亚和埃及行省幸存下来的账目中有详细记载（奥尔斯顿 1995；波拉德 2000）。此外，各个要塞或大型军事设施可以利用包括农场和森林在内的附属军用地产，来至少满足兵营的部分核心需求，尤其是食物、柴火、饲料和牧草（勒博埃克 2000, 219–220）。有关这些军用地产的记录并不充分，因此我们对其知之甚少。但这显然意味着司令和当地的指挥官需要负责组织和管理这些土地。驻军并不只是一群消费者；军队以及范围更大的军事社区还有足够的材料和货物的生产和服务实力（柯林斯 2012, 57–66）。

这样一来，可以将罗马帝国边疆理解为是复杂而精心构建的防御性景观。边疆地区尽管在空间上远离帝国的政治中心，处于外围地区，却与中央在军官和士兵调动以及物资供应等方面保持着密切而快速的联系，并从中受益。的确，庞大的补给网络和巨额军费支持彰显出帝国对外围地区重要性的实质性认可，认可其在帝国及上层社会中的关键地位。将罗马帝国边疆视作经过重塑的景观为我们理解某具体的边疆遗址和古迹所处的环境奠定了基础。这样一来，我们就可以从生态、地理和社会政治的视角来理解像哈德良长城这样的边疆遗址和古迹。

从经济视角看罗马帝国晚期边疆景观

不列颠尼亚的北部边疆集中分布着哈德良长城古迹建筑群，为景观研究方法提供了丰富的数据来源（图1）。不列颠尼亚，尤其是长城，受益于古文物研究者和考古学家数百年的调查研究。一代又一代学者专家不断改进调查和记录方法，深化对它们的认识（布里兹 2014）。然而，要了解帝国的边疆，我们必须放眼长城本体之外。从经济的视角来解读帝国边疆就是方法之一。在这过程之中，景观研究方法也可得到应用。

区域概览

不列颠尼亚的北部边疆很大程度上对应的是罗马晚期的第二不列颠尼亚行省，省会位于约克。这一边疆地区涵盖了如今从亨伯河到哈德良长城的英格兰北部的大部分地区，以及位于苏格兰南部的蛮族领地（马丁利 2006, 228）。行省内目前已知的平民行政区域仅有三个，其中两个位于今天的约克郡，另一个位于卡莱尔，此外还分布着若干个小镇。乡间别墅（即罗马贵族们的广阔乡村地产）几乎全部坐落于行省的东南部。其分布与连续密集、有田可耕的聚落分布基本一致。这一分布规律反映了该地自然地理环境以高地为主，而有耕地的聚落大部分位于行省的东部和最西北端的低地。

不幸的是，农村聚落的调查研究十分受限，目前仅能做到在小范围局部区域内进行调查（史密斯，等 2016），尤其在约克郡，我们可以看到相当密集的村庄和农庄分布，但很少发现乡间别墅。约克郡的这些农业人口使用的是典型的罗马不列颠式陶瓷制品和其他商品。陶瓷以产自今天约克郡的陶器为主。位于蒂斯河畔斯托克顿附近的英告比巴韦克采石场屋农场的乡村别墅尤为独特，让我们得以一窥乡村聚落中的罗马上层社会。这里发现了埃及彩绘的玻璃容器碎片和精美的黄金弩状饰针（亨特 2013, 101；普赖斯 2013, 123–124），表明至少有一位家庭成员在帝国具有很高的地位，能够享有如此贵重的物品。

---

1 Annona militaris，罗马人向农民征收该粮食税，直接用于保障军队的粮食供应。——译者注

Villas (substantial agricultural estates of the Roman elite) seemingly occur almost exclusively in the south-east area of the province. Their distribution corresponds to the distribution of continuous, intensive arable settlement. This distribution reflects the physical geography of the region, which is predominantly upland, with arable settlements mostly situated in the lowlands of the eastern and extreme north-west of the province.

Unfortunately, investigation of rural settlement has been limited, and can currently only be characterised at the sub-regional scale (Smith *et al.* 2016), notably in Yorkshire where a reasonably dense pattern of villages and farmsteads can be found, with less frequent occurrence of villas. These rural populations in Yorkshire had access to ceramics and other goods typical of Romano-British life. Ceramic supply was dominated by the potteries of modern-day Yorkshire. The villa at Quarry House Farm, at Ingleby Barwick near Stockton-on-Tees, provides an exceptional insight to the upper echelon of rural settlement. Fragments of an Egyptian painted glass vessel, as well as an elaborate gold crossbow brooch were found (Hunter 2013, 101; Price 2013, 123–124), indicating that at least one member of the household was of very high imperial rank, with access to prestige goods.

Outside of the province's south-east area, identification of late Roman rural activity is problematic. Settlements appear to retain much of their pre-Roman Iron Age morphology, but the identification of occupation of the later 3rd century and after is dependent on the recovery of coins, ceramics or other distinctive Roman objects, which rarely occur in rural settlements of the later Roman period. Data from metal-detecting (via the Portable Antiquities Scheme[3]) further reinforce the pattern established by more traditional archaeological investigation. For example, the mapping of the find-spots of coins indicates a shrinking distribution of coins through the 4th century, with finds tending to cluster near larger settlements or crossroads (Collins 2012, 58–60, fig. 3.3). This pattern is evident across the entirety of *Britannia* in the 4th century, but is more exaggerated in its north and west (Walton 2012).

In contrast, there is excellent evidence for military settlement throughout the province. Military remains, particularly forts, have been the traditional focus of archaeological investigation in the North of England, and the preponderance of ceramic- and coin-use means that 4th-century activity can be confirmed, even if it cannot always be understood in detail. During the 4th century there were approximately 50 army installations that were occupied, according to archaeological evidence (Collins 2012, 48–51). The Notitia Dignitatum[4] (Not. Dig. Occ. 40) provides the names of the units based at some 40 of these installations, often providing evidence that the same unit had been based at the same fort since the 2nd century, something which can be confirmed through inscriptions (Hodgson 1991). This long-term stability is most notable along Hadrian's Wall and at the legionary fortress at York, whereas the forts lining the roads heading north to the Wall were garrisoned by different units during the 3rd and 4th centuries. Unfortunately, the habit of erecting inscriptions declined dramatically from the later 3rd century and is almost completely absent in the 4th century, making it impossible to verify the claims of the Notitia.

to, say, the capital city or town of a county and its county, and which also indicates the presence of a municipal authority with responsibilities to govern and collect tax in the area. The *civitas* can refer only to the town, or to the entire municipal area of the county.

3 The Portable Antiquities Scheme is a national organization, based in the British Museum, with a network of officers spread throughout England and Wales. These local officers are responsible for meeting with members of the public to record the archaeological objects they have discovered. Sometimes these people have found things when gardening or while walking the dog, but most finders are hobby metal-detector users. More information can be found at: finds.org.uk

4 The *Notitia Dignitatum* is a complicated and intriguing document that is known to modern scholars only through the transcription of the original 5th-century AD text in surviving medieval manuscripts (broadly 14th-16th century). *Notitia Dignitatum* is not the official name of the document, but one given to it as that is what is written on the first page of the manuscript. Translated into English from Latin, it broadly means a Register of Dignities (or ennobled offices – offices that carry with them a noble ranking), but we do not understand the original purpose or intent of the document. It mostly provides some very interesting – if problematic – lists!

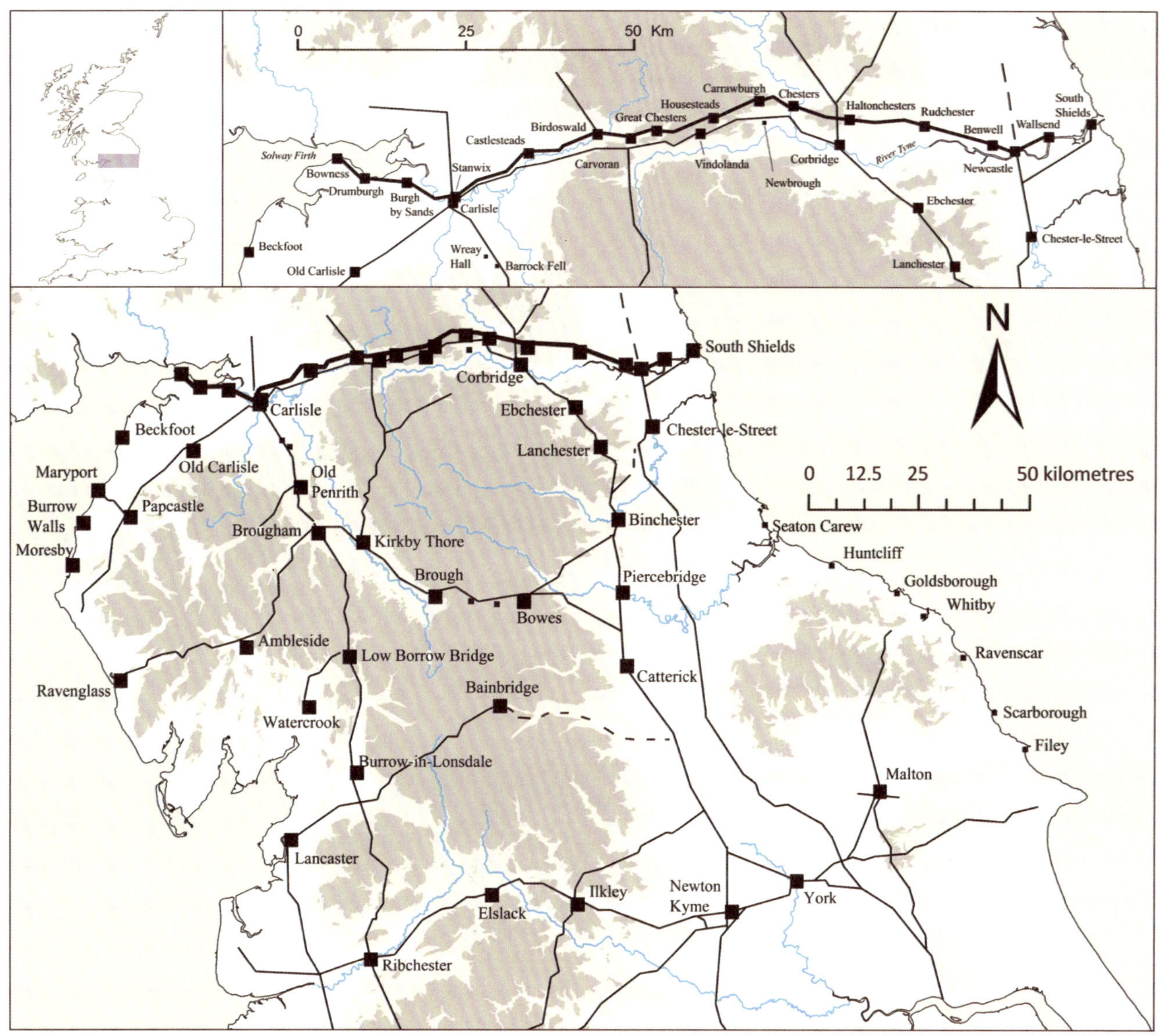

Fig.1 Map of the northern frontier of Britannia showing the location of forts, with the upper panel detailing the sites along Hadrian's Wall (© R. Collins).

图 1 不列颠尼亚北部边疆地图及要塞分布，图上部标明了哈德良沿线要塞的具体位置.（© 罗伯・柯林斯）。

在行省的东南部之外，想要辨别罗马晚期的乡村活动也面临着重重困难。这里的聚落基本保留了罗马之前的铁器时代的形态。而如果要识别3世纪后期及这之后的罗马人占领范围，则要看能否在当地发现钱币、陶瓷制品或其他罗马时期特有的物品，但这些物品往往在罗马后期的乡村聚落非常少见。通过金属探测（据可移动文物计划[2]）获得的数据进一步确认了传统考古调查发现的分布规律。例如，通过标记钱币发

2 可移动文物计划是一个国家机构，总部位于大英博物馆。其官员则遍布英格兰和威尔士各地，负责与公众会面，记录他们发现的文物。有时，民众会在做园艺活或遛狗的时候偶然发现这些宝藏。不过大多数发现文物的人是金属探

Military supply and economy

Analysis of data from forts and other military installations in the frontier to identify the goods used and food consumed, and their possible origins, creates a patchwork of localised data-points that, taken together, provides a more generalised picture for the economic landscape of the frontier.

By the 4th century, the predominant sources of ceramics for the northern frontier of *Britannia* were the potteries in the area of modern-day Yorkshire; fine wares were produced at kilns outside of Crambeck in North Yorkshire, whilst the calcite-gritted coarse-ware kilns have yet to be identified (Bidwell and Croom 2010). Also striking is the dearth of ceramics that originated outside Britain by the 4th century, when supply was being almost completely provided by Romano-British potteries. The fine-ware is found distributed across a range of sites within the greater Yorkshire region of their production, but outside of this area they occur predominantly on military sites. This distribution suggests that the Yorkshire ceramics were strongly tied to military supply in the 4th and early 5th centuries. However, there is however no evidence to show that manufacture was directly tied to the army, or whether their supply was through military contracts or via private merchants (Evans 1988).

Understanding the supply of foodstuffs present a greater challenge, given the issues surrounding their archaeological preservation. Animal bone regularly survives, and it is noticeable that skulls and foot bones are more often encountered in the late Roman faunal assemblages at forts. This indicates animals arriving on the hoof and being butchered locally. Evidence from cattle teeth found at the forts of Carlisle and Birdoswald indicates that cattle at each fort were drawn from the same population or from a breed common to the western sector of Hadrian's Wall (Evans *et al.* 2009, 907; Izard 1997, 366). A widespread programme of stable-isotope analysis has yet to be applied to faunal assemblages from Roman forts, but a small project at the fort of South Shields has suggested cattle consumed there were sourced both locally and from present day northern Cumbria or south-west Scotland (Waterworth 2014). While the sample-size of the project is limited, the results are tantalising and reinforce a hypothesis proposed by Stallibrass (2008), in which lands in southern Scotland and northern England served as a predominantly pastoral zone during the Roman era that produced a surplus of meats, dairy, hides and related products in contrast to the arable surplus of lowland areas.

The sources of cereals, even when there is evidence in the form of macrofossils, are not as easily traced. Archaeological remains of grains have been recovered from granaries at a number of fort sites; as these samples come from a storage context rather than food preparation areas, they contribute more to our understanding of the use of granaries than cereal consumption, but these do permit some tentative patterns to be drawn (Huntley and Stallibrass 2010). First, it indicates that the grinding of grain into flour must have occurred at each fort rather than grain being milled centrally and distributed. Second, in addition to wheat, barley and oats are also present, and these latter grains are found in higher numbers in 4th-century deposits. Third, whilst it is not possible to identify the source of these grains, there is no reason to view them as imported: the upland ecology of much of the frontier favours local production of barley and oats, as does that of the eastern lowlands of the region where barley, oats and wheat have been found. We do not yet know whether cereals were imported to Hadrian's Wall, but the re-organisation of South Shields as a supply depot with at least 17 granaries from the later 2nd-later 3rd century provides clear evidence of their bulk storage at the site of this port.

Evidence for arable agriculture local to forts can be found at Housesteads, in the central upland sector of Hadrian's Wall. Following the abandonment of the *vicus* outside the walls of the fort, the land was redeveloped to include agricultural terraces (Fig. 2). Excavation has revealed that the *vicus* was abandoned *c.* AD 270, and ceramics found in the terrace banking confirm the terracing can be dated to the Roman period, but not earlier than *c.* 160 (Crow 2009, 255, 256; Welfare 2009). This provides some evidence for localized arable production related to a fort in the 4th century. At other locations, field boundaries and agricultural plots simply do not survive, and whilst agricultural implements, such as sickles, forks or hoes sometimes survive, these are more commonly found in strata of the 2nd and 3rd centuries (*e.g.* Allason-Jones and Miket 1984).

现地点，可以看出其分布的范围在公元4世纪期间逐渐缩小，只在更大的聚落或交通枢纽附近分布的更为密集（柯林斯 2012, 58–60, 图 3.3）。这一分布方式在4世纪的整个不列颠尼亚都很普遍，在其北部和西部尤为明显（沃尔顿 2012）。

相比之下，行省内有大量证据能证明军事聚落的存在。特别是要塞这样的军事遗迹一直是英格兰北部考古调查的传统重点。即便无法全部了解细节，通过发现大量的陶瓷制品和钱币的使用也确定了4世纪这些军事设施仍处于活跃状态。考古证据表明，4 世纪期间，约有50处军事设施仍在使用（柯林斯2012，48–51）。《百官志》（Not. Dig.Occ. 40）提供了驻扎在这其中约40处军事设施的部队名单，证明自2世纪以来，同一军事单位会一直驻扎在相同的要塞中，而这一点可以通过碑文得到证实（霍奇森 1991）。这种长期稳定的特征在哈德良长城沿线和约克的军团要塞体现的尤为鲜明。这些要塞沿着向北通往哈德良长城的道路而建，在 3 至 4 世纪由不同的军事单位驻守。不幸的是，从 3 世纪后期开始，立碑树传的习惯大大减少，在 4 世纪几乎消失。这使得《百官志》的内容无从证实。

军事供给和经济

通过分析边疆的要塞和其他军事设施的数据，我们识别了当地使用的货物和消费的食物以及它们的来源。当把这些各地信息点拼凑在一起，我们便能更宏观地了解边疆的经济景观。

至公元 4 世纪，不列颠尼亚北部边疆陶瓷制品主要是产自今天约克郡地区的陶器；精美器皿大多是在北约克郡克拉姆贝克的窑中烧制而成。而至今我们还尚未识别出烧制方解石粗陶的窑址（比德韦尔，克鲁姆 2010）。同样令人吃惊的是，公元 4 世纪的陶瓷制品全部都是罗马不列颠式陶器，根本找不到产自不列颠之外其他地区的陶瓷制品。精美器皿的发现地点主要分布在大约克郡地区内一系列生产地点附近。除此地区之外，则基本都只在军事遗址中发现。该分布特点表明，公元 4 世纪和 5 世纪早期，约克郡的陶瓷制品主要为军用物资。然而，并无证据表明制造者究竟是直接与军队打交道，还是通过军事合同或商人联络（埃文斯 1988）。

由于食品很难留下考古遗存，了解食物的供应来源可谓是难上加难。兽骨通常会留存下来。值得注意的是，在罗马晚期的要塞中更常发现的是成群的动物头骨和足骨堆积。这表明人们先将动物活着运送到当地然后再宰杀。卡莱尔和博得瓦德罗马要塞发现的牛齿证明，每个要塞的牛都来自同一种群或都是哈德良长城西部地区一个常见品种。（埃文斯等 2009, 907; 伊泽德 1997, 366）。目前，我们尚未对罗马要塞的动物族群开展大规模的稳定同位素分析。不过，南希尔兹要塞的小范围研究项目表明当地食用的牛有些来自本地，也有些来自今天的北坎布里亚郡或苏格兰西南部（沃特沃思 2014）。尽管样本量有限，结果却非常有意思，并强有力地支持了斯塔利布拉斯（2008）提出的假设，即罗马时代的苏格兰南部和英格兰北部的土地主要是牧区，肉类、奶制品、兽皮和相关产品产量巨大，超出本地需求。相比之下，低地地区则为农耕用地，也足以满足当地的粮食需求。

要追溯谷物的来源，即便有可辨形化石这样的证据也并非易事。谷物的考古遗存多发现于若干要塞遗址的粮仓；由于这些样本来自仓储地点而非食物的准备区，它们更多地帮助我们理解粮仓的使用，而不是谷物的消耗。但由此我们确实可以得出一些初步的猜测（亨特利，斯塔利布拉 2010）。第一，这意味着将谷物碾磨成面粉的过程一定是在各个要塞中进行的，而并非是集中碾磨而后分配到各地。第二，除了小麦

测器的使用爱好者。欲知详情，可访问：finds.org.uk

Fig.2 The fort of Housesteads, as seen from the south. Note the numerous agricultural terraces that were built up over the demolition and ruins of the second- and third-century extramural settlement (© R. Collins).

图 2 豪塞斯特兹要塞，南向图。注意公元二世纪和三世纪左右塞外平民聚落废弃后原址改建开垦的梯田（© 罗伯・柯林斯）。

Nor was local production limited to agricultural activities. There is abundant evidence for metalworking at military sites: 800 iron arrowheads, an anvil and other iron objects, suggestive of a later 4th century smithy were found at Housesteads (Crow 2004, 96); further evidence of smithing and of metalworking has been found at Binchester (Ferris 2010), at South Shields (Hodgson 1994, 44), and within the legionary fortress at York (Carver 1995, 188). Clay moulds for the casting of spurs, and a sandstone mould for ingots, were found at the fort of Bainbridge (Bidwell 2012); a lead mould of a strap-end, used to create clay moulds for casting, has been found at Stanwix; and a miscast and unfinished copper-alloy strap end was found at South Shields (Fig. 3). Each signifies on-site production (Collingwood 1931, no. 75; Allason-Jones and Miket 1984, no. 3.610). This evidence of metal-working provides clear testimony that although the local frontier soldiers were engaged in production and repair of military equipment and were not reliant on the supply of goods from elsewhere in the Empire, they nevertheless emulated the changing fashions in design of metalwork across the Empire.

CONCLUSIONS

Landscape archaeology methods and perspectives yield a number of benefits in understanding Roman frontiers, and indeed any frontier. Landscape approaches demand that any site or monument is contextualized in both space and time. The economic network of the late Roman frontier of northern Britain outlined above looked almost exclusively at the 4th century, two centuries after the frontier was established. Such an analysis requires the accumulation of considerable archaeological data, but it also requires a super-structural understanding of the Roman Empire as well as of highly localized situations. Landscape archaeology also privileges methods and data consolidated across a number of other disciplines, contesting narratives received from historical texts, the agendas and contents of which rarely match the needs of contemporary heritage managers, curators, researchers, and interpreters.

之外，还有大麦和燕麦，而后两种谷物在 4 世纪的堆积中发现的数量更多。第三，尽管无法确定这些谷物的来源，也无证据表明它们是进口的：大多数边疆地区的山地生态都适合耕种大麦和燕麦，而东部的低地生态适合种植大麦、燕麦和小麦，这与他们的发现地点是吻合的。目前，我们尚不知道是否有谷物进口到哈德良长城。不过公元 2 世纪晚期到 3 世纪晚期，南希尔兹经过改造，建有至少由 17 个粮仓组成的补给仓库，这清楚地证明了该港口巨大的仓储容量。

在哈德良长城中部多山地带的豪塞斯特兹，我们能找到当地农耕的证据。在塞外平民聚落被废弃后，聚落原址进行了改建，以开垦梯田（图2）。发掘工作表明平民聚落在约公元 270 年被遗弃，梯田埂坎处发现的陶瓷制品则证实该梯田可以追溯至罗马时期，但不会早于约公元 160 年（克劳 2009, 255, 256; 维尔法 2009）这也为公元 4 世纪的一处要塞附近的农耕生产提供了一些证据。在其他的地方，农田的边界和农业用地的划分基本无迹可寻。尽管有时能发现镰刀、耙和锄头等农业用具，但它们往往在第 2 或3世纪的地层更加常见（如：阿勒森,米凯特 1984）。

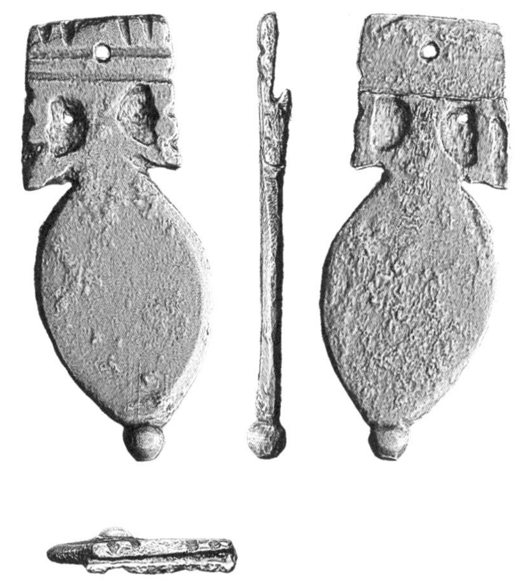

Fig.3 A 3D scan of a locally-made, miscast amphora-shaped strap-end from South Shields (© NU Digital Heritage, Newcastle University).
图 3 在南希尔德当地制造，错铸细颈皮带扣的 3D 扫描图（© NU数字遗产，纽卡斯尔大学）。

而当地的生产也不仅仅局限于农业活动。军事遗址发现的大量证据证明金属加工制造的存在：豪塞斯特兹出土的800枚铁箭镞、一座铁砧和其他铁器表明4世纪后期铁匠铺的存在（克劳 2004,96）；另外在宾切斯特（费里斯 2010）、南希尔兹（霍奇森 1994, 44）以及约克的罗马军团要塞（卡弗 1995, 188）也发现了更多锻造和金属加工的证据。班布里奇要塞出土了用于铸造马刺的黏土模具和用于铸锭的沙岩模具（比德韦尔 2012）；在斯坦威克斯发现了一块带扣的铅模，来制造用于铸造的黏土模具；在南希尔兹则发现了错铸且未完工的铜合金搭扣（图 3）。这些证据都指向铁器为现场生产（科林伍德 1931, 第 75 号；阿勒森,米凯特 1984, 第 3.610号）。这些金属加工的证据清楚地证明，当地的边防士兵也从事军事装备的生产和维修，并不依赖从帝国的其他地区进口货物，尽管如此他们却依然紧跟整个帝国金属制品设计的变化潮流。

结语

景观考古学的方法和视角能够为理解罗马边疆体系，甚至是任何边疆体系，带来若干益处。景观研究方法要求我们要将任何一处遗址或遗迹都置于时间和空间两个环境之中。前文阐述的不列颠北部罗马边疆晚期的经济网络几乎集中于4世纪这一特定时段，比边疆的建立晚了两个世纪。但这类分析所需的不仅是积累大量的考古数据，同时还要对高度本地化状况以外的整个罗马帝国有着非常体系化的理解。景观考古学的优势还在于运用跨学科的方法和数据，验证历史文献中的内容。事实上，当代的遗产管理者、博物馆馆长、研究人员和解译员往往鲜少能从历史文献中获得他们真正想要的信息。

References
参考文献

Allason-Jones, L. and Miket, R. 1984. *The Catalogue of Small Finds from South Shields Roman Fort*, Newcastle upon Tyne.

L · 阿勒森-琼斯, R · 米凯特. 1984. 南希尔兹罗马要塞出土小型文物编目. 泰恩河畔纽卡斯尔.

Alston, R. 1995. *Soldier and Society in Roman Egypt: A Social History*, London.

R · 奥尔斯顿. 1995. 罗马埃及的士兵与社会：社会历史. 伦敦.

Austin, N. J. E. and Rankov, N. B. 1995. *Exploratio: Military and Political Intelligence in the Roman World from the Second Punic War to the Battle of Adrianople*, London.

N . J . E · 奥斯汀, N . B · 兰科夫. 1995. 探索：从第二次布匿克战争至亚德里亚堡战役的罗马世界军事及政治情报. 伦敦.

Bidwell, P. 2012. 'The Roman fort at Bainbridge, Wensleydale: excavations by B. R. Hartley on the *principia* and a summary account of other excavations and surveys.' *Britannia* 43, 45–113.

P · 比德韦尔. 2012. B · R · 哈特利在温斯利代尔班布里奇罗马要塞的发掘：关于基本原理和其他发掘调查的总结 . 不列颠尼亚 43, 45-113.

Bidwell, P. and Croom, A. 2010. 'The supply and use of pottery on Hadrian's Wall in the fourth century AD', in R. Collins and L. Allason-Jones (eds), *Finds from the Frontier: Material Culture in the Fourth–Fifth Centuries*, 20–36, York.

P · 比德韦尔、A · 克鲁姆. 2010. 公元四世纪哈德良长城地区陶器的供应和使用，见于 R · 柯林斯，L · 阿勒森-琼斯（编）边界的发现：四至五世纪的物质文化, 20-36, 约克.

le Bohec, Y. 2000. *The Imperial Roman Army* (trans. R. Bate), London.

Y · 勒博埃克. 2000. 罗马帝国军队（R. 贝特译）. 伦敦.

Breeze, D. J. 2011. *The Frontiers of Imperial Rome*, Barnsley.

D . J · 布里兹. 2011. 罗马帝国边疆. 巴恩斯利.

Breeze, D. J. 2014. *Hadrian's Wall: A History of Archaeological Thought*, Kendal.

D . J · 布里兹. 2014. 哈德良长城：考古思想史. 肯德尔.

Carver, M. O. H. 1995. 'Roman to Norman at York Minster,' in D. Phillips and B. Heywood (eds), *Excavations at York Minster*, 177–221, London.

M . O . H · 卡弗. 1995. 罗马风格到诺曼式的约克大教堂，见于 D · 菲利普、B · 海伍德编，约克大教堂的发掘. 177-221，伦敦.

Collingwood, R. G. 1931. 'Roman objects from Stanwix.' *Transactions of the Cumberland and Westmorland Antiquarian and Archaeological Society*, second series, 31, 71–80.

R . G . 科林伍德. 1931. 斯坦威克斯的罗马时期物品. 坎伯兰与西莫兰文物考古学会会报（第二辑）, 31, 71-80.

Collins, R. 2012. *Hadrian's Wall and the End of Empire: The Roman Frontier in the Fourth–Fifth Centuries*, London and New York.

R · 柯林斯. 2012. 哈德良长城和帝国的终结：四至五世纪的罗马帝国边疆. 伦敦，纽约.

Crow, J. 2004. *Housesteads: A Fort and Garrison on Hadrian's Wall*, Stroud.

J · 克劳. 2004. 豪塞斯特兹：哈德良长城的要塞和兵营. 斯特劳德.

Crow, J. 2009. 'Excavations around the fort,' in A. Rushworth (ed.), *Housesteads Roman Fort - The Grandest Station, Volume 1: Structural Report and Discussion*, 249–263, London.

J · 克劳 . 2009. 要塞周围的发掘，见于A · 鲁什沃斯（编）豪塞斯特兹罗马要塞——最宏伟的一站（卷1）：结构报告和讨论. 249-263，伦敦.

David, B. and Thomas, J. 2008. 'Landscape archaeology: Introduction,' in B. David and J. Thomas (eds), *Handbook of Landscape Archaeology*. Walnut Creek, 27-43.

B·大卫，J·托马斯. 2008. 景观考古：介绍，见于B·大卫，J·托马斯（编）景观考古手册. 27-43. 核桃溪.

ELC. 2000. *European Landscape Convention: Florence, European Treaty Series - No. 176* : http://conventions.coe.int/Treaty/en/Treaties/Html/176.htm

欧洲景观公约理事会（ELC). 2000. 欧洲景观公约：佛罗伦萨，欧洲条约汇编——第176条： http://conventions.coe.int/Treaty/en/Treaties/Html/176.htm

Evans, J. 1988. 'All Yorkshire is divided into three parts: social aspects of later Roman pottery distribution in Yorkshire,' in J. Price and P. R. Wilson (eds), *Recent Research in Roman Yorkshire,* British Archaeological Reports, British Series 193, 323–337. Oxford.

J·埃文斯. 1988. 一分为三的约克郡：罗马晚期的约克郡陶器分布的社会层面研究，见于J·普赖斯，P.R·威尔逊（编）罗马约克郡的最新研究. 英国考古报告，英国系列，193, 323-337. 牛津.

Evans, E-J., Howard-Davis, C. and Bates, A. 2009. 'The animal bone,' in C. Howard-Davis (ed.), *The Carlisle Millennium Project: Excavations in Carlisle 1998–2001, Volume 2: Finds*, 903–921. Lancaster.

E-J·埃文斯，C·霍华德-戴维斯，A·贝茨. 2009. 兽骨，见于C·霍华德-戴维斯（编）卡莱尔千年计划：卡莱尔的发掘工作 1998-2001（卷2）：发现，903-921. 兰卡斯特.

Ferris, I. 2010. *The Beautiful Rooms are Empty: Excavations at Binchester Roman Fort, County Durham 1976–1981 and 1986–1991*, Durham.

I·费里斯. 2010. 美丽的空房间：1976-1981和1986-1991 杜伦郡宾切斯特罗马要塞的发掘工作. 杜伦.

Gamble, C. 2001. *Archaeology: The Basics*, London.

C·甘布勒. 2001. 考古学：基本概念. 伦敦.

Hodgson, N. 1991. 'The *Notitia Dignitatum* and the later Roman garrison of Britain,' in V. Maxfield and B. Dobson (eds), *Roman Frontier Studies 1989*, 84–92, Exeter.

N·霍奇森. 1991. 百官志和不列颠的后期罗马兵营，见于V·马克斯菲尔德，B·多布森（编），古罗马边界研究 1989，84-92. 埃克塞特.

Hodgson, N. 1994. 'The Courtyard House [in Period 8],' in P. Bidwell and S. Speak (eds), *Excavations at South Shields Roman Fort*, volume 1, 44. Newcastle upon Tyne

N·霍奇森. 1994. 庭院式住宅 [第 8 期]，见于 P·比德韦尔，S·斯比克（编）南希尔兹罗马要塞的发掘工作（卷1）, 44. 泰恩河畔纽卡斯尔.

Hunter, F. 2013. 'Non-ferrous metalwork,' in S. Willis and P. Carne (eds), *A Roman Villa at the Edge of Empire: Excavations at Ingleby Barwick, Stockton-on-Tees, 2003–4*, 101–106, York.

F·亨特. 2013. 有色金属制品，见于S·威利斯，P·卡尔内（编）帝国边缘的罗马乡间别墅：蒂斯河畔斯托克顿英告比巴韦克的发掘工作，2003-4, 101-106. 约克.

Huntley, J. P. and Stallibrass, S. 2010, 'Can we see a 4th- or 5th-century diet from the plan and animal remains?' in R. Collins and L. Allason-Jones (eds), *Finds from the Frontier: Material Culture in the Fourth–Fifth Centuries*, 92–95, York.

J.P·亨特利，S·斯塔利布拉斯. 2010. 我们能否从动植物遗骸中看出公元4或 5 世纪的饮食?，见于 R·柯林斯，L·阿勒森-琼斯（编）边界的发现：四至五世纪的物质文化，92-95. 约克.

Izard, K. 1997. 'The animal bones,' in T. Wilmott (ed.) *Birdoswald: Excavations of a Roman Fort on Hadrian's Wall and Its Successor Settlements: 1987–92*, 363–370, London.

K·伊泽德. 1997. 兽骨，见于T·威尔莫特（编）博得瓦德：哈德良长城罗马要塞及其后续聚落的发掘：1987-92, 363-370. 伦敦.

Jones, A. H. M. 1964. *The Later Roman Empire 284–602*, Oxford.

A·H·M·琼斯. 1964 . 罗马帝国后期,284-602. 牛津.

Lattimore, O. 1940 *Inner Asian Frontiers of China*. New York.

O·拉蒂摩尔. 1940. 中国的亚洲内陆边疆. 纽约.

Mattingly, D. 2006. *An Imperial Possession: Britain in the Roman Empire*, London.

D·马丁利. 2006. 帝国的财产：罗马帝国之中的不列颠. 伦敦.

Notitia Dignitatum: Notitia Dignitatum accedunt Notitia Urbis Constantinopolitanae et Latercula provinciarum, O. Seeck (ed.), Berlin, 1878 (new impression, Frankfurt, 1962).

O·希克（编）. 1878. 尊严的通知：君士坦丁堡和拉特库拉省的通知. 柏林（新印象，法兰克福，1962年）.

Pollard, N. 2000. *Soldiers, Cities, and Civilians in Roman Syria*. Ann Arbor.

N·波拉德. 2000 . 古罗马叙利亚的士兵、城市和平民. 安阿伯市.

Price, J. 2013. 'Glass,' in S. Willis and P. Carne (eds), *A Roman Villa at the Edge of Empire: Excavations at Ingleby Barwick, Stockton-on-Tees, 2003–4*, 120–125, York.

J·普赖斯. 2013 . 玻璃制品，见于S·威利斯，P·卡尔内（编）帝国边缘的罗马乡间别墅：蒂斯河畔斯托克顿英告比巴韦克的发掘工作，2003-4，101-125. 约克.

Rushworth, A. 2015. '*Castra* or *centenaria?* Interpreting the later forts of the North African frontier,' in R. Collins, M. Symonds, and M. Weber (eds), *Roman Military Architecture on the Frontiers*, 123–139, Oxford.

A·鲁什沃斯. 2015. Castra还是Centenaria? 阐释后期北非边疆的要塞，见于 R·柯林斯，M·西蒙兹，M·韦伯（编）边疆的罗马军队结构，123-139. 牛津.

Smith, A., Allen, M., Brindle, T. and Fulford, M. 2016. *The Rural Settlement of Roman Britain, vol 1*, London.

A·史密斯，M·艾伦，T·布林德尔，M·富尔福德. 2016. 罗马不列颠的农村聚落（卷1）. 伦敦.

Stallibrass, S. 2008. 'The way to a Roman soldier's heart: Did cattle droving supply the Hadrian's Wall area?' in J. Henriks (ed.), *TRAC 2008: Proceedings of the Eighteenth Annual Theoretical Roman Archaeology Conference, Amsterdam*, 101–112. Oxford.

S·斯塔利布拉斯. 2008. 通向罗马士兵的心：被驱赶的牲畜是否补给了哈德良长城地区，见于J·亨里克（编）TRAC 2008：第十八届理论罗马考古学年会文集，阿姆斯特丹，101-112. 牛津.

Symonds, M. F. A. 2017. *Protecting the Roman Empire: Fortlets, Frontiers, and the Quest for Post-Conquest Security*, Cambridge.

M . F . A·西蒙兹. 2017 . 保护罗马帝国：要塞、边疆和征服后对安全的诉求. 剑桥.

Turner, S., Shillito, L-M. and Carrer, F. 2019. 'Landscape archaeology,' in P. Howard, I. Thompson, E. Waterton, and M. Atha (eds.), *The Routledge Companion to Landscape Studies*, 2nd ed., London, 155-165.

S·特纳，L-M·施力特，F·卡雷尔. 2019. 景观考古，见于P·霍华德，I·汤普森，E·沃特顿，M·阿萨（编）劳特利奇景观研究指南（第二版），155-165. 伦敦.

Walton, P. 2012. *Rethinking Roman Britain: Coinage and Archaeology*, Wetteren.

P·沃尔顿. 2012 . 罗马不列颠再思考：币制和考古. 韦特伦.

Waterworth, J. 2014. *Food for Thought: An Investigation into South Shields as a Major Supply Base in North-West Britain During the 3rd Century AD*. Unpublished MSc. Dissertation, Department of Archaeology, University of Durham.

J·沃特沃思. 2014 . 值得深思的食物：对公元3世纪英国西北部的主要供应基地南希尔兹的调查（未发表的硕士论文）. 杜伦大学考古系 .

Welfare, H. 2009. Survey of Housesteads environs, in A. Rushworth (ed.), *Housesteads Roman Fort – The Grandest Station, Volume 1: Structural Report and Discussion*, 235–249, London.

H·维尔法. 2009. 豪塞斯特兹周围地区调查，见于A·鲁什沃斯（编）豪塞斯特兹罗马要塞——最宏伟的一站（卷1）：结构报告和讨论, 235-249. 伦敦.

Whittaker, C. 1994. *Frontiers of the Roman Empire: A Social and Economic Study*, Baltimore.

C·惠特克. 1994 . 罗马帝国边疆：社会经济研究. 巴尔的摩.

2.5 嘉峪关明代长城修筑工艺及结构特点调查与发掘

张斌
嘉峪关丝路（长城）文化研究院—中国—甘肃

摘要

嘉峪关是明代长城的西端起点，境内长城时代特征明显，防御体系完整，“因地制宜、就地取材”特点突出，类型丰富，在明代西北土质长城中具有典型的代表性。通过对嘉峪关境内明代长城资源的区域环境特征、建筑材料、修筑工艺的田野调查和考古发掘，了解掌握长城构成要素的结构特点和修筑工艺，为长城保护提供可靠依据。[1]

关键词： 嘉峪关 长城 区域环境 结构特点 修筑工艺

嘉峪关是明代长城的西端起点，也是明王朝西部边防的重要门户。明初，宋国公冯胜略定河西，截敦煌以西悉弃之，以此关为限，遂为西北极边，修筑嘉峪关[2]，从此拉开了明王朝修筑长城防御设施巩固政权的序幕。从明洪武五年（1372 年）至万历年间（1620 年），历时 200 多年，明王朝在嘉峪关两翼及周边修筑了由墙体、壕堑、关堡、烽燧等要素构成的长城防御体系。

嘉峪关境内的长城时代特征明显，防御体系完整，“因地制宜、就地取材”特点突出，类型丰富，在明代西北土质长城中具有典型的代表性。

一、长城分布情况及区域环境特征

（一）长城分布情况

嘉峪关境内的长城以土质结构为主，分布有墙体 43.6千米，壕堑 12.94千米，关堡 8 座，敌台和烽火台 49 座，与长城相关的遗存 6 处。

嘉峪关在明代隶属甘肃镇肃州卫管辖。《肃镇华夷志》载：肃州“所属边墙一道，嘉峪关所管讨赖河岸墩起，下古城堡所管东河深止，长一百四十里，其贼由水头哨所分属各堡”；嘉峪关“所管边墙二截，南至讨来河岸墩起，东北至野麻湾界至，长三十五里”；新城堡“所管边墙一截，东至两山口界起，西至野麻湾界止”。嘉峪关境内的长城为嘉峪关和新城堡管辖的三截长城，根据修筑时间和地理位置划分，由西长城、东长城、北长城三段组成（图 1）。

西长城，嘉峪关管辖，位于关城南北两翼。嘉靖十九年（1540 年）肃州兵备李涵请议修筑。全长

1 本文在文集编辑期间，已于 2020 年 7 月在期刊《卷宗》2020 年第十卷发表，标题为《嘉峪关明代长城修筑工艺及结构特点调查研究》

2 肃州，即肃州卫。是明王朝为加强和巩固西北边防，军事防御体系中在甘肃镇管辖区域内设置的地方单位。在长城防御体系中，肃州卫管辖长城沿线的嘉峪关、新城堡、下古城堡等 17 座堡城。

2.5 INVESTIGATION AND EXCAVATION OF BUILDING PROCESSES AND STRUCTURAL FEATURES OF JIAYUGUAN MING GREAT WALL

ZHANG BIN
Jiayuguan Silk Road Cultural Research Institute (Great Wall) - China - Gansu

Abstract

Jiayuguan Great Wall stands at the west end of the Ming Great Wall and has the distinctive characteristics of a complete defensive system of this period. As a typical example of its time, the Wall is built with local materials and follows the topography; it exhibits the rich variety of forms and special features of the earth walls in the northwest part of China in the Ming Dynasty. By summarising the archaeological excavation and fieldwork undertaken of the Ming Great Wall in the Jiayuguan region, the paper aims to characterise its principal structural features, the building processes, and the materials used in their construction and its environmental context, thereby providing a sound basis for future protection.

Keywords: Jiayuguan, Great Wall, regional environment, structural characters, building process

BACKGROUND

Jiayuguan Pass stands at the western end of the Ming Great Wall, and was once an important frontier fortress for the western region in the Ming dynasty. In the early Ming Dynasty, General Feng Sheng pacified the Hexi area and gave up the area that lies west of Dunhuang. Jiayuguan Pass was built to mark the north-western frontier (Huang 1984), and became the starting point from which the defensive system of the Great Wall was built to guard the frontier in the Ming Dynasty. From 1372 to 1620, this defensive system, including the walls, trenches, fortified passes, fortresses, and beacon towers, was gradually built out from Jiayuguan Pass. The Jiayuguan Great Wall presents the distinctive characteristics of its period and of a complete defensive system. The Wall was built with local materials and utilises the local topography; a rich variety of forms and special features are present here among the earth walls in the north-west part of China in the Ming Dynasty.

DISTRIBUTION AND REGIONAL ENVIRONMENT CHARACTERISTICS OF THE GREAT WALL

Distribution of the Great Wall

The Great Wall in the Jiayuguan region is mainly built with earth, including 43.6km of Walls, 12.94km of trenches, 8 fortresses, 49 defence towers and beacon towers, as well as 6 other sites which are associated with the Wall.

In the Ming Dynasty, Jiayuguan was under the jurisdiction of Suzhou *Wei*,[1] Gansu *Zhen*. According to the *Suzhen Huayi Zhi*,[2] one line of the frontier defensive system extended 140 Chinese *li* north and then east, from Taolai River to East River was under the overall jurisdiction of Suzhou. One section of this frontier was under

1 In the Great Wall defensive system, 17 fortresses along the Wall, including Jiayuguan, Xinchengbu Fort, and Lower Guchengbu Fort, were under the jurisdiction of Suzhou *Wei*, itself under the jurisdiction of Gansu *Zhen* (Editors' note).

2 A book recording the history of Suzhou which includes the local economy, military, culture and natural landscape. It was first drafted in 1544 and revised in 1617 (Editors' note).

图 1 嘉峪关市明长城分布图（绘制：张斌）。
Fig.1 Distribution of the Jiayuguan Ming Great Wall (drawn by Zhang Bin).

13.24千米，呈南—北走向，南起讨赖河岸，北至黑山南缘山腰部。沿线修筑有敌台 6 座，关堡 2 座，壕堑 1 道，烽火台 4 座。

东长城，嘉峪关管辖。隆庆六年（1572 年）都御史廖逢节修筑，万历二年（1574 年）完成[3]，全长 18.86千米，呈东北—西南走向，东北在野麻湾堡南侧与北长城相汇，西南在关城附近与西长城相汇，沿线修筑有敌台 9 座。

北长城，新城堡管辖。弘治十五年（1502年）肃州参将彭清创修，嘉靖二十七年（1548 年），巡抚杨博命参将副使赵得祐、参将刘勋重修,全长 11.52千米，呈东南—西北走向，东南与肃州区大面墩长城相接，西北自在野麻湾堡南侧与东长城相汇，沿线修筑有关堡 2 座，敌台 4 座。

另外，在长城外侧还修筑有关堡、烽火台等负责侦查军情和传递烽火报警的系统。该系统是嘉峪关的前沿哨所，以嘉峪关为中心向外辐射分布有三路，嘉峪关境内分布有关堡 4 座，烽火台 25 座。一路是连

the jurisdiction of Jiayuguan, running from the tower by the Taolai River in the south to Yemawan in the north-east; a second section, running south-east from Yemawen to Liangshankou Fort, was under the jurisdiction of the Xinchengbu Fort (Gao 2006).

Today, the Jiayuguan Great Wall encompasses both of these jurisdictions and comprises three elements, namely the West Great Wall, East Great Wall and North Great Wall (Fig.1), which are defined by building date and geographical location.

The West Great Wall, originally under the jurisdiction of Jiayuguan, runs north and south from the strategic pass. In 1540, Li Han, Commanding Officer of Suzhou, sought approval to build the section that extends 13.24km north from the Taolai River towards the southern ranges of the Black Mountain, which includes six defence towers, two fortresses, one section of trench, and four beacon towers.

The East Great Wall was also originally under the jurisdiction of Jiayuguan. In 1572, Censor-in-Chief Liao Fengjie took charge of building the section that runs from south-west to north-east with a length of 18.86km and has nine defence towers; this was completed in 1574 (*A True Record of the Jiajing Emperor* 1539). Its north-eastern end meets the North Great Wall at the south side of Yemawan Fortress, while its south-western end meets the West Great Wall near the fortified pass of Jiayuguan.

The North Great Wall, was originally under the jurisdiction of New City Fortress. The Wall was established by Peng Qing, Assistant Regional Commander of Suzhou, in 1502. It was then reconstructed by Zhao Deyou and Liu Xun, Deputy Envoy and Assistant Regional Commander respectively, under the command of Governor Yang Bo in 1548. With two fortresses and four defence towers, the Wall totals 11.52km, and connects to the Damiandun Great Wall at its south-eastern end in Suzhou District and to the East Great Wall at its north-western end on the south side of the Yemawan Fortress.

Additionally, a signalling system including fortresses and beacon towers was built outside the Wall, to keep watch for the enemy. In the area of Jiayuguan this system ran along three routes radiating out from the strategic pass, and included a total of four fortresses and 25 beacon towers. The first route was a series of beacon towers that connected all passes of the Qilian Mountains to the south of the fortified pass. The second route was a series of beacon towers connecting to the seven *Wei*-forts west of the strategic pass. The third route was along the line of a defensive system outside the Wall which was constructed prior to the wall. In addition, beacon towers were built between the fortresses and between *Bao*-forts and *Wei*-forts.[3]

Regional environmental characteristics

Jiayuguan Pass is situated in the middle of the Hexi Corridor and the narrow east-west channel between the Wenshu Mountain range of the Qilian Mountains to the south, and the Black Mountains range of the Mazong Mountains to the north. This area is long from east to west and narrow from south to north, with an altitude ranging from 1,430m to 2,799m.

Most of the region is in a gravel desert, while only the eastern part is close to the edge of the Jiuquan Basin. It has five types of landscape, including: medium- and high-altitude mountains; long tablelands of varying altitude; alluvial and pluvial fans; alluvial and pluvial plains; and fluvial valleys. With a typical dry temperate continental climate, it has wide seasonal temperature ranges, high hours of sunshine, frequent sand-storms, low rainfall and strong evaporation. Over the last two years, it has had: an annual average temperature of 7.8^{0}C; an annual average precipitation of 131.7mm, and evaporation of 2125.6mm; an annual average wind-speed of 2.9m/s with wind strengths frequently reaching 3-4.

The Ming Great Wall is located in the plains to the west, north and north-east of the city, and includes oases and gravel deserts. Located to the northeast of the city and at the fringe of the Jiuquan Basin, the North Great Wall

3 These were forts of different military status reflecting the rank of the commanding officer stationed at each (Editors' note).

接关城南面的祁连山各关隘的烽燧线。一路是与关西七卫连接的烽燧线。另一路是长城外侧的早期防御体系，修筑时间早于长城墙体。与此同时，堡与堡之间，堡城与卫城之间，也修筑有烽火传递报警的烽火台。

（二） 区域环境特征

嘉峪关地处河西走廊中部，位于祁连山与马鬃山之间的东西向狭长通道中，南有祁连山余脉文殊山，北有马鬃山余脉的黑山，东西长，南北窄，海拔 1430 ~ 2799 米。大部分区域为砂砾戈壁，仅东部紧邻酒泉盆地边缘。地形地貌按其成因分为中高山、长垄台地、洪积冲积扇、洪积冲积平原、河流切蚀谷地等 5 种。气候属典型温带大陆性干旱气候，气候干燥，温差大，日照长，风沙多，降雨量小，蒸发量大。近两年年均气温 7.8℃，年均降水量 131.7 毫米，蒸发量为 2125.58 毫米，年均风速 2.9 米/秒，平常风力多为 3 ~ 4 级。

明长城分布于市境东北部和西部边缘地带，地势平坦。地貌景观分为湿地绿洲和砂砾戈壁两种，气候属典型温带大陆性干旱气候。北长城位于市境东北部，地处酒泉盆地边缘地带，地貌景观为湿地绿洲，地势平坦，植被较好，土壤为灌淤土和草甸土，适于耕种，湿地、农田村庄分布密集。东长城和西长城位于市境东北部和西部，地势平坦，地貌景观为砂砾戈壁，土壤以砂砾石为主。植被稀疏，村庄分布稀少，主要以城市和工厂为主。

二、长城修造工艺及结构特点调查与发掘

2007 年，甘肃省长城资源调查组采取实地测量、周边景观、环境调查和运用景观环境的航拍照片来对长城进行精准测绘等方式，对嘉峪关境内长城进行了全面调查。调查结果显示：嘉峪关长城由人工构筑的墙体、壕堑、关堡、单体建筑（烽火台、敌台）、相关遗存等多种要素组成的防御体系，长城构成要素均因地制宜、就地取材，采用人工夯筑或砌筑、就地挖掘的工艺建造，材质包括黄土、砂石土、土坯、石块、植物根茎等。近年来，为配合长城保护工程的实施，掌握长城构成要素的修筑工艺和结构特点，结合长城资源调查资料，我们又对墙体、壕堑、单体建筑（烽火台、敌台）进行了局部考古发掘。经过实地调查和局部发掘，长城构筑要素因赋存区域环境不同，构筑材料、工艺及结构特点也存在差异。

（一） 墙体修筑工艺及结构特点

墙体均是在地表上直接就地取材夯筑，无其他人工构筑基础。墙体剖面呈梯形，自下而上略有收分，顶部外侧筑有女墙。修筑工艺均为版筑，采用木板、木椽在两侧支模，中间填充土、石等材料，用石杵夯筑，夯层厚 0.18 ~ 0.27米。修建工艺和结构特点归纳有三类。

I 类是黄土或盐碱土夯筑。该类墙体出现在北长城和西长城北段，北长城地处酒泉盆地边缘地带，地貌景观为湿地绿洲，当地土壤为黄土和盐碱土为主，墙体为就地取土夯筑。西长城北段为嘉峪关境内修筑最早的墙体，长城内侧有适宜耕种农田的黄土地貌，修筑时选用黄土夯筑。

II 类是砂石土夯筑，该类墙体出现在东长城。长城沿线地貌景观为砂砾石戈壁，墙体为就地取土夯筑，土质为含有沙粒和少量碎小砾石的粘性砂石土。

III 类是黄土夹页岩石片或卵石夯筑。该类墙体主要出现在西长城南北两端。西长城北端位于黑山边缘，夯筑时采用一层黄土夹一层黑山页岩石片的工艺方式夯筑。西长城南段的二墩长城墙体采用一层黄土铺设一层卵石的工艺方式夯筑。

stands in a flat oasis with good vegetation. Featuring anthropogenic-alluvial soils and meadow soils, the area can be cultivated and there are a great number of wetlands, arable land and villages. The East Great Wall and West Great Wall lie on the flat gravel desert, with sparse vegetation, to the north-east and west of the city where the main landscape is urban and industrial, with only a few scattered villages.

INVESTIGATION AND EXCAVATION OF THE CONSTRUCTION METHODS AND THE STRUCTURAL FEATURES OF JIAYUGUAN MING GREAT WALL

In 2007, the Great Wall Resource Survey Group of Gansu Province undertook a comprehensive investigation of the Jiayuguan Great Wall using methods that included field survey, investigation of the surrounding landscape and environment, and accurate mapping from aerial photographs of the landscape and environment. The investigation showed that Jiayuguan Great Wall is a defensive system including walls, trenches, fortresses and fortified passes, individual structures (beacon towers and defence towers) and other auxiliary structures. All the structures were man-made, using ramming or masonry techniques, the digging of trenches, and by utilising local materials that included loess, mixtures of gravel and earth, adobe bricks, stones, and plant roots. In recent years, in order to facilitate Great Wall conservation projects that need to identify the building techniques and the structural characteristics of various features of the Wall, we have undertaken some archaeological excavation of the walls, trenches, beacon towers and defence towers, basing this on data from the Great Wall Resource Survey. Through survey and excavation, it was found that different features of the Wall have different building materials, structural techniques and forms, and that this diversity is due to the different environments in which they are located.

Building techniques and the structural characteristics of the Wall

The walls were all directly built onto the ground surface, which had been compacted by ramming, and no other man-made foundations were found. The vertical section of the Wall is trapezoidal, on the uppermost exterior of which a battlement was built. The building process involved the use of stone pestles to compact the earth, stones and other materials within shuttering made of wooden boards and rafters. The thickness of the rammed layers can range from 18cm to 27cm. There are three types of building technique and structural form.

Type 1: ramming loess or saline-alkali soils. Such walls are found on the North Great Wall and the north section of the West Great Wall. The North Great Wall, as previously mentioned, is situated at the fringe of the Jiuquan Basin with its oases. The walls were built with local loess and saline-alkali soils though a process of ramming. The north section of the West Great Wall was the earliest one in the Jiayuguan area and had arable loess land to its interior. So it was built with loess.

Type 2: ramming a mixture of gravel and earth. Walls of this type can be found on the East Great Wall. The landscape here is gravel desert, and the walls were built with a local cohesive soil mixed with gravel.

Type 3: rammed loess, with either shale, rubble, or pebbles. Such walls were found at the north and south end of the West Great Wall. The northernmost section of the West Great Wall is situated at the fringes of the Black Mountain, and was built by ramming multiple layers of loess, interspersed with layers of shale rubble from the Black Mountain. The southernmost Erdun section of the West Great Wall was built by ramming alternating layers of loess and layers of pebbles.

Building techniques and the structural characteristics of the trench

There are two techniques and structural types along the trench. The first type is a trapezoidal ditch, wide at the top and narrow at the base, that has a mound of upcast on either side. To the south of Jiayuguan Pass, the area to the exterior of the Wall is flat. So here the trench is dug quite deep, with a mound piled on each side. The inner faces of the ditch and the mounds were faced with pebbles to prevent collapse and the backfilling of the ditch (Fig.2). The

图 2 发掘清理的壕堑原貌（摄影：张斌）。
Fig.2 The trench, after excavation and consolidation (photograph by Zhang Bin).

（二）壕堑修筑工艺及结构特点

壕堑修建工艺和结构特点归纳有二类。

I类是中间挖沟，两侧堆土成垄，壕堑上大下小，剖面呈梯形。经过实地发掘，关城南翼长城外侧的壕堑周边地势平坦，壕堑挖掘较深，结构由地下壕沟，地上土垄组成，修筑工艺为掘地挖壕，两侧堆垄，两垄内侧均用鹅卵石人工垒砌。这种建造工艺可预防两垄堆土塌落回填壕沟。

II类是削山成壕。关城北翼长城外侧为长垄台地，地势落差较大，局部壕堑采用对台地边缘进行削挖，削挖呈“L”状，内侧堆垄。

（三）关堡修筑工艺及结构特点

嘉峪关市内的关堡分为关和堡两类。

关：即嘉峪关，因独特的历史地理背景和重要的边防作用，其构筑方式和建筑结构较为复杂多样。嘉峪关初建时仅为土城一座，墙体均为黄土夯筑。明代从洪武五年（1372 年）至嘉靖二十八年（1549 年），历经 178 年的不断修建和清代数次修缮，形成了由月城、护城壕、罗城、外城、内城、瓮城、城楼及游击将军府、官井、文昌阁、关帝庙、戏台等附属建筑组成的建筑群。城墙的修筑材料为黄土、青砖为主，构筑方式：罗城城墙为内部黄土夯筑，外部青砖砌筑包裹，顶部青砖铺地并砌筑垛墙、女墙；内城和瓮城城墙为黄土夯筑，顶部青砖铺地并砌筑垛墙、女墙；外城城墙为黄土夯筑。

堡：根据地理位置和功能作用的不同，其修筑方式和结构特点也略有差异，归纳为三类。

I 类是结构简单，平面呈矩形，一面开门。修筑工艺为就地取土夯筑堡墙，土质以黄土为主。烽燧线上的堡大多数为该结构。

II 类是在峡谷中用黄土夹石片和植物根茎分层夯筑的墙体封堵峡谷，墙体与峡谷两侧山体共同构成堡城。

III 类是结构复杂，堡由内城和瓮城组成，城墙外侧修筑城台和木结构城楼，堡内修筑有土木结构房屋建筑。

（四）单体建筑修筑工艺及结构特点

单体建筑分为敌台和烽火台。

敌台：均为实心台体，台体与长城墙体连为一体，突出于墙体内侧，平面呈矩形，剖面呈梯形，自下而上略有收分，修筑工艺为自然地表之上就地取材修筑，材质以黄土、砂石土、土坯为主。因敌台所在地域不同，其修筑方式和结构特点归纳为两类。

图 3 暗壁壕堑 2 段"铲崖设险"呈"L"型的壕堑（摄影：许海军）。
Fig.3 L-shaped trench at Anbi Trench No. 2, where the slope is cut as barrier (photograph by Xu Haijun).

second structural type was formed by cutting away the slope of a hill or a mountainside to create a terraced trench. Outside the Wall to the north of Jiayuguan Pass, is a landscape of long tablelands with big differences in altitude. Part of the trench was built by cutting away and digging the edge of the tableland to create an L-shaped trench with one side mound piled to the interior (Fig.3).

Building techniques and structural characteristics of Jiayuguan Pass and the fortresses

Due to its unique historical and geographical background and great defensive significance, the fortified pass of Jiayuguan comprises complex structures exhibiting a great variety of building techniques. At its very beginning, Jiayuguan was simply a city surrounded by an earth wall, which was built of rammed loess. After being constantly developed for 178 years from 1372 to 1549 in the Ming Dynasty, and repeatedly restored in the Qing Dynasty, the fortified pass became a complex consisting of the Moon City, moat, *Luocheng* (perimeter wall), outer city, inner city, *Wengcheng* (barbican and enceinte), gate towers, the General's Mansion, *Guanjing* (the official well in the centre of the city), Wenchang Temple, Guanyu Memorial Temple, theatre tower, and other auxiliary buildings. Building materials for the wall of the fortified pass was loess and black brick. The *Luocheng* was built with rammed loess clad with black bricks. Its top is paved by black bricks with battlements and parapets also clad with black bricks. The wall of the Inner City and the *Wengcheng* was built with rammed loess, with their top paved and battlement and parapet built of black bricks. The wall of the Outer City was built with rammed loess.

The building techniques and structures of the fortresses vary due to their different geographical locations and functions, which can be classified into three types. The first type is a simple rectangular layout with a gateway on one side, and was built of rammed local loess. The construction of most of the fortresses along the lines of the

图 4 嘉峪关（摄影：杨多润）。

Fig.4 Jiayuguan (photograph by Yang Duorun).

图 5 野麻湾 4 号敌台（摄影：张斌）。

Fig.5 Yemawan No.4 defence tower (photograph by Zhang Bin).

图 6 野麻湾 3 号敌台考古发掘出的生活设施遗迹（摄影：张斌）。

Fig.6 Remains of domestic facilities at Yemawan No.3 defence tower revealed by archaeological excavation (photograph by Zhang Bin).

beacon towers were of this form and structure. The second type of fortress were those located in gorges. For these, two parallel walls were built across the gorge, thereby creating an enclosure. The walls were built of alternating layers of loess and stone rubble, and layers of plant roots. The third type is a complicated layout consisting of an internal enclosure and a *Wengcheng*. Outside the fortress walls were horse faces and wooden gate towers. Inside there were buildings and structures built of earth and wood.

Building processes and structural characteristics of defence towers and beacon towers

Defence towers were solid structures connected to the wall and protruding from its inner side. Their plan is rectangular and their sections are trapezoidal. They were built without foundations, using local materials including loess, a cohesive mixture of gravel and earth, and adobe bricks. Since the locations of defence towers vary, their building techniques and structural characteristics can be classified into two types.

The first type was built by ramming local loess with a mixture of gravel and earth (Fig.4 and Fig.5). The second type is those built by layering multiple layers of different materials including loess, a mixture of gravel and earth, and adobe bricks. Through archaeological excavation, remains of domestic spaces, including houses, a *kang* (a traditional bed made of earth), and hearths, were found built on to the sides of the defence towers connecting to the wall. Lines of six to nine small signal beacons were built 10m to 15m from some of the defence towers, parallel to the Wall and to its interior. Either solid or chambered, they were built of local rammed earth.

Beacon towers, which were usually solid structures, were built on the top of hills or other high places outside the Wall. Like the defence towers, they are rectangular on plan and trapezoidal in section. Next to some of these beacon

I 类是自然地表上就地取土夯筑，土质以黄土和砂石土为主（图 5、图 6）。敌台内侧 10-15 米处修筑有 6-9 座燃烟报警燧体，燧体与长城平行布设，燧体构筑方式为就地取土夯筑，结构有空心和实心之分。经过考古发掘，在敌台体连接的两侧底部发现修筑的房屋、土炕、灶台等生活场所遗迹。

II 类是多种材料分层修筑，材料有黄土、砂石土、土坯等。

烽火台：多修筑于长城沿线外侧的山顶等地势较高处，台体均为实心，平面呈矩形、剖面呈梯形。在台体面向长城或关堡一侧修筑有数量不等的燃烟报警燧体。因地貌景观的不同，构筑材料、工艺、结构特点也不同，归纳有五类：

I 类是土坯砌筑，土坯规格为长 36 、宽 22 、厚 8 厘米。修筑工艺为一平一竖砌筑工艺。

II 类是石块垒砌，修筑工艺为用黑山的页岩片石逐层垒筑，垒筑层厚 12 ~ 25 厘米。

III 类是石块和土坯分层砌筑。该类台体下部用石块砌筑，上部为土坯砌筑，土坯规格为长 36 、宽 22 、厚 8 厘米。土坯砌筑工艺为一平一竖方式。

IV 类是砂石土夹植物根茎分层叠筑，修筑工艺为铺夯一层砂石土，再铺设一层植物根茎，逐层向上夯筑。

V 类是外部用土坯砌筑，内部预制木质框架，并用黄土或砂石土填充。经过考古发掘，台体修筑时用 8 根直径 20–30 厘米的圆木在四面埋设立柱，立柱间用方木进行榫卯连接，形成木质框架，框架外侧四周用土坯砌筑 1 米厚的墙体，砌筑工艺为一平一顺方式，内部再用黄土或砂石土填充。

结 语

通过长城资源调查和文物保护工程中的考古发掘，我们详细掌握了嘉峪关市内长城要素的修筑工艺和结构特点，尤其是壕堑原始面貌和烽火台内部结构、修筑工艺的发掘揭示，以及敌台下士兵驻守生活设施的考古发现，改变了我们多年来对长城修筑工艺和结构特点的表象认知，完善了嘉峪关长城建筑的信息资料，对下一步做好长城保护和本体修缮奠定了坚实的基础。

参考文献
References

A True Record of the Emperor Jiajing. 1539. The revised edition of the Institute of History and Language, Academia Sinica, Taiwan, according to the microfilm photocopy of the Hongge manuscript in the national Beiping National Library, (299) 3680-3682. Taibei.

明世宗实录. 1539. 台北：台湾“中央”研究院历史语言研究所校勘本，据国立北平国立图书馆藏红格钞本微卷影印, （299） 3680-3682.

Gao, Q. & Tai, H. 2006. *Suzhen Huayi Zhi [Gazetteer of Chinese and Barbarians in Suzhen Township]*, Lanzhou, Gansu People's Publishing House.

高启安，邰慧丽. 2006. 肃镇华夷志. 兰州：甘肃人民出版社.

Huang, W. 1984. *A Recompiled New Chorography of Suzhou*, Jiuquan.

（清）黄文炜. 1984. 重修肃州新志. 酒泉：甘肃省酒泉县博物馆翻印.

towers were different numbers of small beacons for relaying signals to fortresses, the Wall, and the fortified pass.

There are five types of beacon tower, based on their different building materials, construction techniques, and structural characteristics, each reflecting their different geographical landscapes:

The first type was built of adobe bricks (brick size: 36x22x8cm) in Flemish bond. The second type is built of layers of shale rubble from the Black Mountains. Each layer is 12cm to 25cm thick. In the third type the lower part of the tower is built of stones, while the upper part is built with layers of adobe bricks (36x22x8cm), in Flemish bond. The fourth type is built by alternating layers of rammed gravel and earth with layers of plant roots.

In the fifth type of beacon tower, its interior was constructed by filling a wooden frame with loess or a mixture of gravel and earth, and the exterior was faced with adobe bricks. The archaeological excavation found that these towers were set on eight round wooden piles, with a diameter ranging from 20cm to 30cm, which were connected by mortise-and-tenon joints, thereby creating a wooden frame. The frame was encased by a wall, one metre thick, made of adobe bricks, in Flemish bond, and loess and a mixture of gravel and earth was then filled into the frame.

CONCLUSIONS

Through the Great Wall Resource Survey and the archaeological excavations during restoration projects, we have been able to understand the detailed building techniques and the structural characteristics of different elements of the Great Wall in the Jiayuguan region. Of particular significance has been the discovery of the original appearance of the trench, the internal structures and building techniques of the beacon towers, as well as those of the soldiers' living facilities attached to the defence towers. Together, these discoveries have dramatically changed our understanding of the construction history of the Jiayuguan Great Wall, thereby laying a solid foundation for the conservation and restoration of the Great Wall in the future.

2.6 金山岭长城砖的研究与保护

郭中兴, 贾海麟
金山岭长城文物管理处—中国—河北

摘要

金山岭长城修建于明朝中叶，多采用青砖包砌墙芯方式砌筑。大量青砖构建出不同形式的敌楼、墙体，形成攻守明确、内容丰富的军事堡垒。通过对砌筑于金山岭长城不同部位的长城砖的型制、规格及功能的了解与认识，有助于对长城砖在不同环境下进行有效的养护与管理。

关键词： 明长城　金山岭长城　长城砖

一、砖的历史

砖的出现，可追溯到8000年前。根据考古，在拥有古老文明的美索不达米亚地区，已有经过太阳暴晒得到掺有杂草的干泥块，这种泥块土砖经火堆的烧烤，质地变得坚硬，从而形成早期砖的雏形。

古代中国烧制土坯砖的时间，可追溯到公元前4400年至公元前3300年间，在长江中游地区的新石器时代的大溪文化层遗址，发掘出有陶窑、彩陶及红烧土块等，这种红烧土块拥有砖的质地。

战国时期的建筑遗址中，发现有方砖及空心砖出现。秦汉时期，砖在建筑中逐渐被采用，大量墓内用砖中有实心也有空心砖，也出现了富有特色的画像砖和各种纹饰的瓦当。北魏时期修建的嵩山嵩岳寺塔，是中国唯一的最早见的大型砖建筑物。

砖的原料容易取得，生产工艺比较简单，价格低、体积小，规格统一便于砌筑，成为建筑的基础材料。又因泥土及烧好后的成品砖可塑造性强，可对泥坯砖雕塑后进行烧制或对成品砖进行二次刻画加工，形成精致的装饰而在民用建筑中被广泛使用。明代长城的修建过程中，出于防卫需求只有重要地段，砖才被加使用。

二、金山岭长城对砖的应用

金山岭长城始建于明朝洪武年间（1368–1398），隆庆至万历年间（1567–1620），由明朝著名将领戚继光主持改建扩建完成并保存至今。金山岭长城保护范围内，共有砖砌敌楼67座，关隘5处，烽火台3处。砖、石砌筑墙体长10.5千米。

当前,在开放区域内有敌楼33座,关隘4处，墙体总长5千米，均由长城砖砌筑，其中砖砌拱券结构敌楼12座,砖,木混筑结构敌楼19座,砖砌战台2座。

（一）砖砌拱券结构敌楼

是以条石为基础，由长城砖砌筑墙体、拱券，承托敌楼顶部重量的结构形式。“拱券”即利用长城砖

2.6 RESEARCH AND CONSERVATION OF BRICKS ON JINSHANLING GREAT WALL

GUO ZHONGXING, JIA HAILIN
Jinshanling Great Wall Cultural Relics Management Office - China - Hebei

Abstract

Built in the mid-Ming Dynasty, the Great Wall of Jinshanling was constructed with a technique which uses black bricks to cover the core of the Wall. Different forms of black bricks were used to build various defence towers and walls, forming a series of military structures with explicit defensive or offensive purposes. Knowledge and understanding of the form, specification, and function of the black bricks used in different elements of the Jinshanling Great Wall help to maintain and manage the Great Wall's bricks under different conditions.

Keywords: Ming Dynasty Great Wall, Jinshanling Great Wall, Great Wall bricks

THE HISTORY OF BRICKS

Bricks can be traced back to as early as 8,000 years ago. Archaeological evidence shows that bricks were formed from clay or mud mixed with straw and dried in the sun on the plain of Mesopotamia. Later on, the dried blocks were hardened by fire, thus becoming the prototype of the earliest bricks. The earliest fired bricks appeared in Neolithic China around 4400 to 3300 BCE at one of the settlements of the Daxi Culture in the middle reaches of the Yangtze River. Pottery kilns, painted pottery and fired red clays with a texture similar to bricks have been excavated there (Li and Zhao 2015,7). Square and hollow bricks have been found in architectural sites from the Warring States Period (475–221 BCE). In the Qin and Han Dynasties (221 BCE - 220 CE), bricks gradually became commonly used as building materials. Solid and hollow bricks were found inside graves from this period. Decorated bricks and ornamental eave-tiles with distinct features also appeared. Constructed in 523 CE during the Northern Wei Dynasty, the Songyue Pagoda at the Songyue Monastery on Mount Song in Henan Province was the first large-scale brick structure in China (Liu 1987,7).

Bricks become an ideal building material due to the availability of the raw materials they required, their simple production process, their low cost, their ease of handling and their standardised specifications. In addition, the mouldability of clay and bricks means that adobes can be sculpted before being fired and the fired bricks can be re-sculpted to form refined patterns. Therefore, bricks were also widely used for ornamental purposes in civilian houses. However, bricks were only used in the construction of strategically important sections along the Ming Dynasty Wall.

THE BRICKS USED IN THE CONSTRUCTION OF JINSHANLING WALL

The Jinshanling Great Wall was first built during the reign of Emperor Hongwu (1368-98) in the Ming Dynasty. From the reign of Emperor Longqing to that of Emperor Wanli between 1567 and 1620, the renowned general Qi Jiguang supervised the rebuilding and extension of Jinshanling Great Wall, which stand in good condition today. Within the Jinshanling Great Wall Protection Area, there are 67 brickwork defence towers, five strategic passes and three beacon towers. The total length of the Wall built of bricks and stones amounts to 10.5km.

So far, 33 defence towers, four strategic passes and 5,000m of the Wall have been opened to the public, among

图 1 大量城砖砌筑的金山岭长城（摄影：郭中兴）。

Fig.1 A section of the Jinshanling Great Wall, built of bricks (photograph by Guo Zhongxing).

在砌筑时，砖块之间产生的侧压力，在敌楼内部形成的跨空墙体，常呈半圆形或弧形，也称拱或券。对长而高的拱券称“筒拱”或“主拱”，短而低矮的拱券又称“副拱”。

依据敌楼内部所砌筑的城砖承托上层重量的建筑形式，砖砌拱券结构敌楼有 2 道筒拱或3道筒拱等形式，也有周围回廊式，八角藻井顶式、四角钻天顶式等砖砌敌楼形式。

（二） 砖、木结构敌楼

指以条石为基础，由长城砖砌筑敌楼围墙与内部木构件共同构建成的敌楼结构形式。

砖、木结构敌楼，有木柱梁架与承重砖墙组合形成的双层敌楼建筑，也有木柱梁架、木楼板与承重砖墙组合形成的三层敌楼建筑形式。

砖砌拱券结构、砖木结构敌楼顶部均建有楼橹，楼橹上建有砖木结构铺房或望亭，或由城砖直接砌筑拱券的铺房做为驻守士兵的房屋。

（三） 城墙体

金山岭长城墙体按墙体外皮砌筑材料，有城砖包砌墙体和砖石混砌墙体两种形式。金山岭长城主墙体均由长城砖包裹墙芯砌筑，城砖包砌墙体内部又有夯土墙芯和毛块碎石墙芯等方施工式。仅有的“砖石混砌”墙体位于支墙敞楼与四方台之间，采用就地取材的自然山石砌筑长城墙体，墙体之上用则用长城砖修建垛口墙及铺设地面。

三、金山岭长城砖的种类

长城砖的种类与中国古代建筑用砖样式相关联，结合长城建筑功能应用又形成自身特点。金山岭长城对砖的分类主要有：条砖、方砖和异型砖。条砖用于砌筑长城及楼台墙体，方砖多用于马道及楼台地面铺墁，异型砖则用于墙体、楼台的特殊部位。

（一） 条砖。砌筑于楼体、墙身、马道、垛口墙、女墙等处。长方体，长 38 厘米，宽 19 厘米、厚 9 厘米。

（二） 方砖。用于铺墁敌楼地面、楼橹和马道表面，镶嵌于照壁壁心等。正方体，边长 38 厘米，厚 9 厘米。

（三） 异型砖。这类城砖的制式复杂多样，所处位置不同作用也就不同，形制自然亦不相同，主要包括以下几种：

which there are 12 vaulted defence towers built of bricks; 19 defence towers built of bricks and timber, and two brickwork battle platforms.

Brickwork defence towers supported by vaults

This kind of defence tower was built on the foundation of strip stones. They consist of brickwork walls and internal vaults to support the weight of the upper part of the towers. An vault refers to the arc or semi-circular structure that spans an elevated space by resolving the forces into lateral compressive stresses between two adjacent bricks. Generally speaking, taller and narrower vaults are referred to as main vaults whereas the lower and broader vaults are called sub-vaults.

The defence towers can be categorised into various types according to the different ways that the vaults support the weight of the upper structure, and by their shapes. For instance, there are towers with double or triple barrel vaults. There are also towers supported by four barrel vaults parallel to each side of the square, similar to the layout of a cloister. towers with an octagonal or rectangular pyramid vault in the middle, or towers supported by one pointed vault at each corner can also be found along Jinshanling Great Wall.

Defence towers constructed of brick and timber

This kind of defence tower was also built on a foundation of strip stones. The walls were built of bricks whereas the internal components were made of timber. Among the Towers constructed of brick and timber there are two-storey ones supported by both timber framing and load-bearing brick walls, and there are also three-storey towers supported by timber framing, with load-bearing brick walls and wooden flooring. Sentry houses can be found on top of both brickwork and brick-timber towers. A brick or brick-timber built pavilion, sometimes itself supported by arches, serves as a post for garrison soldiers to keep watch or simply a place to shelter in.

The body of the Wall

Depending on the materials used for the external faces of the Wall, the Jinshanling Great Wall can be categorised into sections of walling that are brick-clad and those that are faced with brick and stone. The majority of Jinshanling Great Wall is clad with bricks. However, the inner core of the Wall can be either rammed-earth or gravel. The only section of the Wall faced with bricks and stones can be found on the section of the branch wall between the Open Tower and the Square Tower. Here the body of the Wall was built with hill stones found nearby, while bricks were used to build battlements and to pave the walkway on top of the Wall.

THE DIFFERENT TYPES OF BRICKS USED ON JINSHANLING GREAT WALL

The different types of bricks used on the Great Wall are closely related to those in the constructions of other ancient Chinese buildings, but have their own unique characteristics for specific functional purposes required on the Great Wall. Bricks on the Jinshanling Great Wall can be classified into three broad categories: narrow, square, and irregular-shaped bricks (including ornamental bricks).

The narrow bricks were used to build and to face structures such as towers, walls, walkways, battlements and parapets. The narrow bricks on Jinshanling Wall are cuboid, 38cm long, 19cm wide and 9cm thick. Most of the square bricks were used to pave walkways, the floors of sentry houses and the floors of the Towers at Jinshanling. Some square bricks were inlaid at the centre of screen walls. The square bricks on Jinshanling Wall are cuboid, 38cm in both length and width, and 9cm thick.

Varying in form, the irregular-shaped bricks were used in different parts of the Wall to fulfil specific functions. Capping bricks are triangular prisms attached on top of the battlement or parapet to throw off the rain. They are usually 38cm long, 40cm wide and 18cm high. Irregular-shaped battlement bricks appear to be the combination

图 2a 长城砖砌筑拱券式敌楼（左）. 图 2b 长城砖与木构件混筑式三层敌楼（右）（摄影：郭中兴）。
Fig.2a A brickwork defence tower supported by arches (left); Fig.2.b A three-storey defence tower built of bricks and timber (right) (photographs by Guo Zhongxing).

封顶砖：砌筑在垛口墙、女墙顶部，防止雨水渗入到墙体之内。三棱体，长 38 厘米，宽 40 厘米、厚 18 厘米。

垛口异型砖：砌筑在垛口两侧，形如一个长方体与一个三棱锥的结合。长宽各 40 厘米，厚 9 厘米。

流水口内侧异型砖：砌筑在女墙底侧流水口内侧，两块砖拼接砌筑，形如倒U（∩）型状。长 35 厘米，宽 28 厘米，高 9 厘米。

流水口外侧异型砖：方砖制成，砌筑在女墙底侧流水口外侧，倒U（∩）型状。长 38 厘米，宽 38 厘米，高 10 厘米。

流水槽异型砖：砌筑于楼橹四周的垛口墙下部，与吐水嘴相连接，或砌筑于女儿墙内侧马道地面，方便排出楼橹或墙体上的雨水。

拦水砖：将条砖的腰身一侧打磨成半圆形的混砖。

（四）砖仿木铺房，柱、梁头、枋、檩、椽构件。文字砖、麒麟影壁等特殊造型的建筑用砖。

四、长城砖的制作

中国古代建筑所用青砖，其制作过程属传统手工技艺。制作青砖的工艺流程全部人工操作，包括砖窑修建、泥砖制作、烧砖、出窑等多个环节，二十几道工序。

选土、晒土、和泥、制砖坯多选春夏秋三季。烧窑则选在春、秋、冬三季。在烧制过程中，春秋用中火，冬天用大火。

（一）砖窑的修建

砖窑选址多选在黄土资源丰富的地方，可以就地取土建窑，制砖坯。要选择就近水源充沛，还要选择燃料近或燃料运输方便之地，也就是建窑烧砖就近取材的“三近”原则。

砖窑有以下几种类型：马蹄窑、罐窑、串窑、排子窑等。砖窑的构造上则具有窑口、砖炕、看火眼、风道、烟筒等功能。

of a cuboid and a triangular prism, sitting between crenellations. They are usually 40cm in length and width, and 9cm thick. Irregular-shaped drainage bricks inside parapets are made by two bricks spliced together to form an 'n' shape. They are usually 35cm long, 28cm wide and 9cm high. Irregular-shaped outfall bricks outside parapets are made of square bricks with an arch, or half of an arch, carved out of the original bricks. They are 38cm in length and width, and 10cm high. Some of irregular-shaped ground gutter bricks were placed underneath the battlement around sentry houses and were connected to the outfalls. There were also gutter bricks laid inside the parapet on the walkway to ensure that the rain on sentry houses and walls could be properly drained. Water-diverting bricks are narrow bricks which have had one of their longer sides rounded by grinding post-firing.

Ornamental bricks were particularly used in sentry houses on the top of towers to imitate features of traditional timber-built structures, including pillars, ends of beams, square columns, joists and rafters. Other ornamental bricks include those used to create the Qilin screen as well as other bricks in unique shapes, and inscribed bricks.

THE MANUFACTURING PROCESS

The manufacturing process of black bricks used as building materials in ancient Chinese architecture is a form of traditional craftsmanship. The whole process consists of over twenty separate manual procedures which are required for the construction of kilns, making of adobes, firing and finishing bricks. Gathering the materials

图 3 采用砖与毛块石混筑的支墙墙体（摄影：贾海麟）。
Fig.3 The branch wall faced with both bricks and stones (photograph by Jia Hailin).

图 4 长城砖砌筑的台阶（左）；长城方砖铺墁的马道地面（右）（摄影：贾海麟）。
Fig.4 Brick stairs on the Great Wall (left); square bricks used to pave the walkway (right) (photographs by Jia Hailin).

（二）砖坯的制作

在长城沿线烧制城砖，首选白沙型黄土，此类黄土的粘性比较大，烧干后不易断裂，适合制作城砖及其他构件。

和泥制砖坯，水要与黄土完全融合焖透，以增加黄土的粘性。无论是何种异形砖样，均须黄泥在模具中填满、砸实，覆扣于晒砖场地，泥砖坯制作完成，凉晒待干。

（三）烧砖出窑

古时取火烧砖，或用柴或用煤，对砖制品生熟均有着严格的检查制度，并制定奖惩。历代砖户总结出烧砖用火的经验加以传承，形成完整的民间工艺。如烧窑时：初期起火去窑内潮气则用小火；中期烧砖烘烤，则用大火。后期则为中小火以把控砖的生熟度；最后为下火，即对窑内各部位泥砖过火烧制到位。烧窑完毕，做水盆上水焖砖，以保证砖证色。

砖体整齐，砖色青莹，声脆如钟方可视为“好砖”。

五、金山岭长城对长城砖的日常管理与养护

当前对长城砖及长城本体存的伤害原因，主要体现在自然因素和人为因素两方面。

自然因素具体包含因气候变化形成的降雨、降雪、狂风、雷电等。作为最大的露天存在的文物本体，也因其年久抗伤害能力减弱，在自然条件下的风、雨、雪、雷电等，所带来影响是直观的、明显的。

雨季：雨水不间断对砌砖所需的白灰或灰土粘合济冲刷，造成大量浮砖出现，浮砖的移位脱落，又使雨水渗入墙体出现开裂、坍塌，或使墙芯土石层流失，造成长城本体伤害。

冬季：表现为冰雪冻融对长城马道墁地方砖的侵扰。雪后，半边受热融化半边冰冻，至使方砖表层受热不均形成炸裂，出现不均匀的表面揭皮现象，伤害面积大、伤痕严重。另外融化雪水流入长城墙体，冻涨后形成撑裂，加大长城本体开裂缝隙形成进一步伤害。

to make adobes, mixing and shaping adobes and air-drying the bricks was usually done in spring, summer and autumn, whereas the firing of the bricks usually took place in autumn, winter and spring. In spring and autumn, bricks were fired with medium temperature. In winter, however, the firing temperature was kept relatively high.

Constructing brick kilns

Usually, bricks kilns were located in loess-rich places to ensure the local supply of raw materials for building kilns and for making adobes. Kilns were normally built near rivers, lakes, reservoirs or any places that had abundant water resources. Ideally, kilns also had easy access to supplies of fuel.

There are brick kilns in the shape of horse's hoof, or a jar or multiple-chambered kilns with several firing chambers lying alongside each other, and parallel kilns with many firing pits can also be found. Each kiln had an access hole, brick floors on which the bricks were laid for firing, an observation hole, a draught passage, and a chimney.

Making adobes

Loess mixed with white sand is the ideal combination of raw materials for fired bricks and other building components. Owing to the high plasticity of this mixture, there is less risk of cracks forming after firing. Water and loess must be thoroughly blended to enhance its plasticity before an adobe is formed. Whatever the designated sizes or shapes of bricks may be, the mixed loessal clay must be compacted and the mould filled to the full before the adobe is completed and ready for air-drying.

Firing and finishing

In ancient China, firewood and coal were both used as fuel for kilns. The temperature of firing and the colour of the fired bricks would be rigorously inspected. There was even a reward and punishment mechanism for manufacturing bricks. Over generations, experience on how to control the heat was accumulated to make firing bricks a form of traditional folk craftsmanship. For instance, in the early phase of firing, craftsmen used a lower level of heat to get rid of any residual moisture in the bricks and in the firing chamber. A high temperature was then used to bake the bricks, after which the heat was reduced to control the colour of the bricks and their finish. At the end of the firing, each brick was only heated from below; finally, a basin of water was placed inside the kiln to ensure that the bricks achieved their desired colour. Bricks with neat shapes, a bright greyish-black colour, and which produced a clear sound when knocked were regarded as 'good bricks.'

ROUTINE MAINTENANCE AND PROTECTION OF BRICKS ON JINSHANLING GREAT WALL

Natural and human factors are the major causes of damage to the fabirc of the Wall. Natural factors include severe and changing weather such as heavy rain, snow, strong winds, thunder, and so on. As the largest cultural relic exposed to the open air, the Great Wall's resistance to damage from natural forces has weakened over time, and damage caused by weather is apparent. In rainy seasons, rains constantly scour the lime or lime and soil mortars between the bricks, causing a large number of them to become loose. Some bricks even fall from the Wall, leading to cracks and collapses as a result of rainwater subsequently seeping into the structure. In addition, without its protective brick cladding, the rammed-earth and gravel core of the Wall suffers further erosion.

In winter, the natural freeze-thaw process poses serious risks to square bricks used to pave horse paths. After frosts, the side of a square brick that is exposed to sunlight will absorb heat and begin to thaw. However, the other side of the brick may still be frozen. As a result of these uneven temperatures, the surface of the brick may peel off, causing widespread and severe freeze-thaw damage. In other scenarios, melted snow seeping into the body of the Wall will induce or enlarge cracks and bulges when it next freezes.

Man-made damage is primarily caused by people climbing on the Wall or carving graffiti into it, as well as the

图 5 女儿墙上的封顶尖砖（左上）；垛口上的尖砖（右上）；排水孔内侧U型砖、外侧U型砖（中）；引水槽型砖（下左）；拦水砖（下右）（摄影：贾海麟）。

Fig.5 Capping brick on top of the parapet (top left); pointed battlement brick (top right); drainage bricks inside (middle left) and outside the wall (middle right); ground gutter bricks (bottom left); water-diverting bricks (bottom right) (photographs by Jia Hailin).

图 6 砖枋木铺房房檐（上）；砖砌麒麟影壁墙（中）；文字砖（下）（摄影：郭中兴）。

Fig.6 Bricks imitating timber eaves (top); Qilin Screen Wall made of bricks (middle); an inscribed brick (bottom) (photographs by Guo Zhongxing).

人为因素具体体现在攀爬、刻画、踩踏磨损等。现阶段刻画现象逐年减少。没有维修过的墙体或地面，多因踩踏造成长城马道铺地砖位移，造成浮砖现象增多。

图 7长城附近的古砖窑遗址（摄影：贾海麟）。
Fig.7 An ancient brick kiln near Jinshanling Great Wall (photograph by Jia Hailin).

针对管理区域内长城砖的病害原因，金山岭长城文物管理处采取具有针对性的保护措施。设立长城保护员加大长城看护力度，保持长城上下干净整洁、制止乱刻乱画行为，避免对长城本体造成损坏。

每年开展长城碎修维护，加强日常保养。排查开放段落的长城安全隐患，对旅游线路内松动、掉落城砖进行归位整理，对墙体、马道地面开裂缝隙进行修补，引导疏通雨水排放，保留古长城马道上原始状态的极小型灌木和野草，已维持天然保护层状态，组织人力在雪后及时清除修复后段落的墙体积雪等多种有针对性的长城本体日常养护。

金山岭长城文物管理处在 2007 年起即开展监测。制定长城“本体监测”、景区“环境监测”、机构“管理监测”、旅游“市场监测”四位一体的监测机制；建立日《监测记录》，月《监测报表》，年度《监测报告》的工作制度；实行每名“长城保护员”即为“长城监测员”的对接工作体系。金山岭长城监测工作多次与中国文化遗产研究院长城项目办及民间长城保护机构“长城小站”合作，所提供的监测数据经分析后成为长城保护研究的有力依据。

参考文献
References

Li, L. & Zhao, L. J. 2015. *Study on Lime Materials in Ancient China*, Cultural Relics Press, Beijing.
李黎，赵林毅. 2015. 中国古代石灰类材料研究. 北京：文物出版社.
Liu, Z. 1987. *China's Architecture Types and Structures*, China Building Industry Press, Beijing.
刘致平. 1987. 中国建筑类型及结构. 北京：中国建筑工业出版社

图 8 冰冻对长城砖的影响（左）；积雪清理（右）（摄影：郭中兴）。

Fig.8 Impact of frost on the Great Wall bricks (left); clearing snow (right) (photographs by Guo Zhongxing).

wear and tear caused by visitor footfall. Fortunately, the carving and writing of graffiti on the Wall is decreasing year by year. The number of loose bricks caused by visitor footfall is increasing at sections that are not properly maintained or repaired.

The Cultural Relics Management Office of Jinshanling Great Wall Office has taken targeted measures to protect bricks according to the causes of damage. For instance, the Office has employed the Great Wall Patrollers to reinforce protection by asking them to keep the Wall clean and tidy, to stop visitors from writing or carving graffiti, or causing any other damage to the Wall. In addition, the repair of broken bricks is carried out annually as a part of the routine maintenance of the Wall. Other targeted measures include: checking for structural risks in sections of the Wall open to public; reinstating loose or fallen bricks along the paths used by tourists; mending cracks in walls and in pavements on horse paths; dredging gutters and draining rainwater; preserving small, original shrubs and weeds on horse paths to maintain a natural layer of protection; organising staff or Patrollers to clear snow from repaired sections of Wall.

The Office has established a monitoring project on this section of the Wall which began in 2007. The project establishes a 'four-in-one' mechanism of monitoring, including monitoring: the state of conservation of the Wall; the condition of the areas open to tourists; the management of institutions involved; and its tourist visitors. In addition, monitoring diaries are maintained, monthly and annual reports are filed, and the Great Wall Patrollers are trained to be monitoring inspectors. The monitoring project has been carried out in coordination with the Great Wall Protection and Conservation Project staff at the Chinese Academy of Cultural Heritage and at the non-government protection organisation, the Great Wall Station. The monitoring data and analysis generated has provided a strong basis for future research on protection of the Great Wall.

2.7 山海关境内明长城及附属构筑物墙体砖简述

冯颖
山海关区文物保管所—中国—河北

摘要

山海关于明洪武十四年（1381 年）建关设卫，以长城为主体，在山、海之间咽喉孔道上，构筑高城深池、以险制塞。山海关踞于明长城九边重镇之一蓟镇东部起点，而蓟镇所辖长城多采用土筑砖包墙，对此，近现代专家学者均有诸多考证研究。本文仅就山海关境内明长城及附属构筑物墙体砖情况做一专题阐述。

关键词：山海关　明长城　构筑物　砖

一、山海关境内长城修筑简况

山海关区今，所辖长城全长26千米，沿线有10座关隘，4座堡城，14 座烽火台，43座墙台（亦称马面台），37 座敌台。按自然区域划分主要为平原长城和山地长城。平原地带多选择地势相对较高台地筑城，山区则选择在山脊分水岭上。建筑形式和建筑结构也是因地制宜，就地取材。由起点老龙头至角山下旱门关段 11 千米平原地段长城本体，绝大多数为土筑砖包墙；由旱门关至一片石关段 15 千米山地长城本体踞重要地理位置地段，多为块石砌筑，内填碎石杂土；而踞于交通要冲之关口及两侧城墙，则为砖石包砌。

作为明长城精华地段，山海关境内长城城墙修筑的既厚且高，平原地段平均高 10 米，厚9米，墙基至城墙顶面均采用素土夯筑，仅在海墁砖下采用三合土夯筑封面，以防止城面向下渗水。经考证，明初修筑的城墙，底部不使用条石，仅以素土夯实作基。明中期以后大部分地段城墙墙体底部为条石砌筑，其上外包条砖，中间亚黏土夯实（图 1）。其城墙顶部用条砖、方砖铺面；内侧砌筑女儿墙，安放吐水嘴；外侧砌筑垛口墙，垛口下设置射孔。其外侧挑挖护城河，宽 10–20 米不等，深度 2 米左右。在平原长城向山地长城过度地段，地势由南向北逐步抬高。山区长城则依地势修筑，就地取材，城墙厚 1.8-4.2 米不等，墙高 2.5-5.1 米不等。

二、长城墙体条砖类型

据《中国长城山海关详考》记载，山海关境内明长城所用城砖从明代初期至中后期有很大变化，每一时期的城砖规格相异，个别的相差仅在 1 厘米左右。今结合出土城砖情况，可大致划分为“明前期、明中期、明中后期、明后期”，且不同地段长城及其附属设施都有具体发现（图 2）。

2.7 AN INTRODUCTION TO THE BRICKS OF THE MING DYNASTY GREAT WALL AND OF ITS ANCILLARY STRUCTURES AT SHANHAIGUAN

FENG YING
Cultural Relics Preservation Office of Shanhaiguan District - China - Hebei

Abstract

Shanhaiguan was established as a Wei[1] and garrisoned in 1381 in the reign of Hongwu, the founding Emperor of the Ming Dynasty. Located to the south of Yan Mountain, and north of the Bohai Sea, the fortified pass guarded the narrow passage through its high walls and deep ditches. Shanhaiguan is situated at the east end in Ji Zhen, one of the nine military command regions along the Great Wall. In Ji Zhen, rammed-earth walls clad with bricks were quite common, and have been much studied by scholars in modern times. This article will focus on the bricks used on the Wall and ancillary structures in Shanhaiguan District.

Keywords: Shanhaiguan, Ming Dynasty Great Wall, axilliary structures, inscribed bricks.

SUMMARY OF THE CONSTRUCTION OF THE SHANHAIGUAN GREAT WALL

The Shanhaiguan section of the Great Wall runs for 26km, along which there are 10 fortified passes, 4 fortresses, 14 beacon towers, 43 horse faces and 37 defence towers. From a topographical perspective, the Wall can be categorised into sections on plains and sections in mountains. The Wall was built on relatively higher grounds on the plains whereas ridges were deemed ideal locations for it in the mountains. Similarly, building structures also depended on the landscape and their building materials were obtained nearby. The Wall built on the plains stretches for 11km, from the very east end of the Great Wall at Laolongtou to Hanmenguan Pass at the foot of Jiaoshan Mountain. This section is mainly built with a rammed-earth core clad with bricks. The more strategically important and mountainous section from Hanmenguan Pass winding 15km west to Yipianshiguan Pass was built with rock facings with mixed gravels and assorted fills. Walls on both side of the strategic passes sitting at strategic transportation gateways were rammed-earth structures clad with bricks.

Reflecting the very essence of the Ming Dynasty Great Wall, the structures at Shanhaiguan were built high and thick. On average, walls on the plains were 10m high and 9m thick. The base and core were rammed earth, on which lime mortar was laid, bedding the bricks and sealing the core to prevent moisture from seeping into the body of the Wall. Research has confirmed that the base of the Wall built in the early Ming Dynasty was only of rammed earth without any strip foundation stones used. After the mid-Ming Dynasty, the base of the Wall was built with strip stones. The upper part was rammed earth clad with bricks bedded in mortar. Narrow and square bricks were used on the top of the wall: on its inner side, parapets with downspouts were built; a battlement was built on its outer side with arrow slits and gunports beneath the crenellation. Externally a ditch, 10m to 20m wide and 2m deep, was dug. The altitude of the Wall gradually rises as it zigzags from the plain in the south to the mountains in the north.

1 A *Wei* was one level of the hierarchy of military commands during the Ming Dynasty, which were, in descending order, as follows: *Zhen, Lu, Wei, Suo, Bu* (Editors' note).

（一）平原长城（老龙头至角山段）

境内仅 11 千米平原地段长城，所用城砖规格众多，究其原因就是，该地段长城曾在不同时期进行过多次修筑所致。明前期规格基本为 48×23×12厘米、45×21×14 厘米、45×21×15厘米；明中期规格为 44 ×22×18 厘米、43×21×16 厘米、43×20×9.5 厘米、43×21×10 厘米；明后期规格为 38×19×9 厘米、38×18×9.5 厘米。

（二）山地长城（角山至一片石关段）

此段长城基本修筑于明中前期及中后期，墙体就地取材，依山就势或铲削，或挑堑，中前期且多使用条石、块石垒砌，砖包墙较少。中后期局部损毁地段及关口险要处包砌城砖。受地形所限，长城所用条砖仅采用两种规格，分别为：38×19×14厘米；38×18×9.5厘米。

（三）长城附属构筑物——墙台、敌台、烽台、墩台

墙台凸出于城墙砌体外侧，台顶面与城墙顶面相平，三面围以垛口墙，其建筑形式基本为方形台，少数为矩形台。敌台有实心和空心两种建筑形制，为两层或三层，骑城墙而建，内外均超出城墙宽度，总高度 8—9 米不等。烽台设置在长城沿线，用于警戒，山海关辖区内烽堠均建在长城内侧。墩台的作用基本与烽台相同，以传递军情为主，建筑结构比较简陋。上述长城附属构筑物分两个阶段修筑，第一阶段为明前期，与平原长城类同，条砖规格为 45×21×14 厘米、45×21×15

图 1 关城西门南侧城墙遗址（中）；北门瓮城西北侧条石基础（下）；夯土层（上）（图片来源：山海关文物保管所）。

Fig.1 The rammed-earth layer at the north-west corner of the barbican of the North Gate; the southern section of the Wall at the west gate of Shanhaiguan Pass (middle); the strip stone foundation of the barbican of the North Gate (bottom) (photographs by Cultural Relics Preservation Office of Shanhaiguan District).

The Wall in mountainous areas was constructed in correspondence to the landscape, and its building materials were acquired locally. This section of the Wall is about 1.8 to 4.2m thick and 2.5 to 5.1m high (Fig.1).

TYPES OF NARROW BRICKS USED ON THE BODY OF THE WALL

As recorded in *A Detailed Research on Shanhaiguan District of the Great Wall* (Guo 2006), there are considerable differences between the sizes of the Wall bricks used in the early Ming Dynasty at Shanhaiguan and those of the mid and late Ming periods, while the differences are less among those used within the same period. Bricks which have been found at different locations along the Wall and in its ancillary structures can be roughly divided according to their date: early; mid; mid to late; and late Ming Dynasty (Fig.2).

The Wall on the Plain: Laolongtou to Jiaoshan Mountain

Although this section of the Wall is only 11km long, it has bricks of various sizes as the Wall here underwent multiple refurbishments in different periods. Bricks from the early Ming Dynasty were basically 48×23×12cm, 45×21×14cm or 45×21×15cm; those from the mid Ming Dynasty were 44×22×18cm, 43×21×16cm, 43×20×9.5cm or 43×21×10cm; and late Ming Dynasty bricks were 38×19×9 cm or 38×18×9.5cm.

The Walls in the mountains: Jiaoshan Mountain to Yipianshiguan Pass

This section of the Wall was mainly constructed in the early–mid to late-mid Ming period. The Wall was built with materials found locally, and by cutting away rock faces in accordance with the topography. Walls constructed in the early-mid Ming Dynasty were built mainly of rammed-earth or gravels clad with dressed or undressed stones. Rammed-earth walls clad with bricks can seldom be found in this period. Then in the late-mid Ming Dynasty, damaged sections and the fortified pass were reinforced with brick cladding. Only two sizes of narrow bricks were found in the reinforcement of this section, respectively 38×19×14cm and 38×18×9.5 cm.

Auxiliary structures of the Great Wall: horse faces, defence towers and *feng* and *dun* beacon towers

The horse face is a square or sometimes rectangular terrace that is attached to the exterior and is the same height as the Wall; the terrace is formed by battlements on three sides. Defence towers are two- or three-storey structures, which can be either chambered or solid, built along the line of the Wall itself. They are 8 to 9m high and wider than the body of the Wall itself, protruding both internally and externally. There are two kinds of beacon towers. The *feng* towers were used as watch towers; all of the *feng* towers along Shanhaiguan section are located on the inner side of the Wall. The other type are the *dun* towers which share a similar function of passing signals but are relatively simple in terms of their building structure.

Construction of these ancillary structures can be divided into two phases. The first phase coincided with construction of the Wall on the plain in the early Ming Dynasty. Sizes of narrow bricks from that period were 45×21×14cm and 45×21×15cm. The second phase of construction was carried out in the mid to late Ming Dynasty, when the sizes of narrow bricks used were 38×21×14cm and 38×21×15cm.

The Shanhaiguan Pass, *Luocheng* and *Buchengs*

There are three types of fort in the military system at Shanhaiguan: the Shanhaiguan Pass, the *Luocheng*, and *Bu*-forts. The *guancheng* or the fortified pass itself is an example of one of the most important features of the Great Wall which guarded key strategic crossing points connecting the interior to the exterior. They stationed troops and stored supplies and were the primary targets for enemy attack. *Luocheng*, or outer forts, were attached to the fortified pass to its east and west to provide further protection to its flanks. *Bu*-forts or *bucheng* were the lowest level of the military hierarchy of forts and which garrisoned military units for mobile deployment.

After it was first built in 1381 in the reign of the Emperor Hongwu, the Shanhaiguan Pass went through many phases of repair and renovation in the Ming period. As a result, various sizes of bricks can be found here. Bricks that are 48×23×12cm

图2 山海关境内出土明代城砖（图片来源：山海关长城博物馆）。

Fig.2 Ming Dynasty bricks discovered at Shanhaiguan (photographs by Shanhaiguan Great Wall Museum).

厘米。第二阶段为明中后期，条砖规格为 38×19×10 厘米、38×18×10 厘米。

（四）关城、罗城、堡城

山海关辖区内有“关城、罗城、堡城”，系山海关长城军事体系重要组成部分，三处重要军事布控，其中关城是长城沿线所设置的重要防守据点，是出入关城的交通孔道，既是驻兵屯粮的重地，也是敌人攻夺的重要目标；罗城系拱卫关城的卫城，位于山海关关城的东、西两侧，为山海关防御重点区域；堡城系长城关口驻防城池，属于最基层军事单位。其中山海关关城自明洪武十四年始筑以来，其后曾经多次修缮，故所用条砖类型最多：条砖规格明早期为48×23×12厘米、45×22×12厘米；明中期43×20×11厘米；明中后期至清代38×19×10厘米。其余城池所用条砖规格基本为三种类型：明前期条砖规格为45×22×12厘米；明中期43×20×11厘米、43×21×9.5厘米；明中后期至清代38×19×10厘米。

三、铭文城砖类型

在城垣建设过程中，城砖是最主要用材。常见的明长城筑墙用砖多为普通长方形烧制青砖，表面并无文字或图案。文字砖仅是明长城用砖中数量很少的一种，出于明确责任和区分不同筑城单位，多印以铭文标记，因此成为特定的长城文化符号。

据实地勘查，山海关境内长城铭文砖全部采用手工模压坯方法烧制，为研究人员提供了重要历史信息。铭文有的仅一单字，如“左”、“中”、“右”、“河”，表示制砖出处；有的标明质地，以示技术等级，如“永固砖”，意为保障城墙永久安全，等等。铭文砖主要集中在东罗城，有的不但有确切纪年，又有烧制单位，如“万历十二年真定营造”等 11 种文字。笔者依据境内长城分布顺序，作进一步调查梳理，以期在规格、年代及筑城历史背景方面找出异同（图 3）。

（一）老龙头长城文字砖

“右”字砖，1985 年修复老龙头滨海段长城时发现，城砖规格：39×18× 9 厘米。“右”字印在砖的大面中部，阳文，楷书体。

“河”字砖，1985 年修复老龙头滨海段长城时在 4 号台附近发现，城砖规格：39×18× 9 厘米。“河”字印在砖的大面中部，阳文，楷书体。

and 45×22×12cm can be dated back to the early Ming Dynasty; bricks from the mid Ming Dynasty were 43×20×11cm and the bricks from the late-mid Ming Dynasty were 38×19×10cm. The bricks found in the rest of forts and fortresses within the area fall into three types: the bricks from the early Ming Dynasty were 45×22×12cm; those from the mid Ming Dynasty were 43×20×11cm and 43x21x9.5cm; and the bricks from the late Ming Dynasty to Qing Dynasty were 38×19×10cm.

DIFFERENT TYPES OF INSCRIBED BRICKS

The most common bricks used in the construction of the Wall are rectangular blue bricks without any inscribed words or patterns; the inscribed bricks are relatively few in number. The bricks were inscribed to denote which unit was responsible for constructing each section of the Wall or its ancillary features. These inscribed bricks have now become important cultural symbols of the Great Wall.

Research has shown that all of the inscribed bricks on the Wall in the Shanhaiguan area were manufactured by hand, using compression moulds, and were then fired in kilns. This manufacturing process provides researchers with important historic information. Some bricks are inscribed with a single character, such as *zuo* (left), *zhong* (central), *you* (right), or *he* (river), to show where the bricks were made. Others are inscribed with words specifying the material or the level of craftsmanship. For example, words such as 'ever-strong brick' were inscribed to convey how impregnable the construction was. Most of the inscribed bricks at Shanhaiguan were discovered at the East *Luocheng*. Some of the bricks were not only inscribed with the exact year of their manufacture but also with the name of the unit that was in charge of their manufacture: for instance, inscriptions such as 'manufactured by Zhending Barrack in the 12th year under the reign of the Emperor Wanli.' Ten similar patterns of inscriptions were also discovered. The author intends to conduct further review and research based on the dates of construction of different sections of the Wall within Shanhaiguan District and to identify similarities and differences in the sizes of bricks, the date of the construction of the Wall, and the other historic information they provide (Fig.3).

Inscribed bricks on the Laolongtou Wall

Bricks, inscribed with the single character for right, were discovered in 1985 when the coastal section of the Wall at Laolongtou Wall was restored. These bricks measured 39×18×9cm and the character was written in regular script carved in relief at the centre of the largest face of the cuboid. Bricks inscribed with the single character for river, were discovered near Defence Tower No.4 at Laolongtou in 1985 when it was under repair. These bricks were also 39×18×9cm with the character written in regular script carved in relief at the centre of the largest face of the cuboid. Bricks inscribed with 'ever-strong brick', were discovered on the inner wall at South Haikouguan Pass in the Laolongtou area in 1987 during refurbishment. These bricks were 40×20×9cm with the characters written in regular script carved in intaglio style at the centre of the smallest face of the cuboid.

Inscribed bricks on the Jiaoshan Wall

Bricks, inscribed with the character for central, were discovered in 1984 when Jiaoshanguan Pass was undergoing a site clearance. These bricks were 39×18×9cm, with the character written in regular script carved in relief at the centre of the largest face of the cuboid. In 1991, bricks inscribed with the character for left were discovered on the face of the Wall on the southern slope of the highest peak on Jiaoshan Mountain. These bricks were 39×18×9cm with the character written in regular script carved in intaglio at the centre of the largest face of the cuboid.

Inscribed bricks at the East *Luocheng*

In the 1960s, 11 types of inscribed bricks were found on the east, south and north walls of the East *Luocheng*, of which ten state that they were manufactured by a particular unit or at a particular place in the 12th year of the reign of Emperor Wanli. Specifically, the bricks manufactured by Zhending Barrack were discovered on the south wall; ones made by Dezhou Barrack and Luanzhou County were found on the east wall The bricks manufactured by

"永固砖"，1987年修复老龙头长城时在南海口关南侧内墙砌体上发现，城砖规格：40×20×9厘米。"永固砖"三字印在砖的小面中部，阴文，楷书体。

（二）角山长城文字砖

"中"字砖，1984年清理角山关遗址时发现，城砖规格：39×18×9厘米。"中"字印在砖的大面中部，阳文，楷书体。

"左"字砖，1991年发现于角山主峰南坡长城城面上，城砖规格：39×18×9厘米。"左"字印在砖的大面中部，阳文，楷书体。

（三）东罗城文字砖

东罗城东南北三面墙砌体上，20世纪60年代以后陆续发现"万历十二年真定营造"（南墙）、"万历十二年德州营造"（东墙）、"万历十二年滦州造"（东墙）、"万历十二年燕河路造"（北墙）、"万历十二年卢龙县造"（北墙）、"万历十二年乐亭县造"（北墙）、"万历十二年迁安县造"（北墙）、"万历十二年抚宁县造"（北墙）、"万历十二年台头路造"（北墙）、"万历十二年建昌车营造"（北墙）等10种铭文砖。还有一种砖仅模印"德州营造"四字（东墙），城砖规格：38×18×10厘米，文字全部印在砖的小面中部，阴文，规整楷书体。时至1984年，位于天下第一关北侧的临闾楼遗址处（明万历十二年建，1986年重建）再次发现"万历十二年石门路造"铭文砖，城砖规格：38×18×10厘米。文字印在砖的小面中部，阴文，规整楷书体。

四、铭文砖烧制的历史成因

（一）单字铭文砖烧制年代解析

山海关境内修筑明长城所用城砖，从明初至中后期有很大变化，那么这是否与明代军事编制存在一定关系？据《明史·职官五》记载："明洪武七年（1374年）审定卫所之制。先是，内外卫所，凡一卫统十千户……。至是重定其制，每卫设前、后、中、左、右五千户。"这里所提到的"中、左、右"千户，系明代初期的军事建制。此三种单字铭文砖均小于明初的城砖规格，因此单字铭文砖为明初"中、左、右"三个千户所负责烧制的可能性极小。

由此分析有两种可能。一为明代中后期隆庆至万历年间（1567-1620年）所烧制。依据是明隆庆元年（1567年），戚继光调任蓟镇总兵，创立车、马、步、辎重四营，又将每一大营分为前、后、左、右、中五营，互为犄角。戚继光镇守蓟镇达十六年之久，曾对长城进行了大规模增筑和修缮，主持加固由山海关至居庸关长达600千米的长城，创建空心敌台1017座。山海关境内长城沿线空心敌台，均系明隆庆至万历年间修筑。参与修筑工程多为长城沿线分防的军队，少数为征调的民夫。所使用的城砖规格与"左、中、右"三种铭文砖的规格相同。据此推断，这些单字铭文砖有可能为这一时期防守本地段的"左、中、右"营的将士负责烧制。

二为明崇祯五年至十三年（1632-1640年）所烧制。依据是，蓟辽巡抚丘禾嘉、杨嗣昌、冯任、朱国栋等驻守山海关时，曾经调整营制，在山海关南部设南海中营、南海左营、南海右营；在山海关北部设北山中营、北山左营、北山右营。这几人在任内多有筑城固疆之举，责成这些驻防的军队负责修缮本防区城墙，因此，"左、中、右"三种单字铭文砖也有可能为这一时期所烧制。

Yanhe *Lu*, Lulong County, Laoting County, Qian'an County and Funing County, as well as bricks made by Taitou *Lu* and Jianchang Che Barrack, were on the north wall. The eleventh type were those bricks inscribed with 'manufactured by Dezhou Barrack' without specifying their date of manufacture; these were also discovered on the east Wall. These bricks are 38×18×10cm with characters written in regular script inscribed in intaglio at the centre of the smallest face. In 1984, bricks inscribed with 'manufactured by Shimen *Lu* in the 12th year of the reign of Emperor Wanli' were found north of the First Pass Under Heaven[2] at Linlu Tower, which was built in the 12th year of Wanli and rebuilt in 1986. The bricks measured 38×18×10cm and had characters written in regular script inscribed in intaglio at the centre of the smallest face.

THE HISTORIC BACKGROUND TO THE INSCRIBED BRICKS

The date of the bricks inscribed with single characters

From the early to mid and late Ming Dynasty periods, the bricks used at Shanhaiguan Great Wall went through huge changes. This raises the question of whether these changes are connected to changes in the structure of the military system during the Ming Dynasty. As recorded in *History of Ming: Treatise of State Offices, Vol.5,*[3] the imperial military system of Wei and Suo was reviewed and revised in 1374, or the 7th Year of the reign of Emperor Hongwu. This resulted in former Wei commands of ten thousand soldiers being reformed into 5 battalions of a thousand soldiers, named front, rear, central, left and right. However, the sizes of inscribed bricks with single character such as 'central', 'left' and 'right' were smaller than the other bricks made in the early Ming Dynasty. Therefore, it is highly unlikely that these inscribed bricks were manufactured by the new divisions mentioned in the treatise.

There are two plausible theories as to when those single-character inscribed bricks were made. One possibility is that they were moulded and fired around 1567 to 1620, in the reigns of the Emperors Longqing and Wanli in the mid to late Ming Dynasty. When Emperor Longqing was enthroned in 1567, General Qi Jiguang was transferred to be the commander-in-chief of Ji *Zhen*. He split the military forces into four divisions, being those for vehicles, horses, infantry, and for logistics and supplies. Each of these divisions, were further sub-divided into smaller units called front, rear, left, right and central battalions. General Qi governed Ji *Zhen* for 16 years, during which he organised a large-scale repair and reconstruction on the existing Great Wall. He oversaw the reinforcement work on 600km of the Wall between Shanhaiguan Pass and Juyongguan Pass and built 1,017 chambered defence towers. All the chambered towers within Shanhaiguan District were built during the reigns of the Emperors Longqing and Wanli. The majority of labour came from forces stationed along the Wall. A few civilian workers were recruited as well. The sizes of single-character bricks coincided with the ones manufactured in this period. As a result, those single-character bricks may have been moulded and fired by soldiers from the local left, central and right battalions.

The other possibility is that these bricks were made around 1632 to 1640, during the reign of the Emperor Chongzhen, the last Emperor of the Ming Dynasty. During the period when Qiu Hejia, Yang Sichang, Feng Ren and Zhu Guodong were respectively Governors at Shanhaiguan they restructured the system of battalions into the Central, Left and Right Southern Coastal battalions, to the south of Shanhaiguan Pass, and the Central, Left and Right Northern Mountain battalions to its north. During their periods of governance, they all sought to reinforce and extend the Wall, and soldiers from these battalions were naturally involved in this work. Hence, it is possible that bricks with single-character inscriptions were made in this period.

2 'The First Pass Under Heaven' is an alternative name for Shanhaiguan Pass (Editors' note).

3 *The History of Ming* is one of the official Chinese historical works known as the *Twenty-Four Histories*. It consists of 332 volumes and covers the history of the Ming Dynasty from 1368 to 1644. The book was edited by Zhang Tingyu (1672-1755) first published in 1739 (Editors' note).

（二）永固砖烧制年代解析

老龙头南海口关南内侧墙砌体上的“永固砖”，其规格即小于明初的城砖，又略大于明后期的城砖，推测应系明中期城砖。这一时期山海卫境内长城较大规模修缮工程有三次。据记载，英宗正统十四年（1449年）修沿边关隘；宪宗成化八年（1472年），右都督冯宗镇守永平、山海，命蓟辽总兵修城堡、边垣、台堑，弘治十三年（1500年），都御史洪钟重修。洪公修置关、营三十八处，皆同此年。由此分析，“永固砖”极有可能为这一时期修筑长城时所烧制。

图3 铭文城砖（图片来源：山海关长城博物馆）。
Fig.3 Inscribed bricks (photographs by Shanhaiguan Great Wall Museum).

（三）东罗城铭文砖烧制年代解析

明万历十二年（1584），永平兵备道与山海关兵部分司负责主持修筑东罗城：“永平等处一带地方切邻边境，当专设兵备官分路经理……。管理燕河营、石门寨二路，监督副、参等官，驻扎永平府。分管该府所属卢龙、迁安、抚宁、昌黎、滦州、乐亭、永平、卢龙、抚宁、东胜左、山海、兴州右屯卫。专一抚处夷情，听理词讼，修葺城池，操练人马，查处主客钱粮，督修关营、墩墙，管理神器、甲仗，修盖营房、仓库。”据此已知，永平兵备道修筑山海关东罗城，征调这些卫、路、营、州、县的军队和民夫是很容易办到的。

“文武各效厥劳”，分段负责。筑城单位在铭文砖中有明确体现。在修筑东罗城的十一个单位中，其中真定营和德州营本不在永平兵备道管辖之内，但这两个营却是奉调到这一地区参加“两防”的军队，因而也参与了修筑东罗城。上述史料证明，山海关境内长城铭文砖应多由永平兵备道所管辖范围内的驻防军队和永平府管辖内各州县所征调的筑城民夫烧制。

五、结语

山海关历经明清两代经营，成为享誉天下的军事重镇。据腾讯网世博频道登载，带有铭文刻记的中国长城砖早于1982年便在美国诺克斯维尔城市举办的国际博览会上被视作文化珍品展出，对于研究明代山海卫的军事防御提供诸多历史信息，具有重要文物价值。时至今日，山海关明长城文字砖经历岁月侵蚀，依然保存较好，应倍加珍视。

The date of the bricks inscribed with 'ever-strong brick'

The ever-strong bricks found on the inner wall of at Nanhaikouguan Pass in the Laolongtou section of the Wall were smaller than bricks made in the early Ming Dynasty period and slightly larger than the ones manufactured in the mid to late Ming period. Presumably, they were made in the mid Ming Dynasty. During that period of time, there were three large scale repair projects carried out on the Wall within Shanhaiguan area. It was recorded that in 1449, during the first reign of Emperor Yingzong, the strategic passes along the border were reinforced. Later on, in 1472, during the reign of the Emperor Chenghua, Feng Zong, the regional military commander, ordered the refurbishment of forts, walls, towers and ditches. Then in 1500, during the reign of Emperor Hongzhi, the imperial censor-in-chief Hong Zhong renovated other related structures, repaired strategic passes and set up barracks at 38 different locations (Dong, 2001). Based on these records it is highly possible that the 'ever-strong bricks' were moulded and fired during this section of the mid Ming period.

The date of the inscribed bricks found at the East *Luocheng*

In 1584, during the reign of the Emperor Wanli, the regional military commander responsible for regulating local forces and managing supplies, and the Shanhaiguan branch of the Ministry of War were in charge of renovating the East *Luocheng*. Below the regional commander, military officers were specifically assigned to manage frontier *Lus* including Yanhe and Shimenzhai. They were also responsible for managing the counties of Lulong, Qianan, Funing, Changli, Luanzhou and Laoting, and they gave orders to units of forces stationed at Yongping, Lulong, Funing, Dongshengzuo, Shanhai and Xingzhou. Their duties included gathering intelligence on ethnic minority populations, administering justice, repairing fortresses, military training, managing local granaries, weaponry and ceremonial materials as well as building camps and warehouses (Dong, 2001). These commanders would have had no difficulty in commanding soldiers and civilians from different administrative units to repair the East *Luocheng* of Shanhaiguan Pass.

Each military unit or county was in charge of one section of the Wall, something which was clearly shown by the inscriptions on bricks. Among the 11 units assigned to repair the East *Luocheng*, those from Zhending and Dezhou Barracks were not under the administration of the regional commander but were ordered to the area to join the spring and autumn shifts of troops to guard the Wall as well as to repair the East *Luocheng*. Based on the historic records mentioned above, it is safe to say that bricks used in the reconstruction of the Wall within Shanhaiguan District were probably manufactured by military forces stationed in the regional prefecture and by civilian workers from counties under its administration.

CONCLUSION

Due to extensive construction, renovation and management in the Ming and Qing Dynasties, Shanhaiguan became an important military complex which is now internationally known. According to the Expo Channel page on the Tencent website, the Great Wall's inscribed bricks were exhibited as cultural treasures at the World's Fair in Knoxville, Tennessee as early as 1982. The inscribed bricks possess significant value as cultural relics as they provide valuable historical information for the study of the military defence system of Shanhaiguan. After long years of weathering and erosion, the inscribed bricks of the Shanhaiguan of Ming Dynasty are relatively well preserved and are deserving of greater academic and public attention and protection.

参考文献
References

Dong, Yaohui (ed.) 2001. *A Compiled Collation and Annotation of Treatises in Qinhuangdao*, Beijing, China Press of Auditing
董耀会（编）. 2001 . 秦皇岛历代志书校注. 北京:中国审计出版社.

Guo, Zemin 2006. *A Detailed Research on Shanhai Pass of the Great Wall.* Tianjin: Baihua Literature and Art Publishing House.
郭泽民. 2006. 中国长城山海关详考. 天津： 百花文艺出版社.

2.8 THE CENTURIAL STONES AND OTHER BUILDING INSCRIPTIONS FROM HADRIAN'S WALL

PAUL BIDWELL
Newcastle upon Tyne - UK

Abstract

The centuries and cohorts of the three legions which built Hadrian's Wall marked their work with inscribed building stones. These stones, which in some ways are comparable to the inscribed bricks of the Ming Wall in China, contribute to an understanding of the overall building programme. They are also a unique collection of centurions' names, some illustrating the origins of officers who served in the earlier years of Hadrian's reign.

Keywords: Hadrian's Wall, Roman inscriptions, legions, cohorts, centurions, building programme

INTRODUCTION

Hadrian's Wall was the most elaborate of all the frontier works that surrounded the Roman Empire. Nowhere along its 134km length does the original Wall stand to its full height, but what remains of its fabric tells us much about its complicated building history. Of special interest are the large number of inscribed building stones: a few of these are still set in the faces of the Wall, but most have been found in the rubble from its collapse or have been re-used in medieval and later buildings. Even though they date to a period more than a thousand years earlier, the building stones have much in common with the inscribed bricks of the Ming Wall. In essence, they simply say 'We built this,' and give the name of the officer commanding the unit of soldiers responsible for the construction.

The reason for including the following brief discussion in this collection of papers is that the British Museum has suggested that we could use these two types of artefacts, the Ming bricks and the Roman stones, as the focus of a UK-China joint exhibition about the design and construction of the two Walls. The lead partner in the UK in taking this forward is Tyne and Wear Archives and Museums, which has been responsible for extensive excavations on Hadrian's Wall and some of its eastern forts.

The study of Hadrian's Wall has produced an enormous body of scholarly literature, and sources more than four centuries old are still regularly consulted by scholars. In the following paragraphs, references are only supplied for specific building stones and for works which refer to the Wall. In the final section, major stages in the development of archaeological understanding of the significance of the building stones are briefly reviewed. The term 'centurial stones' refers specifically to examples inscribed with the names of centuries (see below), sometimes coupled with their cohorts; 'building stones' includes other inscriptions and markings. All the inscriptions are on sandstone, the standard stone used in construction of the Wall across its entire length.

THE BUILDING STONES IN THE ORIGINAL CONSTRUCTION PROGRAMME

The Roman army in Britain during the early second century AD numbered about 40,000 men. It was one of the largest concentrations of military units in the Empire, despite the relatively small size of the province. The three legions in Britain were the elite of the army, and most of the soldiers had the status of Roman citizens. Very few

2.8 哈德良长城百人队勒名石和建筑勒名石

保罗·彼得维尔
纽卡斯尔—英国

摘要

建造哈德良长城的三个罗马军团下属的百人队和步兵大队以勒名石的方式记录下他们的工作。在某种程度上而言，这些勒名石和中国明长城的文字砖可以相互对比，有助于了解长城的建筑过程。勒名石也是了解百夫长姓名的独特来源，其中可以部分揭示哈德良大帝统治早期一些官员的背景。

关键字：哈德良长城　罗马刻字　罗马军团　步兵大队　百人队　建筑工事

引言

哈德良长城是所有罗马帝国边疆防御体系中最复杂的工程。如今，在全长 134 千米的哈德良墙体中，已经没有一处还完整保留着最初的高度，但从遗迹中仍能看出其复杂的修建历史。尤为有趣的是大量留存的建筑勒名石：少数仍然镶嵌在长城墙体表面，但大部分则发现于长城坍塌的碎石废墟中，或被重新用于中世纪及之后的建筑。虽然从年代上，这些勒名石比明长城文字砖早一千多年，但两者有很多共同之处。本质上，两者都在传递“此墙乃我建”信息，并留下了负责修建长城军团的指挥官名字。

之所以在本论文集简要讨论相关内容，是因为大英博物馆建议可以举办明长城文字砖和罗马勒名石的联合展览，通过两者讲述英国和中国长城的设计和建造故事。推进该建议的英国主要牵头机构是泰恩威尔郡档案博物馆，他们长期负责哈德良长城很多墙体的发掘以及部分东部要塞的深入发掘。

哈德良长城的研究形成了大量的学术文献，一些四个世纪前的文献至今仍然被许多学者频繁查阅。本文收录的参考文献仅涉及具体建筑勒名石和针对长城的相关研究成果。本文在最后的部分回顾了考古界对勒名石价值的理解所经历的主要发展阶段。“百人队勒名石”特指刻有百人队名称的石料（见下文），有时也同时刻有其所在步兵大队的名字；“建筑勒名石”包含其他类型的勒名石或标记。勒名用石均为砂岩，是长城全线的标准建造用石。

原始建造阶段的建筑勒名石

公元2世纪早期驻扎在不列颠的罗马军队人数约为 4 万。虽然不列颠行省的面积相对较小，它仍是罗马帝国驻军最多的地区之一。驻扎在不列颠的三支军团为精英军团，即军团的大部分士兵属于罗马公民。士兵中只有一小部分来自罗马或意大利，大多数来自较早建立的行省地区，如西班牙或法国南部，

were actually from Rome or Italy; the majority came from long-established provinces such as Spain and southern France, and from around the eastern Mediterranean. Even though the other imperial soldiers in Britain were of lower status, it was the legions that supplied the labour for building the Wall. The Second *Augusta* legion had its permanent base at Caerleon in south Wales, about 400km south of the Wall; the Sixth *Victrix* at York and the Twentieth *Valeria Victrix* at Chester were closer but still several days' march distant.

A legion consisted of 10 cohorts, each of which was composed of six centuries of 80 men, each with its own centurion and under-officers. The First Cohort, which was the most senior, had only five centuries, also commanded by centurions, including the chief centurion (*primus pilus*) of the legion. The cohort-strength of the legion was thus 4,800, but there were also the senior officers and the legionary cavalry, the latter probably numbering 120. The total strength of the legion was therefore about 5,000 men.

Each legion was responsible for building sections of the Wall about five miles in length, and subdivisions of these allocations were given to the cohorts and further divided between the centuries of each cohort. In the Roman Empire, the erection of military and other public buildings was usually marked by inscriptions dedicated to the emperor; they were often very detailed, including all the Emperor's titles and also the names of high officials such as the governor of the relevant province. On Hadrian's Wall, the ends of the building lengths were marked with a series of much smaller inscribed stones which were probably set into the south face of the Wall. (When the whole system was complete, the north face would have been largely inaccessible because of the obstacles which were placed in front of it, and any inscriptions on it would have been rarely seen.)

The commonest type of inscribed building stones — the centurial stones — either cite the century by giving the centurion's name or have, in addition, the number of the cohort to which the century belonged. The names are preceded by a 'C', or a 'V' standing on its side (a symbol for the word '*centuria*'), and they are often abbreviated, though the full names are sometimes obvious. Stones marking the work of the chief centurion of a legion sometimes give only the title of his post, shortened to 'PP' for '*primus pilus*', rather than his name. Usually, each century seems to have been allocated building lengths of 30 Roman feet (8.9 metres). Having completed its length, the century then moved with its cohort to work on another section of the Wall; this explains why building stones naming the same centurion may occur many miles apart. The building stones might have been a means of checking the quality of the work carried out by the centuries and cohorts. More importantly, they were probably envisaged as permanent memorials to the participation of the units in Hadrian's great building project.

The inscriptions on these stones are usually set within rectangular frames formed by simple mouldings, some with small projections (*ansae*) at their ends, while others carry the text without any decoration. Some examples have carefully carved frames but no inscriptions; it is possible that the lettering had been painted rather than incised. A few of the inscriptions are neatly cut, but many are very rough and can be difficult to decipher. Some more elaborate stones seem to mark the end of the legionary lengths, but they are in a wide variety of styles. Other stones have numbers, crosses or other devices; their significance is unknown. There are also a few carvings of phalluses, symbols protecting the fabric from malign forces.

At least 213 examples of the inscribed stones have been recorded. They were first recorded in large numbers some three centuries ago. Some were preserved in private collections, eventually finding their way into museums, and others were re-used in new buildings. Occasionally some of these old finds are rediscovered, as recently at Walwick Hall on the Wall near the fort of Chesters. New finds are rare, but generally occur when farm buildings or field walls are being demolished or repaired.

THE LATER STAGES OF CONSTRUCTION

The original building scheme for the Wall was soon disrupted by alterations and additions to the work programme. One of the most significant additions was the Vallum, the large ditch flanked by mounds to its north

以及地中海东部各地。即使驻扎在不列颠的其他帝国士兵地位较低，他们仍属于精英军团，成为修建长城主要劳动力。奥古斯塔第二军团的永久基地位于威尔士南部的卡利恩，位于长城以南约 400 千米处；第六凯旋军团和第二十英勇凯旋军团分别驻扎在约克和切斯特，这些地区虽然离长城稍近，但仍需行军数日方可到达。

每个军团包含十个步兵大队，每个步兵大队包含六个百人队，每百人队中由 80 名士兵以及百夫长和副手组成。级别最高的是第一大队，只包含五个百人队，也设百夫长，其中还设有军团首席百夫长（primus pilus）。因此，军团的步兵大队总人数共计 4800 人。此外还有高级军官和军团骑兵，这些共计约 120 人。因此整个军团兵力约 5000 人。

每个军团负责建造约五英里长城区段，该区段会进一步分配给下属的步兵大队和大队中的百人队。罗马帝国中，军事设施和其他公共建筑通常勒名献给帝国皇帝；内容往往非常详尽，包括皇帝的所有尊号以及高级官员的姓名，例如相关行省总督的姓名。哈德良长城上，每段长城的两端都有较小的勒名石标记，通常位于在朝南面的城墙上。（长城完工后，通常城墙北面设有障碍物，北面的城墙难以接近，因此即使在该面墙上刻字，也很少能够被看到。）

百人队石，是最常见的建筑勒名石，通常刻有百夫长的姓名，或再加上百人队所属的步兵大队的编号。姓名前刻有“C”或“V”（指代“百夫长”），姓名本身也常常采用缩写，但偶尔也会看到全名赫然在上。军团第一大队的勒名石标记通常仅包含首席百夫长的头衔，缩写为“PP”(primus pilus), 而非姓名。每个百人队通常负责修筑 30 罗马寸（8.9米）长的城墙。完成该段落后，百人队就跟随其所属大队转而去修筑其他城墙段落。这也解释了为什么刻有同样百人队名字的建筑石会发现于相隔数英里的地方。建筑勒名石可能用来检查百人队和步兵大队工程建造质量。更重要的是，这些勒名石也很可能被视为参与哈德良长城伟大工程建造的永久纪念。

石料上刻字通常置于简单雕刻长方形框内，一些方框周围刻有较小的凸起 (ansae) 装饰，而另一些勒名石则只有简单的文字，没有任何装饰。有些石料上只有精心雕刻的边框但无刻字；文字内容有可能是涂写而非篆刻在石料上。只有一小部分文字是精心雕刻的，大部分刻字非常粗糙，会很难辨别。一些精心处理过的石料似乎标记所在军团建造的工事长度，但这些雕刻风格多样。另一些刻有数字，十字架和其他标记，这些标记的含义则不为人知。还有一些刻有阳具图案，用于抵抗邪恶力量，作为保卫城墙的象征。

目前至少保存有 213 方勒名石的相关记录。在大约三百年前，大批勒名石被首次记录。一些勒名石被私人收藏，并最终进入博物馆。而另一部分则被回收并用于新建筑中。偶尔一些旧的勒名石被重新发现，例如近期在切斯特要塞附近的沃维克礼堂墙体中发现的勒名石。勒名石的新发现现在很少了，通常是在拆除或修复农场建筑或农场界墙时发现。

后期建造阶段

随着工程实施的进展，最初的修建设计很快被突破，进行了修改和添加。最主要添加的是南部壕沟，位于城墙后方，壕沟规模很大，南北两侧堆土为堤。建筑勒名石往往位于南部壕沟两侧的堤岸上，后者由粘土和草被堆成。这些勒名石表明，负责修筑南部壕沟的并非是罗马军团，而是雇佣兵团，即由非罗马公民的士兵组成的小型兵团。长城最西段 31 罗马里的长城（草被长城）段落也是由粘土和草皮修筑的；百人队如何记录该段建造的方式尚不明确，但在草被长城段落中的一座里堡中曾发现有木刻勒名 (RIB 1965)。

and south which ran behind the Wall. Building stones were set into the mounds of the Vallum, which were formed of clay and turf. These stones marked the work not of legionaries but of auxiliary units, smaller units of non-citizen soldiers. The westernmost 31 Roman miles of the Wall (the Turf Wall) had also been built of turf and clay; how the work of the centuries was recorded is uncertain, but an inscription carved in wood (*RIB* 1965) is known from one of the turf milecastles.

About fifteen years later, work began to rebuild the Turf Wall in stone. From the section east of Birdoswald, exposed some sixty years ago, there came one of the best recorded series of building stones which showed that the marking of centurial lengths still persisted (see in particular *RIB* 3415-37). Some later stones are also known, but it seems that the work-parties that were repairing and rebuilding the Wall over the course of the next two centuries only occasionally marked their efforts. Exceptions include the stones of the *civitates*[1], the cantons of the province of *Britannia*: two of these mention the *Dumnonii* who occupied modern Devon and Cornwall in the far South-West of Britain (*RIB* 1843-4). They mark the participation of civilian labour in the rebuilding of parts of the Wall, probably in the later second or third centuries AD.

THE SIGNIFICANCE OF THE BUILDING STONES

There are two reasons why the building stones are of great significance. First, Hadrian's Wall, as well as being the most elaborate frontier work in the Roman Empire, is also now acknowledged as an example of 'exceptional construction' (Delaine 2002). It was one of a series of projects ordered or supported by successive emperors (most of them in civilian contexts and in the Mediterranean areas) which called for huge resources of manpower and materials and a high degree of planning. They were displays of '*magnificentia*', the ability of the emperor and the state to create works of great splendour which were also a public good. Contemporary records of these 'exceptional constructions' are limited and sometimes entirely lacking. The building stones of Hadrian's Wall, combined with the long history of archaeological investigation on the frontier, provide a depth of knowledge about the organisation of a Roman 'exceptional construction' which cannot be matched elsewhere.

Secondly, the stones name at least 130 individual centurions. Even if some of the stones are later in date, they identify a very large number of these officers serving in the three British legions in the AD 120s. Some of their names are recorded elsewhere in the Roman Empire; indeed, some went on to achieve much higher office in the imperial administration. A few others featured in other events. The majority, however, are otherwise unknown or have names so common that when they occur in military contexts elsewhere we cannot know whether they refer to the same person. One example of a name that appears only once on the Wall is Paulius Aper (Fig. 1a). Two building stones are inscribed with the name of Valerius Maximus (Fig. 1b). Although both elements of his name are commonly found across the Roman Empire, they probably represent the same man, but a centurion of this name at the Caerleon fortress, the base of the Second Augustan legion (*RIB* 351– 2) might perhaps have been another individual.

Other centurions have distinctive names which point to their origins. Claudius Cleonicus (Fig. 2a) has a second name with a Greek root which shows that he came from the Greek-speaking eastern parts of the empire (Birley 1979, 75). Another centurion, Gellius Philippus (Fig. 4), has a Greek-sounding name, but it had long been current in the Roman world (Birley 1979,75). He is also known from three other building stones from the Wall, one showing that he had formerly been a centurion in the sixth cohort of his legion (*RIB* 1572, 1668 and 3303). Spain was the

1 A *civitas* (the plural is *civitates*) is a Latin term for a town and its territory with a defined political status, equivalent to, say, the capital city or town of a county and its county. It also indicates the presence of a municipal authority with responsibilities to govern and collect tax in the area. The *civitas* can refer only to the town, or to the entire municipal area of the county.

草被长城修建完成的大概 15 年后，长城开始采用石料重修。在博得瓦德以东的长城段落中，约六十年前发现了一系列保存完好的建筑勒名石，表明百人队标记其所负责段落的做法仍在持续（尤其见于 RIB 3415–37）。一些后期的勒名石也陆续发现，但似乎在接下来的两个世纪中，修复和重建长城的兵团仅偶尔标记他们的工作。也有例外的情况，即在不列颠尼亚行省的民事行政区发现的城邦[1]石，有两处勒名石提到了多姆里人，后者曾居住在现属英国西南的德文和康沃尔地区 (RIB 1843–4)。这些勒名石记录了部分重建长城的劳工来自平民，时间大概是公元后 2 世纪晚期至 3 世纪。

建筑勒名石的价值

建筑勒名石的价值体现在两个方面。首先，哈德良长城不仅是罗马边疆防御体系中最复杂的部分，也被认为是“杰出工程”的典范（迪林 2002）。这些由历任皇帝下令建造或支持建造的一系列工程（这些工程大部分属于民用工程且位于地中海地区），需要庞大人力和财力支持和高度集中规划。这些工程彰显了帝国的“宏大气魄”，体现出皇帝和帝国创建宏功伟业的能力，以及造福人民的慷慨。当时这些“杰出工程”的记录非常有限，有些甚至完全没有记录。哈德良长城的建筑勒名石，和有关哈德良长城的长期考古调查资料积累，加深了对罗马帝国组织杰出工程的理解，这是其他工程所不具备的独特优势。

第二，这些勒名石记录了至少 130 个百夫长的名字。虽然部分勒名石的年代较晚，但它们记录下了大量军官的名字，都服役于公元 120 年代左右驻扎在不列颠的三个罗马军团。其中一些人的名字在罗马帝国的其他地区也有记录。的确，一部分人在帝国统治中达到了更高的地位。另外少数人在其他事件中出现。但是由于大部分人的名字太无名气或者过于常见，以至于我们无法确定在其他军事文件中出现的是否为同一个人。例如 Paulius Aper 这个名字只在长城中出现了一次（图 1a）。而 Valerius Maximus 这个名字在两块建筑石上出现图 1b）。后者的名和姓在整个罗马帝国都很常见，有可能指同一个人。但是也可能有着相同名字却驻扎在凯利昂要塞处第二奥古斯丁军团的一名百夫长（RIB 351-2）是另外一个人。

有些百夫长的名字与众不同可以揭示他们的来历。Claudius Cleonicus（图2a）名字中的第二个词源自希腊，表明他来自帝国东部的希腊语地区（伯利，1979, 75）。另一名百夫长，Gellius Philippus（图4）的名字虽然发音接近希腊语，但其在罗马势力范围已经长久流传（伯利，1979,75）。他的名字还在长城沿线其他三块建筑勒名石中发现，其中一块显示他曾经担任所在军团第六步兵大队的百夫长（RIB, 1572, 1668 和 3303）。百夫长 Terentius Cantaber 则来自西班牙（图2b）。“Cantaber”源自坎塔布里亚（Cantabria）这个词，在罗马时期仍是西班牙西北部一个地区的名字（伯利 1979, 76）。

另外一个有着有趣经历的例子是百夫长 Satilius Solon，他的名字出现在三百年前发现的一块勒名石上，但随后该石遗失（图 3）。几乎可以确定的是，他入伍前加入家乡赫拉克勒亚的一个代表团前往土耳其克拉罗斯参拜供奉着太阳神阿波罗的神谕之所（琼斯 2005, 296）。该神谕之所随后用于献祭诸神，很可能是祈求众神终止二世纪晚期的瘟疫蔓延。有两块勒名石均提到这些献祭，一块来自哈德良长城豪塞斯特兹要塞，另一块来自位于哈德良长城南部的英格兰西北海岸的瑞文格拉斯，它们也证明了罗马帝国内的紧密联系（RIB 1579，托姆林 2019, 49）。Solon 之后提拔为第一辅助军团首席百夫长，驻扎在布里吉第要塞，位于现在的匈牙利境内（伯利 1979, 75, 181）。

1 城邦（civitas, 复数为 civitates）在拉丁文中特指有确定的政治地位和区域的城镇，相当于现在的国家首都或地方首府。这也意味着有自治长官负责该区域的管辖和税收。城邦也可以单指城镇本身，或整个郡县的自治区域。

Fig.1a RIB 1444: coh(ortis) IX c(enturia)/ Paul(i) Apr(i), 'of the ninth cohort, the century of Paulius Aper (built this)', with a neatly cut stop in the form of a leaf between the two elements of the centurion's name. 43.1cm by 25.4cm. Found in the south face of the Wall near turret 26b and removed to Chesters Museum in 1880 (© Humphrey Welfare).

图 1a RIB 1444: coh(ortis) IX c(enturia)/ Paul(i) Apr(i), "第九大队，百夫长 Paulius Aper（建造）"，百人团长名字中间上部精心刻出了树叶形状。43.1 厘米乘 25.4 厘米。发现于长城南墙 26 b号塔楼附近，于 1880 年移至切斯特博物馆（© 汉佛瑞·维尔法。

Fig.1b RIB 1682: *c(enturia) Val(eri)/ Maxi(mi)*, 'the century of Valerius Maximus (built this)'. 33cm by 17.8cm. Found before 1732 between turrets 42a and 42b and now in Chesters Museum (© Humphrey Welfare).

图 1b RIB 1682: c(enturia) Val(eri)/ Maxi(mi), "百夫长 Valerius Maximus（建造）"。33 厘米乘 17.8 厘米。1732 年前发现于长城 42a 号塔楼和 42b 号塔楼之间，现存切斯特博物馆（© 汉佛瑞·维尔法）。

origin of the centurion Terentius Cantaber (Fig. 2b). 'Cantaber' is derived from Cantabria which, as in Roman times, is still the name for a region in north-west Spain (Birley 1979, 76).

One apparent example of a centurion with a fascinating personal history is Statilius Solon, whose name was recorded on a stone which was found three hundred years ago and then lost (Fig. 3). He is almost certainly the man who, before military service, joined a delegation from his city of Heraclea to the oracle of Apollo at Claros in south-eastern Turkey (Jones 2005, 296). This was the oracle which later ordered dedications to the gods and goddesses, probably to avert the spread of a plague in the later second century AD. Two of the inscriptions incorporating these orders are known from the forts at Housesteads on Hadrian's Wall and at Ravenglass to the south of Hadrian's Wall on the coast of north-west England, further instances of the connectedness of the Roman Empire (*RIB* 1579; Tomlin 2019, 495). Solon later rose to become the chief centurion of the First Legion Adiutrix at Brigetio, a fortress in modern Hungary (Birley 1979, 75, 181).

CONSERVATION AND INTERPRETATION

A few stones bearing the names of centurions, or with crosses, numerals or phalluses, remain in the sections of the Wall where they were found. The largest number are visible in a 400m length to the east of the fort at Birdoswald. After this part of the Wall was exposed and consolidated in the late 1950s, the positions of the stones, which can be difficult to find, were marked by metal tags which have now all disappeared (Leach and Whitworth 2011, 113). A centurial stone found near the line of the Wall in the 1980s was placed in the wall of a farm building at Willowford where it is visible to visitors, together with an explanatory plaque.

Fig.2a RIB 1648: *coh(ortis) IIII c(enturia) Cla(udi)/ Cleonici*, 'of the fourth cohort, the century of Claudius Cleonicus (built this)'. Found before 1873 between Housesteads and Cawfields (Wall miles 37–42). 36.8cm by 20cm. Location: Chesters Museum. After Bruce 1875, 213.

图 2a RIB 1648: coh(ortis) IIII c(enturia) Cla(udi)/ Cleonici，"第四大队，百夫长Claudius Cleonicus（建造）"。1873年前发现于豪塞斯特兹要塞和考菲尔德之间（37至42区段）。36.8厘米乘 20 厘米。位于切斯特博物馆。

Fig.2b RIB 1568: *coh(ortis) I/ [centuria] Terenti Cantabr[i]*, 'of the first cohort, the century of Terentius Cantaber (built this)'. 40.6cm by 20.3cm. Found in 1892 built into a field wall and probably removed from the Wall in the vicinity of milecastle 33; now in the Great North Museum. Drawing: Anon. 1893.

图 2b RIB 1568: coh(ortis) I/ [centuria] Terenti Cantabr[i]，"第一大队，百夫长 Terentius Cantaber（建造）"。40.6 厘米乘 20.3厘米。1892 年发现于农田围墙内，很有可能来自附近33号里堡；现存大北方博物馆。阿依绘制，1893。

保护和阐释

有少量勒名石仍保留在发现它们的长城原址处，上面刻有百夫长名字，或还同时还刻有十字架，数字或阳具图案勒名石。其中集中可以看到的位于博得瓦德要塞东边400米长的一段城墙中。这段城墙在1950年代后期被发掘出来并加固，勒名石的位置较难辨认，当时使用金属牌来进行标记，然而这些标记如今已经全部消失（里奇和维特沃斯 2011,113）。20世纪80年代，一块百人队勒名石在长城附近维勒福德的一处农场中发现，该石料砌在农场建筑墙体上，游人可以看到，旁边设有指示牌，对勒名石进行阐释。

在几个世纪之前，当哈德良长城的部分墙体被发掘时，勒名石通常会拆走作为私人收藏或博物馆收藏品。几乎所有早期发现的勒名石现今主要存放或陈列在三个博物馆中：泰恩河畔纽卡斯尔大北方博物馆，切斯特博物馆，和卡莱尔的图利别墅博物馆。2000年，在长城最东端的沃森德要塞处树立起一座石质纪念碑，上面列出了所有勒名石上出现的百夫长的名字。

建筑勒名石的研究

教会牧师约翰·赫斯利奠定了系统研究哈德良长城的基础，他于1732 年去世。他的成就之一是描绘出一系列百人队石并认定这些勒名石的内容是修建记录。另一位对建筑石价值进行系统考古研究的是约翰·克雷顿（1883）。克雷顿驳斥了一些将勒名石意义过分夸大的观点，如认为它们用于土地分界等等，但是他未能意识到勒名石作为建筑记录的作用。约四十年后，R.G. 科林伍德（1926,86–7）重新对赫斯利的观点进行深入研究，依据勒名石在长城上发现时所在的位置，试图推断出分配给步兵大队和百人队负责建造的城墙长度，艾瑞克·伯利进一步发展了这一理论（1939）。

Fig.3 RIB 1439: *coh(ortis) VI/ c(enturia) Statil[i] Solonis*, 'of the sixth cohort, the century of Statilius Solon (built this)'. Found in or before 1725 near milecastle 25, now lost and known only from a drawing in Horsley's *Britannia Romana* (1732, 192, Northumberland XX).

图 3 RIB 1439: coh(ortis) VI/ c(enturia) Statil[i] Solonis，"第六大队，百夫长 Statilius Solon（建造）". 1725 年或之前发现于 25 号里堡附近，原物已遗失，绘图仅存于霍斯利的《罗马不列颠尼亚》（1732.192. 诺桑波兰 xx）一书中。

Fig.4 RIB 3407: *c(o)ho(rtis) V/ (centuria) G(elli) P(h)ilippi*, 'of the fifth cohort, the century of Gellius Philippus (built this)'. 35cm by 17cm. Found in 1986 when a field near Turret 48b was ploughed and built into the side of a barn overlooking the Wall (© Humphrey Welfare).

图 4 RIB 3407: c(o)ho(rtis) V/(centuria) G(elli) P(h)ilippi，"第五大队，百夫长Gellius Philippus（建造）"。35 厘米乘 17 厘米。1986 年发现于 46b 号塔楼附近的耕种的农田里，并砌入于长城相隔不远的谷仓内。

When parts of the Wall were exposed in earlier centuries, the inscribed stones were usually removed and placed in private or museum collections. Almost all of these earlier discoveries are now displayed or are in the stores of three major museums: the Great North Museum at Newcastle upon Tyne, Chesters Museum, and the Tullie House Museum at Carlisle. At the fort of Wallsend, at the eastern terminus of the Wall, a stone monument was erected in 2000 which lists the names of all the centurions known from the building stones.

RESEARCH ON THE BUILDING STONES

The foundations for the systematic study of Hadrian's Wall were laid by John Horsley, a minister of religion who died in 1732. One of his many achievements was to illustrate a series of centurial stones and to recognise that they were building records (1732, 127). The next extensive archaeological discussion of the significance of the building stones was by John Clayton (1883). Clayton rebutted some extravagant theories about the significance of the stones, for example that they were to do with land divisions, but he failed to register their significance as building records. Some forty years later, R. G. Collingwood (1926, 86–7) returned to Horsley's views and attempted to deduce the work-lengths allocated to the cohorts and centuries, relying on the positions where the building stones had been recorded. This line of reasoning was developed further by Eric Birley (1939).

C.E. 史蒂文斯开展了对长城修建规划设计的系统且细致的研究（1966），这些研究大部分基于建筑勒名石提供的证据。他的主要研究成果仍有其价值，但是其中阐释的细节从未获得认可。《不列颠的罗马勒名》(RIB) 第一卷在 1965 年发表，包括了所有在1954年之前发现的建筑勒名石；新的一卷于 2009 年出版，包含了2006年之前的所有发现。此后，仅有两次新发现。这些综合性的出版物为其他学者开展相关研究提供了便利条件，但任务仍然十分艰巨。虽然布里兹和多布森（2000）等其他人所著的若干权威文献对建筑勒名石有所涉及，但勒名石对理解长城修建的潜在贡献还仍有待深入发掘。例如，近期发现了新的证据有助于证明分配给百人队建造的长城段落长度。（霍格森 2017,58; 彼得维尔 2018, 30-1）。

致谢

我非常感谢比尔·格里菲斯和汉佛瑞·维尔法为我推荐了这个中英合作的潜在机会，尤其感谢汉佛瑞在金山岭研讨会上代为陈述我的论文，并为本文和图例提出若干宝贵建议。

References
参考文献

Anon. 1893. 'Donation to the museum', *Proceedings of the Society of Antiquaries of Newcastle upon Tyne, 2nd series* 5, 227.

阿依. 1893. 向博物馆捐赠，见于纽卡斯尔文物考古学会论文集（系列二）, 5, 227.

Bidwell, P. 2018. *Hadrian's Wall at Wallsend*, Arbeia Society Roman Archaeological Studies 1, South Shields.

P·比得维尔. 2018. 沃森德的哈德良长城，见于阿尔比亚学会罗马考古研究1. 南希尔德.

Birley, A. R. 1979. *The People of Roman Britain*, London.

A . R · 伯利. 1979. 罗马不列颠行省的人民 . 伦敦.

Birley, E. 1939. 'Building-records from Hadrian's Wall', *Archaeologia Aeliana,* 3rd series, 16, 219–36.

E·伯利. 1939. 哈德良长城的建造记录，见于纽卡斯尔考古（系列三）, 16, 219-36.

Breeze, D. J. and Dobson, B. 2000. *Hadrian's Wall* (fourth edn), Harmondsworth.

D·布雷兹，B·多布森. 2000. 哈德良长城（第四版）. 哈默兹沃斯.

Bruce, J. C. 1975. *Lapidarium Septentrionale*, London.

J . C · 布鲁斯. 1975. 北石首鱼 . 伦敦.

Clayton, J. 1883. 'Observations on centurial stones found on the Roman Wall, Northumberland and Cumberland', *Archaeologia Aeliana,* 2nd series, 9, 22–39.

J·克雷顿. 1883. 对罗马长城中发现的百人队石的观察，诺桑波兰和坎布里亚地区，见于纽卡斯尔考古（系列二）, 9, 22-39 .

Collingwood, R. G. 1926. 'Roman inscriptions and sculptures belonging to the Society of Antiquaries of Newcastle upon Tyne', *Archaeologia Aeliana,* 3rd series, 2, 52–124.

R . G · 科林伍德. 1926. 纽卡斯尔考古协会的罗马勒名石和雕塑，见于纽卡斯尔考古（系列三）, 2, 52-124.

DeLaine, J. 2002. 'The Temple of Hadrian at Cyzicus and Roman attitudes to exceptional construction,' *Papers of the British School at Rome,* 70, 205-230.

J · 德林. 2002. 基齐库司的哈德良神庙和罗马人对杰出建筑的态度，见于罗马英国学院论文集，70，205-230.

Ambitious and very elaborate studies of the building programme were undertaken by C. E. Stevens (1966) which were largely based on the evidence of the building stones. Much of his work is still of value, but the details of his interpretation have never gained acceptance. It appeared shortly after the publication of the first volume of *Roman Inscriptions of Britain* (*RIB*) in 1965 which included all the building stones found before the end of 1954; a further volume that appeared in 2009 included finds made before the end of 2006, and since then there have been only two new discoveries. These comprehensive publications would make the sort of study which Stevens pursued easier, but it would still be a formidable task. Although standard works such as Breeze and Dobson's (2000) have paid due attention to the building stones, their potential contribution to understanding the construction programme has yet to be exploited fully. One recent development which should prove useful is the emergence of further evidence for the size of the lengths allocated to the centuries (Hodgson 2017, 58; Bidwell 2018, 30–1).

ACKNOWLEDGEMENTS

I am grateful to Bill Griffiths and Humphrey Welfare for information about the potential UK-China project, and to the latter for presenting my paper at the meeting in Jinshanling, for helpful comments on its content and for some of the illustrations.

Hodgson, N. 2017. *Hadrian's Wall. Archaeology and History at the Limit of Rome's Empire*, Marlborough.

N·霍奇森 . 2017. 哈德良长城. 罗马帝国边缘的考古和历史. 马布尔.

Horsley, J. 1732. *Britannia Romana*, London.

J·霍斯利. 1732. 罗马不列颠尼亚. 伦敦.

Jones, C. P. 2005. 'Ten dedications "To the gods and goddesses" and the Antonine plague', *Journal of Roman Archaeology*, 18, 293–301.

C . P·琼斯 . 2005. 供奉众神的十件祭品和安东尼瘟疫. 罗马考古， 18, 293-301.

Leach, S. and Whitworth, A. 2011. *Saving the Wall. The Conservation of Hadrian's Wall 1746–1987*, Stroud.

S·里奇， A·维斯沃斯 . 2011. 保全长城， 见于哈德良长城的保护， 1746-1987. 斯特拉德.

RIB Collingwood, R. G., and Wright, R. P., 1965. *The Roman Inscriptions of Britain. I, Inscriptions on Stone*, Oxford; Tomlin, R. S. O., Wright, R. P., and Hassall, M. W. C., 2009. *The Roman Inscriptions of Britain. III, Inscriptions on Stone*, Oxford.

R . G·科林伍德， R . P·怀特. 1965. 不列颠的罗马勒名石. I， 勒名石， 牛津； R . S . O·汤姆林， R . P·怀特， M . W . C·汉森尔. 2009. 不列颠的罗马石刻. III， 勒名石， 牛津.

Stevens, C. E. 1966. *The Building of Hadrian's Wall*, Cumberland and Westmorland Antiquarian and Archaeological Society, Extra Series, 20, Kenda.l

C . E·斯蒂文斯. 1966. 建造哈德良长城， 坎步兰和维斯特摩兰文物考古会 （ 增补系列 ）, 20. 肯德尔.

Tomlin, R. S. O. 2019. 'Roman Britain in 2018. III. Inscriptions', *Britannia*. 50, 496–524.

R . S . O·汤姆林. 2019. 罗马不列颠 2018. III. 石刻， 50, 496-524. 不列颠尼亚.

Chapter 3:

Survey and Monitoring Technologies

Aerial photograph of Housesteads Roman Fort, taken as part of Historic England's areal mapping of Hadrian's Wall, 27th March 2012 (© Historic England Archive).

豪塞斯特兹罗马要塞航拍，英格兰遗产委员会实施的哈德良长城航拍测绘成果之一, 2012 年 3 月 27日（© 英格兰遗产委员会档案）。

第三单元

长城调查与监测技术

The horse faces on the Wall, Shuozhou, Shanxi (photograph by the Great Wall Resource Survey Shanxi Team I).

墙体与马面，山西朔州（图片来源：山西长城资源调查一队）。

3.1 长城资源调查与明长城的基本构成

柴晓明
中国文化遗产研究院—中国—北京

摘要

2005 年国家文物局启动全国长城资源调查，经过 5 年的调查和测绘，全面掌握了长城的规模、分布、构成、走向及其时代，保护与管理现状，人文与自然环境等基础资料。调查资料显示，明长城分布在中国北部 10 个省（自治区、直辖市）的 202 个县域，在中国历代长城中体系中最完备、保存现状最好，丰富的遗存、因地制宜的构筑方式和布局为我们呈现了以墙体（包括山险、河险等）为纽带，各类关隘、烽燧等设施紧密结合的绵延万里的军事防御工程。

关键字： 长城　全国长城资源调查　防御体系

一、 长城考古调查

横亘在中国大地上的长城遗迹以其绵延万里的规模、古老的修筑历史在历史长河中熠熠生辉，世人对它的兴趣更是由来已久。许多人、许多机构对其做过许多不同形式、不同程度的调查、研究。例如，在中国开展的三次全国性不可移动文物普查就曾对历代长城进行过调查。上世纪 80 年代前后，部分省份对当地长城进行过较为简单的实地调查。这些调查使我们对历代长城的走向、分布、保存状况有了初步的了解，但中国长城究竟有多长，长城的构成是什么等长城的家底依旧不清。

（一）全国长城资源调查

2004 年 5 月，国家文物局在征询国家发展改革、公安、财政、国土、建设、交通、环保、旅游等有关方面和专家意见的基础上，正式编制并向国务院报送了《“长城保护工程”总体工作方案》。其中，以“通过科学调查，全面准确掌握长城现存状况”为目的的长城资源调查工作被列为“长城保护工程”的首项内容。与之前区域性、非专项的调查相比，此次长城资源调查是针对长城的全国性专项调查，具有一定的开创性。开创一，国家统筹规划部署，地方及相关专业机构通力配合。这次调查由国家文物主管部门统一组织并得到了国家财政、测绘等部门的强力支撑与保障。尤其是，国家文物局和国家测绘局首次跨部门合作，联合成立调查专门机构。开创二，制度规范，标准先行。对整个工作进行整体设计的同时，对名称、时代、保存现状，调查、测量方法等关键环节、关键业务和技术也制定了《长城资源调查名称使用规范》、《长城资源调查文物编码规则》、《长城资源保存程度评价标准》等具体的技术标准和工作规范。开创三，多学科合作，大量引入现代科技手段。除了传统考古学调查方法之外，此次调查还充分利用了现代测绘技术对长城进行立体量测。同时，为确保考古田野调查数据质量和方便调查资料的后续使用，还应用现代计算机技术专门设计研发了长城田野调查数据采集、检查与汇交系统。

3.1 GREAT WALL RESOURCE SURVEY AND BASIC COMPONENTS OF THE MING GREAT WALL

CHAI XIAOMING
Chinese Academy of Cultural Heritage - China - Beijing

Abstract

In 2005, the Great Wall Resource Survey was launched by the State Administration for Cultural Heritage (SACH). After five years of survey and mapping, baseline data was collected regarding the scale, distribution, composition, delineation, chronology, protection and management status of the Great Wall, and the surrounding human and natural environment. According to the Survey, the Ming Great Wall was distributed in 202 counties of 10 provinces, autonomous regions, and direct municipalities in northern China; this is the most complete and best-preserved military defence system among all the Great Walls across different dynasties. Stretching for thousands of kilometres, it has rich heritage sites with walls and ancillary facilities, including a variety of strategic passes and towers, and its construction varied in its different landscape settings.

Keywords: Great Wall, Great Wall Resource Survey, defence system

ARCHAEOLOGICAL SURVEY OF THE GREAT WALL

The heritage of the Great Wall has been a bright shining star and has drawn long-lasting interest from people with its vast scale and long construction history. Prior to 2005 many people and institutions had conducted various surveys and researches about it in different forms and with different scope. For example, there had been three nation-wide immovable cultural relics surveys in China that investigated the Great Walls of different dynasties. Around the 1980s, some provinces conducted simple field surveys on their local sections of the Great Wall. These surveys provided a basic understanding of the delineation, distribution, and condition of the Great Wall. However, other basic information, including how long the Great Wall is, or what the Great Wall comprises, remained unclear.

The National Great Wall Resource Survey

In May 2004, after consulting national organisations, including the National Development and Reform Commission, the Ministries of Public Security, Finance, Land and Resources, Construction, Transport, Ecology and Environment, Tourism, as well as many experts, SACH compiled and submitted an Overall Working Plan of the Great Wall Conservation Programme to the State Council. In this plan, the top priority was to conduct the Great Wall Resource Survey (GWRS) which aimed to 'comprehensively understand the current condition of the Great Wall through scientific research (SACH, 2004).' Compared to the previous regional, unsystematic surveys, the GWRS specifically focused on the Great Wall across the country, which was ground-breaking and innovative.

First, it was planned, designed, organised and initiated by the central government, and implemented by the local governments and relevant professional institutions. This survey was managed by the national cultural heritage authorities and supported by other national organisations, including the Ministry of Finance and the State Bureau of Surveying and Mapping (SBSM). In particular, it was the first time that SACH and SBSM had worked across departments and jointly established an organization to oversee the survey. Secondly, principles were stipulated and standards were unified before the work took place. While developing an overall plan for the whole

（二）调查成果

2006–2011年，通过近5年的田野调查，全国长城资源调查获得了丰硕的成果。

厘清了长城资源的分布范围及其具体位置。本次长城资源调查共涉及黑龙江、吉林、辽宁、河北、北京、天津、山西、内蒙古、宁夏、陕西、甘肃、青海、新疆、山东、河南、湖北等16个省（自治区、直辖市），除了湖北省因“楚长城”的性质、年代等分歧较大未获认定外，国家文物局认定长城资源分布于上述除湖北省以外的15个省（自治区、直辖市）的404县域。

明确了长城资源的具体构成与数量。根据《长城资源调查名称使用规范》、《长城资源调查登记表及著录说明》等的规定，本次长城资源调查按照长城墙体（壕堑/界壕）、附属设施、相关遗存等对长城资源各个构成部分进行分类调查记录。

系统了解、掌握了长城资源保护管理现状。此次除了长城本体之外，还对长城公布为各级文物保护单位、保护管理机构的设置、保护范围和建设控制地带的划定、保护标志的设立等长城保护管理状况进行了摸底。

二、明长城防御体系

明长城防御体系在中国历代长城中体系最完备、保存现状最好。明长城的修建几乎贯穿明朝始终，是根据明朝北方军事形势不断变化的情况逐渐完善与整合形成的。

目前，我们所能看到的明长城防御体系表现为以连续、不封闭的高墙为主体，并与关隘、城堡、敌台、烽燧等设施紧密结合的长达数百至数千千米的军事防御工程。墙体无疑是这个防御体系最主要的构成部分，墙体之上有敌台、马面、铺房等建筑以增强墙体的防御功能。墙体之外则由关堡作为整个防御体系的军事指挥中心，烽火台与关堡、墙体相配合形成长城的信息传递系统，除此之外还包括挡马墙、品字窖、壕沟等具有防御功能的相关设施，这些丰富的遗存一起构成了长城整个军事防御体系，属于长城文物的本体部分。长城资源调查还调查、发现了采石场、砖瓦窑、戍卒墓、居住址、古驿站、刻石、碑刻等与长城防御体系相关的遗址遗迹（表1：长城资源调查分类表）。

（一）墙体

中国境内的明长城，分布于北纬42° 52′～35° 50′，东经124° 53～98° 09′的范围内，东起辽宁省丹东虎山西至甘肃省嘉峪关市，横跨辽宁、河北、天津、北京、内蒙古、山西、陕西、宁夏、甘肃等10个省（自治区、直辖市）的202个县域，穿越长白山脉、辽河平原、燕山山脉、太行山脉、永定河谷、阴山山脉、黄土高原、贺兰山脉、河西走廊、青藏高原等地理单元，大致呈东西走向。明长城并不是一道连贯的单线墙体。一方面，明长城防线由墙体与壕堑共同构成；另一方面，根据地形地貌的变化与山川、河流等自然地理要素的分布，常见分叉、并行、交汇、中断等现象，交点、断点极多，而两点之间连续的墙体段落长度 相差悬殊。短者仅数十米，长者可达数千千米。

国家地理信息中心提供的测绘数据显示，明长城总长度为8851.79千米。根据对自然地势的利用情况，可划分为人工墙体、人工与自然相结合的山险墙、自然险、壕堑四大类。人工墙体可根据建造材质的不同，分为土墙、石墙、砖墙；山险墙则利用自然山体、沟壑等，通过人工铲削、砌石或夯土修整形成；自然险可分为山险、河险两类；壕堑是指人工掘壕形成的防御屏障（图1）。

programme, a series of principles regarding technical specifications and working procedures were also formulated. These included: *the GWRS Specifications of Naming; the Resource Coding Principle of GWRS (SACH, 2007);* and *the Guidance of Evaluating Conditions of the Great Wall Resources.* These documents created technical criteria and working guidance for key procedures, practices and technologies for naming, dating, condition assessment, survey, and measuring methods in the Great Wall Resource Survey. Thirdly, multi-disciplinary cooperation and modern technologies were introduced. Apart from the traditional archaeological methods, this survey also intensively used modern mapping technology to measure the Great Wall in all its dimensions. At the same time, to ensure the data quality of the field archaeological research and easy access to that data in later studies, modern computer science technology was used to develop a system to collate, evaluate, and store the Great Wall Resource Survey data.

Results from the survey

The GWRS achieved great results after nearly five years of fieldwork and investigation from 2006 to 2011 (CACH, 2012; SACH, 2016). The distribution and location of most of the Great Wall are now clearly understood. The survey covered 16 provinces, autonomous regions and direct municipalities, including Heilongjiang, Jilin, Liaoning, Hebei, Beijing, Tianjin, Shanxi, Inner Mongolia, Ningxia, Shaanxi, Gansu, Qinghai, Xinjiang, Shandong, Henan, and Hubei. SACH has verified in 2012 that the Great Wall resources are distributed in 404 counties of 15 provinces, autonomous regions and direct municipalities, with Hubei Province excluded. This is due to the divergence of opinions among experts regarding the nature and date of remains found there which were suggested to be part of the Chu Great Wall.

The number and composition of the Great Wall resources have now also been identified. According to the *Naming Principles in the Great Wall Resource Survey* and *the Instruction for the Great Wall Resource Registration Form and Recording* and other regulations, the Great Wall resources were categorised into the wall (including trenches and the Trench Wall), auxiliary components and structures, fortified passes and forts, and ancillary components and structures. Each category was then researched and recorded (State Administration for Cultural Heritage 2007).[1]

The current situation of how the Great Wall resources are conserved and managed is now better understood. Apart from surveying the Great Wall resources, an investigation was also carried out to better understand: the Protected Units of Cultural Relics at different levels that are related to the Great Wall; the designated organizations for its management and protection; the demarcated boundaries of its protected and controlled areas; its protection signage and other aspects of management of the Great Wall.

THE MING GREAT WALL DEFENCE SYSTEM

The Ming Great Wall is the most comprehensive and best-preserved defence system among all the Great Walls built by different dynasties. The Ming Great Wall was under construction almost throughout the entire Ming dynasty, and was gradually refined and consolidated according to the changing military situation in the northern region.

From what we can see today, the Ming Great Wall defence system comprises stretches of continuous high walls, which are integrated with components including strategic passes, fortresses, defence towers, and beacon towers, and which stretches for thousands of kilometres. There is no doubt that the Wall itself is the most important part of this defence system. Components on the Wall, such as defence towers, horse faces, and sentry houses, were built to further strengthen the defence function of the Wall. Fortified passes and fortress are understood to have been the military command centres of the defence system. The fortified passes and fortresses, beacon towers, and the Wall itself, together formed an intelligence communication system. Additionally, other features such as horse walls,

1 The categorisations originally applied in the Great Wall Resources Survey were subsequently amended by SACH for the purpose of the Great Wall Resource Rectification in 2012, which can be found in the Glossary under the corresponding heading (Editors' note).

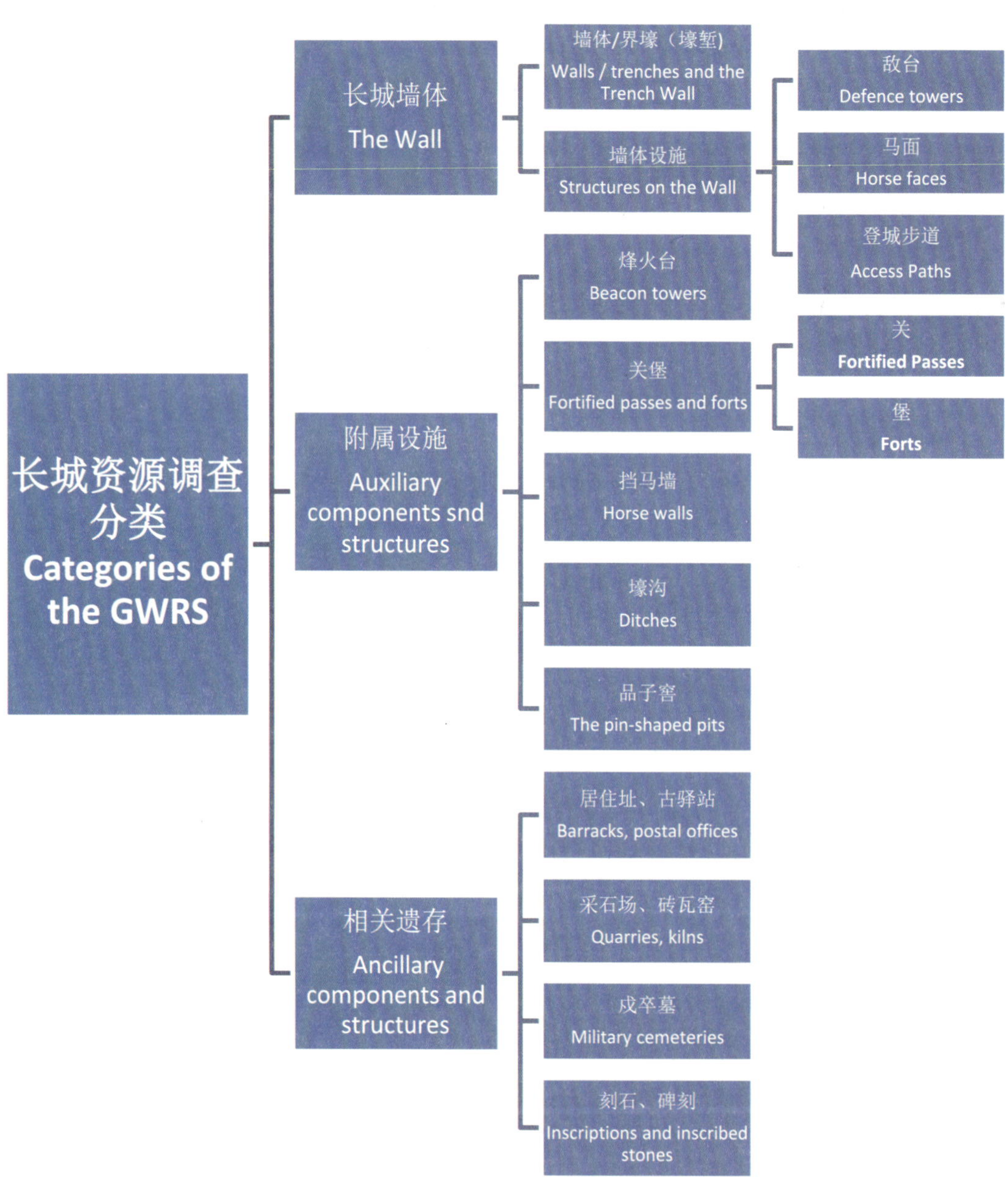

表1长城资源调查分类表。

Table 1. Categories of the Great Wall Resources Survey.

'pin-shaped' pits,[2] and ditches also served defence functions. All of the remains comprise the whole Great Wall defence system, and make up the major components of the Great Wall heritage site. The Great Wall Resource Survey also included ancillary components and structures related to the defence system, such as quarries, kilns for bricks and roof tiles, cemeteries, barracks, postal offices, inscriptions and inscribed stones, etc (Table 1).

The Wall itself

The Ming Great Wall is located in the range of 42°52′ to 35°50′ North and 124°53 to 98°09′ East. It starts in the East, west of Tiger Mountain, Liaoning Province and runs to Jiayuguan City, Gansu Province, in the West, covering 202 counties in 10 provinces, autonomous regions and direct municipalities, including: Liaoning, Hebei, Tianjin, Beijing, Inner Mongolia, Shanxi, Shaanxi, Ningxia, and Gansu. It also crosses multiple geographical areas including, primarily from east to west: the Changbai Mountains, the Liaohe River Plain, the Yan Mountains, the Taihang Mountains, Yongding River Valley, the Yin Mountains, the Loess Plateau, Helan Mountain, the Hexi Corridor, and the Tibetan Plateau. However, the Ming Great Wall is not a continuous linear built wall: firstly, it includes sections of trench wall; secondly, the length of different sections of continuous built wall can vary significantly since they had to be adapted to and integrated with the changing landscape, especially in places where rivers and mountains branch off or meet. The lengths of built wall can be as short as a few dozen meters or stretch for thousands of kilometres.

According to the National Geographic Information Centre, the total length of the Ming Great Wall is 8,852km. It can be classified into four categories according to how the Wall was integrated with the natural landscapes. These are: built walls; cut walls, created by cutting away sections of natural elements; natural barriers; and trenches. According to the use of different building materials, the built walls can be further divided into earth walls, stone walls, brick-clad walls. The cut wall was created by cutting away sections of hills or mountains, and then layering stones or rammed earth above the face created. The natural barriers comprise mountains and rivers which, together with the Wall, constitute a defensive barrier. The trench refers to a defensive system consisting of mounds and ditches. (Fig.1).

Earth walls were built on the flat land using rammed layers of yellow clay or sandy silt; some contained tree trunks, branches and reeds. Stone walls were built with stones that were worked into strip stones, blocks or flagstones, with mortar pointing. Some of the stone walls had cores of rubble and loess. Worked flagstones or coping stones were laid on the top of the wall. On both sides of the top of the wall were battlements, observation holes, and water gutters. Brick-clad walls were filled with rubble, rammed earth, or a mixture of earth and stones, and then covered with bricks, using worked strip stones or hewn stones as a base and mortar as pointing. Their upper surface was paved with black bricks, providing a pavement wide enough for soldiers to walk along with stairs on steeper stretches. On both sides of the top of the wall were battlement parapets, observation holes and drains, built of stones or bricks. In most sections, access to the top of the Wall was provided by a path leading up to concealed doors on the side of the Wall. Elsewhere, trench walls were built by digging a ditch and simply mounding up the spoil on one or both sides of the ditch. Sometimes, these mounds were rammed.

Fortified passes and fortresses

Along the Wall, many gates were provided to allow people and goods to pass through, where not only gates were installed but also forts with multiple military facilities were constructed for defence reinforcement. They are therefore referred to as fortified passes. These fortified passes were usually completed at the same time as

2 These pits were arranged in patterns similar to the Chinese character 品 pronounced 'pin' (Editors' note).

图 1 各类人工长城墙体。自左上图起顺时针依次为：（1）土筑墙—甘肃古浪县圆墩长城（摄影：胡红生）；（2）石墙—辽宁绥中鼓山长城 2 段（摄影：赵普光）；（3）包砖墙—河北阜宁县大帽山长城 7 段（摄影：赵克军）；（4）壕堑—青海省湟中县海马沟壕堑（摄影：张占仓）；（5）山险墙—陕西省神木县杨石畔山险墙（摄影：牛新龙）。

Fig.1 Types of man-made Walls. Clockwise from top left: (1) earth wall Yuandun GW in Gansu Gulang - photograph by Hu Hongsheng; (2) stone wall, the second section of Gushan GW in Liaoning Suizhong photograph by Zhao Puguang ; (3) brick-clad wall, the 7th section of Damaoshan GW in Hebei Funing - photograph by Zhao Kejun; (4) trench wall, Haimagou Trench Wall in Qinghai Huangzhong - photograph by Zhang Zhancang; (5) cut wall, Yangshipan Cut Wall in Shanxi Shenmu - photograph by Niu Xinlong.

the construction of the Wall was finished. They were usually attached to the Wall and provided the main crossing points. Fortified passes, of which 199 were identified during the Survey, also functioned as the central command points of the Great Wall; the military commanding officers were based in them, and from them they directed military deployments and operations.

Fortresses were also an important component of the Great Wall defence system, and were where the soldiers were garrisoned. During the Survey, many fortresses were found to have been damaged and were incomplete. Thus, some of their layouts and internal structures remain unknown. According to the different layout of fortified passes and fortresses, they can be categorised into four types: rectangular fortresses; circular fortresses; irregular-shaped fortresses; and unrecognizable-shaped fortresses. In total 1,081 fortresses were discovered during this survey (Fig.2).

Beacon towers

Beacon towers have many other common names, including: smoke tower, beacon mound, beacon watchtower, smoke platform, smoke signal platform, and smoke signal mound. They are an important component of the Ming Great Wall defence system. A signal was sent by lighting a fire on the top of the tower, creating smoke. Beacon towers are usually located alongside, or along lines into the interior or into the exterior of the Great Wall, and are independent structures linked to it; 8,817 beacon towers were identified along the Ming Great Wall during the Survey. The beacon towers were built with similar materials and techniques as the rest of the Ming Great Wall structures in their region. Based on the building materials used, the towers can be categorised into earth-built, stone-built and brick-built. These beacon towers can also be divided into two types: standalone beacon towers and beacon towers with associated facilities. Most of the beacon towers are standalone ones (Fig.3), whereas some beacon towers have some associated facilities, e.g. a ditched enclosure, attached watchtowers, or accommodation. (Fig.4)

Other auxiliary components and structures

Other auxiliary components and structures in the Ming Great Wall defence system include horse walls, pin-shaped pits, and ditches. Horse walls are also called 'horse stoppers', 'sheep walls', 'minor walls', or 'minor great walls'. They run parallel to the main Great Wall or the ditch, and were built to the exterior of the Great Wall. They were usually built on a gentle slope to increase the defence capability of the Great Wall itself and were used to prevent the cavalry attacks; 83 sections of horse wall were discovered in this Survey, distributed from the east of Liaoning Province to Shanxi Province. Many of them were built with local materials. Due to their wide distribution, the building materials and technique vary. The pin-shaped pits are also called 'horse trap pits' and were located to the exterior of the wall for defensive purposes. Two pin-shaped pits were discovered in this Survey, located in Liaoning Province and Ningxia Hui Autonomous Region. The ditch was a deep man-made trench along the Ming Great Wall defensive line to stop enemy advance; 36 sections of ditch were identified during the Survey. (Fig.5).

CONCLUSION

The building of the Ming Great Wall started in 1368 in the reign of the Emperor Hongwu when general Xu Da started to repair and build Juyongguan Pass and many other strategic passes. The construction of the Great Wall hardly ceased during the 276 years rule of the Ming dynasty. The Great Wall as an important military defence system was a highly regarded achievement of the dynasty. The scale and extent of the construction of the Great Wall at this time represented its historical peak. In particular, the 'Nine *Bian*' defensive command mechanism was established in the Ming Dynasty, and consequently, the principles of operation and construction of the Wall through regional commanders, were also formulated. The entire extent of the Ming Great Wall, of all periods, was covered by the Great Wall Resource Survey. From this Survey, we have a clear understanding of the Ming Great

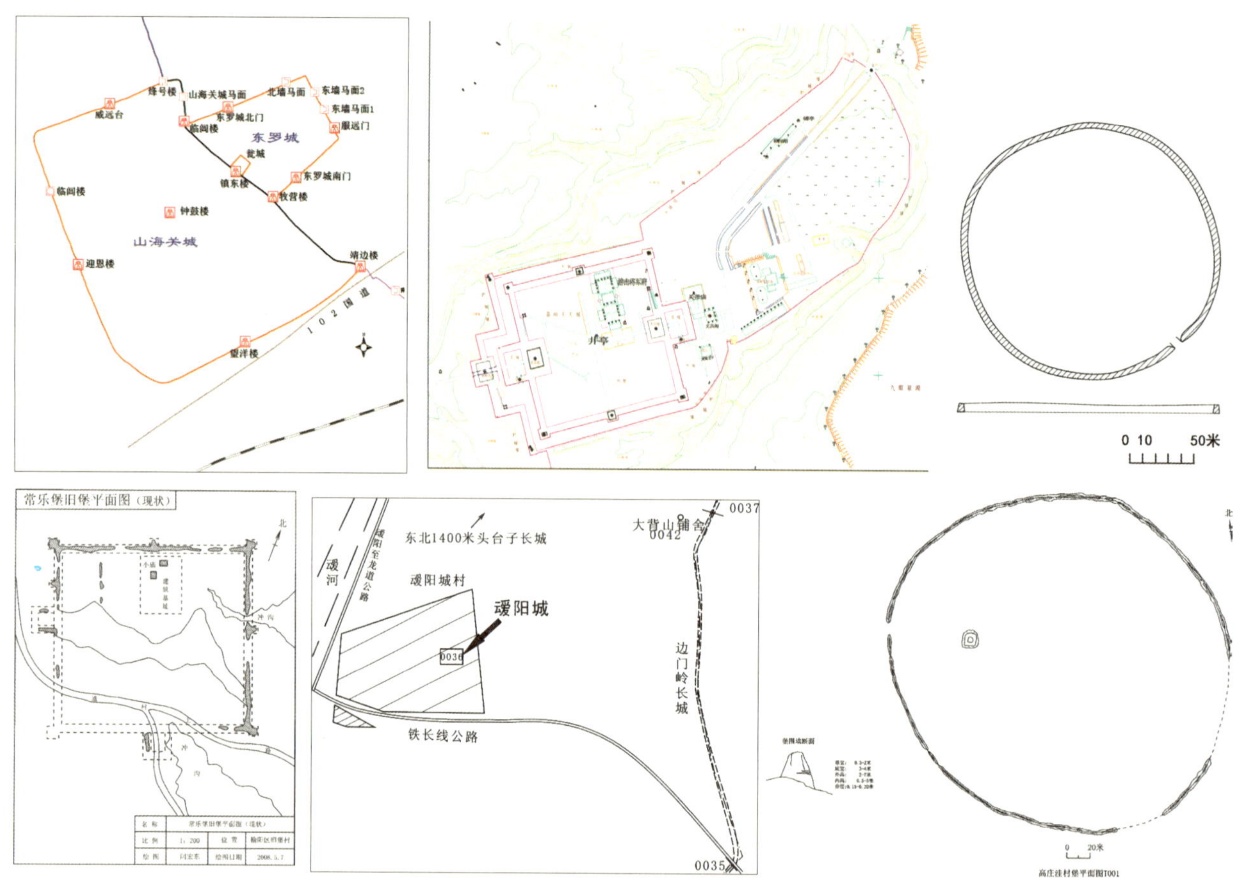

图 2 关堡类型示意图。自左上起顺时针依次为：（1）矩形关—河北省秦皇岛市山海关区山海关（绘图：河北省长城资源调查队）；（2）不规则形关—甘肃省嘉峪关市嘉峪关（绘图：甘肃省长城资源调查队）；（3）圆形关—山西省忻州市繁峙县团城口关（绘图：张永正）；（4）圆形堡—陕西省榆林市定边县高庄洼堡（绘图：王春波）；（5）不规则形堡—辽宁省丹东市凤城市叆阳城（绘图：辽宁省长城资源调查队）；（6）矩形堡—陕西省榆林市榆阳区常乐旧堡（绘图：闫宏东）。

Fig.2 Types of Fortified Passes and Fortresses. Clockwise from top left: (1) rectangular fortified pass, Shanhaiguan Pass in Hebei Qinghhangdao Shanhaiguan - drawn by Hebei GW Survey Team; (2) irregular-shaped fortified pass, Jiayugaun Pass in Gansu Jiayugaun - drawn by Gansu GW Survey Team; (3) circular fortified pass, Tuanchengkou Pass in Shanxi Fansi - drawn by Zhang Yongzheng; (4) circular fortress, Gaozhuangwa Port Fortress in Shanxi Yulin Dingbian - drawn by Wang Chunbo; (5) irregular shaped fortress, Aiyang Port Fortress in Liaoning Dandong Fengcheng - drawn by Liaoning GW Survey Team; (6) rectangular fortress, Old Changle Port Fortress in Shanxi Yulin Yuyang - drawn by Yan Hongdong .

土筑墙，即在平地上用黄粘土、砂土版筑或夯筑。部分墙体内部直接夹杂树干、树枝、芦苇等。石墙，指利用经过人工修整或挑选的石条、石块或石片垒砌而成的墙体，白灰勾缝。部分墙体内部填充碎石、黄土，墙顶片石铺墁。顶部两侧有分别建有垛口墙、女墙和瞭望孔、排水沟等设施。包砖墙，即人工切割的条石或略经打制的毛石砌基，碎石、夯土或土石混筑墙芯，外包砖，白灰浆勾缝。顶面较宽、平坦，部分地段呈阶梯状，可行人马，海墁青砖。顶部有石砌或砖砌垛口墙、女墙、瞭望孔、排水沟等设施，大部分有登城步道、暗门。壕堑，其修建方式是先在平地上挖掘深沟，后将挖出的土简单夯筑或堆筑于壕沟的一侧或两侧。

图 3 单体型烽火台。自上左图顺时针依次为：（1）土筑方形—甘肃临泽县板桥墩（烽火台）东壁（东–西）（摄影：李海涛）；（2）土筑圆形—内蒙清水河县腰2号烽火台（南–北）（摄影：冯吉祥）；（3）石砌圆形—辽宁绥中县顺山堡峰火台西侧全貌（西–东）（摄影：赵普广）；（4）包砖圆形—辽宁黑山县江台北山烽火台北侧（北–南）（摄影：郭东升）；（5）包砖方形—北京密云区密云038号烽火台南面（南–北）（摄影：王化明）；（6）石砌方形—山西平鲁区西虎儿界村烽火台侧面全景（西北–东南）（摄影：刘岩）。

Fig.3 Stand-alone beacon towers. Clockwise from top left: (1) earth built rectangular, east wall of Banqiao Beacon Tower in Gansu Linze (E to W) - photograph by Li Haitao ; (2) earth built circular, No.2 Yaozha Beacon Tower in Inner Mongolia Autonomous Region Qingshuihe (S to N) - photograph by Feng Jixiang; (3) stone built circular, West wall of Shunshan Beacon Tower in Liaoning Suizhong (W to E) - photograph by Zhao Puguang ; (4) brick-clad circular, north wall of Gangtai North Mountain Beacon Tower in Liaoning Heishan (N to S) - photograph by Guo Dongsheng; (5) brick-clad rectangular, south wall of the 38th Miyun Beacon in Beijing Miyun (S to N) - photograph by Wang Huaming; (6) stone built rectangular, Xihuerjiecun Beacon Tower in Shanxi Pinglu (NW to SE) - photograph by Liu Yan).

图 4 复合型烽火台。自上左起顺时针依次为：（1）带围墙的烽火台—山西河曲县船湾2号烽火台东北侧（摄影：郭银堂）；（2）带壕沟的烽火台—河北沽源县李家营南山02号烽火台北侧的壕沟与围墙 （西–东）（摄影：张守义）；（3）带房址的烽火台—甘肃甘州区红泉6号烽火台东南侧10米处地窝 （西–东）（摄影：曹生奎）；（4）带附燧的烽火台—甘肃景泰县索桥堡烽火台东侧与5座燧体（东–西）（摄影：胡红生）。

Fig.4 Beacon towers with associated facilities. Clockwise from top left: (1) beacon tower with enclosure, No.2 Chuanwan Beacon Tower in Shanxi Hequ - photograph by Guo Yintang; (2) enclosure and ditch of beacon tower, on the north side of the second Lijiaying Beacon Tower in Hebei Guyuan (W to E) - photograph by Zhang Shouyi; (3) accommodation structure of beacon tower, the basement on the southeast side of the 6th Li Hongquan Beacon Tower in Gansu, Ganzhou (W to E) - photograph by Cao Shengkui; (4) watchtower with attached beacon towers, Suoqiaobao Beacon Tower and East subsidiary Tower in Gansu Jingtai - photograph Hu Hongsheng.

（二） 关堡

长城墙体是长城军事防御体系的主体，为了人员车马出入方便,长城上往往留下许多豁口，因防御需要，豁口处不仅设门，还要建设具有多种军方设施的城堡，称为“关”、“关城”或“口”，在此统称为关城。这些关城大多是在修建长城的同时完成的，它们的建设依托于墙体，是出入长城的通道。从功能上来说，关城肩负着指挥中枢的作用，关城内一般设有军事长官，是决策的发出地，起到总揽大局的作用。本次调查共发现关城 199 座。堡是军队驻扎的场所，是长城防御体系的重要组成部分。明长城资源调查中，大部分堡城已残破，其中一些内部格局不详。关、堡依平面制形的不同，可以分为矩形堡、圆形堡、不规则堡及形制不可辨堡四类。本次调查共发现堡城 1081 座（图 2：关堡类型示意图）。

图 5 长城相关遗存：山西宁武段残存挡马墙（摄影：山西长城资源调查队）（左）；山西朔城区利民堡长城东侧壕沟（摄影：山西长城资源调查队）（右上）；宁夏省盐池县品字形（摄影：宁夏长城资源调查队）（右下）。

Fig.5 Other auxiliary components and structures: horse wall in Shanxi Ningwu - photgraph by Shanxi GW Survey Team (left); Trench Wall, in Shanxi Shuocheng - photograph by Shanxi GW Survey Team (top right); pin-shaped pits in Ningxia Hui Autonomous Region Yanchi - photograph by Ningxia Hui Autonomous Region GW Survey Team (bottom right).

Wall defence system, including its location, components, and its current condition. Data gathered from the survey has provided us with important materials to understand the whole defence system. Based on these materials and on historical records, we will be able to develop a better understanding of the operational relationship between different components of the Ming Great Wall.

（三）烽火台

烽火台是明长城防御系统的重要组成部分，又有烽燧、墩台、烽堠、烟墩、狼烟台、狼烟墩等多种名称，其功能主要是通过台顶点燃的烟火，起到传递信息的作用。烽火台是依托墙体并独立于墙体之外的一种设施，基本沿长城墙体走向分布或向墙体内外延伸分布。明长城资源调查，统计长城沿线分布的烽火台总计 8817 座。明长城烽火台的构筑材料及建筑方法与同区域内的长城基本相同，依材质大体可以分为土、石、砖三种。各类材质的烽火台又可按照设施构成分为单体和带附属设施两类，大多数为单体建筑，有一定数量复合型烽火台，即与围墙（壕沟）、附燧、居住址等设施共存（图 3：单体型烽火台）（图 4：复合型烽火台）。

（四）其他相关遗存

明长城防御体系的其他防御设施主要包括挡马墙、品字窖、壕沟。挡马墙又名拦马墙、羊马垣、副墙、小长城，是平行于主体长城或护城壕，构筑在长城墙体一侧的短墙。一般建在缓坡处，以便增强长城墙体的防御能力，防止敌方骑兵利用平缓的地形冲上长城。此次调查共发现明长城 83 段挡马墙，从辽东直至山西都有分布，建筑材料多就地取材，因地域广泛，材质便有所差异，垒筑方式也有所不同。品字窖，又名“陷马坑”，是设在墙体外侧用于防卫的陷井，一般呈品字形分布。此次调查中共发现两处品字窖，分别位于辽宁省和宁夏回族自治区。明长城壕沟是用于阻敌的人工挖掘的深沟，共发现 36 条（图 5：长城相关遗存）。

三、结论

明王朝从朱元璋洪武元年（1368 年），大将军徐达修缮居庸关等处关隘开始，明朝 276 年的统治中，对长城的修建几乎没有停止，长城作为军事防御的重要手段在明代倍受推崇，无论在规模还是修建次数上均达到了历史顶峰。尤其是，在明代形成的“九边”分区防守，形成了分段管理和修筑长城的制度。全国明长城资源调查覆盖了历史时期明代长城修筑的全部区域。通过此次调查，我们对明代长城防御体系的分布、构成、保存现状等有了比较清晰的认识，调查所获得的资料为我们复原当时的防御体系提供了重要的资料，通过对这些调查资料与历史文献相结合，明长城各个组成部分的相互作用机理将会得到更加清楚的认识。

参考文献
References

CACH, *The Great Wall Verification Work Completed*, the Cultural Relics News, 2012-06-06

中国文化遗产研究院. 2012. 长城认定工作完成. 中国文物报, 2012-06-06.

The State Administration for Cultural Heritage. 2004. *Overall Working Plan of the Great Wall Conservation Programme (2005-20140*, Beijing.

国家文物局. 2004. 长城保护项目总体工作计划（2005-2014). 北京.

The State Administration for Cultural Heritage. 2007.*The Great Wall Resource Survey Handbook*, Beijing.

国家文物局. 2007. 长城资源调查工作手册. 北京.

The State Administration for Cultural Heritage. 2016. The China Great Wall Conservation Report. http://www.ncha.gov.cn/art/2016/11/30/art_722_135294.html

国家文物局. 2016. 中国长城保护报告. http://www.ncha.gov.cn/art/2016/11/30/art_722_135294.html

3.2 明代长城烽火台的类型与分布–以辽东镇长城为例

刘文艳
中国文化遗产研究院—中国—北京

摘要

烽火台是明代长城防御体系的重要组成部分。辽东镇位于明代九边的最东端，烽火台数量较多，类型丰富。本文通过对长城资源调查中获取的辽宁长城烽火台资料进行系统整理，分析辽东镇烽火台的类型与分布特点。

关键字：烽火台　辽东镇　形制　类型　分布

绪论

明代在北部地区设置9个军事管理区，称为"九边"或"九镇"。辽东镇设立于明洪武年间，是明成祖为加强北京的防御在东北方向设立的军镇，以防御北方的草原游牧地域的地方势力，兼防居于东北的民族政权—女真各部，地域约相当于现在辽宁省大部。

烽火台作为传递军情的设施，很早就已出现，汉代称烽燧、烽堠，明代又称作烟墩、墩台。作为长城防御体系的有机组成部分，多建于长城内、外的高山顶、易于瞭望的岗阜或道路折转处,与墙体、敌台、关堡等设施遥相呼应。《明史》载，绵延千余里的高大边墙就有烽堆三万余处，烽火台上"广积粮草，昼夜轮流看望。遇有急警，昼则举烟，夜则举火，接通情报"。

一、明长城烽火台概述

据明长城资源调查，长城沿线分布的烽火台总计8817座。其中，能辨出原始形制的共有4984座。

从类型来看，明长城烽火台的构筑材料及建筑方法与同区域内的长城墙体基本相同，依材质大体可以分为土、石、砖三种。从形制来看，现在可见的烽火台大多为独体建筑，同时也有一定数量的烽火台台体与围墙（壕沟）、附燧、居住址等其他设施组合，构成复合型烽火台（表1：烽火台类型划分一览表）。

从分布特点来看，烽火台作为长城防御体系的有机组成部分，与墙体、敌台、关堡等设施遥相呼应，其中70％的烽火台分布在明长城墙体内侧，呈线状与墙体平行；或以烽燧线的形式与墙体交叉；另外还有一定数量的烽火台围绕关堡呈群状分布。

辽东镇明代烽火台自东向西分布在振安区、宽甸满族自治县、凤城市、本溪满族自治县、兴城市、绥中县等45个县（市、区），共计1200余座。

按照类型和分布分述如下：

3.2 THE TYPOLOGY AND DISTRIBUTION OF MING BEACON TOWERS: EXAMPLES IN LIAODONG ZHEN

LIU WENYAN
Chinese Academy of Cultural Heritage - China - Beijing

Abstract

Beacon towers play a significant role in the Great Wall defence system in the Ming dynasty. Liaodong Zhen was the easternmost of the nine zhen, or frontier military administrative regions, and had the largest number of beacon towers with the richest variety of forms. This paper presents a systematic review of the beacon towers in Liaoning province based on information from the Great Wall Resource Survey before analysing the typology and distribution of these towers.

Keywords: Beacon towers, Liaodong *Zhen*, design, typology, distribution

INTRODUCTION

The Ming regime (1368-1644) set up nine military administrative regions across the north of the Empire, referred to as the nine *bian* or the nine *zhen*. Liaodong *Zhen* was created during the reign of the Emperor Hongwu (1328-1398, ruled 1368-1398) to reinforce the north-eastern defence of Beijing against the nomadic tribes who had set up a regime that covered the majority of modern Liaoning Province.

Beacon towers had been used for many centuries as a method of sending military signals. They were called *fengsui* or *fenghou* in the Han dynasty. In the Ming dynasty, they were referred to as *yandun* or *duntai*. As part of the Wall defence system, beacon towers were primarily built on peaks on both sides of the Wall, at points on hills with good lines of sight or at significant bends in roads, visually interlinking with each other and with the Wall, defence towers and forts. According to *The History of Ming*,[1] there were over 30,000 beacon towers along the thousands of miles of the Wall. These towers were required to 'be stocked with loads of food and guarded day and night. In a military emergency, smoke will be lit in the day and fire in the night to pass on signals of danger'.

AN OVERVIEW OF THE BEACON TOWERS ON THE MING WALL

The Great Wall Resource Survey shows there are 8,817 beacon towers remaining along the Ming Great Wall. The original designs of 4,984 towers are still recognisable.

Typologically, the beacon towers share roughly the same building materials, i.e. earth, stone or brick, and forms of construction as those of the Wall in the same area. Most of the visible beacon towers were designed to be free-standing, while a considerable number of them were grouped with auxiliary beacons and living quarters and surrounded by a wall and ditch, to form a beacon compound (Tab.1.).

Beacon towers, as part of the Wall defence system, were located in relation to the Wall, towers and forts. Seventy

1 *The History of Ming* is one of the official Chinese historical works known as the *Twenty-Four Histories*. It consists of 332 volumes and covers the history of the Ming Dynasty from 1368 to 1644. The book was edited by Zhang Tingyu (1672-1755) first published in 1739 (Editors' note).

二、辽东镇烽火台的类型

表1：明长城烽火台类型划分一览表

Table 1. Typology of the beacon towers of the Ming Great Wall

Principal Material 类	Type型	Sub-type亚型	Style式
I.Earth I: 土	IA. Free-standing IA：单体	IAa. Square IAa：单体方形	※IAa1. Rammed earth ※IAa1型：夯筑
			IAa2. Adobe bricks IAa2型： 土坯垒砌
		※IAb. Round ※IAb型：单体圆形	—
	IB. With ancillary features IB：带附属设施	IBa. With a wall and ditch IBa～带围墙（壕沟）	—
		IBb. With auxiliary beacons IBb～带附燧	—
		IBc. With accommodation IBc～带居住设施	—
		IBd. With a wall and ditch + auxiliary beacons IBd～围墙（壕沟）+附燧	—
		IBe. With a wall and ditch + accommodation IBe～围墙（壕沟）+居住设施	—
		IBf. With auxiliary beacons + accommodation IBf～附燧+居住设施	—
II. Stone II：石	IIA. Free-standing IIA：单体	IIAa. Square IIAa：单体方形	※IIAa1. Stone clad ※IIAa1型：包石
			※IIAa2. Solid stone ※IIAa2型：垒砌
		IIAb. Round IIAb：单体圆形	※IIAb1. Stone clad ※IIAb1型：包石
			※IIAb2. Solid stone ※IIAb2型：垒砌
	IIB. With ancillary features IIB：带附属设施	※IIBa. With a wall and ditch ※IIBa～带围墙（壕沟）	—
		IIBb. With auxiliary beacons IIBb～带附燧	—
		IIbc. With accommodation IIBc～带居住设施	—
		IIBd. With a wall and ditch + additional beacons IIBd～围墙（壕沟）+附燧	—
		IIBe. With auxiliary beacons + accommodation IIBe～附燧+居住设施	—
III. Brick III：砖	IIIA. Free-standing IIIA： 单体	※IIIAa. Square ※IIIAa：单体方形	—
		※IIAb. Round ※IIIAb型：单体圆形	—
	※IIIB. With ancillary features ※IIIB：带附属设施	—	—

说明：※ 辽宁明代烽火台类型。

Note: Symbol ※ indicates that the type in question is found in Liaoning.

percent of the beacon towers stand on the inner side of the Ming Wall, forming a parallel line to the Wall. In some cases, they are situated along a line that crosses over the Wall. Examples are also found where a group of beacon towers circle around a fort.

Over 1,200 Ming beacon towers have been found in Liaodong Zhen stretching from east to west across 45 counties, cities and districts including Zhen'an District, Kuandian Manchu Autonomous County, Fengcheng City, Benxi Manchu Autonomous County, Xingcheng City and Suizhong County.

TYPOLOGY OF THE MING BEACON TOWERS IN LIAODONG ZHEN

There are 1,212 beacon towers at Liaodong Zhen, including 135 earth towers, 658 stone towers and 397 brick towers, and 22 towers which are so deteriorated that it is not possible to identify their original construction material (Liaodong Cultural Relics Bureau 2011). In terms of preservation, the original designs of 186 towers are still recognisable of which 122 are stone, 57 are brick and 7 are earth. Researchers have only able to identify the construction material of the other 1004 towers because they have reduced to rubble.

In terms of building materials, the stone towers and brick towers are the majority where the original design can be discerned, which is also remarkable, accounting for 47% and 27% respectively on a national basis.

In terms of typologies, Table 1. sets out the different typologies of beacon towers across the whole of the Ming Great Wall. Overall, five out of six of the main typologies and six out of 17 sub-categories can be found amongst the beacon towers in Liaoning. For stone beacon towers, all typologies can be found in Liaoning.

Earth-built beacons

The earth-built Ming beacon towers, are either built of rammed earth or adobe brick, and have a square or circular plan. Among the earth-built beacons in Liaoning, however, only rammed earth beacons have been found. These stand primarily in the Middle-Liaoning Plain, including counties and cities such as Changtu, Tieling, Shenyang and Liaozhong. Most of the 135 rammed earth beacons are poorly preserved and have collapsed into mounds. Some blue bricks can be seen scattered around the towers. These may have been either bricks cladding the rammed earth core or from battlements on top of the beacons.

There are four free-standing square towers built of rammed earth, all in a rectangular plan with a trapeziod elevation. The rammed-earth towers are 7m to 10m square at the base and 3.3m to 10m square at the top, but only remain visible to a height of 0.8m to 4m.

Only one example of a round rammed earth tower with a trapezoid elevation has survived. The diameter is 12m at the base and 6m at the top, and the remains are 5m in height.

Some towers are surrounded by one or more walls and ditches with gateways in some of the walls. Parts of these features have been destroyed due to natural erosion or human activities. Some walls have been flattened and some ditches have been jammed or filled with mud. As complementary defensive structures, it is likely that these walls and ditches would have been constructed at the same time as the towers. The spoil from the ditch would most likely have then been rammed to make the walls. Only two examples that fall into this category are found in Liaoning (Fig.1).

Stone beacons

The stone beacon towers are those built with a stone exterior. Their cores can be rough stones, rubble or a mixture of earth and cobbles which is filled in between a roughly-dressed stone facing, forming a square or a round plan. In Liaoning, this type of beacon is the most widely distributed and the most frequently found. The density is particularly high in the counties of Mingshan, Liaoyang, Fuxin and Zhangwu, the city of Linghai and the districts of Nanfen and Xihu. The original designs of 122 out of 658 stone towers in Liaoning remain recognisable; the rest have reduced to mounds of rubble.

辽东镇烽火台共计1212座，其中土筑台体共计135座，石砌烽火台658座，砖砌烽火台397座。按照保存状况，能够辨认形制的186座；因损毁，仅能辨别材质保留堆状的1004座，还有22座保留遗迹而无法辨认原始构筑材料和形制。

对照明长城烽火台的类型，辽宁尚能辨认构筑形制的186座烽火台，其中石砌122座、砖砌57座，土质7座。从材质看，石砌和砖砌烽火台类型较为齐全，在全国明长城同类烽火台中所占比例也较大，分别达到27％和47％。从形制看，明长城的6大类17亚类中，辽宁烽火台包括了5大类 6亚类，而各种构筑方式明长城石砌烽火台的各种类型在辽宁烽火台中均有发现（表1）。

（一）土筑

明代土筑烽火台为夯筑或土坯垒筑，平面呈方形或圆形。辽宁所见土筑烽火台中未见土坯垒砌，均为夯筑。主要分布于昌图、铁岭县、沈阳、辽中等辽中平原地区。辽宁土筑烽火台保存状况较差，135 座土筑烽火台中大多呈土丘状，部分烽火台周围散见青砖，不能确定是否包砖或顶部垛口砌砖。

土筑烽火台中单体方形共计 4 座。平面呈长方形，剖面呈梯形。烽火台底部边长在 7 米到 10 米之间，烽火台顶部边长在3.3米到10米之间，现残0.8–4米，夯筑而成。

土筑圆形烽火台仅见1例，平面呈圆形，剖面呈梯形。底径12米，顶径6米，存高5米。

带围墙（壕沟）的烽火台，台体四周建有一道或多道围墙（壕沟），其平面多呈方形或圆形，部分围墙可见门。因自然或人为原因，部分围墙已夷平，或壕沟沙土淤积、填埋，仅存围墙或壕沟。从设防考虑，围墙与壕沟应为同时修建，掘土成壕、堆土围墙。辽宁土筑烽火台中仅见2例（图1）。

（二）石砌

石砌烽火台是指墙体外观以石筑为主，其构筑方法主要有毛石干垒或土筑、土石混筑台芯外包块石，平面呈方形或圆形。辽宁境内，该类烽火台分布范围最广，数量最多。其中，明山县、南芬区、溪湖区、凌海市、辽阳县、阜新县、彰武县分布较为集中。辽宁共计石砌烽火台657座中可辨认形制的122座，其余均呈坍塌呈石堆状。

石砌单体方形烽火台共计73座，平面呈方形，剖面呈方锥形。多数为条石砌基，毛石或土石混砌台芯，外包略经打制的毛石；少数用毛石垒砌（图2）。

石砌单体圆形烽火台33座，大部分为内填土、外包石，计有29座，而毛石垒砌的仅存4座。

辽宁石砌烽火台有16座台体四周有围墙（壕沟）,主要集中在开原市、绥中县。大部分围墙均已毁仅存壕沟，围墙宽1–2.8米，高0.8–0.85米；壕沟宽1–4.6米，深0.3–1.2米。

（三）砖砌

砖砌烽火台是指构筑时外观以砖筑为主，内部黄土夯筑或土石混筑，平面呈方形或圆形。

辽宁砖砌烽火台共计397座，可辨认形制的仅57座。其中，单体方形的23座，单体圆形的4座，还有带有围墙（壕沟）的复合型烽火台30座。

砖砌方形烽火台多为土石混筑台芯，外部包砖，并以白灰勾缝。但辽宁此类烽火台保存状况较差。

明代现存圆形砖砌烽火台并不常见，仅有河北、陕西、辽宁3省可见。辽宁的圆形砖砌烽火台非常典型。该型烽火台平面圆形，剖面方锥形，收分明显。条石砌基，黄土夯筑或毛石、土石混砌台芯，外包

There are 73 stone free-standing beacon towers built to a square plan tapering inwards towards the top. Most were built on an ashlar foundation, with facings of roughly-dressed stone filled with a core of undressed stone or a mixture of earth and cobbles. Occasionally, they are constructed completely of undressed stone (Fig.2).

Thirty three surviving free-standing round stone beacons have been found, 29 of which were built with an earth or composite core and a stone-face and four of which had a core of dry and undressed stone.

Sixteen stone-built towers in Liaoning have been found with surrounding walls and ditches, particularly in the city of Kaiyuan and the county of Suizhong. Most of these walls are ruined, and only the ditches have survived. The surviving walls are 1m to 2.8m in width and 0.8m to 0.85m in height. The ditches are 1m to 4.6m in width and 0.3m to 1.2m in depth.

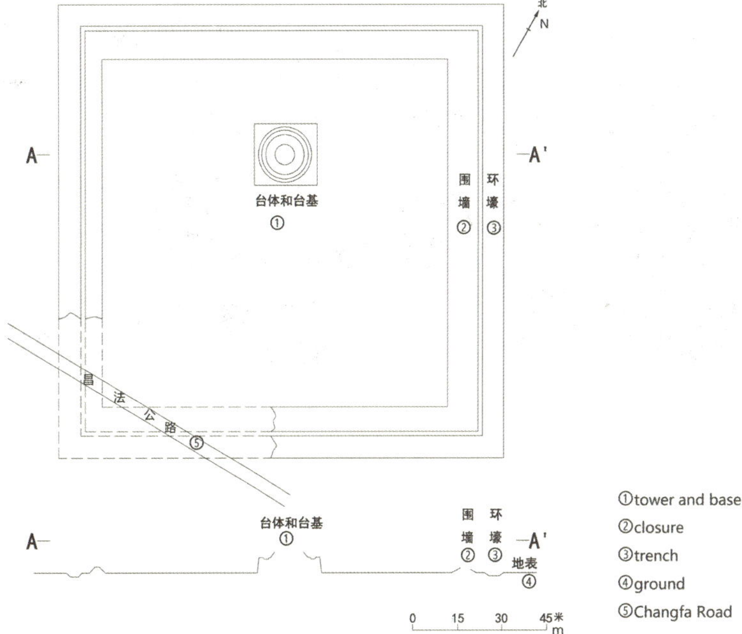

图 1 大台庙烽火台平、剖示意图（图片来源：根据辽宁省长城资源调查资料绘制）。

Fig.1 The plan and section of the Dataimiao Beacon (source: redrawn based on the Liaoning Great Wall Resource Survey).

Brick beacons

The brick beacon towers are constructed primarily of brick outer walls and rammed earth or an earth-cobble composite filling, in a square or a round plan.

There are 397 brick beacons in Liaoning. However, the original design remains recognisable in only 57 of them. Specifically, there are 23 free-standing square beacons, four free-standing round beacons and 30 beacons standing within walled and ditched compounds.

The square beacons are mainly composed of an earth and cobble composite core clad with mortared brick. Unfortunately, such towers are badly preserved.

It is quite unusual to see surviving round brick beacon towers today, as these are found only in the provinces of Hebei, Shaanxi and Liaoning. The beacons found in Liaoning are textbook examples of this type. They have a round plan with a trapezoid elevation. Such beacons were built on a foundation of undressed stone with a core constructed of rammed earth. Alternatively, the core of the beacon wall was undressed stone or earth and cobble composite clad in blue brick and sat on a stone or earth foundation. An example is the Beishan Beacon Tower in the village of Gangtai. The tower has a round plan and tapers inwards towards the top. The tower is 12.5m in diameter at the bottom and 11m in diameter on the top but survives only to a height of 14m. The beacon stands on bedrock and a three-layer ashlar foundation. The body of it is made up of 120 courses of mortared blue bricks. Each brick is 37cm×17cm×9cm in size and mortar joints between the bricks are 2cm wide. A 0.8m wide and 1.5m high entrance to the tower is situated towards the top of its south-east side (Fig. 3).

Generally what survives of the Ming brick beacon compounds is their walls and ditches. Such compounds are often seen on the top or on the slope of a hill. The stone or earth wall is usually built on a square or round plan.

图 2 辽宁石砌单体烽火台（图片来源：辽宁省长城资源调查资料）. 左图：毛石垒砌：冷家沟烽火台；右图：块石包砌：老虎城子山烽火台。

Fig.2 The stone free-standing beacon towers in Liaoning (source: the Liaoning Great Wall Resource Survey). A beacon tower built of random rubble at Lengjiagou (left); a stone-faced beacon at the Laohuchengzishan (right).

青砖，部分建于石砌或夯土台基之上。例如，江台北山烽火台，平面呈圆形，剖面呈梯形，由下至上逐渐收分；底径 12 .5 米，顶径 11 米，残高 14 米。建于自然岩石之上，三层条石砌基，高 0.7 米；青砖砌筑台体，白灰勾缝，共 120 行，青砖 0.37×0.17×0.09 米，灰缝 0.02 米。东南侧顶部有一上下出入口，宽 0.8 米，高 1.5 米（图 3）。

在现存的明代烽火台中，复合型的砖砌烽火台其附属设施仅有围墙（壕沟）1类，多见于山顶或山坡处，该型烽火台围绕烽火台四周建有一道或多道围墙（壕沟）。其平面多呈方形或圆形，围墙为石砌或夯筑，顶宽 0.5 ~ 1.2 米，底宽 2 ~ 6 米。壕沟宽 3 ~ 5 米。辽宁带有围墙 （壕沟） 的砖砌烽火台33座，在明长城分布的各省区中数量最多。例如，七道沟南山烽火台，台体西、北两侧有壕沟，口宽 2.6 ~ 3 米，底宽 0.4 ~ 0.8 米，存深 0.8 ~ 1 米。保存状况一般。

三、辽东镇烽火台的分布

明代烽火台在平面布局上存在三种形式。其一，沿长城墙体走向呈线状分布，是烽火台布局的主要形式，该类烽火台与墙体基本平行且与墙体遥相呼应，其疏密程度和分布数量多寡不一，少数地段未见烽火台遗存，也许与地形地势相关，更多的则是后期损毁所致。其二，独立于长城墙体的烽燧线，这类烽火台呈线状分布，与某段墙体交叉或同时平行于长城墙体，但不连续沿墙体分布。其三，烽火台呈群状（片状）分布，主要集中在长城墙体内侧，一般围绕关堡集中分布，形成烽火台群。或因后期损毁，也有部分烽火台群分布区域内未见关堡遗存。

辽东镇烽火台多沿长城墙体分布，且群状分布是其最大特点。

（一）沿长城墙体分布

这种沿长城墙体走向分布的烽火台在辽东镇境内共有 7 段，按照相邻烽火台间距约 10 千米以上，或因地势影响相邻烽火台不在可视范围为原则划分。其中一种紧邻长城墙体分布（一般在 2 千米以内），共 5 段，距离长城墙体 2 米– 1.4 千米，烽火台间间距 0.1–6 千米，每个段落包含烽火台数量 10–173 座不等。

图 3 江台北山烽火台南侧（南–北）（图片来源：辽宁省长城资源调查资料）。
Fig.3 The south side of the Beishan Beacon at Gangtai, looking north
(source: Archive of the Great Wall Resource Survey in Liaoning Province).

The walls taper from bottom to top, with a width of 2m to 6m at the base and 0.5m to 1.2m at the top. The width of the ditch ranges from 3m to 5m. There are 33 brick beacons with surrounding walls and ditches surviving in Liaoning - the largest number of this type of feature in all the provinces along the Ming Wall. The Nanshan Beacon at Qidaogou, Liaoning Province, is built with ditches on the west and north sides. These ditches are 2.6m to 3m meters wide at the top and 0.4m to 0.8m meters wide at the bottom but survive only to a depth of 0.8m to 1m. This structure is relatively well preserved.

DISTRIBUTION OF THE MING BEACON TOWERS IN LIAODONG ZHEN

The distribution of the Ming beacons falls into three patterns. The first and most common pattern is a linear distribution along the Wall. Here, the beacon towers are essentially parallel and supplementary to the Wall, but in a varying density. In some sections, there are no beacons at all. This could be because of the topography but is more likely to be the result of later destruction. The second pattern is an independent line of beacon towers that can

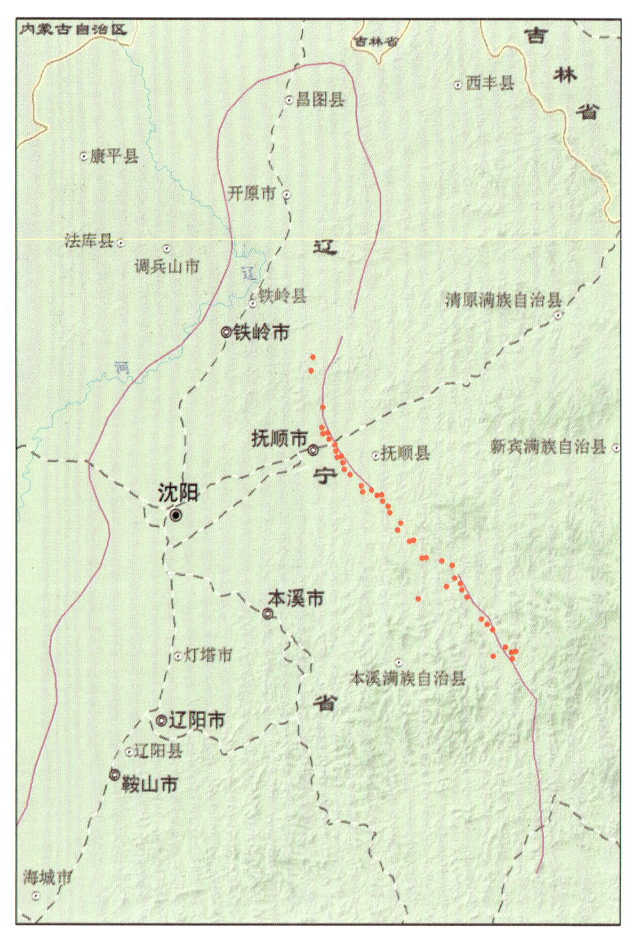

图 4 辽宁沿长城墙体分布的烽火台段落示意图）图片来源：国信司南（北京）地理信息技术有限公司）辽宁沿长城墙体分布的烽火台（左）；辽宁1段沿长城墙体分布烽火台（右）。

Fig.4 A complete map of the beacon lines in Liaoning (source Geo-Compass Information Technology Co. Ltd.); The beacon lines (left): Section 1 of the beacon lines (right).

另一种距离长城墙体较远（一般在 2 千米以外），但与墙体在相互可视的范围内，共 2 段，距离长城墙体 2.8-17千米，烽火台间距0.2-9千米不等。宏观上看，该类烽火台与长城墙体基本是不间断的平行分布（图4）。

（二）群状分布

辽东镇共有8组烽火台台群，其中5组烽火台群围绕某座关堡烽火台，其余3组烽火台群内未发现关堡。这些烽火台群范围、大小不一。烽火台数量从 14 座到 190 座不等。

这些烽火台利用土、石、砖等各类材质，采用夯筑、垒砌、包砌等各种构筑方式修筑而成，并与墙体、关堡等其他防御设施紧密配合，构成了辽东地区的烽传系统。据《全辽志•边防志》记载，辽东镇长城的烽火台共计一千一百五十座，这是嘉靖年的记录。由于历来不断的重建或增建，实际上多于此数。但因为年代久远，且辽东地区长城多分布在丘陵、平原地带，人为生产生活干扰较大，现存形制完整的烽火台

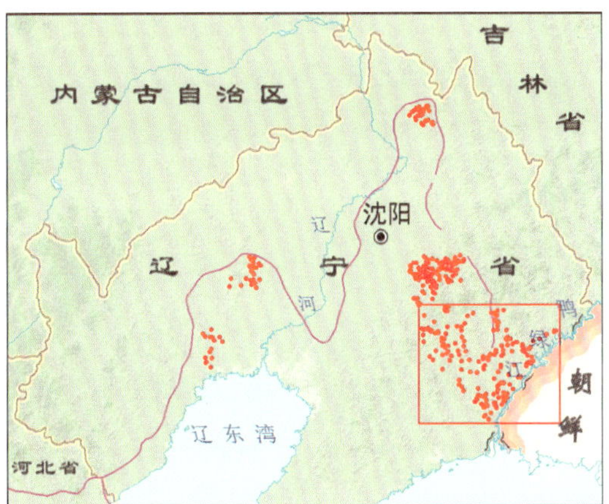

图 5 辽宁沿长城墙体分布的烽火台段落示意图（图片来源：国信司南（北京）地理信息技术有限公司）辽宁烽火台群（左）；辽宁1组烽火台群（右）。

Fig.5 A complete map of the beacon clusters in Liaoning (source Geo-Compass Information Technology Co. Ltd.). The beacon clusters (left); Group 1 of the beacon clusters (right).

cross over the wall or run parallel to it, although often not as a continuous line. The third pattern is beacon clusters surrounding forts, primarily to the interior of the Wall. There are exceptions, however, where there are clusters of beacons without evidence of forts at their centre, which may be the result of the later destruction of these forts.

The beacon towers at Liaodong *Zhen* are usually part of the first pattern – a linear distribution along the Wall. Their most prominent characteristic is that they appear to be grouped up into distinct clusters or sections.

The beacon lines along the Wall

Seven sections of such beacon towers in Liaodong *Zhen* can be discerned, separated either by distances of more than 10km, or by topographical features impeding their inter-visibility. Five sections are built so close to the wall that the distance between them and the Wall ranges from 2m to 1.4km. Within each section, the interval between each tower varies from 0.1 to 6km and the number of beacons varies from 10 to 173. Another two sections are built further away from the Wall, but are still visible from it. The distance between these beacon towers and the Wall ranges from 2.8km to 17km and the distance between each beacon ranges from 0.2km to 9km. Those beacon towers

数量并不多，对研究者直观了解他们的结构、分布等造成一定的困难，因此对辽宁烽火台的分析也仅限于对现有调查资料的分析，深入的研究分析还需要对具有代表性的台体以及附属设施进行系统地考古。

参考文献
References

Liaoning Cultural Relics Bureau. 2011. The Liaoning Great Wall Resource Survey. Beijing: Cultural Relics Publishing House.

辽宁省文物局. 2011. 辽宁省明长城资源调查报告. 文物出版社.

Liu Qian. 1988. A Study on the Ming Wall and Its Defence at Liaodong Zhen. Beijing: Cultural Relics Publishing House.

刘谦. 1998. 明辽东镇长城及防御考. 北京：文物出版社.

that follow this sub-pattern run, in most cases, parallel to the Wall without noticeable interruptions in their lines (Fig. 4).

The beacon clusters

Five out of eight beacon clusters at Liaodong *Zhen* are centred on forts; in the other three clusters no forts have yet been found. The clusters vary in terms of their geographical extent, and the number of beacons they contain ranges from 14 to 190.

Together with the Wall and the forts, these beacon clusters form the signalling system in eastern Liaoning. According to *The Complete Chorography of Eastern Liao: Border Defence*,[2] there were 1,150 beacon towers under the rule of Emperor Jiajing (reigned 1521-1567). It is likely however that due to constant rebuilding and additions many more beacon towers may have existed than the number recorded (Liu 1998). Unfortunately, well-preserved examples are rarely found because of their age and damage caused by the activities of local communities living in the hills and on the densely populated plains of eastern Liaoning. This has made it challenging to understand the structure and distribution of these towers. Analysis on the Liaoning beacon towers is limited to the survey data presently available. More systematic excavations on the towers and their associated features are needed to gain a better understanding.

2 Published in 1565, it is one of the earliest chorographies of northeast China, edited by Li Fu (Editors' note).

3.3 HADRIAN'S WALL SURVEY AND ARCHAEOLOGICAL MAPPING

MATTHEW OAKEY
Historic England - York - UK

Abstract

Between 2002 and 2008 the landscape of Hadrian's Wall and its buffer zone was mapped from aerial photographs. The resulting data are used to better understand and manage Hadrian's Wall and the other historic monuments within its wider landscape. This process followed a set of standards that have been developed over 30 years for the systematic analysis, mapping and recording of archaeological sites and landscapes from aerial photographs and airborne laser scanning (lidar) data. This paper outlines the interpretation and mapping process and also explores the impact of new technologies for recording and understanding archaeological landscapes from aerial survey.

Keywords: Hadrian's Wall, aerial photography, lidar, mapping, GIS, Structure from Motion, cropmark, soilmark, earthwork, structure, monitoring.

INTRODUCTION

Historic England's Aerial Investigation & Mapping (AIM) team comprises landscape archaeologists with specialist skills in the interpretation, mapping and taking of aerial photographs. It is part of a broader Archaeological Investigation team which includes specialists in geophysics, analytical earthwork survey and excavation. The AIM team has two principal roles carried out throughout England: an annual aerial reconnaissance programme, and targeted projects involving systematic interpretation and mapping from aerial photographs and lidar. Most of team's work concerns the second role.

The purpose of the reconnaissance programme is to discover new archaeological sites and to record and monitor known sites and landscapes, including urban areas and buildings. Historic England operates two leased aircraft which are flown by professional pilots employed on a mission-by-mission basis. These aircraft provide coverage over the whole of England - an area of over 130,000km^2, although only a small percentage of this is surveyed each year, Approximately 280 hours are flown annually and an average of around 2,400 sites are photographed each year. The reconnaissance programme is targeted rather than providing complete and systematic coverage. Coverage is determined by a range of factors including soils and geology, weather conditions, the nature and distribution of archaeological remains, and controlled airspace. Aerial photographs taken by Historic England are used for a variety of management and research purposes by internal staff, external heritage professionals and the general public.

Mapping projects use historical photographs, recent reconnaissance photographs and lidar data to create maps of archaeological landscapes. Although projects can be site-specific or cover small landscapes, most encompass larger areas of over 100km^2. This archaeological mapping plays an important role in heritage management, particularly by county councils where it is used on a daily basis to inform planning decisions in advance of development.

Between 2002 and 2008 the AIM team mapped and recorded the landscape encompassing Hadrian's Wall and its buffer zone from aerial photographs - an area totalling 1,693km^2 (Fig.1). The context for this project was provided by the *Hadrian's Wall World Heritage Site Management Plan 1996-2001* (English Heritage 1996). In particular this emphasised that the research strategy for Hadrian's Wall should include 'investigation of the history and archaeology of

3.3 哈德良长城的调查及考古测绘

马修·奥基
英格兰遗产委员会—约克—英国

摘要

自2002年至2008年，哈德良长城及其缓冲区的景观进行了航空摄影测绘。测绘数据用于更好地认知和管理哈德良长城以及其更广袤的地理景观中的其他历史古迹。测绘过程遵循的一系列标准，是经过30多年不断完善而形成的，期间一直致力于通过航拍照片和机载激光扫描（激光雷达）数据对考古遗址和景观进行系统分析、测绘和记录。本文概述解译及测绘过程，并分析新技术对使用航空测绘进行考古景观记录和认识方面的影响。

关键字：哈德良长城　航空摄影　激光雷达　测绘GIS运动恢复结构　作物痕迹　土壤痕迹　土质工事结构　监测

引言

英格兰遗产委员会的航空勘探和测绘（AIM）团队由具备解译、测绘和航空摄影专业技能的景观考古学家组成。该团队是考古调查部门的一个分支，该部门还包括地球物理学、土质工事调查分析和挖掘方面的专家。在英格兰全境范围内，AIM团队主要负责两方面工作：年度航空勘察项目，以及针对特定地点运用航拍照片和激光雷达开展系统性解译和测绘项目。团队的大部分工作都跟第二方面有关。

航空勘察项目旨在发现新的考古遗址，并记录和监测包括城区和建筑在内的已知遗址及景观。英格兰遗产委员会租有两架飞机，由专业飞行员根据需要执行飞行任务。飞行范围可覆盖整个英格兰，总面积超过13万平方千米。实际上，每年仅勘察其中的一小部分，每年飞行时长约280小时，平均拍摄共约2400处遗址。航空勘察项目往往有所侧重，并非面面俱到。具体勘察范围则取决于一系列因素，包括土壤和地质、天气条件、考古遗迹的性质和分布以及管制空域。英格兰遗产委员会将所摄的航拍照片提供给内部员工、外部遗产专家和公众来开展管理和研究方面的各类活动。

特定测绘项目则运用历史照片、近期的航空勘察图像和激光雷达数据来绘制考古景观地图。尽管这些项目可能仅针对某个特定遗址，或涉及景观范围较小，但大多数项目都覆盖了100平方千米以上的较大区域。这类考古测绘在遗产管理中发挥着重要作用，特别是供各郡县政府用来审议建设项目的前期规划，支撑决策。

2002年至2008年间，AIM团队通过航拍照片测绘并记录了哈德良长城及其缓冲区景观，总面积达1693平方千米（图1）。该项目起源于《哈德良长城世界遗产地管理规划1996-2001》（英格兰遗产委员会1996）。其中特别强调哈德良长城的研究策略应包括“将该地区作为一个整体进行历史和考古调查，这对

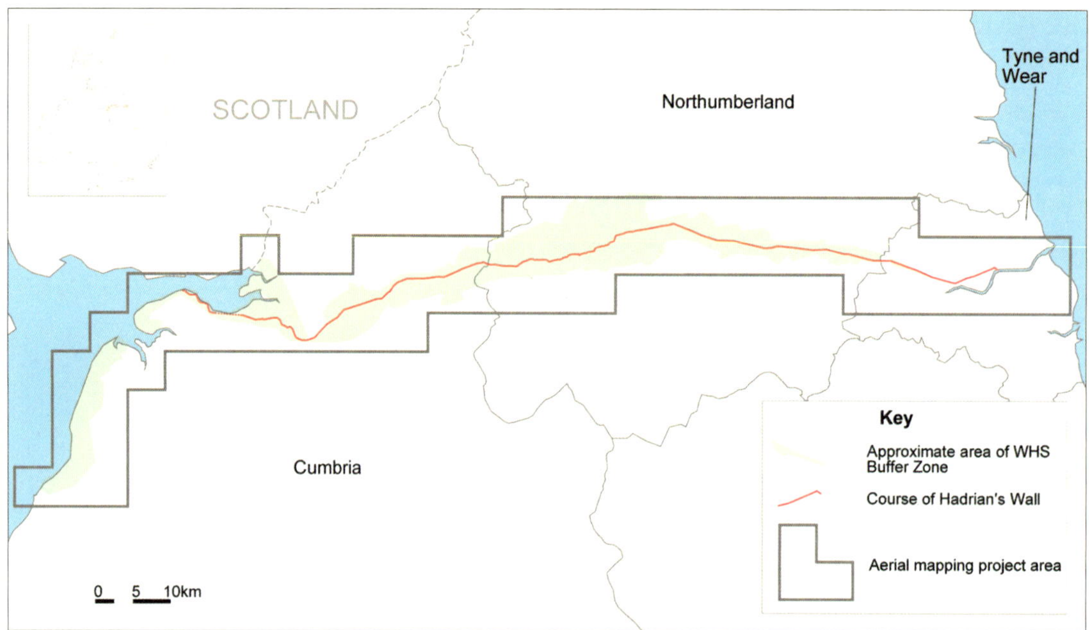

Fig.1 The area covered by the Hadrian's Wall mapping project (© Historic England. Basemap © Crown Copyright and database right 2020. All rights reserved. Ordnance Survey Licence number 100019088).

图 1 哈德良长城测绘项目所涉及区域（© 英格兰遗产委员会.基础地图 © 皇家版权和数据权 2020.版权所有.国家测绘局许可证号 100019088）。

the area as a whole since this is crucial to our understanding of the development of the World Heritage Site.' It also recommended that the strategy should 'relate the Roman military remains within their wider context both topographical and chronological' (English Heritage 1996, 5.2.1; 5.2.7). Digital mapping of aerial photographs was then explicitly listed as a required action in the subsequent 2002 Management Plan (English Heritage 2002, 84).

IDENTIFICATION OF ARCHAEOLOGICAL SITES AND LANDSCAPES

To understand how aerial photographs and lidar are used to create archaeological mapping, it is worth considering how archaeological features are identified on aerial photographs. This can be split into two categories – features that survive above ground and buried archaeological deposits.

Surface features

Surface features are broadly categorised as earthworks or structures. Earthworks are man-made features formed by re-engineering of the natural land surface such as the digging of ditches or the creation of embanked enclosures. Examples within the Hadrian's Wall landscape include Roman temporary camps. Some earthwork sites are formed by collapsed structures, such as stone walls, which have gradually become soil-covered and grassed over. On aerial photographs earthworks are visible from the shadows and highlights that are cast by low sunlight, particularly in the winter months and at either end of each day.

Structures encompass sites constructed of materials such as stone, brick or concrete. In rare circumstances, such as in inter-tidal zones, wooden structures may survive and be visible from the air. Structures would include features such as Hadrian's Wall itself and the exposed remains of forts such as Housesteads.

于我们了解世界遗产地的发展至关重要。”此外，规划还建议研究应“将罗马军事遗迹与其所处的更广泛的环境建立起地形上和时代上的关联”（英格兰遗产委员会1996，5.2.1；5.2.7）。在其后 2002 年颁布的管理规划中，则明确地将航拍照片的数字测绘列为必需开展的任务（英格兰遗产委员会 2002）。

识别考古遗址和景观

要理解如何运用航拍照片和激光雷达绘制考古地图，有必要先了解一下如何识别航拍照片中的考古特征。考古特征可以分为两大类：地上可见的考古特征和埋于地下的考古堆积。

地上特征

地上特征大致分为土质工事和构筑物两部分。土质工事是重建自然地表而形成的人造特征，例如挖掘壕沟或修建有堤岸的围地。哈德良长城景观中的实例则为罗马临时营地。此外，包括石墙在内的一些构筑物在坍塌后会逐渐被土或草皮覆盖，日积月累也会形成土质工事。航拍照片中，斜阳投射形成的明暗对比可以显示出土质工事的位置，这在太阳高度较低的冬季和每天的日出日落之时看得尤为清晰。

构筑物包括由石块、砖或混凝土修筑的设施。在极少数情况下，例如在潮间带，木质结构可能得以存留至今并从空中可见。构筑物的实例包括哈德良长城本体和地上的要塞遗迹（如豪塞斯特兹）等。

地下特征

当考古特征埋藏于地表之下，在适当条件下，我们可以通过土壤或作物痕迹来发现他们的存在。通常，现代犁耕会使考古堆积被揭露到地表，形成土壤痕迹。堆积的组成成分的不同会导致地面土色的差异，从空中可以观察出来。堤岸可能与周围的土壤相比颜色更浅，而由有机和腐殖土填充的壕沟往往颜色更深。

在水分应力下[1]，作物和地下的考古堆积发生反应后，就会形成作物痕迹。生长于壕沟和深坑之上的作物获得了更多水分和养分，于是长得更高，郁郁葱葱的时节也更加长久。而对于那些长在坚硬表面（比如埋于地下的墙体）之上的作物，它们的生长受到了阻碍，跟周围的作物相比个头较矮也成熟得更快（图2）。有时在草地上也会发现后面这种情况，我们经常称之为干枯痕迹。作物痕迹的形成取决于多种因素，包括土壤、地质、土地使用和天气。位于高地的哈德良长城区段基本没有利于作物痕迹形成的条件，但其他地区则有，尤其是西部的索尔维平原。

考古测绘

与任何考古学科领域一样，对航拍照片和激光雷达的解译和测绘也是一项专业技能。据估计，毫无经验的解译员至少需要六个月的时间才能达到一定的熟练水准。尽管过去二十年技术取得了巨大进步，人工解译仍然是整个过程中最为重要而复杂的环节。通过对航拍源进行测绘来记录考古景观不仅效率高，而且成本低。一般来说，有经验的解译员平均一天可以解译、测绘和记录一平方千米的土地，不过这也取决于考古遗迹的密度和复杂程度，以及需要分析的航拍源的数据量（埃文斯 2019, 107）。

1　当植物因蒸腾作用导致流失的水分超过了通过根茎吸收的水分时，通常会产生水分应力。这在夏季长时间干旱的时节最为明显。

Subsurface features

When archaeological features only survive as buried remains, they can be revealed in the right conditions as soilmarks or cropmarks. Soilmarks are formed when buried archaeological deposits are exposed and brought to the surface, often through modern ploughing. The different composition of the deposits can result in colour differences at ground level which can be seen from the air. An embanked feature may show up lighter than the surrounding soil whilst the organic and more humic fill of a ditch will often show as a darker tone.

Cropmarks are formed when a crop under moisture stress[1] reacts to the underlying archaeological deposits. Crops growing over ditches and pits have access to more moisture and nutrients so grow taller and stay greener for longer. Crops growing over hard surfaces such as a buried wall have their growth impeded so grow shorter and ripen more quickly than the surrounding crop (Fig.2). This latter effect can sometimes be observed in grass where it is often referred to as parchmarks. Cropmark formation depends on a variety of factors including soils, geology, land use and weather. The upland sections of Hadrian's Wall do not generally have conditions which are conducive to cropmark formation but other areas do, particularly on the Solway Plain in the west.

ARCHAEOLOGICAL MAPPING

Like any archaeological discipline, the interpretation and mapping of aerial photographs and of lidar is a specialist skill. It is estimated that it takes at least six months for an interpreter with no previous experience to reach an appropriate level of proficiency. Despite considerable technical advances over the last two decades, the human interpreter remains by far the most important and sophisticated part of the process. Mapping from aerial sources is a very rapid and cost-effective method of recording archaeological landscapes. On average it takes an experienced interpreter about a day to interpret, map and record 1km^2, although this will vary depending on the density and complexity of the archaeology, and the number of sources that need to be examined (Evans 2019, 107).

Historic England's Mapping Standards

Aerial photograph mapping projects have been undertaken or funded by Historic England and its predecessors (the Royal Commission on the Historical Monuments of England, and English Heritage) for over 30 years. While some have focused on individual sites or small landscapes, most projects covered large areas of 100 km^2 or more. Just over half of England (*c.* 70,000km^2) has now been mapped. The overarching aim of mapping projects is to provide a visual representation of multi-period landscapes which can be used to better understand how these landscapes have evolved over time. This informs how the archaeological resource can be managed and protected more effectively.

A set of standards and a consistent chronological and thematic scope for all archaeological mapping projects has evolved during this 30-year period to ensure a nationally systematic approach. These standards were used for the AIM team's Hadrian's Wall mapping project. They are based on three underlying principles:

- All available aerial photographs and lidar data are used.
- The chronological scope encompasses all archaeological features visible on aerial photographs from the Neolithic age (typically the first period that leaves traces that are visible on aerial sources) to the 20th century.
- Features are mapped and recorded, irrespective of how they were identified or their current level of survival. This includes features visible as earthworks, structures, soilmarks or cropmarks, and features which were seen on historical photographs, but have since been levelled or destroyed.

---

1 Moisture stress commonly occurs when the amount of water that a plant absorbs through its roots is exceeded by what it is losing through transpiration. This is most pronounced in long dry periods during the summer.

Fig.2 Remains of Corbridge Roman town showing as cropmarks (20559_001 13-JUL-2006 © Historic England Archive).
图 2 作物痕迹之下的科布里奇罗马城镇遗迹（20559_001 13-JUL-2006 ©英格兰遗产委员会档案馆）。

英格兰遗产委员会测绘标准

英格兰遗产委员会及其前身（英格兰皇家历史古迹委员会等）持续开展或资助若干航拍照片测绘项目已有三十多年的历史。有些项目侧重于单个遗址或小景观，但大多数项目的测绘对象都是面积为 100 平方千米或更大的区域。目前，测绘面积已经超过英格兰全境的一半（约 7 万平方千米）。测绘项目的总体目标是呈现景观的多时段视觉形象，有助于更好地理解这些景观是如何随着时间演变的，进而为如何才能更有效地管理和保护考古资源提供参考。

在过去的三十年里逐渐形成了一系列标准以及统一的时间范围和主题范围，应用于所有的考古测绘项目，以确保测绘方法在全国范围内统一而系统。这些标准也应用在了AIM团队负责的哈德良长城测绘项目，主要遵循了三个基本原则：

- 利用所有可用的航拍照片和激光雷达数据。
- 时间范围涵盖所有航拍照片上可见的考古特征，从新石器时代（即在航拍源上留下可见痕迹的最早阶段）到 20 世纪。
- 无论考古特征是如何发现的，也无所谓其残存现状，都对其进行测绘和记录。其中包括可见的土质工事、构筑物、土壤痕迹、作物痕迹，也包括在历史照片上呈现但如今已被夷为平地或遭到破坏的特征。

测绘流程

本节概述解译、测绘和记录的流程。这是一个相对简化的模型，因为实际操作中它并非是一个线性流

THE MAPPING PROCESS

This section outlines the process of interpretation, mapping and recording; it is a rather simplified model as in reality it is not a linear process. Some sequences such as image analysis–rectification–mapping will be carried out several times in the same day. Images are also constantly re-evaluated during mapping, as the significance of some details only becomes apparent as all of the available photographs for that site are digitalised and examined together.

An important point to note is that mapping is not just a technical exercise in digitising features. Throughout the process the interpreter is critically analysing and interpreting the landscape to understand the relationships of features to one another, and how the landscape has evolved. This approach can even affect how features are mapped: the same site could be drawn in a number of different ways, depending on the interpretation of the chronological sequence and how individual elements relate to one another.

Data collation

The first stage of any mapping project is to collate all the available data for the survey area. This data falls into two broad categories. Firstly, primary source material (modern and historical aerial photographs, and lidar). Secondly, other sources of information: for example, existing textual monument records such as those curated by local Historic Environment Records (HERs) or in the national record (see *monument recording*, below), and previous surveys and historical mapping which can help inform interpretation of features seen on the primary sources. Where this information exists as digital spatial data[2], it is usually loaded as layers into the project's Geographic Information System (GIS).

Projects such as the AIM team's work on Hadrian's Wall have access to large archives of aerial photographs and to an ever-increasing number of sources which are becoming available. These can be divided into two categories:

- Specialist photographs – images taken specifically to record archaeological sites and landscapes. These tend to be taken with a handheld camera at an oblique angle to the ground.
- Non-specialist photographs – images taken for other survey purposes but which often coincidentally capture archaeological features. These tend to be vertical photographs taken at 90° to the ground using a specially adapted aircraft.

In England, the largest repository of aerial photographs is the Historic England Archive in Swindon, which contains over 4 million aerial photographs dating from the early 20th century to the present day. Around 250,000 of these are born-digital[3] images which have been produced by the reconnaissance programme since moving to digital cameras in 2006. Although a small part of the Historic England Archive's aerial photograph collection has been digitised, most of the other 3.75 million images are original photographic prints.

The archaeology of the Hadrian's Wall landscape has been discovered and recorded by archaeologists from the air since the first half of the 20th century. The AIM team's Hadrian's Wall mapping project therefore had access to photographs dating as far back as 1930. Over 10,000 specialist oblique photographs and 17,500 non-specialist vertical photographs were examined. Historical aerial photographs were particularly valuable for recording landscape change and for identifying archaeological features that had been levelled or destroyed since the photograph was taken. They were also a unique source for recording short-lived aspects of the landscape, particularly Second World War military features which were often removed soon after the end of the conflict.

2 Spatial data is geographic information about the location, size and extent of an object. In the context of the current paper this specifically refers to points, lines and polygons held in a GIS.

3 The term born-digital refers to photographs taken with a digital camera as opposed to wet film prints that have been scanned and digitised.

程。某些图像分析-矫正-测绘等步骤可能会在同一天内进行若干次。在测绘过程中，图像也会不断得到重新评估。有时将遗址所有的照片都进行数字化处理后再放在一起观察，才会意识到有些细节至关重要。

值得强调的是，测绘并非仅仅是将特征进行数字化处理的技术工作。在整个过程中，解译员都要批判性地分析和解译景观，以了解不同考古特征之间的关系以及景观是如何演变的。该方法甚至会影响到如何对这些考古特征进行测绘：对一处遗址的测绘方式可以有很多种，这取决于解译的年代顺序，以及各个要素之间的相互关系。

数据整理

对任何测绘项目而言，第一步都是整理所调查区域的一切可用数据。这些数据可以分为两大类。第一类是一手资料来源（现代和历史航拍照片及激光雷达数据）。第二类是其他信息来源，包括：现存的古迹文字记录，如记载于当地历史环境档案或国家档案（见下“古迹记录”章节）中的内容；过去的调查和历史测绘，能够帮助我们解译一手资料上观察到的特征。当相关信息是数字空间数据[2]时，通常将其按不同图层加载到项目的地理信息系统（GIS）中。

AIM 团队负责的哈德良长城等若干项目可以获取海量的航拍照片档案，以及越来越多不断开放的资源。这些资源可以分为两大类：

- 专业照片——专门为记录考古遗址和景观而拍摄的照片，通常是用手持相机从与地面倾斜的某个角度采集的。
- 非专业照片——为其他调查目的而拍摄的照片，但恰好捕捉到了考古特征，往往是使用经特殊改装的飞机从与地面垂直的角度拍摄的。

在英格兰，最大的航拍照片资料库是位于史云顿的英格兰遗产委员会档案馆，藏有自 20 世纪早期至今的超过 400 万张航拍照片。其中有大约 25 万张原生数字[3]照片，都是航空勘察项目自 2006 年转而使用数码相机后采集的。英格兰遗产委员会档案馆的航拍档案中有一小部分照片已经进行了数字化处理，但 375 万张照片中绝大多数仍是原始冲印照片。

自 20 世纪上半叶以来，考古学家就通过航空勘察和记录来开展哈德良长城的景观考古。因此，AIM团队负责的哈德良长城测绘项目得以获取最早可追溯至 1930 年的照片。团队仔细分析了超过 1 万张专业倾斜影像和 1.75 万张非专业垂直影像。历史航拍照片对于记录景观变化和识别自照片拍摄以来已经被夷平或破坏的考古特征而言尤为珍贵。它们也是记录该景观的某些短暂存在过的特征的独特资料，特别是二战时期的军事遗迹。通常，它们在冲突结束后不久就会被清除。

图像分析

所有航拍影像和激光雷达图片都会得到系统性的分析，以发现其中包含的任何考古特征。现在有一些其他机构的研究项目正在尝试运用自动化检测方法，但分析过程仍以人工为主。解译员可以使用立体镜仔细查看垂直航拍影像，放大景象并观察到三维立体的景观。在不同的图片上也许会重复看到同一处考古遗址；随后，会从中挑选出最能够清晰展现其特征的那张照片，并对其上面的考古特征进行数字化处理。有

2 空间数据指某个对象的位置、大小及范围的地理信息。本文中，它特指 GIS 中存储的点、线和多边形。
3 原生数字指直接使用数码相机拍摄而成的照片，而并非将冲洗的胶片扫描后再数字化转存的相片。

Image analysis

All of the aerial photographs and lidar images are then systematically examined to identify any archaeological features they contain. Although automated detection is being explored by some current research projects, although not by Historic England, this examination is still a manual process. Vertical aerial photographs are viewed using a handheld stereoscope which enables the interpreter to see the landscape in 3D as well as a magnification of the image. An archaeological site may be visible on a number of different photographs; the image that most clearly shows the features is then selected as the source for the digitisation of the archaeological features. Sometimes it may be necessary to use more than one image as different elements of the site may show better on some images than others.

Image rectification

Before a photograph can be used for mapping, it must undergo a rectification process to accurately remove tilt and height distortions within the image. These distortions are present in both oblique and vertical photographs but are more obvious in an oblique image (features in the foreground appear larger). Rectification also geo-references the photograph to a predefined coordinate system. In the UK this is the British National Grid defined by the Ordnance Survey, the UK's national mapping agency. It is important to note that rectification is not the same as rubber sheeting[4] within a GIS, which simply distorts the image to fit a map.

Rectification is undertaken using specialist software where a number of control points are manually selected that are visible on both the aerial photograph and a digital Ordnance Survey map (which is already geo-referenced). Height data is then added which enables the software to carry out a 3D geometric transformation of the image, accounting for distortions caused by topographic variation. The accuracy of the rectified image is dependent on the accuracy of the map that was used for control, but this can often be within 1m.

Digital transcription

Rectified and geo-referenced images are imported into a drawing package – for Hadrian's Wall this was AutoCAD, but ESRI's ArcGIS software is now used. Individual features are then digitised according to their form, *i.e.* whether they are cut (e.g. ditch, pit), embanked (e.g. bank, mound), or structural (e.g. stone wall, concrete structure). A very limited number of schematic layers are also used. These are used to indicate areas of generic features, such as the remains of medieval and post-medieval ploughing where it would be too time consuming to draw each individual cultivation furrow.

Monument recording

Every feature is assigned GIS attribute data which records key information such as its date, form, and function, and the source that it was mapped from. Attribute data allow the user to quickly access significant information which enables the spatial data to be queried in a GIS environment at feature level. A unique identifier links the spatial data to its associated textual monument record. Monument records are created in a separate recording system; these contain more detailed information about the site and a narrative description. These records often derive from multiple sources and are added to and amended over time. A number of individual archaeological features may be grouped together within a single monument record. For example, a Roman fort (recorded as a single monument) will comprise defensive ramparts, a bath house, barrack blocks, etc. (features).

---

4 Rubber sheeting is a process which stretches and rotates a photographic image so that it fits a map base. This is not as accurate as image rectification which uses complex mathematical formulae to transform the elements of the image onto a common plane, giving a metrically accurate image with a uniform scale throughout. (Herzog and Scollar 1989).

时，可能需要选用多张图像，因为遗址的不同要素在某些图像上显示的比其他图像更加清晰。

图像校正

在将照片用于测绘之前，还必须对其进行校正处理，以精确地消除图像内的倾斜失真和径向畸变。倾斜影像和垂直影像都存在这些变形失真，但在倾斜影像中更为明显（照片前景中的特征看起来更大）。图像校正也对图像进行坐标变换，将其对应到预先定义好的地理坐标系中。英国使用的坐标系是由英国国家测绘机构，即国家测绘局制定的英国国家格网参考系统。重要的是，图像校正并不等同于GIS中的橡皮页变换，[4] 后者只是简单地扭曲图像，使之与地图对齐。

校正是使用专业软件进行的。首先，我们会手动选择在航拍照片和国家测绘局绘制的（已完成坐标变换的）数字地图上皆可见的若干个控制点。然后，添加高程数据。这样一来，软件就可以对图像进行 3D 几何变换，从而解决了由地形变化引起的变形失真。校正后的图像精准度取决于所使用的基础地图的精度，但偏差通常可以控制在 1 米以内。

数字化转录

经过校正和坐标变换的图像随后被导入至绘图软件包中。在哈德良长城项目上，之前我们使用 AutoCAD，目前使用的是 ESRI 的 ArcGIS 软件。随后，软件会根据考古特征的形态进行图像数字处理，换句话说，需要先判断它们是下切的（壕沟、坑）、围堤的（堤岸、土堆），还是构筑的（石墙、混凝土结构）。此外，还使用了若干示意图图层，主要用于标明具有普遍特征的区域，如中世纪和后中世纪犁耕的遗迹，逐条绘制犁沟则会十分耗时。

古迹记录

GIS 赋予了每一处考古特征各自的属性数据，用来记录其年代、形态、功能以及测绘的来源资料等关键信息。属性数据让用户可以快速获取重要信息，从而能够在GIS环境中查询特征级别的空间数据。各个空间数据都通过独一无二的标识符将其与相关的古迹文字记录关联起来。古迹记录是在另一个单独的档案系统中创建的，其中包括关于该遗址更具体的信息和叙述性描述。这些记录的来源十分广泛，且随着时间推移还会添加新的内容并进行修正。一份古迹记录中可能会涵盖多处独立的考古特征。例如，某个罗马要塞（作为单一古迹记录在案）会由防御城墙、一处罗马浴场和若干营房等（特征）组成。

考古测绘的益处

丰富古迹记录数据

古迹记录和测绘数据由国家和地方政府机构负责存档，用于研究和管理。而每次开展新的航空测绘项目平均能使考古古迹记录的数量增长约50%。对个别项目而言，增长比例甚至可以超过 70%（霍恩2011，146）。哈德良长城测绘项目新创建了 2748 份古迹记录，并对原有的 806 份记录进行了

4　橡皮页变换，又称橡皮伸缩法或橡皮拉伸，是指拉伸和旋转图片，使其与基础地图对齐。该方法不如图像校正精准。后者使用复杂的数学公式将图片中的要素转化至一个公共平面上，进而获得一张目标比例尺统一且度量精准的影像图（赫尔佐格和斯考勒 1989）。

THE BENEFITS OF ARCHAEOLOGICAL MAPPING

Enhancement of Monument Records data

The monument records and mapping are curated by national and local government organisations and are used for research and management. When aerial mapping projects are carried out they increase the number of archaeological monument records by around 50% on average, although for some individual projects this figure has exceeded 70% (Horne 2011, 146). The Hadrian's Wall mapping project created 2,748 new monument records and enhanced a further 806 existing records. As noted above, the actual number of *features* added to the archaeological record will be considerably larger than the number of *monuments*.

As well as quantitative enhancement of the archaeological record, mapping of Hadrian's Wall also represented a considerable qualitative improvement in the data. Monuments had previously been identified on maps by a point denoting the centre of the feature or a polygon indicating the location and extent of a site. Aerial mapping, however, provides an accurate depiction of the archaeology which allows the user to better understand sites and landscapes to make more informed decisions on heritage management (Fig.3).

Enhancement of historical landscape analysis

The resulting archaeological maps are a composite of all the available information from every aerial source. The Hadrian's Wall mapping data was created using 3,235 individual photographs, ranging in date from the 1930s to the 2000s. This represents around 17% of the total number of images examined by the project and demonstrates how no one source can provide a full record of the landscape. Those images that were not used during the process of digitising archaeological features will, in many instances, have been essential for aiding the interpretation of sites and understanding how they may have changed over time.

This approach gives a comprehensive view of the landscape, although to get a complete picture it is necessary to combine data from aerial mapping with all other sources of information. It also allows the development of that landscape to be better understood, revealing the spatial and chronological relationships between different archaeological features (Fig.4). Hadrian's Wall and its associated military installations were not constructed in an unpopulated landscape. Mapping and recording of later prehistoric settlements and field systems shows how the Wall related to pre-existing features within the landscape. In turn, the presence of the Wall has influenced post-Roman use of the landscape which has ultimately resulted in the distinctive character of the landscape setting of Hadrian's Wall that we see today. This is a concept that Rob Collins explores in more detail within the current publication.

NEW TECHNOLOGIES

Lidar

Since the mapping of Hadrian's Wall was completed in 2008, new sources of imagery have become available. The most significant has been lidar (light, distance, and ranging) which is now a standard source of information for understanding the historic environment. Hadrian's Wall was used as an early trail of lidar by English Heritage in 2003. It was commissioned for an 8 km^2 transect, centred on Carrawburgh Roman fort. This was undertaken by the Cambridge University Unit for Landscape Modelling and assessed against the information derived from aerial photographs. One of the most significant discoveries from this data was a previously undiscovered Roman camp (next to the fort) that had been masked by the remains of later ploughing (Jones 2012, 68; fig.9).

Extensive lidar data of England is now freely available: it is collected primarily for flood-risk mapping by the public body responsible for England's environment, the Environment Agency. Although a rapid assessment of the Environment Agency's lidar covering Hadrian's Wall was undertaken by Newcastle University (Collins 2015), further systematic analysis and mapping from this source is required.

It is important to note that lidar has not replaced other aerial sources, merely complemented them. An obvious point, but one worth making, is that lidar only records upstanding features. It cannot record sites that have been

补充。如前所述，新添加至考古记录中的实际考古特征的数量会远远超过古迹的数量。

除了带来记录数量上的增长之外，哈德良长城测绘同时也体现出数据质量的提升。过去，古迹在地图上的体现就是考古特征中心处的一个点，或者是指明遗址的位置和范围的一个多边形。然而，航空测绘从考古学角度对古迹进行了精准展现，让用户能够更好地了解遗址和景观，从而为遗产管理决策提供更详细的参考（图3）。

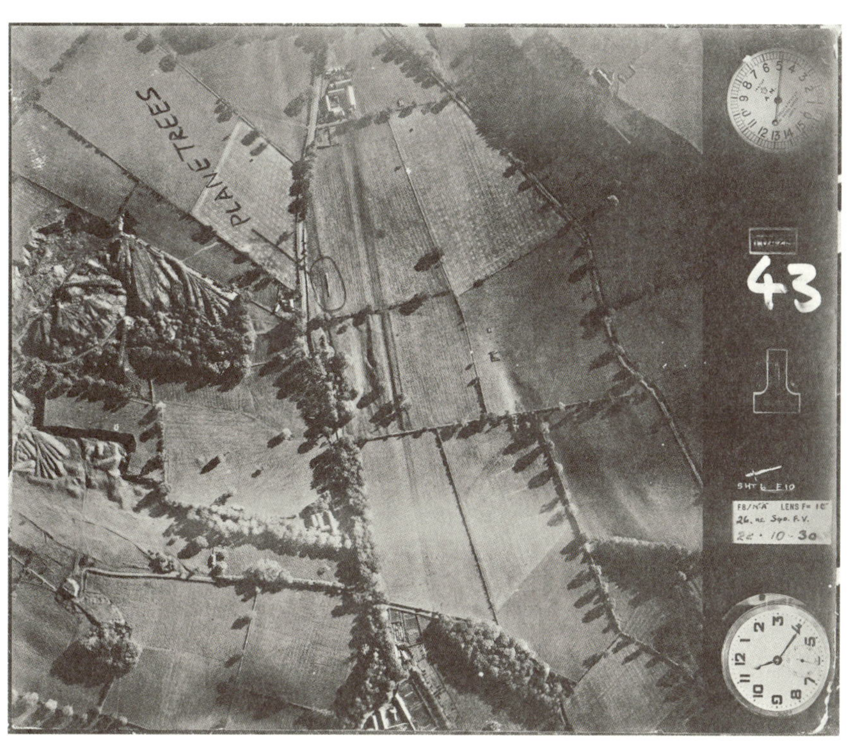

Fig.3 RAF photography from 1930 showing the Wall and the Vallum at Planetrees. To the left of the image are the remains of 19th-century limestone quarries (RAF/26/AC/FV 0043 22-OCT-1930 © Historic England Archive, RAF Photography).

图 3 1930年英国皇家空军（RAF）照片上位于普莱恩特利的城墙和南部壕沟。图片左侧是19世纪石灰岩采石场的遗迹（RAF/26/AC/FV 0043 22-OCT-1930 © 英格兰遗产委员会档案馆，RAF照片）。

推动历史景观分析

绘制出的考古地图可谓集成了所有航拍资料提供的全部可用信息。哈德良长城的测绘数据来自3235 张照片，涵盖时间从 20 世纪 30 年代到21世纪间。使用照片的数量占项目所分析照片数量的约17%。这也同时说明我们不可能仅靠任何单一数据来源得到完整的景观记录。多数情况下，那些在数字化处理过程中未被选中的照片依然起到了必不可少的作用，帮助我们更好地解译遗址，理解他们是如何随着时间的推移而改变。

该方法能够展现景观的综合性面貌，而要获得完整信息还需要将航空测绘的数据和其他的所有信息来源进行整合。此外，它可以帮助我们更好地了解景观的发展变迁，揭示不同考古特征之间的空间和时间关系（图4）。哈德良长城及其相关的军事设施并非修建于无人区。测绘和记录史前聚落和农田系统展示了长城与景观中先前已经存在的特征之间有何种关联。反过来，长城的存在影响了后罗马时期的景观利用，最终形成了今天我们所看到的哈德良长城景观所具有的鲜明特征。本文集中，罗伯·柯林斯在他的文章中就这一概念进行了更详细的探讨。

新技术

激光雷达

自2008 年哈德良长城测绘工作完成后，又有了获取图像的新技术手段。其中，最重要就是激光雷达

Fig.4 Extract of the Hadrian's Wall mapping, showing a multi-period landscape ranging from a Late Iron Age enclosure to a Second World War airfield (© Historic England. Basemap © Crown Copyright and database right 2020. All rights reserved. Ordnance Survey Licence number 100019088).

图 4 选自哈德良长城测绘数据，展示了从铁器时代晚期的围场到第二次世界大战的机场的多个时期的景观（© 英格兰遗产委员会.基础地图 © 皇家版权和数据权 2020.版权所有. 国家测绘局许可证号 100019088）。

levelled (as historical photographs can do), and it cannot identify subsurface deposits that may be seen as soilmarks or cropmarks on conventional photography. Aerial photography is also an important supporting source for accurate interpretation of lidar.

Structure from Motion

One area of current research interest is digital photogrammetry, or Structure from Motion (SfM). This technique creates accurate 3D data from sequences of 2D images. Within Historic England, SfM has been used on drone-acquired images for a number of small sites but the technique is also being applied to much larger areas using aircraft-acquired aerial photographs. At Birdoswald the landscape surrounding the fort was photographed from a light aircraft, resulting in around 1,200 aerial photographs (Fig.5). These were processed to produce an orthophoto (a seamless photographic dataset with all distortions very accurately removed) and a Digital Elevation Model (DEM). The resolution of the data was 9cm for the orthophoto and 18cm for the DEM which is more than adequate for landscape-scale investigation (Knight and Jecock forthcoming).

（lidar, 是 light, distance, and ranging 的缩略词，意即光、距离和范围）。如今，该方法已经成为认识历史环境的标准信息来源。英格兰遗产委员会于2003年曾将哈德良长城作为激光雷达的早期应用对象，以卡洛堡罗马要塞为中心的8平方千米为样带。这项工作由剑桥大学景观建模部门牵头，将获得的成像与航拍照片所获的信息进行了对比评估。其中最重要的发现之一是一处先前未发现的（位于要塞旁边的）罗马营地。它埋藏于在后来的犁耕遗迹之下（琼斯 2012, 68；图 9）。

如今，可以免费获得海量的英格兰激光雷达数据：该数据最初由负责英格兰环境的公共机构英国环境署采集，用于测绘洪水风险。纽卡斯尔大学曾对环境署的覆盖哈德良长城的激光雷达进行过快速评估（柯林斯 2015）,但仍然有必要对此进行进一步的系统分析和测绘。

有必要提醒的是，激光雷达并没有取代其他的航空资料来源，仅仅是起到补充的作用。另外值得一提的是，激光雷达显然只能记录直立的特征。它无法（像历史照片那样）记录已被夷为平地的遗址，也无法识别传统照片中暗示地下有考古堆积的土壤痕迹和作物痕迹。航拍照片也为准确地解译激光雷达数据起到了重要的支持作用。

运动恢复结构

数字摄影测量，又称运动恢复结构（SfM），是目前的又一研究方向。该技术可以从一序列2D图像中创建精准的3D数据。英格兰遗产委员会已经在一些小规模遗址上使用SfM处理通过无人机获取的图像，但该技术也同样被应用于分析航拍照片中的更大规模的区域。在博得瓦德，一架轻型飞机拍摄罗马要塞周围的景观，采集到大约1200张航拍照片（图 5）。这些照片经过处理，会生成正射影像（非常精确消除所有变形生成的无缝摄影数据集）以及数字高程模型（DEM）。正射影像和DEM的数据分辨率分别为9厘米和18厘米，完全可以满足开展景观规模的调查（奈特和杰考克 即将出版）。

测绘技术

自AIM团队于2008 年完成哈德良长城测绘工作以来，测绘技术也在不断进步。GIS 如今已经成为标准的测绘软件。与 AutoCAD 相比，该软件包能够更好地处理复杂的空间数据，并且能够同时查看多层信息和图像。

测绘的常用做法也在不断更新发展。哈德良长城测绘项目综合使用了多边形和单一线条，用来代表狭长的考古特征或陡坡峭壁的顶部。现如今，所有考古特征已经全部多边形化，能揭示更多细枝末节。同时，还使用示意性的T形晕滃线来表示陡坡峭壁[5]。记录的属性数据的数量也在不断增加，有助于对测绘数据进行更为复杂的分析。

数据传播平台

与以往相比，我们得以更为便捷地通过新技术向大众传播数据。线上门户网站能够让公众免费获取过去三十年所采集的全部航空测绘数据。该网站目前正在开发中。公众还有可能通过类似的线上平台免费访问英格兰遗产委员会档案馆的全部数字图像。

---

5 晕滃线是考古土质工事调查中使用的一种标准惯例，它使用一系列细长的短线来表示陡坡的顶部和底部。地形的坡度陡缓等其他细节也可以通过改变线条符号（粗细、疏密和长短）来表示。航空测绘则使用简化的T形符号，其中“T”的横线表示陡坡的顶部，而竖线的末端表示陡坡的底部。

Fig.5 An orthophotograph draped over a Digital Elevation Model of the landscape around Birdoswald Roman fort produced using SfM (© Historic England Archive).

图 5 一张覆盖于SfM制成的数字高程模型之上的正射影像。该高程模型绘制的是博得瓦德罗马要塞周围的景观（© 英格兰遗产委员会档案馆）。

Mapping Technologies

Since the completion of the AIM team's Hadrian's Wall project, mapping techniques have also evolved. GIS is now used as the standard mapping software package. This is much better at handling complex spatial data than AutoCAD and enables multiple layers of information and images to be viewed.

Mapping conventions have also continued to develop. The Hadrian's Wall mapping project used a combination of polygons and single line depictions for narrow features and the tops of scarps. All features are now fully polygonised which reveals more subtle details and a schematic T-hachure cartographic convention is used to depict scarps[5]. The amount of attribute data recorded has also increased which allows more sophisticated analysis of the mapping data.

Data Dissemination Platforms

New technology is also giving us the opportunity to disseminate data to the general public more easily than ever before. An online portal will provide free access to all of the aerial mapping data collected over the last 30 years and is currently in development. The possibility of using similar online platforms to provide access to all digital images held by the Historic England archive is also imminent.

5 A hachure is a standard convention used in archaeological earthwork survey which uses an array of elongated symbols to convey the top and bottom of a slope. Other details such as the steepness of the slope can also be depicted by altering the symbology. Aerial mapping uses a simplified convention based on a 'T' shaped symbol where the horizontal bar of the T indicates the top of the slope and the end of the vertical line denotes the bottom of the slope.

References
参考文献

Anon. 1893. 'Donation to the museum', *Proceedings of the Society of Antiquaries of Newcastle upon Tyne, 2nd series* 5, 227.

阿依. 1893. 向博物馆捐赠，见于纽卡斯尔文物考古学会论文集（系列二），5, 227.

Bidwell, P. 2018. *Hadrian's Wall at Wallsend*, Arbeia Society Roman Archaeological Studies 1, South Shields.

P·比得维尔. 2018. 沃森德的哈德良长城，见于阿尔比亚学会罗马考古研究 1. 南希尔德.

Birley, A. R. 1979. *The People of Roman Britain*, London.

A . R · 伯利. 1979. 罗马不列颠行省的人民. 伦敦.

Birley, E. 1939. 'Building-records from Hadrian's Wall', *Archaeologia Aeliana,* 3rd series, 16, 219–36.

E · 伯利. 1939. 哈德良长城的建造记录，见于纽卡斯尔考古（系列三），16, 219-36.

Breeze, D. J. and Dobson, B. 2000. *Hadrian's Wall* (fourth edn), Harmondsworth.

D · 布雷兹，B · 多布森. 2000. 哈德良长城（第四版）. 哈默兹沃斯.

Bruce, J. C. 1975. *Lapidarium Septentrionale*, London.

J . C · 布鲁斯. 1975. 北石首鱼 . 伦敦.

Clayton, J. 1883. 'Observations on centurial stones found on the Roman Wall, Northumberland and Cumberland', *Archaeologia Aeliana,* 2nd series, 9, 22–39.

J · 克雷顿. 1883. 对罗马长城中发现的百人队石的观察，诺桑波兰和坎布里亚地区，见于纽卡斯尔考古（系列二），9, 2-39 .

Collingwood, R. G. 1926. 'Roman inscriptions and sculptures belonging to the Society of Antiquaries of Newcastle upon Tyne', *Archaeologia Aeliana,* 3rd series, 2, 52–124.

R . G · 科林伍德. 1926. 纽卡斯尔考古协会的罗马勒名石和雕塑，见于纽卡斯尔考古（系列三），2, 52-124.

DeLaine, J. 2002. 'The Temple of Hadrian at Cyzicus and Roman attitudes to exceptional construction,' *Papers of the British School at Rome,* 70, 205-230.

J · 德林. 2002. 基齐库司的哈德良神庙和罗马人对杰出建筑的态度，见于罗马英国学院论文集，70，205-230.

Hodgson, N. 2017. *Hadrian's Wall. Archaeology and History at the Limit of Rome's Empire*, Marlborough.

N · 霍奇森 . 2017. 哈德良长城. 罗马帝国边缘的考古和历史. 马布尔.

Horsley, J. 1732. *Britannia Romana*, London.

J · 霍斯利 . 1732. 罗马不列颠尼亚. 伦敦.

Jones, C. P. 2005. 'Ten dedications "To the gods and goddesses" and the Antonine plague', *Journal of Roman Archaeology,* 18, 293–301.

C . P · 琼斯 . 2005. 供奉众神的十件祭品和安东尼瘟疫. 罗马考古，18, 293-301.

Leach, S. and Whitworth, A. 2011. *Saving the Wall. The Conservation of Hadrian's Wall 1746–1987*, Stroud.

S · 里奇，A · 维斯沃斯 . 2011. 保全长城，见于哈德良长城的保护，1746-1987. 斯特拉德.

RIB Collingwood, R. G., and Wright, R. P., 1965. *The Roman Inscriptions of Britain. I, Inscriptions on Stone*, Oxford; Tomlin, R. S. O., Wright, R. P., and Hassall, M. W. C., 2009. *The Roman Inscriptions of Britain. III, Inscriptions on Stone*, Oxford.

R . G · 科林伍德，R . P · 怀特. 1965. 不列颠的罗马勒名石. I，勒名石，牛津；R . S . O· 汤姆林， R·P· 怀特，M·W·C ·汉森尔. 2009. 不列颠的罗马石刻. III，勒名石，牛津.

Stevens, C. E. 1966. *The Building of Hadrian's Wall*, Cumberland and Westmorland Antiquarian and Archaeological Society, Extra Series, 20, Kendal.

C . E · 斯蒂文斯. 1966. 建造哈德良长城，坎步兰和维斯特摩兰文物考古会（增补系列）, 20. 肯德尔.

Tomlin, R. S. O. 2019. 'Roman Britain in 2018. III. Inscriptions', *Britannia.* 50, 496–524.

R . S . O · 汤姆林. 2019. 罗马不列颠 2018. III. 石刻，50, 496-524. 不列颠尼亚.

3.4 天空地一体化的长城资源监测体系构建

张景
国信司南（北京）地理信息技术有限公司—中国—北京

摘要

本文在综合分析长城资源监测与保护需求的基础上，针对长城资源监测与保护的特点，构建了天地空一体化的长城资源监测体系，旨在为长城资源的监测、保护、管理、合理开发利用等工作提供更好的支持与服务。

关键词： 长城资源　遥感监测

一、绪论

长城是中国乃至世界上最珍贵的文化遗产之一，代表了古代人民的勤劳与智慧，是中华民族精神的象征。但基于长城资源本身的长度长、数量多、分布广的复杂特性，限于当前的管理水平与技术条件，长城资源监测与保护难以全面实现常态化与高效化。以遥感技术为核心的空间信息技术，以及协同地理信息、物联网、大数据和云计算等新一代信息技术，以其宏观性、实时性、周期性及综合性等特征为优势，为提高长城资源监测与保护能力带来了新的契机，在文化遗产监测、保护管理工作中发挥着越来越重要的作用。因此，及时开展基于遥感技术的长城资源监测具有重要的理论与现实意义。

（一）研究缘起

近年来，文化遗产保护的发展日新月异，国内外遗产监测也越来越受到重视。并采取了一系列的遗产保护政策，如：

- 1997 年，世界遗产中心修订发布《保护世界文化与自然遗产公约操作指南》，要求申报世界遗产时提交对遗产地真实性和完整性的监测工作安排。
- 2004 年 2 月 15 日，国务院办公厅转发《关于加强我国世界文化遗产保护管理工作意见的通知》（国办发 [2004] 18号），要求建立世界文化遗产监测巡视制度；
- 2016 年国家文物局发布的《中国长城保护报告》明确了长城保护目标，即实施长城监测预警，加强预防性保护，提升长城资源信息化管理水平；
- 2019 年 1 月 22 日，文化和旅游部、国家文物局联合印发《长城保护总体规划》，明确了坚持价值优先、坚持预防为主、坚持因地制宜的长城保护要求；

长城是中华民族的精神象征，是我国现存体量最大、分布最广的文化遗产，做好长城保护对于展示中华民族灿烂文明，坚定文化自信，弘扬社会主义核心价值观，促进经济社会发展，具有十分重要的意义。

3.4 CONSTRUCTION OF AN INTEGRATED MONITORING SYSTEM FOR GREAT WALL RESOURCES USING SPACEBORNE, AIRBORNE, AND GROUND-BASED REMOTE SENSING TECHNOLOGIES

ZHANG JING
Geo-Compass Information Technology Co. Ltd - China - Beijing

Abstract

This paper describes a monitoring system with integrated spaceborne, airborne, and ground-based remote sensing technologies (ISAGRS) to provide better support and services for the monitoring, protection, management and use of the Great Wall's resources.

Keywords: Great Wall resources, remote sensing, monitoring

INTRODUCTION

The Great Wall is one of China's most significant cultural heritage sites and is of world-wide renown. It not only represents the capabilities and ingenuity of the ancient Chinese people, but is also a symbol of China's national identity. However, due to the complex characteristics of the Great Wall's resources - its great scale, the quantity of its remains, and their wide distribution - and to the limitations of current management capability and technological strength, it is difficult to comprehensively and efficiently standardise their monitoring and protection. With the advantages of being macro, real-time, regularly repeatable, and comprehensive, spatial information technology, based on remote sensing and new-generation information technologies, (including integrated geographic information, the Internet of Things [IoT], big data and cloud computing), has created new opportunities of great scientific and practical significance to improve the monitoring, protection and management of the Great Wall's resources.

Monitoring in heritage management

In recent years, with the rapid expansion of cultural heritage protection activities, heritage monitoring has been receiving more and more attention both in China and abroad. At the same time, a series of heritage protection policies have been stipulated. These include:

- In 1997, the World Heritage Centre revised the *Operational Guidelines for the Implementation of the World Heritage Convention*, requiring that arrangements for monitoring the state of conservation of heritage sites be submitted when applying for world Heritage status.
- On February 15th, 2004, the *Notice of the General Office of the State Council on Transmitting the Opinions of Strengthening the Administration on Protection of World Cultural Heritages of China* (No.018 [2004] of the General Office of the State Council) was released, recommending the establishment of a world cultural heritage monitoring and inspection mechanism.
- The *China Great Wall Protection Report*, released by the State Administration for Cultural Heritage (SACH) in 2016, identified the objectives of the Great Wall protection programme as being to conduct monitoring and risk identification, to strengthen preventive conservation, and to upgrade the application of information technology in the management of the Great Wall.

（二）研究背景与研究目的

根据 2016 年国家文物局公布的《中国长城保护报告》显示，长城的墙壕遗存总长度 21196.18千米，各类墙体、单体建筑、相关遗存等 43721 处。各时代长城资源分布于 15 个省（自治区、直辖市）404 个县（市、区）。因缺少相关技术支撑，对长城资源的监测与保护主要依赖各地方机构的日常巡视，传统的人工巡查方式难以实现监测保护的常态化与高效化。

随着互联网时代的深刻变革，云计算、大数据、物联网、移动互联网等智能化技术的不断发展以及地理信息技术的不断飞跃，“3S+大数据+物联网”将会对行业服务及工作模式产生根本性影响。本文针对长城资源监测与保护的特点，构建了天地空一体化的长城资源监测体系，旨在实现长城资源的精准化监测和多维决策与可视化分析，为长城资源的监测、保护、管理、合理开发利用等工作提供更好的技术支撑。

二、天地空一体化的长城资源监测体系

（一）监测体系定义

天空地一体化的长城资源监测体系是利用遥感卫星、无人机、移动互联网技术，构建了从天空到地面的全方位监测模式，在统一的空间基准下从多尺度多维度观测长城资源变化，从而提升长城资源的监测和保护管理能力。

（二）可行性分析

长城资源的信息已实现数字化和位置化。随着全国长城资源调查工作的顺利完成，特别是利用测绘技术现对长城资源的实精准测绘，目前国家文物局已建设完成了全国长城资源信息管理系统，可提供分米级别的长城资源位置信息服务，天地空一体化长城资源监测的先行条件已满足。

长城分布区域已基本实现网络信号全覆盖。中国互联网硬件基础条件不断完善，长城的分布地区已基本覆盖 3G/4G 甚至是 5G 的网络信号，各种监测技术与设备可在移动互联网的基础上实现无缝集成。

无人机民用化。无人机技术的不断完善，价格便宜且操作简易方便，一般人员经过简单的培训即可上岗，使得远程监测成为可能。

遥感技术的不断发展。随着遥感技术的飞跃发展，遥感影像的空间分辨率越来越高、时间分辨率越来越小，使得获得大范围、高精度、短周期的长城资源影像图成为现实。

其他行业的应用相对成熟。在全国土地调查，林业普查等各类资源调查工作中，遥感、无人机以及地面移动调查系统的结合使用已经普遍应用，为长城资源的监测提供了成熟的行业应用案例。

（三）基础支撑框架

天空地一体化的长城资源监测体系，是在“强安全、控资源、提效率、优管理”的框架下，探索物联感知“一张网”、数据管理“一个库”、智慧管理“一平台”的长城资源监测保护模式。

物联感知“一张网”。这张网是基于统一的基础设施而构建，包括两个层面的内容。一是信息资源获取、存储和处理的承载设备，包括传统的硬件设备、各种监测传感设备、移动终端等。二是承担着信息资源传输重要任务的信息通道，包括以无线网络、互联网为一体的、无所不在的高速传输光纤网络。

- On January 22th, 2019, the Ministry of Culture and Tourism and NCHA issued the *Master Plan for the Conservation of the Great Wall*, reinforcing requirements of value-based, proactive approaches, adaptive to local conditions.

As the symbol of national identity, the Great Wall is the cultural World Heritage Site of greatest size and widest distribution in China. Thus, the effective protection of the Great Wall is of vital importance to demonstrate the splendour of ancient Chinese civilization, to boost cultural confidence, to promote core values and to foster economic development and improve social well-being.

Research background and purpose

According to the *China Great Wall Protection Report*, the remaining walls total 21,196km in length, and there are 43,721 individual elements including various walls, free-standing structures and other structures and components. The Great Wall's resources which were built in different periods are located in 404 counties of 15 provinces, autonomous regions and direct municipalities. Due to the lack of technical support, the monitoring and protection of the Great Wall's resources depends mainly on the daily inspections conducted by local authorities. However, traditional human inspection is not able to ensure regular and efficient monitoring. With profound changes happening in the Internet era, the constant development of intelligent technologies including cloud computing, big data, IoT, and mobile internet, as well as significant breakthroughs in geographic information technology, and the integration of remote sensing, GIS, GPS, big data and IoT, will have fundamental impacts on their potential to serve all sectors and to transform traditional working practices. Given the monitoring and protection requirements of the Great Wall, this paper establishes an integrated monitoring system for the Great Wall's resources utilising spaceborne, airborne, and ground-based remote sensing technologies. This will facilitate accurate monitoring, multi-dimensional decision-making and visual analysis, thereby providing better technological support for the monitoring, protection, management and use of the Great Wall.

THE *ISAGRS* MONITORING SYSTEM FOR THE GREAT WALL

Definition of the monitoring system

The integrated monitoring system utilises remote sensing satellites, drones and mobile internet technologies and establishes an all-round monitoring mode from the sky to the earth. It aims to monitor changes to the Great Wall's resources from multiple dimensions and at different resolutions and thus to enhance the management capability to monitor and to protect them.

Feasibility analysis

The information about the Great Wall's resources has already been digitised and spatially located. With the Great Wall Resource Survey completed, and especially its accurate mapping, NCHA has developed the national Great Wall Resource Information Management System, which can provide decimetre-level location information for each of its elements. Thus, the preconditions for establishing an *ISAGRS* monitoring system are all in place.

Full network coverage has already been realised across the Great Wall. The internet infrastructure in China has been improved continuously, and 3G/4G or even 5G networks have largely covered all areas in which the Great Wall is situated. This means that various monitoring technologies and facilities can be seamlessly integrated based on mobile internet access. At the same time, civilian drone usage has become more popular. With constant improvements in technology, drones have become less expensive and easier to operate and people can learn to control them properly after only simple training. All these make remote monitoring possible. Continuous advances in remote sensing technology have also been made, which, as a result, bring a higher spatial resolution and a higher temporal resolution of remote-sensing images. Thus, it is possible to receive large-scale, high-precision and

图 1 “天空地”一体化监测方法（绘制：张景）。
Fig.1 Integrated monitoring with spaceborne, airborne and ground-based remote sensing technologies (composed by Zhang Jing).

数据管理“一个库”。该数据库包含两部分内容：一是覆盖长城资源的基础地理数据库；另一个是开展长城资源保护、管理、利用等工作的档案库。为完善和加强长城“四有”工作，提高长城保护与监测水平提高坚实有效的信息支撑。

智慧管理“一平台”。该平台运用大数据技术对各类专题数据进行融合分析，结合我国自主研发的互联网地图服务平台天地图，在长城基础数据库的基础上，实现长城信息资源及相关业务数据资源的综合监管与智能决策，达到“动态数据可用、工作流程可溯、风险隐患可控、调度指挥可视、管理形势可判”的目标，实现多元化的长城资源管理体系。

（四）监测方法与应用

天空地一体化的长城资源监测体系主要包含了基于卫星遥感技术的遗产监测预警、基于无人机技术的遗产监测预警、基于移动设备的遗产监测预警三种监测方式，以适用于不同的现实应用场景。

- 天—基于卫星遥感技术的遗产监测预警

在偏远、人烟稀少的长城资源监测区域，利用不同传感器卫星影像对长城资源进行数据获取，可以全面掌握遗产区内土地利用现状、土地覆盖变化、新建项目动态等信息；同时，还可以以遥感影像为基础，结合遗产专题数据制作专题图件。利用卫星遥感进行长城全范围全时段的监测，是对传统摄像头、物联网、人工防护等监测手段的有效补充。

- 空—基于无人机技术的遗产监测预警

在人工巡查困难的长城资源监测区域，无人机监测成本较低、操作简单，能够在恶劣条件下进行低空飞行监测。在无人机远程控制智能平台上进行可以远程控制监测设备，数据获取周期短，时效性高，能够实现自动定时拍照、照片回传、画面对比分析、实时画面直播等功能。以无人机获取的长城遗址大比例影像数据为基础、以遗产要素及巡查任务为框架，精确的模块化监测为长城遗址的格局规划、建设控制等工作提供化的服务。

- 地—基于移动设备采集技术的遗产监测预警

regularly updated images of the Great Wall's resources. These mature technologies have already been applied in many other industries. *ISAGRS* investigation systems have been widely used in the national land survey, forestry census and the surveying of other resources providing examples of their effectiveness.

The basic framework

Under the framework of the objectives of protecting the fabric of the Great Wall, of controlling resources, promoting efficiency, and improving management, the integrated monitoring system of the Great Wall has explored an innovative approach consisting of three components named One Network, One Database and One Platform.

Developed in a unified infrastructure, the 'One Network' is an infrastructure which utilises the concept of the IoT which plays two roles. Firstly, it organizes all related facilities, including traditional hardware, monitoring and sensing equipment and mobile terminals that obtain, store and process information resources. Secondly, it is the channel that transmits information: a high-speed transmission optical network integrated with wireless networks and the internet.

The One Database for data management can be divided into two parts: the basic geo-database of all the Great Wall's resources, and the working documentation relating to their protection, management and use. It can provide effective support to further implement the requirements of the 'Four Haves' and the protection and monitoring of the Great Wall.

The One Platform for smart management utilises big data to conduct fusion analysis of thematic data. Moreover, supported by the Great Wall basic geo-database and Map World[1], it enables the comprehensive supervision and interrogation of the Great Wall information resources and other relevant data resources. As a result, the target of having available dynamic data, traceable working processes, controllable risks, visible project-control systems, as well as assessable condition monitoring, can be achieved, and a diversified management system for Great Wall's resources can be established.

Monitoring approaches and applications

The *ISAGRS* monitoring system for Great Wall includes three principal approaches of heritage monitoring and risk alerts, based on satellite remote sensing, on drones, and on mobile devices, and can be applied to different locations and contexts.

Spaceborne heritage monitoring and risk alerts based on satellite remote sensing technology, which use various sensors and satellites to collect data on the Great Wall's resources in remote areas, can identify current land utilisation, land-cover changes, and new constructions within the heritage zone. Using satellite remote-sensing technology to conduct 24/7 monitoring of all the sections is an effective supplement to the traditional use of cameras, IoT and other monitoring by individuals.

Airborne heritage monitoring and risks alerts are those based on drone technology. For those regions that are less accessible, drone technology can be used for monitoring, the advantages being its low cost and ease of operation. In addition, it can monitor the Great Wall by conducting low-altitude flights even in bad conditions. The monitoring devices can be remotely controlled on an intelligent platform, data can be accessed more quickly, and the whole process is more time-efficient. Furthermore, drone technology also supports timed interval photography, photo transmission, contrastive image analysis, live streaming, and other functions. Based on the high-resolution image data of the Great Wall obtained by drones and the accurate comparison of multi-phased images, changes to the Great Wall itself and the surrounding environment can be identified as they happen, existing and developing problems can be readily understood, and early warning of major problems can be obtained.

Daily inspection is still the most commonly used approach to monitoring. In the Great Wall resource monitoring areas suitable for in person inspection, mobile devices are used to collect monitoring data on the Great Wall.

1 Map World is a network geographic information sharing and service portal developed by the National Geomatics Center of China (Editors' note).

图 2 无人机巡查监测方法（图片来源：基于网络 http://www.v.3023.com/ 无人机航拍箭扣长城 中国历史上最宏伟的军事要塞 – 旅游，原作者不详）。

Fig.2 Inspection and monitoring images by drone at Jiankou Great Wall （based on http://www.v.3023.com/ author unknown）.

图 3 移动巡查监测方法（绘制：张景基于长城巡视巡检系统数据制作）。

Fig.3 Inspection and monitoring, supported by mobile devices （composed by Zhang Jing）.

为了保证建成后的监测预警平台正常运行，有鲜活的实时监测数据输入，日常巡视巡检是最为常用的管理手段。在适合人工巡查的长城资源监测区域，基于移动GIS技术，结合长城移动巡查的特点，进行长城资源的定点巡视巡查，实现长城资源的全方位的实时监测，使遗产本体和环境的安全得到有效的保障，切实使遗产监测成为长城保护管理工作的有力抓手。

三、前景展望

万里长城是我国历史文化与民族精神的象征，是世界知名的重要文化遗产。随着我国对文化遗产的保护意识不断提高，长城资源的监测与保护管理工作将越来越受到社会各界的重视。随着遥感技术的不断发展，数据的精度逐渐提高，获取数据的周期越来越短，成本不断下降，全天候实时的长城高清影像获取将成为可能。基于5G 的物联网技术日益成熟，各类智能传感器将更多取代人工监测。空间信息技术将更广泛、更深入地服务于长城资源保护。

Through ground hand-held or vehicle-mounted mobile devices equipped with geographic positioning and GIS systems, multi-dimensional monitoring can be generated which can pin-point emerging problems in real time. This enables comprehensive and real-time monitoring of the Great Wall's resources, as well as its wider environment and the impact of human activities, which can inform the overall management the Great Wall. This ensures that heritage monitoring will become an important factor in the Great Wall's protection and management.

THE FUTURE

The Great Wall World Heritage Site is not only a symbol of Chinese history and culture but also of Chinese national identity. With the continuous improvement in awareness of the importance of cultural heritage protection, much more attention will be paid by wider society to the monitoring, protection, and management of the Great Wall's resources. In the near future, the constant development of remote sensing technology will improve data accuracy, shorten the time needed to get access to data, and further reduce costs. This will make it possible for us to obtain 24/7 real-time high-definition images of the Great Wall. At the same time, 5G-based IoT technology will become more mature, and the demand for human monitoring will continue to decrease with various smart sensors taking its place. Lastly, spatial information technology will also be more widely and deeply applied to the protection of the Great Wall's resources.

参考文献
References

Chai, Y. 2016. *The Exploration of Architectural Heritage Protection Planning Aided by Airborne and Ground Information Technology*, Master's dissertation, Tianjin University.

柴亚隆. 2016. "空-地"信息技术辅助建筑遗产保护规划探索. 硕士论文，天津大学建筑学院.

Du, P. 2006. *Principles and Applications of Remote Sensing*, Beijing: China University of Mining and Technology Press

杜培军. 2006. 遥感原理与应用 . 北京：中国矿业大学出版社.

General Office of The State Council. 2006. The Great Wall Protection Regulations.

国务院办公厅. 2006. 长城保护条例 .

Hu, P. & Huang, X. 2002. *A Course in Geographic Information Systems*, Wuhan: Wuhan University Press

胡鹏. 2002. 地理信息系统教程. 武汉：武汉大学出版社.

Luo, Z. & Wen, A. 2009. 'Things to Do Before the Great Wall Protection: Knowing What Resources Do We Have', in *Beijing Planning Review*. Issue 06: 81-83

罗哲文，文爱平. 长城保护要先摸清家底. 北京规划建设，2009（06）：81-83.

Shan, J. 2006. 'A Preliminary Study of Large-scale Linear and Serial Cultural Heritages: Breakthroughs and Pressure'. in *Relics from South*. Issue 03

单霁翔. 大型线性文化遗产保护初论：突破与压力. 南方文物，2006（03）.

SACH. 2006. Management Rules on China World Cultural Heritage Monitoring and Inspection.

SACH. 中国世界文化遗产监测巡视管理办法. 2006-12-8.

UNESCO. 1997. *Operational Guidelines for the Implementation of the World Heritage Convention*,1997

联合国教科文组织.1997. 保护世界文化与自然遗产公约.

Zhang, X. 2017. *The Study on Drought Monitoring Oriented Collaborative Method Based on Multiple Satellites and In-situ Sensors*, PhD thesis, Wuhan University.

张翔. 2017. 面向干旱监测应用的星地多传感器协同方法研究. 博士论文，武汉：武汉大学测绘遥感信息工程国家重点实验室.

3.5 箭扣长城保护维修中干预过程管理的数字化途径探索

张剑葳, 尚劲宇, 吴煜楠
北京大学考古文博学院，北京大学中国考古学研究中心—中国—北京

内容提要

基于文物的“现状”、“原状”和“干预”三个重要概念及内在关系，提出了运用数字化技术对长城修缮段落持续进行模型和图像数据采集和追踪，以形成一套数字化数据集的“源场景”概念，进而利用箭扣南段长城修缮工程中的数据成果检验了此种方法的作用和意义。基于“源场景”概念，不仅可有效运用数字化技术对长城保护维修中的修缮和干预进行过程管理，还将推动文物保护工程一系列管理与操作模式的更新。

关键词：长城保护维修　原状　干预　数字化记录　源场景

绪论

长城是中国最重要的文化遗产之一，其保护工作受到广泛关注。从 1952 年开始，国家逐步对多段长城进行保护修缮，在此过程中保护维修的原则和方法也经历了从“恢复原状”到“原状保护”的变化。2014 年国家文物局公布的《长城保护维修工作指导意见》中，明确要求“长城保护维修必须遵守不改变原状和最小干预的原则”。本文结合中国文物保护基金会、腾讯公益慈善基金会资助的箭扣南段长城修缮工程中的数字化保护实践，探讨在长城维修中具体如何实践相关原则，并提出一种运用数字化记录方法对保护工程进行过程管理的数字化新途径。

一、理论基础与方案设计：时间轴上的数字化场景序列

长城或者其他文物古迹，在其“生命过程”中都经历了设计、建造和保存三个阶段。因为自然和人为因素的影响，文物古迹的状态是不断变化的，这些不断变化的状态的累积形成了文物古迹的“现状”。随着时间推移，自然和人为因素不断改变着文物古迹的状态，形成新的“现状”（图 1）。

“干预”是文物古迹的状态改变的原因之一，也是新的现状形成的原因之一。正如《准则》在阐释“最低限度干预”原则时的表述：“对文物古迹的保护是对其生命过程的干预和存在状况的改变。”我们应当关注不同时间点上的干预情况，在干预中关注时间参数，注意时间维度中文物古迹“原状”可能被改变的情况，并及时注意到新“现状”的形成情况。

在长城维修工程中，长城短时间内受到集中的干预，保存状态变动加剧。对于变动中的长城状态，其每一时刻的现状是能被直接记录的。运用数字化手段在不同时刻记录长城维修过程中的现状，可以形成有序的长城状态及其变化的数据，用以支撑评估维修过程和科学管理。

3.5 A DIGITISATION APPROACH TO THE PROCESS MANAGEMENT OF INTERVENTION IN THE PRESERVATION AND MAINTENANCE PROJECT OF THE GREAT WALL AT JIANKOU

ZHANG JIANWEI, SHANG JINYU, WU YUNAN
Peking University - China - Beijing

Abstract

Based on the relationships between three important concepts in the conservation of cultural heritage monuments, 'current condition', 'original condition' and 'intervention', this paper describes the use of digital technology to carry out continuous collection and tracking of 3D and 2D image data on a section of the Great Wall under consolidation. This is used to form a series of digital datasets, collectively referred to as the 'meta scene'. It then describes how the results and significance of this method were tested in the conservation project on the Southern Jiankou section of the Great Wal (the Jiankou Project)l. The concept of the meta scene demonstrates not only how digital technology can be effectively used to manage the processes in the conservation of the Great Wall, but also to drive improvement in management and operational procedures in conservation projects more generally .

Keywords: consolidation of the Great Wall, historical fabric, intervention, digital documentation, meta scene

INTRODUCTION

The Great Wall is one of the most important cultural heritage sites in China, and its conservation has been the subject of considerable concern. Since 1952, repair and conservation projects have been carried out on many sections of the Great Wall. During this process, the principles and practices in conservation projects have shifted from 'restoring to its original condition' to 'conserving its historical fabric' (Li 2013). In 2014, the State Administration of Cultural Heritage (SACH) published a document entitled Guidance on the Conservation of the Great Wall (the Guidelines), which stipulated that the principles of 'no change to the historical fabric' and 'minimal intervention' must be followed in its repair and conservation. This paper discusses how these principles are applied in practice in the conservation of the Great Wall, and proposes a new way to use digital recording to manage projects, based on the experience of their use in the Jiankou Project, which was funded by the China Foundation for Cultural Heritage Conservation and Tencent Foundation.

THEORY AND DESIGN: DIGITISING SCENES ON A TIMELINE

All historic monuments including the Great Wall experience a life-cycle of their design, construction, operational use and maintenance, periodic renovation, abandonment and decay and subsequent conservation. Due to natural and human impacts, the condition of heritage sites is constantly changing, and these accumulated changes have resulted in their 'current condition'. As time passes, this process of change continues and new 'current conditions' are formed (Fig.1).

Intervention is one of the causes of change to the condition of heritage sites, creating a new 'current condition'. In describing the principle of minimum intervention, the *Principles for the Conservation of Heritage Sites in China* (the

因此，在箭扣南段长城修缮工程中首先运用数字化技术记录文物古迹的空间和图像信息，形成每一时刻的数字化场景，主要包括具有纹理、空间信息的模型数据和具有方位信息的图像数据，两者根据高精度的地理坐标信息匹配，形成可视化的数据成果。这样的数字化场景序列反映了时间轴上的文物古迹状态及其变化的可视化数据，我们将其定义为文物古迹的“源场景”。

二、实证：箭扣南段长城修缮工程试验段的“源场景”工作案例

在中国文物保护基金会、腾讯公益慈善基金会资助的箭扣南段长城修缮工程中，基于“源场景”的概念，北京大学考古文博学院的团队综合运用全球卫星导航系统（GNSS）定位、摄影测量和全景摄影等数字化技术，记录了试验段长城在修缮不同阶段的现状。形成的箭扣南段长城修缮工程试验段“源场景”数据成果提供了回溯修缮过程的基础，为科学管理修缮过程、评估修缮工程对长城的干预程度和原状影响提供了一种可行途径。

在箭扣南段长城修缮工程中，我们选取152号敌楼及两侧各50m边墙段作为试验段，分别于2018年5月25日（干预前），9月15日（清理中），10月30日（修缮施工中），2019年5月30日（干预后）对试验段进行数字化记录，形成由四次数据组成的试验段“源场景”成果。

通过箭扣南段长城修缮工程试验段“源场景”的数据成果，可以回溯和分析干预过程，从而实现对修缮工程的过程管理和评估。

以152号敌楼东南雉堞为例：干预前（2018年5月25日）的场景数据反映152号敌楼东南雉堞变形，向内侧倾斜，未坍塌，原构件和原有结构形制完整保留，变形部分有坍塌风险。清理中（2018年9月15日）和修缮施工中（2018年10月30日）两次“源场景”数据成果显示，修缮过程中对152号敌楼东南雉堞变形部分采取了拆砌的干预措施（图2）。《准则》在阐释“不改变原状”原则时指出“不改变文物原状的原则可以包括保存现状和恢复原状两方面内容。……可以恢复原状的对象有：……2.变形、错置、支撑以前的状态”。因此，修缮过程中对152号敌楼东南雉堞的干预行为符合《准则》“不改变原状”原则的要求。

进而，《长城保护维修工作指导意见》对于拆砌的干预措施有较为具体的要求：“确需局部拆砌（筑）时，应在拆卸前详细记录各类长城构件的位置和形制，并在采取结构加固措施后将其按原位置、原形制复位。”但是我们将干预前（2018年5月25日）和干预后（2019年5月30日）两次数据成果对比后发现,152号敌楼东南雉堞变形部分拆砌前后，形制存在一定差别（图3）。

通过“源场景”数据成果发现的修缮过程中的不足，在修缮工程期间已及时反馈给修缮工程的各主要参与方，各方及时、有针对性地对部分修缮措施进行了纠正和改进。综上，“源场景”数据成果能够有效地记录箭扣南段长城修缮工程试验段长城在集中的干预行为下状态的改变，为回溯和分析修缮过程提供了基础，有助于科学地管理和评估修缮工程。

三、讨论：数字化新途径推动的模式更新与公众参与

“源场景”在箭扣南段长城修缮工程试验段中的有效应用，为长城保护维修的过程管理提供了一种数字化新途径，并将对工作模式带来一系列积极影响：

第一，从国家文物局对长城保护维修方案的批复意见看，以往的勘察成果存在一些普遍问题，主要表现在现状测绘不完整、病害分析不全面等方面。大部分勘察成果，现状表达以照片配合线图为主，内容不

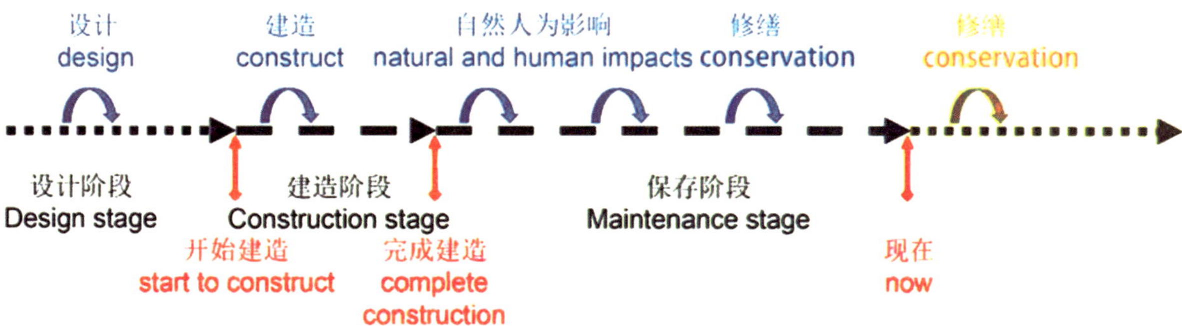

图 1 文物古迹的状态改变体现在时间轴上（绘制：尚劲宇）。
Fig.1 The life-cycle of heritage sites (composed by Shang Jinyu).

Principles) issued by ICOMOS China acknowledged that ‘protecting a heritage site is also intervening in its life cycle and changing its existing condition.’ The Principles recommended that consideration should be given to the impact of interventions at different stages of the life cycle. So attention should be paid to different phases of the intervention process, taking their timing as an integral dimension of the intervention. It should be noted that the ‘historical condition’ can be changing along the time axis while new ‘current conditions’ might be formed at any time.

During conservation projects, the Great Wall is subject to intensive intervention over a short period of time, and its condition can change dramatically. Any ‘current condition’ during the changing process can be recorded instantly at each moment. Using digital ways to record the ‘current condition’ of the Great Wall at different times during the repair can generate comprehensive data of a series of changing conditions. The data collected can then be used to evaluate the repair process and to support its management.

This conservation project first applied digital technology to record the spatial and image information of the monument, and then generated digital imagery at every stage, including 3D imagery with textural, spatial and image data, together with location information. The 3D data and 2D image data, combined with highly accurate geo-location information, eventually generated visual data results. These sequenced digital scenes provided visual data that reflects the changes to the condition of the monument on a timeline, which was defined as the ‘meta scene’ of the monument.

CASE STUDY: THE APPLICATION OF THE META SCENE METHODOLOGY ON TRIAL SECTIONS IN THE JIANKOU PROJECT

In the Jiankou Project, the team from Peking University Archaeology and Museology College applied the meta scene methodology involving technologies such as GNSS location, digital photogrammetry and panoramic photography to record the ‘current conditions’ of the Great Wall during different stages of the conservation. The meta scene data that was generated served as a baseline for reviewing the conservation process; it also provided a possible way to scientifically manage the conservation process, and to evaluate the degree of intervention and impact on the historical fabric of the Great Wall during the process.

We selected Defence Tower No.152 and 50m of the Wall on each side of it as the trial section for the project: we digitally recorded its status on 25th May 2018 (before intervention), 15th September (during clearance), 30th October (during consolidation) and 30th May 2019 (after intervention), forming the meta scenes from the data collected from these four recordings. From the meta scenes we were able to look back and analyse the intervention

图2箭扣南段长城修缮工程试验段“源场景”（152敌楼东南）反映的长城状态变化：干预前（2018年5月25日）（上）；清理中（2018年9月15日）（中）；修缮施工中（2018年10月30日）（下） 模型中红色圆点代表对应全景位置。（图片来源：尚劲宇）。

Fig.2 The meta scenes created for the south-east side of Defence Tower no.152 show the changes in the condition of the Great Wall during the project: before intervention (top); during clearance (middle); during consolidation (bottom). The red dots in the 3D image represent the reference points in the panoramic photography (images by Shang Jinyu).

图3干预前和干预后“源场景”数据对比（东南向)干预前（2018年5月25日)(左)；修缮施工中（2018年10月30日)(中)；干预后（2019年5月30日）（右）（摄影：尚劲宇）。

Fig.3 Meta scene data comparison before and after intervention (south east face): before intervention (left); during consolidation (middle); after intervention (right) (photographs by Shang Jinyu).

process and, in turn, to better manage and evaluate the conservation project.

For example, the data shows that the southeast battlement on Defence Tower No.152 was deformed before intervention (25th May 2018), leaning inwards but still standing. Though the original structure was intact, the deformation posed potential risks of collapse. The two meta scenes generated during the clearance (15th September 2018) and consolidation (30th October 2018) phases show that the intervention measures applied were the removal of the deformed battlement and the reinstatement of masonry (Fig.2). When the Principles explain how to achieve 'no change to the historical fabric,' it suggests either preserving its current condition or repairing it to its historical condition, the latter could be chosen for those parts that are deformed, dislocated or reliant on modern support measures. The intervention undertaken to the battlement of Defence Tower No.152 therefore meets the requirement of the 'no change to the historical fabric' according to the Principles.

In the Guidelines there are specific requirements regarding the dismantling and the reinstatement of masonry of structures: 'for parts that need to be dismantled, their location and forms should be recorded precisely before they are dismantled, and they should then be reinstated according to their original location and shape after the internal structure has been strengthened.' However, when we compared the data recorded before the intervention (25th May 2018) with the data after the intervention (30th May 2019), we discovered that there were some differences in its shape and form (Fig.3).

Problems were discovered by analysing the meta scene data, which were then reported to those parties involved in the conservation project so that they could promptly correct and improve the conservation techniques and measures. To sum up, data from the meta scene was able to accurately record the changes to the monument during the intensive conservation process on the trial section of the Jiankou Project, providing a basis to review and analyse the conservation process and help to scientifically manage and evaluate the conservation project.

DISCUSSION: MODEL UPDATING PROMPTED BY NEW DIGITISATION METHODS AND PUBLIC ENGAGEMENT

The effective use of meta scene methodology in the trial section of the Jiankou Project provided a new digitised way to manage the process of repair of the Great Wall, and will have positive impacts on practical works.

Firstly, regarding the design stage of conservation and repair projects on the Great Wall, there have been some common problems in the past, as indicated in NCHA's assessments of design proposals, principally the incomplete mapping of the current condition of the monument and the insufficient analysis of damage (Li *et al* 2013). Most of the recording undertaken of the current condition of the monument was by means of photos and drawings; these can be incomplete and subject to bias, so that approach cannot be used for the quantitative analysis of damage nor can it provide scientific evidence in developing protection plans. If we combine on-site survey and pre-intervention meta scene data, researchers can analyse and quantitatively assess damage in the digitised scene, thus directly improving the quality of the investigation and resulting in thorough recording and analysis of the condition of the monument.

Secondly, many sections of the Great Wall are in remote areas and are difficult to access, which poses difficulties in the initial survey stage in a conservation project. The general provision in the Principles is that 'the evaluation of the value must be prioritised; and each protection step must be subject to review by experts'. In terms of the survey and design stages of Great Wall conservation projects, the involvement of experts in a review is also applicable. However, currently, the insufficient explanation of the current condition by the survey and design staff leads to incomplete understanding of the Great Wall's *status quo* from the experts undertaking each review. This makes it difficult for the experts to provide appropriate guidance to those designing interventions as the experts are not able to visit every site to evaluate fully the requirements for protection and conservation. If the damage and the designated protection measures are marked clearly in the digitised meta scene, the experts will have much more

充分且主观性强，不能为病害定量分析以及保护措施制定提供科学的现状依据。如果结合现场调查和干预前的“源场景”，勘察设计人员可以直接在数字化场景中对病害进行分析和定量标注，提高勘察质量，实现充分的现状记录与分析。

第二，长城大多地处偏远，部分段落地势险要，保护维修中前期勘察难度大。《准则》总则中规定“保护必须按照本《准则》规定的程序进行。价值评估应置于首位，保护程序的每一步骤都实行专家评审制度”，对于长城保护维修的勘察设计成果同样适用专家评审制度。但是目前在各环节的专家评审中，现状表达不充分造成的勘察设计人员与评审专家对现状信息掌握程度的不对等，使得专家难以真正有针对性地指导勘察设计工作——毕竟专家难以为评审长城保护维修项目而每次都专门赴长城实地调研。如果在“源场景”数字化场景中充分标注病害和保护设计措施，则专家获得的信息量将大大增加。

第三，因为文物修缮工程的特殊性，对隐蔽部位的前期勘察常常有较大难度。箭扣南段长城修缮工程中，因为首次引入数字化记录配合修缮工程的工作模式，数字化数据成果并没有完全向工程参与方共享。但是技术上，现场采集工作完成后，数个工作日内就可以完成数据处理和上线共享。因此，结合修缮过程中的“源场景”数据成果，可以方便设计方及时补充和调整勘察设计方案，提高勘察、设计和施工的协同工作效率；也使专家、设计方在施工过程中能方便掌握施工过程中的干预情况，及时纠正不当措施，加强施工过程监管。

第四，近年来公众对长城保护关注度显著提高，例如2016年辽宁省葫芦岛市绥中县锥子山长城大毛山段抢险加固工程就曾引起舆论极大关注，在全国范围形成了舆情影响。舆情的形成，实际上也与社会公众对于工程性质与进程的不了解有关。如果能够及时沟通、减低信息不对等的情况，将能有效避免误会。利用“源场景”平台，将其中的数据有选择地向社会开放，将有可能直接与公众建立起线上沟通的渠道。

四、结论

综上可见，以箭扣南段长城修缮工程为例展现的“源场景”数字化工作模式是对数字化技术服务于长城保护维修工程新途径的有益探索。新途径之“新”，首先在于对干预过程的记录和可视化有助于对修缮工程的管理和评估，提升长城保护维修质量；也在于“源场景”数字化工作模式所揭示的对勘察设计、施工过程监督、工程评估和公众展示等方面的新的可能性。“源场景”数字化工作模式能够有效记录和反映长城在集中人为干预下状态的改变情况。通过对改变情况的分析，能够实现事中的过程管理和事后的效果评估，提升长城修缮工程的质量和科学性。

information to work with.

Thirdly, because of the particular nature of historic monument conservation projects, it is usually very difficult to investigate the internal condition of structures at the initial stage. In the Jiankou Project, because digital recording was introduced for the first time in order to coordinate the conservation, the data generated by digitisation was not completely shared among the parties involved. However, online data processing and sharing can be completed within a few working days after being collected on site. Therefore, with the meta scene data generated during the conservation process, the design team can add to and adjust the mapping and survey plan in real time, and work more effectively with the construction team. In addition, the experts and design team can easily identify appropriate intervention measures during the repair process, they can correct inappropriate measures and closely monitor the project.

Fourthly, significantly more attention is being paid by the public to the protection of the Great Wall. For example, in 2016, the consolidation project on the Damaoshan section of the Zhuizishan Great Wall in Luanzhong County, Huludao, Liaoning Province, sparked a heated debate among the public nation-wide (*The People's Daily* 2016). This was fuelled by the public's lack of understanding of the nature of the project and its progress. If more accurate information had been communicated to the public more promptly, this misunderstanding could have been effectively avoided. By selecting some data generated from the meta scene and sharing it with the public, it is possible to establish improved and more immediate communications with the public.

CONCLUSION

From what we have discussed, the meta scene digitisation methodology utilised in the Jiankou Project is a positive experiment in the application of digital technology to benefit conservation and repair projects on the Great Wall. The benefits it offers are, firstly, the recording and visualisation of the intervention process to assist the management and evaluation of conservation projects; secondly, it has highlighted new possibilities in applying the meta scene digitisation methodology in surveying, in monitoring the repair process, evaluating the project, and in public engagement. The meta scene digitisation methodology can effectively record and show changes to the condition of the monument after intensive intervention. By analysing the level of these changes, it can help to manage the processes of repair and consolidation and the evaluation of the results, thus improving the quality and scientific basis of Great Wall conservation projects.

参考文献
References

Li Dawei. 2013. 'A retrospective analysis of mapping and design of the Great Wall protection project,' in *China Relic Science Study*, 2013 (04):33-39.

李大伟. 2015. 长城文物保护实践的回顾与思考. 中国文物科学研究 (04)：33-39.

Li Hongsong, Yu Bing, Li Dawei and Zhang Jingke. 2013. 'A retrospective analysis of mapping and design of the Great Wall protection project,' *China Relic Science Study*, 2013 (04):46-53.

李宏松，于冰，李大伟，张景科. 2013. 长城保护工程勘察设计工作回顾性分析. 中国文物科学研究 (04): 46-53.

Xin Yang. 'Visit Zhuizishan Great Wall: the life saving project did not use cement,' in *People's Daily* http://ln.people.com.cn/n2/2016/0925/c346198-29056034.html

辛阳. 2016. 实地探访辽宁锥子山长城：救命工程，没用水泥. 人民日报.

Available: http://ln.people.com.cn/n2/2016/0925/c346198-29056034.html

Chapter 4:

Conservation Principles and Practices

Swarthy Hill Roman fortlet, built of turf and timber: excavated and (unusually) partly reconstructed, it is displayed as an earthwork. Cumbria (© Cumbria Tourism).
斯沃西山罗马小要塞，坎布里亚（© 坎布里亚旅行社）。

第四单元

长城保护维修理念与实践

Most materials for conservation of the Great Wall in mountain areas have to be transported by hand. Conservation work at Jiankou Great Wall (photograph by Zhao Peng).
在山区长城维修工程中，很多情况下需要人工运输材料。箭扣长城维修工程（摄影：赵鹏）。

4.1 长城保护修缮理念与技术措施辨析

汤羽扬
北京建筑大学建筑遗产研究院—中国—北京

摘要

长城作为中国乃至世界现存体量最大、分布范围最广，延续建造年代最久的线性文化遗产,其保护与利用越来越多的受到国家的重视，各项保护利用工作正在陆续展开。无论哪一项工作，涉及到长城保护一定是基础。“保护第一”、“价值优先，整体保护”的原则已经形成共识，但是在保护修缮工程实施层面，“真实性”、“最小干预”、“适宜性”的把握始终存在差异与问题。

关键词： 长城　适宜性　砖石质

一、长城现存真实状态认知

对的长城保护修缮必须正确把握长城现存的真实状态。

中国境内保存历代长城总长度 2 万余千米，墙体、敌台、烽火台、城堡等各类长城遗产超过 4 万处。

在时间维度，长城建造年代自春秋战国始至明清延续 2000 余年，记载了国家社会发展的诸多重要历史事件。同时也反应了不同时代社会经济背景下的建造技艺水平，长城具有很强的时代特征。

在空间维度，长城以总体线性局部立体的形态延续展开，东西延绵中国整个北部地区 5000 余千米；南北自黑龙江到淮河分布近 3000千米。其地质地貌、气候环境及文化背景复杂多样。

在建造类型维度，长城以多个单元、多重纵深、组团式相结合，构成古代防御体系。建造就地取材，虽以土、石、植物为基本材料，却衍生出土坯、土石、土草、砖石、砖草等多种材料变体和组合，涵盖了夯筑、堆筑、坯筑等不同的建构方式。

在人与自然关系维度，长城分布于北方地区农牧交错带，借用河谷山川多类型自然地貌，将人工构筑防御工事与自然屏障完美组合，成就了独特的历史文化景观，长城与环境的依存关系极为深刻。

长城具有土石木草材料简单，地貌气候环境复杂，技艺年代地方性强的突出特点。

正是由于地域分布广，修筑时间长，建造技艺灵活，在长期的自然侵蚀、人类生活影响和历史环境变迁的多重影响下，使得保存至今的长城大多残损乃至坍塌，甚至部分消失的情况。历代长城遗存中，明代长城保存相对完整，但是依然可以看一些已处于快速毁坏的临界状态（图 1）。

《长城保护总体规划》明确了长城的现存状态：“长城是古建筑与古遗址两种遗存形态并存、以古遗址遗存形态为主的文化遗产，并具有突出的文化景观特征。长城这种独特的遗存形态是在 2000 多年不间断的历史演进过程中，人类活动与自然侵蚀共同作用的结果，是长城保存的历史状态，也是现实状态。” 显然，自然侵蚀作用下的古遗址遗存形态留存是保护修缮工程需首先把握的基础。

4.1 A REVIEW OF THE STRATEGIES AND TECHNOLOGIES OF GREAT WALL CONSERVATION

TANG YUYANG
Academy of Architectural Heritage - China - Beijing

Abstract

The Great Wall is China's most significant surviving heritage site in its scale, geographical distribution, and the historical span of its construction. Its preservation and utilisation has become an increasingly higher priority for the national government, and work on its conservation has progressively expanded. Whatever projects are undertaken, conservation must be the first consideration. When it comes to general principles, consensus has been reached on those of: preservation being the first objective; the prioritisation of values based approaches; and ensuring that a monument's integrity is maintained. However, when it comes to practical interventions, there have always been debates and problems on how to define the parameters of authenticity, minimum intervention and appropriateness.

Keywords: the Great Wall, appropriate intervention, brick and stone wall

UNDERSTANDING THE NATURE OF THE WALL REMAINS

A thorough, accurate and objective understanding of the remains of the Wall must be established before any conservation can be done. The total length of the Wall from different periods surviving within China exceeds 20,000km, including over 40,000 towers, beacons, forts, and sections of wall.

Different parts of the Great Wall were constructed over 2,000 years, from the Spring and Autumn and Warring States periods (770-221 BCE) to the Ming and Qing Dynasties (1368-1912 CE). The Wall bears witness to the significant events and changes in Chinese society over the centuries. It also reflects distinctive craftsmanship in different historic social and economic contexts. Therefore, there is great historic richness in the Great Wall.

In its geographical distribution, the Great Wall stretches across the north of China in an overall linear pattern with regional expansions inwards and outwards. It stretches over 5,000km from east to west, and over 3,000km from south to north, from Heilongjiang Province to the Huaihe River. This explains the diversity in its geological, landscape, climate and cultural settings.

In terms of the structure itself, this ancient defence system consists of a sophisticated combination of multiple individual units, multiple linear alignments and clusters. The principal building materials used in its construction were simply locally sourced clay, stone and earth. However, they were used in various combinations such as clay bricks with clay and cobbles, clay and earth, bricks and stones, and bricks and earth. Building techniques such as rammed-earth, mounded stones and mortared courses of brick or stone were used in its construction.

In terms of its relationship with nature, being set in the agricultural-pastoral transitional zone in the north, the Wall is adapted to the various landscapes in which it was built, including valleys and mountains, to achieve a perfect combination of man-made fortifications and natural defences. Therefore, there is a profound and inter-dependant relationship between the Wall and its environment.

The key characteristics of the Great Wall can be summarised as the simplicity of the materials with which it was built, the highly localised and contemporary building techniques used in its construction, and the variety of

图1明代长城一些已出处于快速毁坏的临界状态（摄影：汤羽扬）上图：万全右卫城城墙2014年（左）与2016年（右）垮塌情况对比. 下图：北京某长城敌台2007年（左）与（2019年）残损情况对比。

Fig.1 Parts of the Ming Wall experiencing rapid deterioration (photographs by Tang Yuyang). Top: The collapse of the curtain wall at Wanquanyou Wei Fort in Hebei Province in 2014 (left) compared with that in 2016 (right). Bottom: Damage of a defence tower at one stretch of the Beijing section on the Great Wall in 2007 (left), compared with that in 2019 (right).

二、长城保护修缮理念辨析

我们熟知的“真实性”文物保护理念，在长城保护修缮工程中如何体现呢，是恢复到建造之初的形态与式样，还是建造所用的材料或是工法？

这或许要问一下我们自己，长城已不再有建设之初的防御功能，但为什么人们依然愿意去欣赏她，并被她感动？其真实而又沧桑壮美的物质存在，唤起了人们与过往的联系，有人称之为“令人愉悦的衰落”，这或许是长城的“真实”存在意义，真实的历史物质遗存，岁月留下的斑驳痕迹，与广袤大地的依存关系，以及通过物质遗存所述说的历史故事。由此可以理解“真实性”是指饱含着历史信息，可供人阅读的长城物质遗存。这些遗存越是受到尊重，就会有更多的信息可供后人阅读。保护修缮工作即是如何能够更妥善和精

landscape and climatic environments in which it is situated.

It is these characteristics, combined with natural weathering and human activities over many centuries, that have led to the decay, collapse and even the disappearance of much of the Wall. In comparison with the remains from other periods, the Ming Great Wall is relatively well preserved, but some parts of it are on the verge of rapid deterioration (Fig.1). Therefore, 'the existing nature of the Great Wall should be classified as mainly archaeological sites with strong cultural landscape features, though there are also surviving standing structures', as described in *The Great Wall Protection Master Plan* and 'the unique character of the Wall is the historical result of human activities and natural decay over the past 2,000 years' (Ministry of Culture and Tourism & NCHA 2019). Patently, understanding the Wall's archaeological characteristics is the starting point for any conservation work.

DEBATES ABOUT THE STRATEGIES AND TECHNOLOGIES OF GREAT WALL CONSERVATION

The concept of authenticity has become widely understood. The question remains, however, as to how it should be reflected in conservation practice. Does it mean that the historic form should be authentically restored or that only original materials and techniques should be used?

We may need to ask ourselves why people still value the Great Wall, even though it no longer serves its original purpose as a system of military defence. The original remains convey a nostalgic and perhaps emotional connection to the past. Some call this 'a pleasant decline' (Ashurst 2007), which may reveal the meaning of 'authentic': the physical remains, and the evidence they show of the passage of time, link us to the natural and human events which have shaped and reshaped them over the centuries. Thus, authenticity can refer to the physical remains that contain interpretable historical information and meaning. The more highly valued and respected such remains are, the better their significance and meaning can be preserved for our descendants.

Conservation should preserve this information and meaning discreetly without removal or addition. The best way to achieve that is through regular maintenance instead of intervention, because any degree of intervention will damage the historical information the remains convey. 'Minimum interference' means controlled intervention. Together with minimal disturbance or addition, such an approach allows us to preserve the structure and the remains, as long as the structural stability of the Wall is secured. Appropriateness is the best gauge in determining what level of intervention should be undertaken.

Is a comprehensive restoration of the Great Wall of archaeology necessary? The answer is no. From the perspective of authenticity, most of the remains can be left untouched if no structural risks to its survival are detected. From the perspective of ensuring the future of the remains, only those sections potentially at risk need strengthening. What then if an intervention is necessary? What matters most is the degree, or *du* in Chinese, of the intervention. There are ascending levels of the meaning of *du*: as a physical limit; as an evolving process; and as a state of spiritual perception. The conservation of the Great Wall needs to be based on sophisticated scientific processes to reach an understanding of its aesthetic or spiritual value and authenticity and to determine how that can be sustainably maintained.

The key conservation principles in achieving this may be summarised as follows:

- Make the least amount of addition as possible and do not attempt to restore the original height of structures.
- Refrain from disturbing the surviving archaeological remains when the structural bearing capacity of the remaining components cannot be determined.
- Do not alter the appearance caused by the historical weathering and decay of the monument when the structural stability is not compromised, as they narrate the life of the monument over time.
- No replacement of missing components is needed if their absence does not threaten the structural stability of the remains; new components cannot replace the original historical remains.

心的保留这些信息，而不是移除或是添加其他的信息。将真实的历史信息留存的最好方式是经常维护，而不是干预，任何程度的干预都会损伤原有的信息。“最小干预”既是在保证长城遗存安全情况下控制干预的程度，只进行结构安全和保留遗存的最少介入、扰动、移除或添加，“适宜性”是最好的方法。

古遗址形态为主的长城需要全面修缮吗？回答是否定的。从“真实性”保存角度，只要没有险情，大部分长城遗存可以不扰动；从“延续性”保存角度，仅需要加强对安全隐患部位（点段）的保护加固。

在必须要实施保护工程时怎么办？最需要的是把握好干预的“度”。在新华字典中可以查到“度”的解释：与计量或单位有关，如尺度、刻度等；事物所达到的境界，如程度、高度、风度等；由此到彼，如度日、度假；法则界限，如制度、法度。综合起来可以看到涵盖了一个进阶的过程：界限——过程——境界。长城保护修缮需要有科学依据、精细化的过程，而达到真实延续的境界。

尽少添加新的材料——不要试图通过新增砌——避免过度扰动；

在不影响安全的前提下，留下历史的斑驳与自然力的侵蚀——沧桑感可以讲述历史的故事；

已经缺失但不影响安全时无需补全——新做部分不能够替代历史遗存。

有了“真实性”和“最小干预”，选择技术方法可能是最大的难题，“适宜性”是最好的，加强前期研究性，多手段勘察，精准把握原有的材料构造以及病害病因是一项基础的工作。相比之下，外部支撑优于拆解后重砌、原材料归安优于加配新材料、传统工法优于现代工法，坚实与牢固度与原有部分相配，而不是越强越好。

三、明代砖石长城遗存主要病害分析

目前留存的明代长城墙体 8368 千米，占中国长城总长度的 39.4%，其中砖石质长城墙体 2000 余千米，还有敌台 7300 余座，烽火台 8700 余座，是中国长城的精华。石质长城包括有加工石材和未加工石材，砌筑方法为垒筑和砌筑。砖墙多是土石、碎砖为芯外侧包城砖，或是内侧夯土墙体外侧包砖（图 2）。

通过整理可将长城遗存的病害大致分为 9 类：坍塌、局部塌落、形变、裂缝、滑移、材料劣化、缺失、植物，构造缺陷。

总体看石材垒筑的长城由于未使用粘接剂，在年久自然力的影响下，更多的呈现坍塌形态。局部塌落病害情况较为复杂，独立敌台、烽火台的顶部雉堞、下部转角处坍落较为多见，其原因包括地基缺陷、角部应力、雨水侵蚀等。当内侧为夯土墙外包砖时，常年雨水与冻融作用下，极易产生土体和外包砖石砌体的塌落。

裂缝的情况在长城各类砌体结构中十分普遍，小的裂缝可能仅发生在砌体外层，大的裂缝则有可能贯通砖石砌体乃至整个墙体，带来整体失稳的危险。在一些独立的敌台或烽火台外侧可以看到贯通上下的外八字裂缝，应当是墙顶防水失效后墙芯水土流失引起的破坏。

滑移经常与局部塌落同时发生。由于不同年代对长城加筑和包砌，相同或不同材料之间缺乏拉结，加之水及外力作用，很容易产生分离错位。

在砖石缝隙中生长的乔灌木根系，是造成原有防水破坏及砌体之间粘合失效的主要原因。然而对植物是清理还是保留始终现存在争议（图 3）。

自然营力的反复作用是长城遗存病害发展的主要原因，不同地理和气候环境、不同地质地貌，甚至到某一具体地点其病害情况都有差异，需要详尽的勘察。

Within the principles of authenticity and minimum intervention, the choice of the methodology and materials to be employed may turn out to be the greatest challenge in planning interventions. The best solution is to determine what is most appropriate to each structure. Research-based and multi-technological surveys are necessary. They can help us conduct the fundamental work of obtaining accurate knowledge of the original materials and structures of the monument as well as the causes of damage to it. Comparatively speaking, external strengthening is better than dismantling and rebuilding; replicating using original materials is better than adding new materials; traditional techniques are better than modern techniques. The sturdiness of the new should be consistent with that of the original, and the idea that 'the stronger the better' is not desirable here.

ANALYSIS OF THE PRINCIPAL TYPES OF DAMAGE TO MING BRICK AND STONE WALLS

The Ming Wall, stretching for 8,368km, makes up 39.4% of the total surviving length of the Great Wall, including, most famously, over 2,000km of brick and stone wall, over 7,300 defence towers and over 8,700 beacon towers. Stone structures were built either of mortared courses of dressed or undressed stone or were of irregular dry-stone construction. Brick structures usually had a core made up of clay and cobbles, rubble, or rammed earth (Fig.2).

The forms of damage to the Wall roughly fall into nine categories: collapse, partial collapse, deformation, cracks, displacement, material degradation, the loss of material, invasive vegetation, and structural defects.

The drystone walls tend to collapse under natural forces because no mortars were used in its construction. Partial collapse is more complicated. Collapse of the battlements and the bottom corners of free-standing towers and beacons is commonly seen, as a result of defects in their foundations, stresses on their corners and rainfall. Where the Wall was built of rammed earth clad with bricks, the materials are prone to collapse due to rainfall penetration and the process of freeze-thaw.

Cracks are often found in both brickwork and stonework on the Wall. Smaller ones may only occur on the outer face of the Wall, but larger ones may extend further into or even throughout the structure, resulting in the danger of destabilisation. Vertical cracks can be found on some free-standing towers or beacons and are normally caused by a loss of the core as a result of the failure of the uppermost waterproof layer. Displacement often occurs together with partial collapse. The reason for this is that later additions and facings can lead to a lack of adhesion between materials, exacerbated by moisture penetration and external stress. Trees and shrubs rooted in the gaps between bricks and stones are the primary cause of the failure of the waterproof layer and the mortar. However, it remains controversial whether this vegetation should be removed or not (Fig.3). Constant natural stress is the cause of aggravating structural damage. Yet in-depth investigations are required because different geographical, climatic, and landscape characteristics at specific locations may impact structures differently.

AN ANALYSIS OF THE TECHNOLOGY OF GREAT WALL CONSERVATION

In reflecting on restoration practices over the years on the Great Wall, it can be seen that the preservation of authenticity is facilitated by approaches which are evidence-based, and which utilise surveys, scientifically tested techniques, scientific research and analysis, and process control systems, rather than experience-based conventional practices previously employed.

Firstly, preliminary archaeological surveys and research should be introduced to map out the outline, stratigraphy, quantity and features of the Wall remains. New features and elements are likely to be identified through this process. The deployment of modern surveying technology is important. Cutting-edge methods, such as 3D laser scanning and low altitude aerial photography, can be used to digitally record the condition of the Wall. Geophysical resistivity meters can help survey the interior structures to identify hollows, structural risks and moisture penetration. These techniques provide a more detailed understanding of the location, extent and

图 2 明代砖石质长城的构造特征（摄影：汤羽扬）. 上左图：河卵石砌筑墙体. 上右图：砖石混筑墙体. 下左图：块石垒筑墙体. 下右图：城砖包砌墙体。

Fig.2 Features of Ming brick and stone walls (photograph by Tang Yuyang). Top left: Stone wall built of random rubble. Top right: Brick and stone wall. Bottom left: Drystone wall built of dressed stone. Bottom right: Brick-clad wall.

四、长城保护修缮技术措施分析

反思近些年长城保护修缮工程的情况，突破传统"经验型"的勘察与施工方法，提高"科技型"研判能力与实施过程控制是长城遗存真实留存的重要保障。

首先，需在前期引入考古勘探与研究，以帮助明确长城遗存边界、年代叠压关系、存量和基本特征，或许还会有新的遗存发现。

现代勘察技术方法的引入也非常重要。借助现代仪器设备对长城现存状态进行数字记录，如三维激光扫描、低空近景摄影等。用多功能电法仪进行高密度勘探，可以了解长城内部空洞、垮塌危险部位、地基含水情况，帮助精细化掌握不同部位的病害程度和病害类型和病因。

图 3 明代砖石质长城常见病害（摄影：汤羽扬）上左图：石材垒筑墙体无粘接材料多坍塌. 上右图：构造缺陷带来的外层砌体塌毁. 下左图：雨水导致的局部塌落. 下右图：夯土体与外包砖缺乏链接产生滑移。

Fig.3 Types of damage commonly seen on the brick and stone walls (photograph by Tang Yuyang). Top left: Drystone walls prone to collapse due to lack of mortar. Top right: Damage to the external brickwork resulting from structural defects. Bottom left: Partial collapse caused by rainfall penetration. Bottom right: Displacement due to a lack of attachment between the rammed-earth core and the brick cladding.

causes of damage. Other methods such as geo-technical investigations, hydro-geological investigations, material examinations and structural stability analysis have been successfully employed in surveys. They help us to select appropriate intervention strategies by pinpointing functional weaknesses in the foundations of structures and potential instability in the underlying ground conditions.

Intervention methods which aim to ensure the structural stability of the remains include: for sections with surviving standing structures, adding supports and the reinstatement of original masonry are prioritised to ensure stability and the preservation of historical information; for sections that have already collapsed or are no longer visible above ground, the priority is the prevention of further collapse by partially returning displaced components; for sections at risk of collapse, the priority is to reduce these risks by strengthening or partially restoring components to strengthen their structural stability.

For instance, to avoid disturbing the original components, extra strengthening should be provided to those walls that are at risk of collapse, instead of dismantling and rebuilding them. Thus, the original parts are preserved, the structure is secured, and the intervention undertaken is discernible. Brick built columns can be installed in the core to secure the brick facing when it is prone to tilting or even collapse as a result of a significant loss of a rammed-earth core. Maintaining earth and turf accumulated over time on the top of the Wall can serve as waterproofing

岩土水文工程勘察、材料检测、结构稳定性分析等手段已经被要求用于长城保护修缮勘察工作中，它有助于科学的判断周边地基、岩土性能，以及结构危险的具体部位，从而帮助选择适宜的保护手段。

以长城遗存安全为目标的保护修缮措施包括：地面存有建筑点段应达到结构安全，历史信息最大化目的，以支撑和归安为主要措施；已坍塌或消失段落主要应达到遗址形态安全，以局部整理归安为主要措施；面临险情的段落以缓解风险压力，避免突变性毁坏为目的，以介入支撑加固或局部修复有加固作用部分为主要措施。

例如，对有塌落危险的墙体部位，为减少对原有构件的干扰，应尽量减少拆砌，采用外加结构支撑的加固方法，即保存了原有构件，同时也保证了结构安全，还有可识别性。当内侧夯土墙体大面积缺失引起外包砖砌体倾斜甚至垮塌危险时，可在夯土内增设砖砌构造柱，保证外包砖砌体的安全。当顶部原有地面砖及灰土层缺失时，保留历史形成的土层及地被一方面有防水作用，更重要要的是可以防止冻融。排水是长城保护修缮工程最应关注的问题，容许少量下渗情况下的及时排水，以及基脚排水应受到充分重视（图 4）。

工程实施过程中的实验研究及动态调整是保证初设目标能够实现的关键环节，包括对材料的试验，获取最佳配比、适宜的强度与色彩，通过施工工序和工法的试验，获得与长城原工艺最为接近操作方法与实施效果。

所有工作都指向一个目的：遗存的精心呵护与价值的整体留存。

参考文献
References

Ashurst, J. (ed.) 2007. Conservation of Ruins, London.

J·阿什赫斯特（编辑）. 2007. 遗迹保护. 伦敦.

The Ministry of Culture and Tourism of the People's Republic of China and the National Cultural Heritage Administration. 2019. The Great Wall Protection Master Plan. Beijing.

文化和旅游部，国家文物局. 2019. 长城保护总体规划.

图 4 适宜的保护修缮措施（摄影：汤羽扬）. 上左图：多功能电法仪高密度勘探内部空洞 上右图：介入钢结构加固松散墙体. 下左图：不增加新材料的塌落块石归安. 下右图：学习传统的施工工法。

Fig.4 Appropriate preservation measures (photograph by Tang Yuyang). Top left: Hollows in the interior structures detected by geophysical resistivity meters. Top right: Steel structures set up to strengthen the wobbling wall. Bottom left: Collapsed stone reinstated without adding new materials. Bottom right: Traditional techniques revisited in conservation.

and, more importantly, can provide some protection against freezing and thawing when the original covering tiles and sealing layer are missing. Adequate drainage should be a top priority in conservation, for although a small amount of infiltration is acceptable, the greater part of rainwater must be drained away. Additionally, a similar level of attention should be given to the drainage of foundations (Fig.4).

Adjustments to intervention methods and experimental studies during implementation of conservation work are key to achieve the objectives set out during the design stage. This includes tests on the materials to ensure their best composition, that they are sufficiently sturdy and of an appropriate colour. Experiments on construction procedures and techniques help identify those techniques and procedures that are closest to the original craftmanship of our ancestors. There is a single aim, that is, the meticulous conservation of the site and the complete preservation of its value.

4.2 基于最小干预原则对土长城保护维修方法的探索

兰立志，娄建全，于侠
辽宁有色勘察研究院—中国—辽宁

摘要

本文以中卫姚滩段长城加固工程为例,基于最小干预的原则,对土长城的保护方法进行了初步探讨,强调了文物保护维修中，最小干预决定保护措施的合理性，是真实的、具有价值的历史信息得以延续的基本保证，并取决于保护措施的可行性。通过试验证明了，在土长城维修过程中不采用新材料和新技术的条件下，传统做法的可行性，进一步撑握了关键环节的施工方法，妥善保持了古朴土长城的沧桑感。

关键词：最小干预　历史信息　保护措施　传统做法

一、姚滩段长城的概况

姚滩段明长城位于宁夏回族自治区中卫市沙坡头区迎水桥镇姚滩村，距中卫市城北约7千米，西侧临近大漠边关风景区，西北为千岛湖风景区，东南侧紧靠香山机场。

姚滩段为土长城，采用板筑夯土技术，夯层厚度 150 ~ 180mm，全长 2355 米，现存 1255 米，起点为大漠边关东门的 1 号敌台，向西南从姚滩村北农田中穿过，经 2 号敌台，折向南，沿终点 3 号敌台方向延伸。经检测，夯土成分为粉土，塑性指数 8.1 ~ 9.7，密度 1.63 ~ 1.71g/cm^3，内摩擦角 22.4 0 ~ 28.0^0，凝聚力 18.6 ~ 24.2kp，压实系数 0.89 ~ 0.92，土壤含盐量平均值为 1.5g / kg。

由于长期裸露在不断变化的恶劣的自然环境中，遭受不可抗拒的日照、风吹、雨淋、冻胀等自然力的交替作用和人类活动的蚕食，墙体发育着开裂、剥落、坍塌等病害，失去了原有墙体的稳定性和完整性，使城墙不断残损，直至消失。

现存 1255 米墙体中：基本完好约 375 米、基本消失或呈土垄状约 240 米、残损状约 640 米；主要病害为裂缝、凹槽、冲沟、坍塌。

二、姚滩段长城保护措施

（一）最小干预原则与保护措施的关系

土长城所承载的真实的、具有价值的历史信息得以延续，不仅仅依赖于土长城遗址的物质本体，而且还依赖于保护过程之中，坚持最小干预原则的保护措施。但在现时条件下任何的保护措施都是有损的，都是对遗址本体的干预，对真实历史信息的减损，所以，没有干预的保护措施是不存在的。

4.2 THE CONSOLIDATION OF THE YAOTAN SECTION OF THE GREAT WALL. A CASE STUDY IN EARTH-WALL CONSERVATION METHODS, BASED ON PRINCIPLES OF CULTURAL RELICS CONSERVATION

LAN LIZHI, LOU JIANQUAN, YU XIA
Liaoning Non-ferrous Geological Exploration and Research Institute - China - Liaoning

Abstract

This article takes the Zhongwei Yaotan section of the Great Wall's Reinforcement Project, conducted under the principle of minimum intervention, as an example to provide a preliminary discussion on earth-wall conservation methods. It emphasises how the principle of minimum intervention can be applied as the basis for consolidating and conserving cultural relics and preserving the valuable historic information they contain. In return, the feasibility and effectiveness of conservation methods determines how minimal the intervention should be. Rounds of trials have demonstrated that traditional methods without using any new techniques or materials are feasible. Thus, the key steps of the conservation process can be carried out in traditional ways so as to maintain the sense of time-worn condition of the earth Wall.

Keywords: Minimum intervention, historic information, conservation methods, traditional methods.

AN INTRODUCTION TO YAOTAN WALL

Yaotan Wall, a section of the Ming Great Wall, is situated in Yaotan Village, Yingshuiqiao County, Shapotou District of Zhongwei City in the Ningxia Hui Autonomous Region. It sits 7km north of Zhongwei City, with Desert Frontier Tourist Attraction located to the west, Qiandao Lake Scenic Spot to the northwest, and Zhongwei Xiangshan Airport to its immediate south-east. The Yaotan section is a compressed-earth structure, the rammed-earth layers measuring 15cm to 20cm thick. The overall length of Yaotan Wall was originally 2,355m, of which 1,255m is still standing. Starting at Defence Tower No.1, at the east gate of Desert Frontier Tourist Attraction, the Wall winds its way southwest through farmlands north of Yaotan Village to Defence Tower No.2, and then south to Defence Tower No.3 where it ends. The composition of the rammed-earth has been tested showing it to be silt, with a plasticity index of 8.1 to 9.7; density of 1.63 to 1.71g/cm3; internal friction angle of 22.40~28.00; cohesion of 18.6 to 24.2kp; compaction coefficient of 0.89 to 0.92; and an average salinity of 1.5g/kg.

Exposed to a constantly changing and sometimes harsh environment, and subjected to the inevitable forces of sunshine, winds, rains, frost and human activities, cracking, peeling and collapses have become extensively developed that deprive the structure of its original stability and integrity; this leads to continuous wearing and ultimately to the total disappearance of some of its fabric. Of the 1,255m of the Wall which survives, 375m remain basically intact, whereas 240m has almost disappeared or has been reduced to just a ridge. The other 640m has been damaged, primarily by the formation of cracks, grooves, and gullies, and by collapses.

CONSERVATION MEASURES OF YAOTAN WALL

The relationship between minimum intervention and conservation methods

The preservation of the authentic, valuable and historic information that the Great Wall carries is dependent

最小干预是一个相对的概念，在保护过程中对最小干预很难把握。干预到什么程度才是最小干预呢？总结以前土长城保护工程的经验教训可知，最小干预是建立在消除安全隐患的基础上的，就是说采取的保护技术措施必须符合相关规范，具有有效性和可操作性，即具有可行性。如果措施没有效、不可行，干预性再小，也是无意义的。可以说，干预的力度取决于保护措施的可行性。

但也不能只强调保护措施的可行性，而忽视最小干预的原则，可行的保护措施不是唯一的，只有通过对多个可行的保护措施进行干预程度的比对、评估，筛选出相对干预最小的保护措施，才是合理可行的保护措施，也就是说，最小干预的保护原则决定保护措施的合理性。

只有具有合理性和可行性的保护措施才可应用在土长城维修保护中。

（二）最小干预原则在中卫姚滩段土长城保护维修中的体现

从工程角度而言，土长城遗址可类比于土质边坡。可根据土遗址的形态、破坏类型、危险程度及环境条件等因素，采取削坡、覆土压脚、扶壁柱、锚杆或格构等可行的工程措施。但从文物保护的角度，应从中比选干预最小的保护措施。

1. 长城本体抢险加固、消除长城本体安全隐患是长城保护维修工作的首要任务”，这是进行干预性长城保护维修的基本条件。需不需要采取措施进行干预，取决于土长城遗址的危险程度，取决于对遗址稳定性的评估。经评估，仅对存在安全隐患的 1~3 #敌台及约 1/3 的现存遗址采取了夯补加固措施，对发育较严重的凹槽和裂缝采取了修补措施。
2. 长城保护维修必须保持长城的原形制、原结构，优先使用原材料、原工艺。只有传统工艺作法无法达到长城本体安全的技术要求时，才可考虑采用新技术和新材料”。这是最小干预的基本保证条件。在原形制及现状高度范围内，对危险的、残损缺失的土长城遗址应首选按原质材料、原工艺夯补，既可满足稳定要求，又可达到防护、展示的作用。当原材料、原工艺做法不能满足墙体安全要求或原形制、原结构不清时，可以采用可逆的、可识别的新材料和新工艺的加固措施。

通过施工前考古，基本查清了姚滩段长城的原形制、原材料、原工艺。通过施工前近二个月对材料和工艺进行二十多批次的现场试验（见图 1）得出的结论，采用原质材料和原工艺对土长城遗址进行夯筑补强加固等保护措施，完全可以满足遗址本体安全的技术要求，不必采用新材料和新工艺。但在施工过程中为了提高工作效率，尝试了改进振冲式夯机模拟人工夯筑工艺。

采用夯补保护措施时，应对夯土强度进行检测，夯补的厚度应满足稳定性的要求。对缺失较大的部位，采取随形夯补保护措施；对于缺失较薄的部位，按原形制进行夯补，如果高厚比不足，不能满足稳定要求，辅以木质锚杆（签）补强。木质锚杆（签）的使用也有传统可寻，如山海关城墙发现的木质锚杆、宁夏与内蒙交界处的明长城的木质锚钉（签）等。

三、中卫姚滩段长城保护维修方法

（一）坍塌残损部位的夯补方法

1. 材料配制：晒土和粉碎、泼灰、灰土拌和、闷料醒土。

每个环节都应有质量检测指标，质量检测宜选择对遗址损害较小的现代检测技术。但由于目前对传统作法研究的较少，虽然采用仪器进行了现场检测，但方法还不太成熟，检测数据还不能做为质量的判定标

not only on the condition of the monument itself, but also on the conservation measures being undertaken in accordance with the principle of minimum intervention. However, all conservation methods available today require some intervention into the current condition of any site. Therefore, all repair work is to a degree detrimental to, and reduces, the authentic and historic information that the site contains. As a result, there is no such thing as 'conservation without intervention'.

Thus, minimising intervention is a relative term that can be difficult to define, and the question of how extensive a minimum intervention can be, remains difficult to answer. Past experiences and lessons demonstrate that eliminating identified structural risks needs to be the primary consideration for deciding the appropriate level of intervention. To be more specific, technological conservation measures must be in line with related regulations which require that they must be both effective and feasible. If repair work is neither feasible nor effective, no matter how little intervention is involved, it is completely meaningless.

We should not, however, over-emphasise the feasibility and effectiveness of conservation techniques at the expense of the minimum intervention principle. In each case there is always a range of possible conservation measures. Only through careful comparison and assessment of different feasible alternatives can the plan representing the minimum intervention be identified. That is to say, the minimum intervention principle ultimately determines which conservation measures are most appropriate for a given site. Only feasible and appropriate measures determined in this way should be used in the conservation of the Great Wall.

Minimum intervention applied in the conservation and restoration of Yaotan Wall

From an engineering perspective, similarities can be found between the earth Great Wall and any earth slope structures. Consolidation of both requires an evaluation of their shapes, the types of deterioration, their level of potential risk, and environmental factors. Feasible consolidation measures for both involve such engineering choices as stepped retaining terraces, reinforcing the foot of a slope, adding buttress pillars, rod-bolts, or lattices to support the structure. The difference between these two types of consolidation projects is that for historical conservation projects the measure that involves the least intervention to the site is the most appropriate.

For conservation and restoration interventions on the Great Wall, 'the top priority is emergency stabilisation and consolidation to eliminate structural risks to the Wall's fabric' (SACH 2014). The necessity for intervention measures is determined by the assessment of the level of the risks and the stability of the site. At the Yaotan Wall it was therefore decided based on evaluation that only Defence Towers Nos.1 to 3 and one third of the surviving Wall were at potential structural risk, which were then consolidated with rammed-earth patching, and severely developed grooves and cracks refilled and repaired.

In the conservation and consolidation of the Great Wall, its original appearance, shape and structure must be preserved, and the use of original materials and traditional craftsmanship should be prioritised. Only when traditional craftsmanship cannot meet the technical requirements for structural stability, can new techniques and materials be considered. These principles serve to guarantee minimum intervention. Therefore, consolidation within the bounds of the surviving original structure and its existing height that use original materials and craftsmanship is prioritised which can both address structural risks to the earth wall and display its original structure. In contrast, for sections of the Wall whose original appearance, shapes and structures are unknown or for which original materials or craftsmanship cannot meet stability requirements, reversible consolidation measures using clearly differentiated new materials could be adopted.

With the help of pre-consolidation archaeology survey, Yaotan Wall's original appearance, shape, structure and building techniques were investigated. Based on more than 20 batches of field tests on materials and techniques (Fig.1) in the two months before undertaking the consolidation it was demonstrated that the use of original materials and traditional rammed-earth construction techniques could fully meet the technical requirements

图 1 夯土试验（摄影：邓涛）。
Fig.1 Testing rammed-earth materials (photograph by Deng Tao).

准。技术人员还得依据现场试验的经验积累凭感觉对夯土质量的把控。需要明确的是，再有经验的工匠，也需要现场试验的支撑。如闷料醒土过程中，根据试验确定土料翻倒的间隔时间和次数，使水分润湿土料大致均匀，闷至灰土的微结构发生改变,没有干土或硬土团为止。

2. 夯筑过程：建防护棚、支模、表面清理、洒水湿润、铺土找平压实、人工夯筑、取样检测、拆模、保湿养护，拆除防护棚。

依据清工部《工程做法侧例》土作做法中的记载、相传的夯土传统作法及设计的夯实度，进行试验确定点夯次数、夯距等参数，夯距宜为 0.5 ~ 1 个夯窝，工人之间落杵力量应相近。

夯土的新老界面采用洒水润湿、直接夯筑的处理措施，取消了削坡修阶的有损做法，尽可能多的保留现有遗址本体。对遗址维修加固而言，尽可能用加法取代减法。

（二）裂缝修补方法

裂缝修补过程：裂缝清理、表面封堵、浆液配制和灌浆、表面做旧。

浆液采用夯土同质材料配制，必要时可加入少量的胶质材料，根据裂缝的宽度调整稠度，距离表面一定深度内待初凝后进行捣实做旧处理。裂缝修补不是一蹴而就的，经过一段时间后又会开裂，需再次修补，一般间隔 3 ~ 6 个月修补一次，需修补 3 次以上。

for the stabilisation of the Wall's structures without involving any new materials or techniques. During the consolidation, a modified vibro-flotation ramming machine, which rams the earth vertically, was used to imitate the manual ramming process as well as to improve efficiency.

Different rammed-earth consolidation methods are chosen based on their compressive strength tests so that the thickness of the consolidating rammed-earth layers meet the stability requirement. For parts of substantial losses, complete layers of rammed-earth were added according to their original appearance and shapes. For elements with minor deterioration, patches of rammed-earth were used. If the height-thickness ratio could not guarantee a stable structure, wooden rod-bolts (or pointed sticks) were introduced to enhance stability. Traditional examples of using wooden rod-bolts (pointed sticks) in consolidation work can be found at the Ming Dynasty Walls of Shanhaiguan District, Hebei Province as well as that situated on the border between Ningxia Hui and Inner Mongolia Autonomous Regions.

CONSERVATION METHODS OF YAOTAN WALL

Reinforcing collapsed or severely damaged sections using rammed earth

The preparation of the material for rammed-earth consolidation involves the following stages: air drying and grinding the chosen lime and soil mixture; sprinkling with water; mixing the lime and soil; covering and 'proofing' for further reaction.

Quality test indicators were set up for every step in the process. Modern testing technologies should be chosen with minimum damage to the surviving original fabric. Although equipment has been employed to run on-site quality testing, due to a lack of studies on traditional techniques its results are not yet solid enough for final judgement. Therefore, practitioners still have to control the quality of a rammed-earth construction according to their personal judgement based on past experience. It is necessary to stress that, however experienced practitioners may be, on-site testing is nevertheless indispensable. For example, during the proofing process, soil turning frequency and interval duration should be determined by testing results so that the soil is ensured to be evenly moisturised, the micro-composition of lime and soil has changed, and no dry or hard lumps of soil remain (Xu 2019).

The process of ramming involves the following stages: building an overhead shelter; setting up wooden molds; cleaning and wetting surfaces; spreading, flattening the material; ramming by hand; sampling and testing; removing the molds; sustaining moisturisation for the necessary period of time; and then removing the overhead shelter.

In order to determine parameters such as the frequency and spacing of ramming, reference is made to the designated degree of compaction in the design, to traditional craftsmanship techniques, and to the specifications as set out in the *Engineering Practices and Regulations* published by the Ministry of Construction of the Qing Dynasty in1734 (Wu 2017). Based on modern experimentation, the ramming space should be between 0.5-1 the diameter of the ram used. It is also necessary that workers should maintain consistent pressure throughout the ramming process.

At Yaotan Wall, instead of applying new rammed-earth layers in steps cut out of the slopes of the surviving original structure, the interface between the old and new rammed-earth construction was wetted, after which the new structure was directly attached on top of the original, thus preserving as much of the original structure as possible. This reflects the principle that consolidation work should involve addition to instead of subtraction from the surviving remains.

Mending cracks

The process of mending cracks in the Wall's structures involves the following stages: removing any loose materials or dust from the cracks; surface covering; mixing and injecting the grout; surface tamping.

Theoretically, the composition of the grout should be consistent with that of the rammed-earth structure. A

图 2 二号敌台东南侧加固前、后（摄影：邓涛）。

Fig.2 The south-east façade of Defence Tower No.2, before (top) and after (bottom) consolidation (photographs by Deng Tao).

（三）凹槽修补方法

凹槽修补过程：表面清理、洒水湿润、植木质锚签、夯筑、表面做旧。

凹槽由于深度小、宽度窄，夯补难度较大，一般采用土坯或泥巴修补，但尽如人意的不多。本次凹槽采用夯土修补，将夯土含水率调至塑限，夯杵直径改为 40 ~ 50mm，底部采用斜向夯，将填土夯成向内倾斜的坡面，上部侧向夯实。

（四）墙顶面及冲沟加固方法

墙顶面夯一至二步 4:6 灰土做防水层，再加表层夯一步 2:8 灰土做防护层。

冲沟按现状加固，仍保留其排水通道作用。表面采用二至三步 4:6 灰土夯筑。

small amount of binding substances can be added to the grout when necessary and the viscosity of grout should be adjusted according to the width of the crack. After the subsurface of the grout is half-set, tamping will be conducted on the surface for consolidation, sometimes with certain finishing to ensure a coherent texture with that of the original structure. It is worth noting that repairing cracks is not a single process as new cracks will occur after they are initially mended, and further repair works will be needed. Generally speaking, repairing cracks requires a minimum of three separate repairs undertaken at three- to six-month intervals.

Filling grooves

The process of filling grooves that have been caused by erosion involves the following stages: removal of dust and loose materials; wetting the surface; inserting wooden rods; building up layers of rammed earth; 'antique texturing' of the surface.

Building up layers of rammed earth to fill grooves tends to be relatively difficult because of the shallowness and narrowness of the grooves themselves. Adobe or mud is generally used in such repairs, but the results are not always satisfactory. Grooves in the Yaotan Wall conservation project are filled with rammed earth. The moisture content of the material to be added is increased to its plasticity limit and the diameter of ramming is reduced from 70mm to 40-50mm. The bottom of the grooves is obliquely rammed, so that the added rammed-earth block forms an inwardly inclined slope. The top of the grooves is rammed sideways.

Conserving the top of the Wall and consolidating gullies

This process involves adding one or two layers of a lime-soil compound (in a ratio of 4:6) on top of the wall as waterproof layer, then building a protective layer on top of the waterproof layer with a 2:8 lime to soil mixture.

Depending on their current condition, gullies which have developed over time through rainfall are reinforced, while allowing them to continue to help drain water from the structure. Their surface is rammed with a 4:6 lime-soil in two to three layers.

Dealing with vegetation and related damage

Vegetation that poses no threat to the consolidation work will not be removed or treated, so as to avoid direct damage to the structures during site clearance or the creation of voids caused by dead roots rotting. Tall trees are trimmed or cut short.

CONCLUSIONS AND QUESTIONS FOR FURTHER STUDIES

The consolidation project has realised the goal of 'properly preserving the authenticity, integrity and changed condition of the Great Wall's remains' (SACH, 2014), thus passing the values of Yaotan Wall on to future generations (Figs. 2 to 4).

The Yaotan Wall consolidation project may serve as an initial test and experiment to see how earth-wall sites can be conserved and repaired in accordance with the principle of minimum intervention. It has successfully addressed structural risks to the Wall and conserved what remains of its much changed original structure. There may, however, remain differences in wider understanding of what the principle of minimum intervention means in practice, which need to be addressed. The protection and maintenance measures adopted at the Yaotan Wall may be the subject for further studies. For example, the effectiveness of the conservation measures applied in respect of the upper surface of the structure and the gullies at Defence Tower No.2, will only become known with the passage of time.

图 3 景区段墙体坍塌处加固前、后（摄影：李青松）。
Fig.3 Collapsed Wall at the section by the tourist attraction, before (top) and after consolidation (main image) (photograph by Li Qingsong).

（五）植被处理

对不影响加固工程的植被不进行清理，避免在清理过程中或根系腐烂后对遗址的直接损坏。可对较高的树木进行修剪矮化处理。

四、加固效果及值得商榷之处

加固后基本“妥善保护了长城遗存的真实性、完整性和沧桑古朴的历史风貌”，使姚滩段长城的价值得以延续和传承。（见图 2～4）

基于最小干预的原则，在姚滩段长城加固中，对土长城遗址的保护维修方法进行了初步探索。采取的最小干预的加固措施基本消除了遗址的安全隐患,保持了古朴长城的沧桑感。但对最小干预原则的认知可能还存在偏差，有待修正，采取的保护维修方法可能还存在不当之处。如2号敌台，顶面二步 4:6 灰土加一步 2:8灰土防水层和冲沟三步 4:6 灰土防护层做法，还有待时间的检验。

图 4 残损与基本完好过渡段维修前、后（摄影：李青松）。

Fig.4 The transition between collapsed (red) and substantially intact (blue) sections of the Wall, before (top) and after (main image) consolidation (photograph by Li Qingsong).

参考文献
References

SACH. 2014. *Guidelines on the Great Wall Restoration* (Wenwubaofa No.4, Annex 2).

国家文物局. 2014. 长城保护维修工作指导意见.

Wu, J. 2017. *Notes and Interpretations on Engineering Practices and Regulations issued by Ministry of Works in Qing Dynasty*. Beijing: Chemical Industry Press.

吴吉明. 2017. 清工部《工程做法则例》注释与解读. 化学工业出版社.

Xu, H. 2019. 'Discussion on Construction Techniques of Rammed Earth Wall in Engineering,' East China Technology (General), (4) 0057. http://www.cqvip.com/main/search.aspx?w=许海燕

许海燕. 2019. 对建筑工程中夯土墙施工技术的探讨. 华东科技（综合），57. http://www.cqvip.com/main/search.aspx?w=许海燕

4.3 HADRIAN'S WALL - APPROACHES TAKEN TO CONSERVATION WORKS AND THEIR CONTROL

MIKE COLLINS
Historic England – Newcastle upon Tyne - United Kingdom

Abstract

This paper outlines the underpinning conservation philosophy and approach applied to conservation works on Hadrian's Wall, and the role of the Inspector of Ancient Monuments in implementing the system designed to protect such sites. It then examines the importance of the whole team involved in this work, and their shared understanding of the conservation approach being applied, suggesting that this, and the experience and skills of the team are more important than regulation to a successful conservation project.

Keywords: Hadrian's Wall, conservation, influence

INTRODUCTION

The conservation and repair work on Hadrian's Wall today is based on both an underlying philosophical approach, but also on the organisational structures and the skills and experience of those involved. The aim has always been to produce a high quality of work, which respects the sensitivity and authenticity of the archaeological remains.

However, this work also needs to be informed by very practical and by financial considerations. Finding the way to balance these factors requires both a clear regulatory regime, but also a shared understanding and appreciation of the skills of those involved. This blend of principle and pragmatic reality is the subject of this paper.

CONSERVATION PHILOSOPHY OR APPROACH

Current work on Hadrian's Wall is informed by more than a century of repair and conservation works undertaken by a variety of government and private sector organisations. The approach now taken, our current conservation philosophy, has evolved over this period through our experience in dealing with the broad range of challenges we have faced in the conservation of a wide variety of archaeological monuments. This includes everything from substantial structural repair to save a site or monument from total loss, to works necessary to allow or improve the experience of visitors to sites open to the public, through to routine pre-emptive maintenance.

Four broad principles inform this kind of work on Hadrian's Wall:

Consolidate remains as found

We aim to leave the site in as authentic condition as possible. Whenever possible we repair the site as we find it, without adding anything to or taking anything away from original (Roman) material.

Minimum intervention to secure site from loss

We aim to undertake the smallest amount of work possible to secure the site from loss if its significance, so that we may preserve, as far as possible, the authenticity of the site. It is not, however, always obvious where the limits

4.3 哈德良长城——保护工程方法及管控

麦克·考林斯[1]
英格兰遗产委员会—纽卡斯尔—英国

摘要

本文概述了哈德良长城保护工作的基本理念和方法，以及古迹巡查官在其实施中所扮演的角色。随后，本文考察了整个团队在保护工作中的重要性，以及他们认同和理解相应保护方法的重要性，从而说明对于一个成功的保护项目而言，团队的经验和技能要比管理规定更加重要。

关键字：哈德良长城　保护　影响

引言

今天，哈德良长城保护和修复工作的开展不仅是基于根本的理念方法，而且还以组织架构和所涉人员的技能和经验为基础。其宗旨始终是完成高质量的工作，尊重考古遗迹的敏感性和真实性。

然而，该工作还需要考虑现实需求以及资金因素。要想在这些因素之间取得平衡，既离不开一个明确的管理体制，又需要各方达成共识，并尊重参与各方的技能。本文旨在阐述我们是如何将现实情况与原则相结合。

保护理念或方法

当今哈德良长城开展的工作，是基于过去一个多世纪以来由诸多政府机构和私营机构开展的修复和保护项目成果。我们目前采取的保护方法，或者说保护理念，是从我们保护众多不同类型考古遗迹、应对各种各样的挑战的过程中所积累的经验不断演化而来。具体内容包括方方面面，从使遗址和遗迹免遭彻底损毁的重大结构性修复，到改善游客体验的公众开放工程，再到日常的预防性养护。

此类哈德良长城的保护工作主要遵循四个原则：

按发现时状态加固

我们的宗旨是使遗址尽可能地保持真实的形态。我们会尽可能按发现时的状态进行修复，既不作任何添加，也不移除任何原始的（罗马）材料。

确保遗址免受损毁的最小干预

该方法旨在通过尽可能少的修缮确保遗址价值不遭受损毁，从而做到尽可能持久地保护遗迹的真实性。但在实际工作中，往往并非如此绝对。例如，有时经过深思熟虑后会选择比最初计划修复程度稍高、

1 本文作者为英格兰遗产委员会哈德良长城古迹巡查官——译者注

of such works lie. For example, sometimes a carefully considered decision will be made to do slightly more work, at a higher cost, than originally planned, to thereby reduce the risk of having to return later to do the work again, at which time the availability of funding may be uncertain. In each case, we seek to make decisions which balance different considerations.

Balancing of needs

There are sites on Hadrian's Wall which are primarily managed simply to conserve archaeological sites and monuments. However, the majority of sites on Hadrian's Wall and indeed most other monuments in the UK, are managed to achieve a wider range of purposes and interests. For those sites we need to understand and take account of these wider interests and their needs beyond simply conservation. Such interests will include: those of tourists and tourism organisations; tourism and other businesses, such as farmers; natural environmental conservationists; and of local communities. Further issues which must be considered in undertaking archaeological conservation projects are the needs of owners of sites and the availability of funding to support proposed works.

Each site is different

We seek to apply our conservation philosophy to sites case-by-case basis, so that each site and its issues can be considered individually. This means that we have to take account of its context, its conservation needs and the availability of funding for the work, and to avoid adopting an inflexible and dogmatic approach.

Importance of shared understanding

In addition to these principles, our experience on Hadrian's Wall is that for a successful project there is nothing more important than there being a shared understanding of this philosophy amongst all those involved in the project.

Many of the sites presented to the public on Hadrian's Wall were repaired in the early to mid-20th century by the Ministry of Works, then the government department responsible for historic monuments. These sites represent an outstanding legacy of heritage protection and particularly its presentation to the public. However by modern standards this work often caused a significant level of harm to surrounding archaeological deposits, and have left us a high level of uncertainty about the authenticity of some of the remains which are now presented to the public.

Two factors seem to be responsible for this. First, the works were undertaken without proper archaeological supervision. Second they were undertaken by stonemasons who wanted their work to result in substantial and impressive monuments for presentation to the public visiting Roman sites, and to produce a long-lasting repairs that would not need further conservation for many years. These objectives are quite different from that of conservation.

The key lesson we take from this is not that these aims were wrong or unreasonable, but that they were not balanced with other reasonable aims, such as archaeological conservation and the preservation of authenticity. This is not to say that today we would simply consider only these latter aspects, but would want to collaborate in a much more open and transparent way, and to consider what each interested party needs and can contribute to each project. By this process we look to establish a balanced consensus of the needs of the project and to proceed from there.

REGULATION

Although this balanced approach to conservation has become the established practice in the UK, it is necessarily supported by regulation. This regulation is required to ensure that the discussions necessary to establish agreement on what works may be undertaken take place. It also ensures that if works considered to be too harmful

成本也较高的方案，这是为了避免日后再次返工，而届时能否获得资金支持并非定数。在每种情况下，我们都需要综合考量各方面因素，再做出决策。

平衡各方需求

部分哈德良长城遗址管理的主要目的就是单纯地保护考古遗址和遗迹。然而，绝大多数的哈德良长城遗址，实际上包括英国大部分其他的遗迹的管理都是出于更广泛的目的和满足更多方利益的考量。对这些遗址，我们还需要理解并考虑除了保护之外那些更广泛的利益和诉求。其中涉及的利益相关方包括：游客和旅游组织、旅游业和其他产业（如农业）、自然环境保护者和当地社区等。开展考古保护项目时，还必须考虑到遗址所有者的诉求，以及相关方案是否可以获得资金支持。

遗址各不相同

对每处遗址，我们力图具体问题具体分析，思考如何运用我们的保护理念有针对性地开展对该遗址的保护工作，并解决其存在的问题。这意味着我们必须考虑其环境、保护诉求和项目的资金来源，避免采用僵化而教条的方法。

共识的重要性

除了上述原则之外，我们通过哈德良长城的经验体会到：对一个成功的项目而言，没有什么比确保参与该项目的所有相关人员对保护理念有着相同的理解更为重要。

今天面向公众开放的哈德良长城遗址，许多是在二十世纪初至二十世纪中叶由英国建设部主持修复的。当时，建设部为主管历史古迹的政府部门。这些遗址成为遗产保护的典范，特别是在遗址的公众展示方面。然而，根据现代的标准，这种保护工作往往会给周围的考古地层带来严重损害，也让我们无法确切地回答如今展示给公众的部分遗迹的真实性究竟如何。

造成这一问题的原因似乎有两个。第一，施工过程中缺乏得当的考古监督。第二，修复遗迹的石匠们希望留下雄伟壮观的作品，给前来游览罗马遗址的公众留下深刻的印象。他们还希望修复后的遗址足够坚实稳固，以后很多年都不需要再实施保护。这些目标与遗址保护的宗旨可谓大相径庭。

我们从中得到的经验教训并不是这些目标是错误或不合理的。关键在于，这些目标没有与其他合理目标综合考虑，如考古保护和真实性原则等。这也并非意味着今天我们必须仅考虑后者。相反，我们希望以一种更加开放和透明的方式进行协调，考虑每一个利益相关方的诉求是什么，以及他们如何为每个项目作出自己的贡献。通过这样的方法，我们希望平衡各方诉求并达成共识，在此基础上推进项目的开展。

法规要求

尽管这种平衡各方需求的保护办法已经成为英国的惯例，获得法规支持依然非常必要。法规应当确保就工作方案达成共同意见的讨论程序得以贯彻。同时，法规还应当确保那些太过有害或不合理的方案可以受到权力的制衡，从而阻止其落实。这些法规不仅适用于保护项目计划，还适用于建设项目中考古遗迹的保护方案。

在英国，与古迹保护相关的主要法规为《古迹及考古地区法令》[2]。这是一项主体法令[3]，规定任何要对

2 http://www.legislation.gov.uk/ukpga/1979/46

3 “主体法令”指根据英国《国会法》制定的法律。而其中法律规范未足部分，由英国政府各大臣和其他机关根据主体法令授权制定“次级法令”补充。

or unjustified are proposed, then there are the powers to prevent these happening. These regulations apply not only to planned conservation projects but also to the way that archaeological remains are treated in the context of proposed development projects.

The principal regulation covering the protection of monuments in England is the *Ancient Monuments and Archaeological Areas Act.*[1] This piece of primary legislation[2] requires anyone carrying out works to a protected monument to first obtain the permission of a government minister. Such permissions, known as 'scheduled monument consent' (or SMC), must ultimately be authorised by the relevant minister. In practice, however, advice on applications for SMC, and much of the day to day management of the application process and advice to owners, is devolved to an Inspector of Ancient Monuments from Historic England.[3]

ROLE OF THE INSPECTOR

This advisory role in the SMC process places the Inspector, who almost always has an archaeological background, at the heart of the decision-making process, applying the principles discussed above.

Although they are almost never required to completely refuse permission to undertake works, this possibility, and their wider grant-giving and regulatory powers gives the Inspectors considerable influence in the positive management of change to monuments. This role is not about preventing any change happening to a site, but about protecting what is most significant about it, whilst compromising, where possible, to help maintain a sustainable, living and working historical environment. This positive approach is fundamental to the implementation of our regulatory regime in practice.

The Inspector also has other important duties including: commenting on development proposals; World Heritage management and planning; responding to damage to protected sites (Fig.1). There are around 20 Inspectors across the whole of England who carry out this work.

Clearly, there would be opportunities to manage monuments better if there were a greater number of staff carrying out this work. However, the small number of staff means that although the Inspectors have an important regulatory role, they know they are not going to be able to personally oversee every element of every piece of work in person. For this they need to rely on a wider team, something that requires close co-operation and a high degree of trust in the expertise of others.

VOLUNTEERS

Given how few Inspectors there are, there is a question about how well we understand the condition of sites like the Wall, and therefore their conservation needs. Although as the Inspector I am aware from past work of some elements of the monument where their conservation is problematic, I rely to a great extent on volunteers and the general public for information on its current condition.

At the moment such data is a combination of reports from individual members of the public and from an organised group of volunteers who provide more comprehensive data on the condition of the monument and particular problem areas (Fig.2). This is an area of work currently being developed, with key issues to be resolved on the production of reliable and comparable data, and on providing this in a way that allows prioritisation of conservation work in response.

1 http://www.legislation.gov.uk/ukpga/1979/46

2 'Primary legislation' refers to laws set down by Act of Parliament. It is supplemented by 'secondary legislation' which is created by Government Ministers and other bodies through powers authorised to them through primary legislation.

3 Similar arrangements apply in Scotland, Wales and Northern Ireland through their respective government bodies responsible for the historic environment.

受保护古迹开展的工程，都需要事先获得政府大臣的许可。该许可被称之为登录古迹许可，且必须最终获得相应的大臣批准方可生效。实际上，为登录古迹许可的申请提供意见、绝大部分申请过程的日常管理和向古迹所有者提供建议的工作都是由英格兰遗产委员会的古迹巡查官专门负责的[4]。

古迹巡查官的角色

古迹巡查官通常具有考古背景。上述登录古迹许可过程中的咨询建议职能，使古迹巡查官成为了决策流程的中心。正是通过他将前面讨论过的原则付诸实践。

尽管巡查官几乎从未彻底否决过某些工程，但这种可能性的存在，加之其他资助手段和法定权力，使其在积极管控古迹变化这一方面具有相当大的影响力。该角色的职责并非要防止遗迹发生任何变化，而是要保护其重要价值，并在可能的情况下做出让步，从而协助维护一个可持续的、兼顾生活和生产的历史环境。这一积极举措对于如何在实际工作中执行法规制度至关重要。

此外，巡查官还肩负着其他重要职责，如对建设项目方案提出意见、世界遗产管理和规划、以及处理受保护遗址所遭受的破坏等。目前，全英格兰共计有约 20 名古迹巡查官。

显然，如果有更多人从事这项工作，我们的古迹将有机会得到更好的管理。然而，人手有限便意味着尽管巡查官肩负着管理古迹的重任，他们知道自己无法事事亲力亲为，不可能做到每项工作的每个细节都亲自监督。为此，他们需要更多的团队支持，这要求巡查官与他人能够紧密合作，并对他人的专业技能给予高度信任。

Fig.1 Police and the Inspector of Ancient Monuments launch a project to tackle illegal metal detecting on the Roman site at Corbridge (© Historic England).
图 1 警察和古迹巡查官联合发起一个项目，以整治科布里奇罗马遗址的非法金属探测行为（© 英格兰遗产委员会）。

志愿者

鉴于巡查官的人数如此有限，一个问题随之而来，我们对包括长城在内的众多遗址遗迹的现状究竟能掌握到什么程度，进而对其保护需求又能掌握到什么程度呢？尽管我本人作为巡查官通过既往的工作掌握了长城某些部分存在的保护问题，我仍然很大程度上还是要依赖志愿者和公众提供的信息来了解遗迹的现状。

目前，信息来源主要包括一些公民个人和一个有组织的志愿者团体，后者能够就遗迹的状况和具体的

4 在苏格兰、威尔士和北爱尔兰亦是如此，当地负责历史环境的相应政府机关负责法令的制定。

ARCHITECTS AND CONTRACTORS

Almost all repair and conservation works on Hadrian's Wall are now prepared and carried out by private companies rather than government employees.

Conservation architects are the practical link between what I, as both an archaeologist and an inspector, want to be done and the actual works that take place (Fig.3). They specify works, and are often employed to supervise the contractors on site, to make sure that the work is done according to specification and to the right standard. The Inspector therefore relies heavily on the architect to ensure good quality work, but also to ensure that any variations to the agreed scheme are justified and authorised before it takes place. This role therefore demands a high degree of trust, but also experience of the particular kind of works necessary for the repair of archaeologically sensitive remains.

The contractors, who are usually stonemasons, are the ones actually doing the repair works. This is really the actual work of conservation, turning the aspiration that the Inspector has into an appropriate and long-lasting repair on the ground. Their reputation, and therefore their ability to be awarded contracts for work in the future, depends on achieving this. They are also the people who are on the ground the whole time, far more than the Inspector and even the architect, meaning that we are in reality very reliant on their professional skills and pride. This is again a very important reason why shared understanding of the project and its underlying philosophy is essential.

ARCHAEOLOGISTS

Although not every project will need full-time supervision, perhaps the majority will need some form of involvement from an archaeologist, something which the Inspector will not always have the time to provide. In these cases, work by a private sector consultant archaeologist will need to be a part of the project team and costed into the project budget.

Their work is likely to involve a combination of:

- Supervision to make doubly sure the project specification is followed;
- Supervising any dismantling or ground disturbance to avoid archaeological harm wherever possible, and to record any remains where disturbance is unavoidable and justified;
- Compilation of records of the site both before and after works, so that we know exactly what consolidation has been done to the monuments and what is original Roman remains (Fig.4).

FUNDING

As mentioned above, the availability of funding for conservation works on Hadrian's Wall has a huge influence on the approach that needs to be taken.

Conservation works can be expensive to undertake, and although the majority of the Wall is in private ownership, the site as a monument is usually incidental to the owners' use of the land. Therefore, while the vast majority of owners exercise great care of their section of the monument, it can be difficult for them to justify spending significant sums of money on conservation work.

The availability of public funding to assist owners in such work is increasingly limited, and the State has very little power to force owners to undertake conservation works. The State's powers primarily control new development or alterations to historic sites or monuments, but their owners have no legal obligation to maintain or repair them.

Some owners of sections of the Wall in rural areas have also been able to access funding from farming subsidy schemes for historical environment conservation. In practice however, we have been heavily reliant on the pride that individuals take in owning part of the monument, which has meant that the majority of Hadrian's Wall is in good condition. We have therefore needed to target the limited available funding on those areas at the highest risk of loss of significance. Those have been identified through condition surveys and ongoing monitoring of elements

问题区域提供更为全面的数据。这是当前正在探索的工作领域，也还有一些关键问题有待解决，包括如何形成可靠的、可对比的数据，如何使数据的提供有助于采取相应的优先保护措施。

Fig.3 Conservation architect, contractor and client in discussion on works at Great Chesters, Northumberland (© Historic England).
图 3 保护建筑师、承包商和客户就诺桑伯兰郡的大切斯特工程进行讨论（© 英格兰遗产委员会）。

建筑师和承包商

如今，几乎全部的哈德良长城修复和保护工程都是由私人公司而非由政府雇员完成前期工作和进行实施。

保护建筑师在其中发挥了实际枢纽作用，他们将我作为考古学家兼巡查官应当开展的工作付诸实践。他们负责明确工程方案，还通常受雇在现场监督承包商，以确保工程按照规范和正确的标准进行。因此，古迹巡查官在很大程度上依赖建筑师来保障工程的高质量交付，并确保在没有充分理由和严格审批的情况下，不得对已经商定的方案实施任何变更。也正因如此，该角色不仅需要高度的信任，同时还要有修复敏感考古遗迹的相关专门经验。

承包商——通常是石匠们——负责开展实际的修复工作。他们所做的是实实在在的保护工作，是将巡查官心中的期望落实成为适当的、效果持续的修复工作。他们能否实现这一目标，影响着他们的声誉，因而也影响着他们今后能否承接更多的项目合同。他们也是项目

Fig.2 The Inspector training volunteers in condition monitoring of archaeological remains (© John Scott).
图 2 巡查官对志愿者进行考古遗迹监测方面的培训（© 约翰·斯考特）。

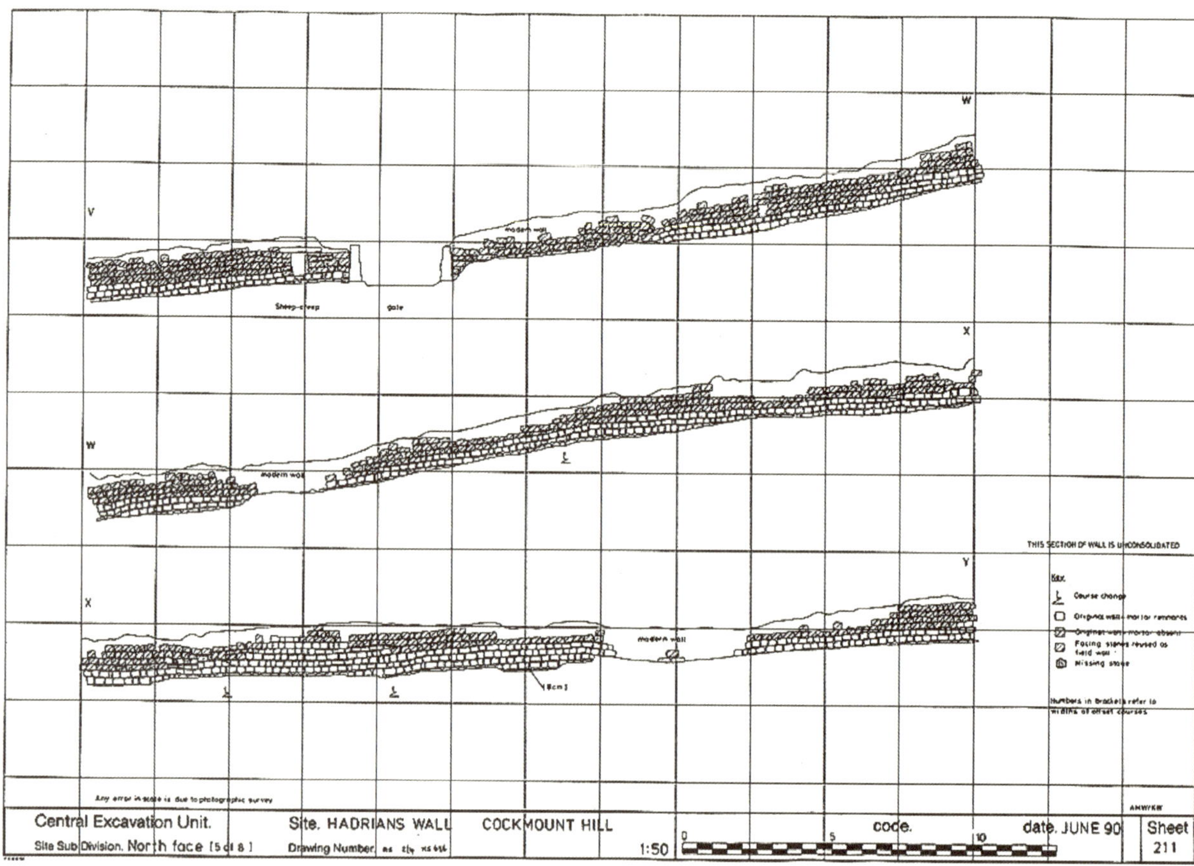

Fig.4 Archaeological drawings of the face of Hadrian's Wall 'as found.' (© Historic England).
图 4 以“原状”呈现的哈德良长城考古图纸（© 英格兰遗产委员会）。

of the monument included on Historic England's Heritage at Risk register. The choice of projects to be undertaken has required a ruthless prioritisation of conservation work to be done - allocating resources only to those works which are absolutely and immediately necessary.

CONCLUSIONS

The experience on Hadrian's Wall is that, whilst there is a need for legislation and for professional staff (the Inspectors of Ancient Monuments) to manage and monitor its implementation, these tools are far from the most important factor in good conservation work.

More important to us are:

1. The shared understanding of project needs and our underpinning philosophy between all those involved in the conservation project.
2. The participation of professional with experience of conservation-led projects.

全过程常驻施工现场的人，在工地的时间远超过巡查官甚至是建筑师。这意味着我们事实上非常依赖他们的专业技能和专业自豪感。这再次说明所有参与人员对项目及其基本理念有着共同理解为何至关重要。

考古学家

尽管不是每个项目都需要全过程监督，或许绝大多数项目还是需要考古学家以某种形式参与其中，对此古迹巡查官有时毕竟精力有限。在这种情况下，就需要为项目团队聘请来自私营机构的考古顾问，所需的相应费用也要纳入项目预算。

他们的工作职责可能包括：

- 监督工程，双重保障按照项目规范作业。
- 监控任何拆除作业或地层扰动，尽可能避免考古损害。当扰动不可避免且理由充分时，对遗迹现象进行记录。
- 对工程之前和之后的遗址记录进行整理汇编，使我们能确切知道古迹的加固内容，以及保留的原始罗马遗迹。

资金来源

如前所述，哈德良长城保护工程的资金来源会很大程度地决定最终采取什么样的保护方法。

保护工程往往耗资甚巨。由于绝大多数长城区段归私人所有，在其使用的土地内存在长城古迹通常纯属偶然。因此，尽管绝大多数所有者都小心谨慎地维护着古迹，很难要求他们在保护工程上投入大量资金。

如今，用于资助所有者用于保护工程的公共资金越发有限，而国家则几乎无权强制规定所有者须承担遗迹的保护工程。国家的权力主要在于对历史遗址或古迹的新建设项目或改造进行管控，但其所有者并不承担维护或修缮的法律义务。

位于乡村地区的部分长城段落的所有者能够获得农业补贴计划的资助，用于开展历史环境的保护工作。实际上，有赖于所有者以拥有长城为荣，哈德良长城绝大部分都状况良好。所以，我们仅需将有限的资金集中用于那些价值受损的高风险区段。这些区段已经通过英格兰遗产委员会的古迹要素现状调查和持续监测得到识别并被列入濒危遗产名录。确定要开展的工程项目需要公正严明地按优先级进行排序，将资源分配给那些绝对需要且迫在眉睫的工作。

结语

谈到哈德良长城保护工作方面的经验，法规和专业人员（古迹巡查官）对于工作实施的管理和监督固然必要，但对于良好的保护工作来说最重要的因素远远不止这些。

对我们而言，更关键之处在于：

1. 涉及保护项目的所有相关方对项目需求和基本理念达成共识。
2. 在保护项目方面有丰富经验的专业人才参与。

4.4 箭扣南段长城抢险工程保护实践

赵鹏
北京国文琰园林古建筑工程有限公司—中国—北京

摘要

在坚持不改变文物原状、最小干预的前提下，加大科技手段，辅助文物保护前期的研究工作，充分合理的评估长城病害，加强日常维护，收集本体的病害发展数据，合理选择保护理念，有效采取保护措施，更好的达到长城保护目的。

关键词： 科技　研究　考古　实践　保护措施

一、绪论

2016 年 9 月，中国文物保护基金会与腾讯公益慈善基金会开展了“保护长城、加我一个”募捐活动，确定将募集款项用于修缮怀柔箭扣南段长城 151 号敌楼至 154 号敌台及边墙。

本项工程于 2016 年 9 月开始进行现场调查，采用无人机航拍及信息分析技术，对本体病害及成因进行分析，于 2017 年 6 月完成设计方案，经批准后于 2018 年 6 月进入现场施工阶段，工程严格遵循“不改变文物原状”的文物保护原则，采用设计驻场形式，并引入田野考古方法指导现场清理，尝试用数字化技术记录施工过程，于 2019 年 7 月验收竣工。

二、项目情况

箭扣南段长城始建于隆庆三年（1568年），戚继光继任蓟镇总兵，并亲自督建完工。

150 号敌楼[1] 至 154 号敌台[2]，该段长城位于北京市怀柔区雁栖镇西栅子村，含 4 座敌楼，4 段边墙，总长度 724 米。分布于两个山峰之间，其中 150 号敌楼的海拔高程约 993 米，154号敌楼海拔高程约 1055 米，最低凹点的海拔高程约为 932 米。

三、形制做法

（一）敌楼的形制做法

151、152、153 号敌楼，基座用大条石砌成，跨城墙而建的中部空豁；中部以筒拱承重，构成相互连通的券室，外侧包砖墙，四面开箭窗。上部为台顶，中央筑有的楼橹现已塌毁，去往台顶的通道，是在楼层间开洞，利用绳梯或木梯上下。

1 敌楼一般由上、中、下三部分组成，下部为基座，中部为券室，上部为台顶，多数在中央筑有楼橹。
2 154 号为敌台形制，长城由山海关方向蜿蜒至此，是内、外长城的分界点，俗称“北京结”。

4.4 THE EMERGENCY STABILISATION AND CONSERVATION PROJECT OF THE SOUTH SECTION OF JIANKOU GREAT WALL

ZHAO PENG
Beijing Guo Wen Yan Garden and Ancient Architectural Engineering Co. Ltd - China - Beijing

Abstract

Following the principles of conserving with no change to the historical fabric and of minimum intervention, we have applied technology to assist initial research before restoration in order to thoroughly evaluate the structural risks and deterioration of the Great Wall, and enhanced routine maintenance and data collection. By doing so, we can balance between following appropriate conservation principles and applying effective methods or techniques in conservation practice, so that the Great Wall can be better protected.

Keywords: Technology research, archaeology practice, protection measures

INTRODUCTION

In September 2016, the China Foundation for Cultural Heritage Conservation and Tencent Foundation jointly started a fundraising event themed 'Protecting the Great Wall, Count Me in', raising funds to repair the south section of the Jiankou Great Wall from No.151 defence tower to No.154 defence tower and the associated lengths of the Wall, which are located in the Huairou District, Beijing.

This project began in September 2016 with on-site survey, using drones for aerial photography in order to analyse the causes of damage to the Great Wall. The project design was completed in June 2017. After the design was approved, repair work started in June 2018. This project strictly followed the principle of 'no change to the historical fabric, as stipulated in Article 21 of the Cultural Relics Protection Law of the PRC, requiring architects to be onsite and adopting approaches used in field archaeology to guide the on-site clearance of debris and vegetation. The whole repair process was recorded digitally, and the project was checked and accepted in July 2019.

Project Brief

The south section of the Jiankou Great Wall was first built in 1568, in the third year of the reign of the Emperor Longqing of the Ming dynasty. Qi Jiguang, general commander of Ji *Zhen*, was in charge of supervising the construction project until it was completed.

This section, from Defence Tower No.150 to Defence Tower No.154, is located in West Zhazi Village, Yanqi Town, Huairou District, Beijing. It comprises four defence towers, and four lengths of the Wall with a total length of 724m. It sits between two peaks, with Defence Tower No.150 and Defence Tower No.154 being about 993m and 1,055m above sea level respectively. The altitude of the lowest point of this section is 932m above sea level.

SHAPE AND STRUCTURE

The shape and structure of the chambered towers

Towers No.151, No.152 and No.153 were chambered towers, the bases of which were built with large strip stones, and they are hollow structures built astride the Wall. Barrel-vaulted bearing walls divide the middle part of each

（二）敌台的形制做法

154号敌台，基本为方形，基座均用大条石垒砌，高度略高于墙体，且有明显收分，呈梯形。墙体顶部用青城砖砌筑垛墙，四周无箭窗，墙顶四周有垛口，垛口上有瞭望孔。中部为台顶，在中央筑有楼橹（现已塌毁）。

（三）边墙的形制做法

箭扣南段长城现存的边墙为双侧包砖城墙。也称一等边墙。其高度根据地形情况而不同，平均5米～8米。墙体宽度，下基厚约6米～7米，顶部厚约4米～6米不等。建筑方法是：在墙体内外两侧首先刨槽夯实，然后根据地形砌数层规整的条石。条石一般长0.5～1.2米，宽0.3米，厚0.4米。条石找平以后，即用大块青砖错缝平铺，垒砌至顶。城砖的尺寸一般长39厘米、宽19厘米、厚9厘米。为使墙体更加坚固，包砖部分随原石墙外皮逐层向上，内收1厘米左右。中芯部位用碎石、泥或灰泥填充。

墙体内侧顶部有宇墙，高0.9米～1.5米，厚0.5米。底部水漫以上有射孔，形状为长方形，高0.3米，宽0.25米。因地势设置石水槽，探出墙体0.3米～1米。水槽形状为长条形，横断面外方内圆，总长1.5米，宽0.35米，厚0.25米不等。墙体外侧宇墙，底部水漫以上均有射孔，尺寸与内侧同。宇墙上部垒砌垛口，垛顶用预制的两面坡青砖遮盖，青砖高0.2米，连宇墙总高1.8米，长0.39米，厚与宇墙同，宽0.4米，高宽与垛同。

台阶地面一般做法为，铺青砖一层或两侧，上一层为方砖地面，绝大部分用特制的方形青砖，尺寸一般为37厘米见方，厚7厘米。遇陡峭之处，上下不便时，用砖石砌出踏步梯道。每阶一般高0.38米，宽0.4米，级数随山岭坡度不等。

四、对病害的调查分析

此次前期采用无人机航拍技术对长城进行了辅助勘察，并利用倾斜摄影测量技术，对长城本体搭建三维模型，直观的反映了此段长城整体病害的分布规律，掌握了长城病害类型、范围的准确数据，为分析病害的成因提供了科学支持。

通过航拍数据统计，此段长城城段的几处大的坍塌部位，基本处在地势较低、雨水冲刷面，城墙地面塌陷、基墙外鼓的病害基本处于两坡汇水点的位置。

由于敌楼（台）、边墙顶部排水不畅，或因大量雨水自上而下的水冲外力造成的表面防护层的缺失、残坏，水由顶部常年渗入敌楼（台）、边墙芯填石层中，石块间的灰土填充部逐渐流失，造成墙芯填石失稳、滑移。内部填充结构失稳对外包砌的基座条石、墙体施加侧向推力，而形成敌楼（台）、边墙下部墙体鼓胀、裂缝。当受力失衡时，产生边墙或敌楼外包墙体坍塌。内部填充结构失稳，同时也造成地面大面积塌陷，形成敌楼（台），城台及边墙上部的垛墙向内倾倒。

本体因冲刷、堆积、局部形成淤积泥土，形成草本植物或灌木类植物生长的小环境，植物根系对本体继续进行侵扰，对本体材料进一步侵蚀，并加快了砖体酥碱、粉化的速度，继而对表层的防水白灰层进一步侵蚀。文物本体的防水层破坏面积逐步加大。

本已脆弱的本体表层，因大量的无序攀爬和踩踏，也是本体病害加速的诱因之一。

五、保护实践

在保护过程中，始终遵循不改变文物原状的原则，坚持对现状最小干预。

tower into several rooms that connect to each other. The walls of the towers were built with bricks, with arrow windows on each of the four sides. The top section of the chambered towers is the platform, in the middle of which a sentry house was built, which are now collapsed and deteriorated. An opening in the floor of the sentry house allowed access from the middle section of the tower via a wooden or rope ladder.

The shape and structure of Defence Tower No.154

The Defence Tower No.154, almost square in its plan, was built with big strip stones at the base. It is slightly higher than the Wall itself, and is obviously in a shape of trapezoid, visible from the side elevation. On the top of the tower was the battlement built with black bricks. No arrow windows were found on any of the side walls, but holes for observation were found on the battlement. The top part of the defence tower is the platform, and the sentry house was originally in the middle of the platform which has now collapsed.

The shape and the building process of the Wall

The existing walls at the south section of the Jiankou are clad with brick on both sides which were classified as 'first class' Wall. Its height depends on the landscape, varying between 5m to 8m. The Wall is 6 to 7m wide at the base and 4 to 6m wide at the top. The process by which it was built was to dig parallel grooves along the lengths of the inner and outer side of the Wall, which were then rammed and on top of which were laid lay several courses of strip stones (depending on the topography). The strip stones usually have a length of 50 to 120cm, a width of 30cm, and a thickness of 40cm. After a flat surface was created with the strip stones, black bricks were then laid in a running bond pattern to the top of the wall. The bricks are usually 39cm long, 19cm wide and 9cm thick. To further consolidate the wall the brick facing tapered inwards by 1cm at each course. Gravel, earth or a lime-soil mix were used to fill the core of the Wall.

A parapet, 0.9 to 1.5m in height and 0.5m thick, was built on the inner side of the Wall. Rectangular gun-ports, 30cm high and 25cm wide, were provided above the gutter. Water-spouts were incorporated in the parapet, projecting 0.3m to 1m from the Wall, depending on the topography. The water-spouts, 1.5m long, 35cm wide, and 25cm thick, are square externally and round internally. A parapet was also found on the outer side of the wall; this had gun ports located above the gutter and these were the same size as the gun ports on the inner side. Above the outer parapet were crenellations covered with black bricks and capped with rectangular bricks moulded so that their upper surface tapered inwards from each side into a central ridge; these are 20cm tall, 39cm long and 40cm wide (the same width as the outer parapet). The maximum combined height of the outer battlement was 1.8m.

In building the pavement of the walkway and the stairs, the usual practice was to lay one or two courses of the black bricks above the core, and then to add another layer of square paving bricks. These square bricks were specifically developed for the Great Wall and were 37cm square and 7cm thick. Bricks were used to build stairs where the walkway was too steep to climb. Each step usually has a rise of 38cm, and a tread of 40cm. The number of steps varies according to the steepness of the slope.

INVESTIGATION AND THE ANALYSIS OF DAMAGE

This project used drones for aerial photography to assist in investigating the condition of the Great Wall. Oblique photography was applied to build a 3D model of the Great Wall which explicitly and accurately shows the distribution and types of damage in this section of the Great Wall; this helps us to better analyse the root causes of these problems.

According to the data collected by aerial photography, the most severely collapsed sections of the Wall are located at lower topographical points where rainwater run-off is concentrated. Problems such as subsidence of the top of the Wall and deformation bulging of the Wall's foundation usually happen where the water run-off from two slopes meet.

Due to insufficient drainage from the top of the defence towers and the walls, or damaged or missing sections of their protective surfaces, water penetrates constantly into the core of the defence towers and the wall, gradually eroding the lime soil fill between the stones and leading to destabilisation of the inner core. The destabilisation of

（一）首先，严格按照田野考古工作的相关规范标准和要求，对长城边墙及敌楼（台）顶面和底面的积土和植被进行清理记录工作。通过这样的工作，即可以清晰全面的记录本体被破坏的初始状态，有利于准确分析本体破坏的原因，确定有价值的遗迹分布情况；又可以防止在保护过程中对本体进行的过失破坏，并极大的保存、收集原始材料，有利于考证原工艺和原做法；还可以准确的发现植物对本体侵扰程度和分析根系生长的趋势。

（二）其次，排除长城本体继续坍塌的隐患。在长城边墙坍塌段落，找出长城遗址的轮廓线，根据现场残存的条石构件数量，归砌3-4层条石基础，现状坍塌后裸露的墙芯填石用白灰浆灌实、注牢，使之不继续扩大坍塌。坍塌部位的上部用白灰浆分层砌筑，增强整体的稳定性及防水性（图 1）。

（三）长城安全性和真实性列为首位。长城本体上的植被，逐棵进行甄别，影响本体安全的、影响排水通畅的一律移除，妥善保护长城周边整体景观风貌，延续本段长城独特的文化景观特征（图 2）。

（四）整修加固墙体，对现状较完整的地面砖、衬砖等进行现状加固保护，并对地面整体做防渗处理。尽最大可能全部保留原面砖、衬砖，有选择的归砌垛墙，充分利用长城原有的排水设施解决给排水隐患，用封护、局部覆盖等方式解决渗水问题（图 3）。

（五）敌楼、敌台裂缝处及坍塌部位采用钢构支护加固。敌楼（台）檐口下部设置钢环箍加固补强，增强敌楼整体性，防止墙体变形歪闪（图 4）。

六、保护实践体会

（一）箭扣南段长城 150 号敌楼至 154 号敌台，是在长城保护工程实践的一次尝试，还需根据实际情况，探求不同环境，不同地域、不同做法、不同年代的长城保护理念是长城保护工作的重要环节。

（二）长城保护，需要加大探索运用科技方法，介入文物本体病害调查，为保护措施提供科学的数据支持，通过数据分析及模拟演示，对一些不可预见的隐患进行提前预判。

（三）长城日常维护工作应加强和提升。文物日常维护以监测为主要工作内容，防范于未然。在日常工作

图 1 坍塌部位加固前、后对比（摄影：赵鹏）。
Fig.1 Before (left) and after (right) consolidating the collapsed area (photographs by Zhao Peng).

the inner core creates a push-force on the strip stones of the foundations and on the structure of the wall, causing expansion and cracks. When there is imbalance of forces, the collapse of the wall and the outer walls of the defence towers can occur. An unstable inner core can also cause large areas of internal subsidence which can lead the battlements on the defence towers and on the curtain wall to lean inwards.

The accumulation of sediment, caused by rainfall and other reasons, on some parts of the Great Wall creates micro-environments for vegetation, the roots of which can damage the Great Wall and its fabric. A consequence is that efflorescence of the bricks is speeded up and the waterproof lime layer is further eroded. Damage to the waterproof layer of the Great Wall continues to spread over time. Frequent and unregulated climbing and walking on the Great Wall is another cause of accelerating damage to the fragile surface.

Practical conservation measures

To protect the Wall, the principles of no change to the historical fabric and minimum intervention have been followed throughout the protection process.

Firstly, relevant standards and requirements of field archaeology have been followed during recording and clearing the earth and vegetation that had accumulated on the top and at the bottom of the walls and defence towers. This work has several benefits. It can comprehensively and clearly record the condition of the Wall where it has been damaged, in order to accurately analyse the root cause of the damage, and can also outline the extent of the monument's original footprint. It can also prevent further unintentional damage to the Wall during conservation, and can collect and store data on the original fabric of the monument, so that the building process and approach can be researched and verified. In addition, it can pinpoint disturbance caused by vegetation and predict the direction of root growth.

Secondly, the structural weaknesses that cause the Wall to collapse are being eliminated. For the collapsed sections, the boundary of the foundations of the Great Wall has been identified. Based on the number of strip stones found around the site, three to four courses of strip stone are rebuilt as the new foundation, the exposed gravel inner core of the wall is strengthened with lime mortar to prevent further collapse. The upper part of the collapsed section is repaired with layered bricks bound together with lime mortar to improve its stability and waterproofing capacity (Fig.1).

The priority is to ensure the structural stability and the authenticity of the Great Wall. Vegetation on the Great Wall is identified and each plant is individually assessed. Those that have negative impacts on the structural

图 2 选择性去除树木整修前、后对比（摄影：赵鹏）。

Fig.2 Before (left) and after (right) partial removal and pruning of the vegetation (photographs by Zhao Peng).

图 3 地面整修加固前、后对比（摄影：赵鹏）。
Fig.3 Before (left) and after (right) consolidating the walkway (photographs by Zhao Peng).

图 4 敌楼清理整修加固前、后对比（摄影：赵鹏）。
Fig.4 Before (left) and after (right) clearing and consolidating the defence towers (photographs by Zhao Peng).

中，加强对长城本体病害发展信息的收集、汇总、分析，这样能够综合分析影响文物变化的原因，有利于更合理的研究，实施及时的保护措施。

（四）前置长城本体考古工作。在长城保护在抢险或修缮工作实施前，有效的、有目的的实施考古工作，有利于设计方案的制订。

（五）加强专项技术工人的培养，探求深入制定文物保护方法的技术细则。制定、规范合理的技术细则，有利于对文物的保护，让文物保护成为一种规范行为，在这个基础上继续探求新的理念，新的技术，让文物保护工作逐步完善。

（六）探讨研究文物保护工程的设计施工一体化制度。文物保护工程在最初的勘察和设计阶段往往是需要根据一种或几种现象综合判断文物病害程度或者病因，而后需要施工阶段去印证，设计图纸所反映的处理办法往往与实际有所不符，这样造成了施工中的不可控因素增加。施工单位是设计理念的执行者，实际操作者对设计理念理解的程度决定保护效果，即对设计人的设计理念的执行也因此增加了不可控因素。若能在文物保护工程中执行设计施工一体化制度，即设计人即是实施者，或实施者提出设计理念，这样的操作方法，也许更符合文物保护的现实情况。

stability of the Wall and on water drainage are removed. The overall landscape character and the unique cultural features of the Great Wall are maintained (Fig.2).

For consolidation of the wall, the principle of no change to the historical fabric is followed for those paving bricks and their underlying brick courses that are well preserved, with an overall water resistance treatment for the paved surface. Most effort was made to keep the original paving bricks, their underlying brick courses, and to rebuild the battlement selectively. The drainage issue was solved by making use of the original water drainage facilities of the Great Wall as much as possible, and water penetration was addressed by sealing and capping certain areas of the Great Wall (Fig.3).

For defence towers, cracks and collapsed areas were supported and strengthened with steel rods. The eaves of the defence towers were strengthened with steel rings in order to maintain the integrity of the structure and prevent deformation and leaning of their walls.

Summary of the protection practices

The project of the south section of the Jiankou Great Wall is an exercise to explore appropriate approaches for conservation of the Great Wall, which may be adapted to different circumstances, locations, and across different construction types and periods.

The protection of the Great Wall requires more use of technological methods and support in surveying the damage to the historic remains. Through data analysis and modelling, precautions can be taken to address some risks that otherwise might be invisible and unpredictable.

The daily maintenance of the Great Wall should be improved and strengthened, in which monitoring is essential in order to minimise risk. Collecting, summarising and analysing information regarding the development of damage to the Great Wall should be enhanced so that we can analyse and identify the cause of changes, conduct research, and apply protection measures more appropriately and promptly.

Archaeological examination of the Great Wall should be conducted earlier in the conservation process. Effective and targeted archaeological work carried out before the emergency stabilisation and conservation work begins can benefit the design stage of the conservation project.

Specialised training and education of technicians should be promoted, and the technical principles of cultural relics conservation methodologies should continuously be explored and stipulated. Formulating standardised technical principles is beneficial to protecting cultural relics in a more regulated way. Based on this, new approaches and new technologies can be further developed gradually to perfect conservation.

The integration of design and construction in cultural relics conservation projects should be further studied. Normally, the initial survey and design can only assess damage and its possible causes on a preliminary basis and judge whether it is due to one or several phenomena. These judgements need to be validated in the construction phase. It is quite common that the solution presented on the design drawing may not be in line with the structural reality; this increases the incidence of unforeseen problems during the conservation work. The construction company executes the project designer's ideas. The effectiveness of conservation work depends on how well the constructor understands the design intent. Thus, how the design intent is implemented and realised is also uncontrollable. If we could integrate the design and construction processes in cultural relics conservation projects, the project designer will also be the constructor, or the constructor may be the person who proposes the design intent. This may be more in line with current good practice in cultural relics conservation.

参考文献
References

Cultural Relics Protection Law of the People's Republic of China (2017 updated).
2017. 中华人民共和国文物保护法（2017 年修正本）.

4.5 RECONSTRUCTING ROMAN BUILDINGS FOR INTERPRETATION AND RESEARCH: THE EXPERIENCE OF TYNE & WEAR ARCHIVES & MUSEUMS

W.B. Griffiths
Tyne & Wear Archives & Museums - Newcastle upon Tyne - UK

Abstract

Although often regarded as contentious, carefully researched reconstructions of Roman buildings not only attract visitors to archaeological sites, but form key elements in their interpretation, enabling a better understanding of Roman architecture than can be derived from the original remains themselves. Such reconstructed buildings also offer opportunities for research, both in understanding their original construction, and in their modern-day usage once complete.

Keywords: reconstruction, interpretation, research, museums, experimental archaeology.

INTRODUCTION

It is important to begin by being clear as to exactly what type of reconstruction this paper will cover. It is not discussing the process of restoring structures when their various architectural elements are visibly evidenced enough to be understood, but rather the reconstruction, or perhaps rather the re-creation, of buildings where little is known of their form, apart from their original ground plan. Tyne & Wear Archives & Museums has reconstructed several buildings at the Roman forts at South Shields (Arbeia) and Wallsend (Segedunum) at the eastern end of Hadrian's Wall.

Three buildings have been reconstructed at the fort site at South Shields, each directly above the original archaeological remains of the Roman buildings they are based on (Fig. 1):

- The South West gateway: as it would have appeared when constructed in the mid-second century AD;
- A barrack block of the third century AD;
- The fourth-century AD commanding officer's house.

Two further buildings have been reconstructed at Wallsend, although there neither is built directly above the archaeological remains of the structures they seek to recreate:

- A section of Hadrian's Wall;
- A typical military bath-house.

It is fair to say that, certainly in Britain, such reconstructions are contentious. Indeed, when the reconstruction of the South West gateway at South Shields was first proposed, archaeological opinion was divided as to whether it should be permitted. The arguments set against it can be grouped into two points:

1. As it was to be set on the site of the original remains, they would not be visible to visitors to the site.
2. There was a concern that this would fossilise one view of a Roman gateway in the public's mind.

The first point is a valid one. The original remains of the gateway cannot be seen. However, they had already been exhaustively excavated and were neither architecturally nor archaeologically significant in themselves. In addition, the remains are still present on site, sealed beneath the reconstruction, so could be displayed again at some point in the future. Furthermore, the more impressive and extensive archaeological remains of the North West gate of the fort can still be seen on site.

The second point has been, in this writer's experience, demonstrably proven to be false. When shown the

4.5 以阐释和研究为目的的古罗马建筑复建：泰恩威尔地区档案及博物馆经验分享

W·B· 格里菲斯
泰恩·威尔郡档案馆和博物馆—纽卡斯尔—英国

摘要

尽管复建古罗马建筑饱受争议，但基于缜密研究的复建建筑不仅吸引游客前往考古遗址参观，更是遗产阐释的重要组成部分。比起遗址原状，复建建筑可以让参观者对罗马建筑本身有更深入的认识。此类复建建筑也为研究提供诸多机会，可以帮助理解建筑最初构筑方式，以及复建建筑完成后的现代使用情况。

关键词：复建　阐释　研究　博物馆　实验

引言

开宗明义，我们首先要界定文章讨论的究竟是何种复建。本文不讨论在建筑构件遗存依据充分情况下的构筑物修复过程。本文讨论的对象是除原始平面图以外，对其形制知之甚少的建筑复建（甚至可能是再创造）。泰恩·威尔郡档案馆和博物馆已进行了数次复建工程，分别位于哈德良长城东端南希尔兹（South Shields）的阿尔比亚要塞（Arbeia）和沃尔森德（Wallsend）的塞盖杜努姆要塞(Segedunum)。

在南希尔兹要塞遗址进行了三座建筑的复建，每一座都直接建于古罗马建筑的考古遗址上（图 1）：

- 依公元 2 世纪中叶初建形态复建的西南门。
- 公元 3 世纪的一座营房。
- 公元 4 世纪的指挥官官邸。

沃尔森德另有两座复建建筑，不过二者都未直接建在考古遗址原址上：

- 一段长城墙体。
- 一座典型的军用罗马浴室。

坦率地说，此类复建建筑在英国可谓饱受争议。的确，首次提出复建南希尔兹要塞西南城门时，考古学界对是否应该允许复建出现了分歧。反对观点主要有两种：

1. 复建建筑直接位于原址上方，致使前来遗址参观的游客无法看到原址。
2. 有人担心复建建筑会在公众脑海中形成罗马城门的固化印象。

第一点不无道理，城门原址确实将无法看到。然而，原址已经经过彻底发掘，其建筑学和考古学价值都已不高。此外，遗址仍然完好地封存于复建建筑下方，未来还是可以再次展出。另外，体量更大、更宏伟的要塞西北城门遗址依然可见。

就第二点而言，笔者的经验已经证明它站不住脚。游客面对复建后的城门时纷纷对其精确性提出疑问，质疑城门的高度、屋顶的构造、窗户等等，相比于面对复建模型或复原图，他们会提出更为具体的问题。从这个意义上讲，复建建筑成为增加公众参与感，共同阐释和理解古代建筑的绝佳工具。

Fig.1 South Shields Roman Fort from the air. The reconstructed gateway can be seen at the upper right, with the reconstructions of the Commanding Officer's house and the barrack block next to each other lower left (© Tyne & Wear Archives and Museums).

图 1 希尔兹罗马要塞俯瞰，图片上部为复建的大门，下部为复建的指挥官官邸及相邻的营房（© 泰恩威尔地区档案及博物馆）。

gateway, visitors question its accuracy in much more detail than they would a model or a reconstruction drawing, challenging its height, roof structure, windows, and more. In this sense it becomes a fantastic tool to engage the public in interpreting and understanding ancient buildings.

RECONSTRUCTING BUILDINGS AS AN AID TO INTERPRETATION

Of course, archaeologists and historians constantly reconstruct buildings as a key way of interpreting them to the public. This can be in the form of an illustration or perhaps as a model in a museum display or, increasingly, a digital reconstruction that the visitor can explore in a virtual environment. I will consider each in turn.

An illustration has the advantage of being relatively quick and cost-effective to produce. It is also possible for areas of uncertainty to be glossed over; for instance, a tree could perhaps hide a section of wall where there is uncertainty as to the position of a door or a window. Further, in a painting the artist is not forced to obey the laws of physics (although many do). Models, although often more expensive to produce than illustrations, provide the third dimension, and often allow researchers to consider how a building might work architecturally.

以辅助阐释为目的的建筑复建

当然，考古学家和历史学家一直在进行建筑复原，作为面向公众进行阐释的重要手段。复原形式可以是绘画，或者在博物馆陈列模型，如今越来越多见的还有数字复原技术，让游客可以在虚拟环境下探索。我将一一分析上述复原方式。

绘画的优势在于制作周期相对较短，性价比较高。对于不确定的地方，绘画也可进行模糊处理。比如，如果不确定某处长城的门或窗的位置，可以用一棵树遮住。另外，绘画时画家并不受物理规律强制约束，尽管不少人还是会考虑物理规律。模型尽管造价比绘画要高，却也带来了立体感，让研究者可以探寻原始结构的建筑特点。数字复建模型使游客可以身临其境地‘穿行’于建筑中，并可以体现建筑随时间流逝而产生的变化。例如，赛盖杜努姆要塞的音像短片展现了要塞布局在 2,000 年间的变化，以及建筑在白天与夜晚、冬季与夏季的不同状态。

复建建筑本质上就是一座 1:1 的模型（格里菲斯 2005，329-330）。相比绘画、模型或数字复建技术，复建建筑一大劣势在于成本，但它胜过其他阐释技术的地方在于它能清晰地呈现建筑原本的体量。沃尔森德要塞的浴室（图2）基于哈德良长城切斯特要塞的浴室复建，不过为与遗址相协调，复建浴室呈现的是原建筑的镜像状态。切斯特罗马浴室现存的西侧墙体有两米多高，是保存最完好的英国罗马时期建筑之一。

当复建者在沃尔森德第一次标出罗马浴室的地面边界时，它看上去比切斯特的浴室小得多。当复建建筑达到接近切斯特遗址浴室现存高度时，能清晰看出两者几乎大小一致。很快，建筑完全掩盖在脚手架中，完全看不出它的真实大小。最后，脚手架拆除。第一次进入完工后的浴室，它看起来比原物要大两到三倍。当然，两者尺寸是完全一致的。因此，只有通过浴室的复建才使我们得以体验到浴室更衣室的开阔，才意识到原来这里对于罗马驻军而言是多么重要的社交和聚会场所。

复建建筑除了可以直观展示建筑及内部房间的大小，还可以启发思考这些房间的原始使用方式及可能的家具布置（克鲁姆，2005）。这样我们有可能布置不同形式供观众思考。比如，在南希尔兹复建的营房中，我们在不同的房间内展现了不同的床位摆放方式，表明我们并不确定营房内的床位摆放情况，也鼓励公众思考可能的形态是什么，从而告诉公众，考古学本身对理解历史也具有一定的局限性。

关于哈德良长城有着诸多未解之谜，其中一个就是墙体当初是否有装饰。有理论认为墙体曾经刷白，而纽卡斯尔以西的丹顿（Denton）发掘的一段墙体表明，墙体可能采用过一种名为“带状勾缝”的装饰工艺。在沃尔森德复建墙体上，其中一段采用了不同的墙面装饰工艺（彼得威尔，2018：161），同样也引发公众猜想，考虑不同的可能性之后，对最可能的工艺作出自己的判断。

以辅助研究为目的的建筑复建

当然，正如任何研究项目，复建可能成功，也可能失败。在泰恩·威尔郡档案馆和博物馆，我们制定了一套原则指导全部复建工程，内容如下：

- 复建必须完整复原建筑高度，否则不得复建。
- 所有复建都必须建到最小的可能高度。也就是说，如果原始建筑高度存在多种可能，我们选择建至最小的可能高度，避免被指责夸大原始建筑高度。
- 复建建筑应当修筑于考古遗迹旁边，以展现只有少量的原始建筑仍有留存。

Digital reconstructions can allow visitors to 'walk' through a building and can also show change through time. For example, the audio-visual display at Segedunum shows the changing layout of the fort site over nearly 2,000 years, and buildings can be shown in day or night, summer or winter, and so on.

Ultimately a reconstructed building is merely a 1:1 scale model (Griffiths 2005, 329-330). Its significant disadvantage over a drawing, a model, or digital reconstructions, is its cost, but its main advantage over other interpretive techniques is that it provides a clear sense of the true size of a building. The bath-house at Wallsend (Fig. 2) is based on the bath-house at Chesters on Hadrian's Wall, albeit produced in mirror image to fit onto the site. The bath-house at Chesters is one of the best preserved buildings from Roman Britain, with the walls at its west side surviving to over two metres in height.

When the builders of the reconstruction first marked out the position that the bath-house was to occupy at Wallsend it seemed much smaller than the building at Chesters. Once the walls of the reconstruction reached similar heights to those surviving at Chesters it was clear that it was about the same size. Shortly thereafter the building disappeared under scaffolding, and it was impossible to form a clear view of its size. Eventually the scaffolding came down. On entering the completed building for the first time it seemed about two to three times larger than the original. It was of course exactly the same size. It was thus only when we built the reconstruction that we appreciated what a large space the changing room of the bath-house would have been, and realised that it would have been a significant social gathering space for the fort garrison.

As well as providing a clear impression of the size of a building and its rooms, such reconstructions also throw up questions concerning what the rooms might have been used for and how they may have been furnished (Croom 2005). This can allow us to set out different possibilities for our visitors to consider. For example, in the reconstructed barrack block at South Shields we have laid out a number of different bed arrangements in the different rooms. This allows us to demonstrate an area of uncertainty in the way the barracks might have been used, and to engage the public in considering how things might have been, and in understanding the limits of archaeological knowledge of the past.

One of the unanswered questions concerning Hadrian's Wall was whether it might have been decorated in any way. One theory is that it might have been whitewashed, and excavations of a section of the Wall at Denton, to the west of Newcastle, suggested that it may have had a specific form of decoration known as ribbon pointing. A section of the reconstructed length of Wall at Wallsend has been decorated with the various alternative facings (Bidwell 2018, 161) again inviting members of the public to consider the various possibilities and make up their own minds as to which was most likely.

RECONSTRUCTING BUILDINGS TO AID RESEARCH

Of course, like any research project, a reconstruction can be done badly or well. At Tyne & Wear Archives & Museums we have developed a set of guidelines which we apply to all our reconstructions which are as follows:

- No reconstruction to be built except to full height;
- All reconstructions to nevertheless be to the minimum possible height. That is to say, where there is a range of posited heights for the original building we build to the lowest of these possible heights, so we cannot be accused of exaggerating the vertical scale of the original structure;
- Reconstructions to be situated alongside archaeological remains, not least to emphasise how little of the original construction actually survives;
- Complete excavation of the archaeology to be undertaken prior to any reconstruction. This enables us to be sure that we are not inadvertently covering any archaeology that should be further explored and understood, and that we have extracted from the site all the available information about the building we are intending to reconstruct;
- All reconstructions must be informed by and contribute to scholarly research. We see our reconstructions

Fig.2 The reconstruction of the bath-house at Wallsend (© Tyne & Wear Archives and Museums).
图 2 沃尔森德复建的罗马浴室（© 泰恩威尔地区档案及博物馆）。

- 复建之前须先进行全面考古发掘。这样可以确保我们没有在无意间掩盖了应当深入研究和理解的考古遗迹，并且确认我们获取了复建建筑遗址现场所有的可用信息。
- 所有复建建筑都应以学术研究为理论依据，并服务于学术研究。我们将复建工程视为加深考古理解的契机，而不仅仅是阐释工具。

我们所有研究都与大卫·艾什（David Ash）和格拉汉姆·滕奇（Graham Tench）两位独立的古迹修复建筑师合作。这就能确保考古学家给出的初始设计中所出现的问题都能得到解决（彼得威尔等, 1988: 221）。

在南希尔兹要塞城门复建中，彼得威尔、麦凯特和福特（彼得威尔等, 1988: 156-157）将要复建方案的考古学研究依据按重要性递减的次序排列如下：

1. 城门遗址的建筑遗迹；
2. 相同类型及年代的城门建筑证据；
3. 罗马时期要塞城门的建筑证据；
4. 罗马雕塑中表现的城门；
5. 罗马城市中的城门遗迹；
6. 罗马时期作品中对其他要塞的形态描绘。

这一考证方法首先从遗址本身的证据入手，逐渐拓展探究其他来源。我们所有的复建工程都采用了该方法，确保通过严密而实际的研究以确定复建建筑最可能的形制。需要指出的是在第 2 点中，我们首先考虑的是不列颠尼亚行省的案例，然后才考虑扩大至更广阔的帝国疆域。

as opportunities to enhance archaeological understanding, not simply as interpretive devices.

For all our research we worked with conservation architects David Ash and Graham Tench. This ensured that solutions were found to problems posed by the archaeologists' initial designs (Bidwell *et al.* 1988, 221).

In terms of the research under-pinning the archaeologists' designs for reconstruction, Bidwell, Miket and Ford set out, in descending order of importance, the sources of evidence used in the construction of the gateway at South Shields:

1. Structural remains from the site of the gate;
2. Structural evidence from gates of the same general type and date;
3. Structural evidence from Roman fort gates in general;
4. Representations of fort gates on Roman sculpture;
5. Structural evidence from Roman city gates;
6. Roman representations of other fortifications.

(Bidwell *et al.* 1988,156-157)

This approach, of working from the primary site evidence first and then gradually exploring other sources, has been taken across all our reconstructions, ensuring sound practical research as to the most likely form of the building in question. It should be noted that at point 2 we will look first at examples for Britannia before considering examples from across the wider Roman Empire.

The rules were applied to all the reconstructions at Wallsend and South Shields, but can be best illustrated with reference to the section of Hadrian's Wall reconstructed at Wallsend. The nearest historical reference to the Wall in time is by Bede writing in the eighth century AD. Bede was based just across the River Tyne from Wallsend, and so would have seen the Wall as it was at that time. He described the Wall as being 12 feet in height (Bidwell 2018, 158). Most archaeological estimates put the original height of the Wall at between 12 and 15 Roman feet, and in reality the height of the Wall may have varied along its 80 Roman mile length. However, following our rules we recreated the Wall at the minimum posited height of 12 Roman feet, so we could not be accused of exaggerating its scale in any way. The fact that the reconstruction sits alongside the actual surviving remains of the Wall serves to illustrate to the public how much it is conjecture.

In one sense the reconstruction is contentious. There is no firm surviving evidence that proves that the Romans patrolled along the top of Hadrian's Wall, and certainly no clear evidence for it having had a parapet wall. While most accept the likelihood of the Wall top being patrolled, some argue that it was not. One element in this argument is the absence of any merlon capstones that one would normally expect to find atop such a parapet wall. Of course these would be some of the first stones to be taken away and reused elsewhere, but it may be that they were never present in the first place. To test this, we used a mortared cap for our parapet Wall, at the time of writing this has been present for almost 25 years, and to date shows no sign of deterioration (Fig. 3). This has allowed us to test an alternative method of construction which could explain the absence of archaeological evidence of capping stones. It is of course not evidence of the Roman practice, but it brings another layer into the debate about the Wall's original design and structure.

RECONSTRUCTED BUILDINGS AS OPPORTUNITIES FOR EXPERIMENTAL ARCHAEOLOGY

The fact that the design and building of these reconstructions have been based on careful research means they can also be regarded as experimental.

The bath-house at Wallsend was built using modern materials. However, it was built to be a working building with an underfloor heating system modelled exactly on Roman hypocaust systems. The bath-house can be heated by a single fire (which we fuel with coal, which would have been readily available to the Romans in this area). We

Fig.3 The reconstruction of a section of Hadrian's Wall at Wallsend, showing the mortared capping of the parapet wall (© Tyne & Wear Archives and Museums).
图 3 沃尔森德哈德良长城墙体段落复建，显示女儿墙顶部石块砌筑（© 泰恩威尔地区档案及博物馆）。

上述规则在沃尔森德和南希尔兹所有复建工程中都有体现，但沃尔森德哈德良长城墙体段落复建是最好的例证。在所有史料记载中，最接近长城历史年代的是公元 8 世纪编年史家比德（672-735）的记录。比德的居所与沃尔森德只有一河之隔，因此他应该见过当时长城的样子。他笔下的长城高度为 12 英尺（彼得威尔，2018: 158）。根据大多数考古学估算结果，城墙原始高度在 12 到 15 罗马尺之间。事实上，绵延 80 罗马里的长城墙体高度可能有变化。不过，在墙体复建过程中，我们遵循上述原则，将高度定为最小的可能高度，即 12 罗马尺，以规避夸大墙体规模的嫌疑。复建墙体就座落于墙体遗存旁，目的是为了向公众展示复建工程有多少属于推测的成分。

从某些层面看，此次复建是有争议的。现存并无确凿证据证明罗马人在哈德良长城顶部巡逻，当然也没有清晰证据证明墙体建有女儿墙。尽管如此，大多数学者都接受有人在墙上巡逻的可能，有些则认为并非如此。反对者的理由是学界尚未发现任何垛口砌石，这种石头一般都应出现在此类女儿墙顶部。当然，它们有可能是最早被拆下挪作它用的材料，但也可能从未存在过。为求验证，我们在女墙采用顶部浆砌方式进行了复建。至本文写作时，砌石已近 25 年，尚未出现任何劣化迹象（图3）。这种做法也使我们得以试验其中一种建造方式，或可解释垛口砌石缺乏考古实证的现象。当然这无法佐证罗马人的做法，但它为城墙原始设计和结构的争论带来了新的层次。

had imagined that we would have had to put a lot of work into keeping the fire burning, but in fact it required very little tending to, and operated very efficiently in terms of heating both the building and the hot water baths. Several archaeological experimentation bathing evenings confirmed that the baths were about as hot as you would want them to be!

The barrack block at South Shields was built, as far as was practicable, under modern health and safety constraints, using Roman construction materials and methods. It was not possible to construct the roof authentically, but the external walls were built of stone with a rubble core bonded with clay, whilst the interior walls were made of wattle and daub. We continue to monitor them to see how well they survive and what kinds of repairs they may require.

South Shields Roman Fort has its own dedicated group of Roman re-enactors, named *Cohors Quinta Gallorum* after the third century garrison of the fort. The group recreates the Roman auxiliary army of that period. Much of their work is experimental, looking at reconstructing and testing various items of military equipment. They have used the reconstructed gateway at South Shields to support this work.

The gateway, complete with the two innermost defensive ditches, offered the ideal opportunity to assess the capabilities of weapons thrown at attackers from the fort wall. The group had several weapons reconstructed using authentic techniques and materials, and threw them from the reconstructed rampart walls adjacent to the gateway. The experiments tested replicas of hand-thrown stones (Griffiths 1992), javelins (Griffiths and Sim 1993), and *plumbatae* (lead weighted darts) (Griffiths 1995). These experiments demonstrated that even in the hands of modern re-enactors, who have not been through the disciplined professional training of the Roman army, the area of the ditches was very much a 'kill-zone' with attackers having no place to hide, even within the ditches.

To ensure the results of the experiments were as accurate as they could be, the weapons were manufactured using, wherever possible, authentic materials and techniques. We were, of course, not able to replicate the training for the Roman soldiers, so we have to accept that our results show only the minimum capabilities of the weapons. It should also be noted that such experiments only reveal what is possible, and they cannot be direct evidence for how the walls of a fort were actually defended. To illustrate this point it is worth studying the experiments involving throwing stones.

There is a series of finds from many Roman sites of rounded stones with slightly flattened sides that will fit into the hand. Traditionally they are viewed as ammunition for artillery pieces. However, Dietwulf Baatz suggested that they would also be useful as hand-thrown missiles (Baatz 1983). As part of *Quinta's* experiments we noted that having stones of the same size and weight made it easier to throw them with some accuracy. The flattened sides certainly helped with grip, but also, as can be seen in Fig. 4, allowed us to stack them on walls ready for use (of course this observation applies equally if they are artillery ammunition). A demonstration of five re-enactors throwing stones from the gateway into the ditches as rapidly as possible showed that this would be a fearsome weapon; effectively you would be caught in a nightmarish hailstorm! This of course only became apparent because we had the reconstruction of the gateway to use for the experiments. The experiments do not prove that the Roman army used such stones in this way, but it does prove they could, and that they would have been an effective weapon if they did.

Our reconstructions are sited at two museums in urban areas at the eastern end of the Hadrian's Wall World Heritage Site. Attracting visitors to archaeological sites in urban areas is a challenge. The reconstructions help draw people to the sites, thus supporting the wider World Heritage Site's aims of increasing visitors to the monument without increasing visitor pressure on the most popular rural sites. They have a significant part to play in interpreting life on the frontier to our visitors. As has hopefully been demonstrated, they are also a research device in their own right, helping move forward academic understanding of the Roman army, its structures and their use.

为实验考古创造契机的建筑复建

以周密研究为基础的复建工程设计与建造意味着工程本身也是实验的过程。

沃尔森德罗马浴室建造采用了现代材料，不过目的是将其建为一座可以使用的建筑，地下供暖系统则完全是依照罗马火炕系统原样设计的。整座浴室只需一处热源即可（在此我们以煤为燃料，因为那是当年罗马人可以就地取材的燃料）。我们原本设想维持热源燃烧需要花费大量人力，但事实上热源并不需要太多照看，无论是加热建筑还是热水浴池，这一供暖系统效率都很高。几次考古实验性晚间洗浴活动已经证实，这些浴池几乎完全可以达到人们期望的水温！

南希尔兹要塞营房的建造在可行且符合现代作业安全规范的前提下采用了罗马时期的材料和工法。屋顶无法原样复制，但外墙仍用石材建造，墙芯填以粘土粘接的碎石，而内墙则采用抹灰篱笆墙建造。如今，我们通过持续监测来观察建筑的保存状况以及可能需要的维修工作。

南希尔兹罗马要塞有自己专属的罗马历史重现剧团，以公元三世纪驻扎于此的高卢第五大队（拉丁文为Cohors Quinta Gallorum）命名，呈现当时罗马辅助军团的生活景象。剧团有不少工作是实验性的，目的是复原和测试各类军事装备。他们也利用南希尔兹的复建城门协助此项工作。

这座城门在建成时于外侧挖有两道离门距离极近的壕沟。若要测试守军于城墙上向进攻方投掷武器的杀伤力，这里是最理想的位置。剧团请人用罗马时期的材料和工艺复制了若干武器，将其从复建城门毗邻的城墙上投掷出去。这一系列实验测试了手掷石块复制品（格里菲斯,1992）、标枪复制品（格里菲斯与西姆，1993）以及重型铅制飞镖（格里菲斯,1995）。实验表明，即便是未曾受罗马军队的严格和专业训练，现代演员也能将壕沟区变成名副其实的“死亡地带”，进攻者即便是躲在壕沟中，也完全没有藏身之处。

Fig.4 Members of Quinta throwing specially shaped stones from the reconstructed gateway. Note the way the stones can be stacked for ease of storage (© W.B. Griffiths).

图 4 高卢第五大队队员从复建城门上投掷形状特制的石块。注意石头摞起的方式为存放提供便利（© W.B·格里菲斯）。

References
参考文献

Baatz, D. 1983. 'Town walls and defensive weapons', in Maloney, J. and Hobley, B. (eds) *Roman Urban Defences in the West* (Council for British Archaeology Research Report 51), London, 136-40.

D·巴茨. 1983. 城墙及防御性武器，见于J·马洛尼，B·霍尔比（编）西部罗马城市防御体系（英国考古委员会研究报告第51辑），136-40 . 伦敦.

Bidwell, P. Miket, R. and Ford, B. 1988. 'The reconstruction of a gate at the Roman fort of South Shields,' in Bidwell, P. Miket, R. and Ford, B. (eds) *Portae cum Turribus: Studies of Roman Fort Gates* (British Archaeological Reports British Series 206), 155 – 231.

P·彼得威尔、R·麦凯特，B·福特. 1988. 南希尔兹罗马要塞城门复建记，见于 P·彼得威尔，R·麦凯特及 B· 福特（编）有塔的大门：罗马要塞城门考（英国考古报告，英国卷 206），155-231 .

Bidwell, P. 2018. *Hadrian's Wall at Wallsend*. South Shields.

P·彼得威尔. 2018. 沃尔森德的哈德良长城 . 南希尔兹.

Croom, A. T. 2005. 'The reconstruction of Roman Military Buildings' in Perez-Gonzalez, C. and Illarregui, E. (eds) *Roman Military Archaeology in Europe*, Segovia 131-136.

A . T · 克鲁姆. 2005. 罗马军事建筑复建，见于 C · 佩雷兹-冈萨雷斯，E · 伊亚勒圭（编）欧洲罗马军事考古 . 塞哥维亚，131-136 .

Griffiths, W. B. 1992. 'The hand-thrown stone', *Arbeia Journal* 1, 1-11.

W . B · 格里菲斯. 1992. 手掷石块 . 阿尔比亚专刊，第1期，1-11 .

Griffiths, W. B. 1995. 'Experiments with *Plumbatae*', *Arbeia Journal* 4, 1-11.

W . B · 格里菲斯. 1995. 重型铅制飞镖 . 阿尔比亚专刊，第4期，1-11 .

Griffiths, W. B. 2005. 'Interpretation of Roman Archaeological Sites for Visitors' in Fernandez Ochoa, C. and Garcia Diaz, P (eds) *Unidad y diversidad en el Arco Atlantico en epoca romana* (British Archaeological Reports International Series 1371), 337-342.

W . B · 格里菲斯. 2005. 为游客阐释罗马考古遗址，见于C · 费尔南德兹-欧查，P ·加西亚-迪亚兹（编）罗马时期大西洋地区拱门异与同（英国考古报告，国际卷 1371），337-342 .

Griffiths, W. B. and Sim, D. 1993. 'Experiments with replica Roman javelins', *Arbeia Journal* 2, 1-13.

W . B · 格里菲斯，D · 西姆. 1993. 罗马标枪复制品实测. 阿尔比亚专刊，第 2 期，1-13 .

为尽可能确保实验结果的准确，制作这些武器时尽可能采用了原本的材料和工艺。我们肯定无法复原罗马士兵的训练方法，所以只能说我们的实验结果展现的只是武器的最小杀伤力。另外应当指出的是此类实验揭示的只是一种可能性，并不能直接证明要塞城墙的实际防御机制。为说明这一点，有必要进一步研究有关投掷石块的实验。

考古学家在多处罗马遗址上发现了一系列圆形石块，侧面稍加削平，适合手持。传统上，这些石块都被视作罗马攻城机的弹药。然而，迪特伍夫・巴茨（Dietwulf Baatz）认为它们也可作为手持投射物（巴茨，1983）。作为高卢第五大队剧团实验的一部分，我们注意到将石块制成（与出土弹药）相同的尺寸和重量更利于增加投掷时的准确度。侧面削平固然有利于手握，不过正如图 4 所示，平面石块便于靠墙摞起。当然，如果这些石块是攻城机的弹药，此推论依然成立。我们进行了一次演示，由五位再现演员尽可能快速地从城门往壕沟投掷石块。演示表明这是一种令人胆寒的武器，进攻者可能会陷入一场噩梦般的石头雨中！我们能有如此发现，也得益于复建的城门为实验提供了条件。这些实验无法证明罗马军队确实如此使用石块，但证明了有这种可能性，并且照这种使用方法，石块将是有效杀伤的武器。

我们的复建建筑位于哈德良长城世界遗产地东端市区的两座博物馆。吸引游客来到城市里的考古遗址是个挑战，而复建建筑有助于吸引人流，以实现哈德良长城世界遗产地的整体目的，即在不增加那些位于乡村的著名遗址景区人流压力的前提下，吸引更多游客到哈德良长城参观。复建建筑在向游客阐释边疆生活方面扮演着重要角色。此外，复建建筑本身还是一种研究载体，帮助推动开展罗马军队、建筑以及其使用方面的学术探索，这正是本文希望向读者展现的。

4.6 RECONSTRUCTION, RESTORATION AND CONSERVATION: THE EUROPEAN PERSPECTIVE, HADRIAN'S WALL AND CURRENT DEBATES

MIKE COLLINS
Historic England - Newcastle upon Tyne - UK

Abstract

This paper explores the approach taken to the issue of physical reconstruction of archaeological and historic remains in the UK and Europe, with particular reference to Hadrian's Wall and the Frontiers of the Roman Empire World Heritage Site. It examines the way that these approaches have changed over the last 100 years, and the main issues that any proposal for reconstruction in the UK would need to address. It goes on to discuss the current approach in the UK, based on heritage values and a balancing of harm with the wider public benefits of any proposal.

Keywords: reconstruction, restoration, conservation, Hadrian's Wall, heritage values.

INTRODUCTION

Approaches to reconstruction, and the related issues of restoration and conservation, have developed over more than 100 years within heritage management in the UK and Europe. Our approach to these issues has gradually evolved, leading to the current position on these issues, as set out in this paper. This process has progressed through debate, and sometimes through controversy. Whilst this has given us a wonderful legacy of sites and monuments enjoyed by the public today, it inevitably highlights work that was done in past which would be approached very differently if undertaken today.

The philosophical and practical approaches that we take to these issues today need to be seen in this context. They represent our current best efforts to balance the sometimes competing demands of managing heritage, and they will undoubtedly continue to change and evolve as our thinking about heritage management itself changes. The potential for this evolution to be informed by exchange and debate with colleagues from other cultural traditions will be a positive part of this.

It is also important to be clear that when we approach the question of reconstruction in heritage management there are no absolute, binary, right or wrong answers. The best that any of us can do is to consider carefully the issues within our general philosophical approach, explicitly balance different considerations in each instance, and document what we conclude and why. We should also acknowledge the different cultural traditions around these issues across the globe. Whilst we all continue to develop our solutions, drawing on the work of others, we need to be clear that no one approach or tradition will be correct in all circumstances.

RECONSTRUCTION: EUROPEAN TRADITIONS FROM THE 19TH CENTURY TO THE PRESENT

Current approaches to reconstruction are, to some extent, a reaction to the practices of the 19th and early 20th centuries. In the UK this period saw the restoration and reconstruction of many buildings, primarily from the medieval period. At this time priority was given to the desire to visually re-create a romanticised version of the past. This was generally undertaken without a great deal of historical or archaeological evidence, and with interventions way beyond the repair needs of the often ruinous structures that were being restored (Fig.1).

4.6 重建、修缮与保护——欧洲视角、哈德良长城与当前争论

麦克・考林斯
英国英格兰遗产委员会—纽卡斯尔—英国

摘要

本文探讨英国与欧洲对考古遗址和历史遗迹进行实体重建的方式，以哈德良长城和罗马帝国边疆世界遗产地为重点。文章回顾过去一百年重建方法的变化，以及评估在英国重建方案需要考虑的主要问题。随后，本文讨论英国目前采取的方式是如何基于遗产价值，同时权衡的遗产伤害与广大公众利益。

关键词：重建　修缮　保护　哈德良长城　遗产价值

绪论

在英国和欧洲，近一个多世纪以来遗产管理领域里关于重建方式及与之相关的修缮与保护问题一直在发展。对相关问题的态度是不断演化的，逐渐形成本文所阐述的当今立场。演进的过程经历了不断探讨，有时甚至不乏争论。它给今天的公众留下壮丽的古迹遗址、提供享受，同时也意味着在现在的情况下会采取与过去截然不同的方式。

因此，需要在这个大的背景下讨论当前处理这些问题的理念与实践。当前的方式体现出在遗产管理中为权衡相互矛盾的需求所做的最佳努力。而且，随着我们对遗产管理的认识变化，相应方式也将继续演变。与其他文化背景的同事们沟通与探讨，也将对未来的演变产生影响，是演进过程中的积极因素。

必须明确的是，在遗产管理语境下的重建问题，没有绝对的、非此即彼、非对即错的答案。我们所能做到的最佳方式就是，认真考虑相关问题应遵循的宏观理念原则，明确列出和充分分析具体方案中涉及的各方面因素，并记录下得出的结论与原因。我们也要承认每个国家的文化传统不同，采取的方法也有所差异。在我们不断完善适合自身情况的解决方式、吸取其他经验的同时，我们需要清楚地认识到，没有任何方法或传统适用于所有情况。

重建：欧洲十九世纪以来至今的传统

当前的重建方式在一定程度上是对 19 世纪和 20 世纪初实践的一种反思。当时英国对许多建筑进行了修缮与重建，主要涉及的是中世纪建筑。那时的主导思想是希望从视觉上重塑浪漫记忆中的过往时代。但实施过程中通常缺乏历史学或考古学依据，其干预程度大大超出了残损结构修复所需的要求。

在欧洲其他国家也出现了类似趋势，其中最著名的案例包括法国的中世纪卡尔卡松城堡，以及德国的罗马要塞萨尔堡的重建。后一个案例对于本文尤其重要。在该案例中，原来残存不足 60 厘米的城墙在几乎

Fig.1 19th century reconstruction, based on very limited ruins, Castell Coch, Wales (© Historic England).

图 1 19 世纪威尔士科奇城堡的重建工程，当时残存遗迹已十分有限（© 英格兰遗产委员会）。

Elsewhere in Europe a similar process had developed, with the notable and famous examples of the medieval town of Carcassonne in France, and the Roman fortress at Saalburg in Germany. The latter is particularly important in the context of this paper. Reconstructed from walls no more than 60cm high, it is almost entirely speculative, but still continues to have a profound influence on our thoughts about what a Roman fort should look like (Fig.2).

In the UK, the period from the late 19th century onwards saw a reaction against this approach, following the establishment of the Society for the Protection of Ancient Buildings (SPAB). This reaction argued that authenticity should be paramount, leaving the original fabric of buildings undisturbed whenever possible, and showing clearly where any new material had been added to provide structural support.

Undoubtedly the work done by our predecessors would today be done in a way that is different to either of these approaches. However, in any criticism of their work we do need to be aware of the great benefit of hindsight that we enjoy. We also need to acknowledge that the decision-making on the reconstruction work undertaken was far from an unthinking process. It was, instead, one that explicitly prioritised the re-creation of the look, atmosphere and detailing of buildings to evoke our medieval past over the principle of authenticity that we would prioritise today. It was simply based on a different balance of heritage values than we would now apply. This balancing, and the need to take account of a wide range of heritage values, is an issue that is returned to below.

THE CURRENT POSITION IN THE UK

There remains a presumption in the UK against reconstruction on the site of original historical or archaeological remains. This presumption is not an absolute ban on such *in-situ* reconstruction, but it establishes the issues that any proposal would need to address and overcome if it were to be allowed. This approach is supported by policy at international, national, and site-specific levels.

World Heritage policy

At an international level it is clear that policies and charters have sought to restrict and limit the reconstruction of archaeological remains, particularly on their original sites. The key advice on reconstruction is that contained in two important documents:

- *'restoration ... must stop at the point where conjecture begins'* (ICOMOS 1965, Article 9)
- *'... reconstruction ... is justifiable only in exceptional circumstances ... on the basis of complete and detailed documentation and to no extent on conjecture'.* (UNESCO 2018, paragraph 86)

Fig.2 Reconstructed Roman fortress, Saalberg, Germany (© Historic England).
图 2 重建后的德国萨尔堡罗马要塞（© 英格兰遗产委员会）。

毫无依据地情况下进行了重建，但至今仍持续深刻影响着人们对罗马要塞样貌的普遍认知。

19 世纪晚期起，自古建筑保护学会 (SPAB) 成立之后，英国开始反思这种方式。反对的观点认为真实性原则至关重要，应尽可能减少对古建筑原材料的干预，若需要添加新材料以加强结构的稳定性，应明确区分出来。

毫无疑问，今天的我们可能不会完全采用先辈们这两种方式中的任何一种。然而，在对“前车之鉴”进行批判的时候，作为后辈的我们应该意识到我们其实是拥有了站在前辈肩膀高度的优势。此外，我们还需要认识到，过去的重建工作中任何决策都不是草率行事的。相反，当时重建工作遵循的首要原则是通过重建建筑物的外观、氛围与细节，以再现中世纪风貌，而绝非如今的真实性原则。根本的原因在于，当时需要平衡的遗产价值标准与当今已经不同。如何平衡、如何将所有遗产价值纳入考量，将在本文后面讨论。

当前英国秉持的原则立场

在英国，对于在历史遗迹或考古遗址原址上进行重建，基本原则是持反对态度。这个基本原则并非意味着绝对禁止原址重建，但成为公认的门槛，如果希望重建方案获得批准，必须首先说服所有的反对意见。这一原则立场在国际、国家和哈德良长城世界遗产地的层面，都得到支持。

This emphasizes that, particularly as concerning World Heritage Sites, there is a clear need to avoid reconstruction which relies to any extent on conjecture. In practice this supports the UK view that there should be a presumption against *in-situ* reconstruction, which should only be undertaken as an exception.

Historic England policy

Beneath the international policy sits Historic England's own policy and guidance. In 2008, under our former name of English Heritage, we set out, for the first time, the principles, policies and guidance that we would apply to all of our conservation work and advice in a document called *Conservation Principles.* The aim of this document was not to produce something which provided detailed answers for every conservation situation, but to provide a set of guidance about what to consider and how those considerations should be weighed-up in conservation decisions. With reference to reconstruction, this guidance says:

- *'Speculative or generalised re-creation should not be presented as an authentic part of a place'* (English Heritage 2008, paragraph 132)

Since this overarching guidance was produced, we have also prepared a series of supplementary advice notes dealing in detail with particular conservation issues, including a draft note on the reconstruction of heritage assets (Historic England 2016). Once more, this makes clear the presumption of avoiding speculative reconstruction, as well as the need for clarity about what is authentic and historic on any site.

Policy in the Frontiers of the Roman Empire World Heritage Site (FRE)

Because Hadrian's Wall is one part of the FRE, it is necessary for policy for issues like reconstruction to be broadly in harmony across the whole of the World Heritage Site, which also includes the Antonine Wall in Scotland and the Upper-German Raetian Limes in Germany. The approach which has been adopted for the FRE is designed to reinforce the established World Heritage policy, whilst allowing for variation because of cultural traditions or legislation:

- *'... reconstruction must follow Historic England guidelines and ... UNESCO decisions and policy'* (Hadrian's Wall Management Plan 2015)
- *'Because of the condition of the ORL, our limited knowledge of it, and its character as part of the cultural landscape, any changes to the monument should generally be limited to works of conservation and restoration'* (Deutsche Limeskommission **2010)**

RECONSTRUCTION: GENERAL CONCERNS

General concerns about the physical reconstruction of archaeological and other historical remains, whether on or off the original site, centre on four main areas of concern. This is not to say that they are insurmountable obstacles in all cases, but they are issues which we need to consider carefully whenever physical reconstruction is being proposed.

Limits of current knowledge

Any physical reconstruction we undertake will need to be based on the best possible research and understanding of the site in question. However, research is always on-going, and our understanding of a site can change quite rapidly. The risk is then that any physical reconstruction can quickly become out of date.

Implied certainty

There is almost always a degree of speculation involved in physically reconstructing an historic building or feature. However, the very fact that something has been given three-dimensional physical form, suggests to many

世界遗产政策

在国际层面，各类政策和宪章都明确限制在考古遗址、特别是原址上进行重建。在两份重要文件中包括关于重建的重要建议：

- "一旦出现主观臆测，修复工作必须立即停止"（《威尼斯宪章》1966年，第九条）；以及
- "重建仅在特殊情况下适用，必须基于完整和详细的记录，摒弃任何臆测"（联合国教科文组织《世界遗产公约操作指南》2018年，第86段）。

上述规定强调了避免任何依靠臆测展开的重建工作，这对世界遗产来说尤为如此。在具体实践中，这些规定也支持了英国反对原址重建、仅特殊情况才可允许的基本原则。

英格兰遗产委员会政策

在国际政策之下，英格兰遗产委员会也出台了自己的政策与指导意见。2008年，英格兰遗产委员会首次发布适用于所有保护工作的原则、政策和导则，在名为《保护原则"》的文件中给出指导建议。这份文件的目的不是对每项具体保护工作给出具体答案，而是制定一系列指导方针，明确需要考量的因素，以及如何在决策时权衡这些因素。针对重建，导则规定：

- "臆测性或类型化的重建不得作为场所原真部分进行展示"（英格兰遗产委员会,2008年，第132段）。

在以上总体指导方针基础上，英格兰遗产委员会还针对某些保护工作中的问题制定了一系列补充建议，其中包含一项有关遗产重建的建议意见（英格兰遗产委员会，2016），进一步明确了避免推断性重建的基本原则，以及区分真实历史遗迹与后续重建的必要性。

罗马帝国边疆世界遗产地政策

哈德良长城作为罗马帝国边疆世界遗产（FRE）组成部分，在重建问题等一系列政策上也应当与整个FRE——还包括苏格兰境内的安东尼长城和德国境内的上日尔曼-雷蒂亚长城——保持一致。FRE采取的政策是强化既定的世界遗产政策，同时尊重各国的文化传统与法律，允许有所变化：

- "重建须遵从英格兰遗产委员会指导意见与UNESCO的决定和政策"（《哈德良长城管理规划》，2015年）；
- "基于上日尔曼-雷蒂亚长城现状、对它的有限了解，以及其与文化景观紧密融合的特点，对其进行的任何改动通常情况下只能限于修缮与保护"（《上日尔曼-雷蒂亚长城管理规划》，2010年）。

重建：普遍问题

对考古遗址及其他历史遗迹的实体重建，无论是原址重建还是异地重建，主要涉及以下四个主要问题。这些问题并不是所有重建项目都必须逾越的障碍，但一旦希望开展体重建，都需要谨慎考虑这些问题。

现有知识的局限性

任何实体重建都需要基于对特定遗址的尽可能详实的研究与理解。然而，随着研究的不断展开，人们对遗址的理解很有可能日新月异。这意味着任何实体重建都可能存在迅速过时的风险。

visitors a high degree of certainty about the reconstruction which then results. This can sometimes be addressed in the way the site is explained and interpreted, but such physical imagery can have a powerful influence on the imagination of the public and of academics.

Single-phase interpretation

Physical reconstruction can often struggle to convey and interpret a multi-phase site. On Hadrian's Wall, many adaptations and changes to its structures occurred over several hundred years of Roman and later occupation. These are comparatively easy to bring to life through reconstruction drawings or virtual reality display. In contrast, physical reconstruction risks showing this dynamic and complex history of occupation as a single unchanging moment in time.

Costs

Put simply, done well, physical reconstructions are usually major and expensive projects. It is very difficult to justify and finance their rebuilding to take account of changes to our knowledge, meaning that once out of date they can continue to influence or mislead popular understanding of our heritage into the future.

ON-SITE RECONSTRUCTION AND THE FRE

On-site reconstruction poses particular issues for heritage management, and these need to be considered in assessing any scheme or proposal. Once more, it is important to emphasise that these are not necessarily barriers to all on-site reconstruction, but they are factors that need to be worked through to come to a balanced decision as to whether the presumption against reconstruction should be overturned.

In addition to the general concerns discussed above, the factors that need to be considered for *in-situ* reconstruction proposals include:

Impacts on archaeological remains

The construction process may cause harm to the archaeological remains of the site to be reconstructed, both directly and indirectly. Such impacts can include:

- Direct damage to the upper strata of remains of later phases on the site by new construction;
- By building over the archaeological remains it may prevent access to them for research purposes in the future;
- The reconstruction may harm the setting of the original archaeological remains in their landscape.

Confusing the public

As discussed in relation to Historic England's *Conservation Principles*, there is a need to be clear to the public which features presented on site are authentic (and in the case of Hadrian's Wall original Roman fabric) and what is a modern reconstruction. This is not necessarily an easy thing to do, especially where the public has an already established expectation about how an 'archaeological site' should look. Particularly problematic in this regard is the approach sometimes seen, where an entirely new 'ruin' is created to represent lost archaeological remains where none survive (Fig.3).

The danger of fossilizing interpretation

As discussed above in general terms, there is a concern that, once constructed, on-site interpretation cannot be easily adjusted when archaeological and historic understanding changes. The potential danger of this is illustrated by the reconstructed Roman gateway at South Shields. Here the detail of the reconstruction was informed by the best information available, at the time of its reconstruction, from the site and sites elsewhere across the former

确定性的误导

对任何历史建筑或历史特征的重建都涉及某种程度的假设与推断。然而，重建展现出来的三维实体形式，很容易使参观者认为重建具有高度确定性。虽然某些情况下这一问题可以通过现场阐释与解读得到解决，但实体形象还是会给公众甚至学术界的想象力产生强大影响。

单一阶段阐释

实体重建很难传达或阐释遗产的多个阶段。对于哈德良长城而言，在罗马帝国数百年以及后续使用过程中，其结构经历了多次改造和变化。通过绘画或虚拟现实等展示方式重建这些变化相对容易。相反，实体重建很有可能将这一复杂与动态利用过程定格在某一特定时间进行展示。

成本

简单来说，高质量的实体重建一般都是大型项目，耗资巨大。因此重建工程往往很难给出充足的理由获得资金支持，特别是考虑到遗址的认知在不断发生变化，一旦过时，它们的存在会持续误导人们对遗迹的理解，影响深远。

原址重建与FRE

原址重建会给遗产管理带来特殊问题，因此审核重建计划或方案时需要加以特殊考虑。再次重申，这并非是所有原址重建项目都会遇到的问题，但在评估过程中需要逐项对照研究，最终才能决定是否可以搁置反对重建的基本原则，做出适度的权衡。

除上述讨论的普遍问题之外，评估原址重建方案还需要考虑以下因素：

对考古遗存的影响

施工过程可能直接或间接地破坏重建范围内的考古遗存，影响包括：

- 新建筑对上面年代较晚的地层造成直接破坏；
- 在考古遗存上加建可能会妨碍未来研究进入遗址的可达性；
- 重建可能损害考古遗存所处环境的原真景观。

使公众产生困惑

正如上文 英格兰遗产委员会发布的《保护原则》所要求，应向公众明确展示现场哪些部分是真实的（具体到哈德良长城，哪些部分是罗马时期的遗迹），哪些部分属于现代重建。这并非易事，尤其是公众对“考古遗迹”的外观总有先入为主的预期。最严重的现象是有些地方用全新建造起来“遗迹”去假冒已经完全消失的考古遗存。

固化阐释的危险

正如在上面普遍问题中所提到的问题，一旦重建完成，原址的阐释便不能随着考古学与历史学认知变化而轻易调整。南希尔兹罗马城门的重建项目便说明了其中的潜在风险。在城门重建之初，当时有关此处遗址与罗马帝国其他地区遗址的最前沿信息为细节设计提供了依据，为此专家们展开了激烈讨论。然而三

Roman Empire, rigorously debated by experts in the field. However, thirty years later, opinions have changed and there is less certainty about what this gateway originally looked like, and even whether there might have been a further storey in its original structure (Fig.4).

The amount of speculation involved in reconstruction

As already mentioned above, there is a concern to avoid speculative reconstruction by basing the details of any such project on archaeological evidence. However, in practice, our experience is that there will always be a degree of speculation when reconstructing based on evidence from fragmentary archaeological remains.

An example of this comes from the watchtowers on the German Limes frontier. Here, there are no examples of the original structures still in existence, and reconstruction has had to rely on their floorplans, derived from archaeological excavation, from details of what appear to be similar structures depicted in commemorative artwork from other parts of the Roman Empire, and from informed interpretation about their likely function, and therefore their form. Inevitably this has involved a significant degree of speculation across the more than 30 watchtowers which have been reconstructed, the majority of which have been constructed since 1970, often with limited archaeological advice. Although they form an impressive collection of structures, which undoubtedly adds to the visitor experience of the FRE in Germany, there remain significant concerns about these reconstructions. The degree of speculation is significant, which is reflected in the great variety of details of their superstructures. The public's understanding of the frontier and its function is now inevitably based firmly on the image of structures re-created from very limited information (Fig.5).

ALTERNATIVES TO ON-SITE RECONSTRUCTION

A further factor needs to be carefully considered if the presumption against on-site reconstruction is to be overturned. This is the question of to what extent the benefits that any such project might bring could be achieved through other interpretive methods. Whilst physical reconstructions can enhance on-site interpretation, the use of traditional reconstruction drawings continues to offer a significant and often underestimated tool in interpretation. It is also fair to say that the ability of virtual- and augmented-reality technologies to bring sites to life, without physical works on site, is considerable, and that these are technologies which are yet to realise their full potential.

The FRE, and in particular the Limes in Germany, has also explored reconstruction of archaeological remains close to, but not on their original site. In these cases some of the same general concerns about all reconstructions discussed above still need to be addressed. However, the considerations to be made in these circumstances are clearly different from those for a proposed reconstruction directly *in-situ*. How successful these not *in-situ* projects have been in addressing those general concerns remains a matter of some debate and controversy. Nevertheless, we do need to acknowledge that all physical reconstructions can be a powerful tool for engaging audiences, particularly for those seeking a physical reality as an alternative to digital reconstruction.

Perhaps most interesting for the future are the on-site alternatives to traditional approaches to physical reconstruction. Germany has a particularly impressive record in looking for alternatives which can evoke the scale and use of space within an archaeological site, but which avoid all of the potential drawbacks of physical replication highlighted above. Amongst recent key examples, I would highlight the Roman Park at Ruffenhoffen (https://www.roemerpark-ruffenhofen.de/index.php/en/), in which planting has been used to present and interpret a Roman fort, its buildings, and the associated civilian settlement (all levelled by ploughing), and the use of frameworks to recreate the scale of Roman fort gateways at places like Pforring, Bavaria (Fig.6).

THE HERITAGE-VALUES-BASED APPROACH

Historic England advocates an approach to change in the historic environment based on heritage values, as set out in our *Conservation Principles,* discussed above. This approach is, we believe, very useful when considering the

十年后，人们的认知发生了变化，对城门原始外观提出许多疑问，甚至怀疑原来城门是否还有一层结构。

重建工程所涉及的推测

上文已提到，所有重建应基于考古证据以避免主观臆断。但在实践中，经验告诉我们基于碎片化的考古遗存所提供的证据进行重建的过程中或多或少还是会出现推测。

例如，德国境内的上日耳曼-雷蒂亚长城瞭望塔重建项目。这些瞭望塔原来的结构无一保留至今，需要参考考古发掘出来的平面布局，罗马帝国其他地区可能类似建筑的艺术作品描绘，对建筑物功能的研究成果以及由此推测的形制等等各种信息。因此这 30 余个瞭望塔的重建无可避免地涉及了大量推测，并且大多数重建都是在 20 世纪 70 年代基于有限的考古证据实施的。虽然重建起来的一系列瞭望塔令人印象深刻，无疑提高了参观FRE德国境内长城的游客体验，但也带来了很多问题。从各个建筑物构造中大量细节的差异就可看出推测程度之大。公众对长城及其功能产生了根深蒂固的印象，毋庸置疑是这些基于有限信息的重建导致的。

Fig.3 Roman 'ruin', reconstructed at Kleinlellenfeld, Bavaria, where no physical remains were present (© Historic England).

图 3 位于巴伐利亚州克莱因莱伦费尔德经重建的罗马遗迹，当时已找不到遗迹实体（© 英格兰遗产委员会）。

原址重建以外的其他方式

若要跨越反对重建原址的基本原则，还需要认真考虑的另外一个因素，即重建的优点多大程度上可通过其他阐释方法得以实现。虽然实体重建可以加强原址展示效果，但传统的复原绘画其实一直以来也是极其重要、但经常被忽视的展示手段。虚拟

Fig.4 Gateway of the Roman fort at South Shields, England, reconstructed in the 1980s (© Historic England).

图 4 英格兰南希尔兹罗马要塞的大门，重建于 20 世纪 80 年代（© 英格兰遗产委员会）。

Fig.5 A reconstruction of a Roman watchtower on the Roman frontier in Germany (© Historic England).
图 5 经重建的德国罗马边疆的瞭望塔（© 英格兰遗产委员会）。

Fig.6 Use of a framework to evoke the scale of a Roman gateway, Pforring, Germany (© Juergen Obmann).
图 6 另一处是采用框架形式，再现位于巴伐利亚州普弗灵市的一处罗马城门通道（© 尤根·奥布曼）。

issue of reconstruction, and is based on understanding of the value of the site, and on an ability to balance harm to heritage against wider public benefits.

Heritage values

At the heart of this process lies the need to understand the heritage values that give any site or monument its significance. These fall into the following broad categories:

- Historic value;
- Archaeological value;
- Architectural and aesthetic value.

Whilst for many parts of Hadrian's Wall, for example, the heritage value may be largely archaeological, we need to consider carefully the contributions its other values make towards its significance.

Public benefit

Once we understand the heritage values of a site, we need to think carefully, logically, and dispassionately about the impact of any reconstruction proposal on those values, and not on any other values which may have become attached to the site. The potential areas of harm that reconstruction could cause to heritage values has been discussed extensively above. Undoubtedly, a well researched and implemented reconstruction will have public value: the value for interpreting the site; the inspiration it gives to visitors; the attraction for more paying visitors, which can add to the sustainability of the site and to the local and national economy. The UK's Planning system is clear that in order to be acceptable the harm that a reconstruction might bring would need to be out-weighed by the public benefits it would generate.

This is not in any way a simple acceptance of any form of reconstruction that provides public benefit; the UK approach is clear that *any* such development which causes substantial harm to a protected heritage asset, such as

现实与增强现实技术可以生动复活遗址，而无需在遗址上进行任何工程作业。相关科技手段可以说极具发展潜力，尚未充分得到发挥。

在 FRE，尤其是德国境内的长城，也尝试在原址邻近区域而非原址之上开展重建。这些尝试仍需要解决上述所有重建都需要考虑的普遍问题，但显然这种情况下需要考虑的问题与直接在原址重建有所不同。当然，非原址重建是否能够有效地解决普遍问题仍存在不同意见和争议。与此同时我们也应当承认，所有实体重建都是吸引观众的有力手段，对那些希望前来看到实物而非数码复原的参观者来说尤为如此。

也许未来最值得关注的是那些基于原址的、但又替代实体重建的其他展示方式。德国在探索替代方式方面的实践令人印象深刻。这些替代方式能够重现考古遗址的体量和空间使用功能，同时避免上文提到的实体重建的潜在弊端。在近期主要实践中，笔者希望推荐以下两个案例。一个是德国巴伐利亚州鲁芬霍芬遗址上的罗马公园（https://www.roemerpark-ruffenhofen.de/index.php/en/），那里用植物展示与阐释因农耕被夷为平地的罗马要塞、相关建筑与附属平民聚落。另一处是采用框架形式，再现位于巴伐利亚州普弗灵市等地的罗马要塞的城门通道。

基于遗产价值的方式

遵循上文提到的《保护原则》精神，英格兰遗产委员会倡导基于遗产价值、关注历史环境变化的管理方式。英格兰遗产委员会认为，该原则对管理重建问题也十分有益。它结合对遗产价值的深入了解，同时加强协调能力，以平衡重建对遗产伤害和使广大公众受益之间的关系。

遗产价值

工作的核心在于对古迹遗址遗产价值的深入认知。遗产价值主要包括以下几类：

- 历史价值；
- 考古价值；
- 建筑与审美价值。

例如，对于哈德良长城来说，大部分点段的遗产价值可能主要是考古价值，但我们仍需要认真考量其他价值对哈德良长城的意义和影响。

公众利益

在理解了具体遗址的遗产价值后，我们需要认真地、有条理地、冷静地分析重建方案对这些遗产价值的影响，还应当排除其他派生出来的价值干扰因素。重建对遗产价值造成的潜在伤害前面已经全面阐述。毋庸置疑，经过精心研究与妥善实施的重建项目具有公众价值：遗产阐释价值，激发参观者灵感，吸引更多付费游客，从而实现遗产地、地方与国家经济的可持续发展。英国的规划系统明确规定，只有产生的公众利益远远大于对遗产造成潜在伤害时，重建方案才可接受。

但是，不是任何形式的重建计划只要能带来公共利益就可接受。英国的原则明确规定，对于受保护的遗产，包括世界遗产，任何造成重大伤害的重建类开发项目通常不予批准，应当被视作极为特别的个案处理。此外还要求任何具有伤害性的方案都必须表明其所带来的公众利益将远远超过损害。只有满足这些要求，重建计划才有可能提上议事日程，反对重建的基本原则才有可能不再坚持。

a World Heritage Site, should not normally be allowed and should be regarded as being wholly exceptional. It also requires that any harmful proposal must show that is will produce a substantial public benefit which outweighs this harm. Only if these tests are met should a reconstruction proposal be considered, and the presumption against this type of development set aside.

CURRENT DEBATES AND THE FUTURE

Historic England believes that we have established a good framework which allows us to think about reconstruction in a robust and transparent way, and to balance harm to heritage against the public good.

However, what should also be clear is that:

- This is the point that we have reached in our thinking on this issue through more than 100 years. This issue is a source of continuing debate, and our thinking will undoubtedly continue to evolve into the future.
- This framework provides us with a set of principles and a balanced approach to considering proposals for reconstructions, rather than a set of rules which provides precise answers in every case.
- Although a presumption against on-site reconstruction still exists, this process needs to be applied on a case-by-case basis, looking in detail at the harm and public benefits of each specific proposal.

References
参考文献

Deutsche Limeskommission. 2010. *Upper German-Raetian Limes Management Plan 2010-2015*. Deutsche Limeskommission, Bad Homburg. https://whc.unesco.org/document/178674

English Heritage. 2008. *Conservation Principles, Policies and Guidance for the sustainable management of the historic environment*, London.

英格兰遗产委员会. 2008 . 历史环境可持续管理的保护原则、政策和指南. 伦敦 .

Hadrian's Wall Management Plan. 2015. http://hadrianswallcountry.co.uk/hadrians-wall-management-plan

哈德良长城管理规划. 2015： http://hadrianswallcountry.co.uk/hadrians-wall-management-plan

Historic England. 2016. *Historic England Advisory Note on the Reconstruction of Heritage Assets*, London.

英格兰遗产委员会. 2016. 英格兰遗产委员会关于遗产重建的建议意见. 伦敦.

ICOMOS. 1965. *International Charter for the Conservation and Restoration of Monuments and Sites (The Venice Charter 1964)*. http://www.international.icomos.org/charters/venice_e.pdf

国际古迹遗址理事会. 1965. 国际古迹保护与修复宪章（威尼斯宪章 1964）

UNESCO. 2018. *Operational Guidelines for the Implementation of the World Heritage Convention*. UNESCO, Paris. https://whc.unesco.org/document/178167

联合国教科文组织. 2018. 实施保护世界遗产公约操作指南. 巴黎. https://whc.unesco.org/document/178167

当前争论与未来

英格兰遗产委员会认为，我们已经建立起相当完备的框架体系，有助于稳健、公开地管理重建问题，也有助于平衡遗产伤害与公众利益之间的关系。

然而，还需要清醒地认识到：

- 我们之所以能达到现在的认识阶段，是经历了一百多年的探索。重建问题是持续争论的主题，我们的认知无疑将继续发展。
- 当前的框架为我们提供的是评估重建方案的一系列原则与权衡方法，而不是针对每个具体方案的确定答案。
- 尽管反对原址重建的基本原则依然存在，但其执行应当遵循一事一议原则，仔细考虑每一具体重建个案在遗产伤害与公众利益的具体情况。

Chapter 5:

Visitor Access and Public Engagement

Visitors walking on the National Trail parallel to Hadrian's Wall, east of Birdoswald Roman Fort (© English Heritage Trust).
游客走在沿哈德良长城并行的国家步道上，博得瓦德要塞以东（©英格兰遗产信托）。

第五单元

长城开放利用与社会参与

Voluntary organisations like the Great Wall Station are promoting greater public engagement in the protection and maintenance of the Great Wall (photograph by Zhang Jun).

长城小站等社会组织积极推动更多社会公众参与长城保护和维护（摄影：张俊）。

5.1 THE GERMAN LIMES ROAD ASSOCIATION MOTORING ROUTE, CYCLEWAY AND HIKING TRAIL

David Brough
Newcastle University - Newcastle upon Tyne - UK

Julia Datow-Ensling
German Limes Road Association - Aalen - Germany

Abstract

The promotion of public access to the Upper German-Raetian Limes World Heritage Site, via the Limes Road, the Limes Cycleway, and the Limes Hiking Trail, is the primary responsibility of the German Limes Road Association. The history of the development of these three routes and their extent and infrastructure is described, along with Association's structure, membership and funding. The aims of the Association and the activities it undertakes to meet those objectives, are then explained. An assessment is offered of how successful the Association has been, and a number of characteristics of its structure and functioning are then suggested as having been key to what it has achieved.

Keywords: public access, tourism motoring routes, hiking trail, cycleway, visitor promotion

INTRODUCTION

The Upper German-Raetian Limes[1] is that section of the Frontiers of the Roman Empire World Heritage Site which runs between the River Rhine and the River Danube; it was inscribed onto the World Heritage List in 2005. It takes its name from the two Roman provinces of Upper Germany and Raetia along whose northerly borders the Roman Empire established a continuous linear barrier. In Upper Germany this mainly consisted of a wooden palisade,[2] whilst in Raetia it was mostly built in stone. Regularly spaced watchtowers constructed of wood and stone were built immediately behind these barriers. Within this boundary a number of forts of differing sizes were built, each connected by a network of roads, and further back there were larger fortresses around which civilian settlements developed. These elements combined to form the Roman military frontier system, along with some ancillary features such as bathhouses, amphitheatres and temples.

The archaeological remains of this system are spread across the German federal states of Rhineland-Palatinate, Hessen, Baden-Wurttemberg, and Bavaria, and each state determines its own regulations for the protection of cultural heritage resources. Local government - rural districts or counties and urban districts (cities or large towns) - is responsible for tourism and public amenities, including museums. Public access along the 550km of the World Heritage Site is facilitated through the Limes Road, the Limes Cycleway and the Limes Hiking Trail, each of which is coordinated and promoted through the Limes Road Association. It is hoped that this account of the German Limes Road Association's experience of developing, operating and promoting the three routes may help to inform current

1 'Limes' is derived from the Latin word for a boundary; it is now used as a generic term for Roman frontiers.

2 For part of the Limes in Upper Germany the middle reaches of the River Main formed the barrier.

5.1 德国界墙之路协会与德国界墙公路、单车道及步道

大卫·布劳夫
纽卡斯尔大学—纽卡斯尔—英国

尤利娅·达托—恩斯林
德国界墙之路协会—阿伦—德国

摘要

通过界墙公路、单车道及步道促进上日耳曼–雷蒂亚界墙的开放利用是德国界墙之路协会的主要职责。本文介绍三条线路的发展历程、长度范围及基础设施，同时介绍协会架构、会员制度及资金来源。之后，本文将介绍协会工作目标及为之开展的活动，并对所取得的成就进行总结。本文认为协会架构和职能方面的众多特点是协会取得这些成绩的关键。

关键词：对外开放　旅游线路　步道　单车道　游客推广

引言

上日耳曼-雷蒂亚界墙[1]是罗马帝国边疆世界遗产地的组成部分，从莱茵河一直延伸至多瑙河。2005 年，该遗址入选世界遗产名录。界墙因罗马帝国的上日耳曼行省（Upper Germany）及雷蒂亚行省（Raetia）而得名。罗马人沿着两个行省的北部边界线修筑了绵延不断的线性防御工事。上日耳曼段主要为木制栅栏[2]，而雷蒂亚段以石质为主。紧挨着墙体内侧建有等间距设置的木石结构的瞭望塔。墙体内则还筑有大小不一的数座要塞，各以路网相连，再深入内地是规模较大的要塞，周围建有平民聚落。这些要素组合起来构成罗马边疆防体系，以及浴室、圆形剧场、神庙等相关设施。

这个罗马边疆防御体系的考古遗迹遍布德国数个州，包括莱茵兰-普法尔茨（Rhineland-Palatinate）[3]、黑森、巴登-符腾堡以及巴伐利亚，而每个州在文化遗产资源保护方面都有自己的法规。地方政府——包括乡村地区或县级行政单位以及都市地区（包括城市和大型城镇）——负责管理旅游和公共配套设施，其中包括博物馆。界墙沿线建成对公众开放的界墙公路、单车道及步道，绵延 550 千米。德国界墙之路协会负责三条道路的协调和推广由。本文将介绍协会建设、运营和推广三条道路的经验，希望可以为中国长城在目前及今后对游客开放方面的工作提供借鉴。

1“界墙”（Limes）一词来自拉丁语，意为界线，如今被用来泛指罗马边疆。
2 上日耳曼界墙的部分区段借助美因河中游共同构成防御工事。
3 德语写作 Rheinland-Pfalz。——译者注

and future thinking in relation to visitor access along the Great Wall of China.

THE LIMES ROAD ASSOCIATION AND THE LIMES ROAD

The Association was established in 1996, nine years before this section of the Roman frontier was inscribed as a World Heritage Site, and its initial focus was the development of the Limes Road as a motoring route for visitors. In 1997 it began work on establishing the Limes Cycleway and the Limes Hiking Trail. Each of these three routes were developed incrementally over a number of years.

The concept of tourist motoring routes had been established in Germany in the 1950s. These routes are each based on a specific cultural or natural theme, and encourage visits to landscapes, villages, cities and towns associated with that theme: these include the Fairytales Road, the Wine Road, the Volcanic Road, and the Asparagus Road. Today there are over 150 such routes in Germany, ranging in extent from under 100km to over 500km. The Limes Road runs for over 820km from Bad Honningen on the Rhine to Passau on the Danube （Fig.1）.

The creation of these routes has generally involved little construction of new roads, and has utilised the existing public road networks. Their 'creation' has essentially been through a process of delineation and signage, and of marketing each one as a coherent 'visitor offer'. Their promotion has included the presentation of potential itineraries for visitors, along with the provision of information about visitor accommodation, local festivals and events, and individual attractions. The German tourist roads have no formal legal status, national designation, or specific regulations which apply to them; they are formed by local or regional associations or by a coalition of local government and tourism organisations. Their common purpose is reflected in their shared branding which is characterised by the brown and white signage that they use to demarcate their routes （Fig.2）.

The Limes Road Association is a non-profit-making organisation, funded by its members. It receives no national government funding. Its institutional membership is made up of over 90 rural and urban district local governments and tourist associations, which pay annual membership fees proportionate to their population. In addition, the Association has 'sustaining members' who are individual members of the public, often local business owners. 'Sustaining members' support the Association's work through a nominal annual subscription fee, in return for which they receive the latest brochures and booklets published by the Association and bulletins from the German Limes Commission.[3] The Association's membership has grown steadily since its establishment and continues to do so, particularly in its individual membership.

The Association has a small number of full-time staff based at Aalen, Bavaria. Its principal aims are to:

- Strengthen interest in Roman history;
- Raise communities' awareness of their local heritage;
- Develop and improve the Limes cultural tourist routes;
- Stimulate usage and enjoyment of the Limes routes;
- Promote the routes and its members' localities;
- Promote sustainable tourism.

The activities which the Association undertakes in pursuit of these objectives are described below.

THE LIMES CYCLEWAY

In 1997 the Limes Road Association began work to develop the Limes Cycleway. It now runs from Rheinbrohl

3 The German Limes Commission was established in 2003 to coordinate the research, management, and presentation of the Roman frontier in Germany. It includes political representatives of each of the German federal states which contain remains of the Roman frontier, together with their heads of heritage services, universities, research institutions, museums, and the German Limes Road Association.

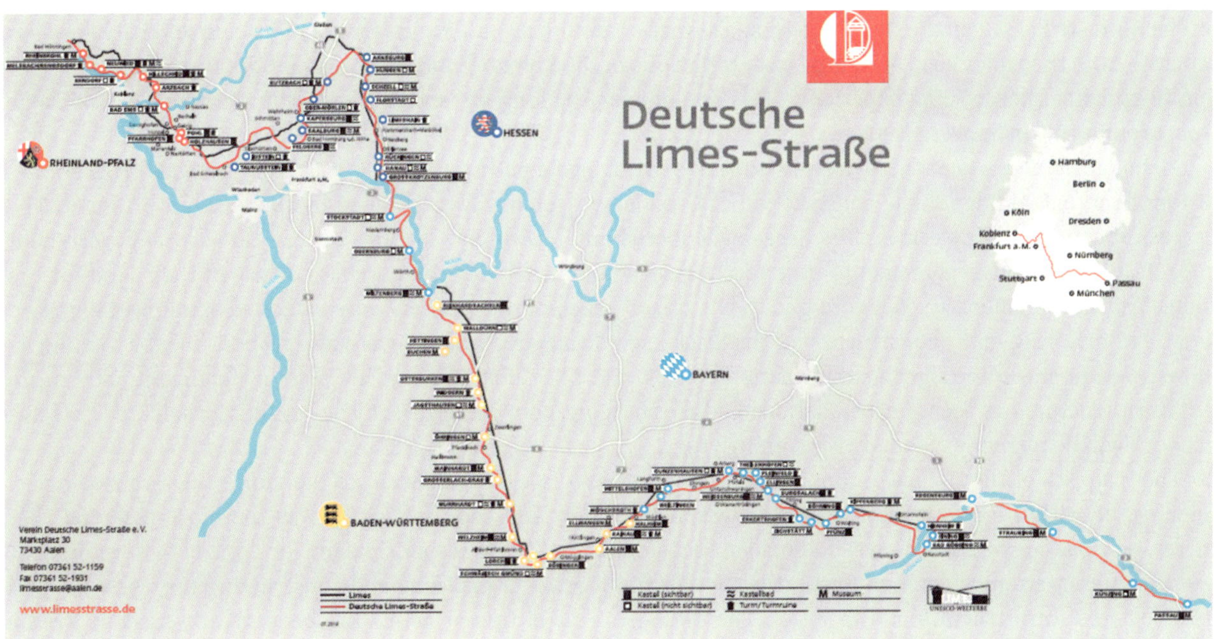

Fig.1 The German Limes Road. The route of the road is shown in red; the line of the frontier is shown in black （© The German Limes Road Association）.

图 1 德国界墙之路 界墙之路以红色标出，古罗马帝国边境线则以黑色标示（© 德国界墙之路协会）。

Fig.2 Signage along the German Limes tourist routes （© The German Limes Road Association）.

图 2 德国界墙旅游线路沿线标识（© 德国界墙之路协会）。

界墙之路协会与界墙之路

界墙之路协会于 1996 年创立，比德国界墙列入世界遗产名录还早九年。协会创立之初的工作重点是建设界墙旅游公路。1997 年，协会启动界墙单车道和界墙步道工作。三条道路分别在数年间循序渐进地发展完善。

在德国，旅游汽车公路的概念诞生于 20 世纪 50 年代。这些公路都各自围绕着特定的文化主题或自然主题，鼓励公众游览与之相关的自然景观、村落和市镇，例如有童话之路、美酒之路、火山之路和芦

on the Rhine to Passau on the Danube, a total distance of around 800km. For nearly all of its course the Cycleway is separate from the Limes Road and runs closer to the line of the Roman frontier. This is for both the safety of cyclists and to enhance their cycling experience. It is one of over 200 long-distance cycleways in Germany, which range from around 100km to over 1,500km.

Although some parts of the Cycleway utilised existing cycle paths, most of it was built to establish the long-distance route. Funding for the construction of these new stretches was provided by the local government. The process of construction was therefore necessarily incremental, with new sections being built as local government budgets allowed, and as agreements were reached with landowners for the purchase or use of their land for the route. This development was not contiguous, but steadily each of the sections were extended and linked together. As well as investing in the construction of the track itself, local governments were also responsible for funding its infrastructure, including signage, information boards, and litterbins. Over recent years a significant addition to this infrastructure has been the installation of e-bike charging-points along the Cycleway; it is anticipated that this network will be further expanded over coming years.

The majority of the Cycleway runs within the World Heritage Site, adjacent to the vulnerable archaeological remains, or within its designated buffer zone and its wider landscape setting. It was therefore essential that there was close cooperation between Roman archaeologists and those responsible for the control of development and the conservation of the monument, throughout the process of planning and constructing the Cycleway and its associated infrastructure and facilities. The establishment of this principle has been greatly assisted by the Association's collaboration with the German Limes Commission and their joint dissemination of information concerning the significance of the monument and its vulnerability.

The Cycleway is presented and promoted as a whole, but also in seven different sections of differing lengths and levels of physical challenge to cyclists. The intention has been to encourage use of the route by people of all ages and of different levels of strength and capacity, from super-fit endurance riders to recreational riders. This variety of sub-routes also caters for visitors who have varying amounts of leisure time, ranging from day visitors to those who can devote several days for their tour.

THE LIMES HIKING TRAIL

The Limes Hiking Trail runs in close proximity to the Roman frontier line from Rheinbrohl on the Rhine to Neustadt on the Danube (including a gap between eastern Baden-Wurttemberg and western Bavaria) and has a total distance of about 700km. As with the Limes Road and the Limes Cycleway, the Trail was developed within the context of an established nationwide network of long-distance Hiking Trails in Germany which now collectively run for over 200,000km. As such, each of the three Limes visitor routes have been obliged to conform to publicly recognised standards in their fabric, signage, facilities and infrastructure, and upkeep.

The route of the Trail was designed to follow the line of the Roman frontier, while also providing hikers with reasonable access to local restaurants, hotels, and campsites at regular intervals along its course. It also sought to provide access to many of the sites of remains of the Roman frontier system which were not adjacent to the linear barrier itself. In the promotion of the Trail, different itineraries are suggested for visitors depending on the length of their visit, with all relevant distances clearly set out.

Most of the Limes Hiking Trail was established by utilising existing paths and trails, many of which had been set up (and were often maintained) by local hiking clubs. Some new stretches of path were required to link up these existing trails so the resulting route could continue to follow the line of the frontier. As with the Cycleway, the costs of the construction and maintenance of the Trail, and of its signage and infrastructure, have been met by local government. Inevitably, the sequence and pace of development of different sections of the Trail was determined by the availability of funding and by progress in the negotiation of new pathways with landowners.

笋之路等。如今德国有超过 150 条旅游公路，长度从 100 千米到超过 500 千米不等。界墙公路总长超过820千米，从莱茵河畔的巴特亨宁根（Bad Honningen[4]）延伸至多瑙河畔的帕绍（Passau，图 1）。

旅游汽车公路的修建一般不是新建道路，而主要利用现有的公共路网。公路的“建设”内容主要是线路设计和标识安装，是将每条公路作为一个“旅游产品”有机整体进行营销宣传。推广宣传活动包括向游客推介各种行程，提供当地住宿、节庆活动及各个景点的辅助信息。德国的这些旅游公路没有正式的法律地位、国家认定或者专门法规，发起者是当地和区域的各类协会，或者是当地政府和旅游机构的合作组织。它们都采用同一种棕底白字标识来标定路线，以反映它们的共同身份（图 2）。

界墙之路协会是非营利组织，由会员提供经费，不接受任何国家政府拨款资助。协会团体会员包括 90 家乡村和城市地区的地方政府和旅游团体，每年根据辖区范围内的人口比例缴纳会费。此外，协会还有“长期会员”（sustaining member），即社会个人，一般为当地企业主。“长期会员”每年象征性地缴纳会费支持协会工作。作为回报，他们会收到协会出版的最新宣传手册，以及德国界墙委员会[5]编制的通讯。协会会员数量自设立起始终稳步增长，尤其是个人会员数量。

协会有少量全职员工，办公地在巴伐利亚州阿伦市。协会的主要目标包括：

- 提升对罗马历史的兴趣；
- 普及社区对本地文化遗产的认知；
- 建设和完善界墙文化旅游线路；
- 鼓励界墙线路的利用和享用；
- 宣传各线路及会员所在地区；
- 促进可持续旅游。

下面详细介绍协会为实现上述目标而进行的活动。

界墙单车道

1997 年，界墙之路协会开始启动界墙单车道建设工作。如今，单车道从莱茵河畔的莱茵布罗尔（Rheinbrohl on the Rhine）延伸至多瑙河畔的帕绍，总长约 800 千米。单车道全线几乎与界墙公路完全分离，而更贴近罗马帝国界墙墙体。这种设计一是保护骑行者的安全，二是提升他们的骑行体验。德国有超过 200 条类似的长途单车道，全长从约 100 千米至超过 1500 千米不等。

部分单车道利用了原有的单车道，但大部分是为了建设长途线路而特别增建的。新增道路的建设资金由地方政府提供。因此，施工是分阶段渐次完成的，每当地方政府有预算支持，与沿线土地所有人达成土地收购或者使用协议，就会修筑一段新路。单车道的建设尽管是分段建设，但各段道路稳步延伸，最终相连。当地政府不光要投资道路本身的建设，还需负责为配套设施提供资金，包括设置标识、信息板和垃圾桶等。近几年，配套设施进行了大规模扩充，主要是在道路沿线加装了电动自行车充电设施。充电网络预计将在接下来数年内继续得到扩充。

4 德语写作 Bad Hönningen。——译者注

5 德国界墙委员会设立于 2003 年，负责组织德国境内罗马帝国边疆的研究、管理和推介。委员会的构成包括境内拥有罗马帝国边疆遗迹的各州的政治代表，以及各州境内遗产保护机构、高校、科研院所、博物馆和德国界墙之路协会负责人。

Through its coordination of their development, the Limes Road Association has been able to establish a high degree of integration between the three Limes routes. Each route has adopted the Association's logo and the consistent livery of brown or dark red and white in their signage and promotional materials, thus making their collective branding stronger. It has also enabled the rationalisation of visitor infrastructure and has minimised duplication of its provision, thereby reducing its overall cost. This has avoided the potential proliferation of signage and information boards which would otherwise have polluted the landscape setting of the World Heritage Site. Lastly, and perhaps most significantly to the benefit of users of the Limes routes, it has enabled intersection points between the routes to be designed and planned to mitigate potential conflicts between motorists, cyclists and hikers.

PRINCIPAL ACTIVITIES OF THE LIMES ROAD ASSOCIATION

The Association currently has four principal areas of activity: co-ordination of the continuing development of each of the three routes; origination and production of print and other advertising materials; public relations and marketing of the routes, including development and maintenance of the Limes Roads website; and support of its membership.

Although each of the three routes is now largely 'complete,' each continues to be gradually expanded, while established sections are subject to maintenance, repair and enhancement. In branding, promotional material, signage and other infrastructure, the Association can use its collective buying power to reduce costs, and by liaising with Roman archaeologists the Association can ensure that information boards along the routes continue to reflect current understanding of all elements of the monument(Fig.3).

The Association's work in these areas is likely to increase with the anticipated forthcoming inscription of the Roman frontier systems along the River Rhine in Germany and the Netherlands, and the River Danube in Bavaria, as part of the Frontiers of the Roman Empire World Heritage Site. Although both the Limes Road and Cycleway already run along the Danube in Bavaria, it remains to be seen whether each of the current Limes routes will be extended to all the potential new sections of the World Heritage Site. Whilst any such extension would increase the Association's responsibility, it would also increase its membership and its financial resources.

The range of promotional materials produced by the Association includes brochures and leaflets, badges, stickers and banners. Brochures are produced for each of the three routes(Fig.4), and leaflets are printed for the Limes

Fig.3 Information boards for visitors along the routes □© The German Limes Road Association□.
图 3 沿线为游客设立的信息板（© 德国界墙之路协会）。

Fig.4 Promotional brochures for the Cycleway (left) and Hiking Trail (right) (© The German Limes Road Association).

图 4 单车道和步道宣传手册（© 德国界墙之路协会）。

单车道大部分处于世界遗产地遗产区范围内，靠近脆弱的考古遗址，或者位于遗产地缓冲区及更大范围的景观区内。因此，在规划、建设单车道及其附属设施时，古罗马考古工作者、建设活动管理者和文物保护人士的通力合作变得尤为重要。这一原则的确立离不开界墙之路协会和界墙委员会的合作，共同宣传遗产价值及其脆弱特性。

单车道既作为一个整体进行展示和推广，同时也划分成七个不同长短、不同骑行难度的段落。这样做的目的是鼓励不同年龄层、不同身体素质的人群充分利用这条线路，无论他们是进行高阶的耐力锻炼还是轻松的休闲出游。不同的路线分段也适应了各个不同出游时长的人群，短则一日，长则数天。

界墙步道

界墙步道的选线紧贴古罗马界墙墙体，起点位于莱茵河畔的莱茵布罗尔，终点位于多瑙河畔的诺伊施塔特（Neustadt on the Danube[6]，其间在东巴登-符腾堡和西巴伐利亚之间有所中断），总长约 700 千米。和

6 德语写作 Neustadt an der Donau。——译者注

Fig.5 The German Limes Road tourism exhibition stand (© The German Limes Road Association).
图 5 旅游展会上德国界墙之路展位（© 德国界墙之路协会）。

Road and Cycleway, not only in German but also in English, French and Italian, reflecting their main international markets. There are other leaflets and maps for sub-sections of the three routes, and hard-copy maps at various scales from route-wide to sectional maps. Printed promotional materials remain popular with both domestic and international visitors. The costs of production of these materials are largely met centrally from the Association's income from membership fees. They are distributed via the Association's membership organisations and are available to visitors free-of-charge at tourist information centres, museums, campsites and hotels, as well as at trade fairs, events and festivals along the Limes. There has been a steady growth in the use of electronic platforms, and a key component of promotion over recent years has been the development of apps for mobile devices, providing audio and visual guidance to visitors along each of the routes. The apps can be rapidly and cheaply updated in the light of new archaeological understanding.

The public-relations and marketing activities of the Association take a number of different forms. Press releases are issued regularly, and media relations are also supported by the provision of access to a photo archive and through promotional tours for journalists. Marketing of the Limes Roads is carried out at local levels, through participation in members' events, and by attendance at national and international tourism trade fairs (Fig.5). Although these trade fairs are important in generating longer-stay (and therefore higher-spending) visitors from other parts of Germany and from overseas, they are expensive to attend and representation of the Limes Roads is only possible due to the collective resources of all its members.

Electronic marketing of the Limes Roads through messaging via its mobile apps and its website is becoming increasingly important. The website promotes each of the three routes on the same platform.[4] Layered maps can be manipulated by users to view each of the routes in more detail, together with other information for visitors in two broad categories. Firstly, information is provided about visitor facilities along the routes, including locations and contact details for over 30 campsites, around 200 hotels and about 50 e-bike charging points, and over 80 nearby large towns and cities. Secondly, there is information about the archaeological features along the routes, including the locations of over 200 watchtowers, over 70 forts, fortlets and other Roman archaeological sites, and the location and contact details for over 40 museums.

The website also provides access to a far wider range of information about the Limes Roads and the Association

4 https://www.limesstrasse.de/deutsche-limes-strasse/about-us/german-limes-road/?L=1

界墙公路和界墙单车道一样，界墙步道也是在建设遍布德国全境长途步道网的大背景下开展的，目前全国整个路网总长超过 200,000 千米。因此，三条界墙线路在材质、标识、配套设施和保养维护等方面也都必须遵循整个路网认同的标准。

步道线路沿罗马界墙设计，同时每隔一定距离为步行者设计出通往当地餐厅、旅馆和露营地的道路。步道设计同时也力求连通离墙体稍远的其他罗马帝国边疆遗址。步道在推广过程中提出了多种行程方案并标明所有相关的步行距离，游客可以此为参照，结合自身时间进行安排。

界墙步道的多数段落利用了现成的小径和小路，它们基本是由当地徒步俱乐部开辟（并养护）的。新建的路段主要是为了连接这些既有步道，使得整条线路可以沿着墙体并行。与单车道一样，步道建设和养护成本，以及道路标识和配套设施建设和养护都由当地政府承担。因此步道各段的建设顺序和速度取决于政府的资金是否充裕，还要取决于新建道路与土地拥有者的谈判是否顺利。

界墙之路协会统筹协调三条界墙线路的建设，使其之间形成高度的整体感。在所有标牌和宣传材料中，三条线路都使用协会会徽和统一的棕（或深红）白配色，增强品牌整体辨识度。同时，协会统筹规划配套设施，避免重复建设，以降低总成本。这样还能避免过多标牌和信息板对世界遗产地景观造成的潜在负面影响。最后就是在三条道路交汇点的选择和设计时尽量减少机动车、自行车和行人的交叉，尽最大可能照顾界墙线路使用者的利益。

界墙之路协会的主要活动

协会当前主要活动集中在四个领域：协调三条线路的后续建设；策划和制作宣传印刷品及其他推广材料；负责线路的公关和推介工作，包括开发和维护界墙之路网站；提供会员支持。

尽管三条线路大体上都已“竣工”，但每条线路都还在逐渐扩展。与此同时，已建路段也需要不断养护、维修和升级改造。在品牌推广、营销材料、标识和其他配套设施方面，协会可以通过集中采购来降低成本。协会还通过与古罗马考古学家合作，确保沿途信息板始终能够反映所有遗产构成的最新学术成果。

由于罗马帝国边疆世界遗产地可能很快会进行扩展，增加德国和荷兰境内莱茵河流域以及巴伐利亚州境内多瑙河流域沿线的罗马边疆防御体系，协会在上述领域中的工作量可能会随之增加。目前界墙公路及单车道已经在巴伐利亚沿多瑙河而建，但三条界墙线路是否会沿未来的世界遗产地继续延伸还未确定。路线延伸固然会加重协会肩负的责任，但同时也会增加会员数量，拓展资金来源。

协会制作了形形色色的宣传推介材料，包括手册、折页、徽章、贴纸和横幅。每条道路都有自己的手册（图 4），其中界墙公路和单车道的折页不仅有德语，还面向主要国际市场印制了英语、法语和意大利语折页。三条道路还另外印有各个区间路段的折页与地图，以及比例不一的印刷版地图，从路线全图到分段地图，应有尽有。印刷版宣传材料仍旧颇受德国国内及其他国家游客的青睐。这些材料的制作费用主要由协会从会费收入中集中支付。材料通过协会的成员机构分发，游客可在游客中心、博物馆、露营地、酒店以及界墙沿线举办的博览会、活动和节庆免费索取。电子平台使用也在稳步增长，近几年的一个重要推广渠道就是移动设备APP，可以为每条线路上的游客提供视听导览服务。一旦有新的考古研究成果问世，APP 可以高效率、低成本的进行更新。

协会的公关和推广活动形式丰富。协会定期发布新闻稿，并且通过开放影像档案、组织记者探访等方式与媒体保持良好关系。界墙之路市场营销则是在地方层面进行的，包括参加会员机构的相关活动以及全

itself. Brochures can be downloaded, and other promotional materials can be ordered in hard-copy free of charge. Details of forthcoming events and festivals along the routes can be accessed together with information on guided tours. Individuals wishing to become 'sustaining members' can also do this via the website. In January 2020 the app 'German Limes Road - Limes to Go' was launched enabling all of the information available on the website to be downloaded to mobile devices.[5]

ASSESSING EFFECTIVENESS

The degree of success which the Limes Roads Association has achieved in fulfilling its aims and objectives is difficult to assess; there has been no formal overall evaluation of its performance, and no comprehensive base-line data was assembled at its inception. It is nevertheless possible to identify three indicators which suggest that it has been successful.

Firstly, the Association has enabled the three routes to be established and each of them to be essentially 'completed' and subsequently maintained. These have been major undertakings and therefore represent major achievements. Although trends in the proportions of visitors using each of the routes are unknown, the establishment of the Cycleway and Hiking Trail have enhanced the Association's ability to meet its aim of promoting sustainable tourism.

Secondly, the levels of usage of its website exceeds those of any other website for comparable long-distance tourist routes in Germany. While this may be partly explained by its presentation of three routes together on one website, it is nevertheless a solid indicator of the Association's effectiveness in stimulating interest in the Limes Roads as a whole.

Thirdly, a more significant indicator may be the development of the Association's membership. Its institutional membership has steadily grown and now includes nearly all of the local government and tourism associations along the course of the routes. This indicates at the very least that these bodies have been sufficiently satisfied with the benefits that the Association has provided that they have continued to pay their membership fees. Whether they regard these benefits as being primarily to their local visitor economy or to the overall well-being of their communities, or both, is unclear.

Similarly, the continuing growth in its 'sustaining members' shows that increasing numbers of the general public wish to support the Association's work. The individual motivations of these members are unclear, but indicate that they approve of what it is doing. Further research concerning perceptions of the Association's performance and the benefits that membership brings, to institutions and to individuals, would help to inform its future strategy and activities.

CONCLUSIONS

Whilst these indicators may not enable either qualitative or quantitative assessment of the Association's success in achieving its objectives, they nevertheless infer a certain level of success. Several features of the Association's organisational structure and functioning may be identified as having been significant in contributing to what it has been able to achieve.

The incremental approach it adopted to developing the routes enabled each of them to become operational early in their development process. It can also be seen as having contributed to the effectiveness of their functioning and promotion, and to the quality of their visitor offer. Had the development of any or all of the routes in their entirety been attempted in a single phase, this would have required a massive concentration and commitment

5 https://www.limesstrasse.de/deutsche-limes-strasse/app/?L=1

国和国际性旅游展会等（图 5）。参展是吸引逗留时间较长（因此消费金额也更高）的德国境内外游客的重要手段。但是参展的成本也更高，只有通过协会成员的集中资源才有可能代表界墙之路参加。

通过手机APP及网站等线上手段进行消息推送对界墙之路推广已经变得日益重要了。网站采用统一平台[7] 对三条线路进行推广。用户可以自由操控分层地图，查看每条线路的细节，同时也能找到另外两大类信息：一是沿途各类游客设施，包括超过 30 座露营地、200 余家酒店、约 50 座电子单车充电设施及周边超过 80 座大城镇的位置和联系方式。二是沿途长城文物古迹相关信息，包括超过 200 座哨塔、70 余座大小要塞等罗马考古遗址的位置，还有超过 40 座博物馆的位置和联系方式。

网站还提供更为丰富的界墙之路及协会的相关介绍。用户可以下载手册并免费订购其他印刷版宣传推广材料，还能找到近期沿路各处举办的节庆活动及专业导游路线信息。如果有意愿成为协会“长期会员”，也可以在网站报名。2020 年 1 月，“掌上界墙”（German Limes Road - Limes to Go）APP[8] 上线，用户可以将所有网站信息下载到移动设备上。

效益评估

界墙之路协会到底在多大程度上实现了自身设立的目标很难评估。目前还没有对其总体绩效开展正式评估，协会在设立时也并未全面收集基准数据。尽管如此，有三个指标可以看出协会的运作是成功的。

首先，协会促成了三条线路的建设，每条线路基本都已“竣工”并且得到正常维护。这些都是浩大的工程，是协会的重大成就。尽管使用各条线路的人数比例变化情况无从知晓，但单车道和步道的设立无疑增强了协会“促进可持续旅游”目标的能力。

第二，协会网站在德国同类型长途旅游线路官网中的访问量最高。部分原因可能是因为三条线路信息都集于同一网站，但它还是有力地证明了协会有效地推动了界墙之路作为一个整体品牌的认知。

第三，协会会员数量可以说是一个更重要的指标。协会的团体会员数量稳步增长，如今囊括了道路沿线几乎所有地方政府及旅游组织。这至少可以说明这些团体机构对协会提供的服务效益是满意的，因此愿意继续缴纳会费。至于他们认为这些效益究竟是造福本地旅游经济还是提升当地社区整体生活水平，或者两者都有，这些问题尚未得出结论。

同样，“长期会员”的持续壮大也体现出有越来越多的公众愿意支持协会事业。此类会员的个人动机尚不清楚，但人数增长意味着公众对协会的认可。进一步研究团体会员和个人会员对协会成效的看法，将有助于指导协会制定今后的发展战略及活动。

结语

前述指标或许不能定性或定量评估协会工作目标完成情况，然而却能一定程度上表明协会的工作是成功的。也许可以从组织架构和工作职能等方面的特点来解释协会成功的原因。

线路建设阶段采取化整为零，循序渐进的方式，使得道路在早期即可投入使用。该方式也有助于协会有效运作与推广，并提高游客服务品质。如果所有线路一次性全部完成，就会需要集中大量管理资源和财

7 https://www.limesstrasse.de/deutsche-limes-strasse/about-us/german-limes-road/?L=1
8 https://www.limesstrasse.de/deutsche-limes-strasse/app/?L=1

of management and financial resources. Assembling such resources would itself have been a major undertaking, which would have been likely to have delayed the start of their development. Instead, the approach adopted enabled progress to be made from the start of the process. This approach also enabled their development to be constantly improved, as the design and structure of the routes, the provision of visitor information, facilities and infrastructure, and associated promotional activities were continuously enhanced through cumulative experience.

As a non-profit-making, internally-funded, membership-led organisation it has been able to mobilise a wide coalition of support between local government, tourism associations, and members of the public. As such it has been accountable to those communities whose interests it seeks to serve. Its objectives and activities have been determined internally, and have not been specified by external governance and funding.

The extent of its membership and the pooling of its members' collective resources have enabled the Association, through the economies of scale, to undertake activities at a far higher level than its members could have done if they had been acting individually. Examples of this include the Limes Roads being able to be represented and promoted at tourism trade fairs nationally and internationally, and being able to afford the costs of translation of promotional materials into several languages. Its aggregation of members' resources has given it greater purchasing power in terms of print and other promotional material, signage and other infrastructure for the three routes.

By establishing a collective budget it has been able to invest in a core staff of marketing, promotional and coordinating professionals, dedicated full-time to the work of the Association. This is in contrast to other collaborative partnerships which rely on collective activities being undertaken through the part-time participation of their members' existing staff on top of their other duties. The activities of the Association's core staff are nevertheless supported by its members' own staff and by staff from other institutions which make up the German Limes Commission. Most significantly, amongst the latter is the archaeological advice and guidance the Association receives in managing development of the routes and in ensuring the accuracy of the archaeological information it presents to the public in printed material and site information-boards.

It is perhaps in its approach to marketing and promotion that the Association's greatest strength lies. This is most clearly seen in its website which provides information about all three routes, together with other important information for visitors, all through the same portal. This greatly facilitates potential visitors' access to all the information they need when deciding whether to visit, and then in planning their visit. More importantly, it also presents a far broader 'visitor offer' and a greater variety of choices of where and how to visit, where to stay and what to do, than would be afforded by separate sites for the three routes, or for the four federal states through which they run.

务资源的投入。集合各方面资源本身可能就是一项浩大的工程，很可能会拖延道路建设开工时间。 现在协会采取的策略可以在开工之初就取得成效。由于路线设计和构造、游客信息、配套设施的提供方式以及相关的推广活动都随着经验的累积而不断更新升级， 化整为零的模式便于协会不断改进建设工作。

作为一个非营利性、自负盈亏、以会员制为核心的组织，协会成功地获得了当地政府、旅游组织及公众的支持。它本身的组织构架决定了它就要为当地社区负责，因为它的使命是为当地社区谋福利。协会的目标和活动都是内部自行决定的，不受外部资本和管辖制约。

会员数量的增加和会员整体资源的集聚形成规模经济，使协会有能力在更高级别范围内开展各会员单独难以开展的活动。例如，界墙之路得以在国内和国际旅游展会上宣传和推广，并且有能力承担翻译多国语言宣传材料的成本。会员资源积少成多，让协会有更强的购买能力投入三条线路的宣传材料印刷、标识设置和配套设施建设。

协会的集中预算也得以聘用专业市场营销、推广和协调等核心岗位的工作人员，全职为协会工作。这与其他合作性组织的做法大不相同，后者需要仰赖会员机构的员工利用业余时间组织团体活动。不过，界墙协会核心工作人员仍然需要得到协会成员及其他德国界墙委员会组成机构工作人员的支持。尤为重要的是，德国界墙委员会提出的考古学意见和建议会帮助协会更好地管理线路建设，并且确保它在印刷材料和现场信息板上向公众提供的信息在考古学方面是准确的。

协会最大的优势或许就在于其营销和推广策略上。能将三条线路及其他重要的游览信息集中在同一网站上，就是最好的例证。这样能让潜在游客获得全部必要信息，帮助他们做出旅行决定，帮助他们规划具体行程。更重要的是，相比于由三条线路或沿线四个州分别各自运营，协会的集中营销和推广方式提供了更广阔的参观空间和更丰富的参观选择，游客可以决定参观什么，如何参观，住在哪里，参加什么活动。

5.2 ESTABLISHING A LONG-DISTANCE FOOTPATH IN A WORLD HERITAGE SITE: THE EXPERIENCE OF THE HADRIAN'S WALL PATH NATIONAL TRAIL

HUMPHREY WELFARE
Newcastle University - Newcastle upon Tyne - UK

Abstract

The long and careful process of establishing a National Trail in the Hadrian's Wall World Heritage Site is described. A particular emphasis was placed upon public consultation on the choice of the route, and upon ensuring that there was a proper and sustainable balance achieved between improved public access and the inevitable impact of an increased number of visitors on the fragile archaeological remains. The importance of monitoring and of the provision of adequate resources for continual maintenance is stressed.

Keywords: National Trail, World Heritage Site, public access, conservation, consultation, maintenance

INTRODUCTION

The Hadrian's Wall Path National Trail, 135km long, provides public access to almost the whole length of the Roman frontier, from Wallsend in the east to Bowness-on-Solway in the west. Opened in 2003, it has been extremely successful in enhancing the public's knowledge, appreciation and enjoyment of this strip of country and of the World Heritage Site that was its inspiration. Paget Lazzari and Mike Collins (2019) have described the management of the Trail, but as it is a classic case of the tension between visitor pressure and sustainable conservation it is worth examining further the painstaking process by which it was established. Some things went well, but other things not so well. This account may assist those along the Great Wall, and elsewhere, who wish to expand and diversify the options for tourists, enabling them to see and experience a World Heritage Site in a different way.

England is a small country, measuring only about 800km from north to south, but it has a dense network of short public footpaths which, taken together, extend for a total length of over 146,000km. In very many cases these paths have been used for centuries by local people. Once each path has been recorded on the 'definitive map' of Public Rights of Way that is held by the highway authority within the local government, anyone has the legal right to walk along that path, even if – as is usually the case – it crosses land that is privately owned. (Other forms of transport, including bicycles and horses, are not permitted on a footpath.)

The pressure for more public access and the right to roam in the English countryside grew steadily during the early 20th century, resulting in the establishment (from 1949) of the National Parks, in which public access was encouraged. Walking in the countryside had become a serious and popular pursuit and, after the Second World War, many walkers wanted some of longer routes such as those that had been pioneered by the Black Forest Trails, in Germany, in 1900, by the 'Long Trail' in Massachusetts in 1917, and by the 3,379km Appalachian Way in 1937. The Pennine Way, the first long-distance National Trail in the UK, stretching for 412km along the upland spine of England – and which runs along the central section of Hadrian's Wall for a distance of 14km between Greenhead and Housesteads - was approved in 1951 but it did not open until 1965. Other National Trails followed.

5.2 在世界遗产地建设长距离步道：哈德良长城国家步道经验分享

汉佛瑞·维尔法
纽卡斯尔大学—纽卡斯尔—英国

摘要

本文介绍了在哈德良长城世界遗产地建设国家步道这一漫长而审慎的过程始末。文章着重阐述如何在路线的选择上征询公众意见，以及如何确保在扩大对公众的开放程度的同时，尽可能减少因客流量增长而对脆弱的考古遗迹带来不可避免的影响，从而达到适度和可持续的平衡。此外本文还强调了在步道的持续维护中，监测以及充足资源保障的重要性。

关键字：国家步道　世界遗产地　公众开放　保护　意见征询　保养维护

引言

哈德良长城国家步道（以下简称“步道”），全长 135千米，东起沃森德，西至波尼斯-索尔维。沿之而行，公众几乎得以参观哈德良长城全线。自 2003 年开放以来，公众对步道沿线地带及哈德良长城世界遗产地的认知、欣赏和愉悦体验与日俱增，实现了建设步道的初衷，可谓大获成功。帕吉特·拉扎里与麦克·考林斯曾在之前介绍了国家步道的管理。然而，作为一个能够体现访客压力和可持续保护这二者之间冲突的经典案例，这值得我们进一步总结步道建设的艰辛历程。其中有些工作进展顺利，亦有些许方面并不尽如人意。对于中国长城、甚至是其他地区希望提供多元化游览方案的同行们，希望本文可以有所帮助，说明如何让游客能够通过一种截然不同的方式参观和感受世界遗产地。

英格兰并非一个地域广阔的国家，从南到北仅约 800 千米长。然而，这里却有着分布密集的短距离公共步行道路网，总长超过 146000 千米。其中多数步行道已为当地居民使用达几百年之久。当一条步行道被地方政府公路管理机构登记绘制进入公众路权的“确认地图”之后，任何人都享有在该步行道上步行的法定通行权，即便路线穿行的土地为私人所有——这种情况十分常见。（步行道上不允许其他交通方式通行，包括骑车或骑马。）

在20世纪早期，民众想要漫步于乡间田野的诉求与扩大公共开放区域的呼声日渐增长。由此，国家公园于 1949 年应运而生，向公众开放。乡间漫步已然成为一项严肃而普及的事业。同时，二战以后，很多徒步爱好者希望有更长的徒步路线可供选择，类似建于 1900 年的德国黑森林步道，建于1917 年的美国马萨诸塞州的长径步道和建于 1937 年、总长达 3379千米的阿巴拉契亚小径（Appalachian Way）[1]。奔宁步道是英

1 美国最长的徒步旅行步道之一，是美国阿巴拉契亚山脉间的一条小路，从缅因州的卡塔丁山（Mount Katahdin）一直延续到佐治亚州的施普林格山（Springer Mountain）——译者注

THE PROPOSALS FOR HADRIAN'S WALL

In the 1970s and 1980s, before the inscription of the Wall as a World Heritage Site, there was little encouragement for anyone but specialists to explore much beyond the sites that had been partly excavated and those displayed by English Heritage, the National Trust, and the Vindolanda Trust. However, that was about to change. The ability to walk across England, from coast to coast, on a continuous public footpath, was an attractive idea, and in 1976 the first formal proposal was made (by the Dartington Amenity Research Trust: DART 1976) that there should be a route that combined this idea with the strong historical theme provided by Hadrian's Wall. The DART Report led to the establishment of a Hadrian's Wall Consultative Committee, the report of which (1984) endorsed the proposal for a Trail as an element in a strategy for the management of the 'heritage zone' represented by the Wall corridor.

The process of defining a route for a long-distance footpath along the Wall proved to be long and complicated; it was not until 1990 that a 'preferred route' for the Trail was provisionally determined and could be sent out for public consultation (Countryside Commission 1990). The issues that were identified for comment were:

- the character of the Path, and the type of audience that its development sought to attract;
- how closely it should follow the line of the Wall, and whether there should be a formal network of linked paths;
- how the 'modest but significant commercial opportunities for local businesses and communities' that the Path might stimulate could be realised;
- how the Path and the wider Wall corridor should be managed;
- the strengths and weaknesses of the 'preferred route', which was briefly described in the consultation documents and illustrated by 18 maps at a scale of 1:25,000.

This care over the consultation was necessary because once the footpath had been established in law it would be difficult to alter or close it. Just as important, local people know their own area better than anyone and are frequently able to make effective practical comments and suggestions. Four factors were particularly taken into account:

- the views of the farmers, landowners and other stakeholders along the route;
- the significance and the vulnerability of the archaeological remains that might be affected;
- the wish to incorporate as many existing Public Footpaths as possible;
- the need to provide a safe and enjoyable walking experience.

(This last factor meant that in the busy urban areas of Newcastle, where there were few remains to be seen, the Path ran along or close to the North bank of the River Tyne for several miles, well away from the line of the Wall itself – much to the frustration of some archaeological purists.)

In the analysis of the responses to this first round of consultation, it was noted that 'many landowners and farmers have demonstrated a generosity of spirit over the granting of access over their land,' but 'there remains a relatively small number of landowners and occupiers whose agreement has not been forthcoming.' The government agency at that time which had the responsibility to set up the Trail, the Countryside Agency, was aware that they were dealing with a World Heritage Site (which had been inscribed in 1987), and that some archaeologists had already expressed concern about the impact of the new Trail on the vulnerable remains of the Roman frontier. With these factors in mind, two particularly important projects were then undertaken. The first was a detailed 'baseline condition survey' which provided a record of the proposed route and identified the work that would have to be done before the Trail could be opened. The second was an Archaeological Impact Study which scrutinised each section of the route, assessing the affect of so many feet on the fragile archaeological remains (especially the earthworks). The database of the archaeological remains was up to date as, between 1988 and 1990, the Royal Commission on the Historical Monuments of England had revised the Ordnance Survey's basic-scale archaeological mapping (1:2500) of the whole of the Roman frontier works (Fig.1). As a result of the baseline and impact studies, some modifications

国境内首条长距离国家步道，沿英格兰高地的山脊绵延，总长 412千米。沿途有14千米伴哈德良长城中部区段而行，从格林黑德起直到豪塞斯特兹。该步道于 1951 年获得批准并得以修建，但直到1965年才向公众开放。随后，其他国家步道也相继建成。

哈德良长城步道建设方案

20世纪70至80年代，在哈德良长城被列为世界遗产地之前，长城沿线只有少数几处经过部分发掘和展示开放的点段，分别在英格兰遗产委员会、国家信托和文多兰达信托管理之下。除专家学者之外，很少提倡公众去探索这些开放点段之外更广大的哈德良沿线区域。但是这样的状况很快便有所改变。能够沿着一条连续公共步道横跨英格兰东西海岸之间，其设想颇具吸引力。于是，第一个正式提案于 1976 年应运而生（达廷顿公共娱乐设施研究信托，DART 1976），提出建设一条将上述设想与哈德良长城的浓厚历史氛围相结合的路线。DART 报告促成了哈德良长城咨询委员会的成立。该委员会在其报告（1984年）中赞成步道建设的建议，并将其作为以长城走廊为代表的“遗产地区”管理战略中的内容之一。

实践证明，沿着哈德良长城规划一条长距离步道的过程既漫长又复杂。直到 1990 年，步道的“优选方案”才初步敲定，可供向公众征询意见（英格兰乡村管理委员会 1990）。征求意见涉及的问题有：

- 步道的特色，和期望吸引的游客类型；
- 步道应该与长城保持多远距离而建，以及是否应与关联道路建起一个正式路网；
- 步道可能给当地企业和当地社区带来哪怕微小但意义重大的商业机遇，如何实现；
- 如何对步道和范围更广的长城走廊进行管理；
- 征询文件中简要概述了“优选路线”的优点和缺点，并标示在 18 幅 1:25000 的地图上。

细致入微的意见征询工作是至关重要的，因为一旦得到法律承认，之后将很难进行改动或关闭步道。与此同时，没有谁能够比当地居民更了解当地的情况，他们经常能够提出十分有建设性而实用的意见和建议。其中特别关注四个方面的因素：

- 沿线的农民、土地所有者和其他利益相关者的意见；
- 可能受到影响的考古遗迹的价值和风险程度；
- 尽可能多地将现存的公共步道整合进来；
- 提供安全而愉悦的步行体验的需求。

（正是因为考虑到了最后一个因素，在选线时，由于繁忙的纽卡斯尔市区中几乎看不到什么遗迹，便将此区域内几英里的步道设在泰恩河北岸沿线或较近的距离，而远离长城墙体，这使得一些考古爱好者颇为不满。）

在第一轮意见征询后，分析表明“许多土地所有者和农民非常慷慨，愿意提供穿行其土地的路权”，然而“也有一小部分土地所有者和占用者尚未同意提供通行权。”当时，负责步道建设的政府机构英格兰乡村署考虑到项目涉及世界遗产地（1987 年列入），同时一些考古学家担心新的步道可能对长城脆弱的考古遗迹带来影响。综合上述所有因素，随即启动了两个重要项目。第一个项目是开展详细的基准情况调查，对提议的路线沿线进行现状记录，并梳理出达到步道开放条件所必须完成的工作。第二个项目是考古影响研究，仔细勘察路线涉及的每个区段，评估大量踩踏对脆弱的考古遗迹（尤其是土遗址）造成的影响。

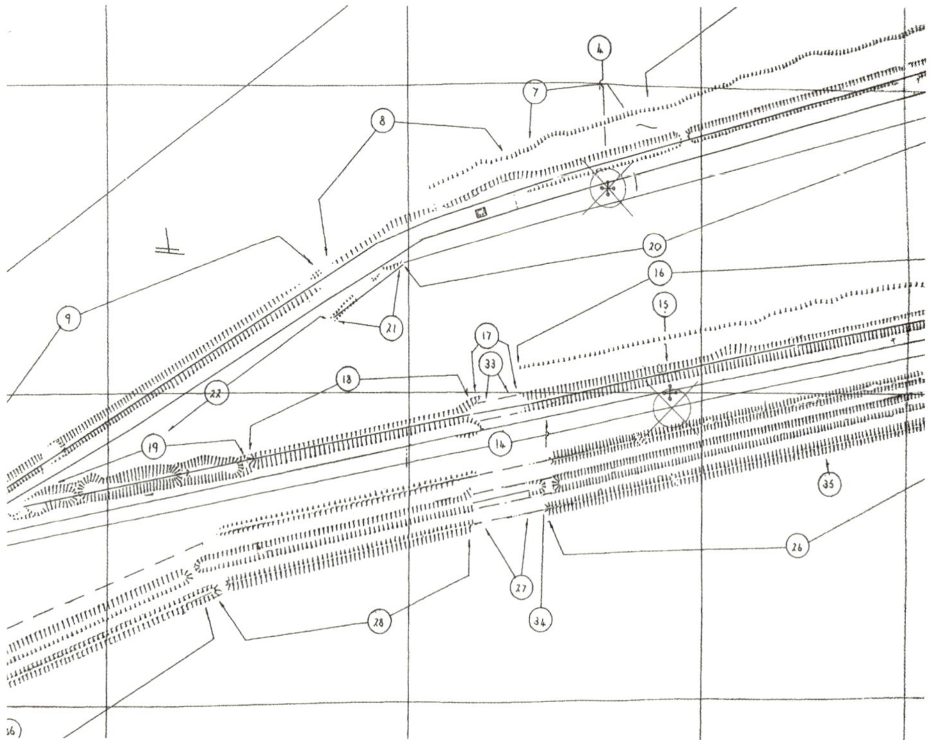

Fig.1 An extract from the detailed annotated mapping (at a scale of 1:2500) produced by the Royal Commission on the Historical Monuments of England in advance of the determination of the route of the National Trail. Each numbered section is linked to an associated textual description. This portion, covering about 600m in Wall-mile 50, to the west of the fort at Birdoswald, shows (from the top): the upcast mound and Ditch of the Stone Wall (which is beneath a modern road); then those of the Turf Wall; and the ditch and flanking mounds of the Vallum (© Crown copyright Historic England).

图 1 详细标注的测绘图节选（比例尺 1:25000），英格兰皇家历史古迹委员会在确定国家步道路线之前绘制。每一个标号的区段都可以找到对应的文字描述。该部分属于区段 50，总长约 600 米，位于博得瓦德罗马要塞的西部，包括（从上至下）：隆起的土堆和石墙的北部壕沟（位于一条现代道路的下方）；草被长城；南部壕沟的壕和两侧的土堆（英格兰遗产委员会）。

to the route were made and a further, more formal, round of public consultation launched in 1992 was based on a new publication which summarised the information that had been gained(Countryside Commission 1992).

Subsequently, the final submission of the proposals to the Government in 1993 revealed strong support for the establishment of the Trail (Countryside Commission 1993). Although many farmers were still concerned about litter, damage, and dogs on their land, the economic and health benefits of the Path were recognised. The baseline condition survey and the archaeological impact study had outlined the steps necessary to mitigate any damage, and had provided the basis for an assessment of costs. The route of the Trail had again been adjusted in detail. A principle concern had been the vulnerability of the archaeological earthworks, especially the ditch on the North side of the Wall, and the Vallum (the ditch and flanking mounds that form a second defensive line on the South side of the narrow frontier zone). The line of the Trail inevitably ran along or beside these linear remains, or crossed from one side to another, so minor adjustments to the course of the Trail were required in order to minimise the risk of excessive wear. Thus, for instance, at Down Hill, beside Milecastle 21, the Path was moved outside the northern edge of the Vallum rather than running along the bottom of the ditch itself. To the west of the Roman fort at Birdoswald, the route was changed (Fig.2) to take the path off the earthworks of the Turf Wall (the first form of the Wall in this area, which was later replaced in stone on a different alignment). There was also a significant alteration in the central sector of the Wall, between the fort at Housesteads and Steelrigg, where visitors had become accustomed to walking on top of the 'Clayton Wall', the long stretches where the faces of the curtain wall had been reconstructed in the 19th century by the landowner, John Clayton. In all but one short section, the National Trust now sought to dissuade visitors from doing this and

在1988至1990年间，英格兰皇家历史古迹委员会[2]重新修订了国家测绘局关于哈德良长城全线的基准考古测绘图（1:2500）（图 1），考古遗迹的数据库也得到了更新。根据基准调查和影响研究结果，对步道路线进行了局部调整，并将最新资料成果汇总出版。在此基础上，于1992 年开展了一轮更为正式的公众意见征询（英格兰乡村管理委员会 1992）。

Fig.2 The route of the National Trail was moved from the line of the Turf Wall (the level area to the right of the fence) to the ploughed-over and less sensitive position of the upcast mound to the left of the fence (© Humphrey Welfare).

图 2 国家步道的路线由原来的紧贴草被长城（栅栏右侧的平坦地带）移至位于栅栏左侧耕翻过且不易受影响的土堆上（© 汉佛瑞・维尔法）。

之后，在1993年向政府提交的最终方案中，步道建设得到大力支持（英格兰乡村管理委员会1993）。尽管许多农民还在担心随之而来的垃圾、破坏和狗对他们的土地造成影响，但步道带来的经济和健康价值得到认可。通过基准情况调查和考古影响研究，已罗列出减小各种破坏所应当采取的一系列举措和步骤，并为成本测算提供了基础。步道的路线再次得到了更细致周密的调整，主要考虑的避让脆弱的土遗址，尤其是长城墙体北侧的壕沟和南部壕沟（中间为壕，两侧为堤，在狭长的边疆地带南侧形成的第二道防御屏障）。步道会不可避免地沿着或紧贴这些线性遗迹而建，或者从一侧穿越至另一侧。因此有必要对步道路线进行细微调整，尽量减少过度踩踏的风险。例如，位于下坡地区里堡 21 附近的步道就被移至南部壕沟的北侧以外，而非沿着壕沟底部铺设。在博得瓦德罗马要塞以西，调整后的步道（图 2）绕开了草被长城的土遗址（即该地区长城的最早期形态，后来被在别处另修筑的石砌长城取代，但遗址得到保留）。介于豪塞斯特兹和斯第尔里格的长城中部区段也进行了重大调整。原来游客来到这里已经习惯登上“克莱顿长城”顶部行走。该段护墙的外部在 19 世纪曾经由当时的土地所有者约翰・克莱顿重新修整过。现在，国家信托[3]试图劝阻游客踏上城墙，因此将步道铺设于城墙旁边，而非在城墙之上，只保留很短一段可供游客登上城墙。该举措不仅控制了旅游带来的影响，还倡导了对考古遗迹的重新尊重。

2 英格兰皇家历史古迹委员会创建于 1908 年，旨在对英格兰境内的古遗迹和古建筑进行盘点记录。1999 年，该机构归入英格兰遗产信托。自 2015 年起，其职责受英格兰遗产委员会统一管理。

3 此段长城所有权属于国家信托，由其负责管理——译者注

the Trail was routed alongside the Wall rather than on top of it. This not only limited the impact of tourism but also engendered a new respect for the archaeological remains.

IMPLEMENTATION, PROBLEMS AND RESOLUTION

As it turned out, only about 50km of new footpaths had to be created; 70km of the route utilised existing Public Rights of Way. Throughout the length of the Trail, new signposts (of a consistent design) had to be put in place (Fig.3). On the new sections, gates and stiles were introduced, and elsewhere they were refurbished. A new footbridge had to be built over the River Irthing, between Willowford and Birdoswald, and a safe crossing had to be ensured across the railway. It seems that little other infrastructure was considered. Strangely, given that it was anticipated (accurately) that about 20,000 people would walk the entire length of the Wall each year, and that more than ten times as many would tackle shorter sections, the provision of toilets was never mentioned; it has been left to pubs, churches, and parish councils to provide these.

The cost of establishing the Trail was estimated at £1.5 million (equivalent to about £3 million in 2019). Thereafter, the costs of maintenance would be shared by those local government authorities (the counties) that had responsibility for highways. Regular photographic monitoring of the Path's condition would enable a programme of pre-emptive intervention to be put in place, thus maintaining the grass surface to the highest standards: spiking and mowing the grass, and repairing worn sections by re-seeding. The annual cost of this cycle of essential maintenance was forecast to be about £100,000; it turned out to be £220,000 in 2004-5, a rate per mile that was nearly double that for any other National Trail.

The new National Trail finally opened in May 2003. However, there was soon trouble brewing. Less than two years later, concern about the condition of the Trail was very publicly expressed in The Times newspaper. An extensive photographic monitoring regime (first begun in 1996) had been in place at 116 points along the route between April 2003 and November 2004 each year, and the results were now analysed by English Heritage, then the national agency for the historic environment. This revealed erosion that could result in an accelerating rate of deterioration; active intervention was required. In consultation with the Countryside Agency, English Heritage issued a response to the publicity (Austen and Young 2005) which set out the considerable strengths, but also the apparent weaknesses of the Trail project, especially the difficult balance that had to be achieved between improved public access and enjoyment, on the one hand, and sustainable conservation, on the other. Most of the Trail already needed some remedial treatment, and although all of the wear was reversible and no archaeological loss had occurred, the response acknowledged that 'the danger signals are there.'

Action followed: not least some welcome improvements in the arrangements for partnership working, the development of generic consents[1] for work within the protected areas, and the appointment in 2004 of a full-time member of staff, and a second in 2006, to do the practical work on the Trail which was informed by the reports of an existing group of volunteers. A further independent review of the condition of the Trail (Fowler 2005) re-ignited the publicity but ensured that the recommendations for improved practice – most of which were already in place - were followed through. Many of the problems had been actually caused by livestock and wild animals, rather than by people's feet, but the improved system of maintenance and the publication of a *Code of Conduct* for walkers (that amongst other things aimed to persuade them not to walk in single file, and thus spread and minimise the damage) were effective. The very positive results of the scheme of grassland management that was put in place has been described by the former Trail Officer, David McGlade (2014).

1 Any work or change to a Scheduled Monument requires specific official consent. The Generic Scheduled Monument Consent mechanism enables a range of defined routine maintenance works to be undertaken without individual consents, and in a timely manner. This mechanism was pioneered and developed by the Hadrian's Wall Path National Trail and was finally codified into UK national conservation policy and practice in 2008.

Fig.3 New signposts had to be put in place to guide walkers. The acorn symbol on the left indicates that this is the line of a National Trail (© Humphrey Welfare).

图 3 设置的新路牌，为步行者提供方向。左侧的橡树果实图标表示这是国家步道（©汉佛瑞·维尔法）。

实施、问题和解决方案

实际上，需要新建的步道总长仅约 50 千米。另有 70 千米长的部分可以直接利用现存的公共步道。沿步道全线都要安置（经统一设计的）新路标（图3）。在新建区段，需要配套修建门和台阶。而其他地方只需翻新即可。还要修筑一座横跨艾辛河、连接维罗福德和博得瓦德的人行桥，并修筑必要的道口使步道能够安全跨过铁路线。除此之外，几乎不需要修建额外的基础设施。据（准确）预测，每年有约两万人会走完哈德良长城的全段，而人数十倍于此的徒步爱好者只会选择较短的区段。奇怪的是，从未有人提议要修建公厕，而由沿途的酒吧、教堂和教区去解决。

步道建设成本估算约 150 万英镑（相当于 2019 年的 300 万英镑）。之后的保养维护成本则由各地负责高速公路管理的地方政府机构（郡）分担。需要对步道状况进行定期摄影监测，以便制定工作计划采取预防性干预措施，使得草皮路面得以保持最好状态，包括刨土剪草，补种磨损的草皮等。这些周期性的基本维护成本最初预计每年在 10 万英镑左右，但实际上在 2004 至 2005 年间花费了 22 万英镑，平均每英里的维护成本几乎为其他各国家步道的两倍。

新一条国家步道最终于2003 年 3 月正式开放。可没过多久，问题便随之而来。不到两年，泰晤士报就公开报道了对步道状况的担忧。1996 年，首次对步道进行了大规模的摄影监测。2003 年 4 月至 2004 年 11 月期间，监测范围则扩大至步道全线共 116 个点，每年一次，共计两次。随后由当时负责历史环境的国家机构英格兰遗产信托对采集结果进行分析。结果表明，侵蚀可能会加速恶化，需要采取主动干预。在征询了英格兰乡村署的意见后，英格兰遗产信托对公开报道进行了回应（奥斯汀，杨 2005），列举了步道项目的巨大优势，也指出了其明显的不足，特别强调平衡两者关系的困难：一方面必须扩大公众开放、改善旅客体验，另一方面还要做到对遗迹的可持续保护。步道的绝大部分已经需要进行修缮。尽管受损的部分都是可逆的，也并没有造成考古遗迹的破坏，但该回应文件也承认“危险信号确实存在。”

随后采取的措施包括：各机构之间的协调合作更为积极；在保护范围内采用通用许可[4]的审批制度；2004年任命了一名全职工作人员负责步道维护工作，2006 年又增加一名。当时已经有志愿者队伍，他们发现问题及时报告，由工作人员采取相应措施。之后又对步道状况开展了一次独立评估（福勒 2005），确保建议的改进措施得到贯彻落实（绝大多数彼时已经实施）。报告再次引发了公众

4 任何对登录古迹的开发工作或变更都需要先获得特别的官方许可。登录古迹一般性变更许可（Generic Scheduled Monument Consent）这一机制允许相关方无需等待申请逐个获得批准，就可以及时开展一系列规定的例行维护工作。该机制由哈德良长城国家步道首创，最终于2008 年被编入英国国家保护政策和实践。

With hindsight, we can see that the baseline condition survey was too optimistic about the wear and tear that the Trail would cause. The intention was – and is – to maintain a grass surface throughout, but in some areas more hard surfacing (in the form of natural stone slabs) has been required than was originally envisaged (Fig.4). Another measure that was intended to reduce the impact of the Trail was the development of an associated network of footpaths that would lead walkers into other parts of the landscape, away from the Wall. Despite a number of attempts, this has never really become established, and the vast majority of walkers stick to the Trail itself. More positively, another key factor in the original Submission to the Secretary of State for the establishment of the Trail was the availability of public transport throughout the Wall corridor: trains, buses, and the Metro system within urban Tyneside. The Hadrian's Wall Bus Service, number AD122, which runs during the summer season between April and the end of September, has been particularly important. Although it has been affected by cuts in some linked scheduled services, and has required subsidies, this has proved popular, especially with overseas visitors. It runs along the Wall between the railway stations at Hexham and Haltwhistle, and has made a visit wholly by public transport eminently possible. As an alternative, many taxi firms and baggage-carriers have built up a solid business in ferrying walkers and their belongings, especially in the far west between the railway station at Carlisle and the western end of the Wall at Bowness-on-Solway.

Other commercial companies have benefitted from the success of the Trail. Before it was established, the choice of accommodation in the area was poor; now, however, there are many guesthouses, bunk-barns, and campsites for walkers to choose from, and standards have risen. Village shops, tea-rooms and pubs have also seen an increase in business, sustaining the rural economy and thus aiding community cohesion.

CONCLUSIONS

Although it may be more expensive per mile to establish and to maintain than other National Trails, a long-distance footpath in a World Heritage Site can provide great benefits in allowing walkers to reach parts of the Site that were previously inaccessible, and thus to improve awareness of the historic environment, to stimulate public education and well-being, to ensure sustainable conservation, community involvement and participation, and to provide support for the local economy. The experience on Hadrian's Wall suggests that the following factors contributed to success:

- thorough public consultation, in more than one phase, to determine the optimum route;
- a detailed survey of the physical conditions along the route;
- good quality data derived from an archaeological impact survey, as appropriate;
- a ground management regime appropriate to the local vegetation (walkers prefer a natural surface wherever possible);
- regular and sustained monitoring of the condition of the route and of the affect on the archaeological remains;
- the establishment of a partnership of local government and specialist organisations to manage all aspects of the Trail;
- the provision, before opening, of the necessary infrastructure: fences and walls, gates, bridges, and signage;
- an operational strategy for the coordinated provision of public transport to give access to the route;
- a website that provides the walkers with all of the information that they will need;
- the centralised promotion of a range of accommodation;
- the provision of an associated network of linked routes that can take the pressure off the main Trail;
- a code of practice for walkers, aimed at ensuring the minimum impact on the countryside, i.e. not walking in single file, and discouraging mass-participation events;

Fig.4 More sections of hard surfacing – here, stone slabs in the poorly drained Peel Gap (Wall-mile 39) - had to be laid than had been anticipated, increasing the cost and introducing a significant visual intrusion (© Humphrey Welfare).

图 4 若干铺设硬质路面的部分，此处是位于排水不畅的皮尔谷口（位于区段 39）石板路。该方案不在原本最初的规划中，因此带来了额外的成本并造成明显的视觉上的突兀感（© 汉佛瑞·维尔法）。

的关注。很多问题实际上并非因人类的足迹，而是由家畜和野生动物导致的。但是，步道维护体系的完善和步行者《行为准则》的颁布（其中一条建议游客不要前后纵列而行，而尽量并行，以分散踩踏范围，降低磨损）是卓有成效的。草皮管理计划取得的积极成效在前任步道管理官员大卫·麦克格莱德

- the commitment to deliver realistic resources to maintain the route, in staff, cash, contributions in kind, and the support of volunteers;
- the encouragement of authors and publishers to produce guidebooks of good quality, and accurate maps at a suitable scale for walkers (1:25,000 in the UK).

References
参考文献

Austen, P. and Young, C. 2005. 'Finding the Way,' *British Archaeology* (July/August 2005), 42-45.

P·奥斯汀，C·杨. 2005 ."路在何方"英国考古 (2005 年 7/8 月)，42-45.

Countryside Commission. 1990. *The Hadrian's Wall Path: Proposed National Trail from Wallsend to Bowness-on-Solway. Informal consultation (CCP319)*, Cheltenham.

英格兰乡村管理委员会. 1990. 哈德良长城步道：从沃森德至波尼斯-索尔维的国家步道方案.非正式征求意见稿 （CCP319）. 切尔滕纳姆.

Countryside Commission. 1992. *The Hadrian's Wall Path Proposed National Trail. Formal Consultation (CCP391)*, Cheltenham.

英格兰乡村管理委员会. 1992. 哈德良长城国家步道方案. 正式征求意见稿 (CCP391). 切尔滕纳姆.

Countryside Commission. 1993. *The Hadrian's Wall Path. Submission to the Secretary of State for the Environment (CCP409)*, Cheltenham.

英格兰乡村管理委员会. 1993. 哈德良长城步道. 提交环境内阁大臣稿 (CCP409)，切尔滕纳姆.

DART Report 1976 Dartington Amenity Research Trust. *The Hadrian's Wall Strategy for Conservation and Visitor Services (CCP98)*, Countryside Commission, Cheltenham.

DART 报告. 英格兰乡村管理委员会. 1976. 达廷顿公共娱乐设施研究信托，哈德良长城保护及访客服务策略 (CCP98). 切尔滕纳姆.

Fowler, P. 2005. *Hadrian's Wall and the National Trail: a note on a visit, 18-18 July 2005* (unpublished).

P·福勒. 2005. 哈德良长城和国家步道：游记，18-2005 年 7月18 日（未出版）.

Hadrian's Wall Consultative Committee. 1984. *The Strategy for Hadrian's Wall. Countryside Commission*, Newcastle upon Tyne.

哈德良长城咨询委员会. 1984. 哈德良长城战略. 泰恩河畔纽卡斯尔：英格兰乡村管理委员会.

Lazzari, P. and Collins, M. 2019. 'Hadrian's Wall – tourism, access and its consequences: managing the Hadrian's Wall Path National Trail,' in Yu B. and D. Brough (editors), *Wall to Wall: the Hadrian's Wall and Great Wall of China Management Seminar Proceedings*, CACH and Historic England, Beijing, 272-282.

P·拉扎里，M·考林斯. 2019. 哈德良长城的旅游、通道及其后续效应：如何管理哈德良长城国家步道，见于于冰，D·布劳夫（编）双墙对话：哈德良长城与中国长城保护管理研讨会文集，中国文化遗产研究院及英格兰遗产委员会，北京，272-282.

McGlade, D. 2014. 'Hadrian's Wall Path National Trail and the World Heritage Site. A case Study in Heritage Access Management', in P. G. Stone and D. Brough (editors), *Managing, Using, and Interpreting Hadrian's Wall as World Heritage*, Springer, New York, 47-61.

D·麦克格莱德. 2014. 哈德良长城国家步道及世界遗产地遗产开放管理案例研究，见于 P . G·斯通，D·布劳夫（编）哈德良长城世界遗产管理、利用和阐释. 纽约：斯普林格，47-61.

（2014）的报告中有所所总结。

事后来看，我们可以发现基准情况调查对步道可能造成的损害估计得过于乐观。最初的——包括现在的——设想是步道全线均铺设草皮路面，但在某些区域还是需要铺设硬质路面（石板路），对最初的设想做出调整（图4）。另一个旨在减少步道影响的设想是与建设国家步道连通的路网，引导行人远离长城，去探索其他地貌景观。然而几经尝试，这个想法至今尚未真正实现。绝大多数的徒步者还是坚持沿着国家步道走到底。但也有些设想取得可喜的成效。在提交给内阁大臣的步道方案中，有一项有关步道的重要任务是在长城地带建立通达的公共交通体系，包括火车、公共汽车、和泰恩赛德市区的地铁系统。其中哈德良长城公交专线 AD122 通常在每年夏季的四月到九月底运行，发挥了重要作用。该线路大受青睐，尤其是海外游客，尽管因部分关联线路班次取消而受到影响，并且需要补贴。它沿着赫克瑟姆和霍特惠斯尔的火车站之间的长城区段往返，使游客仅依靠公共交通就能够游览长城。此外，很多出租车公司和行李承运公司已经开拓了稳定的业务，接送步行者并运送他们的物品。这项业务在最西端的卡莱尔火车站和波尼斯-索尔维的长城西端之间尤为受欢迎。

其他商业公司也纷纷从国家步道的成功中受益。步道建设前，该地区的住宿选择十分有限。可如今，这里有许多宾馆、由谷仓改造的青年旅社和露营地供游客选择，住宿标准也得到了提升。乡村商店、茶室和酒吧的生意也越来越好，支撑了乡村经济的发展，从而提升了社区的凝聚力。

结语

尽管每英里的建设和维护成本可能要比其他国家步道昂贵，在世界遗产地建设长距离的步道所能带来的益处还是很大的。它使步行者能够游览之前无法进入的区域，提升对整体历史环境的认识，推进大众教育并提升其幸福感，加强可持续遗迹保护，扩大社区参与，促进当地经济发展。哈德良长城的经验表明，步道的成功得益于如下因素：

- 通过数轮公众意见征询，确定最佳路线；
- 对步道沿线的实际状况开展详细调查；
- 必要时开展考古影响研究，获得高质量的数据；
- 建立适用于当地植被状况的路面管理制度（只要条件许可，徒步者更偏爱自然路面）；
- 定期持续监测步道的状况和考古遗迹影响；
- 当地政府和专业机构建立合作关系，对步道进行全面的管理；
- 开放前修建必要的基础设施：栅栏和围墙、门、桥和路标；
- 配套协调公共交通系统，制定运营策略，提供抵达步道的便利条件；
- 创建能够为步行者提供所有所需信息的网站；
- 对住宿设施进行集中改造和提升；
- 将主步道和周边的步道打通，建立互联的路网，从而缓解主步道的压力；
- 制定步行者行为准则，确保对乡村的影响最小化，例如，不要成一列纵队行走，避免群体性聚集活动；
- 为步道维护提供切实可行的资源保障，包括工作人员、资金、实物支持和志愿者的支持；
- 鼓励作家和出版商提供高质量的旅行指南，以及比例尺适于徒步者使用的精准地图（英国通常为1:25000）。

5.3 长城的旅游利用现状与发展趋势

周小凤，陈晨，张朝枝
中山大学旅游学院—中国—广州

刘文艳，于冰
中国文化遗产研究院—中国—北京

摘要

作为我国体量最大、分布最广、问题最复杂的文化遗产，长城的旅游利用现状、问题与趋势是我国文化遗产利用的缩影。本研究将长城的旅游利用分为接触型利用和非接触利用，发现这两类利用对长城的综合效益、保护状态均有积极影响。但是，接触型利用的综合效益明显高于非接触型利用，在将来的长城保护利用中需要加以关注。

关键词：长城　文化遗产　利用　旅游

旅游利用是遗产利用的重要组成部分。然而，究意何谓文化遗产的“旅游利用”，到底有哪些利用方式，各种利用方式各自存在什么问题，目前仍然不清晰。长城既是国家形象与民族精神符号，又是我国最受游客欢迎旅游景点之一，因此长城的保护与旅游利用工作重要性不言而喻。鉴于此，本研究拟以长城为例，分析文化遗产利用的概念与内涵，并对长城旅游利用的分类、现状特征、发展趋势等问题进行了讨论。

一、文化遗产旅游利用的定义与内涵

旅游是文化遗产利用的一种重要方式，也是促进遗产保护的一种有效手段。依据相关国际宪章与国内相关法规，本文将文化遗产的“旅游利用”定义为“在不影响文化遗产安全和真实性、完整性的前提下，以传播文化遗产价值为目标，利用遗产本体进行遗产价值阐释、展示、教育、体验等实践活动”。

二、长城旅游利用的分类与特征

（一）利用的分类

根据实际情况，本文将长城“旅游利用”分为接触型和非接触型两类。其中，接触型指利用者在长城开放状态下可直接与长城本体接触开展活动，如攀爬、登临、建设等活动形式。非接触型指利用者利用长城的景观价值但不直接接触长城本体开展活动，如远眺、旁观、俯瞰等活动形式。2018–2019年，中国文化遗。

5.3 THE GREAT WALL: CURRENT PATTERNS AND FUTURE DEVELOPMENTS IN THE UTILISATION OF HERITAGE FOR TOURISM

ZHOU XIAOFENG, CHEN CHEN, ZHANG CHAOZHI
Sun Yat-sen University - China - Guangzhou
LIU WENYAN, YU BING
Chinese Academy of Cultural Heritage - China - Beijing

Abstract

As the largest and most widely distributed cultural heritage site in China, the Great Wall is faced with many complicated management problems. The challenges of its protection and of managing its use by visitors epitomise those facing many cultural heritage sites in China. This study divides tourism uses on the Great Wall into two categories: direct visits and indirect visits. Each of these types of visiting have positive effects in delivering economic and social benefits and in conservation. However, these benefits are higher from direct visiting than indirect visiting, and this needs to be taken into account in future work to enhance both the social and economic value of the Great Wall and its protection.

Keywords: Great Wall, Cultural Heritage, Use, Tourism

INTRODUCTION

The utilisation of heritage for tourism is an important dimension of heritage management. However, it is still unclear what is meant by the utilisation of cultural heritage for tourism, what are the different ways in which it can be utilised for tourism, and what are the challenges of these different forms of use for tourism. The Great Wall is not only a national icon and a national spiritual symbol, but also one of the most popular tourist attractions in China. Therefore, the importance of both protecting the Great Wall and of optimising the benefits from tourists visiting it is self-evident. This study takes the Great Wall as an example to analyse the concept and implications of utilising cultural heritage for tourism, discusses how such use might be categorised and the characteristics of its current use for tourism. It also looks at factors that will influence future patterns of tourism on the Great Wall.

MEANINGS OF CULTURAL HERITAGE TOURISM USE

As an important way in which cultural heritage is used, tourism is also an effective means to promote cultural heritage conservation. According to the relevant international charters and domestic regulations, this paper defines tourism use of cultural heritage as practices which without affecting the safety, authenticity, and integrity of cultural heritage, have the goal of spreading the value of cultural heritage, and of using the heritage itself to interpret, demonstrate, educate and experience the value of heritage.

CLASSIFICATION AND CHARACTERISTICS OF TOURISM USE OF THE GREAT WALL

Classification of tourism uses

This article identifies two types of tourism use of the Great Wall: direct visiting and indirect visiting. Direct

产研究院联合中山大学旅游学院开展长城保护与开放利用专项研究》[1]，通过调研、问卷等形式对162处长城段落的开放利用形式、管理机构、经营状况、本体保存等内容进行广泛调查。这162处基本涵盖所有已知长城开放长城段落，可以较为全面了解长城开放利用现状。这些长城段落分布在北京、河北、山西、山东、宁夏、黑龙江、甘肃、辽宁、陕西、天津、内蒙古、河南、新疆等13个省市（见图1）。分析表明，长城的利用以接触型为主，共128个，占比达到79%，以攀爬、登临等活动形式为主的长城场所，如北京慕田峪长城、北京八达岭长城等；以生产、生活等活动形式为主的长城，如北京岔道城、辽宁兴城古城等。非接触型利用场所共34个，占比21%，如天津八仙山国家级自然保护区、山东药乡国家森林公园等区域内的长城场所。

（二）利用的特征

资源分布区域广，但利用区域集中。我国长城文化遗产资源呈线性分布，跨越了我国15个省（自治区、直辖市）。在利用方面，162处以长城点段为主体的开放与利用场所共涵盖13个省31市77县。其中，接触型利用长城主要分布在我国华北地区，以北京、河北、山西为主，分别有39、25、22处（见图2），三省的接触型利用长城资源占比已超过总数的1/2；其次是东北地区，以辽宁、黑龙江为主；再次是西北地区，以宁夏、陕西、甘肃为主。而非接触型利用长城主要分布在山东、河北、北京等省市。总体来看，长城遗存分布与利用的区域差异大。

资源遗存量大，但利用对象集中。根据长城资源调查数据（国家文物局，2016），我国各类长城资源遗存总数达43,721处（座/段），总长度达21,196千米。其中，墙体和壕堑/界壕共11,815段；单体建筑共 29,510座；关堡共2,211座，其他相关遗存185处。在实践中（见表 1），接触型利用以墙体和关堡为主，其次是敌台；非接触型利用的长城本体以墙体为主，其次是敌台和烽火台。总体来看，长城虽然体量大，但主要是对关堡、敌台的直接利用，其他部分利用较少。

表1 长城资源本体的利用状况统计。
Table 1 Statistics of Great Wall Resource usage

本体资源 Great Wall components	利用类型 Use types	数量 Number
墙体	接触型/Direct	297km
The Wall	非接触型/Indirect	340km
敌台	接触型/Direct	296
Defence Towers	非接触型/Indirect	16
关堡	接触型/Direct	83
Fortified Passes	非接触型/Indirect	5
烽火台	接触型/Direct	171
Beacon Towers	非接触型/Indirect	7

遗产保护等级不一，但利用多的地方保存良好。据表2统计，在162处长城开放利用场所中，接触型利用长城的国保与省保占比分别为51%、25%，非接触型利用长城的国保与省保占比分别为13%、4%。从长城保存的状况来看，接触型利用保存较好的长城本体的比例多于非接触型利用，且其保存较差或存在安全隐患的长城本体比例少于非接触型利用。总体看来，遗存保护好就利用多，或者说利用多的遗产保护状态也相对好。

1 2018年，中国文化遗产研究院“中央级公益性科研院所基本科研业务费”支持《长城保护与开放利用对策研究》。2019年，中国文化遗产研究院“专项业务费”支持中国文化遗产研究院和中山大学旅游学院共同开展《长城开放利用与旅游专题研究》。

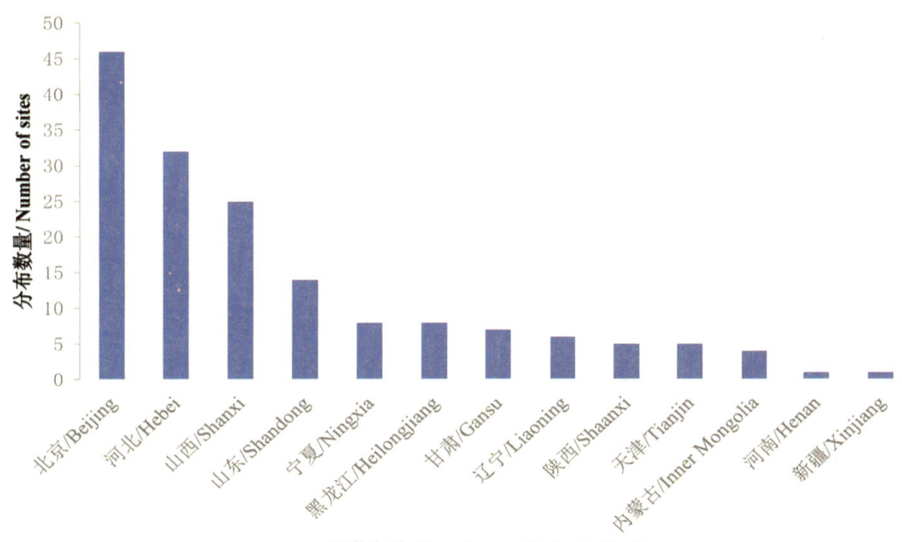

图1中国长城资源开放利用的空间分布及其占比图(数据来源：中国文化遗产研究院，《长城保护与开放利用对策研究课题报告》，2018）。

Fig1. Distribution of Great Wall sites open to the public (source CACH, Policy Research Report on Great Wall Protection, Opening-up and Utilisation, 2018).

visiting means that visitors have physical contact with the Great Wall itself, by visiting those sections which are open to the public, walking along the Wall and visiting beacon towers and associated structures. Indirect visiting is where visitors appreciate the landscape value of the Great Wall without physical contact with the Wall itself. For example, this includes appreciating the panorama of the Wall as a landscape feature from nearby viewpoints and through other activities associated with the cultural heritage of the Great Wall. Between 2018 and 2019, the China Academy of Cultural Heritage (CACH) and the School of Tourism at Sun Yat-sen University carried out research on public access to and tourism on the Great Wall[1]. Through field interviews, questionnaires and other survey methods, this study investigated 162 sections of the Great Wall, looking at their accessibility, how they are used by visitors, their management and operation and their level of conservation. These 162 sections comprise all known sections of the Great Wall that are open to the public, and provide a comprehensive understanding of the current level and nature of tourism on the Great Wall. These Great Wall sections lie in 13 provinces, direct municipalities and autonomous regions including Beijing, Hebei, Shanxi, Shandong, Ningxia, Heilongjiang, Gansu, Liaoning, Shaanxi, Tianjin, Inner Mongolia, Henan, and Xinjiang (see Fig.1). The analysis shows that there are 128 sections (79% of the total) open for direct visiting. One form of direct visiting is climbing and walking on the Wall, for example, in sections such as Beijing Mutianyu Great Wall and Beijing Badaling Great Wall. Another form is mostly using the fort villages as places for tourists to visit and stay at to experience local historic cultures and traditions, for example in forts such as Chadao Fort in Beijing and Xingcheng Ancient City in Liaoning. There are 34 Great Wall sites, comprising 21% of the total, which are primarily part of an indirect visit, for example, the Great Wall section in Tianjin Baxian Mountain National Nature Reserve and Shandong Yaoxiang National Forest Park where the wider

1 In 2018, CACH funded the research on Policies of Protecting, Opening up and Utilising the Great Wall via the Central Government Funding Foundation for research projects for public benefit. In 2019, CACH supported the Special Study of Great Wall Opening up, Utilisation and Tourism, which was carried out jointly by CACH and the School of Tourism of Sun Yat-Sen University.

表 2长城资源本体利用的保护级别与保存状态,(数据来源：中国文化遗产研究院, 2018)。
Table 2 Protection level and preservation status of the Great Wall in use (source China Academy of Cultural Heritage, 2018).

保护级别 Protection level	利用类型 Use types		保存状态 Preservation status					合计 Total
			好 Very Good	较好 Good	一般 Satisfactory	较差 Bad	不详 Unkown	
国保 National	接触型 Direct	数量(处) No.	1	47	7	24	4	83
	非接触型 Indirect	数量(处) No.	0	8	5	6	2	21
省保 Provincial	接触型 Direct	数量(处) No.	0	13	14	3	10	40
	非接触型 Indirect	数量(处) No.	0	2	1	2	2	7

旅游景区发展等级不一，接触型利用高于非接触型利用。据图3统计，162处长城开放利用场所中已经有66处成为不同等级的旅游景区，其中接触型利用长城的A级旅游景区占80%，远远高于非接触型利用长城的A级旅游景区（20%）,景区等级越高，这一特征越明显。

旅游效益显著，接触型利用高于非接触型利用。据表3统计，接触型利用长城旅游景区的年游客接待量与年收入整体高于非接触型利用长城景区，且优势明显。根据专家对长城利用效益的评分（表4），经济与社会效益较好的接触利用型景区普遍多于比非接触利用型多。这表明接触型长城的利用效益优于非接触型长城的利用效益。

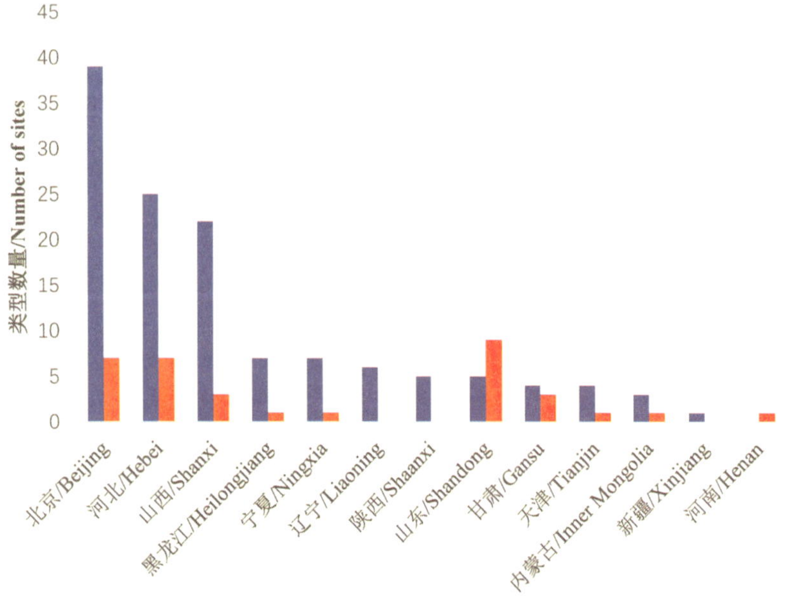

图 2 各地长城资源利用方式比较图（数据来源：中国文化遗产研究院, 2018）。
Fig.2 Number of sites directly and indirectly visited on the Great Wall by region (source China Academy of Cultural Heritage, 2018).

表 3长城相关旅游景区的年游客接待量与年旅游收入统计。
Table 3 Statistics on the Annual Tourist Visits and Tourism Revenue of the Relevant Tourist Attractions of the Great Wall.

长城旅游景区的年游客接待量 The number of annual tourists to Great Wall tourist attractions						
年均游客量（万人次） Average annual tourists (10,000s)	0-10	11-50	51-100	101-500	501+	合计 Total
景区总数（处） Total number of tourist attractions	16	18	4	7	2	47
非接触型（处）/ Number of Directly visited	3	3	0	0	0	6
接触型（处） Number of Indirectly visited	13	15	4	7	2	41

长城旅游景区的年旅游收入 Annual tourism revenue of the Great Wall tourist attractions							
年旅游收入（万元） Annual revenue (RMB 10,000s)	0-50	51-100	101-500	501-1,000	1,001-5,000	5,001+	合计 Total
景区总数（处） Total number of tourist attractions	10	4	8	7	13	4	46
非接触型（处）/ Number of Directly visited	2	1	2	0	3	0	8
接触型（处） Number of Indirectly visited	8	3	6	7	10	4	38

数据来源：中国文化遗产研究院,2018。
Data source: China Academy of Cultural Heritage, 2018.

landscape is the main reason for visiting.

Characteristics of tourism use of the Great Wall

While the Great Wall covers a large area, tourism is focused in certain hotspots. China's Great Wall spans 15 provinces, autonomous regions and direct municipalities in China. The 162 sections that are open for tourism are in 13 provincial, 31 city and 77 county level administrations. Direct tourism to the Great Wall is mainly in North China, with Beijing, Hebei, and Shanxi provinces, comprising 39, 25 and 22 sites respectively (see Fig.2). Direct visiting to the Great Wall in these regions represents more than half of all direct visits followed by Northeast China (primarily in Liaoning and Heilongjiang) and then by Northwest China (mainly in Ningxia, Shaanxi, and Gansu). Indirect visits to the Great Wall are mainly in the regions of Shandong, Hebei, and Beijing. Overall, there are major differences in regional distribution and usage type of the Great Wall for tourism.

While the Great Wall is an enormous heritage site, the number of sites along it which are currently open to and

表 4 长城旅游景区的利用效益评估（数据来源：中国文化遗产研究院，2018）。

Table 4 Evaluation and comparison of benefits in Great Wall in use as Tourist Attractions (source: China Academy of Cultural Heritage, 2018).

经济效益评估 Evaluation of economic benefits					
效益评分Score on usage benefits	0	1	2	3	合计 Total
景区总数（处）/Total number of tourist attractions	12	1	13	62	88
非接触型（处）/Number of Directly visited	4	0	0	6	10
接触型（处）/Number of Indirectly visited	8	1	13	56	78
社会效益评估 Evaluation of social benefits					
效益评分Score on usage benefits	0–2	3–4	5–6	7	合计 Total
景区总数（处）/Total number of tourist attractions	30	27	20	11	88
非接触型（处）/Number of Directly visited	3	1	2	4	10
接触型（处）/Number of Indirectly visited	27	26	18	7	78

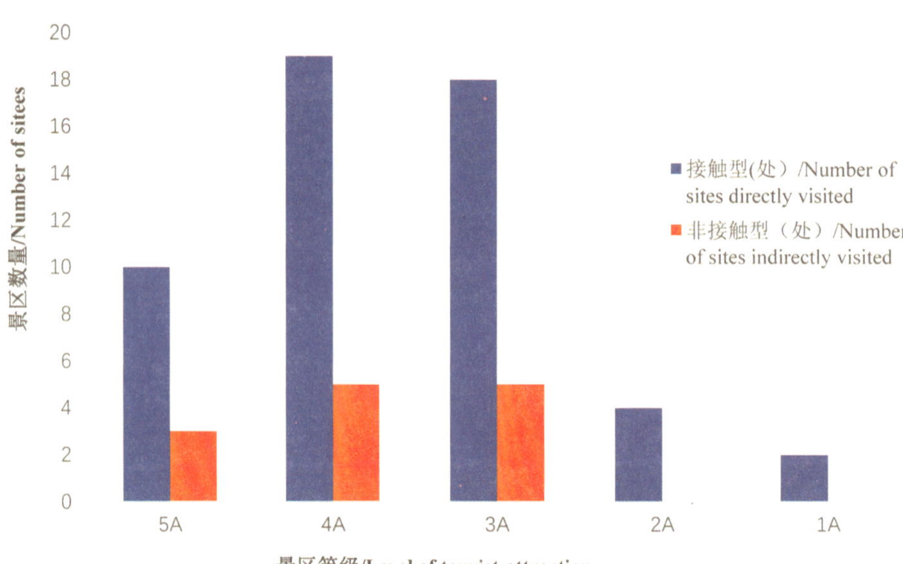

图 3 长城旅游景区利用的等级划分示意图（数据来源：中国文化遗产研究院，2018）。

Fig.3 Breakdown of Great Wall tourist attractions by level of designation (source China Academy of Cultural Heritage, 2018).

三、利用的趋势与策略

随着文化自信战略、资源管理体制改革、文旅融合、文物活化利用等工作的不断推进，未来长城的旅游利用将面临四大发展趋势：

（一）在国民文化自信建设中承担更重要的功能。《长城保护总体规划》（2019）与长城国家文化公园建设方案已明确提出要求未来长城遗产工作的核心任务是展示与传播遗产价值以坚定国民的文化自信心；

visited by tourists is relatively small and are concentrated in certain areas. According to data from the Great Wall Resources Survey (State Cultural Relics Bureau 2016), there are 43,721 elements of the Great Wall with total length of 21,196km. Among them, there are 11,815 sections of walls and ditches; 29,510 free-standing buildings; 2,211 fortified passes and 185 other related sites. In practice (see Table 1), direct visiting is mainly to the Wall itself, to fortified passes, and defence towers; while indirect visiting focuses on the Great Wall itself, defence towers and beacon towers. Generally speaking, although the Great Wall is big in scale and has a large variety of components, it is mainly used for direct visiting to the wall and defence towers and visitor numbers at other parts of the Great Wall are low.

While levels of heritage protection vary, sites visited frequently are usually well protected. According to the statistics in Table 2, among 162 sections of the Great Wall open to public, sites with CRPUs (Cultural Relics Protection Units) at national and provincial level represented 51% and 25% respectively of those directly visited, compared with 13% and 4%, respectively of those where visiting was indirect. Those sites which are regularly visited by tourists are generally in a better state of preservation than those which form part of the wider landscape and are not directly visited. Generally speaking, the better the heritage is protected, the more it is used. Or in other words, the more heritage is used, the better it is protected.

As shown in Fig.3, 66 out of the 162 sites along the Great Wall which are open to the public, have been designated tourist attractions of different classes. Of those, 80% of which are designated as A-level tourist attractions[2] where the Great Wall is visited directly, in contrast with the far smaller proportion of number of A-class tourist attractions in which the Great Wall forms part of an indirect visit. The higher the level of the scenic area, this characteristic is more obvious.

The overall economic and social benefits which the Great Wall generates are significant, and the benefits from direct visiting are higher than those from indirect visiting. Table 3 shows the annual tourist visits and annual income of those Great Wall tourist attractions which are a focus for direct visits compared with those that are indirectly visited. According to the experts' overall evaluation of the benefits of tourism on the Great Wall (Table 4), the tourist attractions with better economic and social benefits from direct visiting are generally more than those indirectly visited.

FACTORS INFLUENCING FUTURE TOURISM USE

In the context of the continuing development of the national Cultural Confidence Strategy, the national reform of resource management systems, the national programme of cultural and tourism integration and the 'Bringing Relics to Life' initiative, future developments in tourism use of the Great Wall can be foreseen:

Tourism use will play a more prominent role in the Cultural Confidence Strategy. Both the Master Plan of the Great Wall Protection (2019) and the Construction Plan of the Great Wall National Cultural Park place a greater emphasis on the display of heritage values and the sustainable use of heritage becoming the core of Great Wall protection;

Tourism will need to make greater progress in reform of its management systems. The structural reform of natural and cultural heritage resources management and the creation of the Great Wall National Cultural Parks in China will significantly contribute to the reform of the Great Wall management system and further promote greater integrated use of the Great Wall;

Tourism will play a greater role in heritage protection. Experience shows that tourism can not only make an

2 A-levels are a measure ofthe tourist attractions' quality rating. In China, the tourist attractions rating system is used by the China National Tourism Administration and local tourism administrations to score the quality of the attraction in terms of safety, cleanliness, sanitation, shopping, transportation, number of visitors, attractiveness of resources, conservation of resources, reception service, public service, operation and management. There are five levels: A (or 1A, the lowest level), AA (2A), AAA (3A), AAAA (4A) and AAAAA (5A, the highest level).

（二） 在管理体制改革方面将进行更大的突破。我国自然与文化遗产资源管理体制改革与国家文化公园的建设要求深化长城管理体制改革，进一步促进综合利用；

（三） 旅游利用在遗产保护中将发挥更大的作用。实践表明，旅游利用是遗产保护的一种重要方式，能够产生重要经济、社会效益，需要更加关注旅游对遗产保护的综合影响；

（四） 接触型利用需要受到更多关注。实践表明，接触型利用是长城遗产利用的主体，在产生显著旅游效益的同时对长城本体的潜在影响也大，需要更多关注以更好地平衡保护与利用的关系。

最后，结合长城利用的现状问题和发展趋势，本文提出将“优先保护、分级管理、选择开放、差别利用”作为新时期长城文化遗产活化利用工作的指导方针。

（一） 优先保护遗产价值突出的长城点段。对于绝大多数长城点段，重点做好日常维护管理、局部抢险和标识说明。保护好长城的本体及其与周边人文、自然环境的完整性，处理好全面保存与重点保护的关系。

（二） 分级管理长城资源本身与周边环境资源。将长城本体包括长城墙体、壕堑/界壕、单体建筑、关堡、相关设施等各类遗存分为城墙主体、城墙上附属设施与城墙外配套设施等三大类，归属于核心管理层。而长城本体外的自然与人文资源列入外围层次进行管理。

（三） 选择性开放不同点、段的长城资源。对于尚未开放的长城，依据资源保存状态、发展潜力与周边的可达性进行科学规划、选择性开放。对于已开放但缺乏规范性的长城依据规范性开放的条件逐步转变非规范性的局面，将其对长城物质形态与价值信息的危害降至最少。

（四） 差别性地采取利用方式展示长城的遗产价值。接触型利用对长城本体及其整体环境干预程度与影响力度较大，需要建立定期监测、评估及反馈利用的影响结果，必要条件下将其转化为非接触型利用，以维持长城遗产价值的原真性与完整性；而非接触型利用对长城本体及其整体环境干预程度与影响力度较小，在影响人与长城遗产互动深度的情况下可能不利于广泛地传播遗产价值，同时可能导致长城本体在自然与时间因素的损耗下逐渐消失殆尽。为此，针对非接触型利用的长城，需要加强对本体的防护、加固及抗风险等举措，同时在适当条件下按可承载、可接受的范围转化为接触型利用。

References
参考文献

Chinese Academy of Cultural Heritage. 2018. Policy Research Report on Great Wall Protection, opening-up and utilisation, 2018.

中国文化遗产研究院. 2018. 长城保护与开放利用对策研究课题报告.

State Cultural Relics Bureau. 2016. Report on the Great Wall Protection of China.

国家文物局. 2016. 中国长城保护报告.

important contribution to heritage protection, but can also provide significant economic and social benefits. In particular greater attention should be paid to the overall impact of tourism on heritage protection;

Direct visiting on the Great Wall will be more closely managed. Practice has proven that direct visiting is the main form of use of the Great Wall heritage, which not only generates remarkable tourism benefits, but also has a great potential impact on the Great Wall itself. Therefore, more attention should be paid to the sites directly visited in order to better balance the relationship between protection and public access.

In conclusion, in the light of these factors, this article proposes 'prioritising protection, management according to resource classification, selective opening up and designating different sections of the Wall for different forms of tourism' as guidelines for enhancing the Great Wall's benefits to society in the new period. This article therefore proposes the following actions:

- Give priority to the protection of the outstanding values of the Great Wall. For most sections of the Great Wall, the focus should be on daily maintenance with only limited intervention, and on values interpretation. The integrity of the Great Wall and its surrounding human and natural environment should both be preserved and a balance between routine works for the overall preservation of the whole site and concentrated interventions on some specific sections should be carefully maintained.
- Classify the resources of the Great Wall and the surrounding environment for the purposes of applying different management policies according to the particular conditions of different sections of the historic remains and of different sections of their landscape settings.
- Select different sections of the Great Wall resources to be opened up. For sections which have not yet been opened, careful feasibility studies and scientific planning should be carried out according to the conservation status and development potential of the Wall and the accessibility of surrounding areas. While for those which have already been opened but are not well regulated, more effort should be made to minimise activities harmful to the tangible and intangible authenticity of the Great Wall.
- Differentiate tourism uses to display the heritage values of the Great Wall. Direct visiting has greater impact on the fabric of the Great Wall and on the overall environment, so it is suggested to establish regular monitoring, evaluation and feedback on the impact of tourism. Conversion of access to indirect visiting might be necessary as a result. Conversely, even though indirect visiting has less impact on the Great Wall itself and its overall environment, the interaction between people and heritage is also reduced which might result in lower public understanding of and participation in its protection. It is therefore necessary to improve the protection of sites while opening them for direct visiting within acceptable limitations and under appropriate conditions.

5.4 PROMOTING TOURISM: UNDERSTANDING WHAT VISITORS WANT

JOE SAVAGE
English Heritage - York - UK

Abstract

Interpretation Development in museums and in heritage has advanced considerably in the UK over the last two decades. Where once a curator's expertise was foremost as the basis of all collection and site narratives, it is now supported by the professional application of audience insight and pedagogical practice, ensuring that the visitor experience is engaging and enables the audience to learn in the way that is best for them.

Recent investment in interpretation at English Heritage's visitor sites has been guided by enhanced understanding of our visitors, which has been established through audience research and through visitor segmentation models. This paper describes how this process has been applied at English Heritage's visitor sites along Hadrian's Wall, and the changes which have resulted in visitor interpretation at each of them.

Keywords: interpretation, exhibitions, audiences, visitor research.

INTRODUCTION

English Heritage is a charity formed in 2016, entrusted with the guardianship of the National Collection of historically significant monuments, buildings and sites. It is responsible for all historical sites in state care, amounting to over 400 sites across England, including castles, abbeys, prehistoric monuments, country houses, and industrial sites, and for public statues in London and elsewhere.

The historic sites that the British public most closely identify with English Heritage are: Stonehenge, the best known prehistoric monument in Europe; the Blue Plaques which commemorate the birthplaces or residences of famous people; and the Hadrian's Wall World Heritage Site. On Hadrian's Wall there are four staffed and ticketed sites within English Heritage's portfolio: the Roman forts at Housesteads, Birdoswald and Chesters, and the Roman Town at Corbridge, as well as 26 free-to-enter sites.

Housesteads Roman Fort is managed in partnership with the National Trust. It is considered to be a flagship site for English Heritage and a perfect gateway to introduce visitors to the picturesque central section of the Wall. Of English Heritage's four principal sites along Hadrian's Wall, Housesteads arguably provides the visitor with the best combination of the Wall and its landscape setting.

Birdoswald Roman Fort sits amidst the longest continuous stretch of Hadrian's Wall still standing today. Within a short walk of the site, visitors can discover many of the components of the Roman Northern Frontier defences, revealing a considerably more complex system than is visible elsewhere along the Wall.

Chesters Roman Fort is claimed to be the most complete Roman cavalry fort in Britain. Set within an idyllic landscape and home to some of the first archaeological finds made from along Hadrian's Wall, Chesters tells the story not only of the Romans who built and operated the fort, but of the antiquaries and early archaeologists who discovered it and first investigated its remains.

5.4 旅游推广：了解游客诉求

乔·萨维奇
英格兰遗产信托—约克—英国

摘要

近20年来，英国博物馆与文化遗产领域的阐释出现了长足的进步。过去，文物专业在博物馆策展和遗产现场展示中发挥着举足轻重的作用。如今，观众意见与教育实践成为这一领域的两大专业支柱，以确保游览体验更加具有吸引力，也确保参观者能够以其自身最适宜的方式有所习获。

在英格兰遗产信托（以下简称“遗产信托”）管辖的旅游景区，近期投入的遗产阐释项目都立足于对游客更加深入的理解，开展了观众调研和游客细分模型分析。本文将探讨这些方法如何应用于遗产信托管辖的哈德良长城遗址，以及各个遗址在阐释方面做出了哪些改变。

关键词：阐释　展览　参观者　参观者调研

引言

英格兰遗产信托是一个于2016年组建的慈善组织，负责监管国有资产中的重要历史古迹、建筑与遗迹。遗产信托所监管的国家所有的历史遗迹，遍布英格兰全境，包括400多处城堡、修道院、史前古迹、乡间住宅、工业遗产地等，也包括伦敦等地区的公共雕塑。

英国民众认知度最高的几个属于遗产信托的历史遗迹有：欧洲最著名的史前时期遗迹巨石阵；纪念名人出生地或故居的蓝牌建筑；以及哈德良长城世界遗产地。在遗产信托负责监管的哈德良长城遗产点中，有四个景点配备工作人员并且需要购票进入，分别为豪塞斯特兹罗马要塞、博得瓦德罗马要塞、切斯特罗马要塞、科布里奇罗马小镇，还有26个可以免费参观的遗址。

豪塞斯特兹罗马要塞是由遗产信托和英国国家信托合作管理的，它被视作遗产信托的“旗舰遗产地”，是一处最佳门户，从这里游客可以开启风景如画的哈德良长城中部之旅。在遗产信托旗下四个主要哈德良长城遗产点中，豪塞斯特兹罗马要塞可以说是将长城与周围的地貌景观结合完美呈现给游客的最佳典范。

博得瓦德罗马要塞位于现存哈德良长城中连续墙体最长的一段。在步行距离内，游客就能参观到罗马北部边疆防御体系中许多类型的防御工事，相比于哈德良长城其他遗址，这里更能展现出复杂的防御体系。

切斯特罗马要塞被称作英国现存最完整的罗马骑兵要塞。坐落于田园风光之中的切斯特要塞是最早一批哈德良长城考古发掘点，它不仅讲述了建造和使用这座要塞的罗马人的故事，还诉说了最早发现和调查研究切斯特要塞的古董收藏者和考古工作者的故事。

Roman Corbridge's rich collection was largely discovered between 1906 and 1981, through 45 seasons of excavation. This collection of artefacts reveals a story of life within a primarily civilian settlement, and so helps broaden the narrative of the Roman frontier. Despite its extensive collection, it is a small compact site and is not currently as well-known as other sites but, situated in a pleasant market town which is becoming more of a holiday destination, it has the opportunity to appeal to a museum-going, culture-seeking audience.

HERITAGE INTERPRETATION

Within the context of heritage management, the word "interpretation" is defined as follows:

> 'Interpretation is a communication process that helps people make sense of, and understand more about, a site, object or collection. It enhances visitor appreciation and promotes better understanding.' （UK Association of Heritage Interpretation）.

For English Heritage, interpretation is the process of bringing history to life. The charity employs an interpretation team within a large curatorial department; the role of this team is to lead the development and design of new visitor experiences, to act as advocates for the visitors, and to bridge the knowledge-gap between experts and audiences. The media that the team develops are informed by thorough research of the current and potential audiences.

Since 2015, English Heritage has invested nearly £2 million in improving interpretation at its sites and museums along Hadrian's Wall. This investment was central to the new charity's business objectives. These were: to create high-quality visitor experiences; to improve its offer to its membership; and to encourage repeat visits. Although the charity's business model is dependent on income from ticket sales, membership subscriptions and retail spend, there was not an expectation of a high financial return on this investment. Rather, the developments were focused on creating marketable and recognizable destinations which strengthen public awareness of English Heritage's identity and of its role.

The multiple public, private and commercial stakeholders involved with Hadrian's Wall are perhaps more numerous and diverse than those of any other heritage and landscape partnership in the country. Consequently, there is a long history of partners working together to jointly promote the World Heritage Site. In 2011 the Hadrian's Wall Trust launched a shared Interpretation Framework which set out an agreed set of principles for visitor experiences throughout the World Heritage Site. These formed the foundation for the development of its interpretation.

The Interpretation Framework proposed that all developments, large or small, should be based on three key principles:

Each site should contribute to an overall narrative of the Wall. Although each site is marketed and managed as a discrete attraction, they are all fundamentally part of the same monument and archaeological resource. Collectively, they inform a narrative of the whole Wall, its defence systems and even the wider Northern Frontier of the Roman Empire. Each reveals evidence that can be scaled to interpret the wider story and they present the opportunity to inspire visitors to explore the span of the Wall from the Tyne to the Solway.

Each site should present a unique visitor offer based on its location, facilities, significance and stories. Holiday makers have many different attractions competing for their time and, because they tend to prioritize variety, they avoid repeating an experience. One Roman fort sounds much like another to these visitors, and if visitors are to be encouraged to explore the region more thoroughly over more than one day, it is necessary to communicate what is unique or distinctive in feel and experience at each site, not just the differences in historic significance.

Focus should be on the type of interpretation and activities which appeal to visitors, not just the stories we want to tell. This sounds straightforward but it is not always so. The first step is to recognize that we, the

科布里奇罗马小镇出土文物十分丰富，主要来自于1906年到1981年之间45次考古发掘。这些文物以反映平民聚落生活为主，因此丰富了罗马帝国边疆遗产的阐释内容。虽然科布里奇罗马小镇的文物数量众多，但相关遗址却小巧而紧凑，目前知名度也不如其他遗址。科布里奇罗马小镇位于一座宜人的集市小镇之中，市镇成为越来越多游客的度假目的地，具备吸引博物馆爱好者与文化爱好者的潜力。

遗产阐释

在遗产管理语境下，“阐释”一词的含义为：

“阐释是一个沟通的过程，它可以帮助人们更多发现和理解一处遗址、一件文物或藏品的意义。阐释可以加强参观者的鉴赏能力，增进理解”。（英国遗产阐释协会）

对于遗产信托来说，阐释是一个赋予历史以活力的过程。遗产信托在遗产保管部门内设立了一个阐释团队。阐释团队负责开发与设计新的游客体验，代表游客需求发声，沟通专家和游客之间存在的认知差距。基于对当前和潜在参观者的透彻调研，阐释团队开发了遗产阐释的不同方式。

自2015年以来，遗产信托投资近200万英镑，用于提升其管辖哈德良长城遗产点与相关博物馆的遗产阐释。上述投资对遗产信托实现其新组建之后设立的业务目标至关重要，即为游客创造高质量的游览体验，为会员提供更加丰富的服务，鼓励游客成为“回头客”。尽管遗产信托运营模式中的收入来源主要依靠门票销售、会费收入和零售商品，但初衷却并不是提高投资的财务回报。恰恰相反，这些新的投资项目侧重于创建具有营销价值与知名度的旅游目的地，加强民众对遗产信托及其作用的认识与了解。

与哈德良长城相关的政府机构、私人与商业企业利益相关方的数量与差异性或许超过了英国其他任何遗产和景观地。因此，哈德良长城世界遗产地长期以来一直致力于与合作伙伴共同发展。2011年，哈德良长城信托制定了一个共同阐释框架（以下简称“框架”），为哈德良长城沿线所有游客活动制定了各方认同的原则规范，这为遗产阐释开发奠定了基础。

框架提出所有遗产阐释开发，不论大小，都必须基于以下三个关键原则：

每个遗产点都应对哈德良长城的总体阐释有所贡献。尽管每个遗产点作为独立景点进行运营和管理，但从根本上来说，它们都是同一古迹与考古资源的组成部分。它们集合在一起，才共同构成了哈德良长城整体及其防御体系、乃至罗马帝国北部边疆的遗产阐释。每个遗址所提供的线索，都可以放在更广阔的故事背景中加以解读，可以激发游客去探索从泰恩河到索尔韦湾的哈德良长城全线。

每个遗址都应基于其地理位置、设施、历史意义和故事呈现独特的游客体验。度假的游客有许多选择，但由于时间有限，他们倾向于参观多元化景点，不愿重复性的游览体验。在游客印象里每个罗马要塞都大同小异。如果要鼓励游客利用一天以上的时间在同一区域进行更深度的游览，就需要向游客宣介每处遗产点能够带来的独特、与众不同的感受和体验，而不仅是向游客介绍它们具有不同的历史意义。

重点应放在吸引游客的阐释方式和活动，而不只是关注专业人士想要介绍的内容。这听起来很简单，但实际上并非如此。第一步是要认识到，我们作为遗产地的管理人员，与游客的背景或兴趣并不相同。通常情况下，考古或文化遗产行业的工作人员往往对历史抱有极大的热忱，有能力从各种不同的碎片证据中构建起完整的信息链条，喜欢沉迷于大量细节而不厌其烦。然而一定要记住的是，完全按照遗产专业人士意见做出的阐释通常不能为普通游客带来美好的体验。为了营造成功的游客体验，管理人员必须意识到游

managing officers of the sites, do not necessarily have the same background or interests as our audiences. Generally, the people who are employed in archaeology and heritage are enthusiastic about the past, are able to readily make intellectual connections between different pieces of cultural evidence, and are tolerant of large amounts of detail. It is important to remember that interpretation which is based solely on the expectations of heritage specialists does not always result in a good day out for other visitors. To be successful, those managing the World Heritage Site must recognize that visitors actually have many different motivations for visiting the area.

Some might want to explore the natural landscape, maybe as part of a multi-day trek or a short family walk accessible from a car park. They might simply want to capture the best shot of the Wall for posting on social media while en-route to another destination. They might be part of a study group and have a deep personal interest in Roman history and archaeology. Others they may be looking for something fun yet educational to do with their children. For some the Wall is simply a backdrop to their holiday. They may also differ in their expectations and requirements of visitor facilities.

When this is all better understood, we can create experiences that best work with the type of visit that the majority of visitors are looking for, whether it is a good introduction to Hadrian's Wall as part of a walk through a landscape or an in-depth exploration of its stories through its world-class collections.

AUDIENCE RESEARCH AND SEGMENTATION

English Heritage's response to the Framework started with a major piece of audience research across all four of its Hadrian's Wall sites to assess the profile of its visitors and their perceptions of its existing offer. This showed that Hadrian's Wall was attracting many more holiday makers and day-trippers from over an hour's drive away than local or regional visitors. Only one in ten visitors were local to the site they were visiting and, for each site, over 64% were on a holiday from outside the region. Apart from at its most famous sites such as Stonehenge, this visitor profile is relatively rare within English Heritage's properties.

It was clear that Hadrian's Wall was attracting visitors into the region. However, unlike Stonehenge, visitors were not coming to visit a specific site but with a more general idea of seeing the Wall. Financially, this was a challenge to English Heritage because there was very little awareness about the ticketed sites as potential places to visit. As a result, visitors were coming to see the Wall itself without necessarily visiting these sites. This highlighted a need to present these sites within a narrative about the World Heritage Site as a whole, so that visiting them would be incorporated into the planning that these visitors would make about their holiday.

Of the four main sites, Housesteads enjoyed the greatest level of visitors' pre-visit awareness. It was perceived as a 'must-see' site, and consequently the decision to visit Housesteads was typically made further in advance than for any of the other three sites. For most of the sites, visitors were only deciding to visit on the day of their visit, rather than when they were planning their holiday. For English Heritage this short lead-time in visitors' planning of their holiday made it harder to promote visits that were centred around events and activities. This also meant that these visitors had limited opportunity to understand and consider their options on what they might see, and which experience would be best for them.

The audience research identified that when visitors were asked about the interpretation of a site, the two lowest-scoring indicators were against the questions: 'Does it provide a lively, fun and engaging experience?' and 'Does it offer a genuinely unique experience?' At that time the interpretation of the sites was based on graphic panels, which had a slightly academic tone, and on crowded displays of objects. The museum displays were based around a traditional taxonomic arrangement of objects, appealing more to an expert than to a non-expert or to someone who was new to the subject. In all instances the interpretation of the site was dependent on guidebook information for more depth, for images and for any stories about people. The displays and graphics were not just of little interest to children, but non-specialist adult audiences were also struggling to engage with them. Consequently, the

客参观哈德良长城景区的目的和动机各不相同。

有些游客希望享受自然景观，这可能是延续几天的远足活动的一部分，也可能只是在停车场周边短暂的家庭散步。他们可能只想在前往其他旅行目的地的途中，照一张哈德良长城的绝好照片，上传到社交网站。有的游客可能是某个学术团体的成员，对罗马的历史和考古具有深厚兴趣。另一些游客或许只是希望和孩子们一起做些有教育意义并且有趣的活动。对于一些游客来说，哈德良长城只不过是他们度假的背景环境而已。游客们对旅游设施的预期和要求也可能不尽相同。

对上述情况有了更清醒的认识后，我们才能创造可以最好满足大部分游客需求的游览体验，或者使在自然美景中漫步的游客更好地了解哈德良长城，或者提供深度探索世界一流遗产地的历史之旅。

观众调研与细分

框架发布以后，遗产信托便开始对四个主要的哈德良长城遗产点的参观者进行大型调查，分析他们的情况，以及他们对现有的游客活动抱有何种期待。调研显示，哈德良长城的观众主要以度假或短期游客为主，他们多来自一小时车程以外的地方，而本地或附近区域的居民较少。只有十分之一的游客来自他们参观的遗产地所在地区。在接受调研的四个主要哈德良长城遗址中，超过64% 的游客都是从别的地区来到哈德良长城度假的。除了巨石阵以外，这种情况在所有遗产信托管理的遗产地都是相对少见的。

调查也清楚地显示出哈德良长城是其他地区的游客到访参观的主要吸引物。但与巨石阵不同的是，到访哈德良长城的游客并不是来参观某一特定遗址，而是抱着更加笼统的“看看长城”的想法前来参观的。这对遗产信托的收入构成了影响，这是因为很少有人将这些收费的景点作为参观目的地。往往游客只是来参观一下哈德良长城的墙体，不一定会去那些收费的遗址。因此，特别有必要将上述遗产点作为哈德良长城整体的一部分加以阐释说明，以促使游客在制定旅行计划时就将参观这些哈德良长城遗产点纳入进去。

在遗产信托的四个主要哈德良长城景点中，豪塞斯戴兹罗马要塞享有最高知名度，更多游客在参观哈德良长城之前就知道它。豪塞斯戴兹通常被视作“必去”景点，因此相对于其他三个景点，游客通常会更早决定参观豪塞斯戴兹要塞。然而更多的情况是游客在当天才决定要去参观，而不是提前将参观纳入度假计划中。对于遗产信托来说，游客的这种临时决定行为增加了以活动为主要形式吸引游客的推广难度。这也意味着游客很少有机会充分了解并选择参观内容、充分考虑哪种参观体验最适合他们。

观众调研发现，当被问及对于遗产点阐释感受时，参观者对以下两个问题的反馈评分最低，即“是否提供了生动、有趣、参与度高的体验”以及“是否提供了真正独特的体验”。当时遗址现场阐释的主要形式是图板，配以略带学术口吻的文字以及密集的文物图片。博物馆的陈列方式主要基于传统的文物分类陈列方式，这更符合专家的视角，但对于普通参观者或是对展示主题毫无了解的观众并非如此。当时，在所有的遗址现场阐释都是借助游客指南提供更加深入的信息、更多图像介绍以及相关的人物故事。不仅儿童对其内容兴趣寥寥，非专业的成年观众也很难提起兴趣去阅读。因此，游客们的普遍认为，只有喜爱或已经对罗马历史有所了解的人才会认为遗址有趣，对于其他参观者来说，如果没有遇上活动，参观体验十分乏味。在四个哈德良长城的主要景点都出现了上述反馈，参观者很难分清他们参观的景点有何特别之处。由此明确了展示提升的重点是确保每个遗产特色鲜明，并且能够提供更加生动和互动的游客体验。

由于所有游客都有不同的参观目的、兴趣与需求，如何运用这项调研成果协助推动遗产信托的阐释提

overriding impression from visitors was that the sites were only interesting if you already liked or knew something about the Romans, but otherwise, unless there was some form of activity or event, the experience was dull. This was reflected across all of the four sites, at each of which visitors struggled to identify what was special about the site they were visiting. So the main areas for improvement were identified as ensuring that each site delivered a distinctive offer and a more lively, engaging visitor experience.

Given that all visitors have different motivations, interests and needs, how has this research been used in English Heritage's development of interpretation? In common with most audience-focussed organisations, English Heritage has developed its own audience-segmentation model that identifies groups of visitors by their motivations and interests. There are a number of broad segments in this model, from the people who are looking for in-depth historic information, to those who are simply seeking a relaxing day out. On Hadrian's Wall, the two dominant segments are defined as 'Culture Seekers' and 'Shared Explorers'.

Culture Seekers are looking for 'self-improving' days out. They see a visit as being of benefit to them, believing that they will leave knowing more or having experienced something of high quality. They have a very high interest in history. They do not like crowds or noise or being told what to do. In order to truly engage them, the interpretation must draw them in and feed their fascination in an appropriate manner and environment.

Shared Explorers seek exciting learning experiences, for them and their families or companions. They are specifically inspired by things they can enjoy together. They don't just want something to keep the children entertained while they pursue their own interests. They like interactive, hands-on interpretation but will also create their own experiences. This may include a mixture of indoors experiences and exploring within the outdoor environment.

ENGLISH HERITAGE'S RESPONSES ALONG HADRIAN'S WALL

The subsequent redevelopments of interpretation at each of English Heritage's four Hadrian's Wall sites, described below, were based on the findings of the audience research. They each focused on creating experiences that would appeal to a particular balance of these two primary audience segments, while not alienating those secondary audience segments which the research had identified. This was achieved by using the audience research to focus on specific messages (the knowledge and understanding that visitors want to develop) and visitor outcomes (more intangible benefits like inspiration and fun).

Housesteads Roman Fort: Visitors can see for miles from Housesteads, making it a perfect location for photographs for posting on social media. To a visitor, enjoying a bracing walk through a dramatic landscape, the site perfectly plays into the image of a remote military posting to the edge of an empire. As one of the most complete Roman forts in Britain, Housestead's extensive remains are easy to comprehend, interpret and wrap into story-telling, creating a perfect base from which to introduce a picture of a soldier's life on the Roman frontier. The site's museum collection, while interesting, is not as extensive or illuminating as that of nearby Vindolanda, so here the objects are used to convey how experts have been able to piece together our understanding of life on the Wall rather than try to illustrate it. Overall, the site is designed as an introduction to the central section of Hadrian's Wall including a focus on its natural landscape setting.

Birdoswald Roman Fort: Just as Housesteads introduces the Wall to visitors arriving from its eastern end, Birdoswald fulfils a similar function to visitors coming via Carlisle and the Lake District in the west. The audience research suggested that this site was of particular appeal to families (Fig.1). There are a number of public paths nearby which perhaps provide more freedom to roam the surrounding area than elsewhere along the Wall.

Family focus-groups informed the audience research team that they enjoyed this sense of outdoor exploration, and the opportunity for children to get muddy and to be able to play hide-and-seek. This felt compatible with the rugged state of the site, only a small part of which has been excavated for display. It all suggested an experience

升？与大多数以参观者为重的机构相同，遗产信托根据观众和兴趣开发出自己的观众细分模型。这个模型包括几大观众类别，从希望深入了解历史信息到只是寻求休闲放松不等。其中参观哈德良长城的游客主要被分为两大类，即“文化独行者”与“共同探索者”。

“文化独行者”希望通过出行获得“自我提升”。他们认为参观能够带来收获，相信在参观结束时能够了解更多知识，或者通过参观获得高质量的体验。这类参观者对历史有着浓厚的兴趣。他们不喜欢人群与嘈杂的环境，也不喜欢被说教。为了真正吸引这种游客参观，遗产阐释必须通过合适的方式、营造适宜的环境满足他们的好奇心。

“共同探索者”希望和家人朋友一起获得刺激的学习体验。他们对集体参与的活动尤其感兴趣。这类参观者不希望以满足大人自己的兴趣为主，孩子只能自娱自乐，而是倾向于既能满足自身体验，又能与孩子互动、让孩子更多参与的阐释方式。这类观众可能喜欢将室内体验与户外探索活动相结合。

遗产信托在哈德良长城各遗产点的调整

随后，遗产信托旗下四个主要的哈德良长城遗址的遗产阐释都经历了重新设计开发，这些都是在参观者调研结果的基础上展开的，下文将展开介绍。针对调研发现的两个主要细分类别的游客，每个景区都着力打造能够平衡各自需求的参观体验，同时还尽量兼顾其他次级细分类别中小众游客的需求。要实现这一目标，需要特别关注观众调研分析出来的具体信息（那些参观者希望了解的知识）及参观预期（更多是无形的收获，诸如获得灵感、体验快乐等）。

豪塞斯戴兹罗马要塞：站在豪塞斯戴兹，游客可以极目远眺数英里之外，是一处可以在社交媒体平台炫耀的绝佳拍照地点。漫步在壮丽的自然环境中，游客特别能够体验到处于帝国偏远边疆的军事哨所的感受。作为英国最完整的罗马要塞之一，豪塞斯戴兹遗迹众多，易于理解，便于以娓娓道来的故事进行阐释，参观者可以在此对罗马帝国边疆士兵生活的景象产生初步了解。豪塞斯戴兹罗马要塞遗址博物馆的馆藏文物虽然重要，但不如附近的文多兰达要塞博物馆出土文物那么丰富和生动。因此，豪塞斯戴兹的文物展陈主要用来说明专家是如何通过这些线索开展哈德良长城历史的研究，而并没有试图通过这些文物去展现哈德良的历史面貌。总之，豪塞斯戴兹景区的设计定位是向观众介绍哈德良长城中部地段情况的起始点，并着重凸显其自然的地貌景观。

博得瓦德罗马要塞：如果说豪塞斯戴兹遗址是来自东部地区游客开始参观哈德良长城的起始点，博得瓦德则是从卡莱尔和湖区等西部地区来参观长城的起始点。参观者调研显示，博得瓦德景区对以家庭形式出行的游客特别具有吸引力。博得瓦德景区附近有几条公共步道，游客可以在周边区域更方便地游览，相较于其他哈德良长城遗址可活动范围更大。

家庭游客在接受观众调查时表示他们喜欢这种户外探索的感觉，孩子们可以尽情摸爬滚打玩得脏兮兮，还能大玩捉迷藏，不亦乐乎。这种体验与博得瓦德相对原始粗犷的风貌十分相称，其中只有一小部分遗址进行了发掘和展示。上述调查反馈说明，博得瓦德的核心体验是娱乐、探索和发现。因此，博得瓦德景区以“共同探索者”为目标人群，阐释主要围绕一些常见问题展开，例如“为什么建造长城”？景区以直截了当的方式解答这些问题，而不是将答案隐藏在大段描述性的文字中，以使参观者能够迅速了解长城的功能。在一系列简短的阐释说明引导下，游客可以继续探索更加广阔的罗马历史和景观，并对他们将要前往的目的地有了更多的预期和了解。

that had fun, exploration and discovery at its heart. Specifically targeting 'Shared Explorers', the interpretation was based around frequently asked questions such as 'Why was the Wall built?' Addressing these explicitly, rather than hiding the answers in more descriptive text, has created an experience that enables the audience to quickly build an understanding of the possible functions of the Wall. Equipped with these bite-sized pieces of interpretation, visitors can go on to explore the wider Roman landscape, knowing what they are looking at.

This target audience likes to visit as a group, so the theme of working together as a team to establish understanding which wouldn't be possible to do individually is threaded throughout the site. The narrative focuses on the Roman Empire's technical capabilities and ability in coordinating manpower to build epic structures. It also focusses on Roman ingenuity, turning this into an opportunity to promote problem-solving through interactive exhibits which allow for creative responses rather than demanding right or wrong answers.

Birdoswald's visitor centre is one of very few within the World Heritage Site that is located directly on the National Trail. Its visitor facilities were therefore reconfigured to meet the needs of people walking the Trail. The café and toilet were relocated outside the perimeter of the ticketed site, to accommodate those people that wanted a brief stop without paying for a full visit. A family space, tolerant of muddy boots, now allows for a wider audience of visitors. Most of the structures in the interior of the fort are underground. This makes this site less easy for visitors to comprehend than Housesteads, so at Birdoswald large-scale re-enactment events are staged to bring the site to life （Fig.2）.

Chesters Roman Fort is one of the more accessible Hadrian's Wall sites, particularly for coach parties. Set within an elegant, quiet pastoral landscape, a visit might involve a peaceful stroll, tea and cake, and the sense of having discovered a hidden gem. The key objective behind the repositioning of its presentation was to enhance its unique atmosphere, without destroying it （Fig.3）.

Chesters was discovered in the garden of the antiquarian and archaeological pioneer, John Clayton, who in the 19th Century led some of the earliest excavations along Hadrian's Wall. Many of Clayton's finds were originally displayed in his gardens and subsequently in a museum that was built there shortly after his death. The John Clayton Museum is an atmospheric treasure trove, with a very rare Edwardian layout and feel. Every effort has been made to preserve this atmosphere. The interpretation, whilst modern in its tone, is inspired by the structure and appearance of Edwardian presentation; a digital catalogue is presented on elegant monochrome e-readers rather than on LCD screens.

Conveying the image of a busy fort is a challenge in a quiet parkland setting, where the open spaces, solitude and birdsong make it hard to picture an ancient military base, most of the remains of which are now buried below today's grassland. Viewing posts around the site enable visitors to visualise the structure and scale of the original military installation and its inhabitants （Fig.4）.

Families are not the identified primary target audience for Chesters. Nevertheless, the dwell-time of family visitors has been increased through the creation of a story-based quest to encourage visitors to explore all the buildings in the fort.

Corbridge Roman Town is a less well-known site although its museum holds an internationally significant collection of artefacts. Unlike many of the archaeological sites along Hadrian's Wall, Corbridge wasn't just a base for the Roman army, it was also a Roman town. Its collection therefore also reveals the story of civilian life at the edge of the Roman Empire.

The renewed interpretation of the site is designed to appeal to a culture-seeking audience. It features dramatic displays, a multi-layered story, and high-quality materials and mounts for the objects. Despite the small size of the museum, the new interpretation aspires to create a world-class display to reflect the importance of the finds and to appeal to a discerning audience （Fig.5）.

The Corbridge collection, one of the largest in the region, is housed just metres away from its architectural and

这类目标游客喜欢以团队方式进行参观，所以在整个景区各处都设计安排了不能仅靠个人力量而必须通过团队合作才能完成的活动。这些活动着重展示罗马帝国在组织调动集体力量建造宏伟建筑的技术水平和能力。阐释还特别突出罗马人的独创性，籍此设计互动式展陈，鼓励以各种新奇方法解决问题，而不是设定固定的正确答案。

Fig.1 Birdoswald exhibition space（© English Heritage Trust）.
图 1 博得瓦德要塞的展览空间（© 英格兰遗产信托）。

博得瓦德罗是哈德良长城沿线少数几个将游客中心直接建在国家步道上的遗产点之一。鉴于此，游客设施也进行了重新调整，以满足国家步道的游客需求。咖啡厅与卫生间被迁到收费景区外围，满足短暂停留但不想购票参观景区的游客需求。游客中心还配置供家庭休息的空间，即使踩着泥泞的鞋子也可以进入，扩大了使用人群的范围。博得瓦德要塞内部大部分建筑结构都在地下，这意味着相较于豪塞斯戴兹要塞，游客理解博得瓦德遗址的难度更大。因此，博得瓦德景区组织了大型的表演重现活动，为遗址注入活力。

Fig.2 Birdoswald Roman Fort live interpretation（© English Heritage Trust）.
图 2 博得瓦德罗马要塞阐释（© 英格兰遗产信托）。

切斯特罗马要塞是哈德良长城遗址中交通最方便的景区之一，对乘坐大巴参观的游客来说尤其便利。切斯特坐落在典雅宁静的田园风光之中，游客在参观时可以安静地散散步，享用茶点，感受觅得“沧海遗珠”的喜悦感。重新定位这里的呈现方式是为了在不破坏气氛的情况下，突显切斯特独特的氛围。

切斯特遗址是在古董收藏者与考古学先驱约翰·克莱顿的花园里发现的。哈德良长城沿线开展最早的一些考古发掘就是由克莱顿于19世纪率先组织的。起初，很多出土文物都陈列在他的花园里对外展示。在

archaeological context. A key aim of the project was to help visitors make the link between the many objects in the museum and the site from which they came. Architectural objects mounted on large plinths are sited near large windows, allowing visitors to think of the archaeology in the context of a large, richly decorated public space.

The museum is curated using themes inspired by everyday life. It explores the changing appearance of the town over its long life, and the stories of its residents, to which visitors can personally relate: their desires to make a settled home, ply a trade and live a comfortable life.

The text in this museum has more detail and nuance than in the exhibits at Birdoswald. The culture-seeking visitors are typically happy to make their own connections between stories and are prepared to spend longer exploring the exhibits in depth.

Each of the small **free-to enter sites** in English Heritage's guardianship have received new interpretation signage in the last three years. Though simple in comparison to the larger projects, the scheme of each of these has been designed to the same principles. Each panel introduces the whole Wall, in order to allow it to provide context for a visitor who might only visit that site. However, every panel also highlights an aspect of the site's archaeology that is unique, revealing, or even puzzling; this approach helps to build a developing picture for the visitor, especially those who are walking along the Wall and who will be visiting several sites. Vivid new representations allow visitors to quickly get a sense of how a site may once have looked, while a walker's guide at the top of each panel links the sites together.

All the panels follow the same template so the interpretation can enhance English Heritage's visibility across the Wall. Illustrations of all the smaller sites are repeated within the Birdoswald visitor centre, and consistency in presentation helps to link the individual small sites into a larger experience for walkers.

Broadly, all the new interpretation has been recognised as an improvement to visitors' experiences, scoring particularly highly in the evaluations received from English's Heritage's primary target audiences. There is still work to do to broaden the interpretation for secondary audiences: at Birdoswald, in particular, the interpretive experience for independent adults, visiting without families, could be enhanced. However, the increased engagement of the visitors at all sites shows the benefit of talking to your audiences, understanding what they are looking for, and tailoring their experiences to meet their needs.

Further Reading
深入阅读材料

Interpretation practice
阐释方法

Brochu, L. 2003 Interpretive Planning, InterpPress.

L·布罗楚 . 2003. 遗产阐释规划 . 遗产阐释出版社.

Brochu, L., & Merriman, T. 2002 *Personal Interpretation: Connecting your Audience to Heritage Resources*, InterpPress

L·布罗楚， T·梅里曼 . 2002 . 个性化阐释：连接观众与遗产资源 . 遗产阐释出版社.

Ham, S. H, 2013 *Interpretation - Making a Difference on Purpose*, Fulcrum Publishing.

S . H · 海姆. 2013 . 遗产阐释——目标的意义 . 支点出版社.

Ward, C & Wilkinson, A. 2006 Conducting Meaningful Interpretation: A Field Guide for Success, Fulcrum Publishing.

C · 瓦德， A · 威尔金逊 . 2006 . 进行有意义的遗产阐释——成功的实践指南 . 支点出版社.

Slack, S. (due 2020) *Interpreting Heritage: a Guide to Planning and Practice*, Routledge *[contains a case study of Birdoswald Roman Fort]*

他去世后不久，建起了一座博物馆将这些文物收藏展陈。约翰·克莱顿博物馆是一个氛围奇特的珍宝馆，富有爱德华时期[1]的布局与特色，十分罕见。为了保留这种氛围，我们下了许多功夫。虽然阐释的内容具有现代感，但展陈的布局和外观都保留了爱德华时期的风格。数字展品目录以单色的电子书形式展示，而没使用液晶显示屏幕。

Fig.3 The beautiful landscape of Chesters Roman Fort (© English Heritage Trust).
图 3 切斯特罗马要塞的美丽景观（© 英格兰遗产信托）。

在一个拥有开放空间、适合独处、鸟鸣声不绝于耳的绿地公园背景下，重现一个古老的军事基地的繁忙景象颇具挑战性，而且大部分遗迹如今还埋藏在草地下面。在切斯特遗址周围设置的瞭望点可以令参观者直观地领略原来的军事基地的布局和与规模，及其原来使用者的活动。

家庭并不是切斯特确定的目标参观人群。尽管如此，故事性的寻找任务鼓励参观者去探索切斯特要塞中的所有建筑，增加了家庭游客在此停留的时间。

Fig.4 Overlaying an artist's impression onto a view of Chesters Roman Fort (© English Heritage Trust).
图 4 在切斯特罗马要塞安装一件艺术作品（© 英格兰遗产信托）。

科布里奇罗马小镇的知名度不高，但它的博物馆却拥有世界一流的文物馆藏。与哈德良长城其他考古遗址不同的是，科布里奇不仅是罗马军队的基地，还是一座罗马时期的城镇。因此，科布里奇的文物还呈现居住在罗马帝国边界地区平民的生活。

在经过更新后，科布里奇的遗产阐释寻求吸引“文化独行者”型游客前来参观。阐释方式以引人注目的陈列展品、层次丰富的故事与高质量的陈放设施为特色。虽然博物馆体量不大，但新的阐释方式致力于以

1 爱德华时期的博物馆主要通过玻璃展柜展陈，通常配有手写的展品介绍。——译者注

S · 斯莱克.（预计2020年出版）. 遗产阐释——规划与实践指南. 罗德里奇出版社（书中包含博得瓦德罗马要塞案例）.

Audience insight
游客意见

Morris Hargreaves Mcintyre 2006 Audience Knowledge Digest https://www.culturehive.co.uk/wp-content/uploads/2013/04/audience-knowledge-digest1.pdf
莫里斯·哈格里夫斯·麦金太尔. 2006. 参观者知识摘要https://www.culturehive.co.uk/wp-content/uploads/2013/04/audience-knowledge-digest1.pdf

English Heritage Trust
英格兰遗产信托

www.english-heritage.org.uk/about-us/our-priorities/
www.english-heritage.org.uk/about-us/our-priorities/

Hadrian's Wall
哈德良长城

Adkins, G. and Mills, N. 2011 *Frontiers of the Roman Empire World Heritage Site - Hadrian's Wall Interpretation Framework*, Hadrian's Wall Heritage Ltd, Perth.
G · 艾德金斯，N · 米尔斯. 2011. 罗马帝国边疆世界遗产地——哈德良长城遗产阐释框架.哈德良长城文化遗产有限出版社. 珀斯.
Adkins, G. and Holmes, N. 2011. *Frontiers of the Roman Empire World Heritage Site - Hadrian's Wall Interpretation Framework: Public Engagement Appendix*, Hadrian's Wall Heritage Ltd.
G · 艾德金斯，N · 霍尔姆斯. 2011. 罗马帝国边疆世界遗产地——哈德良长城遗产阐释框架：公众参与附录. 哈德良长城文化遗产有限出版社. 珀斯.

Online resources
网上资料

Association for Heritage Interpretation (UK) https://ahi.org.uk/
遗产阐释协会（英国） https://ahi.org.uk/
European Association for Heritage Interpretation http://www.interpret-europe.net
欧洲遗产阐释协会http://www.interpret-europe.net
National Association for Interpretation (USA) www.interpnet.com
国家遗产阐释协会（美国） www.interpnet.com
Boys, D. 2017 *We'll Do The Content Ourselves*, Association of Heritage Interpretation https://ahi.org.uk/wp-content/uploads/2017/12/journal-22-1.pdf p.18
D · 博伊斯 . 2017 . 内容由我作主 . 遗产阐释协会.

世界一流的展陈，突出文物的重要价值，以此吸引独具慧眼的参观者。

科布里奇的文物数量在地区名列前茅，藏品就存放在距离其出土的建筑与考古遗址数米之遥的地方。阐释项目的一个关键目标是帮助参观者将博物馆中诸多展品与其出土的遗址联系起来。放置在大型基座上建筑构件，陈列在大幅窗旁，使观众可以在一个开阔并且精心装饰的公共空间中体验考古遗址并思考相关问题。

Fig.5 Corbridge Roman Town museum (© English Heritage Trust).
图 5 科布里奇罗马小镇博物馆（© 英格兰遗产信托）。

博物馆利用日常生活的主题进行策展，介绍了漫长历史过程中小镇面貌的变迁，以及居民的故事，游客可以与罗马时期的居民产生共鸣，切身体验他们想要安家立业、过上舒适生活的愿望。

相比博得瓦德要塞的展品，科布里奇博物馆的解释文本具有更多细节信息。“文化独行者”类型的参观者通常乐于自行品味其中的内涵和背景，也愿意花费更长的时间深入观赏各个展品。

近三年以来，由遗产信托为其监管的每个免费参观的小型遗迹都设立了新的阐释指示牌。虽然与大型阐释项目相比，这些阐释设施更加简单，但其设计都遵循着相同的原则。所有指示牌都包含了对哈德良长城的整体介绍，这样即使只参观一处遗址的游客也可以掌握更全面的背景。与此同时每块指示牌还突显了相应的考古遗迹的独特性、包含的独特信息，以及还存在哪些未解之谜。这种方式有助于为游客构建一个动态展示图景，对于沿着哈德良长城徒步和参观多个遗址的游客来说尤其有帮助。生动而新颖的图示令游客能够很快领略遗迹原貌，指示牌上方的步行者指南则将各个遗址联系起来。

所有的指示牌都采用相同模板，这样一来也可以突显遗产信托在哈德良长城遗产中的品牌认知度。在博得瓦德罗马要塞的游客中心，所有小型遗址的指示牌再次集中统一展示。这种展示的一致性和统一性有助于将各个小型遗迹与完整的游览体验联系起来。

总体来说，所有新的阐释都获得了认可，提升了游客的体验，尤其在遗产信托的主要目标参观者中广受好评。当然拓充遗产阐释、吸引小众参观者方面还有许多工作需要完成，特别是在博得瓦德要塞，对没有与家庭一同出行的成年游客来说，阐释质量有待提升。不论如何，通过与参观者沟通、了解他们的诉求、尊重游客体验，使游客在各个遗产点的参与度均得到提升，取得积极效果。

5.5 REDISCOVERING THE ANTONINE WALL

Patricia Weeks
Historic Environment Scotland - Edinburgh -UK

Abstract

The Rediscovering the Antonine Wall Project is a three-year programme aimed at enhancing local community engagement with the World Heritage Site. It consists of both capital projects as well as a range of initiatives targeted at increasing community participation. This paper outlines how the programme was developed and reviews the progress made in achieving its objectives in the first year of its operation.

Keywords: community engagement, community participation

INTRODUCTION

The Antonine Wall marks the North-Western frontier of the Roman Empire in the second century AD. It was built on the orders of the Emperor Antoninus Pius, the successor to Hadrian, but only occupied for a generation before troops retreated south to the former frontier of Hadrian's Wall. The Antonine Wall cuts across central Scotland, running for some 41 miles between the Firth of Clyde and the Firth of Forth. It runs through the jurisdictions of five local governments each of which, along with Historic Environment Scotland, are Partners in the Antonine Wall Steering Group which oversees and directs the management of the World Heritage Site. Each of these Partners is actively involved in the management and promotion of the Wall.

The Rediscovering the Antonine Wall Project emerged from the five-year Management Plan for the Wall, published in 2014 (Historic Environment Scotland 2014a). The Plan set out the objective of Steering Group Partners for the communities living along the Wall to more be actively engaged with the World Heritage Site. The project aims to use our Roman heritage for the benefit of local communities and their economies, and to make the Antonine Wall interesting, exciting and accessible to everyone. In particular it seeks to engage with people who have not traditionally been interested in heritage.

A key element of the project is to raise the profile of the Wall, as earlier research had revealed that few people knew much about it (Historic Environment Scotland 2014b). The sites that comprise the Wall are very diverse and only some sections are publicly accessible. Although all these sections are open access (free to enter) sites, they can often only be reached via a muddy walk, or up a steep hill. While visitor interpretation on each site has recently been updated, in many cases the ephemeral nature of the visible remains makes it difficult for general visitors to understand the remains. Although the Wall runs through some of the most heavily populated areas of Scotland, these areas include some of Scotland's most deprived communities. One of the challenges facing the project has been how to engage everyone. Many local communities are not actively engaged with the Wall even though it lies on their doorstep, and many areas suffer from a lack of amenities and are in need of regeneration.

PROJECT DEVELOPMENT AND FUNDING

The project-development phase began with a series of around fifteen community consultation events, across all of the five council areas. We strongly believed that all elements of the project should be co-designed and co-curated

5.5 “安东尼长城再发现”项目

帕特丽夏·威克斯
苏格兰遗产委员会—爱丁堡—英国

摘要

“安东尼长城再发现”是一个为期三年的项目，旨在加强安东尼长城沿线社区与世界遗产地的联系。项目包含若干建设项目，以及一系列社区参与活动。本文概述项目的立项过程，并总结在项目运行的第一年里为实现目标取得的进展。

关键词：动员社区　社区参与

绪论

安东尼长城确立了罗马帝国边疆的西北边界，建于公元 2 世纪。长城由哈德良大帝的继任者安东尼·皮乌斯皇帝下令修建，建成后罗马军团仅在此驻守几十年，之后便向南回撤至原哈德良长城的边界。安东尼长城横亘苏格兰中部，西起克莱德湾，东至福斯湾，全长约 41 英里[1]。现在安东尼长城途经五个行政区。这五个地方政府与苏格兰遗产委员会一起成立了安东尼长城领导小组，负责监督和指导安东尼长城世界遗产地的管理。领导小组中的每个成员机构都积极参与长城的管理与宣传。

“安东尼长城再发现”项目是在 2014 年发布的为期五年的《长城管理规划》（苏格兰遗产委员会，2014a）中提出来的。在《规划》中，安东尼长城领导小组提出目标，希望长城沿线社区更加积极地与安东尼长城世界遗产相融合。项目旨在利用罗马时期的文化遗产造福地方社区，带动地方经济，并且将安东尼长城的形象打造成对所有人都生动有趣、富有吸引力和可以密切接触的遗产地。项目尤其希望能够吸引那些原本对文化遗产不感兴趣的受众。

项目最希望实现的关键目标是提高长城的认知度，因为之前研究表明公众对安东尼长城知之甚少（苏格兰遗产委员会，2014b）。安东尼长城遗址类型多样，但大部分段落人迹罕至。尽管长城全线都是开放的（可自由进入），但往往需要穿过泥泞的道路或攀登陡峭的山坡才能抵达。此外，虽然近期更新了长城各处的遗产说明标志牌，但由于大多数可见的遗迹现象十分零散，普通参观者理解的难度还是很大。安东尼长城一些段落经过苏格兰人口最稠密的地区，而这些地区恰好也是最贫困的社区。因此，项目面临的挑战之一是如何动员每一个人参与其中。虽然长城近在咫尺，许多地方社区却缺乏参与的热情，还有很多区域则急需配套设施与重建。

项目前期工作与资金来源

项目开始阶段，在长城沿线所有 5 个行政辖区内开展了 15 个社区征求意见活动。我们坚信项目的每项

1　约合 66 千米。——译者注

with the local communities, so we were open to all ideas that they might bring forward. This work led to a series of capital and community projects being developed and submitted for consideration by the National Lottery Heritage Fund (NLHF), our main funder.

The NLHF bid was approved in 2018 and the project began in November that year. It is a three-year project with a total cost of £2.1 million, with the funding from the NLHF being supplemented by financial contributions from LEADER[1], several landfill tax[2] funds, and from Partners' funds. Our project manager had been in post for over a year by the time the funding package was approved, and the appointment of the rest of the team quickly followed in the early half of 2019. There are two development officers plus a part-time administration officer. To meet the diverse range of projects proposed by the local communities during the consultation process, the project has been split into several sections.

CAPITAL PROJECTS

There are two important capital project strands: children's playparks and the erection of replica Roman distance-stones.

We are constructing five Roman-themed playparks, one in each council area. Each design is unique, telling the story of their local section of Wall: they were initially designed by local schoolchildren, and then adapted by play companies to meet health and safety and construction standards. Together, the five sites create a 'playpark trail' along the Wall and offer an opportunity to engage families and encourage them to visit the archaeological remains of the Wall nearby and further afield.

The first playpark, at Callendar Park (Fig.1), opened in August 2019 and takes its inspiration from the nearby fort at Falkirk. 'Attack and defence' are the themes here (trampolines replicate the defensive *lilia*[3] pits of the original Wall), and there are allusions to the hoard of Roman coins found in the area. Provision is made for those with special access needs, including wheelchair access to the sandpit and picnic benches and a wheelchair-friendly roundabout.

The second capital strand is the production and installation of five replica Roman distance-stones, one in each local authority area. The distance-stones are a distinctive feature of the Antonine Wall: elaboratively carved stone slabs which were set up by the legionary soldiers who built the Wall to mark the length of the barrier that they had completed. An important part of this project is about regenerating areas along the Wall which suffer from deprivation and lack of financial investment. The idea stemmed from a community project in 2013 to place an exact replica of the Bridgeness distance-stone in Bo'ness, Falkirk, at the east end of the Wall. For each stone, the community has been involved in the creation of its design and that of its landscape setting.

Each distance-stone will be a unique response to the site on which it is being placed, and two stones will feature sculptures of Roman soldiers, to improve their visibility in the landscape (Fig.2). The work is backed up by academic research at Glasgow University, funded by Historic Environment Scotland, to examine the residual colour that has been identified on the original distance-stones; the aim is to develop a colour palette, so that at least one stone can be recreated to reflect its original full colour.

Coloured digital versions will also be recreated in collaboration with students from City of Glasgow College who have created waterproof 3D digital models for us. This work has been run as a student design competition with the College's Computing Department, and further collaboration is taking place with the College's stonemasonry

1 LEADER is a programme funded from the European Union which aims to support environmental, community and regeneration initiatives in deprived rural areas.

2 Landfill taxes are paid by waste-disposal companies and are used to support natural and cultural environmental conservation projects.

3 *Lilia* are pits which were dug immediately in front of the Antonine Wall as additional obstacles to attackers, and which archaeological evidence suggests contained wooden stakes.

Fig.1 Callendar Playpark (© Crown Copyright: Historic Environment Scotland).
图 1 卡伦德主题游乐园（© 皇家版权：苏格兰遗产委员会）。

内容都应该与当地社区共同设计与策划，这有助于更好地吸纳社区所提出的建议。征询到的意见最终汇集成一系列建设项目和社区活动方案，提交到主要出资方英国文化遗产彩票基金会（National Lottery Heritage Fund，缩写为NLHF）进行审议。

2018 年，申请 NLHF 资助的方案获得批准，项目于同年 11 月正式启动。该项目历时3年，经费共计210万英镑。主要资金来自 NLHF，部分资金则来自欧盟LEADER项目[2]，填埋税[3]基金和领导小组成员机构捐助。项目方案获批时，已经有一名项目经理上任超过一年，团队其他工作人员的聘用工作也很快在2019年上半年完成。团队共包括两位全职的项目管理人员和一位兼职行政管理人员。由于征求意见阶段社区提出的需求类型差别很大，项目分成多个板块。

建设项目

建设项目主要由两项内容组成，一是兴建儿童主题游乐园，二是竖立复制的罗马里程石碑。

项目建造了五个罗马主题乐园，五个行政区每区一个。每个主题乐园的设计都别具匠心，根据各自长城区段的特点分别讲述不同的故事。乐园由当地学校的学生操刀设计，再由相关公司根据安全、健康和工程标准进行调整。五个主题乐园在安东尼长城沿线串联成一条“游乐园线路”，吸引举家出游的参观者，鼓励他们去参观临近游乐园或者较远的长城考古遗迹。

2019 年 8 月，首个主题游乐园卡伦德乐园（见图 1）正式开放，其设计灵感来自于附近的福尔柯克要塞。卡伦德乐园以“攻防”为主题，利用蹦床还原了长城上原有的防御工事“防御坑”[4]。设计中还包括附近发现的罗马金币宝藏元素。为了满足特殊需求，乐园设置了通往沙坑和野餐长椅的轮椅通道，以及方便轮椅通行的环形路线。

建设项目的另一项重要内容是在每个辖区内制作并竖立一块复制的罗马时期里程石碑。里程石碑是安东尼长城独有的标志。它由石板精心雕琢而成，是负责建造长城的军团士兵为了标记已经完成的墙体长度而竖立起来的。项目最重要的目标之一是复兴长城沿线贫困、缺乏投资的地区。设置石碑的提议来源于2013年的一个社区项目。该项目在安东尼长城东端福尔柯克辖区博内斯镇设置了一座 1:1 复制的布里根

2 LEADER是一项由欧盟出资的项目，目标是支持贫困农村地区的环境、社区和复兴计划。
3 填埋税是一项由废物处理公司支付的税款，用于支持自然与文化环境保护项目。
4 “防御坑”（拉丁语为 lilia）是紧贴安东尼长城墙外挖掘的深坑，以增加攻城的难度与障碍，考古证据表明坑内曾竖有木桩。

students to create the actual stone replicas. Wherever possible, the project is providing opportunities for training and the development of craft skills for students and apprentices.

COMMUNITY PROJECTS

We are also working to develop a strong volunteer programme, called the '21st Century Legion', to offer people skills training and engagement opportunities, and building individuals' capabilities along the Wall. There are several roles in which people can participate: these include being researchers, tour guides, or ambassadors for the Wall, each of whom will work alongside communities and project staff. To help them understand the wider context of the Antonine Wall (as part of the Frontiers of the Roman Empire World Heritage Site) additional funding was secured from LEADER to allow us to take some of these volunteers to visit our sister sites at Hadrian's Wall and the German Limes.

As well as managing these core projects, the project team engages in other outreach and learning events. This is proving to be a valuable way of targeting harder-to-reach audiences and including them within the scope of the project. Working with Scout groups along the Wall will include a 'Big Roman Camp Out' event, where they will live under canvas like Romans and will explore cooking and living in period style using specially sourced replica utensils. We have also been promoting existing resources to schools, such as our worksheets and the downloads available on our website. These include an app with 3D models and augmented reality (Historic Environment Scotland 2019a), and an interactive game called 'Go Roman' (Historic Environment Scotland 2019b) which can be used in the classroom alongside more traditional hands-on resources (Fig.3). Throughout the project, opportunities will be taken to further develop material for educational audiences and to add these to the resources on the Antonine Wall website.

Perhaps the part of the Rediscovering the Antonine Wall project that will have the most impact has been the thirty co-designed and co-curated community projects, six in each of the council areas. To reach out to a youth audience we have taken forward a mural street-art project, employing contemporary urban art and design specialists to work with young people to create five new murals. As well as allowing young people to share their responses to the Wall, the project will give them the chance to work with internationally renowned artists. The final works, located in towns and communities with areas of high footfall, will create yet another positive advertisement for the Antonine Wall.

At the other end of the age spectrum, we are collaborating with an organisation called Cycling Without Age, to fund electric trishaws for elderly residents in communities on the Wall. Based on an original concept from Denmark, the aim of the work is to encourage residents in local care-homes and sheltered housing, who may not otherwise be able to get out and about, to have the chance both to socialise and to visit local heritage sites. In one of the trial sessions, one of the participants had not left their care home for nearly a year but took two trips out on the trishaw and loved every moment of the experience.

Other community projects are based on improving local areas around the Wall. At Bearsden there are the remains of a Roman bathhouse, currently run by Historic Environment Scotland as a visitor attraction. One key problem is that it is only part of what was a much wider Roman site: the fort itself is now hidden under housing. We were approached by the Baptist Church who own the adjacent house and grounds to help them with an interpretation / community space project that would benefit both locals and visitors. They are working to create mosaics, with designs based on the evidence of Roman dietary practices that was revealed by the bathhouse excavations; these will be added to a Roman themed garden, growing plants evidenced from the excavations. The Church is also developing ideas for art and interpretive installations - such as an immersive sound-cloud that will suggest noises that may have been heard in the Roman fort - and other ways to enable local schools and tourists to enjoy the gardens.

内斯里程石碑[5]。在每一块石碑的图案设计和周边环境设计中，社区都参与了进来。

因此，每块里程石碑都以独特方式与周边环境相呼应，其中两块里程碑将雕刻为罗马士兵形式（如图 2所示），使其从周围环境中凸显出来。里程石碑的复制工作获得了格拉斯哥大学的学术科研支持与苏格兰遗产委员会的资助。科研确定了里程石碑原件上残留的色彩，以此为基础研发出来一套色板，以确保至少有一块复制的石碑可以还原其原来的色彩。

此外，格拉斯哥城市学院还将与我们合作重建彩色数字石碑。早先的3 D数字模型就是由他们制作的，由学院的计算机系以学生设计竞赛的方式展开。随后，还将继续与学院石艺专业的学生合作，共同制作石碑的实体复制品。总之，项目竭尽所能地为学生与工匠提供培训和精进技艺的机会。

Fig.2 Design for sculpture at Croy Hill (© Rediscovering the Antonine Wall Project).
图 2 克洛伊山 雕塑设计图（© 安东尼长城再发现项目）。

社区活动

我们还致力于打造一个名为“21 世纪军团”的重磅志愿项目，为人们提供技能培训和参与活动的机会，协助长城沿线居民提升个人能力。人们可以选择参与不同性质的工作，包括长城相关的研究、导游或者宣传工作，同其他社区志愿者和项目团队并肩工作。此外，为了帮助参与者更好地了解安东尼长城作为罗马帝国边疆世界遗产一部分的重要价值，LEADER 项目还提供了额外资金，使我们得以带领部分志愿者参观姊妹遗产地哈德良长城和德国上日尔曼-雷蒂亚长城。

除了组织上述核心活动以外，项目团队还组织了诸多外延活动与教育活动。事实证明，这些活动可以有效地鼓励更多的人参与到项目之中。通过与长城沿线的童子军组织合作，举办了“罗马大露营”活动，组织孩子们像罗马人一样住在帆布帐篷之中，用特别复制的罗马时期餐具烹饪，复原罗马时期生活的原貌。与此同时，我们还寻求在校园推广现有的学习资源，例如团队编制的安东尼长城小练习，以及官网上不少可供下载的资料。具体来说，官网上提供了三维立体模型与增强现实的应用程序（苏格兰遗产委员会，2019a），名为“出发吧罗马人”的互动游戏（苏格兰遗产委员会，2019b），可用于辅助课堂中的传统动手练习（见图 3）。随着项目的推进，团队着力深入开发更多教育资源，新资源也将上线安东尼长城官网，以供教学使用。

安东尼长城再发现项目中可能最具公众影响的活动将是共同设计、共同策划的下面三十个社区项目，均衡分布在五个行政辖区。为了吸引年轻参与者，我们推出街头壁画艺术活动，聘请当代城市艺术专家与设计专家与年轻人在每个社区创作一幅壁画新品，该项目共产生五幅新的壁画作品。这不仅为年轻人抒发长城情怀提供了平台，还给予他们与国际知名艺术家共事的机会。这些壁画设置在城镇与社区人流密集的

5　布里根内斯里程石碑（Bridgeness distance-stone）：为罗马时期里程碑，在位于苏格兰博内斯福尔柯克辖区博内斯镇的布里根内斯被发现，被视为苏格兰现存雕刻最精细、保存最完整的里程碑。——译者注

Finally, along the Wall we hope to work specifically with asylum-seekers and refugees who have relocated to Scotland, so as to better understand how their stories relate to the Wall, weaving them into its wider narrative. The Romans typically moved soldiers around the Empire, often sending auxiliaries far from their native provinces to reduce the risk of localised rebellion. As a result, there were significant numbers of Roman soldiers, as well as traders and their families, living on the Antonine Wall from Syria, from north Africa, and from other countries across Europe. The project will explore some of their stories and experiences, comparing these with those of the communities living near the site today.

At the end of the first year of the project, community feedback has been very positive. As they have helped to design the projects and significant elements of the capital strands, the communities feel a strong sense of ownership of both the project and, increasingly, of the Wall. Social media has shown improved awareness and mention of the Antonine Wall online, and this is growing steadily. The wide range of projects that have been brought forward by the communities is impressive, and has opened up the Wall to a whole new range of audiences. Whilst the project team has faced many challenges in delivering such an ambitious project, the supportive feedback we have received and the happy faces we have seen have made it all worthwhile.

References
参考文献

Historic Environment Scotland. 2014a. *Antonine Wall World Heritage Site Management Plan*, Edinburgh, available at <https://www.antoninewall.org/system/files/documents/494733_283836_Antonine_Wall_MP_WEB_20131125134011.pdf>

苏格兰遗产委员会. 2014a. 安东尼长城世界遗产管理规划. 爱丁堡. 可见：<https://www.antoninewall.org/system/files/documents/494733_283836_Antonine_Wall_MP_WEB_20131125134011.pdf>

Historic Environment Scotland. 2014b. *Antonine Wall World Heritage Site Interpretation and Access Strategy*, Edinburgh, available at https://www.antoninewall.org/system/files/documents/Interpretation%20Plan%20and%20Access%20Strategy.pdf

苏格兰遗产委员会.2014b安东尼长成世界遗产地阐释与开放策略. 爱丁堡. 可见：<https://www.antoninewall.org/system/files/documents/Interpretation%20Plan%20and%20Access%20Strategy.pdf>

Historic Environment Scotland. 2019a. Antonine Wall World Heritage Site, Antonine Wall App, available at <https://www.antoninewall.org/visiting-the-wall/download-the-app>

苏格兰遗产委员会. 2019a. 安东尼长城世界遗产地. 安东尼长城 app.可见：<https://www.antoninewall.org/visiting-the-wall/download-the-app>

Historic Environment Scotland. 2019b. Antonine Wall World Heritage Site Go Roman Game, available at <https://www.antoninewall.org/learning-centre/primary/digital-game>

苏格兰遗产委员会. 2019b. 安东尼长城世界遗产地"出发吧罗马人"游戏. 可见：<https://www.antoninewall.org/learning-centre/primary/digital-game>

位置，完成后将成为安东尼长城又一亮丽的广告宣传。

针对年长的参与者，项目团队与“单车兜风无年限”组织合作，集资为长城沿线社区的长者提供了电动三轮车。这一理念源自丹麦，目标是鼓励当地养老院与护理机构中原本无法外出的老人参与社交，参观当地的文化遗产地。活动测试阶段，一名近一年没有踏出护理中心半步的参与者两度搭乘三轮车兜风，十分享受这份体验 。

还有其他社区活动以改善长城周边社区境况为目标。在贝尔斯登，有部分罗马浴场遗迹作为旅游景点对公众开放，目前由苏格兰遗产委员会运营。一个关键问题是，这些遗迹只是范围更大的罗马遗址的一部分，其中要塞遗址目前还埋压在附近的房屋之下。房屋与土地的所有者浸礼教会与我们取得联系，希望协助他们一起开辟一个展示空间和社区活动空间，使当地居民和参观者都可获益。基于浴室遗址考古发掘证据，教会组织设计制作了与罗马时期饮食习惯相关的马赛克图案。马赛克将装饰在罗马主题花园中，还将参照考古发掘证据种植罗马时期的植物。此外，教会还尝试利用装置艺术解读遗产，比如安装沉浸式环绕音响重现当年在罗马要塞可能听到的声音，以及其他方式使当地学校和参观者在花园获得更好的体验。

Fig.3 Educational resources developed for the Antonine Wall (© Crown Copyright: Historic Environment Scotland) .
图 3 安东尼长城相关教育资源（© 皇家版权：苏格兰遗产委员会）。

最后，项目团队还特别希望与移居苏格兰的难民与避难者展开合作，让他们更好地理解其经历与安东尼长城之间的联系，融入安东尼长城更宏阔的背景中。罗马帝国通常在帝国境内大范围调遣士兵，尤其是将辅助军团士兵调离故土，以此减少地方叛乱的风险。正是因此，有大量罗马士兵以及商人与家眷聚居于安东尼长城脚下，他们来自叙利亚、北非和欧洲各个国家。项目挖掘他们的故事和经历，将其与今天生活在长城附近的族群联系起来。

项目开展的第一年年末，社区的反馈十分积极。遗产地附近的社区共同参与了项目策划，参与了建设项目很多内容的设计，因此对项目产生很强的主人翁意识，从而对安东尼长城的主人翁意识也与日俱增。社交媒体显示居民对安东尼长城的理解越来越深入，关注度持续提升，并且还在稳步增长。社区设计的一系列活动令人耳目一新，印象深刻，也将安东尼长城推向了全新的受众群体。虽然在实施这样一个目标宏伟的项目时团队遭遇了诸多挑战，但收到的积极反馈和参与者幸福洋溢的笑容令一切付出都有了回报。

5.6 中国长城保护员纪实

刘文艳
中国文化遗产研究院—中国—北京

梁庆立
长城保护员—中国—河北

摘要

为解决长城遗产特点与管理条件之间的矛盾，中国探索实施了长城保护员制度，在一定程度上解决了长城看护难的问题。本文通过对梁庆立——名有着6年长城巡查工作经验的年轻长城保护员进行跟踪访谈，真实记录他的实际工作，并提出长城保护员工作需要思考的现实问题。

关键字：长城保护员　巡查

一、背景—中国长城保护员制度

中国长城保护员制度的前身是各地根据《文物保护法》，对尚未设置专门文物保护机构的古遗址、古墓葬、古建筑等不可移动文物以聘请文物保护员的形式进行看护管理。

长城分布地域广，且多位于人迹罕至和经济欠发达地区，完全依靠政府、文物部门现有的力量对其进行全线实时监控和管理难度极高。各地探索在长城沿线居民中以聘请保护员的方式，让他们担负起定期巡查、及时发现和反映问题、向当地群众宣传长城保护的责任。1980年代起，一些地区开始聘请看护长城的文物保护员，但这些保护员通常需要看管除长城外的其他文物。

2003年河北秦皇岛试点施行长城保护员制度。2006-2011年全国长城资源调查，包括长城保护员在内的长城保护管理工作得到各级国家文物行政管理部门的重视。2006年国务院颁布了《长城保护条例》，明确规定“地处偏远、没有利用单位的长城段落，所在地县级人民政府或者其文物主管部门可以聘请长城保护员对长城进行巡查、看护，并对长城保护员给予适当补助”，以法律形式正式确认了长城保护员制度。为规范长城保护员的聘用、管理等，2015年下半年，国家文物局委托中国文化遗产研究院开展了长城保护员信息汇总、核实、审查工作，完成了当时所有长城保护员信息的备案。2016年，国家文物局出台了《长城保护员管理办法》，明确了长城保护员的聘用条件、责任等，为各省文物主管部门聘请长城保护员提供了更具针对性的制度依据。

长城保护员既可以弥补文物管理工作人员不足，保护管理覆盖不及时的问题，又能调动和发挥长城沿线居民认识、宣传、保护长城的积极性。截至2016年4月，长城沿线15个省（自治区、直辖市）备案长城保护员共3403人。

5.6 THE STORY OF A GREAT WALL PATROLLER

LIU WENYAN
Chinese Academy of Cultural Heritage - China - Beijing
LIANG QINGLI
Great Wall patroller - China - Hebei

Abstract

The geographical spread of the Great Wall across many remote regions presents enormous managerial challenges, particularly in terms of monitoring, inspection and protection. The scale of these challenges is far beyond the collective capacity of the government departments with responsibility for its management. To address this problem, China has developed the Great Wall Patroller Mechanism. This has greatly enhanced the capacity to inspect and protect the Great Wall. This paper describes the work done by Liang Qingli, a young man who became a Great Wall patroller in 2013. It presents a number of issues identified by Liang Qingli from his experience, which can inform future thinking about the work of the Great Wall patrollers.

Keywords: Great Wall patroller, inspection

BACKGROUND - THE CHINA GREAT WALL PATROLLER MECHANISM

The China Great Wall Patroller Mechanism grew out of the established practice, according to the Cultural Relics Protection Law, of local authorities recruiting patrollers to help protect immovable cultural relics, including archaeological sites, ancient tombs and historic buildings, which do not have dedicated management institutions.

Many sections of the Great Wall are in remote and underdeveloped areas. It was therefore extremely difficult to conduct real-time monitoring and management using only the existing capacity of the government and cultural relics departments. As a result, the local authorities explored recruiting residents along the Wall as patrollers who would be responsible for inspecting the Wall regularly, the early discovery and reporting of problems, and promoting protection of Great Wall to local people. Great Wall patrollers were recruited as early as the 1980's in some regions, though at that time their responsibilities extended beyond the Great Wall to include other cultural sites.

In 2003, Qinhuangdao City in Hebei Province launched a pilot project of the Great Wall Patroller Mechanism. In 2006, the Great Wall Protection Regulation was promulgated by the State Council, specified that 'for sections located in remote areas without identified users or owners to rely on, the local county-level People's government or the relevant cultural relics department can recruit Great Wall patrollers to inspect and maintain the Wall, and pay them appropriate allowances.' By this, the Great Wall Patroller Mechanism was officially recognised in law. To regulate the recruitment and management of the Great Wall patrollers, the Chinese Academy of Cultural Heritage (CACH), commissioned by the State Administration for Cultural Heritage (SACH), collated information about and established records for all the Great Wall patrollers active in the second half of 2015 and kept the records. In 2016, SACH promulgated Measures for the Management of the Great Wall Patrollers (MMGWP) defining the recruitment requirements and responsibilities of Great Wall patrollers, which provided provincial cultural relics departments

二、纪实——个长城保护员的故事

（一）从长城保护的志愿者到长城保护员

梁庆立，河北省唐山市迁西县金厂峪镇榆木岭村村民，一位80后长城保护员。

据他的祖辈说，明代万历年间，梁姓家族和叶姓、邢姓家族从山东一个叫做大柳树村的地方迁居至此修筑长城，而“梁姓”家族主要负责泥木工种。至今，在村子后山上存留的记事碑上还写着他的祖先—梁先业的名字。

与长城特殊的渊源，使梁庆立从小就着迷于关于长城的各种故事，村子里的老人们经常会讲起关于长城的战争、传说。世代口耳相传，让他从小就认为保护长城就是在继续祖先们的责任。2004年初中毕业后，他成为了一名长城保护的志愿者，从那时起他就经常在闲暇时间走上长城巡视，并多次制止破坏长城的事件。梁庆立的家步行至长城只需要半小时，地理位置的“优越性”加上长城保护志愿者的经历，2014年迁西县文物管理所就将他聘用为长城保护员。

（二）一名长城保护员工作职责

作为一名长城保护员，聘用他的迁西县文管所与梁庆立签订了聘用书，并根据他生活居住范围划定了他的“责任田”。梁庆立的看护范围是15千米的榆木岭长城墙体，以及17座位于墙体上的敌台，榆木岭长城附近的3座烽火台，和1座名叫榆木岭的关城。按照《长城保护员管理办法》，梁庆立需要履行主要的职责包括：巡查、看护长城以及长城保护标志和防护设施；定期向迁西县文管所报告长城保护状况和工作情况；及时报告长城自然损坏或者遭受环境地质灾害情况；发现破坏长城，或者在长城保护范围和建设控制地带内违法建设，擅自移除、破坏长城保护标志和其他有关防护设施，盗窃长城构件等违法犯罪行为，以及法律法规禁止在长城上从事的活动，及时向迁西县文管所和当地公安部门报告。

每隔3-5天，梁庆立就会骑着自己的摩托车来到榆木岭长城脚下，花3-4个小时沿着长城将自己的“责任田”巡查一遍。遇到雨季等特殊天气，或者旅游旺季，他还会增加巡查频率。成为一名长城保护员以来的6年里，他已经数十次次向迁西县文管所报告了长城受到破坏的情况。

除了巡查之外，遇到游人集中的时段或者长城容易出现险情的雨季梁庆立会在必经的“关卡”劝阻到访的旅友，不要攀爬危险的段落。每次巡查，他都会带着垃圾袋随手清理旅友遗留在长城上的垃圾，遇到游人踩踏滑落的砖石，他也会进行简单的归安。他也会利用自己巡查长城的机会，收集很多散落在长城附近以及周边村民手中的长城建筑构件（图1）。

（三）参与长城监测试点

让梁庆立感到自豪的是，他的工作为长城的专业“监测”提供了重要的支持。2016年，为加强长城日常监测的规范化和信息化，中国文化遗产研究院和国信思南合作开发了“长城监测巡查 APP”并着手在长城巡查工作中使用。梁庆立作为一名80后长城保护员，具有较好的学习能力，中国文化遗产研究院开始委托他进行APP的监测试点，选取他所巡视的长城点段中未对游客开放的5.9千米长城墙体及附属的敌台，每3-5天1次进行一次监测数据的采集，并将现场采集到的照片、记录等上传。2016–2018年试点期间共完成巡查249次，采集特定监测角度监测照片13,415张（图2）。不仅如此，通过他的反馈长城监测巡查APP功能更加完善，使用更符合一线工作的需要，并实际检验了利用手机APP开展长城日常监测的可行性和必要性。

with a more specified guidance.

Recruiting Great Wall patrollers increases the capacity and effectiveness of protection, and also promotes the engagement of local people along the Wall in understanding and protecting the Great Wall. By April 2016, there were 3,403 recorded Great Wall patrollers in 15 provinces, autonomous regions and direct municipalities along the Wall.

THE STORY OF A GREAT WALL PATROLLER

From volunteer to patroller of the Great Wall

Liang Qingli, a resident of Yumuling village, Jinchangyu town, Qianxi County, Tangshan City in Hebei Province, is a Great Wall patroller who was born in the 1980s.

According to his ancestors, between 1573 and 1620 in the Ming Dynasty, the Liang family together with the Ye and Xing families, who originally lived in the Big Willow village in Shandong Province, moved to Yumuling to build the Great Wall. The Liang family were mainly specialists in masonry and carpentry work. Today, the name of one of his ancestors, Liang Xianye, can still be found on a tablet standing on the mountainside behind the village.

Since his childhood this personal connection to the Great Wall has attracted Liang Qingli to immerse himself in various stories related to the Wall. The older people in the village always told stories of battles and legends related to the Wall. Liang Qingli has long believed that protecting the Great Wall is a way of continuing his ancestors' responsibilities. He became a volunteer to protect the Wall after graduation from junior high school in 2004. In his spare time he made his rounds along the Wall and dissuaded people from damaging it. His house is only half an hour's walk from the Wall. With such an advantage and his experience as a volunteer, he was recruited as a Great Wall patroller by the Qianxi County Cultural Relics Management Institute (QCCRMI) in 2014.

The Responsibilities as a Great Wall patroller

The QCCRMI signed a recruitment note with Liang Qingli and designated the area for which he would be responsible based on his location: a 15km-long section of the Yumuling Great Wall with 17 defence towers, 3 nearby beacon towers and the Yumuling Fortress. In accordance with MMGWP, Liang Qingli is mainly responsible for inspecting and taking care of the Great Wall, its official plaques and barriers preventing access to vulnerable sections of the Wall, and regularly reporting on its state of conservation to QCCRMI. He is also responsible for the early reporting to QCCRMI or local police authorities of any natural, environmental or geological damage to the Great Wall, and any illegal activity including damage to the Wall, illegal construction within the Great Wall protected area and the development control area, damage to signage and safety facilities, and theft of components and building materials from the Great Wall.

Liang Qingli rides his motorcycle to the foot of the Yumuling Great Wall every 3 to 5 days and hikes for 3 to 4 hours inspecting the section for which he is responsible. He checks the Wall even more frequently in at particular times of year such as the rainy and the tourist seasons. Over the past six years as a Great Wall patroller, he has reported dozens of instances of damage to the Great Wall.

Apart from inspecting the Wall, he also discourages visitors, as they approach the Wall, from climbing the most dangerous sections, particularly in the tourist and rainy seasons when visitor accidents are most likely to occur. Whenever he carries out his inspections, he brings a rubbish bag with him to pick up the litter that visitors have left on the Wall, and replaces any bricks and stones dislodged by people walking on the Wall. He also takes the opportunity to collect the pieces of the Great Wall he finds near the Wall or in villages in the surrounding areas (Fig.1).

Participation in the Great Wall monitoring pilot project

What makes Liang Qingli proud is the contribution he has made to the professional monitoring of the Great Wall.

图 1 梁庆立巡查中搜集的长城建筑构件和碑刻（摄影：梁庆立）。
Fig.1 Component parts and inscribed stones of the Great Wall collected by Liang Qingli during his inspection (photograph by Liang Qingli).

（四） 职责之外—为长城保护开展社会活动

梁庆立工作的场所不仅在长城上，他还将自己的"责任田"延伸到了长城周边。多年来，他利用巡查长城的便利，向居住在长城周边的村民宣传保护长城，在他的影响下，长城脚下的村民们自发地来到长城捡垃圾，来自唐山、天津、北京等各地越来越多的公益人士以各种方式参与长城保护（图 3）。长城脚下的学校也会邀请梁庆立，为小学生进行长城保护专题讲座，影响下一代保护长城的理念。

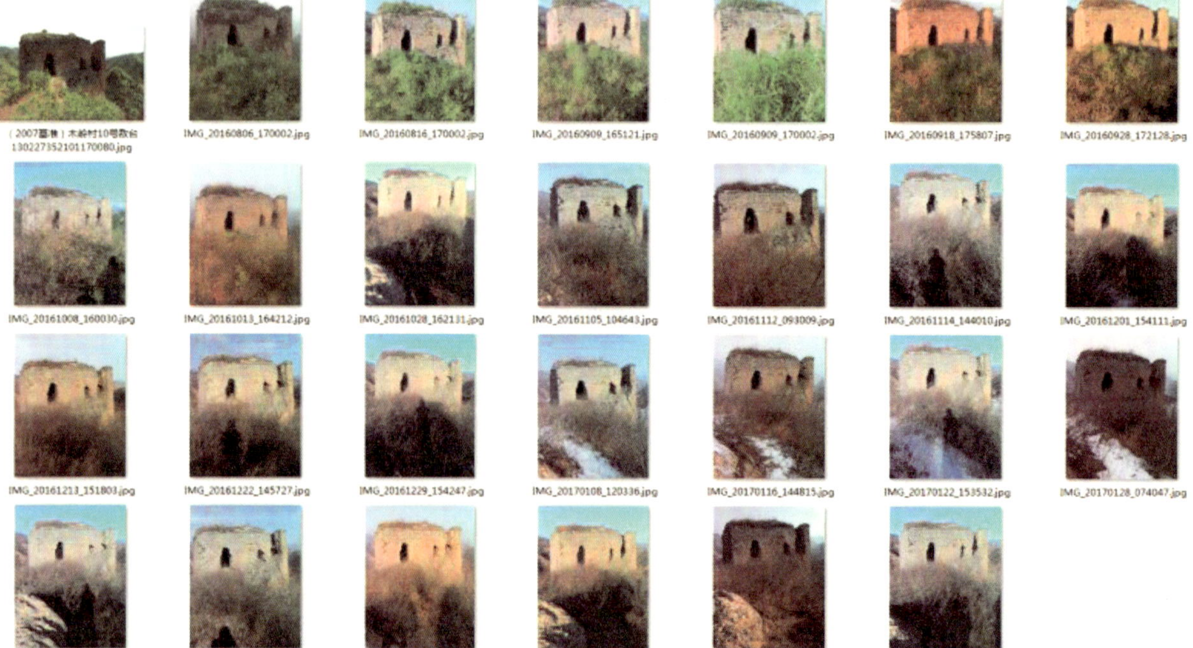

图 2 2016–2018 年梁庆立配合中国文化遗产研究院采集的监测数据（图片来源：张依萌）。
Fig.2 Monitoring data collected by Liang Qingli from 2016 to 2018 commissioned by the CACH (provided by Zhang Yimeng).

图 3 英国长城爱好者–威廉林赛捐赠垃圾袋（摄影：梁庆立）。
Fig.3 Garbage bag (above) donated by William Lindsay (below, second left), a UK Great Wall enthusiast. (Photographs by Liang Qingli).

In 2016 CACH cooperated with Geo-compass to co-develop a mobile phone application for Great Wall monitoring and inspection, to enable immediate recording and uploading of data onto a central system for analysis. As a rare youngster among Great Wall patrollers, Liang Qingli was chosen by CACH to pilot test the application. He was asked to collect monitoring data for a 5.9km section of the Wall and its auxiliary defence towers every 3 to 5 days, and then upload the photos, records and other information collected on site to the application. The section of the Wall chosen for the pilot is not open to visitors. During the period of the pilot project from 2016 to 2018, Liang Qingli completed 249 inspections, collecting 13,415 monitoring photos from specific angles (Fig.2). His feedback has also facilitated the functional improvement of the application, enabling the application to meet the demands of workers on the front line, and validating the feasibility and benefits of using mobile applications to conduct daily monitoring of the Great Wall.

Beyond core responsibilities: community activities for the Great Wall

Liang Qingli's footprints can also be found beyond the area for which he is responsible in surrounding areas of the Great Wall. For many years, he has been visiting villagers living near the Wall to raise public awareness of protecting the Great Wall. Under his influence, many villagers have voluntarily picked up the rubbish on the Wall, while an increasing number of public-spirited enthusiasts have participated in the protection of the Great Wall in various ways (Fig.3). Schools situated at the foot of the Great Wall invite him to deliver speeches to students, to foster interest in protection of the Great Wall among younger generations (Fig.4).

REFLECTIONS

As a result of the Great Wall Patroller Mechanism, almost every single section of the Great Wall, extending over 20,000km, now has a person assigned to act as its guardian. These patrollers are indispensable to the protection of the Great Wall, playing an important role in the early identification of risks to the monument, allowing appropriate action to prevent damage to be undertaken more immediately. However, with the development of digitisation and standardisation of the Great Wall inspection, patrollers need to keep improving their professional competence, to learn to use modern IT methods in their work, and to understand laws and regulations as well as technical specifications related to the Great Wall. Each of these actions enable them to make proper assessment of any risks on the spot.

三、思考—写在后面的话

截止目前，通过设置长城保护员，绵延2万多千米的长城全线基本实现了看护的全覆盖。为及时发现长城险情，第一时间阻止长城破坏事件的发生起到了重要的作用，是长城保护不可缺少的力量。随着长城巡查工作逐步科学化和规范化，长城保护员也需要不断提升自己的工作水平，学习使用现代信息技术手段开展工作，了解掌握长城保护的法律法规、技术规范，以便能在第一时间对长城发生的破坏事件等进行判断。

梁庆立表示自己非常自豪是一名长城保护员，因为年轻，艰苦的巡查没有带给他太大的压力，学习利用手机APP开展具有一定专业要求的监测工作他也能得心应手。像梁庆立这样有热情、有学习能力的年轻人无疑是长城保护员的最佳人选。但长城大多分布在经济欠发达的地区，甚至有很多长城所在的地区是贫困县，地方政府能够给付长城保护员的补贴十分有限。这样的“补贴”很难对年轻人产生吸引力。根据目前备案的3403名长城保护员信息，大部分集中在1960年代出生,即50-60年龄段。“老龄化”、“待遇低”还需要通过开通除政府补贴外的其他社会渠道来解决。

梁庆立说，长城面临的主要破坏之一就是日益增加的游客数量，这时常让他感到只凭自己一双眼睛、一张嘴巴难以看护、劝说那些破坏长城的行为。长城保护与周边居民生活关系密切，只有让更多生活在长城周边的人更加自觉自愿地长城保护员队伍才能让长城得到切实的保护。

近年来，长城保护员队伍建设工作取得较大进展，天津、北京、河北等地都在积极开展对长城保护员的培训，使他们能够更加胜任长城保护的一线工作。2018年10月国文物保护基金会发起“长城保护员加油包”项目，通过腾讯公益平台向社会募集资金，给贫困县区的长城保护员提供“户外保险、装备和能力培训”，为长城保护员的巡查工作提供支持和保障。截止目前已筹集资金121439.44元。作为一名普通的长城保护员，梁庆立的工作也得到了社会认可（图5）。相信政府与社会的联手行动，会让更多家住长城边的居民愿意加入长城保护员队伍。

References
参考文献

Website of “Great Wall Patroller Support Package” on Tencent's fundraising platform, https://gongyi.qq.com/succor/detail.htm?id=203859

腾讯公益平台“长城保护员加油包”网站，https://gongyi.qq.com/succor/detail.htm?id=203859, 2020.01.16

Xu, H. 2018. Current Situation and Issue Analysis of the Great Wall Patroller Mechanism. China Cultural Heritage, 1.

许慧君. 2018. 长城保护员制度的现状和问题分析. 中国文化遗产，1.

图 4 梁庆立为村里的小学上长城公益课（摄影：梁庆立）。

Fig.4 Lesson given by Liang Qingli to students of the local village primary schools (photograph by Liang Qingli).

图 5 梁庆立获得迁西县“十佳青年公益执之星”称号（图片来源：长城小站）。

Fig.5 Liang Qingli won the title of the “Top Ten Young Role Models for Public Welfare” of the Qianxi County (photograph by the Great Wall Station).

Liang Qingli says that being a Great Wall patroller makes him proud. As he is relatively young, this demanding job has not brought him too much pressure and it is not difficult for him to learn how to use mobile applications to conduct professional monitoring. Young people like Liang Qingli who are passionate and have the ability to learn are undoubtedly the best candidates for the Great Wall patrollers. However, most sections of the Great Wall are in underdeveloped, even impoverished, areas. Many local governments can only provide very limited allowances to the patrollers, making the role less attractive to young people. Most of the 3,403 patrollers on record were born in the 1960s, which means their age ranges from 50 to 60. Aging and low income need to be overcome by leveraging other social channels rather than depending solely the subsidies provided by local governments (Xu 2016).

According to Liang Qingli, one of the major risks to the Great Wall is brought by the increasing number of tourists, which makes him feel it is more and more difficult to protect the Wall and discourage visitors on his own from behaviours that harm the Wall. The Wall is closely related to the life of local communities. It is only by involving more people who live near the Wall in the work of the patrollers' team in a more active way that the Great Wall can be adequately protected.

Efforts to address this concern have been recently undertaken. Direct municipalities and provinces including Tianjin, Beijing, Hebei have provided training to the patrollers to develop their skills and competencies. In October 2018, the China Foundation for Cultural Heritage Conservation (CFCHC) initiated a “Great Wall Patroller Support Package” project to raise funds from the public via Tencent's fundraising platform, providing the Great Wall patrollers in impoverished counties and districts with outdoor insurance, equipment and training, and giving support and protection in their inspection. So far, it has already raised over RMB120,000 in total (gongyi.qq.com, 2020). Work by ordinary patrollers, including Liang Qingli, has been recognised more and more by society (Fig.5). It is firmly believed that the joint efforts brought by the government and by wider society will encourage more residents living near the Great Wall to join the team of the Great Wall patrollers.

5.7 VOLUNTEERING AT VINDOLANDA

BARBARA BIRLEY
Vindolanda Trust - Northumberland - UK

Abstract

As part of the ongoing archaeological excavations at Roman Vindolanda, the Vindolanda Trust has developed a comprehensive volunteer programme. This paper sets out the process through which the programme has developed, its challenges and the benefits that volunteer working on the site has brought not only to the Vindolanda Trust but to the volunteers themselves.

Keywords: Vindolanda, Hadrian's Wall, Roman frontiers, museums, volunteers, excavation, community archaeology

INTRODUCTION

The Vindolanda Trust was founded in 1970. Since then over 10,000 people have volunteered their time on the excavations, and on other projects and programmes which have helped the Vindolanda Trust in achieving its aims and objectives. The Trust is an independent charity which was set up with the objective of completely excavating one of the fort sites along Hadrian's Wall, and to then conserve, research, publish and display that fort site and the artefacts found there to the general public. Enshrined in the foundation of the Trust was a clear educational purpose, and this was taken forward from the 1970s by encouraging students and other volunteers to help with the excavation of the site.

ROMAN VINDOLANDA

The Roman site of Vindolanda was established in *c.* 85 CE and was a central fort on the line of the Stanegate road. This road lies just to the north of the site and demarcated the first Roman frontier in what is now Northern England. The road linked the Roman military bases and towns of Carlisle in the west to Corbridge in the east. In around 122 CE, the Roman army started the construction of Hadrian's Wall, a mile to the north of Vindolanda, and the site became both a construction base and a garrison for the new frontier developments. Over Vindolanda's long history, nine separate forts were constructed, one on top of the other, representing several periods of occupation. The forts varied in size and shape depending on the strength of their garrisons. By the time that construction on Hadrian's Wall started, Vindolanda had been completely re-built five times. Thanks to its proximity to the main transportation route of the Stanegate road and to the line of the Wall, Vindolanda remained a garrisoned site until the end of Roman Britain.

Today's visitors can see the excavated 3rd and 4th century remains including the rectangular fort with central military buildings, military bath house and the extramural settlement outside the fort walls （Fig. 1）. What cannot be seen, unless directly under excavation, are the two to seven metres of occupational material which is underneath these remains. Through recent work, the dating of the last post-Roman occupation of the site has been

5.7 文多兰达志愿者项目简介

芭芭拉・博利
文多兰达信托基金—诺桑伯兰—英国

摘要

作为古罗马文多兰达要塞持续性考古发掘工作的一部分，文多兰达已发展出一套全面的志愿者项目。本文将介绍项目的发展历程，所面临的挑战，以及志愿者在现场的辛勤劳作给文多兰达信托基金，更是给志愿者自身带来的诸多效益。

关键字：文多兰达　哈德良长城　罗马帝国边疆　博物馆群　志愿者　发掘　社区考古

引言

文多兰达信托基金成立于 1970 年。成立至今，超过1万人志愿参与考古发掘以及其他各类项目，帮助文多兰达信托基金完成其使命和目标。文多兰达信托基金是独立的公益组织，设立的目标是完整发掘哈德良长城沿线的这处要塞遗址，并在发掘后保护、研究、面向公众出版和展示遗址及遗址出土的文物。信托基金的目标很清晰，那就是教育，这也是信托基金所珍视的立身之本。为推动这一目标，上世纪70年代以来，基金始终鼓励学生和其他志愿者协助发掘遗址。

古罗马时期文多兰达简史

公元85年前后，古罗马文多兰达要塞设立，是石路（Stanegate）沿线一处中心要塞。石路紧临要塞北侧，在如今的英格兰北部标定了最早的罗马帝国边疆。石路连接若干罗马军营和城镇，西至卡莱尔（Carlisle）,东至考布里奇（Corbridge）。公元 122 年左右，罗马军队开始于文多兰达以北一英里处[1]修筑哈德良长城。于是文多兰达要塞成为了新边疆修筑的工程基地和军事驻地。文多兰达使用时间跨度很长，期间分别建造了多达九座要塞，层层叠压，代表了不同使用时期。各时期要塞依照戍守军队的兵力形成了各不相同的大小和形状。仅在哈德良长城开工前，文多兰达就已完全重建五次之多。得益于毗邻石路交通主干道以及长城主线，文多兰达一直作为军营使用，直到古罗马帝国在不列颠的统治结束。

今天，游客可以看到已发掘的3世纪和4世纪遗址，包括建有中央军用建筑和军用浴室的长方形要塞和要塞墙外的聚落（图 1）。在游客看不到的遗址下方，还有厚达两米至七米的堆积层尚未开展考古发掘。通过近期的考古工作，要塞在后罗马时期最后的使用时间得以重新确定，大致为 9 世纪初。

然而，让文多兰达蜚声国际考古界的却是要塞早期的使用年代层。这一时期从公元 85 年左右开始，

1 约 1.6 千米——译者注。

Fig.1 Aerial photograph of Vindolanda 2019（© Adam Stanford and the Vindolanda Trust）.
图 1 2019年文多兰达航拍图（© 亚当·斯坦福德和文多兰达信托基金）。

re-established close to the start of the 9th century.

However, it is the earliest occupation levels at the site that have helped to propel Vindolanda into international archaeological fame. During this period, from roughly AD 85 to the mid 1st century when a garrison was ordered to move on, the garrison pulled down the timber walls of their forts. New garrisons would then level the land with turf and clay to provide a good foundation for their new base. This process of destruction, covering and rebuilding to provide new foundations quickly created anaerobic or oxygen-free environments, which water and other decompositional organisms could not reach. This has resulted in the largest single site collection yet found of organic material from Roman Britain.

Examples of this preservation include over 8,000 Roman leather objects, most of which are shoes, as well as artefacts such as tent panels and horse gear. Preservation extends from items like large structural timbers to small and personal wooden objects and textiles including a child's woollen sock. The most famous set of artefacts to be unearthed at the site are the Vindolanda writing tablets. These are letters written in cursive Latin script on thin pieces of wood and about the size of a modern postcard, which represent the personal and military correspondences

至 1 世纪中叶军队收到转移命令撤离。军队撤离时，拆除了要塞周围的木制围墙。当新驻军到来时，他们将土地平整后覆以草皮和泥土，作为新军营的基础。这一拆除、覆盖及重建奠基过程很快就形成了厌氧环境，使水和其他分解性有机体难以侵入。于是文多兰达成为了迄今发现有机物遗存最丰富的单座罗马时期不列颠大型遗址。

这些遗存中有超过8000件罗马时期皮具，大部分为鞋子，也有帐篷垂帘和马具之类的文物。遗存品种多样，大到木制建筑构件，小到私人使用的木制品和纺织品，比如儿童羊毛袜子。遗址出土的文物中，最著名的当属文多兰达木简。木简内容为信件，以草体拉丁文书写于木制薄片上，大小相当于今天的明信片，反映了要塞早期驻军的私人信件及军事通信往来。

志愿者发掘项目

自20世纪70年代启动以来，志愿者发掘项目历经发展和变化，包容性越来越强，允许万里之外，来自不同背景的人们参与其中。每年参加该项目的志愿者人数也有明显增长，从最初参加发掘的寥寥数人，到如今图 2所示的庞大规模。通过更深入地了解志愿者与信托基金相互之间的期待与要求，志愿者项目的成效也日益显著。

过去五十年间，对志愿者参与考古活动的态度也发生了巨大变化。比如鼓励16-18岁学生参加考古发掘，过去曾遭诟病，被视作纵容"未经培训人员"参与（博利，2016），如今却成为学术研究的延伸对象。与此同时，公众志愿参加遗产项目或参与公共考古活动的热情也越来越高。

前来遗址参加志愿活动的人群构成以在职或退休成年人为主，他们素有体验考古发掘的夙愿。他们的背景多样，来自各行各业，包括医生、律师、教师，有些仍在职，抽出休假时间来参加。有很多学生以个人形式申请参加，不过项目也接受少量高校田野实习的申请。2019 年，信托基金接待了两个国外高校的田野实习，分别隶属于美国密歇根州安·阿博尔学院（Anne Arbour College, Michigan, USA）以及加拿大西安大略大学（the University of Western Ontario, Canada）。每年还有一些专职考古学家申请参加，只为体验在文多兰达的发掘工作。

除了发掘志愿者，文多兰达信托基金同样招募发掘后期工作志愿者。这些志愿者负责清理古罗马陶器、织物及动物骨骼，整理器物以供专家进行分析和记录。这个团队人数较少，根据不同的发掘区域，一般每周由3到6人组成。参加这类工作中的不少人是感到自己体力不足以支撑发掘工作，但仍然希望为信托基金及其正在进行的研究出一份力。

自2003年，文多兰达信托基金将志愿者项目正规化，并开始通过官方网站招募志愿者。从那以后，总能招募到发掘需要的志愿者人数，从未遇到任何问题。信托基金的国际影响力拓宽了招募渠道，形成规模较大的人力资源库。遗址本身是旅游目的地，通过与社交媒体、影视纪录片合作，全英国及世界范围内对信托基金的兴趣日渐浓厚。在文多兰达，每个人都能为揭开历史、探索发现、研究考古做出直接贡献，这些都是强有力的驱动力。该项目持续吸引着英国以外的参与者前来，包括欧洲、美国、加拿大、澳大利亚和新西兰。

发掘的报名流程通过文多兰达信托基金的官方网站（www.vindolanda.com）进行，报名开始日期及报名相关信息都发布在该网站上。报名流程一般于11月上旬启动，所有名额在启动后30分钟内就会报满。迅速的周转使信托基金对志愿者人数与工作目标心中有数，从而有时间计划和准备下一年要开展的研究工作。

of the early garrisons stationed at the fort.

THE VOLUNTEER EXCAVATION PROGRAMME

Over the years since its inception in the 1970s, the volunteer programme has developed and changed. It has become more inclusive, allowing people from further afield and from different backgrounds to participate. The number of people joining the programme each year has also grown significantly. From initially only a few volunteers joining the excavations, it has now reached the large scale of volunteer participation summarised in Table 1. The volunteer programme has also become more effective, through an increased understanding of what the volunteers expect from the Trust, and at the same time, what the Trust requires from its volunteers.

Over a fifty-year period, attitudes to volunteering in archaeological heritage have also changed significantly. Practices that had been criticised for engaging 'untrained labour', such as the participation of 16-18 year-old students on the excavations (Birley 2016), are now the subject of extensive academic research. At the same time volunteering in heritage projects and in public archaeology has become increasingly popular.

The demographic make-up of the people who come to volunteer at the site largely consists of working or retired adults who have always wanted the experience of excavating. They come from different backgrounds and professions which include doctors, lawyers and teachers, some of whom are still employed and who use their holiday time to take part. Though there are many students who apply independently, the programme accepts a limited number of field schools linked to universities. In 2019, the Trust hosted two international field schools, affiliated to Anne Arbour College, Michigan, USA, and the University of Western Ontario, Canada. Every year a few professional archaeologists apply simply to have the experience of excavating at Vindolanda.

In addition to the excavation volunteers, the Vindolanda Trust also recruits post-excavation volunteers. These volunteers work to clean the bulk of Roman pottery, tile and animal bone, and to prepare the material for specialist analysis and recording. This is a smaller team, usually of three to six people per week, depending on what area is under excavation. Many of these individuals do not feel that they are physically fit enough to do the work on the excavations but still wish to contribute to the work of the Trust and its active research.

From the moment that the Vindolanda Trust formalised its volunteer programme and began to recruit volunteers via its website in 2003, it has not experienced any problems reaching the number of volunteers it needs to support its work. The international profile of the organisation gives it a large reach and a pool of people to draw from. The site is a tourist destination and by working with social media, film crews and documentaries, national and international interest in the work of the Trust has steadily grown. Vindolanda is a place where individuals can directly contribute to uncovering history, making discoveries and to archaeological research, all of which are powerful motivators (Fig.2). The programme continues to attract people from beyond the United Kingdom including from Europe, US, Canada, Australia, and New Zealand.

Table 1: 2019 Excavation volunteer statistics.
表1：2019 年发掘活动志愿者统计数据。

Volunteers per two-week programme 每期（两周）志愿者参与人数	30-35
Return rate per year 每年志愿者回归率	60%
Minimum age 最小年龄	17
Maximum age 最大年龄	None - depending on physical fitness 无 - 取决于个人体力
Average age 平均年龄	47
Total number of volunteers 志愿者总人数	279
Gender split 性别占比	54% women to 46% men 女性占54%，男性占46%

Fig.2 Volunteers in action (© The Vindolanda Trust).
图 2 工作中的志愿者（©文多兰达信托基金）。

信托基金聘用两名全职考古学家及一名兼职发掘后期工作导师。他们的工作是在现场监督和培训志愿者。此外，发掘主管会为没有经验的发掘小组配备两至三名有经验的志愿者，这些志愿者会协助工作人员培训其他志愿者。这些有经验的人员可能本身即为专业考古学家，或已经在遗址上工作多年。发掘新手会和有经验的志愿者结对，这样可以相互帮衬，共同协作。

每年信托基金会为三名志愿者提供青年资助计划，该计划覆盖两周内全部发掘费用，以及遗址现场海德利中心（Hedley Centre）的全部食宿费用，任何16-25岁的全日制学生都可申请。资助名额由数位捐赠人赞助，其中不少都在遗址有志愿发掘的经历，希望能给他人提供同样的机会。

志愿服务的效益及动机

为了每年保持对志愿者的吸引力，文多兰达信托基金定期评估自身提供的项目体验，确保能照顾到每一个人。发掘志愿者参加两周的发掘需交纳160英镑[2]，发掘后期工作志愿者每人交纳50英镑[3]。参加信托

2 约合人民币1400元——译者注。
3 约合人民币440元——译者注。

The process of joining the excavation is administered through the Vindolanda Trust's website www.vindolanda.com, where the date the application process opens and joining information is posted. Usually, the application process goes live early in November and all of the places are filled within 30 minutes after launch. This quick turn-around allows the Trust time to plan and prepare for the research and work to take place the following year, knowing how many volunteers it has and what can be achieved.

The Trust employs two full-time archaeologists and a part time post-excavation supervisor. It is their role to supervise and train volunteers while on site. In addition, the Director of Excavations places two to three experienced volunteers within non-experienced groups and they support the role of the staff in training other volunteers. These are either professional archaeologist themselves or volunteers who have already worked on the site for an extensive period. New excavators are then paired up with more experienced volunteers so that they can work together and help each other.

A young person's bursary scheme is offered to three individuals every year. This includes full board accommodation for two weeks in the Trust's on-site Hedley Centre and covers all their accommodation and excavation fees. Anyone in full-time education between the ages of 16-25 can apply. These places are sponsored by several donors, many of whom have experience of working at the site as volunteers and want to give others the same opportunities.

THE BENEFITS OF VOLUNTEERING AND ITS MOTIVATIONS

In order to continue to attract volunteers every year, the Vindolanda Trust periodically reviews the experience it offers, to make sure that each person is catered for. The excavation volunteers make a contribution of £160 for their two-week experience, and the post-excavation volunteers contribute £50 per person. Volunteers to other Trust volunteer programmes do not make such financial contributions or donations towards their experience and work. All the volunteers are encouraged to join the Friends of Vindolanda, a scheme which gives them free admission to the site even outside the excavation period, discounts in the shops and an invitation to an annual Friends' Day and dedicated yearly report on the Trust's work. The fees volunteers pay provide them with several benefits: they are used to part-fund equipment such as wheelbarrows, trowels and shovels, as well as producing a volunteer t-shirt each year for every participant. The t-shirts become collectors' items for many who come year after year but are also a form of advertising for the Trust. While there are many tangible benefits to volunteering with the Vindolanda Trust, it is also important to consider what intangible benefits may bring people to volunteer.

When looking at what volunteers get out of their experience, an outcome that is apparent and easy to comment upon is the enormous sense of wellbeing that many volunteers experience. They become part of the team (Fig.3) and during their two weeks they develop friendships, camaraderie, and a wish to stay in touch with the people they have met. Several lifelong friendships and relationships have developed out of their experiences digging in the Northumbrian countryside. These benefits are clearly expressed by the volunteers during their stay and have a quantifiable manifestation in the high rate of returning volunteers every year. However, more research is yet needed on volunteer motivations across Hadrian's Wall (Weekes *et al.* 2019).

The Vindolanda Trust is aware of the importance of exploring volunteer motivations and their relationship with continued commitment to a cause and is pursuing this avenue by sponsoring the PhD research of one of its employees. The research is being conducted at Newcastle University and involves using both quantitative and qualitative methods to assess the motivations not only of individuals who volunteer at Vindolanda, but of volunteers more widely across the World Heritage Site.

CHALLENGES TO THE VOLUNTEER PROGRAMME

The Trust does have challenges when it comes to maintaining the excavation programme. The actual process

基金其他志愿项目的志愿者无需缴费即可参加工作。信托基金鼓励所有志愿者都加入“文多兰达之友”计划。加入该计划后，他们可以在发掘期以外的时间免费参观遗址，享受商店消费折扣，受邀参加年度会友日活动，并获赠信托基金特制的工作年报。志愿者缴纳的会费也用于会员福利：这些款项部分用来购买独轮手推车、泥铲和铁锹等工具，以及每年为每位志愿者制作纪念T恤。对不少每年都参加的志愿者而言，纪念T恤已然成为收藏品，它也是信托基金广告宣传的载体。这些固然是文多兰达信托基金参加志愿服务的实际效益，不过参加志愿工作的无形效益也非常重要。

诸多志愿者从服务经历中得到的收获，有一方面非常明显，那就是志愿者们体验到的幸福感。他们成为了团队的一员（图4），在两周的发掘过程中，他们结识了朋友、战友，并希望和新朋友保持联系。在诺桑伯兰乡村的发掘经历，让不少人结下了终生情谊。这些益处是志愿者在参加项目期间就经常提及的，每年志愿者的高回归率也是对此的量化体现。不过，哈德良长城沿线志愿者的动机仍有待进一步研究（Weekes 等, 2019）。

文多兰达信托基金意识到认识志愿者动机及长期服务之间关系的重要性，目前正资助一位工作人员攻读博士学位从事这方面的研究。该研究在纽卡斯尔大学进行，采用定量和定性方式进行评估，评估不仅涉及文多兰达志愿者，而且涉及更大范围内世界遗产地志愿者的动机。

志愿者项目面临的挑战

文多兰达信托基金在持续开展发掘项目时确实遇到各种挑战。要获得《登录古迹许可》耗时日久，而它却是在英国受保护古迹上开展任何项目的必须文件。要开展考古发掘，信托基金必须向英国文化、媒体和体育部申报，陈述信托基金本次发掘的研究目的、预期成果，以及本次发掘的资金来源和出版规划。文多兰达信托基金与英格兰遗产委员会及多所高校和专家合作，对其研究项目流程进行了优化，每五年开展一次评估。当前开展的项目是“理解当地社区与身份认同：文多兰达塞维鲁时期要塞与圆形建筑群”，计划 2022 年结项。

Fig.3 One of the volunteer teams in 2019 (© The Vindolanda Trust).
图 3 2019 年的志愿者队伍之一（© 文多兰达信托基金）。

文多兰达信托基金为发掘、保护、研究和出版提供的资金，募集渠道包括遗址及博物馆门票收入和零售及餐饮收入。信托基金不接受外部资金资助其工作。因此，文多兰达信托基金为参观者开发出系列服务产品，从教学活动到各种项目，从而使信托基金的工

of obtaining Scheduled Monument Consent is a lengthy but key requirement of any project working on a protected ancient site in Britain. To conduct its archaeological excavations, the Trust must apply to the Department of Culture, Media and Sport, outlining the Trust's research aims and objectives for the proposed excavations and how this work will be funded and published. Working closely with Historic England, as well as a number of universities and specialists, The Vindolanda Trust develops and refines its research process, with a major review every five years. The current project is *Understanding Communities and Identities: the Severan fortlet and roundhouse complex at Vindolanda,* which will be completed in 2022.

The Vindolanda Trust funds the excavations, its work in conservation, research and its publication through the sale of admission tickets to the site and museums as well as retail and catering sales. The Trust does not receive outside funding for its work. As such, the Vindolanda Trust has developed a comprehensive visitor offer from educational activities to events, so that its work is sustainable. It has managed to maintain this balance between the demands of research and those of the visiting public for over 50 years. The excavations, and the ability of visitors to interact with the specialists working on the site are vital parts of this offer, as many of the visitors to the site come to view the archaeologists and volunteers as they work. Rather than a grass park and manicured monument, the work at Vindolanda brings the site alive and creates a sense of excitement. The excavations and research are profiled on social media and through the website to raise awareness of what is being undertaken as it happens.

The greatest challenge, to both the archaeological work and the visitor flow of Vindolanda is the changeable weather. Depending on the depth of the area under excavation this can be a significant problem. Wet weather can make conditions muddy and dangerous for the volunteers to work in. Too much rain can also make it difficult to see the archaeology in the ground, therefore raising the risk of damaging the fragile anaerobic conditions. Hot, dry weather also creates its own problems, as it can damage the damp layers of deposits and cause trouble for the volunteers if they are not protected from sunstroke and dehydration. The changeable weather can also be very demoralising for the volunteers, and the archaeologists must work to keep the team motivated. A wet-weather programme, including lectures, workshops, and educational hikes along the Wall, allows the archaeological team to maintain morale even when excavation is not possible.

BENEFITS TO THE VINDOLANDA TRUST AND TO THE VOLUNTEERS

The benefits of the volunteer excavation programme to the Vindolanda Trust are numerous. They include the labour it provides to help undertake the excavations and the inspiration and training it gives to future Roman archaeologists, researchers and museum specialists. The programme helps the Trust in other ways (Fig.4). Many excavators join the Trust's other volunteer programmes as Heritage Tour Guides or Educational Guides. These volunteers mostly come from the local community and they deliver different types of tours to the site ranging from 20 minutes to 1 hour. To become a guide requires an extensive training to make sure they are delivering the best possible tour of the site, and regular feedback is received from the public as well as from the guides themselves. Each guide provides the Trust with between 8 to 30 days of volunteering per year.

The Vindolanda Trust has a small but dedicated team of museum volunteers. All of this team started as volunteers on the excavations and they work closely with the Curator to catalogue the growing collection. They help with other activities such as the annual museum cleaning exercises at both Vindolanda and at the Trust's nearby Roman Army Museum, and with one-off projects like the installation of temporary displays or moving stores.

Activity and events volunteers often overlap with other categories of volunteers and therefore have an understanding of Vindolanda and its wider context. They deliver 'finds handling' sessions at which the general public have the opportunity, under supervision, to hold and examine objects from the excavations which are

作可持续开展。过去 50 多年，信托基金也成功地平衡了研究与公众参观的需求。发掘活动，特别是参观者可以在遗址现场与专家交流的机会，是系列服务产品的核心组成部分。因为许多游客来到遗址现场正是为了一睹考古学家和志愿者的工作场景。文多兰达不是草坪优美的公园或是修整精良的古迹，而是一个充满活力、激发兴奋感的地方。发掘和研究的情况会在社交媒体和官网上发布，实时宣传活动进展。

对考古工作和游客管理工作而言，最大的挑战是多变的天气。根据发掘的不同深度，问题可能很严重。多雨的天气会让地面泥泞湿滑，志愿者在此条件下工作存在安全隐患。雨水过多会使得埋藏于土中的考古遗存难以识别，也加剧了本就脆弱的厌氧环境遭到破坏的风险。炎热干燥的天气也有问题，因为那会损坏湿润的堆积层。对志愿者的工作也会带来麻烦，志愿者没有遮挡，可能会中暑或者脱水。多变的天气也会影响志愿者的士气，考古学家必须努力让团队保持振奋的精神。针对雨天状况，基金会就组织讲座、工作坊，或沿长城进行科普徒步活动，使考古团队在无法开展发掘工作时依然士气高昂。

Fig.4 Non-excavation volunteers include site guides (top); museum volunteers (middle); volunteers assisting with the replica pottery kiln project (bottom) (© The Vindolanda Trust).

图 4 非发掘类志愿者，包括讲解员（上）；博物馆志愿者（中）；协助陶窑复建志愿者（下）（© 文多兰达信托基金）。

对文多兰达信托基金及志愿者的益处

志愿者考古发掘项目为文多兰达信托基金带来的益处数不胜数，

explained to them by staff. They also help staff during Family Days in organising games activities or craft sessions for children to participate in. They talk to the public by the trench-edge, telling them about what they are working on and what has been found. These activities greatly improve the engagement of the visitors and provide them with the best possible experience on the site.

Many volunteers continue their own personal journeys to better understand the Roman Empire and archaeological practice. Some do this by joining the workshops and courses which are run by the Trust. This not only expands their knowledge but is a further source of revenue for the Trust. Courses may include diverse topics such as archaeological illustration and learning how to identify different type of Roman ceramics. Volunteers can attend the Trust's lecture series or outside lectures at local history societies, Hadrian's Wall events or they can become volunteers at other Wall or other historic sites. This community aspect contributes to the whole of the Hadrian's Wall World Heritage Site and its management, the benefits of which are seen in a wider context than that of the Vindolanda Trust itself.

There are less obvious advantages of the programme that were perhaps less expected but have become just as useful. The Trust has developed relationships with professionals outside the archaeological world. As an example, the archaeologists have been working with a retired chemist who, after he excavated as a volunteer, became fascinated with the anaerobic layers on the site and their preservation of organic artefacts. He put the Trust in contact with his colleagues to better understand and research the chemical and microbiological environments which create the oxygen-free conditions which preserve the organic layers. This has resulted in three PhD projects about the site.

This mutually beneficial environment means that the Trust has a wider community of expertise to call on when assistance is needed. A case in point for this was the building of a replica pottery kiln in the museum's gardens. The volunteers helped the Trust's freelance provider of technical assistance in this field to build the kiln and now often come back to help him fire it. This becomes an engaging, public-facing event for the visitors on site undertaken with the help of the volunteer team.

In conclusion, the Trust gains both local support and the volunteer's enthusiasm. They help the Trust to meet its requirements and they become positive advocates, not only for Vindolanda but for the World Heritage Site, both in the local area and beyond. Every year the Trust looks forward to the coming season not only for its archaeological discoveries, but to be able to welcome friends back to help to uncover them. Their contribution helps to make the Vindolanda Trust what it is today.

References
参考文献

Birley, A. 2013. 'Vindolanda,' in Walker, C. and Carr, N. (ed.) Tourism and Archaeology: Sustainable Meeting Grounds, New York: Routledge, 127-42.

A · 博利. 2013. 文多兰达要塞，见于 C · 沃克，N · 卡尔（编）旅游与考古：可持续的聚集地.纽约：劳特利奇，127-42.

Weekes, J., Watson, S., Wallace, L., Mazzilli, F., Gardner, A. and Alberti, M. 2019. 'Alienation and Redemption: The Praxis of (Roman) Archaeology in Britain', Theoretical Roman Archaeology Journal, 2(1), p.7.

J · 威克斯，S · 沃特森，L · 华莱士，F · 马其利，A · 加德纳，M · 阿尔伯蒂. 2019. 异化与救赎：英国境内（古罗马）考古实践，见于古罗马考古理论期刊，2(1), 7.

不仅提供了发掘工作所需要的人力，还吸引和培养了未来的古罗马考古学家、研究人员及博物馆专业人士。志愿者项目也在其他方面帮助信托基金（图5）。不少发掘人员还参加了信托基金的其他志愿者项目，比如遗产之旅讲解员或教育讲解员项目。这些志愿者大多来自本地社区，设计了不同类型的遗址游览路线，时长从20分钟至1小时不等。要成为讲解员，得先经过全面培训，确保他们提供最优质的遗址讲解，同时会定期征询公众及讲解员自身的反馈。每位讲解员每年都为信托基金志愿服务8到30天。

文多兰大信托基金还有一支小而专业的博物馆志愿者队伍。这些志愿者起初都是发掘志愿者，他们与博物馆馆长紧密协作，为日渐庞大的藏品编目。他们还参与协助其他的活动，比如文多兰达博物馆以及信托基金附近罗马军队博物馆年度大扫除，以及为临时展览或移动商店布展装卸。

活动志愿者常和其他类别志愿者重叠，因此对文多兰达及其宏观背景有更多的了解。他们会组织“触摸出土文物”活动，让广大公众有机会在专业监督的前提下把玩和研究出土文物，并由工作人员进行讲解。他们也在“家庭日”协助工作人员组织各种游戏、小制作活动，让孩子们参与进来。他们在考古探沟边上向公众讲解目前工作进展及发现。这些活动增进了游客的参与度，为游客提供了遗址参观的最佳体验。

不少志愿者也继续着个人对古罗马帝国和考古学实践的深入探索。为此，有些参加了信托基金举办的工作坊和课程。这不仅扩展了他们的知识，更为信托基金开拓了又一收入来源。课程涵盖丰富多样的主题，诸如考古绘图、古罗马陶瓷制品种类鉴别等。志愿者可以参加信托基金的系列讲座，或参加当地历史协会组织的外部讲座、哈德良长城活动，亦或在其他长城或历史遗址担任志愿者。这一社区特性为整个哈德良长城世界遗产地及其管理作出贡献，其效益之深远，超出了文多兰达信托基金的范畴。

志愿者项目额外带来一些意想不到的收获，它不那么显眼，却也变得有用。信托基金与考古界以外的专业人士建立了关系。比如，信托基金的考古学家一直与一位退休的化学家保持合作。这位化学家参加了志愿发掘项目后，迷上了遗址的厌氧层及对有机文物的保护。由他牵线，信托基金联系上他的同事，并得以深入理解和研究创造无氧条件保存有机层所需的化学和微生物环境。这项研究已经催生了三个与遗址有关的博士学位研究项目。

这一互惠互利的氛围使信托基金拥有广泛的专业社群，一旦需要即可加以利用。在博物馆花园里复建陶器窑址就是一例。信托基金的一位自由职业技术专家在志愿者的帮助下把窑修建起来，现在志愿者们还经常回来帮助烧窑。烧窑活动也成为在志愿者帮助下面向公众的一个互动项目。

总结来说，信托基金得到了本地社区支持及志愿者的热情响应。他们帮助信托基金完成工作要求，在本地及更大范围内成为了宣传文多兰达甚至世界遗产地的使者。每年，信托基金都期待着新一季的来临，不仅是因为会有新的考古发现，更是因为能迎接朋友的回归来帮助揭开这些发现的面纱。他们的奉献，成就了文多兰达信托基金的今天。

CONCLUDING REMARKS: REFLECTIONS ON WHAT WE HAVE LEARNT FROM THE WALL TO WALL COLLABORATION TO DATE

YU BING
Chinese Academy of Cultural Heritage - China - Beijing

If we consider conservation work as a cycle, it involves survey, research, preservation, monitoring, public access and social engagement, which are not necessarily linear but overlapping and interactive. The papers by UK and Chinese authors show different emphases on different phases of the cycle for Hadrian's Wall and for the Great Wall.

Major work on the Great Wall has been focused on survey and conservation, while research, public access and public engagement have received greater attention on Hadrian's Wall. This contrast is partly illustrated by the preponderance of Chinese authors in Chapter 3 (survey) and of British authors in Chapter 5 (visitor access and public engagement).

One of the sharpest contrasts within the Wall to Wall dialogue is the role archaeology plays in the conservation and management of the two Walls. Even though archaeology has received more attention on the Great Wall in the last few years, too little has yet been done; only four archaeological excavations have been undertaken along the 20,000km of the Wall in two years (Yu Bing, et. al.). In contrast, archaeological research plays a much more significant role in the conservation and management of Hadrian's Wall, developing from its long research history (David Breeze) to systematic involvement across the full cycle of research-framework planning (Tony Wilmott), the multidisciplinary approach of landscape archaeology (Rob Collins) and wide engagement through community archaeology (Barbara Birley).

Another difference in the cycle is the overwhelming emphasis on intervention (consolidation, repair, conservation) projects carried out on the Great Wall, which has seen dozens of projects every year over the last decade (Yu Bing, et. al.) compared to the number undertaken on Hadrian's Wall. The difference is not just the amount of work on the Great Wall, which is understandable and will continue for a long time, taking into consideration its size, the natural threats it faces, development pressures and soaring tourism demand. A difference in approaches is also apparent. Several Chinese authors concentrate on discussions of the conservation principles 'no change to the historical fabric' and 'minimum intervention' and indicate how controversial debates are concerning how these commonly accepted principles are applied in practice. Management approaches for the Great Wall, however, are still led by engineering and architectural perspectives (Tang Yuyang, Lan Lizhi, Zhao Peng, and Zhang Jianwei), whilst for Hadrian's Wall, more emphasis is placed on archaeological, visitor and managerial perspectives (Mike Collins, Bill Griffiths).

Contrasts are also demonstrated in public access and social engagement between the two Walls. Even though some sections of the Great Wall have become very popular and established tourist sites for domestic and international visitors, the process of heritage and tourism integration both in terms of policy and research is only in its early stages (Wang Yuwei, Zhou Xiaofeng et. al.). By comparison, considerable progress has been made on Roman Frontiers in alternative forms of public access such as trails, in interpretation, signage schemes and re-enactments in addition to huge capital projects at tourist sites. More importantly, these practices have been based on careful visitor analysis and have been organised in a more collaborative way through heritage-tourist and public-private partnerships (Julia Datow-Ensling and David Brough, Humphrey Welfare, Joe Savage, Patricia Weeks, Bill Griffiths). It can also be observed that communities and the third sector are engaged with Hadrian's Wall over the whole heritage cycle from archaeology (Barbara, Birley), planning (David Brough), conservation and reconstruction (Mike Collins), public engagement project design (Patricia Weeks) and promotion (Julia Datow-Ensling and David Brough). In comparison, too little effort, at least from academic perspectives, has been made to follow and study the practice of social engagement on the Great Wall. The systematic analysis of cases, including not only Liang Qingli, the patroller on the Great Wall (Liang Qingli and Liu Wenyan) but also other voluntary groups and wider community participation, could better inform public access and social engagement policy decision-making and operation.

These differences and contrasts provide the most valuable lessons from the Wall-to-Wall dialogue, and also help identify potential areas for future mutual learning and cooperation.

结语：双墙对话交流中的思考

于冰
中国文化遗产研究院—中国—北京

如果我们将保护工作视为一个周期链，它涉及调查，研究，保护维修，监测，开放利用和社会参与。当然这些自上游向下游延伸的环节不一定是线性的，而可以相互交叉和循环。文集中英国作者和中国作者的论文从一个侧面表现出哈德良长城和中国长城保护管理工作在这个周期中不同的侧重点。

中国长城的主要关注点仍集中在调查和保护维修上，而哈德良长城在研究、开放利用和社会参与方面取得了更多的进展。这从文集各章中两国论文的数量上可以反映出结构性差异。例如，第3章（调查）以中国论文为主，而第5章（开放利用和社会参与）以英国论文为主，部分地说明了这种对比。

通过交流对话，其中最鲜明的差别之一就是考古在双墙保护管理中所发挥的作用。尽管最近几年考古在中国长城开始受到一定的关注，但做得仍然还很有限。 在两年的时间里，沿长城20,000千米仅开展了四次正式考古发掘（于冰等）。相比之下，考古学研究在哈德良长城的保护管理中起着更为重要的作用，有着悠久的研究历史（大卫·布里兹），发展到现在已经发挥系统作用，渗透到保护工作周期链各个环节，从编制实施研究框架规划（托尼·威尔莫特），开展多学科视野的景观考古学（罗伯·柯林斯），直到鼓励支持社区考古学（芭芭拉·博利）。

在这个周期链上，另一个显著差异是中国长城的保护维修权重远远高于哈德良长城，近年来每年都有数十个项目在进行（于冰等）。其中的区别不仅仅在数量上，因为考虑到中国的规模、长期破坏的积累、面临的自然威胁、发展压力和旅游需求的飙升，亟需实施大量抢险维修，当然这种差别还会长期存在。更重要的差别是在方法上。有好几位中国作者都讨论了“不改变原状”和“最少干预”的保护原则，表明这些公认原则在实践中应用仍存在很大争议。可以看出中国长城保护维修的讨论还主要集中在工程技术层面（汤羽扬，兰立志，赵鹏，张剑葳）为主导，而对于哈德良长城，则更加注重考古，游客体验和管理因素（麦克·考林斯，比尔·格里菲斯）。

在周期链上的下游端，双墙在开放利用和社会参与方面也存在明显差别。尽管中国长城的个别点段已经成为国内外知名旅游景点，但长城文化遗产和旅游融合无论从政策还是研究方面还处于初期阶段（王玉伟，周小凤等）。相比之下，罗马边疆除了主要旅游景点开发的形式外，遗产道、阐释标识系统、历史情景再现等多种形式的开放利用已取得了可观的进步。更重要的是，开放利用的策划是基于详细的游客细分研究，而且遗产部门和旅游部门、政府与社会的合作形式更为紧密（朱莉娅·达托–恩斯林和大卫·布劳，汉佛瑞·维尔法，乔·萨维奇，帕特里夏·周，比尔·格里菲思）。另外，社会参与也覆盖于哈德良长城保护管理全周期链各个环节，包括考古（芭芭拉，伯利），规划（大卫·布劳），维修和重建（麦克·考林斯），开放利用项目设计（帕特里夏·周）和营销推广（朱莉娅·达托·恩斯林和大卫·布鲁夫）。相比之下，至少从学术角度而言研究总结中国长城社会参与实践的成果还很不够。如果能够更系统地开展象梁庆立这样长城保护员（梁庆立和刘文艳）研究，开展针对其他社会团体长城社区研究，将有助于更好地为中国长城开放和社会参与的政策制定和实施提供支撑。

这些差异和对比是“双墙”对话交流的宝贵收获，也有助于确定未来双方相互学习与合作的潜在领域。

HUMPHREY WELFARE
Newcastle University - Newcastle upon Tyne - UK

The papers presented in this publication are of great importance in allowing all of us to think about the heritage of the Walls for which we are responsible and how we discharge that responsibility. We hope that the papers will be informative and stimulating for our readers too.

Thanks to the kindness of our hosts, those who attended the seminar at Jinshanling were not confined to the seminar room and we were able to do and see other things as well. After the end of the presentations on the first day we visited the fine new museum in Luanping to see the objects from the Great Wall that it holds; this was an opportunity to discuss museum development, how the displays can be linked to the remains that can be visited, and the needs and expectations of visitors of all ages from home and abroad. The next evening we were treated to a very different event that will stay in the memory for the rest of our lives: this was an extraordinary pyrotechnic display, traditional to Luanping County. (We were warned, wisely, that we should stand well back from the rotating buckets of red-hot iron filings.) It reminded us of the importance of intangible heritage for the communities along the Walls, and, for the UK party, it prompted the thought that we do not do enough about this kind of heritage along Hadrian's Wall. For the UK party this display was particularly appropriate as it was performed on 5th November, a traditional night for fireworks.

After the seminar, a number of us went to see another section of the Great Wall at Jiankou. On our way we stopped at Gubeikou which has a special place in UK-Chinese relations and in the study of the Great Wall. It was there, in September 1793, that Lord George Macartney, who was leading the first embassy from Britain to China, crossed the Great Wall in his journey to see the Emperor Qianlong at Jehol. Lord Macartney was hoping to increase and simplify trade between our two countries, and he brought gifts that he thought might be examples of the sort of things that might be traded in the future. The embassy was not a success for the British; the Emperor was not particularly impressed by what he saw and he was content for China to stay as it was; there was no change in the trading relations. Neither side had done enough preparation for the visit: they did not understand each other. Nevertheless, the British had been able to learn a little more about China, and Lord Macartney knew that better knowledge of each other was the key if the two countries were to work together. He was greatly impressed by what he saw at Jehol, and he described the Great Wall as 'the most stupendous work of human hands ... built by ... a very powerful empire... and a very wise and virtuous nation.' At Gubeikou, one of the soldiers in his party, Henry Parish, took the opportunity to make detailed and accurate drawings of some of the towers of the Great Wall. His fine watercolours were the first high-quality technical illustrations of the Wall that came to the West, and they made a great impression.

In 2019, during the seminar, we too were able to expand our knowledge, seeing at first hand the huge amount of work that had been done at Jinshanling since 1984 to repair and to maintain the Wall. We saw how access for the public had been made possible, and how the routine care of the structures had made them safer for tourists to visit. However, there are always new problems to address and work still to be done: we were privileged to see the decorated brick Qilin panel and we discussed how such a special survival might be best conserved and presented. The care and maintenance of brick and masonry structures is a topic to which we will return in our future work together. After Jinshanling, on the steep slopes at Jiankou, we admired the results of the recent, very successful, programme of repairs, following the principle of 'conserve as found.' Here, as elsewhere - on the Great Wall as on Hadrian's Wall - the challenge is to achieve a sustainable balance between access for visitors and the damage that they can do, quite unintentionally, to the structures that they have come to see. Heritage and tourism can work well together, hand in hand, but each has to understand and to respect the needs and aims of the other.

Finally, a few of us were very lucky to be able to visit some sections of the Great Wall in Gansu Province, around Jiayuguan and in Yumen County. Here, some stretches of the Wall were very much earlier, dating from the Western Han Dynasty, and were built of rammed earth. The conservation problems for this material are very different, especially in a changing environment. There are also major challenges in explaining remains of this kind to visitors, and in protecting these fragile structures from the impact of tourists so that our grandchildren - and their grandchildren - can marvel at them.

The places that we visited were fascinating and instructive examples of the problems that we all face in conserving our

汉佛瑞·维尔法
纽卡斯尔大学—纽卡斯尔—英国

撰写这些论文集结成册，促使我们思考所肩负的长城文化遗产保护责任以及如何履行这一责任。也希望这些论文也能对读者有所裨益，启发思考。

感谢金山岭研讨会各主办方的精心安排，与会代表不仅在室内展开讨论，还参与了丰富多彩的体验和现场交流。第一天大会发言结束后，我们参观了滦平县新落成的博物馆，欣赏长城馆藏文物的同时，还探讨了博物馆建设，如何使博物馆展陈与现场参观的实物遗迹相结合，以及国内和国外不同年龄段观众的需求和期待。第二天晚上，我们得见此生难忘的民俗展示：滦平县传统的抡花表演，精彩绝伦，让人大开眼界。（表演开始前主人一再提示我们注意保持安全距离，当装有滚烫铁浆的转筒加速旋转起来时，我们意识到主人的明智）精彩的表演提醒着我们长城附近社区现存的非物质文化遗产的重要性，也使英方代表意识到哈德良长城周边的这类文化遗产未曾获得足够重视。特别令英国代表团感到亲切的是，表演恰好安排在11月5日，与英国传统节日——烟花之夜神奇巧合。

研讨会后，我们去箭扣长城途中在古北口下车参观。这里是见证英中两国关系和长城研究的特殊地点。1793年9月，乔治·马戛尔尼爵士带领英国第一个访华使团，正是从这里越过长城去承德避暑山庄觐见乾隆皇帝。马戛尔尼爵士期待加强两国贸易，简化贸易流程，并把他认为可在未来与中国进行贸易的产品作为礼物进献。这次外交出访对英国来说并不成功；乾隆皇帝对所呈礼物颇不以为意，认为中国可以保持自给自足；因而双方的贸易关系没有取得任何进展。中英双方都没有对这次访问作充分准备：他们彼此互不理解。即使如此，英国开始对中国有所认识，马戛尔尼爵士知道若两国共同合作，双方需要对彼此有更好的了解。在热河的见闻给他留下了深刻印象，他笔下的长城是“人力所及了不起的工程……唯有强大的帝国和聪明正直的人民方能建造。”在古北口，英国使团中一名随行的士兵亨利·帕瑞斯精确描绘了一些长城敌楼。通过他的水彩画，中国长城的真实清晰形象第一次展现给西方世界，引起轰动。

2019年的研讨会中，我们也进一步加深了对中国长城的认识。我们实地参观了金山岭长城自1984年以来开展的大量保护工作，包括不同阶段的维修和养护，以及在面向公众开放的同时加强长城日常维护，确保长城安全。当然，长城也始终面临新的问题和未竟的工作：我们非常荣幸地见到有着华丽装饰的麒麟影壁，并讨论如何最好地保存和展示这一珍稀遗存。砖石质长城保护将是我们未来探讨共同合作的领域之一。金山岭研讨会结束后，在巍峨陡峭的箭扣长城上，我们考察了依照“原状修复”原则圆满完工的最新修复成果。在这里，和其他地方一样——无论是中国长城还是哈德良长城——都需要在开放参观和保护遗迹避免游客（大部分无意地）造成损坏这两方面保持平衡。文化遗产和旅游可以携手共赢，但两个领域间需要互相理解和尊重对方的需求和目标。

最后，英国代表团中的少数几位有幸参观了位于甘肃省的嘉峪关和玉门县内长城。这里的一些长城段落建造时间较早，可追溯至西汉时期，使用夯土建造。夯土长城的保护问题不同于砖石质长城，尤其在持续变化的环境之中。这类夯土长城还面临另外的挑战，即如何向游客阐释，以及如何保护其脆弱结构以减少游客带来的消极影响，使我们的子子孙孙都能够欣赏它的壮丽。

这些实地参观既引人入胜也让我们获益良多，同时显示了我们面临的共同问题：如何保护文化遗产，如何向公众说明这些遗产的重要性以及它们为什么应该受到珍视。交流研讨也揭示出一些可共同合作的潜在领域。研讨会的最后我们邀请到会同行提议未来可以共同合作的项目。提议的项目数量众多，如果能够

cultural remains, and in explaining to the public why these things are important and should be cared for. What we saw also highlighted some of the topics on which we can collaborate. In the last session of the seminar we had invited colleagues to suggest projects on which we could work together in the future. A very large number of suggestions were made, and it would be wonderful if we could take forward all of them. This will not be possible in the short term, but since the seminar we have been discussing which options should be treated as our joint priorities and which should be included because they are unilateral priorities. Particular importance is attached to those potential projects in which we can learn together.

In 1793 Lord Macartney was warmly appreciative of the great generosity shown to him and his colleagues by his hosts. The hospitality and kindness that we were all shown during our time in Jinshanling and Jiayuguan demonstrated how little has changed in human values over the last two centuries.

全面推进将令人鼓舞。当然这不可能在短期内实现，但在研讨会后双方仍在继续讨论，哪些是双方共同关注的重点项目，哪些单方感兴趣的重点项目。有利于促进双方相互学习的潜在合作项目特别受到重视。

1793年，马戛尔尼爵士深深感激东道主对他及代表团的宽容大度和周到接待。我们在金山岭和嘉峪关同样得到了热情款待，这也显示着虽然两个世纪过去，人心相交的温暖不会改变。